SPIRITUAL
INDIA
HANDBOOK

SPIRITUAL INDIA HANDBOOK

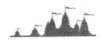

A GUIDE TO TEMPLES, HOLY SITES
FESTIVALS AND TRADITIONS

STEPHEN KNAPP

JAICO PUBLISHING HOUSE

Ahmedabad Bangalore Bhopal Chennai
Delhi Hyderabad Kolkata Lucknow Mumbai

Published by Jaico Publishing House
A-2 Jash Chambers, 7-A Sir Phirozshah Mehta Road
Fort, Mumbai - 400 001
jaicopub@jaicobooks.com
www.jaicobooks.com

© Stephen Knapp

Published in arrangement with
Stephen Knapp
180 Lenox Street
Detroit, Michigan
48215, USA

SPIRITUAL INDIA HANDBOOK
ISBN 978-81-8495-024-3

First Jaico Impression: 2009
Fourth Jaico Impression: 2011

Printed by
Pashupati Printers (P) Ltd., Delhi-95

Dedicated to all Pilgrims
Who carry with them
The hope and intention of
Reaching a higher perception of
Who they really are

Contents

Introduction

Reading about Eastern philosophy is one thing, but going to Eastern lands and actually experiencing it is quite another. Seeing the local people who understand and practice this knowledge in their customary surroundings can be quite enlightening, but it can also be perplexing if you do not know what is happening or the reasons behind what people do.

India, like other places in the world that have unusual mystical traditions, is a land that can be both physically and mentally demanding. India is an exotic, beautiful, and wondrous country, depending on what aspects of it you see. Living and traveling there can be pleasant and exciting, but it is also likely to provide you with many trying situations. It can be terribly hot, dry, and dusty. Good food and water may not always be readily available. And living conditions and transportation can often leave much to be desired. But it is a total experience on every level: a testing ground that is not for everyone. It can separate the serious from the frivolous; the real truth-seekers from the superficial and worldly sight-seeing tourists. But if you want the real treasure of India, the spiritual heritage of the East, it can be found if you are determined. But you have to know where to look and how to find it.

When entering India, you will most likely go through one of three places: Kolkata, Mumbai, or New Delhi. Like any big city, they can be somewhat overwhelming if you do not know where to go or how to handle the various situations that one is likely to encounter, especially in such a different culture. Some people may handle it quite easily, while others will find that the difference in lifestyle will make them ask, "Why did I ever think I wanted to come to this place?" For those, India may be a country where they stop long enough merely to see the Taj Mahal, the Jaipur Palace, and a few other places before going on to some other part of the world. Then they can say that they have been to India. But whether they actually see the real life of the people is another thing.

When visiting India, you have to be willing to readjust the way you see the world. It is a country that moves slowly. For example, trains and buses are often late. So you must have patience and plenty of tolerance, otherwise you may experience much to complain about and little of the beauty and wonder that exists there. You have to look beyond the poverty, the dirt, dust, smells, and overcrowded living conditions in the cities if you expect to enter into the mysteries of India's spiritual culture.

If you are attached to your Western ways or particular standards of comfort and are not willing to adjust, then, quite honestly, you have no business going to India, not at least if you are looking for its spiritual aspects. To do that requires you to drop your guard and your pretenses, and get out amongst the people, especially the *sadhus* or holy men, and see them as they are, doing their regular business, visiting their temples and attending their religious festivals. Whether you understand it all or not, it is bound to awaken a part of you that you never knew existed or have rarely experienced. You may either be confused by it, or you may find that you are quite at home with it, feeling a spiritual tranquility, the likes of which you have hardly realized before.

Attaining this spiritual serenity is a matter of evolving your consciousness. And how can your consciousness evolve if you do not decondition yourself from the habitual materialistic thought patterns in which you have grown accustomed? You must set aside your normal (or is it unnormal?) everyday ways of thinking in order to look at things from an entirely new perspective, a different state of mind. This is what expanding your consciousness and becoming aware of higher realms of existence is all about. And this is the real spiritual heritage of India. It offers an individualistic process of personal transformation and development for understanding yourself, your position in the universe, and your relationship with the Supreme. However, let us remember that the goal of Eastern philosophy or yoga is not to escape or cut yourself off from the outside world, but it is to BRING IN the awareness of self, the understanding of your real identity. Upon attaining this perception, one is never shaken in any situation. Of course, this does not mean that if you go to India you will see everyone intensely absorbed in this aspect of life. Like any place else, most people will simply be engaged in the struggle to survive, work, career, or ways to make money. Nonetheless, the people of India, generally speaking, are the most spiritually oriented people in the world.

In one's attempt to see the spiritual side of India, it is very important to know where to go and what to see in order to maximize whatever spiritual experiences you are looking for. Naturally, some places have more to offer than others, and certain towns are more sacred to specific religions or spiritual paths.

There are places in India like Vrindavan, Mathura, Mayapur, Dwarka, Varanasi, Puri, and others, as well as rivers like the Ganges or Yamuna, which exist and can be experienced in the normal three dimensional way. But these places are said to also exist in the spiritual realm, the higher dimension. This means that these places are where the material and spiritual energies overlap. Although the spiritual energy may pervade the universe, at such holy places or *tirthas* the experiences of higher dimensions are easier to attain. This is what gives these places special meaning amongst those who can perceive or know of this multidimensional aspect. This depends, however, on how receptive and elevated the person is in spiritual knowledge and awareness.

For those who are not spiritually aware, these cities and rivers will appear as no different from any other. Such people will say that the Ganges is not a holy river, that the Deities in the temples are merely stone idols, and that the sages are ordinary men. But the Vedic texts say that people with such a vision have a hellish mentality. They are forced by their own limitations of consciousness to be aware of nothing more than the most base level of existence and cannot perceive the higher realms of life that are all around us. For them this three dimensional material universe holds more mysteries than they can imagine, what to speak of the spiritual dimension which they cannot see at all.

From the gross sensory perspective, many of the values the people of India have, as well as activities they perform in the name of spirituality, will be completely bewildering for an uncultured tourist who lacks the spiritual knowledge that India has to offer. Such people may see a variety of activities, customs, and traditions that people enthusiastically perform in their abandonment for unity between the soul and God. Yet the average tourist will have no idea of why or what is the meaning of such customs. Then, as to be expected, they will view everything as being very strange. Therefore, only for those who are spiritually elevated does the higher dimensional realm of India exist, not simply as something to observe or study, but as a reality to be experienced. For others who lack such spiritual awareness, this aspect of India will forever remain a peculiar mystery. However, with the proper knowledge they can understand what is going on and the purpose of the numerous traditions that have existed for many hundreds and thousands of years.

Spiritually, the temples are like launching pads where one performs those activities that assist in reaching higher dimensions. They are the doorways to more advanced realms and where pilgrims and devotees go to make an outward display of their devotion to their deities. Though God is within us all, and religion or yoga is very often an inward process, God can manifest externally as the deity, the *arca-vigraha* incarnation, through which He accepts the devotee's service while he or she is in the material realm. These devotional activities, such as simple *darshan* (seeing the deity and being seen by the deity), are considered purifying for one's life and consciousness. The goal is to continue on this path until one's thoughts are purified to the point where one sheds his or her materialistic consciousness and can enter the spiritual realm, at least by the time of death if not before. Thus, everyone tries to visit the nearest temple a few times a day, or tries to make pilgrimages to the famous holy places.

The temples usually have a main shrine with smaller temples or shrines surrounding it. These shrines may have *murtis* or carved images of important spiritual masters, or deities of various demigods, such as Parvati (Lord Shiva's wife), Durga (the warrior aspect of Parvati, sometimes called Kali, Tara, etc.), Sarasvati (goddess of knowledge and intelligence), Lakshmi (goddess of fortune, Lord Vishnu's wife), Ganesh (a son of Shiva, said to destroy obstacles and offer good luck), Murugan (meaning divine child, the Tamil name for Subramaniya, another son of Shiva, especially worshiped in the South), Brahma (born from Lord Vishnu and who engineered the creation of the living beings within the universe), and Shiva (the benevolent one, part of the triad of Brahma, Vishnu, and Shiva who continually create, maintain, and destroy the universe), and other deities of the Supreme, such as Vishnu (incarnation of the Supreme appearing as the All-pervading One, the preserver or maintainer of the universe), or Krishna (the Supreme Being, source of all other incarnations, such as Rama, Vishnu, Narasimha, etc.). The temple is usually dedicated to a particular form of God or demigod which you will find on the main altar.

It is explained that the deity is not a product of someone's imagination, but is made in accordance with the ancient Vedic texts, called the *Shilpasutras*, which deal with the science of iconography. Everything about the deity, such as its proportions, the postures, hand gestures, weapons (if any), the emblems, etc., all mean something. Therefore, it is very important that every part of the deity is formed properly. The deity may also have different features which represent different aspects, abilities, powers, or pastimes. After the deity is formed, there is the elaborate installation ceremony during which the deity is installed in the temple. At this time the devotees and priests petition the personality of the demigod or Supreme Being to take up residence in the form of the deity. Only then does the deity become the *arca-vigraha*, or a worshipable incarnation of the Supreme Being or particular demigod.

It is considered that since God is the controller of both material and spiritual energies, He can turn something material into spiritual energy or vice versa. Thus, the deity, which may appear to be made of common material elements, becomes spiritual and allows us to see spiritual form with our material senses. Out of the causeless mercy of the Supreme, He agrees to reside within the form of the deity to accept the worship of His devotees. Of course, we should not think He is forced to remain there. If He is neglected or if harm is allowed to come to the deity, He may leave the form of the deity at any time.

There are many stories in both traditional Vedic writings and local legends that relate how various deities have reciprocated with devotees. Such relations have taken place in dreams as well as in the awakened state in which the deity has come to life to show Himself or Herself as He or She is, or partake in pastimes with their devotees. There are also some instances when Krishna or Shiva spontaneously manifested themselves as stone deities. Such deities are called self-manifested because they were not formed by any artist or priest. Lord Venkateshvara at Tirupati, Vishvanatha Shiva at Varanasi, and several Krishna deities at Vrindavan are a few examples of this. Of course, most Westerners of little faith cannot explain such occurrences, and can hardly accept that the Supreme would exhibit Himself in this way, which many would call miracles. They would rather look for some "logical" or non-mystical explanation for such things. But for the devoted and the sages who have glimpsed and understand the spiritual dimensions of existence, the deities are a living reality. Even if one cannot accept the concept of deities, then even in the most abstract sense the images, such as in Buddhism, represent cosmic principles which affect us all. Therefore, they remain a part of the reality we experience at every moment. In this way, the temples are the places where one can see and even experience the Divine.

Furthermore, many of the temples are built at locations where ancient historical or holy events involving the incarnations of God or the demigods have occurred. Such temples give evidence for the legends that are described in the *Puranas* which explain how the Supreme Being appeared there. Therefore, these sites become very sacred, even spiritualized for having been the site of the pastimes of the Supreme. It is for this reason that people can acquire great spiritual merit by visiting these places. Thus, these sites become important centers on the pilgrimage routes for many of the devout. In this way, the temples are the most significant of the surviving monuments where religious, social, cultural, and, in many cases, political aspects of history have been preserved.

Historically, the temples were also major centers for education. The larger ones would maintain priests and students for the recitation of the Vedic and Puranic texts to the people at large. Thus, both literate or illiterate people could be provided with a cultural education. The villages, however, had schools for basic study and learning, but beyond that the temples often had libraries full of books from all branches of learning and teachers who taught all these subjects.

The temples also served as centers for the arts since they would employ many artists to paint scenes from the Puranic legends or carve beautiful sculptures. There were also jewelers and goldsmiths who would make articles and ornaments for the deities. Musicians and singers were also employed, and dancing girls would perform exotic dances in times of worship, especially during festivals.

The larger temples had hospitals and doctors and areas for feeding and caring for the poor and destitute. In order to do all this, the temples consumed large amounts of fruits and grains. Thus, the temples were given plots of land that were used mostly by the farmers for growing food for the offerings in the temples. These offerings, however, would then be redistributed amongst the temple employees and the poor who needed food. The temples also had systems of banking. Thus, with such a variety of activity centered around them, the temples played a very important part in Indian culture, and in preserving that culture and distributing knowledge. In many cases, the temples are still the center of cultural and spiritual activity in the towns.

PURPOSE AND BENEFITS OF PILGRIMAGE

There are several reasons why many people go on pilgrimage tours of holy sites and temples. One, of course, is to dovetail our interest in traveling and seeing foreign lands into a way of acquiring spiritual merit. Most everyone likes to travel and see new countries and sights and inspiring places, and some of the most stimulating places are those of spiritual importance where historical events or miracles have taken place, or where significant spiritual incidents have happened as described in various spiritual texts and epics, such as the *Ramayana*, *Mahabharata*, etc.

One of the most important reasons for going on pilgrimage tours and seeing the places of spiritual importance is to meet other saintly people who follow a spiritual path and see how they live. This is especially the case with saints and sages who can help us by giving their association and sharing their spiritual knowledge and realizations. This is of prime importance for us in order to align our lives in a similar manner so we can also make spiritual progress.

Also, by staying in such spiritually vibrant holy places, even for short periods of time, or by taking bath in the spiritually powerful rivers, such experiences will purify and enliven us and give us a deeper understanding of how to live a spiritual lifestyle. Tours like this can give us an everlasting impression that will inspire us for years to come, maybe even for the rest of our lives. Such an opportunity may not happen often, even after many lifetimes. So if such a possibility does come into our lives, we should seriously take advantage of it.

Pilgrimage is a sacred journey. It is a process that is not meant simply to get away from it all, but to allow oneself to encounter, see, and experience the Divine. This is accomplished by associating with holy people, visiting the holy places where the pastimes of the Divine have taken place, and where the sacred temples allow *darshan*: The vision of the Supreme. *Darshan* is the process of approaching the deity in the temple in a state of spiritual communication, open and ready to receive sacred revelations. It means to the see the Absolute Reality, and also to be seen by that Supreme Reality, God.

Pilgrimage means living very simply, and going toward what is holy and most sacred, and remaining focused on the opportunity of having a life-changing experience. In this way, we will undergo voluntary austerities for purification to relieve ourselves of lifetimes of karma. This process will help change our consciousness and our perception of our spiritual identity and how we fit into this world, and help us gain access to the spiritual dimension through enlightenment.

When you are traveling in harmony with the Divine, it is not unlikely that you will experience spontaneous help from others when you may need it. This has happened to me in many ways and many times. In such a state of consciousness, seeming obstacles will quickly disappear. However, other challenges may be there to test our sincerity, but usually it is nothing so great that prevents us from reaching our goal, unless we have some serious karma to work out. It is divine guidance that assists us in our mission and prepares us for higher and higher levels of spiritual perception. Perceiving this assistance is another form of experiencing the Divine and the spiritual progress that we are making.

The objective of pilgrimage takes on more meaning when we realize the purpose of life. Life is meant for becoming free from the wheel of *samsara*, which means the continuous cycle of birth and death. It is for making spiritual advancement and to perceive our real identity. For this, we need to continue performing our regular religious practices to acquire virtue and freedom from sins and karmic reactions. It also requires purification of the mind, which then paves the way for clarity in perceiving who we are and the importance of spiritual progress. It leads to the destruction of ignorance of reality and the means to see beyond the illusion of material existence.

Such a practice to elevate our mind and consciousness is a type of yoga, which means the process to link ourselves to God. And the *yatra* or pilgrimage to holy places can be a step in that yoga process. Thinking about, arranging to go to, or even the process of reaching holy places is a process to elevate our consciousness and realign it to be more aware of God and the higher dimensions of the spiritual strata. *Sadhus* and saintly people may go on such *yatras* on a regular basis. But to do a pilgrimage can be especially rewarding and beneficial for householders who are often closed up in their daily business, cares, anxieties, and concerns. On such a *yatra* they can give up their ordinary concerns and replace it with the joy of traveling to the places that give spiritual merit. Such holy sites are often where great and sacred events have taken place. Then people can remember the purpose of life and experience a mental and spiritual rejuvenation. They can also find uplifting association with other *yatris*, or pilgrims, and with *sadhus* and sages who can share their own experiences and wisdom. This association with saintly people and the spiritual atmosphere is the main goal of pilgrimage. We can gather that impression in our conciousness and take it with us wherever we go.

The devotee may start out with God's name on his lips, or the thought of reaching the Divine, yet take the process of traveling as a form of penance that they undergo for a higher purpose. The pilgrim may also stop along the way to visit sacred rivers and shrines, or be elevated and blessed by having *darshan* of the deities at the temples one visits. Of course, the level of tolerance and endurance will also have to increase as one undergoes the usual difficulties of traveling in places that are foreign, strange, or unfamiliar, and sometimes crowded with other pilgrims. And where there may be little in the way of modern amenities. You may also have to travel lite, without many of the things you would like to take with you. Yet, that is the idea, to free your mind from many of the usual attachments and concerns of life. This will also help you take in the higher vibrations of the holy places that you visit, which is the main focus during pilgrimage. But take it slow if necessary, and be sure to keep the meaning of it in the forefront of your purpose.

The holy places may be a mountain like Mount Kailash or Arunachala Hill, a holy lake such as Manasarovara or Pushkar, a temple town like Vrindavana or Dwaraka, a sacred river like the Ganges or Yamuna, or other place or area like the Char-dham route consisting of Yamunotri, Gangotri, Kedarnath, and Badrinath. All of these are sanctified by tradition wherein historical and spiritual events have happened. Or we may go to places where there are still traditions and rites to be performed that offer spiritual credit. Such pilgrimages can be done any time on an individual basis, or with a small group. Or they may be done at special times during the year when a huge gathering or festival may take place. The holy site may be a short distance away, or it may be reached only after a long drive or walk, under easy circumstances or after undergoing difficult physical austerities. Some simply walk around the hill, while others may do a *dandavat parikrama*. The latter is when you bow down and prostrate on the ground a full body length and then move forward that same distance to bow down again. This continues all the way around the hill. Others undergo a particular vow they have made. It is all for spiritual merit.

The significance of pilgrimage is that the *yatri* or pilgrim does not consider the physical aspect of the journey, but focuses on the spiritual power of the place, the Divine presence, or the sacred events that have happened there, and the opportunity to tap in and experience that dimension. Through faith and dedication, you make yourself receptive to the higher vibrations of the holy site. The waves of spiritual energy can purify and uplift all levels of our being, destroying the dark elements in our consciousness and bad karma, and awakening our dormant spiritual tendencies. Or if we already have strong spiritual inclinations, they will become ever more apparent. By traveling to and associating with powerful holy places, the divine atmosphere and energy, and the saintly people who live there, if we are receptive to it, will bring us to a heightened state of awareness and unity with the Supreme. This is the importance and the inner effects that can take place through such pilgrimage.

As we begin our travels, we should bear in mind that India, at its present place in time, may be materially less advanced than the West but is far more spiritually developed. Of course, India is changing rapidly and is acquiring many material amenities. The average person in the streets of India knows more about spiritual science than most educated Westerners. Though someone from the West may know about religion, they still may know very little about real spirituality, which includes the knowledge of the soul, what happens at death, reincarnation, karma, etc. Try to have a conversation with a Westerner on these topics and it usually will not last long. But take any person from the East and the talk may go on for hours. Thus, there is a difference in cultures from the spiritual point of view.

To truly understand spiritual topics requires a change of consciousness, not simply a change of intellectual disposition or viewpoint, as many academicians tend to think. It requires one to rise above the bodily concept of life. Thus, even a poor man who superficially might appear to be uneducated may still attain great levels of spiritual realization. But some people may not agree with or understand spiritual knowledge because they, quite simply, might be incapable of changing their consciousness or of rising above the material conception of life. The ability to do this is a qualification that is far removed from simply acquiring a material education. Thus, regardless of one's position in life, everyone can try to understand spiritual knowledge. And one of the best ways, aside from studying spiritual texts, is to travel and experience the special nature of the sacred places that exist in India.

By entering deeply into the mysteries of spiritual India a person may experience a culture shock. Not a culture shock merely in the sense of having to deal with strange new situations and customs that you find in a different country, but also in the sense of taking a new look at yourself and the world and what your position really is in this universe. When you are traveling in the East, you are occasionally forced to be somewhat defenseless to new ideas, values, and perceptions. You may not have the easy access to Western forms of escapism. In India, life and death as it is stares you in the face, and you can either come to terms with it or simply try to avoid thinking about it. But by understanding the transitory nature of life through the spiritual knowledge that India is known for is something that can give you levels of realization you never had before. These may be simple realizations that you might reflect on from time to time, or they might be the kind that makes you change your way of seeing yourself, the world, and the way you want to live. So in spite of customs or traditions that you may not be used to or able to fully accept, you may still attain a new understanding of your real identity. Or you may also get a clearer glimpse of the infinite realm of divine consciousness. What you find within yourself depends on you and how open you are to new perceptions.

So let us begin our journey and see what happens. (I must clarify that when I say *we*, I mean *I* the traveler and *you* the reader. Together on this tour in the following pages *we* see these places.) In this journey I also tend to be very nonsectarian, and I visit and will describe many important holy places of many religions. I believe that all spiritual places have potency, some more than others. Yet, they all have something to offer. As you travel, you can also purchase the small books that more fully describe the history and legends that are connected to each location. I regularly do this to get additional information about each place which increases my appreciation for it.

TAKING THE TRAINS

Traveling from one part of India to another is often accomplished through the use of trains. Taking the train during our travels in India can be quite an adventure. You can definitely see some great landscapes as you go through hills, valleys, or travel past the lakes, cities, villages, farmlands, rice fields, and groves of fruit trees. At the train stations there are often vendors who will come through the train cars or call through your window selling anything from bananas, biscuits (cookies), cool drinks, magazines, nuts, salad, etc. And, of course, there are the tea sellers with their loud and often annoying shouts of "Chai, chai". There may also be children (or old men and women) who seem to live at the train stations by begging. Or a blind beggar will use his cane to find the door to the train car, board and carefully walk down the aisles asking for donations while playing an instrument and singing songs as the train goes on to its next stop, where he will get off.

There may also be village children who sing songs or play with monkeys as a form of entertainment outside your train window in the hope of getting a few rupees. Or maybe they will perform some acrobatic tricks to gain your favor. And while traveling, the people you meet on the train are often friendly and willing to share conversation, ask you questions, or even share their food. On the average, Indian people are much friendlier than Westerners. But if you are a Westerner you may have to get used to people staring at you, especially when in smaller towns. There were many times when I was the only white person on the train or the bus, and the people could not help but be curious and watch every move I made. One time in a small town in Central India I got off the bus to buy a few apples. When I had made my purchase and turned around, I was facing a large crowd of local people who had gathered behind me simply to watch what I was doing. Who knows when the last white man went through their village.

When using the trains, if it is available, always travel in the first-class or second-class AC section where it is a little cleaner (most of the time) and more organized and roomier. People are also likely to be more trustworthy, and traveling with them will make you less susceptible to theft or robbery, of which you must always be careful. In third-class, anything can happen and people sometimes squeeze in until there is standing room only. It also creates easier pickings for pickpockets. One time I was sitting in the crowded third-class section and with each stop more and more people left the train. So I got on an upper bunk to take some rest. Just as I was getting to sleep the train stopped at a place where the whole village must have tried to get on. There were eight people sitting on benches that were meant for four. I did not get much sleep that night. Another time I was at a train station waiting for a train when one train pulled out that was completely full. There were no more seats available, the aisles were full, and there were people hanging onto the doors and windows on the outside of the train. How long they could hold on like that I don't know. But these kinds of things are not unusual to see while traveling by train. Now, about the buses ...

When traveling shorter distances, buses are the usual form of transport. However, there are some areas and routes where trains simply are not available, and long distances must be made by bus, unless flying is a possibility. Going through the mountains or the highlands of north India are areas where you must take buses, unless you choose to go by taxi. I have had fairly good luck taking buses in India. They are also an adventure, although generally slower, less safe, and much bumpier.

BE CAUTIOUS

No matter how you travel, you must be careful. In spite of India being a place where you could have some of the most extraordinary experiences you could ever find, there are certain precautions of which you need to be aware. Crime here is still an ongoing thing. There are police here, but they are not as efficient as in the West, and in some areas they just don't care, which makes crime easier to get away with. There are also elements of darkness, meaning those individuals who will view Westerners with envy and as a source of money, even if it must be acquired through cheating, robbing, or even killing. In all my travels of India, I have heard great stories from travelers as well as tales of horror.

You must also keep in mind that India is not a place where women should be left to travel alone. I have known and met some women who have traveled by themselves to find great adventures, but I have also heard of those who have met with much trouble for having done so. Even upon arrival in India one needs to be careful. Taxi drivers are usually good and dependable, but some people have died at the hands of taxi drivers who have robbed or killed newly arriving tourists, especially women traveling by themselves. I have even heard of one man being taken to a dark area of Delhi instead of the place he requested, and had to flee the taxi with his possessions to get away. This is not likely when you travel with others. So if you are traveling alone, try to have someone meet you at the airport and give you a ride to your destination. Or call an organization or temple that you are affiliated with to make arrangements for your pick up. Iskcon members can especially call the New Delhi temple and have a dependable taxi driver take you to the temple where you can stay in the guest house, and then sort out your travel plan or itinerary.

I have also heard where a single woman went to Kashmir to stay on a houseboat and returned to Delhi two weeks later with absolutely no money, not even enough to get back to Finland, where she was from. She had arrived in Delhi and was immediately convinced by a Kashmiri tourist agent to go to Srinagar. The owners of the boat where she stayed intimidated her into buying things she did not want, to give money for their son's so-called education, and using her credit cards to the maximum. Only with the help of an Indian friend who gave her some money was she able to get back to Finland.

Let me say that Kashmir is now much safer than it once was, but in the past, such as in the 1990s, there have been kidnappings of Westerners by the Islamic insurgents for ransom money. This has also gone on in Nepal where the Maoists, who often lived in the jungles, have kidnapped trekers and held them for ransom, which they use to fund their cause. Another time a tourist in Delhi was looking for the best rate he could get in changing his money and looked for a black market exchange. [This was back when you could get more rupees to the dollar on the black market than what banks were giving. This is not the case anymore.] Someone talked him into going down an alley where several others then came out and stole everything he had. He was lucky they did not beat him up, but he was left with begging for money for the rest of his trip in India.

I have also heard where one Western lady was kidnapped in India and kept as a sexual hostage for months until someone found out and released her. This kind of stuff goes on everywhere, even in America, but when you are in a country like India, tourists are not always given the protection they need, or their unfamiliarity with things makes them an easy target for cheaters or robbers. And don't wear fancy or high-priced clothing or jewelry or camera bags. It only sends out a red flag that you have money or are wealthy to those who are looking for someone to cheat.

Some minor cheating is par for the course when you travel in India and you may not be able to avoid it all the time, but prior preparation, such as what I'm trying to give you in this book, can help prevent as much as possible. Remember to always protect your money and passport as much as practical. Do not keep money or valuables in loose pockets that allow a hand to easily enter them, even in the holy places or temples. I am one of those who has lost a wallet and money because of this, even while at a holy place. Just because you are at a sacred site does not mean that all the people there are of the same mindset. A criminal has no religion. This is why I usually wear fairly tight fitting pants while traveling so I can feel anyone's hand going into my pockets if someone tries such a thing. A money belt can be useful, but make sure no one sees you taking money from it. I heard of one person who went to sleep on a train with a money belt around his waist under his shirt, only to wake up the next morning to find that someone slit the bottom of the money belt and all his money was gone.

So if you take the proper precautions, you can still have a life-changing and positive experience while visiting India. Except for losing my wallet once or twice, or having to pay a Westerner's tax (a slightly higher price on things) from time to time, with proper precautions I have never had much trouble, even when I have traveled to numerous out of the way or even questionable locations. In general, Indian people are often much friendlier and more hospitable than you find in many western countries. And you are less likely to be robbed or held up in India than in places like London or New York City.

AVOIDING SCAMS

As much as we would rather not talk about this possibility, we must understand that there are always people waiting for those who are unfamiliar with India and who want to take advantage of them. So we must know a little about what to watch out for. Some cheating is bound to take place, and we just have to accept that as part of the expense of traveling. But we can keep it to a minimum if we are careful. So, for example, if you are entering India through Delhi, there are a few things you need to do. You can keep this in mind for any city that you are entering.

1. Have a reservation somewhere in a hotel or guesthouse to at least spend the first night or two. Years ago it used to be easy to fly into Delhi from overseas and find a room without having a reservation, but those days are gone. There are so many more travelers within India, and the consumer class of India is growing, so more people are traveling.

This means it is harder to find a hotel without a reservation in places like Delhi, Mumbai or Kolkata. Once you get to India and spend the night somewhere, you can always look around and find a different or better place the next day. But if you come into Delhi at night, and most flights do arrive at night, most hotels can be booked up by then, especially on the weekends. So have a reservation somewhere. This will help avoid the second point:

2. Do not go to a government tourist office if trying to find a hotel when you arrive in Delhi. First of all, they usually are not really government offices. They just call themselves that to get you in and gain your trust. Then they try to sell you a package trip or something. Taxi drivers, if they know you have no prior reservation or arrangement to spend the night somewhere, will often try to drive you to such an office, working with the people in them to get your money. Or they may be willing to get you a hotel, but it is usually at a more expensive price.

If you do go to such a tourist office, they are usually just regular travel agents looking for a good profit from you. This is especially the case if they know you have just arrived and have all of your travel money to spend, or if you are unfamiliar with the prices of things in India. Thus, if they quote you a price, it won't seem as expensive as it really is because you have not done any or enough price comparisons yet. In other words, you won't suspect so easily that you actually may be getting ripped off.

A common ploy is that if you have not booked a reservation in a hotel, they may call some hotels for you but actually they may only be calling their friends who pose as the hotel manager or something who say the hotel is full. Then as this goes on, you don't know what to do and become more vulnerable to considering their advice to quickly leave on a package tour, like to Srinagar, Kashmir or somewhere. If you decide to book it, you have just bought yourself a trip that is more expensive than it needs to be. It still may be fun and worthwhile, but it will be for more than what you could have spent if you had gone about it differently. Of course, if you were planning to go to a place like Srinagar anyway, then if you don't mind paying the prices they want, it may all work out.

3. Do not go to a travel or tourist agent to buy a bus ticket. Just go to the Interstate Bus Terminal in Delhi, which is near the old train station, not the station at Paharganj. If you are going south, say to Agra, and want a government bus, then go to the Veer Hakikat Rai ISBT (Interstate Bus Terminal) on the south side of the city. Buying a ticket directly from the station or on the bus is always cheaper than buying it through an agent. Or if you are indeed going to someplace like Srinagar, check with the Jammu & Kashmir State Road Transport Corporation, which has a separate station a ways away from the Interstate Bus Terminal. Any taxi or auto-ricksha driver can take you there. Just be persistent in telling them that you are not interested to go someplace else. They offer direct buses from Delhi twice a day for the nonstop, 25-hour trip to Srinagar. Or you can always take a regular bus to places north, stopping at places to see along the way, until you get to a place like Jammu, and from there easily get a bus on to Srinagar. Or if you are in a tourist office and they won't help you in any other way, then just walk out. You can get another taxi, auto-ricksha, or just walk down a busy street to the next hotel you find.

4. You can also take a train to most places you want to see. If you are a foreigner to India, you can get your train tickets for the best price available at the International Office on the second floor at the main train station near the Paharganj area of Delhi. Don't fall for a scam and get lead somewhere else, or think that you have to go through an agent or something. The people at the station are usually very helpful and can book your tickets to several places at once if you know where you want to go and the train on which you want to book a reservation. However, you will be expected to pay for the ticket in dollars or Euros, or in rupees if you can show a certificate of where you exchanged your money, although this may be changing.

5. Don't listen to anyone, but only go to these bus or train stations to get your tickets if you want the best prices for them. And if you have a hotel reservation, don't fall for the trick of the taxi driver at the airport or train station telling you that you have to reconfirm it once you arrive in Delhi. If you fall for that, it is likely that you will only be told by someone on the phone that the hotel is full and you have no reservation. Or that the taxi driver knows a reliable and trustworthy government tourist office that can help you. If you listen to that, then you will be spending more money than necessary, or you have got more money than I do. If you have a reservation, then just get a prepaid taxi at the airport and have them take you to your hotel. Then you are set for the night and can take care of things the next morning without being exposed to these kinds of scams. You can always make changes, or even choose a different hotel the next morning.

6. If you do arrive in Delhi without a reservation, the problem is that many flights arrive late at night, which is a bad time to be looking for a room at various hotels for safety reasons. Also, many hotels are indeed filled up late at night, especially if it is a week-end when there are generally more travelers coming in to town.

If you do arrive without a reservation, and if you are going for the cheaper end and don't mind staying in the busy Paharganj area where many of the cheaper hotels are located, you can ask your driver to just drop you off at the train station and then just walk down the street of the main bazaar at Paharganj and stop at each hotel (there are many) until you find a room. And if you try them all and there's nothing to be found, find a taxi or auto-ricksha and go to the Karol Bagh area, which is not far away and where there are plenty more hotels. Somewhere there is likely to be a room available. Then the next morning you can scout around again and find something more to your liking, or just book your bus or train ticket out of town. And of course if you come in by train, especially before late afternoon, then just cross the street to the Paharganj area to look for a room, and it should not be a real problem.

Also, taxis from the train station to a place in Delhi are always more expensive than getting a taxi from somewhere to the train station. They always try to take advantage of you in this way, no matter whether you are a foreigner or an Indian national.

If you are going to be staying in Delhi for a while, once you have seen what you want to see in Delhi and hit the road to other places, things usually get easier. So don't fret too much about what happens in Delhi if things are not what you expected. Nonetheless, Delhi can also be a very interesting place once you begin to know your way around.

BEING PREPARED

One of the most important things you can do for yourself is to be prepared, which is one of the main purposes of this book, to help you be prepared and know where you want to go in India. Yet, this means to not only be knowledgable about what can happen and what to expect, but also have an idea of what you want to do and where you want to go. If you have a hotel reservation when you first get into town, as previously recommended, then you can get settled and plan your itinerary. However, if you already know where you will be going, that will help you avoid making such decisions at the last moment, or being tempted by touts that are making business of pushing you into accepting ideas of going to certain areas of India.

Delhi has many touts from Kashmir, for example, and they will try to lure you into going to Kashmir by any means. If you plan to go there anyway, then it may be fine, but they usually charge more than you need to pay. The point is that if you have already done your homework and have an idea of where you want to go in India, that will help you avoid suggestions that may not be in your best interest once you reach India.

Places like Thomas Cook is also available in Delhi where you can get assistance and can change money, etc. Some hotels have information desks that can also provide information for you to decide where to go and how best to get there. They may be there mostly for assistance to their guests, which can be helpful to you. But remember to get your tickets at the train or bus stations themselves rather than through an agent. Getting them through an agent may be less hassle, but the cost will be higher, and sometimes considerably higher.

DEALING WITH RICKSHA OR TAXI DRIVERS

I want to offer a few words of caution which may save you some money and aggravation when visiting the bigger cities and dealing with ricksha and taxi drivers. You will sometimes find that in some cities motor-ricksha drivers have formed a syndicate and charge exorbitant prices to foreigners. Locating drivers away from major tourist hotels or attractions, or train or bus stations, will help you find drivers who charge more reasonable rates. A few rules to follow are:

1. Find out what the going rates are before getting a ricksha or taxi, if you have time. The manager of your hotel can often be of help in this regard. Ask him or her how much it costs to go to a certain place before getting an auto-rickshaw or taxi. Or he may have someone to recommend. Where travelers are especially susceptible to being cheated in this way are places when they come into a town for the first time, like coming into Delhi. Often times tired travelers just want to quickly get to a hotel and are willing to pay a higher rate without questioning or bargaining. Or they simply don't know what the proper rate is or where to get a reasonable taxi. That is why so many taxi or ricksha drivers seek out foreign travelers at the airports or train stations. In Delhi, you can get a prepay taxi as you leave the airport waiting area (where people are waiting to pick up friends and relatives) and go <u>outside</u> just as you enter the parking area. There will be a booth on your

right. Go to the window and book a taxi to where you want to go, preferably to your hotel or guesthouse and not a travel agent office. The prepay taxi services <u>inside</u> the airport still charge higher prices, sometimes by a few hundred rupees.

2. In other situations, <u>always</u> set the price first before you get started. If the driver does not set a price, don't go with him. Find someone else who will set a price so you know what to expect.

3. Don't be afraid to bargain. If he says one price, set a lower price and see if he will go lower, or find someone who will.

4. If you do go with him and he says "Pay as you like," then make sure you stick with that and if he asks for more than you want to pay, don't pay more. First, before paying or bargaining, get out of the ricksha or taxi, take your bags with you, and only then begin any discussions about the price to pay. That way you are not still in the auto-ricksha or taxi and he does not have your things inside it. If there is a problem, if possible, check with another driver what the going rate may be. However, if the drivers are working together they will both say a high price. Or better yet, simply tell him that you want to find a policeman to settle the issue. If the driver knows the rate is too high, he'll immediately drop it. If you're still not satisfied, then go find a policeman to see what he says, or simply go off and get lost in the crowd (if there is one) and disappear without paying anything, as long as he doesn't know your hotel. Otherwise, you'll find him there waiting for you. This last suggestion may sound a little dishonest, but chances are that if he is ripping you off, you are not the first person to whom he's done this.

When you are a Westerner and unfamiliar with rates of travel, it is not unusual for drivers and shop keepers to suddenly raise their rates when they see you coming. Someone told me that when you deal in dollars, the prices tend to be very high because Americans are used to higher dollar rates. But say, for example, you want the price in French Francs, the costs are comparably less.

Another point to remember is that drivers are often compensated by shop owners in money or gifts for bringing foreigners to their shops, which in turn will cost you in the form of higher prices on the items you buy. I went to a shop and was interested in buying a particular miniature painting. They wanted 1200 rupees. But after negotiating with them and when they learned I had no driver outside waiting for me and they would not have to pay any driver a commission, I finally bought the painting for around 700 rupees, almost half the original price. So it is often better when you go to a popular shop to have the driver simply drop you off, sometimes a little distance from the place, pay him for the ride and then let him leave. Thus, there is no driver for the shop to pay. Then after doing your business, simply find another driver to take you elsewhere.

CURRENCY EXCHANGE

If you are traveling with a group tour, they will often make arrangements for your currency exchange. They will probably provide arrangements for your travel from the airport to the hotel, so you wouldn't need to have money for taxi or the hotel to start off with.

However, if traveling alone or with a few friends, things will be different. So this is what I do.

When I first arrive at the airport in Dehli, or any other big city, I will first stop at the bank exchange window that one of the banks will have not far from the luggage pick up area and exchange $100 or $200 of cash or traveler's checks into rupees. It is better to do it there than at the hotel, where exchange rates may not be as good, although this is not the problem that it used to be. After I'm in town, later I'll go to a bank where I can exchange more money if I need to. You can go to the American Express office for America Express Traveler's Checks, or to the Thomas Cook Travel Agency, or one of the prominent banks.

Another consideration is that I usually bring about $1000 for every month I'll be traveling in India. I don't usually spend that much on travel, and I certainly intend to bring the rest of it back home, but if there is an emergency then I've got enough to handle whatever may come along. If you stay in cheaper hotels, and use less expensive means of transportation like buses, you can easily travel and stay in India for anywhere from $5 to $15 a day, or around $400 to $550 a month. Of course, it is more expensive while staying in the bigger cities and in bigger and more sophisticated hotels, or when traveling with a tourist group, but smaller towns can be especially affordable. If you are not doing so much traveling and staying in affordable places or smaller villages, you can get by on less. However, prices are always going up, on both travel and accommodations in India. And, actually, India is not the travel bargain it used to be, yet it is still cheaper than traveling in many other parts of the world.

A little less than half of the money I bring, I bring in cash. As I travel, I use the cash first and then depend on the traveler's checks later, since they are more secure. If you want, you can bring more money in checks. But I've found that unless you are careless, a person is not likely to be robbed in India. Besides, while traveling to small towns or villages, some places I've gone to do not have a bank with facility for exchanging traveler's checks, and could only exchange cash or the foreign currency. So you better have some cash on hand when you run out of rupees in such places, or make sure you plan accordingly. However, always keep enough dollars on hand for when you return to the US for taxi or other expenses until you get back home.

These days a safer way to handle your money is to use bank cards with ATM machines, which are in numerous places all over India. Then you only get what you need as you need it, and don't worry about carrying so much in cash or traveler's checks. In fact, when I was in Ujjain I could not cash any traveler's checks, but an ATM machine was available.

Another thing I do is spread my money in different places between my wallet, shoulder bag, and camera bag, and I don't carry too much money on my person. I've had my wallet pickpocketed once, and lost it once. Both times I did not lose that much money and had money elsewhere, making it possible for me to keep traveling in spite of the loss. On my person I keep my wallet in the front pocket of my pants, which are somewhat snug, making it impossible for someone to reach in to take it without me being aware. If I do wear loose fiting pants, I make sure they have a pocket that fastens shut. I only keep several hundred rupees in my wallet at any one time, or maybe 1000 or so. Yet, if you keep most of your money in a money belt, do not let anyone see you taking money from it. It is better to show a wallet with a small amount than to reach in a money belt, because then people will know you have a bundle. Then someone will know where the majority of your money is. That's not good. Robbery can result. Of course, even in America or other countries such precautions are necessary, not just in India.

FOOD PRECAUTIONS

This is easy advice, but is probably the most important if you want to have a good trip. Watch what and where you eat. Please drink only bottled water in India, even for brushing your teeth, which is available most anywhere. Don't think that you can go up into the mountains and let your guard down because the water must be cleaner, at least in the restaurants. Not true. Even with all the experience I've had, and I've drunk water from a variety of places while in India, still one time I drank water from a restaurant in Gangotri and by that night I was sick, and was mildly sick and weak with a protozoa infection for the next five weeks. Bad move. As I've said, I always buy bottled water and sometimes keep a canteen with additional water in my shoulder bag. Whenever something goes wrong with my health during my travels in India, it's because I failed to follow these rules, unless I get a cold. It takes only one drop of bad water to cause stomach problems. You can increase the variety of foods you eat when at reputable vegetarian restaurants or at the *sattvic* ashramas and temples where they are strict about serving vegetarian foods.

Also, watch out for drinks that use ice, unless you are sure where the water for the ice comes from. You should eat only hot, cooked food or peeled fruits and vegetables. Do not eat cooked food from street vendors! And at bus or train stations, only eat fruits that can be peeled by you and certainly no salads. You never know where the water came from that they used to wash the salad.

Strictly following this simple advice will help a lot. You have to be in India a good while for your body to acclimatize, so to speak, to be able to drink water from various places, which you may not want to do anyway. When I first started going to India, I always lost weight. Now I'm so used to it that I may even gain weight. I love that Indian vegetarian food.

HEAT STROKE OR HEAT EXHAUSTION

This can happen more easily than you think. Make sure when you visit India that you keep your head covered while in the sun. Make sure you wear a hat or a cloth, or use an umbrella. Too much sun or heat in India can kill you, or put you seriously out of action for days. If you start getting overly hot, tired, or dizzy while in the sun, take a break in the shade, and don't forget to drink plenty of water.

EXPECT PERSONAL CHANGES IN YOURSELF

There is no way to prepare for what India may do to you! It can be magic! You just have to be open to whatever may happen and go with the flow. This will be one of the most memorable and possibly most profound experiences in your life! Go for it!!!

WHAT IF TEMPLES DO NOT LET US IN?

I must say one thing regarding temples that are restrictive about who they let inside. First of all, I can understand why those who are disrespectful should not be allowed entrance. And there is certainly a history of the white Christian missionaries who came to India to preach and blaspheme against the "pagan gods." But for those who are sincerely trying to understand Eastern philosophy and have respect and veneration while in the temple, I see no reason why they should not be allowed inside. Otherwise, the local priests are simply keeping the temples to themselves without any concern for the spiritual well-being of others. This is due to their callous blindness and a tendency toward exclusiveness. They do not see the soul that exists within everyone. All they can see is that this person is Indian or Hindu, and that person is white or a Westerner. This person can come in, and that person must stay out. This is not proper. Spiritual understanding will not spread like that. They should be happy that people other than Indians are interested in their culture and philosophy, but if they don't want to assist in this exchange, then their selfishness and lack of concern will be all that is recognized. It will only limit the growth or future of their culture.

Maybe Westerners in general have engaged in what to the brahmana priests are very low activities, such as eating meat, or taking intoxicants, not bathing daily, etc. But God is God of everyone, the Supreme Pure, and, obviously, must be able to purify anyone who comes before Him. So any old brahmana who feels that Westerners will only disturb or spoil the atmosphere of the temple lacks real spiritual understanding. And who can say who is really worthy of entering a temple? While riding the trains I have seen Indian brahmanas eating eggs and smoking cigarettes. This kind of activity certainly does not give them the qualities that differentiate them from anyone else. It merely shows their hypocrisy. In fact, according to the orthodox view, once a brahmana eats such food, like eggs or meat, he immediately is considered to have lost his caste or *varna*. He can no longer be a brahmana. So how can they enter a temple to see the deities when other Westerners who may be following a more pure or virtuous lifestyle cannot go in? This is ludicrous. I have seen many Westerners adopt a spiritual path that includes no meat-eating, no intoxication, no illicit sex, etc., habits that many Indians as well as some brahmanas cannot give up. Yet they hold sway over their temples to exclude these sincere souls from entering. So this should be changed.

As far as we are concerned, if a temple does not let us in, we can understand their limited mentality and their prejudice against our skin color, and then simply move on to those temples that do let us in. And I have been to both. I have been rejected numerous times from being able to enter a temple in India, and I have also been graced many times to enter a temple and to be able to have truly amazing experiences between me and the people there, or me and the deity, in which I was raised to a completely new and unique perception of our spiritual connection. There will be plenty of such opportunities if you are receptive to it. Just be ready for it.

▼

The Major Holy Places in East and Central India and Nepal

For most people who visit India, they will either arrive at one of a few ports of entry, such as New Delhi, Kolkata, or Mumbai. Since we will begin our journey of India in the East and Central part of India, New Delhi will be a good place to start our descriptions of what to see.

You may arrive in New Delhi late at night, as many people from the West often do. You will need to go through customs, pick up your luggage, change some money into rupees at a bank desk within the airport, and then go to your hotel. I strongly suggest changing some of your money into rupees before you leave the airport simply because it will be easier for you and you will be less likely to be cheated in common transactions where you need to calculate the difference in currencies. State Bank of India, one of the most common, and another bank or two will have desks across from the luggage claim at the airport. Once you pick up your luggage, it takes little time to go over to change some money. I often change about $200 to $400 into rupees to get me started. I also change my dollar currency before starting to change my traveler's checks. The checks can always be changed later, and if they are stolen you can replace them. But I change my dollar currency first because if they are stolen, you are simply out of luck. However, if you are in small towns and need to change money, sometimes these small towns do not change checks, or are particular about which ones they do change. So without some currency, you may find yourself in difficulty at times when you are in a rural area and are running low of money.

After that you need to find a hotel, and there are desks that will help you do that with phones to call certain hotels. I never do that because often they are misleading and will try to direct you somewhere that you may not want to go because they are getting a commission from certain hotels that they recommend you to use. These days I make reservations with a guesthouse or hotel that I know since many hotels are often booked up by the time I can reach them. Otherwise, I simply go to fiind a hotel in the Paharganj area. This is right across from the train station. There are lots of hotels in this area and they are the least expensive in town. Unfortunately, all hotels have gone way up in costs over the last several years, and the Paharganj area still offers the best values in town, although some of the hotels do not have the best of facilities. Besides, when we are ready to start our journey, the train station is not far away, which is a convenience by itself.

The next thing to know is that the best taxi service to use is the prepaid taxi just outside the door of the airport, as you enter the parking area. If you book a prepaid taxi inside the airport, and they will be hawking you to do so as you walk past their desks, the prices are higher. So wait until you exit the door of the airport and the last prepaid taxi desk will be on your right. Prepaid means you pay for it before you leave and there is no further question about how much it will cost. Just go up to the window and book a taxi to wherever you want to go, and name your hotel that you are interested in, and they will take you to a taxi and drive you there. If you are interested in a hotel that you find is booked full, the taxi driver will know of others to take you to. It is not difficult. And the prepaid drivers are often the most honest as opposed to those who are not prepaid. But don't let them take you to a Government Tourist Office. This is often merely a regular tourist agent that they may be working with to get you to book a tour package to someplace.

Once you settle in somewhere, and if you plan to follow our tour of East and Central India, then get ready to visit many of the various temples, holy places, and sacred towns that India is know for, some of which are considered by several religions to be the most holy in all of India, if not the world.

NEW DELHI

Unless I have to be at a certain place at a certain time, I stay in Delhi for a day or two just to get used to being back in India, and to pick up whatever else I may need for my travels. Delhi is often the starting point for wherever else you may want to go.

When you have decided on where your next destination will be, you can walk to the train station and go to the Foreigner's Office up on the second floor. This is quite helpful and they can book most of the tickets you may be interested in purchasing. They also accept foreign currency for payments, and you can buy the Indrail Passes here in foreign currency. The Indrail pass used to be a great bargain, but over the years they have raised the prices on them to such a degree that they are no longer the best way to go. They are way too expensive. So now I buy train tickets only as I need to.

In the meantime, Delhi is a great place to get your first taste of India if you have not already been here. New Delhi, a city of 13 million at the time of this writing, is not necessarily a place of pilgrimage, but an innumerable number of people from all walks of life, holy and otherwise, come through this city. New Delhi is also a city that shows how much India has changed through the years, and is perhaps as modern as most any part of India we will find. New Delhi is where we can get most of whatever we need for continuing our travels. There are plenty of tour offices, banks, airline companies, and shops of all kinds for most anything we'll need, including bookstores where we can get additional information on places to see, or photo books on places we have visited to take home. And if you are looking for souvenirs, shops around Connaught Place have art work, sculptures, deities, religious items, carved wood figures, jewelry, textiles, etc., from all over India, Nepal, and Tibet. And there is a great deal one can learn about India and its culture just by investigating the many interesting places within the Delhi area. So while we are here, we can spend a few days seeing the sights before continuing our journey through another part of India, or before taking our flight back to our home country if we are finishing a tour.

New Delhi has much history connected with it that goes back 5000 years to the time when the Pandavas, as related in the *Mahabharata*, founded Indraprastha along the Yamuna. The ruins in the area of the Purana Qila are said to be all that remains of the ancient city of Indraprastha. This is surrounded by massive stone walls, entered through three gateways. The fort we see today at Purana Qila is said to have been built by Sher Shah, an Afghan ruler who held sway over Delhi for a time (1538-45) before the Moghul Humayan took control again. A small archeological museam exists inside the main gate. It is also interesting to note that the small octagonal tower, the Sher Mandal, made of red sandstone, was where Humayun slipped from the staircase while descending them and later died from his injuries. He had been using the tower as a library. Nearby is the Qila-i-Kuhran Mosque.

Several other locations also have ruins where different phases of the city's development took place. But aside from ruins, there are many monuments and places of interest that are worth a visit for tourists and pilgrims alike, depending on your own special concerns. New Delhi has something for everyone.

Most of the monuments in the area, however, have an Islamic link. It was the last great empire that held sway over the city before the British rule. There is, of course, the Red Fort along the Yamuna at the end of Chandni Chowk Road. It is said to have been built by Shah Jahan and completed in 1648. However, there is evidence that shows that it was a pre-existing building merely captured by Shah Jahan. It is a massive structure and inside is an assortment of interesting and decorated buildings. There are pools, fountains, meeting halls, rooms for infantry, courtyards, and inlay work on ornate columns that indicate how opulent was the lifestyle of the ruler when it was built. You can pick up a guidebook on the place when you visit that will explain each building.

Not far from the Red Fort is the Jami Masjid mosque, also said to have been built by Shah Jahan, completed in 1658. On what grounds this is established may be questioned because here again there is evidence that has revealed that it was a pre-existing temple building before Shah Jahan ever invaded the area. For example, Tamerlain (Taimurlang), one of Shah Jahan's ancestors 10 generations prior to him (about 230 years), gives his own testimony that the Jama Masjid mosque was previously a Hindu temple. He relates that in his memories entitled *Malfuzat-i-Timuri* wherein he describes the take over of Delhi and how many of the resisting Hindus assembled in the Masjid-i-Jami (meaning the Chief Temple) of Old Delhi prepared to defend themselves. Thus, the Jama Masjid had to have been a Vedic temple prior to its Muslim takeover.

As of now, it is the largest mosque in India with a capacity of 25,000. You can go in with a camera and look around. For a fee, climb one of the minarets that stand 40 meters high. This gives a good view over the old part of Delhi. This place can be quite busy at times, especially during Muslim holy days.

Not far from the mosque along the Yamuna River is Raj Ghat park where Mahatma Gandhi, Jawaharlal Nehru, Indira Gandhi, and, more recently, Rajiv Gandhi were cremated. People still go there out of respect to such people.

Just south of Purana Qila is one of a number of Muslim tombs in the New Delhi area. This one is the tomb of Humayun, the second Moghul emperor, said to have been built in the 16th century by his wife, Haji Begum. It has lovely architecture with a domed building in the middle of a large garden, entered through large gates, one on each side in the walls that surround it. The building is another that could have been a pre-existing Vedic Lakshmi temple before the Muslims arrived. The style of the building, with the bastions, numerous gateways, surrounding annexes, guest houses, guard rooms and walls all point to a typical Vedic temple structure. There is even a Shakti Chakra, and overlapping triangles that adorn its top facade. Humayun is not even buried there. Abul Fazal says Humayun is buried in Sirhind while Farishta says he is buried in Agra. There are only a couple side rooms which have a few cenotaphs. And for that the whole structure is designated as a Muslim tomb.

Furthermore, French writer G. Le Bon has published in his book, *The World of Ancient India*, a photo of marble footprints that were found in the building. He describes them as the footprints of Lord Vishnu. This is also very typical of a Vedic temple, to have the footprints of the main Divinity of the shrine. In this case it is the husband of Lakshmi, Lord Vishnu. So it has all the elements of a temple, except for the added Muslim graves that are there now.

Across the road from Humayun's Tomb is the tomb of the Muslim saint Nizam-ud-din who died in 1325, along with a few other graves, such as that of the Urdu poet Mirza Ghalib. If you look at all the elements, you will notice that the Nizam-ud-din is also Vedic in design. The saffron colored tall archway under the tree at the left hand top is evidence of the Vedic origin of the site. The whole area, under Muslim occupation for the last few centuries, has a magnificent spacious stepped well which is a typical Hindu feature. The so-called Amir Khusro tomb with a white dome is part of that great Vedic temple complex. The lotus-petal border of the terrace and the lotus cap above the dome are strictly Vedic features.

The Nizam-ud-din complex contains Muslim graves because the area, being a Vedic temple complex, came under repeated Muslim attacks with carnage every time. Muslims would station themselves in captured Vedic ruins and lay claim to it by burying their dead leaders in such buildings and say it was Muslim property or Muslim constructed.

Since Islam existed only from 622 C.E., most Muslims in the area are the descendants of Hindu ancestors who were captured and forcibly converted to Islam.

Heading west from here we find the Lodi tombs, containing graves of some Lodi and Sayyid rulers. These are also interesting domed buildings that have been made into a pleasant park, but it does not take long to look them over. Though they try to maintain the serenity of the place, it is somewhat small and crowds can often gather here on Sundays.

Farther southwest of the Lodi tombs is the tomb of Safdarjang, said to have been built in 1754 by his son who was the Nawab of Oudh. However, again it has all the elements of a pre-existing Vedic temple before the Muslims came to capture the building and make it into one of their mausoleums. Any visitor can see the typical Vedic design of the four towers, one in each corner of the complex (usually held for different deities that are viewed before going into the main sanctum), the walls of which are inlaid with marble, with a main shrine in the middle. If the evidence regarding this place is true, then it is originally another Hindu building. The point to consider is that there were two mounds of loose red-brick powder which would get blown away and which the archeology department would need to keep replacing fraudulently to maintain the pretense of the graves. The other mound is supposed to be Safdarjang's wife, but which wife is hard to say since he had a full harem. There are an additional two mounds in the basement but only one unlabeled cenotaph on the first floor. It is also known that Safdarjang was buried at Paparghat in Uttar Pradesh. Therefore, the tomb in the building at Delhi may not be real and only an attempt to give the Muslim claim some credibility.

Farther south, 15 km from New Delhi, is the Qutab Minar tower, 73 meters tall, that represents the Muslim victory over the last Hindu kingdom in the area. Most history books on this place say that the construction began in 1193 by Qutab-ud-din and was completed a few centuries later. Near the base of the tower is the first mosque built in India, the Quwwat-ul-Islam, or "Might of Islam" mosque. It is said that it was made on the foundation of a Hindu temple and constructed of material and parts gathered by destroying 27 other "idolatrous temples." If you understand architectural designs, you will recognize Hindu and Jain elements within the structure of the mosque. There is even a seven-meter tall iron pillar standing in the complex, known for not having rusted after 2000 years of being exposed to the elements, and for being a Garuda *stambha* taken from an ancient Vishnu temple.

One of the reasons why the mysterious iron pillar has not rusted for so many years is that it has been discovered that it was made with high levels of phosphorous in the 99.2 per cent pure wrought iron used to build the structure. Some feel that it was also not cast iron, but was constructed by a welding process. In either case, this shows the expertise of metallurgy that had been reached during the reign of King Chandra II, Vikramaditya of the Gupta dynasty, when the pillar is said to have been built. However, one of the legends behind the pillar is that the mighty Bhima, one of the five Pandava brothers in the *Mahabharata*, lifted the pillar in his right hand and impaled it into the ground. It is also said that an image of Vishnu surrounded the pillar, which was probably removed by the invading Muslims who left the pillar in place.

The Qutab Minar tower is also known to have been a pre-existing Vedic temple dedicated to the study of the planets. Different people suggest a variety of theories about its origin. Such theories range from it being built by Kutubuddin Aibak, the Muslim slave ruler who controlled Delhi from 1206 to 1210. Or it was built by his son-in-law and successor Iltmash. Or it may have been built or partly constructed by Allauddin Khilji. Feroz Shah may also have helped build it.

Mr. P. N. Oak gives some hints to the background of this building on page 30 in his book *Some Blunders of Indian Historical Research*: "The township adjoining the Kutub Minar is known as Mehrauli. That is a Sanskrit word *Mihira-awali*. It signifies the township where the well-known astronomer Mihira of Vikramaditya's court lived along with his helpers, mathematicians and technicians. They used the so-called Kutub tower as on observation post for astronomical study. Around the tower were pavilions dedicated to the 27 constellations of the Hindu Zodiac.

"Kutubuddin has left us an inscription that he destroyed these pavilions. But he has not said that he raised any tower. The ravaged temple was renamed as Kuwat-ul-Islam mosque.

"Stones dislodged from the so-called Kutub Minar have Hindu images on one side with Arabic lettering on the other. Those stones have now been removed to the Museum. They clearly show that Muslim invaders used to remove the stone-dressing of Hindu buildings, turn the stones inside out to hide the image facial and inscribe Arabic lettering on the new frontage."

On page 291 of the same book he goes on to explain that, "Even the Arabic term Kutub Minar signifies an astronomical tower. Kutub and Kutubuddin was a subsequent unwitting mix-up. Around the tower were 27 constellation temples which Kutubuddin's inscription vaunts to have destroyed. The tower too has 27 flutings. Near the first storey ceiling are 27 holes—one in each is likely. True to the significance of the term Kutub, this tower's entrance faces due north."

On page 538 of *World Vedic Heritage*, Mr. Oak describes a little about the way the temple used to be. He explains that underneath (the tower) lay a giant statue of Lord Vishnu reclining on Seshanaga. At the top of the tower on the seventh storey was an image of Lord Brahma sitting on a lotus flower seat. But the Muslims destroyed both of those images.

The mosque at the base of the Kutub Minar, the Quwat-ul-Islam, is also said to be the very first mosque in India, built with the remains of numerous destroyed Hindu temples. However, the ornately carved columns provide proof that this was once a Hindu temple. Besides, if the tower was a Hindu observatory, it is in line with tradition that there would be a Hindu temple nearby and other shrines for the nine planets.

This is confirmed by Sir Sayyas Ahmad, father of the Muslim League and a founder of the Akigarh Muslim University. He has said, "The current tradition which ascribes the Minar and the adjoining temple to the Hindu period appears to be correct."

In this way, Hindus have been robbed not only of credit for the architectural structures that they had made, but also for much else that is good and artistic, including music, poetry, literature, styles of painting, color decoration, gardens, fountains, pottery, porcelain, carvings, etc., even when found in India. Thus, the glories of the original Vedic culture has been humiliated and made to appear small and puny by these outside forces. Or that anything really good in India was brought in by someone else. Thus, it is time for people to realize the immense contribution that the Vedic culture and the ancient people of India have given to the world. Furthermore, Muslim inscriptions on such Indian buildings, mosques, or tombs, should not necessarily be mistaken to signify the original builder, but only the captor, occupier, or usurper. Even Muslim chronicles may mention the building of such things as canals, giving themselves the credit, when actually the canals were already there.

To visit a few of the more modern buildings, another interesting place in the southern part of Delhi is the Lotus temple, which belongs to the B'hai religion. The architecture is totally unique in that it is built to resemble a huge lotus blossom. The B'hai religion is an offshoot of Islam, but they are very open and respectful of all faiths. As with any B'hai temple, anyone can come in to see it or use it for prayer. But this place does not remain very quiet because of the hundreds of people who flow through it. Most of them come simply to see the place. So if you would like to visit it, you must be prepared for the occasional long lines of people who are waiting to get in.

Not far from the Lotus temple is the beautiful "Glory of India" temple, one of Iskcon's Sri Sri Radha-Krishna Mandirs. This is a new and interesting temple, with a wonderful temple room with beautiful deities of Gaura-Nitai, Radha-Parthasarathy, and Sita-Rama-Lakshmana and Hanuman. There are also popular diorama exhibits and museum, giftshops, and a lovely vegetarian restaurant. Many people visit this temple, especially on weekends and weekday evenings. So it is worth the time.

Back in the city there are some fine museums, such as the National Museum on Janpath Road, which I personally feel is one of the best in India. It has some very good exhibits of paintings, costumes, jewelry, ancient culture, sculptures of wood, bronze, terra cotta images, and many deities, etc.

There is the Nehru Museum on Teen Murti Rd., which was Nehru's residence turned into a museum if you are interested in his life. Not far away is also a Rail Transport Museum if, after riding the trains all over the country, you are interested in India's old trains. There is also a crafts museum on Mathura Road at the exhibition grounds that shows traditional arts and crafts of India. A doll museum is on Bahadur Shah Zafar Marg with over 6000 dolls from all over the world.

Not far from Connaught Place is a Hanuman temple with a variety of deities and worship that can be done, and a small Shiva-Parvati temple, both of which are regularly visited by local people. They often stop on their way to or from work to pay homage or say prayers.

A little walk away is the Jantar Mantar, one of Jai Singh II's unusual but very interesting observatories. A larger one is found in Jaipur. Though the instruments look peculiar, they are quite accurate in predicting eclipses and plotting the course of stars.

The one thing to understand about such sites as Humayan's tomb, the Kutab Minar, and now the Jantar Mantar and others, is that there is an entrance fee. It used to be the same price for everyone. But the Indian government has decided that foreigners can afford to pay more. So the Indian nationals can pay 5 or 10 rupees for some of these places, while the Western foreigners can $5 or $10. Some of these places may be worth it, but others are definitely not worth seeing for that amount of money. You can decide what is right for you.

Walking west on Ashoka Road we will find an important Sikh temple which is very active. There are several Sikh temples in the Delhi area, but this one is called Gurudwara Bangla Sahib. It is named after the bungalow of King Jai Singh where the Eighth Sikh Guru, Harkrishan Ji, stayed during his visit to Delhi. It is said that, in his concern for the sufferings of common people, he put his feet in a water reservoir and then offered the sacred water to the sick and ailing who got cured of their grief and sorrows. Even today devotees visit the temple and drink the water that is served in a special area just outside the temple. Many Sikhs stop by in the morning and evening to listen to recitations of their holy scripture, the *Granth*, in the temple or over the loudspeakers. The Sikhs are very nice to everyone here, and you can go in, providing you leave your shoes at the stall and wear a cover on your head. There is also a guest office that may be open to help explain things to you. In the morning they distribute delicious halava near the temple exit door.

Farther west on Ashoka Road we find the large and beautiful Lakshmi-Narayan temple on Mandir Marg. There are some lovely deities of Sri Sri Lakshmi-Narayan (Vishnu), as well as Shiva, Ganesh, and others, with a side temple to Buddha. It is another temple built by the Birla family in 1938 and anyone is allowed in. It is definitely worth a visit. Before the threats of terrorists, you used to be able to photograph the temple and deities, but now that has changed and they have been very strict about no photography.

For Jains there is the Lal Mandir on Chandni Chowk across from the Red Fort. It is a small temple but has a very ornate interior and altars with images of their *tirthankaras*. At this temple they take care of many sick birds that are brought to them. But they have received some criticism for not giving more help to the local needy people.

Farther down Chandni Chowk is the Gauri-Shankara temple dedicated to Shiva, and there are altars with a variety of Vedic gods and goddesses as well as Lakshmi and Vishnu. Though this temple does not have a fancy exterior, it is very busy inside with people continually coming and going. Not far from here is another Sikh temple built where the ninth Sikh guru, Tegh Bahadur, was martyred by orders of the fanatic Muslim Aurangzeb because of not adopting to Islam.

Another lovely new site in Delhi is the pink sandstone and white marble temple complex of the Swaminarayan sect (BAPS), called Akshardham. It took 11,000 craftsmen and volunteers five years to complete this huge $44 million project and temple for a grand opening on November 6, 2005. It is located on 105 acres near the banks of the Yamuna River. The temple complex itself covers about 30 acres. It has a center on Indian culture, exhibition on the origins and philosophy of the Swaminarayan sect, an IMAX theatre, gift and book shop, theme gardens, along with 120 ornate pillars and 1200 images of the Vedic gods and goddesses.

What I have given here is just a short description of the major points of interest in New Delhi. A variety of other sites and facilites can also be seen here. Not all of them may be for you, and certainly not all of them may be for those with spiritual interests, so you can take your pick. But there is much that New Delhi can reveal in regards to the history, culture, and spiritual practices of India. So it is worth spending a few days here. Unfortunately, it has become one of the most polluted cities in the world. If you take a *ricksha* through the old section of town, the air can be so thick with exhaust fumes, dust, and so forth, sometimes you'll hardly be able to breathe. The outskirts of the city are not so bad, but in the summer when it is hot and there is hardly a breeze, it can be horrendous no matter where you go. So be prepared to be tolerant of this factor.

MATHURA

As we begin our tour of the holy places of East and Central India, the first major holy place to see is only a short three hour ride by train or bus ride south from Delhi. Now that they have built a nice highway through the area, the road is much faster than it used to be. Vraja, which has a perimeter of 168 miles and is composed of many villages and towns, is considered nondiferent from the holy places of Mayapur (Navadvipa), Jagannatha Puri, and Dwaraka. The same spiritual nature is manifest in all of these places. But Vraja is considered the holiest of all holy *dhams*. In many places in the *shastra* are descriptions of the glories of Mathura and Vrindavan. The glories of Mathura are elaborately explained in the *Varaha Purana*, chapters 152 through 180. One verse states: "A moment in Mathura is worth a thousand years spent in Kashi (Varanasi)." And simply by bathing in the Yamuna River in Mathura one can be freed from all sins. Residing here for only a few weeks qualifies one for liberation from material existence. And each step taken in Mathura is equal to visiting a holy place elsewhere. It is explained that those who die here attain Vishnu-loka, the abode of Lord Vishnu in the spiritual sky of Vaikuntha, and do not take birth again.

The descriptions of the glories of Vrajamandala go on and on, but they are known only to a few rare souls in this world. Only the most fortunate get to hear about it, what to speak of getting the opportunity to visit this holy place. And since it is only a few hours away from Delhi, anyone who is spiritual inclined must visit this sacred place.

Many holy men can be seen visiting the temples, walking in the streets, singing or chanting as they go. Though they may seem destitute, they are often very jolly because of their spiritual wisdom and freedom from materialistic problems. Here the holy men and saintly women enter into a higher reality that makes their bodily condition less significant. Many *bhaktas*, sages, and mystics have experienced unimaginable levels of spiritual ecstasy here, though superficially the area may look like any other part of India where people are engaged in the struggle to survive. But as you look deeper, if you are capable of it, you will find quite another aspect of Vrajamandala that draws pilgrims by the thousands from all over India.

Basically, Vraja is the land of Krishna. If you really want to understand the pastimes of Krishna, you have to know Vraja. And if you want to know the significance of Vraja, you have to understand Krishna's pastimes. Krishna was born in Mathura 5,000 years ago but lived in Gokula for three years, then moved to Chatikara and Vrindavan for three years, then lived in Nandagram for three years, and from age 10 to 28 He lived in Mathura. After this He moved to the western coast of India where He lived in Dwaraka for over 96 years. Thus, He stayed in this world for 125 years, but some of His sweetest and most attractive pastimes were performed in Vraja. To fully explain these pastimes and where they took place in this present volume is impossible, unless we wanted to greatly extend the length of this book. There are other books that you can acquire that will explain these pastimes much more fully. But there are some significant sites and temples that I'll try to briefly describe so you can visit and understand their significance. We will start our tour at Mathura since that is usually where we get off the train or bus.

Mathura is the largest city in Vraja with around 325,000 residents. It is a very busy, noisy, and dusty town with a large railroad junction. Nonetheless, it is an important town for pilgrims. Besides being the birthplace of Lord Krishna, Srila Vyasadeva also took birth here at Krishna Ganga Tirtha on the banks of the Yamuna, where there is a small temple to Ganga Devi and many Shiva *lingas*. It was also at Ambarish-tila where the great devotee King Ambarish fasted while waiting for the sage Durvasa Muni to return from being chased by Lord Vishnu's chakra, as described in the *Bhagavata Purana*. Not far from Krishna Ganga Tirtha is Vishrama Ghat, the best known of all the bathing ghats on the Yamuna in Mathura. Anyone can direct you to it. It was here that Lord Varaha rested after saving the earth from Hiranyaksha and spoke the *Varaha Purana*. Lord Krishna also bathed and rested here after killing Kamsa, the demoniac king. And Sri Chaitanya also bathed here while visiting Mathura. So many pilgrims come here to perform various rituals and take a purifying bath. You can also watch the aratika to the Yamuna River that takes place every evening around seven PM.

The most important temple in Mathura is the beautiful Keshava temple that represents the place where Krishna was born. It stands next to a mosque that the fanatic Muslim Aurangzeb built where the original Keshava temple stood before he tore it down in 1669. Nowadays it is all fenced in and you have to go through security gates to enter the temple. The present temple has lovely Radha-Keshava deities and paintings of Krishna's pastimes cover the walls and ceiling of the large interior. It is said that simply by seeing this deity of Keshava, within a second a person is relieved of the sins of one's past seven births and will not take birth again. You can also enter the mosque building to see where the original Krishna Janmastan temple stood. There is a nice little altar there now with Krishna deities. The real spot where Krishna is said to have been born is a few blocks away, represented by a very small temple building, past the Potra Kund. The Potra Kund is said to be the location where Mother Yasoda would wash Krishna's baby clothes. Then down a side street is the place where King Kamsa's prison was located in which Lord Krishna first appeared. The building is not very well kept because it is located on property owned by Muslims. But this may change in the future.

Other important temples in Mathura include the Dwarakadish Mandira which is not too far from Vishram Ghat. It has a small, beautiful black deity of a four-handed Dwarakadish, similar to the deity in the huge temple at Dwaraka. This temple is quite popular and many people crowd to see the *arati* ceremonies. Nearby is a temple of white Sweta-Varaha, and another of Adi-Varaha which was supposed to have once been Lord

Indra's deity in Swarga, his heavenly abode. The deity was later taken by Ravana to Sri Lanka and then to Ayodhya by Lord Ramachandra when Rama defeated Ravana. Lord Ramachandra gave it to His brother Satrughna who brought it to Mathura. This story is more fully explained in Chapter 163 of the *Varaha Purana*.

Downstream from Vishrama Ghat is Prayaga Ghat where the ancient temple of Veni Madhava is located. It is said that by bathing here one gets the benefit of bathing at the *sangam* (where the three rivers of the Ganga, Yamuna, and underground Sarasvati meet) in Prayaga (Allahabad). A little farther is Bengali Ghat where Vasudeva is said to have crossed the river when taking baby Krishna in his arms from Kamsa's prison to Mahavana after His birth. Next there is Dhruva Ghat where there is a temple on a mound called Dhruva Tila which marks the spot where Dhruva performed austerities to get the *darshana* of Lord Narayana, as described in *Srimad-Bhagavatam*.

Across the river from Vishrama Ghat, about 200 metres from the river, is the small village of Isapur. Here you will find a temple with an image of Durvasa Muni which marks where the great mystic performed many austerities and meditated during Satya-yuga.

Mathura's most popular Shiva temple is the Rangeshwara Mandira, one kilometer south of Vishrama Ghat. This is one of four main Shiva temples of the city, which includes Bhuteshwara to the west near Krishna Janmastan, Pipaleshwara in the east near Vishrama Ghat, and Gokarneshwara in the north. Near the Rangeshwara Mandir is the Keshava temple of the Gaudiya Math where Srila A. C. Bhaktivedanta Swami took sannyasa, the renounced order of life. The temple has beautiful deities of Radha-Keshava and Sri Chaitanya.

During the afternoon when the temples are closed you can visit the Government Archeological Museum. It has a good collection of Hindu, Jain, and Buddhist sculptures and art work. Mathura was a major Buddhist center with as many as 20 monasteries when the city was visited by Fa Hian around 401 C.E. and Hiuen Tsang in 634. But things drastically changed for Hindus and Buddhists alike when the Muslim invaders, like Mahmud of Ghazni, arrived in 1017. After that Buddhism practically disappeared from Mathura.

Another place open all day is Ranga Bhumi, the area which was the wrestling arena of King Kamsa located across from the Main Post Office. On a hill, Kamsa-tila, is where Krishna killed the demoniac Kamsa, and just beyond it is where Krishna crowned Ugrasena as King of Mathura.

GOKULA

Six kilometers south of Mathura is the small town of Gokula next to the Yamuna River where Krishna lived during part of His childhood. There are several temples here, such as the Gokulnathji Mandir and the temple in the reconstructed fort, Nanda Qila, of Krishna's father, Nanda Maharaja. Across from the temple are diorama displays of Krishna's Gokula pastimes. These temples are interesting to visit, but the priests often act like they simply want to make a business of doing special *pujas* for you and then charge you high prices for them, like 125, 250, 501, or 1001 rupees. So if you do not want this, be sure to tell them you simply came for *darshan* and then leave a small donation you can afford. Nearby is also a shrine that is the entrance to an underground chamber, located down a few flights of stairs, that has the deity of Mayadevi, who appeared as Krishna's sister. She appeared from Mother Yasoda but was put into the arms of Mother Devaki by Vasudeva, Krishna's father, to fool Kamsa into thinking that their seventh child was actually a girl. King Kamsa was waiting for their seventh child to kill Him since he had heard that he would be killed by their seventh child, who would be Lord Krishna. However, when Kamsa learned that their seventh child was born, he went to the prison where he had kept them to see this child. But, instead of Lord Krishna being there, it was Mayadevi who rose up into the air and escaped his clutches. She warned him that the child he was looking for was born elsewhere, and then she disappeared.

Two kilometers south of Gokula is Mahavana where there is the Nanda Bhavan temple on a small hill. Inside are large images of Nanda, Mother Yashoda, Balarama, and baby Krishna. The pillars are said to have come from the original palace of Maharaja Nanda. This is also near the *janma-bhumi* or appearance place of Lord Balarama. A short ride away is the Yamalarjuna Bhanga, also called Ukal Bandan, where you can see an ancient grinding mortar said to be the one Mother Yashoda tied to baby Krishna in order to try and get Him to stay in one place. But He dragged it between two yamalarjuna trees and caused them to crash to the ground. When the trees fell, two demigods were freed who had been cursed to live as these trees for offending Narada Muni. However, Narada Muni had also blessed them to eventually be freed by Lord Krishna. Then the two demigods were allowed to return to heaven. The *Srimad-Bhagavatam* explains all of these pastimes.

A kilometer further south is Brahmanda Ghat, which is not only a beautiful and serene bathing spot on the Yamuna, but also where Krishna's mother suspected Him of eating dirt. When she looked in His mouth she saw the whole universe. This place is a quiet place much of the time, but when you go during the month of Kartika (Oct-Nov) when many people come to Vrindavana for pilgrimage, the place can be very crowded with busloads of people doing their sacred bath and getting *darshan* of the local Krishna deity.

A short ride further south is Chinta-garam Ghat. This is indeed a very quiet and lovely spot along the Yamuna. Only a few sages live here with their cows and a small temple with a few deities of Krishna and a Shiva *linga*. It is soothing under the tree and sitting in the sand. This is the place where Mother Yasoda visited in order to sooth her mind after being confused by seeing the universe in her son's mouth. She could not fathom that such a sight could be seen in Krishna, so she had to come here to calm herself. So even today it is a nice and quiet place with the only sound coming from the wind and the birds in the trees.

Seven kilometers further south is the Dauji temple. Dauji is the deity of Lord Balarama that was originally installed 5,000 years ago by King Vajranabha, Krishna's great-grandson. In fact, he established a number of Krishna deities in the area. The present temple was built 200 years ago by Shyama Das of Delhi. Many people also attend this temple to get *darshan* of the single deity of 6 feet tall Lord Balarama. From the other side of the temple you can see the diety of Revati, Lord Balarama's wife. Nearby is the Balabhadra Kund or Kshira (milk) Sagara (sea) where the deity of Lord Balarama had been hidden during the Moghul invasion. Near this kund is a temple to Harideva and in the bazaar is another temple to Banke Bihari.

VRINDAVANA

Back in Mathura we start toward Vrindavan and soon find the Gita Mandir, a very nice temple built by the Birla family. The temple has a very good standard of worship for the deities of Lakshmi-Narayana, as well as Sita-Rama. The central deity is of Lord Krishna explaining the *Bhagavad-gita* to Arjuna. In the courtyard is a column called Gita Stambha that has all the *Bhagavad-gita* verses engraved on it.

Twenty minutes away we find the Pagal Baba temple complex. It has residential facilities surrounding the courtyard, and a large temple with many dioramas of the different incarnations of Krishna on the bottom level. As you go to each higher floor there are altars with deities of Lakshmi-Narayana, Sita-Rama, Vamanadeva, etc. On the top floor you can look out and get a good view of the town of Vrindavan in the distance. Across the road nearby is a path leading to Akrura Ghat, which used to be along the Yamuna River until the river changed its course, as it often does in this area. Akrura Ghat is where Akrura, Krishna's uncle, got to see Krishna and Balarama as Vishnu and Ananta lying on the surface of the Yamuna. Akrura had stopped there to chant the *gayatri* mantra while taking Krishna and Balarama to Mathura. What the vision signified was that Krishna never leaves Vrindavan, He eternally resides there, but Krishna's expansion as Vishnu was going to Mathura.

Now we continue to the most holy town of Vrindavan which has many temples to see. In fact, it is said that there are over 5,000 temples in this town, both large and small. Out of all of these, I will describe the most important. Vrindavan is not a place you go to and expect all its secrets to become easily revealed. It is said that you do not get to Vrindavan simply by purchasing a ticket. Vrindavan is not only a geographical place, but it is a state of spiritual consciousness, without which you will not comprehend the special nature of the place. Thus, as you become qualified through bhakti-yoga, and by receiving the blessings of the resident devotees, Vrindavan will gradually reveal itself to you. I have personally experienced this. Only after staying in Vrindavan for several weeks was I able to find and understand the meaning of certain places and temples that I had been looking for from the time I arrived. Slowly I began to have my own realizations about the spiritual characteristics of this holy town.

For me, Vrindavan is my favorite place in all of India. I love to walk around the village visiting the temples and holy places, seeing the beautiful deities, dealing with the friendly residents, and watching the pilgrims who also tour the temples. Of course, this does not mean that you should not be careful as in other places in India. There may still be plenty of ricksha drivers and store keepers who are too willing to raise the price on their services and merchandise when they see a foreigner. And some tourists are easy prey for such people. But after having done as much traveling as we have throughout the rest of India (unless you have come straight to Vrindavan from Delhi upon your arrival in India), we will find that Vrindavan is a small and very sweet village that is easy to get to know.

The spiritual nature of this place can be very apparent if one is able to perceive it, and some people feel it right away. But there can be plenty of things that can hinder your absorption in such spiritual bliss. Things like misquitoes, noisy monkeys that fight in the night that keep you from sleeping, incredibly hot summers, cold winter nights without central heat, and so on. For the average person it is not an easy place in which to live. That's why it is recommended to keep your visits in Vrindavan short so you do not lose respect for the place and consider it an ordinary, mundane town, and, thus, become critical and offensive. Such an attitude makes one lose all ability to enter into even the most basic level of Vrindavan's spiritual atmosphere. In the proper consciousness, one can perceive that everything about Vrindavan is spiritual.

Rupa Goswami explains in his book *Sri Upadesamrita* that Vridavan is spiritually superior to Mathura because this is where Krishna's highly esoteric *rasa-lila* pastimes take place. Rupa Goswami was the top literary disciple of Sri Chaitanya Mahaprabhu and chief of the Goswamis who lived in Vrindavan about 500 years ago. He wrote many books about the art of devotional service to Krishna and restored many of the holy places in Vraja, re-establishing its spiritual importance. The *rasa-lila* is the pinnacle of transcendental loving exchange between Krishna and His purest devotees, the *gopis* or cowheard girls, as explained in *Srimad-Bhagavatam*. The rasa dance is purely spiritual and not easily understood by mundane scholarly interpretations. If one is not a *bhakta* (devotee engaged in bhakti-yoga), one cannot comprehend such elevated love of God.

The *rasa* dance took place in the forest of Seva Kunj, which used to be a much bigger area than the small enclosed forest it is today. Nonetheless, it is considered the center of Vrindavan, and is where, according to *shastra* or the Vedic literature, the *rasa* dance takes place every night. In fact, it's said that Krishna never leaves Vrindavan; the spiritual pastimes are eternal. We will understand this more clearly as we visit a few of the temples and relate the pastimes connected with them. Just one thing about visiting Seva Kunj is watch out for the monkeys. There is quite a pack that lives there and they can be aggressive in ways such as stealing your glasses, which has happened often, or your camera, shoes, etc.

There are a number of important temples in this area. Just north of Seva Kunj is Imli Tala. Here we find a very old tamarind tree that has existed since the days of Krishna in the courtyard of a Radha-Krishna temple that was built by Bhakti Saranga Maharaja. Krishna used to sit under this tree and His body would turn golden from ecstatic separation from His dearmost devotee, Srimati Radharani. Five hundred years ago, Sri Chaitanya would sit under the tree and due to His love for Krishna His golden body would turn blackish.

Heading east we visit the Radha-Damodar Mandir. The original deities of Radha-Damodar were installed by Rupa Gosvami in 1542, but were later taken to Jaipur where they are now worshiped. The present deities are considered equal to the original. There is also a stone or *shila* from Govardhana Hill in the temple that has an actual footprint of Krishna on it. Krishna personally appeared to Sanatana Gosvami to give him the *shila*. He told Sanatana that because he was having difficulty from old age he should stop his daily circumambulation of Govardhana Hill and simply circumambulate the *shila*. The footprint became part of the stone when Krishna stood on it and caused the stone to melt from the sweet sound of His flute playing. Now pilgrims circumambulate the temple four times, which is equal to walking once around the 15 mile path of Govardhana Hill. You can ask the *pujari* (priest) at the temple for Giriraja *darshan* and for two rupees he will bring the Govardhana *shila* for you to see.

On the left side of the Radha-Damodar temple, through a doorway, are the *samadhi* tombs or representative tombs of Jiva Gosvami, Krsnadas Kaviraja Gosvami, Bhugarbha Gosvami, and a *puspa samadhi* (flower or representative *samadhi*) of Bhaktisiddhanta Gosvami. Through a door on the right side of the temple is the *samadhi* and *bhajan kutir* (small and private place for worship) of Rupa Gosvami. On the right side of the courtyard are the rooms where Srila A. C. Bhaktivedanta Swami Prabhupada lived for several years from 1959 to 1965 and wrote his commentary on the First Canto of *Srimad-Bhagavatam*, which he later brought to America.

Not far away is the Radha-Shyamasundara temple, which is one of the seven main temples of Vrindavan and has some very beautiful deities. It was established by Shya-mananda Prabhu who was a disciple of Sri Chaitanya and a very elevated *bhakta*. In fact, one time he saw Srimati Radharani. He would regularly clean the little forest area of Nidhibana and happened to find an anklebell. He thought it must be Radharani's since he knew Krishna and Radha often spent Their evenings there. When Radharani discovered one of Her anklebells was missing, she sent Lalita to find it. At Nidhibana Lalita saw Shyamananda Prabhu and asked him if he had found an anklebell. He said he had and asked if it was hers. Lalita said it belonged to her sister and asked to have it. Shyamananda said he would not give it to her but only to her sister. Lalita insisted that he give it to her, and Shyamananda continued to refuse. So Lalita returned to Radharani and Radha decided to personally go for the anklebell Herself. Approaching Shyamananda, Radha asked for the anklebell and he was happy to give it to Her. Radha, being pleased with his service, revealed Her identity to him and by impressing Her anklebell into his forehead personally gave him a *tiloka* mark. Later, the other *bhaktas* criticized him for wearing a new style of *tiloka*. But that night Srimati Radharani appeared to Jiva Gosvami in a dream and told him that She was the one who gave Shyamananda the *tiloka* mark. Then all the devotees went to Shyamananda to ask for forgiveness and accepted that he actually saw Srimati Radharani. This is another story signifying that the eternal pastimes of the spiri-tual realm are continually taking place in Vrindavan.

A little walk (half-block) from the Radha-Syamasundara temple is Loi Bazaar, one of the main shopping areas in the village. Here you can find all the necessities for living in Vridavana. There are shops of all kinds, for clothes, medicines, utensils, food, deities and worship paraphernalia. Walking eastward through the bazaar we next see the Shahji Mandir which was built in 1876 by Shah Kundan Lal of Lucknow. This is an attractive temple that has small Radha-Krishna deities, and shows how Shah Kundan Lal, a rich jeweler, appreciated service to Krishna in Vrindavan. To the left of the temple and down a lane is a small but pleasant Krishna temple of the famous poetess Mirabai.

On the eastern side of the Shahji Mandir is another enclosed park called Nidhibana. This is where Radha and Krishna performed many pastimes. Even now it is considered that They still take rest here in the evening. Thus, there is a small temple of Radha-Krishna sleeping on a bed located here. This was also the place where Haridasa Gosvami found the deity of Banki Behari, another famous temple in Vrindavan which we will visit shortly.

Another important temple nearby is the Radharamana Mandir, founded by Gopala Bhatta Gosvami. Gopala Bhatta had been worshiping a *shalagrama-shila*, which is a stone form of Krishna that he had gotten while on pilgrimage in Nepal. However, he longed to have a deity of Krishna to worship and dress. One day the deity of Radharamana manifested from the *shalagrama-shila*, thus fulfilling Gopala Bhatta Gosvami's desire. You can still see the stone form on the back of the deity, from which He manifested Himself. This is one of those miracles of *bhakti*.

A short walk farther down the lane is another of the seven major temples, the Radha-Gokulananda Mandir, founded by Lokanatha Gosvami. On the altar of this medium sized temple are the Radha-Vinoda deities of Lokanatha Gosvami (though his original deities were moved to Jaipur), along with Radha-Vijaya Govinda of Baladeva Vidyabhushana, Radha-Gokulananda of Vishvanatha Cakravarti Thakura, and a Sri Chaitanya deity that belonged to Narottamadas Thakura. The temple also has a small Govardhana *shila* that was rubbed smooth by Sri Chaitanya who used to hold it while chanting Krishna's holy names. The *shila* had been given to Raghunatha Dasa Gosvami. Across from the temple in the courtyard are the *samadhis* of Lokanatha Gosvami, Narottamadas Thakura, and Vishvanatha Chakravarti Thakura who were all important Vaishnavas in the Gaudiya line. The Radha-Vamsi Gopala temple is also nearby, farther down the street, and is where Srila A. C. Bhaktivedanta Swami Prabhupada lived from 1954 to 1962 and wrote his first commentary on *Bhagavad-gita*.

Following the street to the Yamuna River we come to Keshi Ghat where Krishna performed the pastime of killing the Keshi demon. Keshi was a henchman of the demoniac King Kamsa and took the form of a huge horse to terrorize the residents of Vrindavana. Krishna, therefore, killed the demon and then washed Himself in the Yamuna.

The *Adi Varaha Purana* establishes that by taking a holy bath at Keshi Ghat brings the results of bathing at all the holy places, and is worth 1,000 baths in the Ganges. Therefore, Keshi Ghat is one of the holiest ghats in Vrindavan. Not far from Keshi Ghat is Bhramar Ghat where Bilvamangala Thakura, the author of *Krishna Karnamrita*, performed austerities years ago. Lord Krishna used to appear in Vrindavana just to serve His great devotee Bilvamangala by supplying him with a cup of milk everyday.

As we head back into the village, not far from the Radharamana temple is the Radha-Gopinatha Mandir. It is another of the seven original temples and was founded by Madhava Pandita. The original deities were transferred to Jaipur and similar deities were again installed in this temple. Around the corner is the New Radha-Gopinatha temple with deities of Srimati Radharani, Gopinatha, and Srimati Jahnava. Jahnava was Lord Nityananda's wife and this deity of her was brought from Jahnava's native Bengal by a man who said the deity appeared by Divine Will. This was years after she had left this world. Then the deity of Gopinatha appeared to the temple priest in a dream and told him that Jahnava was actually the elevated *gopi* Anangamanjari, and that the deity should be placed on the altar next to His left side. So this is why the deities in this temple are now arranged in this way.

Farther into the eastern part of town are many other temples; including the large and ornate Lala Babu Mandir with Radha, Krishna, and Lalita deities. Then at the corner where we turn off from Loi Bazaar to go toward the Banke Bihari Mandir, we find the Gopishwara Mahadeva Shiva temple with a Shiva *linga*, said to have been originally installed by Krishna's great-grandson, Vajranabha, and is the place where Lord Shiva did austerities in hopes of entering the *rasa-lila* dance as a *gopi* (cow-herd girl). In the morning devotees wash the *linga* with milk and other items, and then later the *pujaris* dress the *linga* in bright colored clothes.

Retracing our steps just three shops back, on the left we can find the Pishima Gaura Nitai temple. This small temple has the deities of Gaura-Nitai which had belonged to Murari Gupta. They are about three feet tall, with eight inch Radha-Krishna deities and some Govardhan *shilas* in front.

From the Gopishwara temple heading south, other temples we can find include the Tikarirani Radha-Krishna temple; the especially beautiful Thakura Yugala Kishora temple, which has many small cut mirrors embedded in the walls and a sleeping Krishna deity on a swinging bed; and the large Rangaji temple with its South Indian style *gopurams*. This temple is a major landmark along the road and modeled after the Sri Rangam temple near Trichy in Tamil Nadu. It has three gates you go through to get to the central temple. Presently, Westerners can go in as well, but it used to be that they were not allowed past the third gate.

Not far from this temple is Brahma Kunda where the demigod Lord Brahma prayed to Krishna for forgiveness after testing Him to see if He was actually the Supreme. The story is that one time Brahma took away all of Krishna's friends and cows. After a moment he came back to see what Krishna's reaction was and to his amazement saw all of the boys and calves still there. Krishna had expanded Himself into the forms of all the boys and calves. Realizing his insignificant position, Brahma returned all the boys and calves he had taken and prayed for Krishna to excuse his ignorance.

Next is the Radha-Govindaji temple that is another of the seven major temples of Vrindavan. It is across the road and a little farther down the street from the Rangaji temple. It was established by Rupa Gosvami where he discovered the Gopala deity. The beautiful temple is made out of red sandstone and was completed in 1590. The temple is now only two storeys tall but once reached up to seven storeys. The Muslim fanatic Aurangzeb, doing his dirty work once again, dismantled the upper five storeys of the temple due to his envy. While his men were destroying the temple, there was a loud thunderous noise that shook the ground. This put fear into the hearts of the men and they immediately stopped and ran away. Due to fear of the Moghuls, before they arrived the devotees moved the original deities to Jaipur where today many pilgrims go to see them. So the temple now has *pratibhuh* deities, or representative expansions, of the original

Radha-Govindaji that are worshiped. The original Govindaji deity is said to have been installed thousands of years ago by Vajranabha.

A hundred yards northeast of the Govindaji temple is a mound that has the ruins of the Sakshi Gopala temple. The present Sakshi Gopala temple is just outside of Jagannatha Puri. Sakshi Gopala had been discovered and installed in the temple in Vrindavan, but walked over 1000 miles to Vidyanagar to bear witness for one of His devotees. This story is told in our coverage of the Jagannatha Puri temples. Following the road going south and then west from the Radha-Govindaji temple, you can find many more temples and ashramas of Vrindavan.

Back at Seva Kunj, we now head west to the Radha-Vallabha Mandir. This is a temple that is the center of the Radha Vallabha sect founded by Sri Hit Hari Vamsa, a disciple of Gopala Bhatta Gosvami who was known for his poetry about Radha and Krishna. After this we see the Banki Behari Mandir, one of the most popular temples of Vrindavan. Haridas Gosvami found Banki Behari at the bottom of Visakha Kunda in Nidhiban after Haridas had a dream in which the deity told him where to look. When you visit the temple you will see that the curtain in front of the deity is closed for a few seconds every minute. This is because the deity once walked off the altar and out of the temple to follow a great devotee who had come for *darshan*. Apparently the devotee and deity gazed at each other too long and the deity became fond of the devotee and later walked off the altar to find him. When the temple priests found the deity of Banki Behari, they placed Him on the altar again but began closing the curtain at short intervals to keep the deity from getting too attached to any of the visiting devotees. This tradition has continued ever since then.

Not far away, located down a lane, is the Asta-Sakhi Mandir, a lovely eight-sided, dome-topped temple. This temple offers *darshan* of not only Radha-Krishna (Radha-Rasabihariji in this case), but also of eight important *gopis*. They include Rangadevi, Champaklata, Chitra, and Lalita on the left, and Vishakha, Indulekha, Tungavidya, and Sudevi on the right. From this temple you can easily see the old temple of Radha-Madan Mohan to the west.

The Madan Mohan temple, located on a hill near the old river bed of the Yamuna, was established by Sanatana Gosvami. This was one of the first temples erected after Sri Chaitanya's visit to Vrindavan. The deity is said to have been found in the hill by Sri Advaita who gave the deity to a Mathura priest. The priest treated the deity like one of his children and when Sanatana Gosvami saw this he criticized the priest for not following the many rules and regulations for deity worship. Then in a dream Madan Mohan told Sanatana that He had been happy with the priest's spontaneous love, but now He was no longer happy with all these rules that were supposed to be followed. So Sanatana went to see the priest who then gave the deity to Sanatana. At first Sanatana used to keep Madan Mohan in a tree because he had no where else to keep Him. Then one time the deity asked for some salt with the dried bread that Sanatana offered to Him. Sanatana only said, "I am an old man. What can I do? Please accept it the way it is." Just then a rich merchant was taking a boat loaded with salt down the Yamuna. By Krishna's will the boat became stuck in the shallow river. Madan Mohan changed into a cowherd boy who led the merchant to Sanatana. Sanatana could do nothing to help the merchant, so the merchant prayed to Madan Mohan that if his boat became free he would sell his salt and return to use the money to build a nice temple. After praying, the merchant returned to his boat and found that it was no longer stuck. When the merchant sold the salt, he returned to build the temple. So this is how the temple was erected. Later, this was the deity from which Krishnadas Kaviraja got the inspiration to write the *Caitanya-caritamrta*.

Unfortunately, in 1670, due to the threat of fanatic Muslims, the original Radha-Madan Mohan deities were moved to Jaipur, and then again moved to Karauli where a nice temple was built for them. *Pratibhuh* deities were later installed in the Vrindavan temple. You can still see the *bhajan kutir*, or place of worship, of Sanatana Gosvami, along with a well said to have been dug by Krishna Himself for Sanatana's water. While you are here, you can have a drink from the well. Sanatana Gosvami's *samadhi* tomb is on the hillside behind the temple. Walking east along the old river bed we can reach Kaliya Ghat marked by the old Kadamba tree from which Krishna lept into the Yamuna to chastise the multi-headed serpent-demon, Kaliya. This is described in *Srimad-Bhagavatam* as is most of Krishna's Vrindavana pastimes. Farther down the trail is Varaha Ghat where Krishna manifested His form as Varaha for the amusement of His friends.

Varaha Ghat is in the area of Raman Reti on the outskirts of the village of Vrindavan. Raman Reti means cooling sands and is where Krishna and Balarama would come and play amongst the large trees, flowers, chirping birds, and peacocks. Raman Reti is where the ISKCON temple of Sri Sri Krishna-Balarama is located along the road called Bhaktivedanta Swami Marg. This has become a very popular temple amongst pilgrims who visit Vrindavan. You will find the most beautiful deities of Krishna and Balarama on the center altar, with Sri Nityananda and Sri Chaitanya on the left altar, and Sri Sri Radha-Syamasundar on the right. The tamal tree in the courtyard is said to be where the tree was under which Srimati Radharani would wait for Krishna to return from herding the cows. The temple was founded by Srila A. C. Bhaktivedanta Swami Prabhupada, and his lovely *samadhi* is in front of the temple where his body was interred.

Located along the main road from the Raman Reti area or Krishna Balamara Mandir heading toward the downtown area of Vrindavana is the Vrindavana Research Institute. This place has many old manuscripts and along with original leaves with the hand writing of Sanatana, Rupa, and Jiva Gosvamis.

Some of the additional ashramas that you can find in Vrindavana include the Neem Karoli Baba Ashrama, near the main road on the *parikrama* path. His *samadhi* shrine, along with temples to Hanuman, Sita-Ram and Durga are here. The Ananda Mayi Ma Ashrama is the ashrama of the renown woman saint, on the main road. And Jagadguru Dham along Raman Reti Road is the ashrama of Swami Prakashananda Sarasvati, when he's not staying in his Austin, Texas ashrama. He also has places in Barshana, near Vrindavana, called Rangeeli Mahal and Vishwa Kalyan Kendra.

Today, Vrindavana is gaining in popularity. Construction and development is an ongoing thing. More apartments and temples, and guests houses with temples, are always being built. So there are many more temples in Vrindavana that you can easily visit simply by wandering around the town. This is where you cannot easily forget Lord Krishna, and most anything you do will give spiritual progress. But respect for the holy *dham* must be maintained, or offenses committed here can also bring harsh results.

GREATER VRAJAMANDALA

Some other very holy places are located elsewhere in the greater area of Vrajamandala, such as Radha Kund, the bathing place of Radharani and Her most elevated assistants, the *gopis* or cowherd girls. Radha Kund is located on the northern end of Govardhan Hill. Sri Rupa Gosvami explains in verses 9 and 10 of his *Sri Upadesamrita* that out of all the places in Vraja, Radha Kund is superior to them all because it is flooded with the ambrosial nectar of Krishna *prema*, ecstatic love of God. Therefore, those who live here are the most fortunate in the universe. The *Padma Purana* also explains that just as Radharani is most dear to Krishna, Her bathing place of Radha Kund is also dear to Him.

Across from Radha Kund is Shyama Kund, Krishna's bathing place. Krishna dug Shyama Kund when Radharani insisted that He purify Himself by bathing in all the holy rivers after He had killed the Aristasura demon who was in the form of a bull. So rather than going to all the sacred rivers, He simply dug His heel into the earth and called the presiding deities of the various holy rivers of India to merge their waters into the pool. After bathing, He explained to Radharani and the *gopis* that the bull was actually a demon, so they should also take a purifying bath to rid themselves of the sin of siding with a demon. Radharani became upset and decided She could also make a *kund* or lake. Thus, She and the *gopis* broke their bangles and dug a hole, but it remained dry to Krishna's amusement. However, by using water from the nearby Manasi Ganga lake and the waters from the presiding deities of the holy rivers who appeared, Her *kund* also filled up. Thus, these *kunds* are very special to pilgrims who visit. It is said that anyone who bathes here will get the perfection of Krishna *prema*, which is far beyond mere liberation from material existence. It is said that Radha Kund is the liquid form of Radharani's ecstatic love for Krishna. And since Radha Kund is Lord Krishna's favorite bathing place, anyone who bathes in Radha Kund gets the mercy of Lord Krishna and will attain Krishna *prema*, ecstatic love for Lord Krishna. Similarly, Radharani also said that anyone who bathes in Shyama Kund will get Her special favor. Therefore, Radha Kund is difficult to attain.

To recognize the spiritual significance of Radha Kund may not be so easy for neophytes. As I said earlier, in order to perceive the spiritual atmosphere in Vrindavan you have to receive the blessings of the resident devotees and become qualified so that Vrindavan reveals itself to you. An example of this was related to me by a friend. When he visited Radha Kund he met an old *sadhu*, a saintly man who had retired from material life and was now living at Radha Kund. My friend asked the *sadhu* some questions and at first the man hesitantly explained that he did not work or attempt to maintain himself. He simply depended on Krishna and chanted the holy names at Radha Kund. How he got his food was that a small boy would come by and give him some food every day. The man explained that as a person becomes more and more spiritual, he will recognize the eternal atmosphere that pervades Vraja, especially at Radha Kund, and he will not feel the need to take so much care of the body. My friend then asked him if he could actually see the spiritual world or if he had ever seen Krishna at this holy place. The old man said he had not seen Krishna, but sometimes he could here the *gopis* talking with Krishna or discussing amongst themselves how Krishna looked and what He was doing.

My friend then asked the old *sadhu* how it was possible for him to perceive such things? The man then began talking quite readily and convincingly told my friend that Radha Kund was indeed the spiritual world; you simply had to remove your materialistic vision. Then the old man took my friend's hand and pushed it flat to the ground on the banks of the Radha Kund and said, "Just touch this land and you can feel the spiritual nature of it." My friend told me that at that moment a charge went up his arm from the ground and he could actually feel the difference, that this was indeed a spiritual place. But before my friend got the blessings of this sage, he could not really feel the difference. And that is what is necessary. Until you can actually perceive it, all you can do is to try to understand with your mind and imagine how Krishna performed so many pastimes here, and how this place is spiritual. But the actual realization of such things goes much further than that. It is a matter of re-establishing your spiritual identity and connection with the spiritual realm. It is the reawakening of your spiritual consciousness and actually perceiving the subtle nature of spiritual reality.

In the area of Radha Kund as you circumambulate the area, you can find numerous temples and important places. To describe a brief tour around Radha and Shyama Kunds, we first enter the area from the bus stop, and on our way along the road we come to the Radha-Gokulananda temple, which has the *pratibhu* or representational deities that belonged to Visvanatha Chakravarti Thakur. Going farther along, we next come to the Kundesvara Mahadeva temple and the sacred peepul tree. Mahadeva Shiva is one of the guardians of the holy *dham*. Then we soon get our first view of Radha Kund, and pay our respects by bowing our heads toward this form of Radharani. Farther down across from the vegetable market is the lane on the left that goes to the Purana Mandir, which has a lovely set of Radha Krishna deities. These were found by Raghunatha dasa Goswami when he was excavating the *kunds*. Continuing on, we come to the road that leads to the left. This can take us to the Gaudiya Math temple with the beautiful deities of Radha-Kunjabihari. Farther on we can also reach the Shiva Khor or *kund*, and the Ramesvaram Shiva temple.

Back to the main *parikrama* path, we can next see the Radha Kanta temple right at the corner of Radha Kund. Across from that on the left of the road is the Sri Gopal temple. Then just down the street on the right is the Radha-Gopinatha temple, which also has at the far end the *samadhi* tomb of Raghunatha dasa Gosvami. Exiting through the door on the south side, we are now along the water of Radha Kund where many people take a holy bath. This is near the private bathing place of Jahnavi, the wife of Lord Nityananda when She lived here at Radha Kund nearly 500 years ago, which you can see there.

Going farther along the main *parikrama* road, we next see a circular platform, which is a *rasa-sthali* where dances are performed at times. There we take a right turn. Going down the path we can find the *bhajan kutir* of Gopal Bhatta. Around the corner is also

Krishna dasa Kaviraja's *bhajan kutir*, the small living quarters where he wrote the *Caitanya-caritamrta* and several other important spiritual books. Then there is Raghunatha dasa's *bhajan kutir* and the cremation place of these Swamis used when the Muslims were coming into the area. Rather than taking the chance of having their bodies disturbed in case the Muslims would dig them up, they cremated them instead. On a side road there is the *bhajan kutir* of Bhaktivinoda Thakur where he and Bhaktisiddhanta would stay when visiting the area. Farther along the *parikrama* road we next find Lalita Kund on the left, across from which is Jiva Gosvami's *bhajan kutir*. Next along the road and down a lane on the right toward Shyama Kund there is the place of Madhavendra Puri's sitting place, and around the curve we come to Lord Chaitanya's sitting place. This used to be like a little hut or *bhajan kutir*, but now they have expanded it and put a roof over it. After that we continue our walk down the lane and other temples can also be found, such as Asta Sakhi Mandir, Nitai Gauranga Sitanatha Mandir, Manipur Maharaja Mandir, Radha Gopinatha Mandir, a Gaura Nitai Mandir, Radha Govindaji Mandir, and other temples that are located around the *kunds*. Then we go to the *sangam* or meeting place of the two *kunds* where many people take a holy bath or do some special worship or *pujas* to the *kunds*, since they are non-different from Radha and Krishna. If it is not crowded and somewhat peaceful, it is also nice to sit and meditate or chant *japa* for a time, contemplating our good fortune to be here. Then returning to the path and going through some shops we pass a deity of Hanuman and pray that he relieves us of whatever offenses we may have committed while visiting, and then we return to where we started.

These temples and holy places can be located with the help of local residents, or guides may present themselves to show you around or to help you do some rituals or *puja* to Radha Kund and Shyama Kund. They are called Tirtha gurus, or the local pandits who know all about these special *tirthas*, holy places. This is alright, but be sure to establish a price before you accept their service. Presently you can also get guidebooks of these specific areas. You can find them at the Krishna-Balarama Mandir, or in a few of the shops in Loi Bazaar at Vrindavana. These will have photographs, maps to show you around, and more detailed stories of the pastimes that have taken place here. You must definitely visit these places if you are in the area.

One word of caution: this is certainly a holy place but when there are crowds of people here, do not take any valuables with you or keep wallets in your pockets, especially if you will bathe in the water. It is not uncommon that such things end up missing. And the road between Vrindavana and Radha Kund is closed at night because of thieves and dacoits. So if you plan on visiting Radha Kund, do not wait too late at night or you may up having to spend the night or taking a longer route through Govardhana to Mathura to get back to Vrindavana.

Next we see Govardhana Hill which is the hill Krishna lifted with the little finger of His left hand for seven days to shelter the residents of Vraja from the torrential rains that Indra had sent. Indra sent heavy rains when he became angry after seeing the residents of Vraja worshiping Govardhan Hill instead of him, according to the directions of Lord Krishna. Only later did Indra realize his great mistake. The hill is also considered a manifestation of Krishna Himself, just as the hill at Barsana is a manifestation of Brahma, the hill at Nandagram is Shiva, and Charanpari is Sesha. Therefore, many pilgrims circumambulate Govardhana as an act of worship, a route that is about 15 miles long and passes near many other holy spots along the way. I will describe a few of the main places along the route.

Usually devotees start their *parikrama* or circumambulation of Govardhana near Kusum Sarovara. This is a great swimming spot and where Radharani used to pick flowers before meeting Krishna here. It now has beautiful *chatris*, or small temple enclosures, at one end, which has beautifully painted ceilings. These have many beautiful illustrations of the pastimes of Radha and Krishna. The story of how these came to be built is quite interesting. When the Moghuls ruled over Delhi, the King of Bharatpur, Suraja Mal, attacked them, but lost his life doing so. However, his son, Jawarchar Singh, decided to attack and vowed that if he won, he would return and develop Kusum Sarovara in glorification of Lord Krishna. So he assembled an army and attacked Delhi and defeated the Muslim tyrants. Therefore, he returned and built the temples around Kusum Sarovara with his newly victorious wealth.

Nearby Kusum Sarovara in a separate compound across from it is a temple to Uddhava with a deity dating back to the days of Krishna. Across the road and down the lane is also a temple and *kund* of Narada Muni where he wrote the *Narada Bhakti Sutras*. There is a little image of Narada Muni in the small temple there.

From here we walk down the road until we reach Manasi Ganga, which is a lake where Krishna made the Ganges appear, and which has a small township around it. There are several little holy spots to see here. So as we make our way around it we can see the places such as the Makharvinda Mandira which stands out along the waterfront on the southeastern corner of the lake. The Chakra Tirtha area on the eastern side of Manasi Ganga has the Shiva temple called the Chakalesvara Mahadeva Mandir. Across from that is one of the *bhajana kutirs* of Sanatana Gosvami, and a small Mahaprabhu Mandir. On the western side of the Manasi Ganga you can see the Manasi Devi Mandira and the Harideva Mandira is located up a few lanes. Your local guidebooks or maps, or traveling with someone who knows the area, will make finding these places easier. Or also asking the local people how to reach them as you walk along will also work. I've been to these places several times, but the first times I would go with someone else to show me the way.

Walking farther down the road, or through the small alleys from the Harideva Mandir, we next come to Govardhana town. We make our way to the Dana Gatt Giriraja Mandira, the temple where we pay our respects to Govardhana Hill because this is where He starts to actually become visible. The hill itself has been shrinking for hundreds of years, and the first part of the *parikrama* we really cannot see Him because of being underground. But now the hill becomes visible and we can see the rocky formation. As we start this part of the *parikrama*, there is also a place that shows Radharani's footprint. As we approach the southern end of Govardhana Hill, we arrive at Govinda Kund. This is a good place to rest for a few minutes. This *kund* was created when Indra, the king of heaven, performed the bathing ceremony for Lord Krishna. After Indra realized his mistake for harassing the people of Vraja with heavy rains that he had sent, he returned and performed a bathing ceremony for Lord Krishna in order to try and pacify the Lord and obtain His forgiveness. The accumulated water from the bathing ceremony gathered to form this *kund*.

As we start again, there are other smaller temples and little *kunds* and forests along the way that we walk through. A person could actually spend several days just going to each holy place and hearing or reading about the pastimes that took place there. Finally, we reach Naval and Apsara Kundas, which are at the far end of Govardhana Hill and near the half-way point when we start heading back to the north along the other side of Govardhana Hill. Therein we continue through the small forests and past more small and occasional temples and *kunds*. Along this part of the route there is also a place called Aparadha Kund, which is a small pond just off the path where Indra atoned for his offense to Lord Krishna for having sent the torrential rains over Vraja. As we keep going, if we are with a group, someone will likely be guiding us to the most important places and will explain the meaning and history behind each one. Of course, we cannot slow down too much if we expect to get back in time to catch our return ride to Vrindavana.

Finally we reach Uddhava Kund, and stop for a few minutes at the small temple here. The temple has Radha Krishna deities, believed to have been originally installed by Vrajanabha, Krishna's grandson. A new set of Radha-Krishna deities has also been installed now which is famous for being formed out of one piece of marble. Behind the temple is the Uddhava Kund, the water of which is said to have originally come from the tears of Krishna's queens when they were consoled by Uddhava at this place.

Then we move on past a new Mahaprabhu temple, and on around Radha Kund and Syama Kund again. After going around them we head west back to Kusuma Sarovara. This completes our *parikrama* walk around the hill of Govardhana. Doing this provides immense spiritual purification and merit for our devotional advancement, not to mention a real adventure into the spiritual land of Vraja.

Again, many of these places around Govardhana can be found with the help of special guidebooks and maps. But the easiest way is to come to Vrindavana for a visit during the month of Kartika (Oct-Nov). This is the time when devotees celebrate Govardhana Puja, or the worship and respect of the sacred hill. Then you can easily go on one of the Govardhana *parikramas* when groups of devotees gather in buses to go to Govardhana Hill early in the morning and walk around the hill and stop to visit these particular holy places along the way.

North of Govardhana is Barsana, 30 miles from Mathura, the town where Radharani grew up and the capital city of her father, King Vrishabanu. Once we arrive, we walk up the steps to get to the main temple of the town that looks like a fortress on the hilltop which can be seen from miles away. This is the Shriji or Larily Mandir, a local name for Radha. It is very ornate and the walls of the interior are covered with paintings of Krishna's pastimes. Lovely Sri Sri Radha-Krishna deities are on the altar. A short walk away is the Radha-Kushal Behari Mandir, another majestic temple on a different peak of the hill, with Rajasthani style architecture. A little farther away on another peak is the Mayur Kuti temple that has a painting of Krishna dancing as a peacock for Radha's pleasure. The painting was done by a blind saint who had the divine vision of the pastime as long as he was working on the painting. On another of the hill's peaks is Man Kutir, a temple marking where Krishna made Radharani angry for fun, but She left Him to lament and look for Her. Then the other *gopis* brought Them back together, much to their celebration. The four peaks of this hill represent the four heads of Brahma, and the hill is considered an expansion or incarnation of Lord Brahma.

A few miles from Barsana is Nandagram, another place where Krishna performed many childhood pastimes described in the *Bhagavatam*. On top of the hill is the main temple that has deities of Krishna, Balarama, Nanda Maharaja (Krishna's father), Mother Yashoda, Srimati Radharani, and two of Krishna's friends. There is also a Shiva *lingam* in a small shrine across from the temple called Nandisvara, said to have been installed by Vajranabha many hundreds of years ago. It is considered that this hill is an incarnation of Lord Shiva. From the top of the walls that surround the temple we can get good views of the area, and someone who is familiar with it can point out other nearby places connected with Krishna's pastimes that we may want to visit.

As I've said, this is by no means a complete description of Vrajamandala and the holy places within it, such as Vrindavana, Mathura, Govardhana, etc. And there are too many to mention for this discourse which covers all of India. However, there are already full length tour books dedicated to doing this, which I recommend you to purchase. The significance and the history of Vrindavana is a full topic by itself. Nonetheless, this description of Vraja will certainly give you a start for finding the important places to see if you're ever fortunate enough to visit. It is explained that all the holy places of India are manifest in some way in Vrajamandala. Thus, Rupa Gosvami writes that anyone who leaves Vraja to go to other holy places achieves nothing but the trouble it takes to get there. Nonetheless, I will be describing many of the holy places throughout India anyway.

AGRA

As we continue our way around India, just south of Vrindavana or Mathura is Agra, only an hour bus ride away. We can either visit this place as a day trip, or stop for a night as we make our way to other destinations. Decent hotels are not far from the bus station. Agra is not really a pilgrimage center, but many people flock here to see the Taj Mahal. The general story is that the Taj Mahal was built between 1632 and 1653 by Shah Jahan as a memorial to his wife Mumtaz Mahal. It is said that as many as 20,000 craftsmen helped work on the building. The tombs of Mumtaz and Shah Jahan are in a lower chamber, while the upper chamber has the representational tombs. Years ago you could also go into the lower chamber, but they have since blocked it off from visitors. The Taj Mahal is an impressive building and many come to see it on the full moon nights. The quietest time to see it is around sunrise. After 9 AM it starts filling up with many tourists, all wanting to stand in the same place to take the same photograph or to see the same thing from the same angle. In the summer, however, as can be expected, there are far fewer tourists that visit since foreigners tend to stay away from the hot season.

However, there is also a different story to the Taj Mahal that many people do not know. There is evidence that shows the Taj Mahal is actually much older than Shah Jahan, the person who has been given credit for building it, and is, in fact, not Muslim but a Vedic contribution to the world. As explained in *World Vedic Heritage* (p. 836) by Mr. P. N. Oak:

"In a paper that professor Mills read in Chicago on November 4, 1983 at the 17th Annual Meeting of Middle East Studies Association of North America, based on his preliminary research endeavors involving an archaeometric analysis of the so-called Muslim buildings in ancient Spain, Mr. Mills observed, 'Two specific potentially fertile monuments for the application of archaeometry are the Taj Mahal and the (so-called) Mosque of Cordoba. Neither face Mecca. The (so-called) mosque that is part of the Taj complex faces due west whereas Mecca from Agra is 14 degrees 55 minutes south of west. It is oriented to the cardinal directions as would be typical of a Hindu temple in India.'

"Prof. Mills then describes how a wood sample he took from the rear, river-level doorway of the Taj and had it tested for carbon-14 dating by Dr. Evan Williams, Director of the Brooklyn College Radiocarbon Laboratory, provided that even the door was pre-Shahjahan. Similar samples taken from Fatehpur Sikri also proved that that township, usually attributed to the 3rd-generation Mogul emperor Akbar, is also much more ancient."

The Taj Mahal gets its name from its original name, Tej-Mahalaya, which is said to have been a resplendent shrine housing a Shiva *linga*. So before it was converted into a Muslim mosque, it very well could have been a Hindu palace, part of which was a Shiva temple.

Further obvious evidence, most of which any tourist can witness for themselves, is explained in *Some Blunders of Indian Historical Research* on pages 304-5: "Its octagonal shape and the cupolas and four towers at the plinth corners are all Hindu features. [You can still see many temples in India, such as those at Khajarao, that are built on a platform with small temples or towers at each corner.] Havell, the English architect, has all along stressed that the Taj is entirely a Hindu structure in design and execution. Within its three floors—basement, ground and first floors—the marble structure has a nearly 25-room palace suite. The four towers used to sport multi-colored lights. The Taj precincts are a huge building complex encompassing over three hundred rooms. The locality was known as Jaisinghpur. It was surrounded by defensive structures like moats, hillocks and massive walls. Chronicles give the indication that Babar, the founder of the Moghul dynasty and his grandson Akbar, used to sojourn in the Taj. Babar even died there. But being a new-comer to India he had expressed a wish that he be buried in his native country. But for that fortuitous happening the Taj would have been known to posterity as Babar's (grand) mausoleum instead of Mumtaz's since all Muslim royal personages have been buried in conquered and occupied Hindu buildings.

"The ornate trellis work, entirely in the Hindu style, now encloses two tombs believed to be those of Mumtaz and Shahjahan. The network was stuffed with rare gems. Traditional accounts tell us that this enclosure had silver doors and gold railings to boot. Even Shahjahan's and Mumtaz's palaces never boasted of such fabulous fixtures when the pair was alive and kicking from the imperial throne. How come then that when Mumtaz died (1630) all this wealth descended on earth all of a sudden. Far from that, this expensive and resplendent enclosure was made to house the dazzling Peacock Throne. That throne, wrongly credited to Shahjahan, came into his possession when he dispossessed the Taj Mahal's last Rajput owner, Jai Singh, of this fabulous ancient Hindu palace. So far from spending anything on the Taj Mahal, Shahjahan utilized the somber occasion of Mumtaz's death to enrich himself with Jai Singh's wealth."

Other evidence that the Taj Mahal was a Hindu temple is that once a Mr. P. N. Sharma, who lives in the Safdarjang Development Area in New Delhi, had a peek inside a chamber underneath the marble basement of the Taj Mahal. With the help of a light he was able to see through a hole in the crumbling brick work with which Shah Jahan or Cunningham of the Archeological Survey of India sealed the chamber. This was in 1932 when he saw in the chamber a number of Vedic deities that had obviously been secretly dumped after having been dislodged from the various parts of the Taj Mahal.

This is not unlike the case in which an employee of the Archeological Survey of India, named E. R. Sathe, who wrote to Mr. Oak describing that around 1959 S. R. Rao, who was in charge of the Taj Mahal, noticed a big crack in a wall. To repair the wall, a number of bricks had to be removed. When this happened, out popped several images of Vedic goddesses known as Ashta Vasu. Rao referred the matter to Delhi to know whether he should probe other walls for other deities. The education minister, Abul Kalam Azad, and Prime Minister Jawaharlal Nehru simply told him to shut up the walls as well as his mouth. This shows that though Vedic images and Sanskrit inscriptions have been found from time to time at the Taj Mahal, everyone prefers to maintain silence rather than finding out the real truth of the matter.

Other points to consider include that there is a doorway in the Taj Mahal premises that is kept locked by the Archeological Survey of India. This door leads down a stately staircase to a massive, octagonal, seven-storied water well. The well is enclosed in the tower near the peripheral wall to the left as you stand below the marble platform facing the Taj. Surely for a mausoleum there is no such need for so much water. There are also several dry latrines in the well-house that shows many people once lived there. This is all kept from the eyes of visitors and shows that the building was equipped for being more than a simple mausoleum, and more like a palatial Hindu palace and temple.

A great proof of Shah Jahan's taking this building from another rather than building it himself is found in Shah Jahan's own official chronicle, *Badshahnama* (Bibliotheca Indica series of the Asiatic Society of Bengal publication, page 403, Volume I). Therein he admits that the Taj Mahal is Raja Mansingh's mansion which, when taken over for Mumtaz's burial, was set amidst a majestic lush garden. This is an obvious proof that the current history of the Taj Mahal as we know it, that it was built by Shah Jahan for his wife, is completely false.

In a letter written by prince Aurangzeb in 1652 to his ruling father, emperor Shah Jahan, Aurangzeb reports doing an urgent repair to the cracked dome and leaking seven-storeyed complex. This is a blatant contradiction in the modern historical theory, especially considering how the archeological sign at the Taj asserts that it was first built in 1653.

Shah Jahan left no records, receipts, building plans, or expense accounts regarding the building of the Taj Mahal. The Taj itself is built in the manner of a palatial palace, not as a tomb. Thus, it had to have been first a palace converted into a tomb.

Had Shah Jahan really conceived and built the Taj himself, he never would have had to remind his paid court chronicler not to forget describing its construction in the official chronicle. Such an event would not have been forgotten by anyone. Furthermore, if a stupendous monument like the Taj is built for a consort, there certainly would be a burial date that would not go unrecorded. However, the burial date is not only unrecorded, but the date of the time in which Mumtaz must have been buried in the Taj varies from six months to nine years of her death. Mumtaz being a commoner never deserved a palatial monument. Even historically there is no record of any special out-of-the-ordinary attachment or romance between Shah Jahan and Mumtaz during their life.

Furthermore, Shah Jahan was no patron of the arts. The decorative patterns that cover the Taj are not only entirely of Indian flora but also of sacred Hindu motifs like the lotus. Such "infidel" characteristics, according to Muslim beliefs, would never allow any peace for the departed souls lying buried underneath.

Cunningham also played his part in destroying colossal Vedic evidence of its origin by destroying or displacing deities and Sanskrit inscriptions that once adorned the Taj. For example, a massive black basalt Stone with Sanskrit inscriptions was found at the Taj. It testified to the erection of the Taj as a "peerless, crystal-white Shiva temple," but was misleadingly and deliberately branded by Cunningham as the Bateswar inscription. It was then taken away from the Taj to the attic of the distant Lucknow Museum, as can be inferred from noting Cunningham's own not-so-cunning assistant, Carlleyle. Carlleyle's report on Agra (pp. 124-5, Volume of 1871-72 C.E.) records, "the great square black basaltic pillar which was the base and capital of another similar pillar once stood in the garden of the Taj Mahal."

It is also apparent from Carlleyle that the original ancient Vedic documents and drawings of the Taj Mahal did exist. They passed into Moghul possession from Jai Singh when Shah Jahan suddenly took the Taj Mahal with all its fabulous wealth for himself. Later, with the expulsion of the last Moghul, the Taj Mahal documents passed into the hands of the British Viceroy in India in 1858. Cunningham, having been chosen by the British administration to head the Archeological Society, took charge of the Taj Mahal papers along with those of many other monuments throughout India. He deliberately burned them all so he could have an open field to ascribe all historic towns, cities, towers, bridges, forts, canals, and water tanks to Muslim authorship. More evidence of the way Cunningham credited the building of the Taj Mahal is found in a well-documented booklet recently published by an intrepid and courageous Hindu scholar, Mr. V. S. Godbole who resides in Bedford, England.

Another point that disclaims the idea that the Taj Mahal and buildings like it are of Islamic origin is that the arch and dome in architecture was pre-Muslim and Vedic in design. This is described in *Encyclopedia Britannica*, (14th edition, Vol. 15, page 651). It is related that, "When in a victorious advance the Arab followers of Mohammed subdued the old civilizations of Asia and Africa, Persians, Turks, Byzantines, Syrians and Copts, their own civilization was not yet much developed and in many respects dependent on those of neighboring countries. The architecture of the Mohammedan world, therefore, was created by members of those overthrown peoples who were clients of the Arabs and had themselves turned Muslim."

Furthermore, in Volume 12, page 221, it continues to describe, "As both arch and dome were known to the Sumerian builders in the 4th millennium B.C., there is nothing surprising in the fact that both appear in India long before the Mohammedan period and in fact from the Mauryan period onwards." Even as late as 1910 the *Encyclopedia Britannica* said that the Taj Mahal was a pre-existing building before Shah Jahan came along. So at best, maybe he did some renovations on it but not much else.

Another point is that Sumeru and Mount Meru are names that occur frequently in ancient Vedic literature. By understanding that Sumerians were Vedic people, it becomes obvious that the architecture that is most noted as Islamic in India actually contains elements in design that were known long before Islam ever came to India. They were Vedic in design, and used elements described in the Vedic *Shilpashastras*. Furthermore, the methods of construction were unknown to the invading Muslims. Thus, they were essentially incapable of building such structures anyway. So there is no way that such buildings can be given credit to the Islamic invaders.

The other most prominent building in Agra is the Red Fort, the twin of the Red Fort in Delhi. This is also an interesting combination of buildings. However, it also bares evidence that it was built before the Muslims arrived in India. In fact, the name *Agra* itself is a Sanskrit name that indicates this was a flourishing Rajput city before the Muslims invaded. Thus, it had to have a fort. The fort itself is built in typical Rajput style. The architecture of the main halls bears a close resemblance to the main halls and interior apartments in the Amber Fort near Jaipur. Even its gates bear Hindu names, such as Amar Singh Gate and Hathipol Gate. On the archways are also stone flower emblems, which display the usual ornamental style of Vedic temple *mandaps* (halls). Elephant images exist at the gateways of both forts. This is hardly what you will find on Muslim architecture since Islam frowns on such images. There is also no documented evidence that it was built by any Moghul emperor.

Other interesting buildings in Agra include the Itmad-ud-daulah, another tomb, though smaller than the Taj, said to have been built between 1622 and 1628. Nowadays it is a memorial for Mirza Ghiyas Beg and several family members. Guides are willing to take you around the place but some of them have such poor English you can hardly understand a word. The walls are covered with similar inlay work as the Taj and is considered a prototype.

Nine kilometers north of Agra is Akbar's Mausoleum in the middle of a huge garden at Sikandra. It is a combination of Hindu and Muslim styles of architecture and has four gates that lead to it. One gate is Muslim in design, one is Hindu, one Christian, and one is a mixture that is supposed to show Akbar's respect for all religions. It is said that although Akbar had a Muslim background, he had a Hindu guru for a teacher and renounced hunting and tried to adopt a vegetarian diet because of the influence. However, before this time he had displayed much favoritism toward his own religion at the expense of others.

Ten kilometers north of Agra is the Dayal Bagh temple which belongs to the Radha Soami religious sect. Their practices and philosophy are very similar to the path of bhakti-yoga. The temple has been under construction but much of it is finished. If you want to see some of the most beautiful carved marble and inlay work in India, this is the place to see it. It might not be as big as the Taj, but the quality of work is the best I have seen anywhere.

FATEHPUR SIKRI

One place that some people say you should not miss in your visit to Agra is the deserted but well preserved city of Fatehpur Sikri, 20 miles west of Agra, said to have been built between 1570 and 1586. If you like to wander around exploring old buildings and architecture without many restrictions, this is a place where you can let yourself go. The place is divided into two sections. There is the mosque, and there is the residential section. In the mosque, which you enter through the huge gateway on the south side called the Buland Darwaza, or Gate of Victory, buildings include the Dargah Mosque, that is supposed to be a replica of the one in Mecca, and the tomb of Saint Shaikh Salam Chisti, which is visited by many women who want children. This is because the saint foretold the birth of Emperor Akbar's son when the emperor, without heir, went to see the saint in hopes of getting his blessing to have a son. In the back are the tombs of Islam Khan, Shaik Hajji Husain, and other family members. As you leave the mosque on the left side of the main gate you'll find an inscription that refers to the teachings of Christ. It states that the world is a bridge, pass over it but build no residence on it. He who hopes for an hour may hope for eternity. The world endures but an hour. Spend it in prayer, for the rest is unseen.

The story is that the city came into existence when Akbar decided to move his capital to Sikri. Akbar spent 12 years building the city and put up a palace for each of his three queens. One was Muslim, one was Hindu, and the other was Christian. Akbar was known for being liberal towards all religions and even had a Hindu guru, at least in his later years. The residential section also included a hall of public audience, a treasury house, a huge sleeping chamber, a swimming pool, a big bath house, a stable for 200 horses, a large outdoor pachisi game board played with slave girls dressed in different colored outfits as the pieces, and a harem of over 600 concubines with a hospital to handle all the pregnant women. The buildings are all interesting and quite ornate. But only four years after the city was completed the water went salty, or may have been poisoned, and Akbar had little choice but to abandon the place.

However, once again there is evidence that Fatehpur Sikri was built many years before Akbar. For example, Muslim chronicles pertaining to the reigns of rulers preceding Akbar list the city as Fathpore, or Sikri, or even Fathpore Sikri. The book titled *Akbar* by Justice J. M. Shelat (published by The Bharatiya Vidya Bhavan, Bombay) carries a painting on page 82 captioned "Humayun's troops entering Fathpore." Humayun was Akbar's father. So how could Akbar build Fatehpur Sikri before his father's time?

Akbar lived in the township but it had already been attacked and damaged by the battle between Rana Sanga and Babar, Akbar's grandfather. Babar's troops were killing innocent civilians and ravaging the county-side, forcing Rana Sanga out of the city to do battle. This is also when the water supply of Anup Lake was poisoned. Thus, Fatehpur Sikri had been conquered by Babar two generations before Akbar.

The typical history of this place is that Jala-ud-Din Akbar began building this town in 1571 and completed it in 1585. It is often said, and any tourist will hear this story, that Akbar left the city several years after completing the construction because the water supply went bad. However, the water supply already had been poisoned before that. The gaping holes in the surrounding walls are proof of the battle and attack by Babar's troops. The name of the lake itself, Anup, is Sanskrit which also indicates that it was built by Rajputs in pre-Muslim times. The lake being old and neglected, finally burst in 1583 which made Akbar permanently leave Fatehpur Sikri. If it had been newly constructed as a water-reservoir, it should not have burst.

Further evidence is that an Englishman, Ralph Fitch, visited Fatehpur Sikri in September of 1583. In his notes he considered the city to be very old, comparing it to ancient Agra. Therefore, it was not a new township as Muslim chronicles try to indicate. Even the Muslim chronicles are not in agreement with the start of the city's construction, mentioning dates from 1564, 1569, 1570, or even 1571. The date of 1583 is recorded as when the city was completed. However, why would Akbar have left only a few years later in 1585 if the city was in good shape. He should have stayed and simply made a few repairs. But no, he left because he did not have the skilled men who knew such construction repair.

Furthermore, there is not one piece of paper that provides any evidence that this city was built, commissioned, or designed. Nor are there any to show that materials were ordered or transported, or that any laborers were paid in order to build this city. Contemporary Jesuits at Akbar's court have recorded that not one stone-cutter's chisel was ever heard or any building materials ever seen during the time when the city was supposed to have been built. Therefore, either the city had already been built years ago, or it was constructed overnight. And the idea that such a city could be built overnight without any building supplies scattered about, or any records of construction, is typical of the sentimental nonsense used to manipulate historical truths.

The township's intricately ornamental workmanship is in the traditional Rajput style. The two huge Rajput style stone elephants flanking the Hathpol gate bear the marks of Muslim defacing since their heads have been chiseled away. The elephant has always been a symbol of royal and divine might in Hindu iconography. The so-called tomb of Salim Chisti within Fatehpur Sikri is actually an ancient Hindu temple that was for the family deity. It shows the delicate and ornate stone work, as well as an ambulatory passage for circling the deity, common in all Vedic temples, which would serve no function in a tomb. On page 321 of *Akbar the Great Mogul* by Vincent Smith, he says, "It is surprising to find unmistakable Hindu features in the architecture of the tomb of a most zealous

Musalman saint, but the whole structure suggests Hindu feeling, and nobody can mistake the Hindu origin of the columns and struts of the porch."

The one verandah that is designated as a mosque has many Hindu features in its intricate workmanship, as noted by the western historian E. W. Smith. Even in front of the Panch Mahal building is a huge Chaupat (Backgammon) board on the paved redstone floor. The tourists are told that Akbar would play the game using girls as the life-size game pieces. However, this is an exclusively Hindu game of ancient origin, very popular in mediaeval times, which is not played in Muslim households.

Another point is that the name "Sikri" is of Sanskrit origin, which comes from the Sanskrit word *Sakata*, which means sand. From this a native principality in Rajasthan is known as Sikar. The diminutive feminine form of Sikar is "Sikri." This lends credence that the original founders of Fatehpur Sikri were a clan of Rajputs, probably from Sikar. The suffix "Pur" also indicates a township in Sanskrit. The prefix "Fateh" signifies a captured township. Thus, the name makes it obvious that it was an earlier Rajput township captured by invading Muslims.

In any case, if you visit Fatehpur Sikri you may want to hire one of the local guides to take you around to better understand all the buildings and their purpose, according to the typical tourist stories of the place. But the guides always try to sell you things when they show you the shops near the mosque, so be prepared for their hard sell techniques. However, the prices on the marble items are not too bad compared to prices on similar things sold in Agra. You can go to Fatehpur Sikri quite easily by waiting for a bus at the Idgah bus station, but getting back to Agra may be another matter. There is supposed to be a bus every hour between the two towns, but it doesn't quite work that well. The buses are usually overloaded and the people who are waiting to get back to Agra swarm the bus when it pulls in. Tactics to get a seat can get pretty extreme. Aside from the normal pushing and shoving, one thing I learned was to toss something like a water bottle through the window onto a seat to reserve it. Then when you get on the bus you can say it's your bottle and your seat. Or, if it comes to the worst, give a lift to a small Indian boy so he can climb through the window into the bus as people are getting off. Then he can save you a seat as everyone else gets on, for a few rupees of course. Other people just climb on top of the bus for the hour ride back to Agra.

GWALIOR

Gwalior is a city of around 850,000 south of Agra. This will be another overnight stop in which we will arrive in early afternoon from Agra, spend a few hours seeing what interests us, and then head out again the next morning. What we want to visit is Gwalior's unused fort that is enclosed by a massive wall and sits on a hilltop that is almost two miles long and rises 330 feet overlooking the town. Though it is not a place of pilgrimage, a paragraph describing it is not unnecessary. The best way to start your tour of the fort is by walking up the southwest road which passes a number of impressive Jain sculptures along the cliffs of the ravine that were carved in the 1400's. The biggest of them is image number 20 of Adinatha, which stands 17 meters tall. As we wander around the fort, some of the things we will see are the 9th century Teli-ka-Mandir, a tall Hindu temple that rises 75 feet high and is covered with carvings, and has an unusual design for a temple. There is also the Suraj Kund, a lake that cured Suraj Sen of leprosy after the hermit Gwalipa made Suraj drink from it. The Sasbahu temples are along the east wall, dating back to the ninth century. The larger one was once a Vishnu temple and the interior is especially interesting with pillars and walls covered with carvings. Other old buildings can be found, but the Man Singh palace, or Man Mandir, built from 1486 to 1516, is still in fairly good condition. It has four storeys, two above and two below ground. It has a wide variety of roofs, balconies, ornamental friezes, paintings, and rooms that make it a fascinating place. As you walk through the archway toward the northeast entrance to the fort, you'll hear the many voices and sounds of the town below. At first I thought there was a large crowd of people in the palace, but then I realized what it was when I came to the wall overlooking the city. There are some good views from up here. On the northeast side of the fort are other Jain and Hindu sculptures, but they are not as impressive as what we find at the other entrance. At the base of the hill there is the Gujari Mahal that has a museum with a good collection of Jain and Hindu sculptures dating from the first century B.C.E. to the 11th century C.E., but closed on Mondays.

JHANSI TO ORCHHA

A short bus ride south of Gwalior is Jhansi, and from Jhansi we take a bus or a tempo to go a short distance to the small and remote village of Orchha. Orchha is not really a holy place, but some people do stop here for a visit and there are some impressive temples and palaces that you can see. It is quiet and peaceful, reached through lovely forests and gentle hills. It is also 170 kilometers from Khajurao, which will be our next place of interest. So we can stop here for a short visit, or merely take a look at it as a day trip from Jhansi if we want.

Orchha was built during the 16th and 17th centuries by the Bundela rulers of the area. Visiting Orchha is like stepping back into time. Little modernization has occurred. The Bundela Rajput chieftain, Raja Rudra Pratap (1501-31), chose this site as his capital as it was situated on an island of rock along a bend in the Betwa River and elevated above the surrounding area. He built a wall around the existing settlement and his successor Raja Bharti Chand completed the city walls and citadel, as well as the first of three palaces. Rulers that followed also added to Orchha to make it a prosperous city.

The first of the three palaces is the Ramji Mandir. It has a central rectangular courtyard with apartments sitting on receding platforms. Blue tiles glitter on the outer walls. The Raj Mandir is the second palace built between 1554 and 1591 by Madhukar Shah, who was deeply religious. Its plain exterior is topped by the *chhatris*, the umbrella-like cenotaphs. This gives way to the royal chambers where you find exquisite murals from the Vedic legends on the walls and ceilings. The attendant may have to unlock some of the rooms for you.

The Jehangir Mahal is the third and most imposing of the three palaces. It was built by Raja Bir Singh Ji Deo. It is 70 square meters with a smaller interior courtyard. This has a central fountain surrounded by apartments and terraces in three storeys. You will see hanging balconies along the exterior walls topped with delicate *chhatris*, which offer good views over the countryside. Windows and terraces overlook the Betwa River. The interior displays excellent examples of Bundela painting.

The fort also has numerous shrines and monuments. The Rai Praveen Mahal is a brick palace two storeys tall, built by Raja Indramani (who ruled in 1672-76) for a beautiful musician courtesan. The Ram Raja temple, which is still a functioning temple, was originally a palace turned into a temple. After Madhukar Shah had a dream of Lord Rama, he brought a deity of Rama from the holy place of Ayodhya to his capital and placed it in this palace while the Chaturbhuj temple was being built. However, the deity was impossible to move once it was installed, so Madhukar Shah left the deity there, recalling the edict from the deity in the dream that He should remain where He was first installed. Thus, the palace, with its soaring spires and ornate architecture, became a temple.

The Chaturbhuj temple was also built by Madhukar Shah for his queen Kunwari. It has delicate lotus motifs and religious emblems, with a tall spire rising up over the sanctum.

The Lakshmi Narayana temple is reached by a stone path from the Ram Raja temple. It has an impressive fort-like structure, and its interiors show beautiful Bundela murals and wall paintings.

A few other places worth visiting includes the Phool Bagh garden complex, with a central row of unused fountains with an eight-pillared palace pavilion. An underground apartment was used as a summer retreat for the kings. The Shahid Smarak is a memorial that honors the freedom fighter Chandrashekar Azad who lived here in 1926-27. This is now a library and museum. The Sunder Mahal is also a small palace but mostly in ruins. It belonged to the grandson of Bir Singh Deo, Dhurbjan, who converted to Islam after having married a Muslim girl and spent the latter part of his life in prayer. This is now a place of pilgrimage for Muslims. The Siddha Baba ka Sthan, Jugal Kishore Mandir, and the Janaki Mandir are also noteworthy temples to see.

There are a few decent hotels in this town, and if it is open, you can even stay in the Hotel Sheesh Mahal, which is a wing of the Jehangir Mahal Palace.

KHAJURAHO (or KHAJURAO)

From Jhansi we can get a direct bus to Khajuraho. Along the way the bus makes many short stops at little towns that are so small they are not even on the map. And at most towns, vendors will pull their carts along the side of the bus to sell fruits, sweets, or other snacks. Sometimes little children will come up to the windows asking for rupees, or older children will walk through the bus with a tray of grapes or something else to sell. And, of course, there is always the tea vendor carrying a pot of tea and some cups, yelling in the most abrasive voice, "Chai, chai." Sometimes they keep walking through the bus until you're almost ready to tell them, "Alright, already, nobody wants any, so get out of here." But soon the bus is rolling again and you can settle back to watch the scenery.

When we get to Khajuraho, we are again greeted by men who want you to see their hotel. There was even one little boy who asked me if I wanted to stay in his father's house. He assured me it was very clean and for a very low price I could stay and his father would cook my meals, too. I opted for a hotel closer to the center of town.

Khajuraho is a very small village but is world famous for its wonderful temples. Lots of tourists come through this town even though it is out of the way and reached only by bus, plane, or taxi. Yes, it does have an airport because of the number of tourists. One evening I watched the skies and counted five airplanes that landed and took off from the airport, all within a half-hour. And as you wander around the town and temples, you will see not only Indian but also Western tourists from such places as Britain, France, Germany, Italy, America, and everywhere. I also saw a group tour of Japanese who were totally fascinated by the temples. So why do so many people come to this very small village just to see the ancient temples? Because these temples are in such good condition and have some of the most outstanding carved stonework you will find anywhere.

Khajuraho is a good distance from the main lines of travel, which is one of the reasons why the temples were not destroyed or defaced by Islamic invaders like many of the other ancient temples in northern or central India. Here we get a good look at the Indo-Aryan architecture and the exceptional stonework that covers the exterior. The carved stone shows many scenes of what life was like 1000 years ago, and includes carvings of musicians, gods, goddesses, warriors, animals, beautiful ladies, and erotica. They have captured the interest of the world through magazine articles, travel brochures, and tours. Now many people include this town in their travels through India. And only a couple of these temples are still used for worship, so we can look at them to our heart's content without restriction.

Most of the temples were constructed between 950 and 1050 from blocks of sandstone and built so the entrances face east. On the East side of town there are three Jain temples dedicated to Parsvanatha, Adinatha, and Shantinatha. Although not as big, these temples are just as ornately embellished as the other temples of Khajuraho. On them are carvings of scenes and gods from the Jain scripture as well as images of Vayu, Bhairav, Shiva, Vishnu, Brahma, and others from the Hindu *shastras*. This indicates that many of the Jain gods are the same as the Vedic, or they were heavily influenced by the Vedic tradition, or these temples were part of the Vedic tradition before they were converted to the use of Jains. Some of the local people told me the latter was the case.

Historically, it is explained that Khajurao was a major center of the later Chandella kings from the 9th to 14th centuries. It was under their patronage when the temples were developed. It is believed that 85 temples were built out of which 25 still remain in varying degrees of preservation. The oldest temples, namely the Chausath Yogini and Lalguan Mahadeva, were built during the reign of King Harshadeva (900-925) who had succeeded his father, Rahilya. Under Harshadeva's son, Yasovarman or Lakshavarman (925-950), the Lakshman temple, dedicated to Vishnu, was built. An inscription found among the ruins of the Lakshman temple, dated to 954, established that Yasovarman built it. It was under his son Dhanga's rule (950-1002), when both the Parsvanatha (954) and the Visvanatha (1002) temples were built. Since he was following his predecessors who were all associated with the Vedic culture, it is unlikely that he would build a Jain temple, as the Parsvanath temple is now. Furthermore, both temples were constructed in a similar design. They have towering roofs over the sanctums, which consist of a series of peaks around a central point that resembles the Kailash mountain abode of Lord Shiva, as does the Kandariya Mahadeva, the most prominent Shiva temple. Therefore, again it is most likely that the Parsvanatha temple was originally dedicated to Shiva. In fact, the image of Parsvanatha, the 23rd in the line of Jain *tirthankaras*, was placed in the sanctum only in 1860.

Dhanga's son and successor was Ganda (1002-1017). He had a short reign and the Jagadambi (Vishnu) and the Chitragupta (Surya) temples are attributed to him. Ganda's son was Vidyadhara (1017-29). He continued the building tradition of his ancestors, during which time the grand Kandariya Mahadeva temple was constructed. After Vidyadhara's death, the political significance of Khajurao began to wane. His successors continued their rule over the area for the next century, but moved to hill-forts elsewhere in the kingdom. Nonetheless, the temples continued to be active until the 14th century, patronized by pilgrims and yogis. By the 16th century, Khajurao was but a simple and obscure village, having lost all importance. It was only in 1838 when British army engineer Captain T. S. Burt happened to discover what was left of the temples.

Nowadays, we can easily visit and see what remains of this great temple town. To begin a little tour of the temples, we can start with the east side of town, we can start with the Parsvanatha temple. This is the largest of the Jain temples here. As you go inside, the interior is also richly carved, as with many of the temples at Khajuraho. The interior doorway has figures of elephants, lions, goddesses, and guardians. On the altar is the black stone image of Parsvanatha, the 23rd *tirthankara*. Nearby is the Shantinatha temple. This presents many good examples of Jain sculptures and has 12 altars in it, including one with a highly polished image of Lord Adinatha that is 14 feet tall. This temple was constructed about 100 years ago using the remains of other ruined Jain temples. A museum is also nearby with a larger collection of ancient images and stonework gathered from the area.

From here we turn south. A kilometer down the road is the Duladeo temple, which stands alone and is still used for worship by some of the local people. Inside is a unique Shiva *lingam* with 999 *lingams* carved on its sides. This way when a worshiper circumambulates it once, it equates with going around it 1000 times. Farther south beyond the river in the village of Jatkari is the Chaturbhuja temple. Above the doorway are the images of Vishnu, Brahma, and Shiva. The temple is ruined but still has an exquisitely carved deity of Vishnu that stands three meters tall.

Closer to the village is the Jain Ghantai temple which is interesting, but not in very good condition. On the other side of the village near the Khajur Sagar lake is a small Brahma temple with a four-faced *linga* inside. It is actually a Vishnu temple and one of the oldest structures in town. Farther up the road is the Vamana temple, which was under repair when I visited. It is an interesting temple with a single tower above the sanctum. Inside the temple is an image of Lord Vamanadeva, plus images of Narasimha and

Varaha. A little ways south of the Vamana temple, in the field, is the small Javari temple, dedicated to Vishnu and dating back to 1100.

As we make our way back through the village, some of the people who are very friendly may ask you if you would like to see their house. So if you want, you can visit, take some photos, and leave some *baksheesh*, rupees. On the road heading toward the most impressive group of temples is a very small shrine to Hanuman. This shrine dates back to 922 and has an 8 feet tall deity of Hanuman which is covered in vermillion.

The western group of temples are the most fascinating and exceptional showpieces of temple architecture in Khajuraho and Central India. Except for a few temples, they are all found within a fenced enclosure. The park-like area is well maintained with watered and trimmed lawns. The temples are of various sizes and are covered with the usual carved figures. Starting in the front right corner of the enclosure is the Visvanatha temple, built around 1002, dedicated to Shiva with a stone *linga* inside. The north stairway leading to the entrance is flanked by two stone lions, and the south stairway has two stone elephants. The temple exterior and its tower are covered with rich carvings of a variety of subjects and designs. Across from the entrance is a temple for a huge Nandi, Shiva's bull carrier. Nandi is six feet high and seven feet long. You can sit in this little temple and easily look out over the rest of the park. Across from the Visvanatha temple is the smaller Parvati temple which now has an image of Parvati as Gauri. It is believed this was originally a Vishnu temple.

In the front left corner of the park is the Lakshmana temple, which dates back to 930 to 954. This temple is dedicated to Vishnu and is in the best condition of any of the temples. Above the entrance are images of Lakshmi, the goddess of fortune and Lord Vishnu's wife, and Brahma and Shiva on either side of her. On the doorway are carved stone illustrations of Puranic pastimes. There are four smaller shrines at each corner of the temple's terrace. One is for Lakshmi, wife of Lord Vishnu, and another is for Varaha, an incarnation of Vishnu. These five temples are exceptionally rich with elegant sculptures both inside and out. The sanctum has niches with other Vaishnava deities in them amongst the many carvings that fill the interior. The main deity in the sanctum is a four-armed and three-faced Vishnu. The central face is Vishnu while the other faces are of Narasimha and Varaha. The deity was obtained from Devpal, the Pratihar king of Kanauj, and originally came from Tibet.

In the very back of the park starting on the left is the Kandariya Mahadev temple, the grandest of all the temples. It represents the culmination of temple art in Central India. The central tower reaches a height of over 100 feet, and the temple has as many as 646 sculptures on the exterior and 226 inside, most of which are two and three feet in height. The panels of sculptures depict the usual assortment of figures, including gods, goddesses, maidens, warriors, hunters, dancers, and erotica, for which these temples seem to be especially known. The main focus of worship is a Shiva *linga*, and deities of Vishnu and Brahma on either side. The temple is made to look like a mountain and the word *kandariya* means a cave, which symbolically represents Shiva's cave abode in the Kailash mountain. At one time it had four smaller shrines at the corners of the terrace, but they have since perished.

On the same raised terrace as the Kandariya temple is the Devi Jagadambi temple and smaller Mahadeva temple. The Mahadeva temple, between the larger ones, still stands though its sanctum is ruined. It now houses a *sardula*, or a sculpture of a man or woman holding a lion. The Jagadambi temple was originally dedicated to Vishnu, but now has an image of a black painted Parvati in the sanctum who is generally called Kali, but in this case is called Jagadambi. Across from this temple is the large Chitragupta temple which is the only local temple dedicated to Surya the sun god and has a Surya deity inside that is five feet tall. On the south wall of the exterior in the central niche is a fine carving of an eleven-headed Vishnu. The central head is Vishnu and the others represent His ten incarnations.

If you prefer to see these temples with few people around, the best time is at 6.30 A.M. when the ticket booth opens. No one is there at that time and you have the whole enclosure to yourself. It is quite fascinating to walk around or be in one of these temples in the quiet and coolness of the morning while the sun is coming up. The place takes on a special mystical atmosphere that is quite unlike the way it feels when all the tourists show up a few hours later. By nine or ten o'clock all the group tours start arriving and some of the temples can get rather crowded as people shuffle in and out.

Outside the park and right next to the Lakshmana temple is the Mantangeshvara temple, dedicated to Shiva, and is still used for worship. It dates back to about 900 and is much simpler in design than the other temples and is not covered by the usual stone carvings. This temple is very busy with devotees coming and going. In front of the temple to the left is a deity of Ganesh that many of the women worship by offering incense and flowers.

Then climbing the steps you enter the cave-like temple and make your way to the back of the huge circular (20 feet) and raised Gauri-patta upon which is a polished Shiva *linga* over a meter in diameter and 2.5 meters (about eight feet) tall. People go up the stairs onto the Gauri-patta and splash pots of water onto the Shiva *linga* and then continue down another stairway that leads out a side door. The water is brought from the nearby Shivsagar Lake. Sometimes, especially on holy days, you can see people continually repeat the process of getting water from the lake, go through the temple to worship the *linga* by pouring water on it, exit out the side door, and then go back to the lake for more water.

In front of the Mantangeshvara temple is the Varaha temple. This is built merely as a *mandap* hall about 20 feet by 16 feet, but has a huge deity of Varaha, the boar incarnation of Lord Vishnu. The body of the deity is carved with rows of small figures on it, as many as 764, that consist of various members of the Hindu pantheon.

Another temple is located past the Shivsagar lake and across the field. It is the ruined Chausath temple, dedicated to Kali and the 64 yoginis who tend to the goddess. It is built on a terrace 18 feet high, but has no ceiling or tower over it. You can see the 65 little cells where the small images used to be kept, but there is really little else to see. Another 600 yards to the west is the small, ruined shrine to Shiva, the Lalguan Mahadeva temple next to the Lalguan Sagar lake. This is another ruined temple with little to see.

Across from the Shivsagar lake is the Archeological Museum. It offers an interesting assortment of ancient sculptures and deities from the area and is worth checking out. Entrance used to be free with your ticket to the western group of temples, but now or at least the last time I was there they are charging $10 to Westerners. It is not worth it at that price, but it is up to you. Hopefully they will change it. Around the corner from the museum is the main street with a number of shops that sell the usual variety of nick-nacks from which you might find some souvenirs if you are so inclined. This area gets pretty busy in the evening, mostly with Indian shoppers and tourists. It's an interesting place to hang out and watch the people for a while. However, if any local person comes up to you to start talking, regardless of how friendly they may be, it is usually because they have a shop they want you to see, or there is some way they can make some money from you. The more touristy this place becomes, then the more this type of business will increase. Nonetheless, if you are a little careful, this is certainly a town worth visiting.

CHITRAKUT

When we are finished seeing the temples of Khajuraho, we can take a pleasant bus ride through the forested hills to our next major place of pilgrimage. Chitrakut (*Citrakoot*, meaning beautiful mountain) is 132 kilometers west of Allahabad by the border of Uttar Pradesh and Madhya Pradesh. It is also about halfway between Khajuraho and Varanasi. Many pilgrims come here every day and as many as 100,000 on major festival days. Once when I visited it was right after the Kumbha Mela in Allahabad in 2001, and the place was packed.

The significance of this place is that Lord Rama and Sita stayed here for 11 of their 14 years of exile. This is also where Lord Rama's brother Bharata came to beg Rama to return to Ayodhya. The Mandakini River, which flows through Chitrakut, is considered as sacred as the Ganges. The story is that the sage Atri and his wife Anusuya live nearby. Because the sage needed sacred water for his austerities, Anusuya made the Ganges appear in the form of the Mandakini. Lord Rama bathed here every day. Sita also took bath here at Janaki Kund where Her footprints are said to still be on the rocks there. There are numerous bathing ghats along the river. You will find over 30 temples in this area.

In the central part of town along the river is Ramghat, the main and busiest *ghat* in this small town. Many pilgrims gather a little water from the Mandakini and some flow ers from one of the vendors nearby, and then walk up the steps to the Shiva temple. There we can see the main Shiva image, as well as a few other images of Vedic divinities. Being on the high steps give a great view over Ramghat and all the people and boats on the river. There are also temples to Sita-Rama, a few for Krishna and Narasimha, one for Lord Jagannatha, and a number of other Shiva temples.

From Ramghat you can get boat rides to a few of the other sacred places along the river. For other places you can walk to some or simply take a ricksha to others. You can also hire a jeep nearby. Upstream by about 2 km is Sita's main bathing place, Janaki Kund, named after Sita as Janaki, daughter of Janaka. You can see the Rama Janaki Raghuveer temple and the Sankat Mochan Hanuman deity nearby. It is a beautiful place and has a most soothing atmosphere. The water is especially clear. You will not want to leave.

A few km farther upstream is the Sphatik Shila. This is the boulder that is said to have the footprints of Lord Rama, and where He would bathe everyday. Another nearby boulder is said to be the sitting place of Sita as well as Lakshmana. It is also where Sita was standing when pecked by Jayant who appeared as a crow.

For the places that are farther away, there are the Char Dhama buses. You can get these near the Madhya Pradesh Tourist Hotel, and they will call out when they are trying to get passengers. They leave in the morning and afternoon. So just hop on and pay the ticket and away you go. However, they do ride around a while trying to pick up more passengers, even though the bus I was on looked fairly full anyway. Then we are on our way over bumpy roads.

The first place we go to is about 18 km out of town. This is Gupta Godavari where you will find two caves. One is a narrow but long cave, the end of which is where Rama and Lakshmana would meet for discussions. It has a narrow entrance, but is roomy with a high ceiling once inside. At the end of the cave, you will find a small pond said to be equal to the Godavari River, fed by natural springs. However, in the other cave you will have to wade knee deep in water to get through it.

We then go to Sati Anusuya where the ashram was located of Atri Muni and his wife Anusuya. Their three sons were the incarnations of Lord Vishnu, Brahma, and Shiva. The temple here has diorama doll displays depicting the story of Atri Muni and his wife, and a deity of Anusuya swinging her babies. This is a pleasant and somewhat wooded area with the Mandakini River flowing nearby.

After this the buses also take you to Sphatik Shila and then to Janaki Kund. A tour on one of the buses takes about three to four hours, so take the early buses so that you are not still touring while it is getting dark. If you are on a tour, once it starts getting dark, they will try to rush you through everything and you do not get as much out of it.

Another holy place of interest in Chitrakut is Hanuman Dhara, which is a spring made by Lord Rama to refresh Hanuman after he returned from Lanka after setting it on fire. Sita had told him that at Chitrakut there is a spring that is quite cool. You will find it after a tough climb up a rocky hillside, several hundred feet up, which gives a great view over Chitrakut in the distance. Be careful of the monkeys. Also on the hill is the five-headed (Panch Mukhi) Hanuman Dhara deity, as well as Sita's kitchen (Sita Rasoi) on the hilltop. A few little shrines are there and refreshment stalls are at the base of the hill.

About a half-hour out of town is another place called Bharata Koop, a well where Lord Rama's brother, Bharata, stored the holy waters from all the sacred places of India.

Another place that is worth visiting is the modern Ram Darshan Mandir. It is a beautiful temple and garden, with an excellent museum of paintings and dioramas that tell the pastimes of Lord Rama and the *Ramayana*. I have to admit that it is one of the best of such displays I have seen. There is also a huge outdoor image of Hanuman shown opening his chest to reveal Sita-Rama inside his heart.

Perhaps the most sacred place in Chitrakut is Kamadgiri Hill. This is considered the original Chitrakut where Lord Rama was supposed to have lived during His exile. It is, thus, considered an expansion of Rama. Because of this, many people walk barefoot around the hill on the 5 km pilgrimage path. It's a pleasant and easy walk. Temples are along the path around this forested hill, which includes the Shree Kamatanath temple (considered to be the tongue of Kamadgiri Hill) and the Bharat Milap temple, where Bharata is supposed to have pleaded with Rama to return to Ayodhya. Just past this temple is a path that will take you to Lakshman Pahadi, which are the places where Lakshmana stayed while guarding Ram and Sita. You will find the Lakshman temple on the hilltop. A visit to Chitrakut is not complete without visiting this hill. It is said that anyone who circumambulates the hill gets his wishes fulfilled. There are also many monkeys around the hill, as well as many beggars, both male and female. They simply depend on the mercy of the pilgrims. Yet it seemed to me the visitors were more interested in feeding the monkeys than they were the poor people.

If you want to wander around the town on your own, you can get a brochure about the holy sites in English at the Madhya Pradesh Tourist Bungalow. Be sure to bring your flashlight to this town, or have candles ready in your hotel because it seems that lights go out quite regularly.

ALLAHABAD (PRAYAGA)

Once our tour of Chitrakut is finished, we can walk a ways out of the city to the bus station to catch the next bus to Allahabad.

Allahabad, though more spread out and less congested than Varanasi and most big cities in India, has little in which the general tourist would be interested. So if your time is limited, there are other cities far more fascinating to see. However, there are some important times of the year in which the spiritual pilgrim will want to visit. For places of interest, there's the huge fort, which foreigners are not allowed to enter, that has an Ashoka Pillar inside. But through a side door you can see the undying banyan tree that is over 1000 years old and still looks in good condition. Visit the Hanuman temple with a reclining Hanuman, open to non-Hindus, located on the Sangam side of the fort. The nearby Adi Shankara temple has nice carvings and a Balaji deity. Also in the city is the Anand Bhawan, a two-storey mansion with a collection of personal items of the Nehru family. There is also the Allahabad Museum. The Sri Rupa Gaudiya Math temple on Mallaca Street is in the Madhavapur area, by the Ganges River on the way from downtown to the *sangam* or meeting place of the Ganges and Yamuna Rivers. This temple is where Srila A. C. Bhaktivedanta Prabhupada took initiation from Srila Bhaktisiddhanta Sarasvati Thakura.

The name Allahabad, which was given to the city by Emperor Akbar in 1584, means the city of Allah. But prior to this the name was Prayaga or Prayaga Raja, which meant the place where the sacred rivers meet and where great sacrifices are performed. So for the pilgrim it is an important site since this is the confluence (*sangam*) of the sacred Ganges, Yamuna, and the mystical Sarasvati Rivers. The *Mahabharata* relates how Lord Brahma performed a sacrifice here thousands of years ago. Lord Ramachandra, His wife Sita, and brother Lakshmana visited this place in Treta-yuga. They stayed at the ashram of the great sage Bharadvaja, which is now the location of the Allahabad University. There are temples of Bharadwajeshwara Mahadeva, Rishi Bharadwaja, and Kali there. The five Pandava brothers also visited this *sangam*, as described in *Mahabharata*. And 500 years ago Sri Chaitanya also stayed for 10 days at the *sangam* and visited the Bindu Madhava temple, one of the important Krishna temples in Allahabad located several kilometers upstream. Sri Chaitanya's footprints can also be found nearby at a place called Dashashvamedha Ghat, near the Triveni Sangam. This is where He imparted His teachings to Srila Rupa Gosvami on the science of bhakti-yoga for several days. It is called Rupa Siksasthali. And across the river from the *sangam* is another temple on a small hill that Sri Chaitanya visited. About two miles downstream is the house of the saint Vallabhacarya, where Sri Chaitanya had lunch with the saint.

Forty km out of Allahabad on the Ganges is Ramchaura-Shringverpur where there's a platform called Ram Chabutara where Lord Rama stayed before crossing the Ganges to go into exile and go toward Chitrakut. There are also temples to Panchmukhi (five-faced Hanuman) and Shring Rishi Lakshagriha (45 km out) where the Pandavas' house of lac was located, marked by a big mound. This house of lac is described in such ancient books as the *Mahabharata* and *Bhagavata Purana*.

The one thing that Allahabad is noted for is the *sangam* or confluence of the Ganges (Ganga) and the Yamuna Rivers. Hundreds of people come to the *sangam* every day to bathe in the spiritually purifying water. But thousands of people come to the *sangam* area when there is the annual festival known as the Magh (January-February) Mela. And every 12 years the Magh Mela becomes the Kumba Mela which lasts for 41 days in which millions of pilgrims join together to bathe at the *sangam* and to perform other types of spiritual activities. In fact, during the Kumba Mela festival in 1989 nearly 30 million people attended. But at the last Mela in January-February of 2001, an estimated 71 million people attended over the course of its duration, and more Westerners came to see it than at any other time in history. It is by far the largest festival, what to speak of religious festival, in the world. The Kumba Mela alternates every three years between Allahabad, Nasik, Ujjain, and Haridwar.

During the Magh and Kumba Melas the 3600 acres called the Kumba Mela grounds that surround the *sangam* become its own city with roads, street lights, markets, medical facilities, and areas for food distribution, etc. Hundreds of large tents are erected as far as you can see to accommodate the thousands or millions of people. And it is not uncommon to see whole families, including babies, children, parents, and grandparents, come to the festival from any part of India. Some come by bus, train, plane, or even by foot.

Not only do ordinary pilgrims attend, but many of India's most elevated mystics, sages, and yogis also attend. Some of these sages are hundreds of years old, live in the pure atmosphere of the Himalayas, and are never seen except at such festivals. In fact, one of the most important aspects of the festival is to allow ordinary pilgrims the opportunity to associate with saintly persons for instruction in attaining spiritual realization.

During the festivals some of the large tents also become the temporary dwellings for various ashrams or spiritual groups. You can often walk by the entrance and hear over the loudspeaker the lecture that is being given inside. This may attract people who then go in and sit and listen to the lecture and ask questions. At other times there may be a play on the Puranic pastimes being performed on the stage. At other times there might be devotional music being performed that people can listen to or join in singing.

Wherever you go during the festivals there is something spiritual to watch, listen to, or engage in. With all the uplifting activities, such as lectures, plays, *bhajans*, worship, rituals, the presence of highly learned and experienced sages and yogis, and the holy *sangam*, the Mela festivals are a highly energized and spiritual event for one to attend. However, many of these lectures and songs are not in English. But regardless of whether you are a serious pilgrim, businessman, teacher, student, housewife, or curious Western tourist, it is an event you will never forget.

THE TRADITION OF THE KUMBHA MELA

The significance of the *sangam* is related in the *Puranas*. It is told that many millions of years ago there was a battle between the demigods (*devas*) and the demons (*asuras*). Due to an offense to the powerful sage Durvasa Muni, the demigods had lost all of their power. So the demigods sought advice from Lord Vishnu who told them to make an agreement with the *asuras* to churn the ocean of milk together in order to get the nectar of immortality. After everyone agreed to it, they churned the ocean of milk and from it came various items and personalities. Finally, Lord Dhanvantari appeared carrying the *amrita-kumbha*, the jug filled with the nectar. The demons grabbed the jug and fighting immediately broke out between the *devas* and *asuras*. Over a period of twelve days of fighting some of the nectar was spilled from the jug onto four places: Nasik, Ujjain, Haridwar, and the *sangam* at Allahabad. In the end the demigods got possession of the nectar, but the nectar, which can spiritually purify all who come in contact with it, is said to become manifest in those four cities during certain auspicious times that are astrologically calculated. Thus, many people come to these cities for the Kumbha Mela festivals that signify the presence of the immortal nectar. To bathe in the *sangam* on the peak days, one of which is Amavasya or the time of the new moon, purifies one's existence and relieves one from the continued cycle of birth and death in the material world after this life. Thus, the importance and good fortune for those who can do this is taken very seriously. Many of the devout try to go at least once in their lifetime.

Before anyone else bathes in the *sangam*, the saints go first. Down the road through the middle of the crowd the saints parade past the people and enter the water once the astrologically auspicious moment has arrived. Usually the first group of mystics given the opportunity is the *naga babas*. These men wear no clothes and live in the mountains, but no one sees them traveling to the festival or going back to the mountains afterwards. It is as if they simply appear by mystic power. When they are done bathing, the other sects each have their turn to come down to the river. First there are the Vairagis, the Shaivites, Shankarites, Ramanujas, Madhvas, Nimbarkas, and the Gaudiya Vaishnavas.

After all the prominent saints bathe in the *sangam*, everyone else rushes in to do the same. Then the *sangam* becomes a river of bodies, a roar of voices, all clamoring to get to the water while reciting or even shouting invocations to the deities and to the Ganges and Yamuna Rivers. Each person blends in with everyone else regardless of race, caste, or sect, all with the intent of spiritual purification. But as you can imagine, when so many people gather in a relatively small area like this, safety can be a major concern. There have been instances in the past when hundreds of people have died when there is a rush to the river. Of course, newer arrangements have been made to help prevent this. But it is considered that to leave one's body during the Kumbha Mela or while in the *sangam* is especially auspicious and denotes liberation from material existence.

Where the Ganges and Yumana meet can be seen in the difference of the color of the rivers. The Ganges is shallower, muddier, and yellowish or whitish in color, while the Yamuna is deeper and dark green. Many pilgrims enter the water from the shore in between the two rivers, while others take boats out to where the rivers actually mix. There are small wooden platforms for people to get out of the boats and dip into the water. Then they change into dry clothes on the boats. Some people also bring big jugs to fill so they can take the holy *sangam* water back with them to their homes.

If you want to take a boat out, find one that is very close to the *sangam* where you can get the cheaper prices. There is usually a dock where all the boats pick up people. However, in the annual Magh Mela season, the boatmen might want to charge a Westerner as much as 200 rupees or more to take you out to the *sangam* area. But if you get closer on the shore, you can find boatmen looking for customers who will charge only 10 or 20 rupees. And if you do not mind taking a boat filled with other pilgrims, it may only cost you three to five rupees to ride with them. Of course, you will have to wait until everyone else is ready to come back to shore. In any case, be careful about prices. But do not forget the value of being here.

It was a festival that truly changed my life. You will never experience anything quite like it. And after my dip in the holy *sangam*, the waters of the Ganges and Yamuna during the Amavasya time, I could certainly feel a big difference, like being liter and ten years younger, but I could not explain what had happened.

VARANASI

An easy train ride east of Allahabad is available for us to take to the next holy town we will visit, which is Varanasi. Varanasi is a city of many legends and numerous temples. Books have been written exclusively on the life, legends, and significance of the city. Many tourists from around the world come here to see the culture, the *ghats* along the Ganges River, and to experience various aspects of the living religion which has gone on for thousands of years. Varanasi is known for its silver, copper, brassware, and art work, as well as the excellent textiles, such as carpets, saris, and especially silks that are made here. There is an interesting museum showing some of the best examples of these kinds of craftsmanship at the Banaras University, the Bharat Kala Bhawan, and at the old palace in the Ramnagar Fort. Varanasi has been a center for learning and spiritual pilgrimages for over 2500 years, and attracts many students and scholars on religion, philosophy, and music, and has some of the world's best astrologers. If you're interested in having your horoscope read, this is a good place to have it done. Tulsi das, who wrote the Hindi version of the *Ramayan* (the *Ram Charit Manas*), also lived here years ago. Many noted Indian musicians also have homes here. Especially important for the pilgrim are the many temples. But many of the temples, unfortunately, will not let foreigners inside. Nonetheless, there are still many important temples that do.

For the general tourist from the West, Varanasi, out of many Indian cities, is a town that is probably least understood. The traditions of this town go back well over 2000 years, and most foreigners, when seeing these practices for the first time, can hardly comprehend what exactly is happening or the intent of it. But everything has its purpose and meaning. To understand the importance of Varanasi, you must familiarize yourself to some degree with its legends. For example, Varanasi is often referred to as the city of Shiva, but it was not always Shiva's city. The *Kashi Khanda*, a text that explains some of the glories of Varanasi (or Kashi, "the city of light"), explains that at one time many, many years ago, all the gods lived here. However, the rule of the city was given over to King Divodasa who made all the demigods leave. After a while Lord Shiva wanted to come back, but everything he tried in order to return failed. Finally he asked Lord Vishnu to help him. So Lord Vishnu went to Varanasi and first arrived at the confluence of the Varana and Ganges Rivers where He bathed. Now there is the Adi Keshava ("original Keshava" or Vishnu) temple at that location to commemorate the incident, which is now an important *tirtha* or holy place. Sri Vishnu then made His way into the city and again bathed at the Panchaganga Ghat. Then by His trickery He caused the departure of King Divodasa and gave Varanasi back to Lord Shiva, and Lord Vishnu and Shiva, along with other demigods and goddesses, have manifested themselves here in many ways ever since. Therefore, Varanasi (the city between the Varana and Asi Rivers) has always been a center for pilgrimage. More legends of Varanasi could be explained, but there are so many that they easily could fill a separate volume. So I will only relate a few as we tour some of the many temples.

You can find temples dedicated to any personality of the Vedic pantheon in this city. Thus, they say that all the gods reside here. And it is said that all of the holy places of India can be found in certain portions of the town. Mathura is found in one part of the town, Ayodhya in another, as well as Badrinatha, Dvaraka, and so on. In fact, some of the ancient texts say that Varanasi is not of this earth, but is a holy place and part of the spiritual realm. Therefore, dying in this city brings salvation from future material existence. So there is a strong atmosphere of devotion here as many pilgrims come from all over to spend their last days living in this city, bathing in the sacred Ganges, visiting temples, and having *darshan* of the deities, all for spiritual purification.

Probably the best way to get to know Varanasi is to take a little tour of the important temples and river ghats. Many of the temples are not very important to the general tourist, and not all of them are so interesting or necessary to see, unless you are a serious pilgrim who wants to spend some time here. So I'll simply explain where many of the temples are located. The easiest way to find them is to have your motor or cycle ricksha driver take you. But some of the temples in the old section of town can only be reached by foot because the lanes are too narrow even for cycle rickshas. Yet drivers can park their rickshas somewhere and lead you the rest of the way. The real adventure of finding these temples is not only seeing what they are like, but simply wandering around the town to experience the place and observe how the people live.

We can start our tour by taking a motor ricksha to the New Visvanatha temple in the Banaras Hindu University at the southern end of the city. This very nice temple was established by the Birla family, thus anyone is welcome. This is the temple that all Western tourists should visit if they want to see an authentic Shiva temple. It is well kept, clean, and surrounded by fountains, pools, and nice grounds. It was made in the architectural style of the original Visvanatha temple that was in the heart of the old section of town before the Muslims invaded and tore it down. This new temple has a large central room for a Shiva *lingam* that is attended by a priest. There are also two shrines in separate rooms, one for Parvati and Ganesh, and the other for a five-faced Shiva *lingam*, Mahadeva. It is a very interesting temple and is easily reached without having to find your way through dark and dirty alleys that can be crowded with people, children, and wandering cows, which is the case in much of the old section of town. And the Banaras Hindu University is like a spacious park that is pleasant to walk or drive through.

From here we take a ricksha to Sankat Mochan on the south side of town, one of the most important Hanuman temples in the city. The architecture of this temple is not very elaborate, but it is a lively place and many people visit and offer respects to the deities of Sita-Rama, Hanuman, Ganesh, etc. This is not far from Durga Kund Road where, heading farther north, we can walk to the Tulsi Manas Mandir; a large temple that has beautiful Sita-Rama deities and the complete Hindi *Ramayan* by Tulsi Das written on the inside walls. This temple marks the place where Tulsi Das lived while he wrote it. This is another temple that welcomes anyone, and Western tourists should also visit this clean and well kept temple to view the beautiful Sita-Rama deities.

About a block or two farther down the road is the Durga temple beside the Durga Kund. Many pilgrims go to this temple, which is commonly called the Monkey temple because of the many monkeys of which you have to be careful. Anyone can go in and see the temple that is in the middle of the courtyard and houses a small deity of goddess Durga. This temple is completely filled with pilgrims during the Durga-puja festival. From here we take the road that leads toward the Ganges until we find Asi Ghat, where the small Asi River joins the Ganges. From here we leave our rickshaw and begin walking.

The best time to see the *ghats* is in the morning when you will find the most activity, and also before it gets very hot from the sun. The Asi Ghat is busy in the morning with bathers, women collecting water for worship and washing, and others worshiping the Hanuman deity and the Shiva *lingams* under the nearby pipal tree. Some men will be practicing yoga, sitting in meditation, eyes closed, facing the morning sun. Others sit near the river chanting the Hare Krishna mantra on beads, or will be doing other morning rituals. In fact, one old renunciant, seeing my own bead bag hanging from my neck, came up in a most friendly manner to tell me the glories of chanting the holy names. In essence, he stated that to always be chanting the names of God means that one is liberated from material life. But mostly he was expressing his happiness to see a Westerner taking to the process since he had obviously attained his own experiences of enlightenment through the chanting process.

The next *ghat* along the river as we head north is Tulsi Ghat, above which is Lolarka Kund and the house and temple of Tulsi Das. It is also advised to visit the temple of Ganesh that overlooks the Ganges here for your good fortune since Ganesh is believed to take away obstacles.

Next is Shivala Ghat where we find on the banks the massive 17th century palace of Maharaja Chet Singh. After that is Hanuman Ghat which is where the great philosopher and Vaishnava Vallabhacarya was born. There is also a Ruru Bhairav temple above it on the hill. Next along the river is Harischandra Ghat which is sometimes used for cremations. There is a platform here, the top of which is reached by a small stairway. On the top is an interesting copper Shiva *lingam* that many pilgrims and local devotees visit to worship or pay tribute. After that is Kedara Ghat where pilgrims bathe in the Ganga before climbing the steps to the Kedareshvara temple, with the red and white stripes on the outside of the building, which is one of the most important Shiva temples in Varanasi. The *Kashi Khanda* states that just deciding to come here destroys the sins accumulated in this lifetime, while seeing the temple destroys the sins of seven lifetimes. Bathing in the Ganga River and then worshiping the Kedareshvara *lingam* is said to destroy the sins of 10 million lifetimes. The temple also has deities of Durga, Ganesh, Shiva, etc., and Westerners are allowed inside for *darshan*. It is very important, so do not miss this temple.

Farther along we come to Chauki Ghat with a huge tree at the top of the stairs sheltering many stone *nagas*. Then there is a quiet section at Manasarovara Ghat and Chaumsathi Ghat, above which is the Chaumsathi temple dedicated to the 64 yoginis along with images of Kali and Durga.

Next we enter the busy Dashashvamedha Ghat where the bather gets the results of ten *ashvamedha* sacrifices or special rituals for spiritual power and advancement. It was here that Lord Brahma performed ten *ashvamedhas* many, many years ago in order to attain the purity to see Lord Shiva at Varanasi. At this ghat people gather from all over the world, from all walks of life. Here they take their holy bath, or perform rituals to the Ganga, or consult with local priests found sitting under the rattan umbrellas and discuss their lives, horoscopes, and their spiritual progress. It is by far the busiest *ghat* in Varanasi and the most easily reached. Many foreign tourists come here as well, and in the morning you can see group tours or individuals climbing into the boats to float past the *ghats* and to watch the activities of the local people who use the *ghats* each morning along the riverside. A boat ride down the Ganga at Varanasi can be a very relaxing and interesting experience that should not be missed.

In the evening there is also an elaborate Ganga *puja*, when five priests on five platforms simultaneously perform the worship of the Ganga River. They offer incense, large ghee lamps, large camphor lamps, and yak tail fans. It is a great site to see and makes for good photography or video to take back with you. Many people also come here in the evening to merely sit on the steps, socialize, watch other people, and enjoy the cool breeze. Some people also come to worship in the nearby temples. You can hear the bells as this happens. Popular temples along the *ghat* include one to Shitala and the Dashash-vamedheshvara Shiva *lingam*. Another temple is the Shulatankeshvara, and one of Brah-meshvara, which is a Shiva *lingam* said to have been installed by Brahma himself during his stay here.

Above the *ghat* along the steps near the temples you will see lines of beggars sitting in the shade. Some of them are deformed from leprosy and nearly invalid. They try to get your attention by reaching out with their begging bowls to you in hopes of receiving a donation. For many of them, handouts are their only source of income, especially for those who can do nothing else, like the lepers who have cloth rags covering their hands which have been eaten away by the disease. In other areas of Varanasi you may also find renunciants or poor widows spending their last days here who live only by begging. It can be shocking to the Western tourist, but such sights are common most anywhere you go in India. But begging is not always the last resort only for those who can do nothing else. In India, begging is also accepted by those who have renounced most of their earthly connections and now live by this most humble of means, which is to depend merely on the mercy of others, which is the mercy of God.

Farther above Dashashvamedha Ghat along the street are many stalls that sell souvenirs, beads, incense, brass pots to carry Ganga water, etc. There is also the scent of incense and perfumed oils in the air, and ricksha drivers that ask you where you want to go. Farther up the road are many more shops, restaurants, and stalls that sell snacks and create the strong aroma of fried foods. From here one gets into the business area of Varanasi, which is much more congested with pedestrian as well as motor traffic, and seems to leave the spiritual life behind.

Back along the Ganga, the next *ghat* is Man Mandir, above which we find the small but unique observatory of Jai Singh. Jai Singh was known for being a great king, musician, and astronomer. He built more elaborate observatories in New Delhi, Jaipur, and two smaller ones in Mathura and Ujjain. Not far from this observatory above Man Mandir Ghat is the temple of Someshvara, which has a *linga* said to have been established by Soma. Above Mir Ghat is the well known Vishalakshi temple, one of the forms of Parvati. Not far away are the Shiva temples of Dharmesha (where it's said that Yamaraja received his authority over the dead), Divodaseshvara (the *linga* said to have been established by King Divodasa before he left Kashi), and the Dharma Kupa or Well of Dharma.

These temples are in the Godaulia area or the old part of the city which is a maze of narrow and crowded alleyways through decaying buildings that lead past many little shops, temples, guest houses or hotels, and homes of the local people. In the residential areas children often find just enough room to play in these alleys, but if a stray cow comes walking through, it can sometimes take up the whole lane. The dust and smells in this area can be overwhelming, especially in the heat of summer. But, nonetheless, there are new discoveries and experiences to have amongst these alleys if one is open to them. You are never quite sure what you will find next. You may see astrologers consulting clients, guides offering you their services (in hopes of getting you to their shop where they can sell you something), flower peddlers, a funeral procession, or people simply sitting together sharing tea and conversation.

In the middle of this area is the temple of Visvanatha, Shiva as Lord of the Universe. This is a temple all pilgrims visit, although foreigners generally are not allowed inside. However, there are times, such as during the holiday of Shivaratri, they do allow many more inside to see the Shiva *lingam*.

The present temple was built in 1776 by Ahalya Bai of Indore after the original temple was torn down by the fanatic Muslim Aurangzeb who built the mosque in its place. The mosque on the other side of the courtyard is separated from the temple by the Jnana Vapi well (Well of Wisdom) where the original Shiva *linga* was hid in order to keep the Muslim invaders from harming it. Some people say the original *linga* was never recovered from the well and is still at the bottom. Needless to say, with the temple and mosque so close, police patrol the mosque continually to prevent disturbances. The courtyard and temple are situated behind a large wall making it difficult to see from the outside, and the south entrance into the courtyard is for Hindus only, while the Muslims enter from the north entrance. But the towers of the temple that are plated with three-quarters of a ton of gold can be seen from a rooftop across the street, or from the rooftop of a hotel near the courtyard. For Westerners it may be the best view of the temple you are going to get.

Inside the temple is the Visvanatha *linga*, a smooth black stone sitting about a foot tall on a silver altar on the floor. Many other *lingas* are clustered around it. There are several other shrines around the temple, including one of Vishnu that must be worshiped as one enters the temple. The temple interior is not very ornate, but it can be quite crowded and filled with an intense mood of devotion. On the street just outside the courtyard entrance are many shops selling all kinds of religious paraphernalia, such as beads, flowers, incense, pictures of Shiva, etc. The street, Visvanatha Lane, has seen millions of pilgrims from all walks of life. And when they leave Visvanatha they stop at the small temple of Annapurna (Goddess of Plenty) across the street. She is considered the Queen of Varanasi, another aspect of the wife of Lord Shiva.

Making our way back through the alleys and down to the river, we find Lalita Ghat where there is the Ganga Keshava Vishnu shrine, and a Bhagirathi Devi or Ganga shrine. Bhagirathi is another name for the Ganga or Ganges River. There is also an ornate Nepali temple with an image of Pashupateshvara, like the one in Kathmandu. Next is the Jalasai cremation *ghat*, which is often referred to as part of Manikarnika Ghat. You can see piles of logs stacked on the steps ready for cremations, and sometimes there can be as many as five or six cremations taking place at once. The fires can easily be seen at night from a long distance away, and the smoke can fill the air of the *ghat* by day. Anyone can watch, but this is no place for photography which you will soon discover if you try taking photos. The fact that death is ever-present is obvious in India. Disease and death are not hidden away like in America, but are a fact of life that is dealt with on a daily basis; a reminder of the reasons why people are more spiritually inclined in India.

The cremations seem to be a morbid tourist attraction for foreigners, many of whom seem to think this is one of the most unusual sights in India. But there is a reason for the cremations at this location. The deceased are brought to the cremation ground by family members, and the eldest son shaves his head and dresses in a white cloth and, when everything is ready, lights the funeral pyre. The family stays until the body of the deceased has burned, and then the son throws the part of the body that does not burn into the Ganga, and douses the last embers with a pot of Ganga water, thus purifying whatever is left of their relative. Then they turn and leave. An excessive display of sorrow by family members at this time is said to be inauspicious for the dead, who is entering a new realm of existence.

The Doams are the low caste people who manage the cremation grounds and collect fees for tending the fires and supplying the wood. They gather the ashes of the deceased to be put into the Ganges. By cremating the body of the deceased, it is believed that the disembodied spirit will be more likely to go on to the next realm of existence. If the person had been very attached to life in the material body, the spirit may want to cling to the body in some way. If the body is cremated, then the spirit will be forced to move on. Furthermore, by pouring Ganga water on the body and the ashes, it is believed to help spiritually purify the deceased from past karma. It is said in *shastra* (the Vedic texts), such as the *Kashi Khanda*, that people who leave their bodies here will attain liberation and will receive spiritual existence. This is why it is the desire of many people to die and be cremated in Varanasi. It is also said that Lord Shiva whispers the mantra of liberation into the ear of those who die here, thus assuring them of a higher existence in their next life.

The next *ghat* is the Manikarnika, the most auspicious of all the *ghats*. Here Lord Vishnu's footprints are set in a circular marble slab in a little shrine, the holiest spot in Varanasi. It is said that here is where the process of universal creation and annihilation begins. The little 20 foot square spring-fed pond or *kund* that is also found here above the *ghat*, which used to be a lake many years ago, is said to have been dug out by Lord Vishnu with His disc near the beginning of creation and was filled with the water of His perspiration. Inside on the north steps is a small shrine with little deities of Vishnu. It was also here that Lord Shiva's jeweled-earring (Manikarnika) fell into the pool. But the *Shiva Purana* explains that it was Vishnu's earring that fell into the pool when the water expanded, upon which Lord Vishnu floated while bringing forth the cosmic egg or universe and the process of universal creation. It is also said that all the gods and goddesses come here to bathe in their subtle forms on a daily basis. Also on the *ghat* is the Tarakeshvara *linga* temple, which represents Shiva who whispers the mantra of liberation into the ears of those who die here. On the northern side of Manikarnika Ghat is a Shiva temple that has tilted and is no longer used. The foundation seemed to have given way during the construction of the Sindhia Ghat next to it. During the monsoon season the water level of the Ganga can rise quite high and flood the entrance to this temple.

Above Sindhia Ghat, the pilgrim walks up the hill and through the narrow streets to visit some more important temples. These temples are not easy to find but are well known to the locals, so only the more serious of the touring pilgrims will try to find them. These are temples dedicated to Vireshvara, Agnishvara, Nirriti, Upashanteshvara, and the goddess Sankata Devi above Sankata Ghat. Then there are temples of Katyayani Devi, Siddheshvari Devi, and the Lakshmanabala temple and Mangala Gauri temple above Lakshmanabala Ghat, just north of Rama Ghat.

The next important *ghat* is Panchaganga Ghat, a most holy confluence of the five (*pancha*) rivers, which include the Ganges, Yamuna, Sarasvati (which joined in Allahabad), and the Dhutpapa and Kirana, which are but trickling streams. Here we find many little niches on the steps housing various deities on the steps, one with a reclining Vishnu. It was here that the famous poet Kabir was initiated by Ramananda.

Above the steep and narrow steps leading through the buildings is the Bindu Madhava temple, one of the most significant Krishna temples in Varanasi. On the altar is a beautiful Krishna deity that stands about two feet tall, and smaller Sita-Rama and Lakshmi-Narayana deities. The temple room is somewhat small, with walls interspersed with windows and prints of Krishna's pastimes. The present Bindu Madhava temple is in a quaint building but still visited by many pilgrims. It is known to have been rebuilt several times from the 12th to 16th centuries, and used to be a marvelous structure and a very rich temple in which the deity, that had been quite large at that time, was dressed in a wide array of jewels. But the Muslim ruler Aurangzeb tore it down and built a mosque in its place. The huge mosque dominates the skyline, but is now unused and locked up. You can, however, get the guard from the nearby house to unlock the door to the mosque for you for a small donation. After climbing the steep stairs inside, you reach the rooftop for a good view of the Ganga River as it flows past the city. In the back of the mosque you can see remnants of the old Bindu Madhava temple that the Muslims used for building the mosque.

The Bindu Madhava temple, along with the Adi Keshava temple, was where Sri Chaitanya Mahaprabhu stayed and preached to the residents by chanting and dancing during His visit to Varanasi. When He first arrived He bathed at the Manikarnika Ghat and visited and preached at the Visvanatha temple where people lined up to see Him. He also held huge *kirtanas* (congregational singing) at *ghats* such as the Panchaganga.

From the Bindu Madhava temple we go farther into the city in the Chaukhamba district where some other Krishna temples are located. There is a Gopala temple and another Radha-Krishna temple. Both have small deities but are well known amongst devotees in this part of town. However, in order to reach them you must find your way through many narrow alleys that make giving directions useless. It is best to use a guide or someone who will take you there.

Back at the river we next come to Brahma Ghat, then Durga Ghat, and farther on is Gaya Ghat with nearby temples of goddesses Nageshvari Devi and Mukhanirmalika Devi. Next is Trilochana Ghat with the Trilochana temple in the alleyways above it, which contains a very old and famous *linga* in Varanasi, and also has a deity of Varanasi Devi. Nearby is the Mahadeva temple.

After this lies nothing but a long walk to the Adi Keshava temple. Several hundred years ago this area had many important temples before the Muslims invaded. The Adi Keshava temple, next to the confluence of the Varana and Ganga Rivers, has a very ancient significance. As mentioned earlier, Lord Vishnu first appeared here when He came to get the city back from King Divodasa for Lord Shiva. Unfortunately, because of its distance from the other temples, and due to people forgetting its importance, few pilgrims from outside Varanasi visit, so they are glad to see anyone. The Sangameshvara *linga* in a shrine next to Adi Keshava is said to have been installed by Lord Brahma, as was the four-faced Brahmeshvara deity next to it. The *Linga Purana* states that those who bathe in the confluence of the rivers here and then worship Sangameshvara need never fear taking rebirth. After having *darshan* and offering our respects to the deities, we take the long walk back to Manikarnika Ghat. Or if we want, we can begin walking along the river until we find a boat for hire and just ride a boat back.

Many other temples and holy sites exist in this city, such as the Kapalamochana Tirtha which is in the north part of town and is very auspicious to visit. This is where Shiva bathed and was purified from his sin of decapitating Lord Brahma's fifth head. He had carried this sin in the form of a skull, and after bathing at Kapalamochana the skull fell, meaning he had become purified. The legend behind this relates as follows:

Once Brahma disputed Lord Vishnu's superiority over himself. In connection with this, Shiva appeared between them in the form of a fiery column and asked both Brahma and Vishnu to reach the respectively upper and lower ends of the column. Lord Vishnu expressed His inability to do so, while Brahma falsely claimed to have accomplished the feat. On committing this offense, Shiva severed one of Brahma's five heads, reducing his heads to four. Thus, Brahma became wiser at the expense of one of his heads. However, for severing one of Brahma's heads, Shiva was charged with the sin of Brahma-hatya, or killing a brahmana, and the head stuck to his hand. At the bidding of Brahma, Shiva then went to Lord Vishnu for advice, and Vishnu told him to proceed to Kashi, Varanasi. There Shiva was purified of the sin of Brahma-hatya after bathing in the holy pond of Kapalamochana Tirtha.

The pilgrims who take the route to the five main holy *tirthas* along the river start at Asi Ghat, then stop at Dashashvamedha Ghat, then go to the Adi Keshava temple, then back to Panchaganga Ghat, and at last the Manikarnika Ghat. Then they go to pay respects to Visvanatha at the Golden temple. After touring the many *ghats* and temples along the river and elsewhere, and after seeing the Visvanatha temple, our pilgrim's tour of Varanasi is complete. Other temples of Varanasi could be described, but for most people I think this is enough.

Though Varanasi is a special town, it is losing its spiritual atmosphere. When I was there, I talked with a few wandering mendicants who were disillusioned with the city. One was an old man who told me that things were changing too fast, prices had gone way up in the past several years for things like food and basic necessities. Why? Because of the growing number of tourists who have less respect for the spiritual culture that Varanasi has always been known for, and who are willing to pay more for everything, which makes it more expensive for the local people to live as they had. He also said the local priests were primarily concerned about business and family, though they may take some time for spiritual activities. He said that real *sadhus* in Varanasi and places that accommodate them are decreasing.

Then I talked with another monk who was standing nearby and who was from the south, Ramesvaram, where the standard of Vedic or brahminical culture remains high. He said that a few years ago a monk could sleep at night on the steps of the *ghats* along the river and not be disturbed. He had done that the previous night and awoke to find his belongings had been stolen. He was also upset that many priests in Varanasi had now given up their strict brahminical diet and were eating forbidden things, like eggs, fish, or even chicken and goat, and were also smoking *bidis* (Indian cigarettes). He told me that all he wanted to do now was collect enough money to leave Varanasi as soon as possible.

So if you want to visit this city to see the spiritual side of it, you might want to go soon before it continues to lose more than it already has. But then I met another old *sadhu* who had just retired from being a teacher and moved to Varanasi and loved the place. He was staying at a local temple and had taken up some asceticism by eating only unspiced rice and dahl, nothing else. And he loved swimming in the Ganga River. He had just moved here from Dacca, Bangladesh, where he said the Muslims were creating so much political trouble and terrorism that he no longer wanted to stay there. So compared to that, I suppose Varanasi was a big improvement, especially now that he wanted to utilize his final years to concentrate on spiritual life.

SARNATH

From Varanasi we catch a bus or a motor ricksha for a 10 kilometer ride to Sarnath, a holy place for Buddhists and one of the four main towns in regard to the life of Buddha. This is the place where Buddha, after having attained enlightenment in Bodhgaya, gave his first sermon about reaching nirvana through the middle way. Lord Buddha stayed for one rainy season here, but never made a permanent residence at Sarnath. Yet, Sarnath became an important Buddhist center by the end of the fourth century B.C.E. when Ashoka ruled the area. It greatly flourished between the third and seventh centuries and was said to have as many as 1500 priests. During the 10th century the place declined and by the time the Muslims invaded in the 11th and again in the 12th centuries, it was practically destroyed.

As we approach Sarnath, we first see the Chaukhandi Stupa on the left which is the remains of an ancient stupa from the second or third century. On our right is the Archeological Museum that has a nice collection of ancient relics from the area. Across the road from the museum is a Jain temple built in 1824 which contains images of Shreanshnath, the 11th *tirthankara* of the Jains. Behind the Jain temple are the excavations of the old temples and monasteries. This includes the main shrine, Kumara Devi's temple, and other things like the Ashoka Pillar, built around 250 B.C.E., which may mark the site of Buddha's first sermon. Beyond the ruins is a pleasant garden area called the Deer Park.

Near the Jain temple is the massive Dhamekh Stupa, built in the fifth century and stands 98 feet high. East of this stupa is the Mulgandha Kuti-Vihar, a modern replica of the Mahabodhi temple in Bodhgaya built by the Mahabodhi Society in 1932. Inside are very colorful murals of Buddha' life, and a beautiful image of Buddha on the altar. Next to the temple is a life size diorama exhibit of Buddha giving his first sermon to his first disciples under a Bo tree. This tree is a transplant of the tree in Sri Lanka, which is a descendent of the original Bo tree that Buddha sat under when he became enlightened. Not far from here is the Chinese temple which contains a beautiful white marble Buddha.

There is also a Tibetan Monastery at Sarnath. Everything at Sarnath can be seen in a few hours.

AYODHYA

From Varanasi it is an easy train ride up to Ayodhya. We take the train to Ayodhya from Varanasi because it is easier to find a direct train more regularly than at Allahabad. And besides, Varanasi is just east of Allahabad and is a town not to be missed. So now it is time to move on.

A pilgrimage to Ayodhya is considered most auspicious since it is the birthplace of Lord Ramachandra. By visiting the temples in this town we rid ourselves of many life-times of karma. This place is a small and simple town that does not cater much to foreign tourists, but it is a very spiritual place with more temples than you can mention. The nice thing about it is that Western pilgrims can enter almost every temple in town and see the deities and watch the ceremonies, so you do not get that feeling of being excluded from the spiritual activities that go on here. Some people say that in Ayodhya every house is a temple, which means there are more than 8000 temples. And there are temples where you least expect to find them. You can be walking down the street at night passing by a plain looking building and be surprised when you look inside and see the flames of ghee lamps being swung in the air for the *arati* ceremony in front of the deity of Lord Rama, while the sound of ringing bells and singing voices accompany it. As you wander around, you have to be willing to stop and check out unexpected temples that can often have beautiful deities and interiors to see. You just never know what you will find. Everywhere you go Lord Ramachandra is the central point of the lives of the people who live here. But it is also said that Buddha stayed in Ayodhya for some time, which became an important place for Buddhism for a while. Plus, Ayodhya is the birthplace of the first and fourth Jain *thirtankaras*.

The town is located on the Gogra River, where there are some nice temples at the *ghats* of Rama ki Pauri. This is a very pleasant area to walk and visit the various temples and see the numerous deities, among which are the Sri Nagyshwarnath temple, which has a Shiva *lingam* that is said to have a connection with Lord Rama. Around the corner is the Sri Kaleram Mandir that has nice Sita-Rama deities. As you walk along the *ghats* and the river inlet, you can easily go in one temple after another to view the lovely deities.

Elsewhere in Ayodhya is the Sri Valmiki Ramayan Bhavan that has the complete *Ramayan* written on the inside walls. At this temple they hold regular discourses on the *Ramayana* in Hindi, and the temple fills up with many devotees, young and old alike, who will sit for hours to listen. Nearby is the Sri Charoo Dham Mandir that houses older male devotees and brahmanas. The Kanak Bhavan or Golden temple is one of the older and more important temples in town. Many people gather here to perform *bhajans* and *kirtanas* in front of the most beautiful deities of Sita-Rama, Lakshmana, Satrughna, and Hanuman. This temple even has bedrooms for the deities.

The Vasistha Mandir is a recently remodeled temple that marks the place where Rama and His brother Lakshmana studied in their youth under the great sage Vasistha. This temple has paintings and dioramas that tell the story. Plus, there is a well (Vasistha Kund) in the middle of the courtyard that is supposed to be the well where Rama and Lakshmana got water for bathing and drinking.

One of the most important Hanuman temples in all of India is also found in Ayodhya, the temple of Hanuman Ghri. Hanuman was the dear monkey servant of Lord Rama. The temple is up a flight of stairs in a small fortress on a hilltop. Many pilgrims, some pushing their way through the crowds up to the altar, come to see the deity of Hanuman, which is so decorated with flower garlands and jewelry that you can only see his vermilion covered face. Around the small courtyard are other altars for deities of Durga, Shiva, Ganesh, and Sita-Rama. In the evening some of the older people attend the discourses that are held in one of the rooms in the courtyard.

Other fascinating temples you can visit include the Sri Tulsi Smarak Bhawan, Sri Raj Sadan, the Dasaratha Mahal, and places like the Sarooj Kund, Sri Tulsi Park, Sri Janki Bhag, along with other temples you will find as you wander through the town. There is also a Jain temple here, though it is not so impressive, and the Birla family, the industrialists who are noted for building very nice temples in many major towns and cities, also have a nice temple here dedicated to Sita-Rama-Lakshmana and Hanuman. The people are very friendly and, though they may stare at you out of curiosity, if you simply greet them by exclaiming "Jaya Rama" or "Sita-Rama ki jaya!" they will easily smile and similarly respond.

There is, however, some political trouble here, and it evolves around the place called Sri Ram Janma Bhoomi, or the location where Lord Rama is said to have taken birth in this world during Treta-yuga, many years prior to the appearance of Lord Krishna. The problem stems from the fact that there is a 500 year old mosque (Babri Masjid) at the spot. I was told that there used to be a Rama temple there but it was torn down by the fanatic Muslims, led by Aurangzeb, who then built a mosque in its place. This is not the only town where the Muslims have done this. They have also torn down the famous Visvanatha (Shiva) temple in Varanasi, and the Sri Krishna Janma Bhoomi temple in Mathura and built mosques at the sites. They also cut five storeys off the seven-storey tall Govinda temple in Vrindavan. Incidents of Muslims destroying Hindu and Buddhist temples are known to have happened all over north and central India.

Anyway, the Hindus have always resented what the Muslims did in Ayodhya and now want to replace the mosque with a Rama temple as it had been years ago. But the Muslims do not want this, so there is trouble until some arrangement is made. In fact, there were big demonstrations here in which people were killed shortly after I had visited Ayodhya in early 1990. And this sparked off bitter demonstrations in other parts of India as well. So this explains why I saw so many police patrolling the streets and important temples.

When I first saw the mosque in 1990, which was considered the Ram Janma Bhoomi (birthplace of Lord Rama), we were not allowed to bring in any cameras or shoulder bags or even metal belt buckles into the mosque, and you had to pass through metal detectors. The mosque itself was highly fortified with barricades and barbed wire fencing, and police were all over the place, and still are. But once you got inside it did not seem like a mosque at all. Two of the three domed rooms were used as a Sita-Rama temple and had altars with small Sita-Rama deities, which were installed in 1986, along with many pictures of Lord Rama. They still did the *arati* ceremonies several times a day, and many devotees visit from all over India. Only the third room had a few pictures of Muslim saints on the walls. So it certainly was not used very much as a mosque and had not been used in such a way in years. So the question would be; why not let the Hindus build a nice temple to Lord Rama?

The next time I visited this place was in 2001, when the mosque had been torn down by angry Hindus. Then when I wanted to see the Ram Janma Bhoomi, I had to wait at the security office while they took my passport number. Without a passport you cannot get in. Some of the security guards were pleased to meet me. After about a half-hour, a security man who spoke English came along and He took me through the area. You had to leave your camera bag at a certain checkpoint, go through security checks and get padded down with metal detectors, and then follow a narrow aisle that is fenced in with heavy barbed wire. You follow that along with numerous other pilgrims. This took you near the hilltop where the Ram Janma Bhoomi is, and where the mosque used to be. Then you see the deity of Lord Rama for about five seconds. He is in a tent attended by a few priests, and then you are moved along. Then as you shuffle back to the security checkpoint, you pick up your camera bag and head off to another place. After seeing these and other temples concludes our visit to Ayodhya.

Another town not far away that is certainly worth visiting is Faizabad, six kilometers from Ayodhya. It is a much bigger town of 210,000. What we are looking for is Gupta Ghat. Our auto-ricksha driver can take us there. This is where we find a very plain looking temple which honors the place from where Lord Ramachandra left this world. Inside is an altar which has several sets of Sita-Rama deities, along with numerous *shalagram-shilas*, and Hanuman deities. Not many people visit this temple, so the priest is glad to see any visitors and is very friendly. There is a special room which houses a little shrine marking the place from where Lord Rama ended His appearance in the material world. Remember, this site goes back thousands of years.

NAIMISARANYA (TIRUNAIMISARANYAM)

Being in Ayodhya, and while we are this close to another holy town, we might consider going to Naimisaranya. So we get a train that goes directly to Sitapur, or one that goes to Lucknow, and then get a three-hour train or bus to Sitapur. Once we arrive in Sitapur, if we have arrived by train, we can get a room at a simple hotel that is not too far away, such as the Tourist Lodge. This town does not have many hotels, but a much nicer and more expensive one is located farther into town, called the Mayur Hotel.

Naimisaranya is the place we are interested to visit, but these days the name has been shortened to Nimkhar, which is the name you will find on the map, located 80 km northwest of Lucknow along the Gomati River. It is located at the junction of the roads from Sitapur and Khairabad, 20 miles from Sitapur and 24 miles from the Sandila railway station, and 45 miles north of Lucknow in Uttarpradesh. Even though it has guest houses and *dharamshalas* for pilgrims to stay, they did not seem all that plentiful to me. That is why we can stay at Sitapur and then take a bus for a day trip to Nimkhar.

Naimisaranya is an important place of pilgrimage. It is mentioned frequently in both the *Mahabharat* and the *Ramayana.* It is noted for being where Saunaka Rsi and 60,000 other sages performed a sacrifice to help ward off the deteriorating effects of Kali-yuga. It was also here 5,000 years ago, at the junction of Dvapara and Kali-yugas, when Suta Gosvami spoke the *Srimad-Bhagavatam* (*Bhagavata Purana*). The specific place where this is said to have happened is now called Suta Gaddi. This is also where Lord Balarama killed Romaharshana Suta for being so conceited that he did not stand to offer respects when Lord Balarama approached the sages. Thereafter, Balarama decided that Romaharshana's son, Ugrasrava Suta or Suta Gosvami, would recite the *Bhagavatam* in place of him.

Chakra Tirtha Kund is the center of attention at Naimisaranya, and is also said to be the center of the universe. The *Vayaviya Tantra, Vayu Purana* and the *Brahmanda Purana* explain that Lord Brahma imagined a great wheel that enclosed the whole universe, the hub of which was here. Also, it is said that 88,000 *rishis* and sages went to Brahma to ask where is the best place for them to perform *tapasya*, spiritual austerities. Brahma said that his chakra would indicate the location of such a place. Brahma sent out a great chakra which moved around until it reached Naimisaranya where its rim was shattered. It thus formed the Chakra Tirtha Kund. The sages, following this wheel, bright as the sun, stopped at Naimisaranya and also settled here. However, the chakra was still moving, which worried the sages who approached Brahma about it. Brahma then sent his *shakti* in the form of Lalita Devi who stopped the chakra. This quelled the fear of the sages, and Lalita Devi became an important part of the legend of Chakra Tirtha Kund.

The *kund* is a huge spring of sweet water which has no bottom. The proof of this happened when the British wanted to show the falsehood of this legend years ago. They lowered a cable into the *kund* to find the bottom but quit and gave up when they ran out of cable after reaching a depth of 3200 feet.

Legend has it that if on a full moon day on Monday you bathe here and make an offering to Lalita, the main female deity in the nearby temple, and then bathe in the *kund*, you are relieved of all the sins of a lifetime. However, more important than that is bathing here on the twelfth lunar day, which takes you to the abode of Vishnu, in spite of however many sins one has committed. You can witness as many as 10,000 people who visit on such days. It is also explained that if a person walks eight miles along the Ganga River, he will acquire the merit of performing one *ashwamedha* ritual. In Kashi (Varansi) one gets the same result by walking only four miles, and only two miles when walking in Kurukshetra. But when one walks in Naimisaranya, every step is equal to such merit.

Nimkhar is an hour bus ride west of Sitapur. The Nimkhar bus stand is on the other side of the Sitapur township. So we get a motor ricksha from our hotel to the Nimkhar bus stand. The bus ride is extremely bumpy, so try not to sit in the back of the bus, which makes the bumps all the worse. The bus makes stops along the way at various towns and villages to pick up and drop off passengers. Finally, as you approach Naimisaranya, you will pass under an arch which welcomes you. Soon the bus stops and everyone gets off. You will find cycle rickshas waiting for passengers. But these are more like cycles pulling small flatbed carts. Nonetheless, if you want to see all the main temples fairly quickly, just climb in and use it, after negotiating a price. Otherwise, you can easily walk to the Chakra Tirhta Kund without any ride.

Many pilgrims walk to the Lalita Devi temple first. On our way down the road, we will pass a Gaudiya Math temple with beautiful deities of Radha-Vinoda Vihari and Lord Chaitanya. This was established by Srila Bhaktisiddhanta because he felt this town was so important that it should have a Gaudiya temple. They also have a free *prasada* distribution program at lunch time, and many pilgrims attend. I also visited at that time and the cook was glad to give me a plate of *maha-prasada*, remnants of the deity offering, which was quite good.

As we walk farther down the road, we pass numerous pilgrims who are also visiting this holy place. As we reach the Lalita Devi temple, we approach an area of vendors just in front of the temple and purchase flowers and paraphernalia for doing worship and making a little offering to the deity of Lalita. This area has several little shops for this purpose so the shop owners often compete in trying to get us to go to one or the other. When we pick one, they put everything we need together quickly, and give it to us as they take our money. Then we go into the Devi temple where the priests are more than happy to help us through a little worship ceremony. As we leave, other priests want us to throw holy offerings into the sacred fire, at a cost of more rupees. But we need to be careful. All these priests will try to get us to give a large amount of money as a donation, *backshish*. And if we are too kind, we may find that in the first five minutes of being at Naimisaranya we have already spent several hundred rupees, and we have not even gone to Chakra Tirtha Kund yet.

After paying our respects to Lalita Devi, then we go to Chakra Tirtha Kund. This is a round pool or *kund* with eight sides. There is an inner circle cordoned off, which is the deep part of the *kund*. So everyone stays outside that circle. Then we can take a holy bath, or sprinkle some water on our heads. In any case, there will be some priests of the *tirtha* to guide us through a little ceremony at the *kund*. Again we will need to put a limit in the amount of money we can give the priest, or they will ask for a donation for each thing they do. However, giving something is proper because they can show us how to do it, and how many times might we ever return to this place? On one side of the *kund* are small shrines to various divinities, and you can see the priests engaging groups of people in various rituals.

Once we have taken our holy dip in the water, we can take the short walk to visit the nearby Vyasa Gaddi. This is said to be where Vyasadeva sat under the big, 5000-year old banyan tree and divided the *Vedas* into four parts. A central mound in the little temple is said to mark the spot, while there is also a deity of Vyasadeva on one side and another of Shukadeva Gosvami on the other. Right across from this little temple is the *yajna pitha*, or spot where the 60,000 sages had gathered with Saunaka Rishi to perform sacrifices or rituals for warding off the darkness of Kali-yuga. Vyasa later provided 17 *Puranas*, yet was still not satisfied. After being approached by Narada Muni who instructed him to write one more *Purana* about Lord Krishna, Vyasa composed the *Bhagavata Purana*. He did this at his Badarika Ashrama, now near Badrinatha. Only after having done this did he feel complete in accomplishing his purpose of explaining this highest of all spiritual knowledge for the benefit of humanity.

From here we can move on to visit a number of other temples. It is said that within the 16-km circumference of the *parikrama* path of Naimisaranya one can find all the sacred places of India. The *Varaha Purana* explains that this is a powerful place in which we can become free of demonic influence by the performance of *yajna*, or austerities. Many great personalities have taken advantage of the potency of Naimisaranya, or given more power to it, such as Lord Ramachandra, Lord Balarama, Dadhici Muni (when the demigods asked him to sacrifice his body so they could use it to make a weapon to kill the demon Vrittrasura), the Pandavas, Shankaracharya, Lord Nityananda, Surdas, and Ramanujacharya.

As we go around the *parikrama* route, we can go to the Gomati River. This is a pleasant area, and there is a little *kund* next to the river called Gangotri Kund, and another called Brahma Kund. As we tour some of the temples, we also visit Hanuman Garhi. This has a self-manifested deity of Hanuman that is 18-feet tall. This commemorates the time when Hanuman appeared here after rescuing Rama and Lakshmana from being captured by the demon Ravana and kept in Patalaloka, the bottom of the universe. This is described in the *Ramayana*. You can see the deity of Hanuman with Rama and Lakshmana on either shoulder. Pilgrims put sweets in between his lips.

Other places to see include the Panch Pandava, the temple dedicated to the five Pandavas. There is also the 1008 Shiva Linga temple, which is basically a courtyard with a central shrine. This is surrounded by 1008 small *lingas* on the shelves of the wall that makes the courtyard. It is also said to have copies of the four *Vedas* and many *Puranas*. A small Ramanuja temple is also in town. Modern temples are also here and more are being built. A Narada Deva temple is also worth seeing and has 108 altars. There are also temples to Chakranarayana, Ganesh, Rama, Lakshman, and others.

Back at Chakra Tirtha Kund, we take a different path that leads us to the Suta Gaddi. This is an old building that sits on a small hill. This was another important place for me to visit since this is where Suta Gosvami spoke the *Srimad-Bhagavatam* that we study today. He spoke this to the large group of sages who had gathered here at that time to thwart the approaching difficulties of the age of Kali. You have to knock on the door so they will let you in, but they are glad to see you. The interior is a little run down, and they are trying to rebuild it. There is a little sanctum that has an altar with small Radha-Krishna deities, with a sacred seat nearby which commemorates the location where Suta Gosvami sat when he spoke. This is also the place where Vyasadeva spoke the *Puranas* that he had composed. So this is a very important place.

It takes a few hours to see the main places of interest, so it is best just to take a day trip out of Sitapur. To help find your way around you may want to use a guide since the places are spread out and some are not easy to find. Try to get a guide who knows English, which most people do not speak here.

It is easy to get a bus or a share-taxi back to Sitapur. And once we are back, we can make arrangements to catch the evening train to our next port of interest, which in this case will be Gorakhpur.

GORAKHPUR/KUSHINAGAR

Gorakhpur can be easily reached from Sitapur or Ayodhya, in case you did not want to venture to Naimisaranya. This town is named after the Shaivite yogi, Gorakhnath. Its main spiritual attraction is the temple of Gorakhnath, which is large and on a sizable piece of property. When I visited it, a fair was going on, so there were lots of people. Families were arriving to see the temple and also enjoy the atmosphere. There are lots of booths in the front grounds that sell sweets, various food items, what looked like extra large and sweetened puris, as well as devotional paraphernalia. There were also boat rides in the nearby *kund*, and the lines to go into the temple were quite long. In another part of the grounds were other rides like a Ferris wheel, etc.

The temple is a lovely structure with three towers. After entering the doorways, people form lines, men and women are separate. Then they let groups of the men go up to have *darshan* of the deity, and when they leave groups of women go up next. Around the main temple building are other smaller shrines, including a small temple for Radha-Krishna. Gorakhpur is also the home of Gita Press, which publishes many books on Hindu or Vedic philosophy.

Another of the main reasons why we want to visit this place is to see Kushinagar, which is known for being where Buddha left this world, thus entering Mahaparinirvana. Pilgrims will take an eastbound bus from Gorakhpur to Kasia (Kushinagar) 55 km away. You can get the bus at the stand near the train station. This is why when staying in Gorakhpur, it is best to stay in a hotel across from the train station for ease of making travel arrangements. Buses to other locations can be had at the Katchari bus stand 1 km south of the train station. You can also take a taxi if you want, which is more convenient since the bus drops you off, but the taxi will continue to take you to the various sites or temples you want to see and bring you back whenever you are ready. It is a one-and-a-half hour ride there.

Once you arrive in front of the main temple, you make your way in through the gate and down the sidewalk to the Mahaparinirvana Stupa. This is considered to be the place where the Buddha left his body. Actually, I was told that there are two Sarasa trees in front of the shrine and between them is the actual spot where this happened. Anyway, the present shrine has been reconditioned and looks much nicer than it did before. The front building is made in a half-barrel design, and has an image of Buddha reclining in the position he was supposed to have taken when he passed from this world. The image is carved out of one piece of chunar stone and measures 20 feet in length. Buddha is lying on a platform and draped with a long red cloth.

Behind this building is the Mahaparinirvana Stupa which commemorates the place where the Buddha left his body. It was here that Buddha selected as the place of his passing after having announced his approaching disappearance three months in advance to Ananda, Buddha's first disciple. This *stupa* originally dates back to 413-55 BC, but was rebuilt in 1927 by the Burmese. However, the present structure is a new outer building that houses the older *stupa* inside it. Around the area you can see the ruins and foundations of a few old monasteries that are being excavated.

About three-quarters of a mile away there is also the old brick Ramabhar Tila (or Angara Chaitya) that is said to mark the spot where the Buddha's body was cremated. It is said that years ago vandals bore into the *stupa* to steal whatever valuables they could find. Through this passage the bottom of the *stupa* can now be reached where one can still see the scorched earth, thus confirming that a cremation took place here.

Nearby and along the main road are other modern monasteries that you can visit, such as the Thai, Burmese, Japanese, and Chinese temples. They are quite lovely and ornate, and have images of the Buddha, some of which are quite large.

GOING TO NEPAL AT SAUNALI FOR LUMBINI

Now you have a choice, you can travel north to Nepal, which I recommend everyone to do if you get the chance, or you can head back to Varanasi and go on to Patna, where we will continue our journey through East India. For those of us who are going to Nepal, we may first want to get a passport photo here in Gorakhpur for our Nepali visa, and make arrangements to take a bus to the border town of Saunali. Our hotel can usually help us with this if we ask.

Once we are ready, we can take a bus to Saunali. If we take a morning bus, there will be plenty of time to cross the border into Nepal. It is only about a three hour or more bus ride to Saunali. Once we reach the bus stand we can get a cycle ricksha to carry our bags and take us to the points of entry. This area is really crowded. The street is narrow and the traffic is thick. So that alone can slow us down.

Before taking a ricksha, make sure you agree with the driver on the price of the ride BEFORE you go anywhere. If the driver does not agree to that, then walk along and find another driver even if you are tired from your long ride, unless you just don't care. And don't agree to let him exchange Indian rupees for Nepali rupees for you. He may take a chunk of the change and say there was a charge or tax. He may also say he needs 75 rupees for the tax that is charged on rickshas crossing the border. There is no ricksha tax. And although not all drivers may try these tricks, some of them will tell you anything in an attempt to get your money if you look like you don't know the procedure for crossing the border. Don't listen to any of this and just give him the agreed price for the ride and nothing else, or find another driver.

First we go to the Indian Customs and Immigrations offices to fill out forms on any outstanding purchases and to have our passport stamped. Then we head for the border, which we cross and go to the Nepali immigration office where we get our visa. We simply have to fill out a form, give them our passport photo and $30, and we are soon on our way. The usual visa is for three months but you can easily get them extended later if you want to. For us, three months is more than enough. We will be here only for a few weeks at the most.

The next thing we want to do is have our ricksha driver take us to a hotel. We can continue on our way if we want by going to the bus stand and booking the next bus to either Pokhara or Kathmandu, depending on where we want to go. The only thing is that if we leave on the next bus, some of the trip will be during the night, which means we will not see as much of the landscape. And as we get farther into Nepal, the scenery gets quite interesting. So I spend the night here. I can have my hotel book my bus ticket for me, which will naturally cost a little more to let them do it. But while they do that, it is one less thing to worry about while I go visit Lumbini.

Most hotels here are connected with a travel agency, so they are only too happy to help you with such things, and it does make your trip easier. So we also book a taxi to take to go to Lumbini as soon as it can arrive. Then when we return they will also have our bus ticket ready for us. Also, the hotels and businesses here take Indian rupees as well as Nepali rupees, but you should exchange some money into Nepali rupees here so you will be prepared for the rest of your trip. There are offices around town for changing your money, so this is easy.

GOING TO NEPAL THROUGH RAXAUL TO BIRGANJ

If you decide not to go to Gorakhpur or Lumbini and decide to go to Kathmandu from Varanasi or Patna by bus, then you will go into Nepal through Raxaul and over to Birganj, which many people do. The difference is that the ride from Patna or Varanasi to the Nepal border takes several hours, so if you do not start early enough, you will get there after dark. I do not like going through unfamiliar places like this after dark. That is why crossing the border at Saunali was easier.

Crossing the Nepal border through Raxaul and to Birganj takes about 45 minutes from the time we get off the bus. Our first stop will be at the Indian immigration office to check out of the country and get our passport stamped. If it is during the evening, the mosquitoes are so thick as we and the clerks fill out the forms in these offices that we practically have to dance to keep them from biting. Stop moving for a second and they've got us. When we leave this office we ride our cycle rickshaw through the night along the dark, quiet, and deserted road and cross into Nepal. The next stop is to the Nepali immigration office to get our Nepal visa, if we don't already have one. So we fill out the forms, and give them a passport photo and $30. We get our visa and check into the country, then continue our ride on to Birganj, the Nepal bordertown, and our hotel, the standards of which depends on the travel company with which we booked our "through" ride. It could end up being very basic accommodation at a rinky dink house where we spend the night fighting mosquitoes instead of sleeping. [In many cases, however, it is cheaper to book your own ticket to the border, then cross the border, and then book your own ticket on a bus of your choice, rather than booking a ticket from Patna or somewhere and all the way through to Kathmandu.] By the time morning comes we'll be relieved just for the chance to get the heck out of town and on our way to Kathmandu. The buses leave Birganj between 6.00 and 9.00 AM. If we get the faster Japanese-made bus and leave around 7.30, we can expect to arrive in Kathmandu about 4.30. From Patna, taking the 45 minute flight to Kathmandu and avoiding the two days of travel is much easier, unless you are on a low budget.

LUMBINI

While we are crossing into Nepal from Saunali, the nearby town of Lumbini is considered to be the birthplace of Gautama Buddha. So for many Buddhists and Hindus alike, this is a place of pilgrimage. When the taxi arrives to pick us up, it may only be a van and a driver. But it is a 45 minute drive to Lumbini, about 22 km away. You can also take the bus, which leaves every half-hour and is cheaper, but it moves rather slowly and is not all that convenient. So I take a taxi. There is not much to see in Lumbini, so it is best to simply see it as a day trip from Saunali. However, as with any such place like this, as the tourist and pilgrim trade increases, there are more buildings and temples with monasteries that are being built.

We first arrive to see the Japanese Peace Pagoda, which is on the outskirts of town. It is a lovely pagoda, with a different form of Buddha facing in each of the four directions. There is a small monastery just across from it. Then we can visit some of the other newer temples and monasteries in the vicinity. These often represent the different Buddhist countries, such as Thailand, China, Japan, or Tibet.

One of the main points of interest here is the Ashoka pillar, built in 244 B.C.E. by Emperor Ashoka near the site where Buddha was born. Near that is a small temple that has a slab of rock with the scene of Buddha's birth carved on it. It shows Maya Devi holding onto a tree while Buddha is emerging from her side. There is also another smaller rock under glass with Buddha's footprint on it, which is held in a shrine wherein many people go to see it. Modern excavations have discovered the foundations of an old monastery, the ruins of which you can see nearby. There is also the *kund* or pond where Buddha's mother, Maya Devi, bathed before she gave birth to Buddha, and where ablutions were performed after his birth. This is also near a Tibetan Buddhist monastery that you can visit that has beautiful wall murals and a huge image of Buddha in its temple building. There are some joyful and young Buddhist monks that also stay here.

Our whole visit to Lumbini will take no more than a few hours. Then it is back to Saunali. We should be booked for an early morning bus so we can get to Pokhara and still have time to explore the town. This should be easy since the bus ride only takes about six-and-a-half hours. The scenery through the Nepali hills is great.

As we proceed, we will notice a difference between the Indian and Nepali cultures right away. And the further we get into Nepal, the bigger the differences we'll find. At first the landscape is nothing special as we ride through the plains. But later we'll ride past steep hills with terraced slopes and little cabins precariously built on them that look as if they could tip over and roll down at any minute. As we make our way into Nepal, the hills get quite big and the landscape is very beautiful; breathtaking in some parts. We will also ride next to rivers, some of which have swift rapids, flowing through the mountainous hills. Sometimes we'll go over a hill that allows us to see some snow capped peaks in the distance. This is why we decided to come by land instead of plane.

POKHARA

This is not a place of pilgrimage, but I liked visiting this town. It is like a little version of Kathmandu, and has everything but on a smaller scale. There are a variety of shops for Nepali art, carpets, books, embroidered T-shirts, travel agents, boat rides on the calm Phewa Lake or to the Shiva temple on the little island, or even hang-gliding from Sarangkot hill. Pokhara is a rather quiet town. There is the main bazaar area in the city, but most tourists stay in the lake area, which is much different. There are a wide variety of hotels, so you can shop around and take your pick from small and low budget, to more sophisticated and high-end. The main street by the lake has everything you will need, and then some. You can also visit restaurants in the evening that have shows that display local folk dances and songs, if you want a taste of some of the Nepali tradition. This is a nice place to sit back and relax without all the traffic of the big cities. You can also rent bicycles or motorcycles to get around the area. But be careful. There is no insurance on these bikes so if any thing happens and you have a serious accident, you are out of luck for any compensation. Of course, you can just take very pleasant walks for miles into the countryside. Most everyone speaks English and is quite friendly.

Pokhara is especially known for its great views of the incredible snow-capped Annapurna mountain range, with the peak of Machapuchhare being most notable. It is also known for the treks that start from Pokhara. For starters, you can take an easy three hour walk up Sarangkot hill. Or take a taxi early in the morning. At an elevation of 1592 meters, this is a great place to view the mountains, especially at sunrise. The best trek of all Nepal is the one that goes to the Muktinatha temple. It takes about two weeks, is relatively safe, not too rough, and provides a good adventure. A friend of mine went on this trek and liked it enough that he hopes to go back to Nepal sometime to do some more trekking. The sunsets here are also world famous, especially when viewing the colors reflected off the lake with the mountains in the background.

Around town you can see several interesting sites, such as Devi Falls (also called David's Falls). This is about 2 km southwest of the airport on the main Siddhartha Highway, just before arriving at the Tashiling Tibetan Village. The Pardi Khola is the outflow from Phewa Lake, and at Devi Falls it suddenly drops into a hole in the ground and disappears. Its alternative name of David's Falls comes from the story of a tourist named David who went too close and disappeared down the hole, taking his girlfriend with him. They were never seen again.

A little ways down the road on the other side you can visit the Guptaisar Mahadeva Cave. You get your ticket and flashlight, and then go down the stairs until a most humid and warm draft of air hits you. This is a cave with a small shrine to Shiva. And if you can unlock the gate past the shrine with the key they give you at the ticket counter, you can go farther into the cave, making your way through the narrow passageway and down the rocks to get a different view of the Devi Falls. This time you are looking up at it as the water descends to form a stream in the cave. However, this cave is only accessible during the dry season. Otherwise the water flow is much greater and the cave floods. The river emerges from its underground route and joins the Fusre Khola before flowing into the Seti River. The Seti River also carves out a gorge that in parts are over 100 feet deep.

If you want, you can also go to the Pokhara museum. It is small and simple but gives some insight into the nature of the culture and history of the tribes in this area.

You can also visit some of the Tibetan settlements in the area. Tashiling Tibetan Village is where they weave carpets, and is only 2 km south-west of the airport. Other settlements are also outside of the lake area, down the road a ways. You will see Tibetans selling their wares in town and in the lake area. They are quite friendly, but that may be because they are hoping for a sale. Nonetheless, I met one Tibetan lady who was born near Pokhara shortly after her parents left Tibet. She said she had never seen her own country of Tibet.

Another temple includes the Bimbasani (Bimbodayaisan) temple, dedicated to the Goddess that is said to live in the hills. Smaller shrines to Shiva and Ganesh are also located here.

If you want to stay a while and see more of the area, you can easily acquire more information from any of the travel shops, and then plan accordingly.

When our visit to Pokhara is finished, we can fly to Kathmandu, which offers excellent views of the mountains. Or we can take a bus, which lets a person see the wide variety of landscapes in Nepal. The busses leave around 7 AM or so, and arrive in Kathmandu about seven hours later. Once again, we can book our bus ticket through our hotel and also reserve a taxi to come and pick us up in the early morning. Once the bus fills up, we are on our way.

MUKTINATH

There are some people who like to walk up into the hills, or even find their own *shalagrama-shilas* at the Gandaki River. So Muktinath may interest you. You can go there by a combination of bus and trek. Many people like the trek. Otherwise, you can take a bus up to Jomsom, 250 km northwest of Kathmandu, north of Pokhara, and then a day's walk up to Muktinath. The journey can also be done on a pony. But be sure to take warm clothes and rain gear.

Muktinath has a Vishnu temple that is one of the Divya Desams, or one of the 108 most holy places of Lord Vishnu. It is at an elevation of 12,000 feet (3749m). So it is not unusual to be very cold here. So pick the season carefully when you want to visit. Muktinath is a name of Lord Vishnu which means "Lord of Liberation." The temple itself is called Jiwala Mayi, and has an oriental look to it. Interestingly, it is managed by some Buddhist nuns. Inside, no photos are allowed, but they may have a photo you can purchase of the central shrine. For a little donation you can also see the sacred natural gas flames that burn on rock and water, hidden behind a curtain. These are also mentioned in the *Mahabharata*. Off to the side from the temple is a spot that has 108 water spouts of sacred water that you can bathe in, if the cold does not stop you.

For those who want to find their own *shalagram-shilas*, Damodara Kund, or Forbidden Lake, is about a nine or ten day trek from Muktinath, best undertaken in late summer. It is considered the source of the Gandaki River and is a major and popular source of the *shalagram-shilas*. These are the self-manifested stone deities of Lord Vishnu. They are small black stones found in the water here, and the special features that each one has can distinguish it for being a particular form of one of the *avataras* of Lord Vishnu. They are accepted as direct manifestations of the Lord, which can be worshiped without any further installation or preparation, except the worshiper must be serious and attentive to continue it once started. So this is the place to find them.

The holy town of Ridi Bazaar is also a place where *shalagram-shilas* can be found. It is at the confluence of the Ridi River and the Kali Gandaki, which is a tributary of the Ganges. This is about 28 km, or a two-hour bus ride, from Tansen, and about 75 km from Pokhara. There is a significant Vishnu temple here that has a large *shalagram-shila* that represents Lord Hrishikesh. It is said that all of your sins can be washed away if you fast here and then worship the diety, after which you take a holy bath in the Kali Gandaki.

GOING TO KATHMANDU

The ride feels long and the bus is often filled with too many people, and the seats often do not give much leg room. A few times we'll stop at small Nepali towns and get out to stretch and buy some fruit, or have a noon stop for a vegetarian lunch at a little village restaurant where we can converse with the local people and our fellow travelers. Invariably there will be other Westerners on the bus, and it can be fun to talk and share stories of our journey. Again, between Pokhara and Kathmandu, the landscapes are very beautiful and inspiring. We travel through small towns, steep hillsides, and swift rivers. It is a great journey.

As we creep up the last and biggest hill on the winding and narrow road that has a steep drop on one side, we hope the driver knows what he is doing. One wrong move and we are all finished. The roads here have no guardrails. Nonetheless, as the bus turns this way and that, it gives us a chance to look out over the picturesque landscape of Nepal. But soon we are over the top of the hill and we slowly start down the other side, riding past houses and little businesses or shops on the outskirts of Kathmandu valley. After about another 45 minutes or so, we make the last few turns into the city and here we are, on the other side of the world in that strange and exotic city of Kathmandu.

When we arrive, whether by bus or by air, many agents from hotels will be there to greet us and offer their rates and services. Some may even provide a free ride just for us to come and see the hotel. If it sounds good, check it out. It could be worthwhile. When I go to Kathmandu, rather than staying in the Thamel area where the newer hotels are located, I like to stay near Durbar Square in the old section of town. Things may not be quite as modern, but we readily find much more of the old culture, which is the real Kathmandu as far as I'm concerned.

KATHMANDU

Kathmandu, the largest city in Nepal, has many things of interest for any tourist. For those who wanted to get away from the heat of the plains of India and cool off near the Himalayan mountains, Kathmandu is far more interesting than Darjeeling, another hill station of India. In fact, Kathmandu has so many things to see while we are in town that the best thing to do is get a detailed guide book that tells us all about the area so we can decide what to see and do. One of the things Kathmandu is known for is the treks that people can take up into the foothills of the Himalayas. There are many small travel agencies in the city that can make arrangements for you to trek solo or with a guide or with groups. And there are many routes one can take. I talked with one man who had just returned from the Everest trek and said that the views were fantastic. This is one of the better known treks of the area, but can be fairly rough, takes three weeks, and goes up to the base camp of Mt. Everest. So you should be in good physical shape if you want to go on this one.

Kathmandu has a wide variety of people from ethnic groups that include Tibetans, Indians, Sherpas, Rais, Limbus, Gurungs, Magars, Chetris, and the Newars, Kathmandu's original inhabitants. We will also see tourists from all over the world, some of whom may live close to our own home. Near the Freak Street area there are still plenty of hippies wandering about who look like they are right out of the '60s era and haven't changed in 40 years. There are also local guys who come up to you and discreetly ask if you are interested in any grass, hash, opium, or in changing money. Kathmandu is a mixture of people and things the likes of which we will see no where else.

Buddhism and Hinduism are the two main religions here, and they sometimes blend together so closely that it's difficult to tell where one leaves off and the other begins. Unfortunately, many of the Hindu temples are strictly off-limits to foreigners, although Buddhist temples are open to all and usually allow photography inside. In this way, the Buddhists, who are some of the friendliest people you will ever meet, do far more to promote inter-cultural understanding than the Hindus. Therefore, Buddhism will continue to grow as they allow foreigners to enter their temples and look or participate in the activities and learn more about them, whereas the exclusiveness of the Hindu temples does nothing to increase cultural exchange. Nonetheless, whether we are allowed in all the temples or not, we will see and appreciate the unique architecture of the many temples and older buildings.

There are many colorful shops in the area and vendors sell all sorts of items that include food, jewelry, Buddhist masks and deities, Tibetan carpets, caps, jackets, bags, lots of *thanka* paintings, and many other things, much of which is geared toward the tourist trade. There are a few designated streets that block all motor traffic in the morning to allow people to come in from the countryside and set up stalls to sell their fruit and vegetables. Such a marketplace always provides an interesting blend of local people to see. By noon they all go their way and the streets open up to traffic again.

There are also a number of vegetarian restaurants or cafes, some of which will remind us of the little cafes that were in San Francisco back in the '60s. Tourists from all over will come in and out of these cafes talking in all sorts of languages, but especially English, and will have a meal or tea and a desert to the background music of Western rock & roll. Some hotels that you might stay in will have a rooftop restaurant where we can eat outside while hearing the sounds of the town below and viewing the sunset over the city skyline with the mountains all around us.

On the nearby corner of New Road and Surkha Path is the Super Market, which is like a small mall with a variety of stores where we can get some of the more practical things we might need, from flashlights, alarm clocks, locks, luggage, trekking clothes, or whatever. Nearby are banks for changing money as well. I mention this because by this time in our travels things that have become broken or lost, as things sometimes do when traveling, can easily be replaced here. Some of these items are not so readily found while traveling in India. And if you are interested in having custom jewelry made or embroidery work done on your jacket or jeans or something, there are shops that will offer this service in the Indrachowk area, north of the Teleju temple. These people can do it fast and for a very reasonable price.

As we walk through the streets of Kathmandu toward Durbar Square, we pass Basantapur Square, which is like an open flea market. It is used by the local people who set up dozens of tables to sell every sort of nick-nack from old Nepali or Tibetan jewelry, coins, deities, prayer wheels, beads, lots of khukris or decorated Nepali knives, metal pots, and anything else they think a tourist might like. Many of these tables are run by family members as an additional or only source of income. It's a great place to shop for souvenirs or little presents for friends back home, but we have to bargain. And if we ask about a price on something and then tell them it's too much and walk away, they will follow us and keep asking how much we will offer. As long as they think they might make a sale, they won't give up. This can become a real nuisance. But sometimes we can say a ridiculously low price and they will accept.

Tourists, however, must be careful in buying certain items if they want something genuine. For example, the Buddhist *thanka* paintings are of two kinds: the Nepali paintings which may be detailed and interesting, but often have little philosophical basis; and the Tibetan *thankas* which are usually simpler in design but are painted by an authoritative artist or Tibetan monk. The Tibetan artist may gather herbs and semi-precious stones to grind into dust for making his own paints rather than using synthetic colors. The Tibetan style of painting is a science, and each painting may take the artist up to three months or longer to do, depending on the size, and is philosophically genuine. What this means is that every detail of the painting has a specific purpose and significance, whether it be the color of the deity, the hand gesture, the sitting posture, etc. Everything can be interpreted according to Buddhist philosophy, whereas the Nepali *thanka* tourist paintings, though more readily available and sometimes less expensive, often have no real esoteric meaning. Therefore, they are not genuine Buddhist *thankas*, but merely a conglomeration of designs and figures to attract the eye of the foreigner. Of course, if you see something you like and want to buy it, it's your decision.

Authentic Tibetan paintings are valued in three ways. Aside from the condition and size of the painting, it is also valued according to who painted it. There are paintings by monks who occasionally make a painting to sell. Then there are monks who paint only because they love to and do not sell the paintings but only give them to special friends, which make such paintings more valuable. The most valuable paintings are those painted by monks because of their love of the paintings and who keep them, which means the paintings go into circulation only after the death of the monk. Such paintings are the most rare and most valuable. There are also young monks who go to school and learn to paint as part of their training to become self-supportive, or to contribute their talents for the benefit of the monastery.

In seeing the sites around town, Kathmandu valley has quite a number of temples, and you may not want to visit all of them, but I will describe some of the most interesting and you can take it from there. Next to the flea market of Basantapur Square is the Kumari Chowk temple. This is the temple that houses a living goddess, Kumari Devi, considered to be an incarnation of Durga. She is a girl from a Newar family and is installed on the throne in a grand ceremony when the spirit of the goddess Kumari is said to enter the girl's body. The girl resides as a goddess in the temple until she reaches puberty when it is considered that she again becomes human. Then a new girl is chosen. Once a year during the Indra festival she is taken on a chariot around the city for all to see.

Beyond this temple is Durbar Square where there are many temples of various sizes. Around the year 2000 or so, the local government decided to set up toll booths for visitors going into Durbar Square. At this writing, foreigners are now expected to pay 200 rupees to enter Durbar Square, as part of the means to maintain its upkeep. They also do this in Patan and Bhaktapur, too. They have four of them on the main streets as you go into the Square. However, if you know the area, it is easy to take a back alley in Kathmandu and avoid the toll booths.

Anyway, some of the temples in Durbar Square are very small, which allows you to easily see the deity just inside the doorway. Other temples are larger, but entrance may not be allowed for foreigners except in the Buddhist temples. Durbar Square is continually filled with the bustle of Nepalese life, whether it be men or women selling fruits, vegetables, spices, etc., from small shops or curbside stands, or children going off to school, devotees visiting temples, or the many tourists roaming through the streets. As we enter Durbar Square we face the Trailokya Mohan Vishnu temple, behind which is an image of Vishnu's bird carrier, Garuda. Behind this is a temple to Lakshmi-Narayana, and small Ganesh and Shiva temples. To our right is the three-roofed Maju Deval, and further right is the Shiva-Parvati temple where the images of Shiva-Parvati are looking out the window over the square.

Around the corner is the entrance to the old palace. At the gate is an image of Hanuman covered with red vermilion. To our left as we enter the courtyard is a beautiful deity of Lord Narasimha in the act of killing the demon Hiranyakasipu. Across the courtyard is the Basantapur Tower covered with very ornate wood carvings. We can climb the stairways up inside the nine-storey tower to get a view over Basantapur Square, Freak Street, and the city skyline. When we leave the old palace we face an area with many temples that are dedicated to Vishnu, Krishna, Sarasvati, Jagannatha, and Shiva in his forms as Sweta Bhairab and Khaila Bhairab, and others. The beautiful three-storey Taleju temple is one of the oldest, built in the 16th century, dedicated to Taleju, the Nepalese form of Bhairab.

Past the Taleju temple on the left is a temple similar to the Pashupatinath (Shiva) temple, which we will visit later in Bhaktapur. On the left at Indrachowk is the temple of Akash (sky) Bhairab. The deity here is a large, five foot tall mask of Bhairab. Bhairab, or Bhairav, is the fearful form of Shiva who protects his devotees. I actually entered this temple, not sure if I could or not, and though the people inside looked at me oddly, they said nothing, so I kept going. I got right up to the deity before someone said I had to leave. Oh, well, sometimes you have to take a chance. But you can see the deity through the second floor window from across the street when the sun shines on it in the early morning.

Another block up the road is Kel Tole where the Machendranatha temple is located on the left. This temple has a shrine dedicated to Avalokiteshvara and is one of the most sacred Buddhist temples in the area. Many of the devout visit this temple every day early in the morning between six and seven. After this is Asan Tole, a square that has six roads intersecting it and is a major market place, especially in the morning. There are two pagoda style temples here; the three-storied one is to the goddess Annapurna, and the two-storied temple is to Ganesh. These are interesting and busy little temples, and are fascinating to watch as people continually go in and out. They are especially mystical after it has become dark and the temple lights go on, which also allows you to see inside from the street.

Walking through Durbar Square can be a most fascinating experience. It's like taking a trip back through time and seeing a city the way it was hundreds of years ago, except for the occasional motor vehicle and the Western tourists. The customs and ways of the people really haven't changed that much, which makes it like a living museum. Although modern amenities are now available in the form of cars, buses, planes, phones, electricity, etc., it's a place where age old customs that still exist meet the 20th century. This is the unique thing about Kathmandu. Although Nepal is still a developing country with much poverty, and over 16 million people with an average lifespan of only 45 years, and an illiteracy rate of about 70% among males and higher among women, it still has a high regard for its old ways and spiritual customs. Of course, modernization is bringing standards of life and education upward.

Outside of Kathmandu city are many temples in the surrounding towns and villages. To the west is one of the oldest (2500 years) and most famous of the Buddhist *stupas*, Svayambunatha, with the painted eyes which can be seen from anywhere in the city. It is located on a hilltop that may have been an island when Kathmandu was a lake many years ago. It's about 20 minutes away from Durbar Square by taxi or ricksha, or a 35 minute walk. As we go we can pass by the Nepal Museum that you may find interesting. Arriving at the hill, we see the steep stairs leading up to Svayambunatha that takes us past statues and small *stupa* shrines. Lots of monkeys are also loitering about, which is why this *stupa* is sometimes called the monkey temple. Getting to the top provides a great view of the valley, especially at dusk. In front of the *stupa* is a huge *dorje* or thunderbolt, and around the sides are many prayer wheels that are turned by the visiting devotees. In the four directions along the sides are also small shrines to other forms of Buddha. Nearby there is a large image of the Buddha and in a pagoda style temple on the northwest side is an image of the goddess of smallpox, Hariti. Many people continually line up to enter this small temple while a priest performs rituals in front. It is said that Hariti used to consume children, as smallpox, until the Buddha stopped her and kept her at his side.

There are many smaller *stupas* here, and further back are many shops that sell all kinds of Buddhist paraphernalia and souvenirs. There is also a room where many monks who live here gather to chant *sutras*. When I was here a group of people were preparing vegetables for a large feast, and I passed by a room where two men were cutting up a dead animal for meat, while three dogs were outside looking in and waiting for scraps. Many Buddhists are vegetarian, but some still eat meat and hire others to do the butchering since they don't want to partake of the animal killing. Unfortunately, as the *Vedas* point out, anyone connected with killing, distributing, or eating animal flesh also partakes of the bad karma that comes from killing the innocent animals.

Also around the Svayambunatha *stupa* is one of the power places of Kathmandu. In a chamber on the north side of the *stupa* is a locked doorway. This is the Shantipur cave. Past this doorway are three gates into the cave, which has eighteen rooms filled with tantrik deities. It is said that the room is so powerful that only the experienced tantrik priests can enter. Once a king wanted to show his bravery and forcefully entered the doors. However, he soon retreated out of the cave because as soon as he went in he became blind.

Once we have seen enough of the Svayambunatha *stupa*, we can go back down the hill and turn to our right. Walking up the road and into the neighborhood for 30 minutes, passing a number of other Buddhist temples, we come to a street corner on the other side of the hill where there is a huge, 30-foot-tall outdoor image of Amitabha Buddha. He is golden in color and many Buddhists who spend their evening chanting on their beads will also walk here to circle the image while chanting. There are benches where monks and families alike stop and rest or absorb the atmosphere.

Another place we want to see to the north of Kathmandu by 11 kilometers is Budhanilkantha at the foot of Shivapuri hill. Here we find the large deity of sleeping Vishnu, carved out of solid rock in the 11th century. One legend relates that the deity was found when a farmer was tilling his field and saw blood oozing up from the ground after his plough struck something. The people dug into the ground and found the deity. Many pilgrims come here, but not so many tourists. We reach it by getting a bus near the National Theatre, a pleasant ride, but the bus stops often to pick up passengers. When the bus makes its final stop, the deity is only a few minutes away. Anyone is allowed in the courtyard and can see the deity, but the central pool, where the deity is reclining on Seshanaga, is for Hindus only, which means those who are born Hindu. At the feet of Lord Vishnu the devout chant their prayers and make offerings of rice, where the pigeons wait to eat it up. It is considered that the deity sleeps continuously for four months in the rainy season, and in November there is a festival when thousands of devotees come to participate when the deity wakes up.

A two minute walk further west is the Hare Krishna temple that we can visit that has beautiful Jagannatha deities. At the very end of the road they have purchased some land where they are slowly building a nice temple. Getting a bus back to town is easy, but the smaller commuter buses that serve the valley get extremely crowded.

East of Kathmandu, reached by bus, is one of the most important Shiva temples in Nepal, the Pashupatinatha temple. As we approach the temple from the front we pass by many stalls that sell items like rudraksha beads, incense, and supplies for worship, like flower garlands that pilgrims buy to offer the deity inside the temple. The main deity of Pashupatinatha (Shiva as Lord of the animals) has four heads and is said to be over 600 years old, installed after the Muslims destroyed the original deity in the 14th century. There are also deities of Vishnu, Narasimha, and others of Shiva, some dating back to the fifth century. Although foreigners are not allowed inside, you can cross the Bagmati River to get a good view of the temple and the many people who visit. On the hillside is a row of many small shrines with Shiva *lingams*. Along the walkway by the river are other small shrines, and sometimes there are cremations taking place on platforms near the river behind the temple. All in all, it's a very mystical place. Across the road from the temple is a care facility that gives free medical assistance for the elderly and sickly, and meals to those who need it.

Farther east by bus is the Bodnatha Stupa, the largest in the world. This *stupa*, dating back about five centuries, is said to house the bones of Kashyapa, a Buddha who preceded Gautama. This is where Tibetan culture is centered in the valley, and the people who live nearby and run the shops that surround the *stupa* are primarily Tibetan. People who want to study Tibetan Buddhism come here for extended stays. There are nearby monasteries, such as the Jamchen Lhakhang that has a huge (about 30 to 40 feet tall) deity of Maitreya, the coming Buddha, that is very beautiful to see. Many Westerners come to study Buddhist meditation at the Kappan monastery, located a little ways north of Bodnath.

Patan is south of Kathmandu, easily reached by bus, tempo, or bicycle if you are renting one. We first see the beautiful Hiranya Varna Mahabihar Buddhist monastery, which has a very ornate three-storied temple with a deity of Buddha. A walk north of Durbar Square in a little enclave is the Kumbhesvar Shiva temple. It has a seven tiered roof with a Shakti temple nearby where women come to pray for their husband's safety. The architecture is quite uniquely Nepali in style. South of that is Patan's Durbar Square. Here we find interesting architecture in the forms of several temples dedicated to such deities as Ganesh, Shiva, Krishna, Narasimha, etc. There is also a temple to Durga in one of the side wood palaces, the Mulchwok Palace, where they still offer buffalos during the annual celebration of Durga *puja*.

Most of these temples were built in the 17th century and have many stories about them. South of Durbar Square is the temple of Rato Machendranatha that has a beautiful image of Avalokiteshvar. About ten minutes walk southeast of Durbar Square is the Mahaboudha temple. This is a small monastery with a central Indian style temple building resembling the Mahabodhi temple in Bodhgaya. The exterior is covered with 10,000 images of Buddha. Inside is an image of Buddha's mother, Maya Devi. This is not far from another temple called Rudra Mahavihar, built in the 6th century. The temple itself was not open but the courtyard was filled with many elaborate stone and metal sculptures.

Patan is also known for its bronze and brass work. There are many shops in the area where you can get some fantastically detailed and beautiful images of the Buddhist pantheon. But these higher quality images are not cheap, although very interesting to look at.

A short walk away is the Golden temple, with a Tibetan monastery on the right and a Newari monastery on the left which has been closed due to damages from an earthquake some years back. Built in the 12th century by the King Vaskar Deva Varma, much of it is covered with gold. Many local people attend this temple to offer worship. It is full of art and architecture of Nepali pattern. The main pagoda on the main floor is occupied by the image of Shakya Muni Buddha. The most ancient structure is the Svayambhu Stupa in the courtyard. The holy text of *Pragya Parmita*, written in letters of gold, is also preserved here since ancient times for recitation.

Bhaktapur is a distance farther east, reached by bus or taxi, a city that has probably changed the least in the valley. The Durbar Square of Bhaktapur is an open area with various sizes of temples of Krishna, Shiva, Pashupatinatha, Vatsala, etc. There is also an art gallery with some old and rare Nepali manuscripts and paintings depicting types of Hindu and Buddhist Tantrism. Next to this is the golden gate, a most interesting piece of art that is the entrance into the pathway leading to a Hindu temple, all part of the "55 windowed palace." Through an alley past the Pashupatinatha temple we find the Nyatapola temple, a good example of Nepalese architecture that is often seen on postcards or in travel brochures about Nepal. This five-storied temple was built in the 18th century by King Bhupatindra and is the tallest in the valley. The Bhairabnath temple across from the Nyatpola is where they still occasionally sacrifice animals, such as goats or buffalo, to the deity on special days. A ten minute walk to the other side of town is another square where we find a Dattatreya temple, an image of whom can be seen looking out of the upper storey window. And the Pujahari Math is nearby, which is known mostly for its finely carved peacock window located in the small alley beside the monastery.

Nagarkot, east of Bhaktapur (20 km out of Kathmandu), is reached by taxi or a special tour bus by following the winding road up into the hills located on a ridge. This is where many people go for the best view of the Himalayan mountains. Most people come at dawn or sunset. Unfortunately, when we leave Kathmandu for Nagarkot we can not be sure of how the weather will be in the mountains. If it is cloudy, we will not be able to see much. If it is clear, we will get a fantastic view from Dhaulagiri to our west all the way to Kanchenjunga and Everest to the east, although they are very far away. It can be cool and windy at Nagarkot, so we must dress warm. Plans for building some big hotels there are now in the making.

There are other noteworthy temples in the area, such as the ornate pagoda style temple of Vishnu at Changunarayan, reached by foot two hours north of Bhaktapur. And one of the most important temples of Goddess Kali is at Dakshinkali in the southern part of the valley. This is reached by car or taxi. On Saturdays and Tuesdays many local people who eat meat take their goats or chickens there to be sacrificed to the deity of the Goddess under the direction of the priests. It's a bloody scene, after which they finish butchering the animals outside and take them home to eat later. This is, according to *shastra*, actually the way animal killing is supposed to be done for those who have to have meat to eat. It was never meant that animals were to be raised on factory farms and then conveniently killed in mass quantities at the slaughter house. The *shastra* explains that animals are supposed to be raised by their owners who then make their own arrangements to offer the animals in sacrifice, but only to Goddess Kali, since other deities do not accept animal sacrifices. Some Vedic texts explain that even Kali does not accept meat offerings, but she gives it to her ghostly servants who accept it. Afterwards the people can take the offered carcass home, while understanding that by the dictates of the law of karma the offered animal may get the opportunity to kill them in their next life. That is the meaning of the Sanskrit word for flesh, *mamsah* (me he). During the ritual the person who is offering the animal in sacrifice is supposed to say in the animal's ear, "*Mamsah*, me he will kill in my next life." Thus, the habit of thoughtlessly eating meat does not go without its consequences.

This is a basic introduction to Kathmandu. It is a fun town and there is much more one can find here if a person spends the time.

JANAKPUR

We have already visited the birthplace of Lord Rama on this tour, so Janakpur is the birthplace of His wife Sita. It is also here where Lord Ramachandra married Sita. This town is 128 kilometers southeast of Kathmandu near the border with India, north of the Indian cities of Darbhanga and Sitamarhi.

Another way to see this town is if you stop here on your way to or from the Nepali border town of Kakarbhitta, as when you have visited or going to visit Darjeeling. Or if you are traveling south along this highway from Kathmandu, you can turn south at Dhalkebar from which Janakpur is 25 km away. There are few tourists here most of the time, so you can peacefully see the places that are related to the pastimes of Sita-Rama. It is called Janakpur since it is the city of King Janak, as described in the *Ramayana*. He adopted baby Sita when he found her while tilling the soil with a golden plow. Then Lord Rama, an *avatara* of Vishnu, married her there after he was able to bend the great bow of Shiva, which none of the other princes could do.

The present temple to Sita is a rare example in Nepal of Moghul architecture, built in 1911 over the place where Sita's image had been found. Pilgrims have been coming to this site for some time but especially after some ascetics found the images of Sita and Rama and a piece of Shiva's bow, along with other artifacts in the jungle in the 16th century. The deities are of Sita, Rama, and Rama's brothers Lakshmana, Bharata, and Satrughna.

Next to this temple is the Vivaha Mandapa, a temple that pays tribute to the wedding of Rama and Sita. They are shown in full wedding attire. Not far away to the southeast is the Nepalese Rama Mandir, built in 1882. This plays a major part in the RamNavami festival. Next to the Rama Mandir are the Dhanush Sagar and the Ganga Sagar water tanks. They are said to be located at the spot where one of the pieces of Lord Shiva's bow fell after Lord Rama had broken it to show His strength and capability for marrying Sita. The Sankat Mochan temple is for worship of Hanuman. Here Hanuman is represented by a live rhesus monkey, kept in a cage and fed by the pilgrims. It is also called the big monkey temple. Another place that may interest you is Dhanusa, about 15 km north of town. This is said to be where Rama strung Shiva's bow before He later proceeded to brake it.

Naturally, the holy day of RamNavami or celebration of Lord Rama's birth is a major festival here, as is Biha Panchami, the day that marks the wedding celebration of Sita-Rama. They attract thousands of devotees here, many of whom also take holy dips in the 24 water kunds scattered throughout this holy town. Janakpur was also the capital of Videha, which is the ancient kingdom of 3000 years ago that covered an area from northern Bihar to Sapt Kosi to the Gandaki River. This was home to the Mithila culture, which had its own language and customs. It still exists today in the uniquely colored paintings that the Mithila women do in the same way as ancient times.

WHERE TO GO NEXT?

When our visit to Nepal is over, there are a few different directions we can take. Some people can take a plane back to Varanasi or to Patna, while others move on farther east toward Darjeeling.

For those who want to go to points farther east, we will leave that to a special section on Far Northeast India. Once we head into Darjeeling, it is not too difficult to keep going into Sikhim and on to Assam and other states in that area. That is a whole tour by itself, but the one consideration is that you cannot visit some of these areas without a permit, although getting a permit to Sikhim is easy. So some of these places are not only off the beaten path and out of the way, they also may not be accessible for those who cannot or do not want to bother with trying to get a permit to visit. So we will leave this for a special section. So, for the moment, we will take a flight from Kathmandu to Patna where we will continue our tour of East India.

PATNA

We reach Patna by bus from Varanasi, or by the 45 minute flight from Kathmandu, at least on this tour. This city is the capital of Bihar, what used to be the ancient Pataliputra. It is built along the western banks of the Ganga (Ganges) River. It is a busy city with over half a million residents. It is not really a great tourist town or a pilgrimage site, but it does have a few interesting things we can see before we move on. The Patna Museum near High Court has many Hindu and Buddhist sculptures in stone, terra cotta, and bronze. Not far from the Maidan Park is the Golghar, a beehive-shaped building that was construced in 1786 by Captain John Garstin after a famine. It was to be used as a granary holding up to 150,000 tons of wheat. It was hardly ever used, but now people come to climb the steps up the 25 metre tall building to get good views of the city and Ganga River.

In the old section of the city is one of the most sacred places for Sikhs, the Har Mandir, where Gobind Singh was born in 1660. He was the 10th and last Sikh guru and made their scripture, the *Granth*, the spiritual authority in place of personal gurus. The

Har Mandir is a pleasant temple and has a little museum as well. Anyone can go in as long as you leave your shoes outside and put a cover on your head. The easiest way to get to Har Mandir is to hire a motor ricksha from the east side of Maidan Park. We will go through the very narrow streets of the old town, which are hopelessly crowded with people, bicycle rickshas, ox carts, cars, motor bikes, etc., all trying to get through. And the exhaust fumes from other vehicles are horrendous. Also in the old town area is the Khudabaksh library, started in 1900, that houses rare Arabic and Islamic manuscripts, Moghul paintings, and other things.

Patna is mostly a place from which we arrange to go to our next points of interest, such as any of those that follow:

VAISHALI

Some Jain pilgrims may want to divert their trip to see Vaishali, a town 40 kilometers north of Patna where the Jain saint Mahavira was born. The Second Buddhist Council was also held there in 383 B.C.E. However, there is really not much to see, except for an Ashok pillar and the ruins of some Buddhist *stupas*.

NALANDA

From Patna we can take a bus or train to Bihar Sharif and then a short ways to Nalanda, which is 90 km southeast of Patna and 15 km from Rajgir, and has a train station. Nalanda has much history to it. The Jarasandha-ka-Akhada is where Bhima and Jarasandha fought for 28 days before Bhima tore Jarasandha's legs apart. This was when Rajgir was the capital of Magadha and Jarasandha ruled.

Nalanda is not really a holy place like most of the other towns I have mentioned, but it does have some importance for Buddhists and Jains. Buddha and Mahavira, the last Jain *tirthankara*, visited and taught at this place often, and the Nalanda University became famous because of its exceptional professors and high standard of teaching. At one point, when Hieun Tsang visited in the seventh century, the students numbered over 10,000 and there were 2,000 teachers. The local princes supported the college, thus enabling it to accommodate the students' room, board, and education without charge. And many of the Gupta Kings built monasteries for the resident monks. The university started to decline during the eighth century because of political changes in India. But when the Mohammedan invaders arrived, they killed many of the monks and ransacked and burned the university. The library is said to have had over two million volumes and burned for six months.

Presently, the ruins of the university, the main point of interest in this town, can still be seen, and from a distance it looks like a huge fortress. You can go through what is left of some of the monasteries and temples and see how big they were, with rooms for students, lecture halls, kitchens, libraries, bathrooms, and wells. Most of it is now merely what is left of the foundations. West of here is the Sariputra *stupa*, which was built by Ashoka in honor of Ananda, the first disciple of Buddha. Nalanda also has Jain, Japanese, and Burmese rest houses, as well as Thai and Chinese temples. There is also a research center on Buddhism and Pali literature set up by the Bihar government.

RAJGIR

We now take a bus to Rajgir, another small but holy place with much history for Buddhists and Jains just six miles south of Nalanda. The Buddha spent five rainy seasons here and did much teaching. After the Buddha's death, the First Buddhist Council was held here at Saptaparini cave. The Jain Mahavira also taught here for 14 rainy seasons, and the 20th *tirthankara*, Muni Suvrata, was born here. This was also the place where Mahavira's earliest disciples died.

Across from the small square in town is Venuvana, the bamboo park where King Bimbisara built a monastery for the Buddha and his disciples. In the park is Karanda Tank where the Buddha used to bathe. Just south of the park are 22 hot springs with Jain and Hindu temples around them. A path leads to some natural caves on Vaibhara Hill where the first Buddhist Council took place. On top of the hill are several modern Jain temples. Gridhrakuta Hill has two natural caves where Buddha lived and is where he did much of his preaching. And on Ratna Giri hill is the World Peace Stupa built by the Japanese which can be seen from miles around. There are other things you can see here, including the Thai, Japanese, Burmese, and Jain temples. There are a number of things to see in Rajgir, and the best thing to do is stop at the Tourist Office and buy a guidebook to all the places of importance.

PAWAPURI

Another sacred place for Jains is the very small town of Pawapuri. This is 25 km from Nalanda and 13 km south of Bihar city. Lord Mahavira is said to have attained salvation and was cremated here. A white marble temple in the center of a lotus pond marks the place. Five more Jain temples are located nearby.

GAYA

Gaya can easily be reached by bus from Rajgir, or we can take a train straight from Patna. It is a very important holy place and many Hindus come here. The significance of Gaya is described in chapters 43 through 50 of the *Vayu Purana*. In a conversation between Narada Muni and Sanat Kumara it is related that many, many years ago the demon Gaya performed a severe penance at Brahmajuni Hill. The penance caused such a disturbance throughout the universe that the demigods went to Lord Vishnu for advice. After conferring with Him, Lord Brahma went to Gaya and asked him to give his body in sacrifice, which he agreed to do. Then Gaya lay on the ground at Kolahala (Brahmajuni) Hill and Dharma placed a stone slab on the head of Gaya on which Brahma would perform the sacrifice. The stone, however, kept moving and many demigods who came to participate in the sacrifice put their feet on the stone to help steady it. Still it could not be kept steady, so Lord Vishnu also appeared and placed His foot on the stone to steady it. Thus, the slab of rock, that was once Dharmavrata, wife of Marici, was touched by Vishnu and all the demigods, including Brahma, Shiva, Dharma, etc. Then Brahma performed the sacrifice at the beginning of the day of Brahma called the Sveta Varaha Kalpa.

Because Vishnu and the demigods were pleased with Gaya, they asked him if he wanted a boon. He asked that the city be named after him and that Lord Vishnu and the demigods continue to reside in the town of Gaya forever in manifest and unmanifest forms. He also asked that those on whose behalf the *sraddha* ceremony is performed go to Brahmaloka, and that the sins of all those who visit Gaya perish. Lord Vishnu replied that all he had asked for would be granted. Thus, as stated in the *Vayu Purana* (45.55), "It is certain that a man who performs *sraddha*, etc., uplifts thousands of Pitris (ancestors) of his family, including himself, and leads them to Vishnuloka, the region of Vishnu." In this way, by performing the *sraddha* ceremony in the city of Gaya in which *pinda*, balls of rice *prasada*, is mystically offered to one's forefathers, they are relieved of any hellish existence.

The person to whom the *pinda* is offered through the ceremony can then be liberated from material life. Furthermore, it is stated that if a son stays in Gaya for three fortnights, or fifteen days, or at least three nights, he sanctifies seven generations of his family.

The opportunity to go to Gaya is considered very rare to achieve, and dying here confers salvation, even to Brahma. It is also stated that each step one takes on his journey to Gaya equals a flight of steps toward Svargaloka, the heavenly region, for one's ancestors.

For those who want to perform the *sraddha* ceremony, shops around the Vishnupada temple in the old part of town sell articles for the ritual and priests are ready to help the pilgrims perform it properly. Actually, some pilgrims may have started the ritual as far away as Varanasi where they might have cremated a relative. Then they come to Gaya to perform the *sraddha* ceremony in front of the Vishnupada temple on the banks of the Phalgu River. Sometimes cremations also take place here. The river flows during the monsoon season but completely dries up in winter. The *sraddha* ceremony also includes visiting several temples and sites of this town for spiritual purification. Before commencing the ritual, one crosses the river to the small Sitaji temple to offer garlands and respects to the deities of Mother Sita, Lord Rama, and His brothers Laxman and Satrughna. Then they go back to the Vishnupada temple to continue. Thus, with the help of a priest, a person or family will be assisted in performing the ritual and chanting the mantras, and making the beneficial offerings to help relieve their deceased ancestors of any suffering they may be enduring.

The Vishnupada temple is the main temple in Gaya. It was built in 1787 by the Maharani of Indore and houses the stone that has a 40 cm impression of Lord Vishnu's footprint. It is generally not open to Westerners, but I visited it while wearing a *dhoti* and *kurta* and was allowed inside. I was also guided through the process of offering sweets to the footprint of Lord Vishnu. During a previous visit I was also guided through the *sraddha* ceremony, which I've briefly described. This is a tradition that goes back hundreds and thousands of years and is very rare for a Westerner to be able to participate in such traditions, unless they are noted for being connected with the Vedic path. However, being affiliated with Iskcon and familiar with the Vedic customs, there are priests there who have guided many such devotees through the *sraddha* ceremony.

Just north of the Vishnupada temple is a temple to Surya, the sun god. A kilometer southwest of Gaya is the Brahmajuni Hill. We can walk the steep 1000 steps to the top of the hill where there are a few small shrines to Narada, Buddha, and Mother Durga. From the top we get a good view over the area.

This town is also the place where Sri Chaitanya Mahaprabhu was initiated by Iswara Puri. He had been a great logician and debater, and was known for defeating anyone with His great knowledge of Vedanta. But after He was initiated, Sri Chaitanya gave up the debating process and simply engaged in *kirtana*, the congregational chanting of the holy names. Through this process He spread the glories of the Holy names of Lord Krishna to everyone He met, and changed the lives of millions. This influence continues to expand through His sincere followers.

BODHGAYA

Bodhgaya is 13 km from Gaya and is reached by taking a ride on a bus or minibus. Bodhgaya is one of the most sacred places of Buddhism for it was here that Buddha became enlightened and where Buddhism really began. Many Buddhists as well as Hindus come here from all over the world. The most important place in this very small town is the Mahabodhi temple which has a pyramidal tower rising 180 feet, situated next to the Bo tree. The present Bo tree is a direct descendent of the original tree that Buddha sat under in meditation when he became enlightened. On the north side of the temple is a platform marking where Buddha walked in meditation. It has lotus markings on it which is said to show where he stepped during his walk. In the tall spired temple, which is supposed to be similar to the original one that was built by Ashoka in the third century B.C.E., there is a large gilded image of the Buddha on the altar. Behind the temple is a lotus pond that the Buddha was supposed to have bathed in. It is pleasant to take some time here and sit under the Bo tree or near the lotus pond and meditate on its significance. By the shoe stall are men who sell guidebooks that contain information on Buddha's life.

There are several monasteries and temples in this town, most of which are interesting to see, such as the Tibetan monastery with a large wheel of law; the Thai monastery built like a typical Thai *wat* with a beautiful altar inside; and the Japanese monastery with a beautiful deity of Buddha from Japan. The active temples allow you to go in and watch the rituals and proceedings. There are also regular conferences here that draw large numbers of Buddhists and monks from all over the world. On this tour, visiting Bodhgaya completes our visit to the four most holy places of Buddhism, which includes Sarnath where he gave his first sermon, Lumbini where he was born, and Kushinagar where he left this world. Bodhgaya is probably the most important because of it being where Buddha became enlightened and where Buddhism began.

BARABAR HILL

While we are in the area, if we are interested we can also visit Barabar Hill where there are seven cave temples, locally known as Satgharas that were described in E. M. Foster's "A Passage to India." These are located 20 km north of Gaya and date back to 200 B.C.E. Two of them have inscriptions by Ashoka. They also served as retreats for Jain monks, and the inside walls are known for their polished surfaces. The interiors consist of vaulted roofs and sloping sides. The most noteworthy of these caves are the Sudama and Lomasa Rishi Caves. The latter has an oval chamber and a dome roof and the most elaborate doorway of all the caves. The interior stone is cut to resemble a hut with sloping timber supports and curved eaves carved in relief.

DEOGHAR

Deoghar is a three or four hour bus ride 180 km southeast of Gaya. It is settled in the Santal Parganas region of Jharkhand, in what used to be Bihar. It is a little out of the way, but has the Vaidyanath Shiva temple, which is one of the 12 important *jyotirlingas* in India, which are the naturally formed *lingas* and not man-made. This one is said to have manifested from light. However, some schools of thought consider the real Vaidyanath or Baijnath *jyotirlinga* temple is actually found in Parali in Andhra Pradesh. So you can also see that town as well if you want. The Vaitheesvaran Koil temple in Tamil Nadu also contains a Vaidyanath Shiva *lingam*, but it is not a *jyotirlingam*.

The temple is nicely situated in a large courtyard surrounded by stone walls. Near the entrance, the Chandrakoopa water well is said to have been constructed and consecrated by Ravana using the water from several holy tirthas. Within this complex are 22 other shrines and temples. The main Vaidyanatha temple faces east. The top of the Shiva *lingam* is slightly broken, connecting it to the legend that it chipped away when Ravana tried to uproot it.

The story is that Ravana meditated on Shiva and requested that he come to Sri Lanka to add power to his capital and become invincible. Ravana had attempted to carry away Shiva's abode of Mount Kailash, but Shiva crushed Ravana with his finger. So Ravana prayed to him and sought his mercy, after which Shiva blessed him with one of the *jyotirlingams* with the condition that wherever he sat it down, it would take root immediately. Thus, Ravana carried the *lingam* toward Sri Lanka, but on the way, Varuna, the god of water, entered Ravana's belly and made him feel the need to relieve himself. Then Vishnu appeared as a boy and volunteered to hold the *lingam*, but before Ravana could return, the boy had set the *lingam* down on the ground and it rooted itself to that spot. Ravana, disappointed at this turn of events, did severe austerities to again appease Lord Shiva. He cut off nine of his ten heads, but Shiva revived him and rejoined the heads to the body like a Vaidya or physician. Thus, this *jyotirlingam* goes by the name Vaidyanath. This same legend goes for the *lingam* at Gokarna in Karnataka, as well as for the temple in Parali. Since the *lingam* is manifested from Shiva himself, it is considered non-different from Shiva. Another legend is that the temple was rediscovered by a cowherd Baiju, from which there is the name Baijnath.

Vaidyanath is also considered one of the 52 Shaktipeeths of Sati, and where her heart fell to earth. This was when Sati's body was being carried by the angry and lamenting Lord Shiva, and was cut to pieces by Lord Vishnu to squelch Shiva's attachment to Sati, Durga. This temple is quite important and attracts as many as 100,000 pilgrims every day of its month-long annual *mela* or festival.

From here we can take a bus farther southeast and make our way to Vishnupur.

VISHNUPUR

Vishnupur is our next stop before heading into Kolkata. It is on the train line heading from Gaya, about 150 to 200 km west of Kolkata, south of Bankura. It is in this town that West Bengal's temple culture was enriched during the reign of the Malla kings. Vishnupur's exquisite temples have made it a major tourist center. The artistic and architectural appeal of these temples is quite surprising. Vishnupur became well known while ruled by Bir Hambir, the Malla ruler. He became a Vaishnava through Srinivasa Acharya, and then built the Rasa-manch temple in the town center where he began the worship of Krishna as Madana Mohana. There are over 30 brick and stone temples here, dating from the 17th century, most of which are Radha-Krishna temples. Some of the major temples in town are the Radha-Govinda temple, Madhava temple, Kalachand Sri Mandir, and Nandalala temple, all of which are on the south side of the Lal-bandh. Other interesting temples include the Patpur temple on the Krishna-bandh, and Madana Mohana, Madan Gopal, Lalji, RadheShyam, Shyam Raya, the Krishna Raya temple, and the Shridhara temples. Other noteworthy temples are the Madana Gopal, Lalgiri, and the Jorbangla temple. All are known for unique styles of architecture with terra cotta panels and carvings that illustrate the pastimes of Krishna and various Puranic episodes.

The Radhe-Shyam temple is one of the famous temples, built in 1758. The interior is designed in the Challa style, typical of Bengal. The 10th century Sri Mandir is also unique. The temple of the Madan Mohana deity is rich in terra cotta work and architecture, however the main deity, made of Ashtadhatu metal (combination of eight metals), now resides in Kolkata. The Ramascha temple, just opposite the Tourist Lodge, constructed with overburnt bricks, has a combination of Charchala and Egyptian pyramid style. The temple has three extraordinary galleries comprising of 3 tiers with 64 compartments and a 35-feet high and 80 feet wide stage. The Shyam Rai temple has illustrious decoration that follow the Charchala Pancharatna style of art. The walls depict Lord Krishna's Rasa-lila with His *gopis* carved in terra cotta.

If leaving Kolkata for Vishnupur, it's best to take a bus from the Esplanade Bus Stand on Chowringhee Rd. There are 3 before 9 A.M. and it's a five hour ride. Or take a train from Howrah station to Tarakeshwar and get a bus.

A few other interesting places north of Kolkata include the Tarakeshwar Babu temple, 57 km west of Kolkata, for those who may have the time to stop and see it. The main deity here is a black stone Shiva *lingam*. The architecture is nothing outstanding but many pilgrims visit this temple, especially for the Shivaratri or Kasta-mela festival when they may carry pots of water all the way from the Ganges River (22 miles away) to pour on the *lingam*. The place of Karmarpukur is further west where the philosopher Ramakrishna was born. There is a temple with a marble statue of him that marks the spot where he took birth.

Shantineketan is north of Vishnupur and some 130 km from Kolkata. This place is where the poet Rabindranath Tagore established a university from what began as an ashram that his father started in 1861. Nearby is Kendubilwa where the great poet and Vaishnava philosopher Jaidev was born. Each year in mid-January many come here for a few days to perform non-stop recitations of Jaidev's poems. Fifty-eight km north is Bakreshwar, and about 20 km farther is Tarapith, both small towns that are sacred to Shiva and Kali worshipers.

KOLKATA

Coming into Kolkata by train can be somewhat intimidating. Kolkata is not the beautiful city it once was. Now it has many areas that are slums, and much of it is dirty, smelly, and hopelessly congested. If we have decided to stay for a few days, there are a few things that we can see. However, if we are just passing through, then we can keep moving on to our next destination. We can get on our next train to head farther south, or get a taxi to go to Mayapur, in which case you can skip this section and go to the next segment on Mayapur. But in our description of India, we can stay for a couple days here at Kolkata.

Arriving at the Howrah station, which is a big and busy place, we make our way through the crowds and out onto the streets where we find a taxi to take us downtown to the Sudder Street area. Staying at a hotel in this area of town allows a person to walk to many of the points of interest one may find here, such as the Victoria Memorial, the Indian Museum (probably the best general museum in India, though I still prefer the ones in Delhi and Chennai), the Birla Planetarium, the Maidan Park, and the downtown shops and bazaars. There's also decent restaurants in the area, and South Indian style vegetarian *thalis* are available at the Hindustan restaurant nearby.

Many young tourists like this area of Kolkata because it is a good meeting place and a lively area. But over the past few years that I've been coming through this city, I've noticed a great deterioration. The city seems like it just keeps getting more run down and dirtier with each visit. Though there are many people who seem to take it in stride, I personally no longer look forward to coming through this city as much.

Kolkata, like any big city, has many things a tourist may want to see. But for the pilgrim there a few places of particular interest. However, one significant temple in this city is the Kali temple, also called Kalighat from which the name Calcutta originated, but now called Kolkata. The temple is said to be about 200 years old and many local people visit it every day. It is surrounded by shops that create a dark narrow lane that a person walks through in order to enter the temple. Many people continually surround the altar to see and offer respects to the deity, which is a large form of Kali. The Ganges used to flow not far from the temple where it would carry away the bodies from the cremation ground.

But now the stream is only a small canal of stagnating water. It is said that human sacrifices used to take place here many years ago in the worship of Kali. But now only a buffalo is occasionally sacrificed, and a goat is offered to Kali every morning in a sacrifice that is sponsored by a family who then take the offered meat home to eat as Kali *prasada*. This form of worship, however, is said to be in the mode of darkness. The *Bhagavata Purana* explains that goddess Kali does not actually accept offerings of meat, but that she allows her demoniac associates to accept these offerings. Thus, these animal offerings do not become Kali *prasada*, but are only remnants of lower beings in the mode of darkness. Therefore, one does not often see worshipers of Krishna or Vishnu visiting this temple. Other temples to Shiva, Vishnu, and Radha-Krishna are along Alipore Chetla and Tollygunge roads.

There is also the Dakshineshwar Kali temple ten km north of town. This is another important temple, built in 1847. The temple complex has a central temple with a deity of Kali, plus two shrines dedicated to Radha-Krishna, and a smaller one for Ganesh. Across the courtyard are 12 smaller Shiva temples with a *linga* in each one. The Indian mystic Ramakrishna was a priest here, and there is a room commemorating his stay. The headquarters of the Ramakrishna mission is downstream across the river at Belur Math, which is a building made to look like a combination of a church, mosque, and Vedic temple to represent the unity of all religions.

Durga is the goddess of both terror and placidity and is known by many names. Her terrible aspect is in the form of Chandrika or Chamunda and Kali. Mahishasuramardini is her most terrible form, said to personify the collective strength of the demigods who prayed for her to destroy the demons, such as Mahishasura. Durga is also called Gauri, Uma, Parvati (daughter of the Himalayas), and Ambika (the embodiment of feminine beauty and motherly affection).

If you are in Kolkata in late summer or early fall, you may want to see the festivals of Durga, Kali, and Lakshmi *puja*. Durga and Kali are both forms of the wife of Lord Shiva, and Lakshmi is the wife of Lord Vishnu. During the festivals the temples dedicated to these goddesses become very crowded with pilgrims. There is a grand celebration all over Kolkata, but especially near Babu, Outram, and Princep *ghats* where they take the deities of Durga to the river and celebrate. Durga *puja* begins on the seventh day of the bright half of the month of Aswin (Sept.-Oct.) and ends on the tenth day when processions take the images to the *ghats* and immerse them in the Ganges or other local lakes or rivers.

For the Muslims, Kolkata has the Nakhoda mosque, said to be able to accommodate up to 10,000 worshipers. For Christians, there is the beautiful St. Paul's Cathedral, completed in 1847, but redesigned after 1934. It is one of the most important churches in India. For Jains, there is the Sitambara temple, which is in a complex of four beautiful Jain temples, each built by one of four rich brothers. The main temple is extremely ornate with the interior walls covered with mirrors, colored stones, and mosaics. In fact, the deity, Sheetalnathji, the 10th of the 24 Jain *tirthankaras*, has a 10 carat diamond on its forehead. There is a garden in the middle of the temple grounds which is very pleasant and clean. All the temples are very richly decorated with lots of gold and silver.

The new imposing Shri Radha Krishna temple in the heart of upscale Ballygunje has emerged as the prime spiritual destination for the people of the city. The grandiose structure—a classic blend of temple architecture of Orissa and South India—attracts more than 2.5 million devotees a year. Spread over 22,000 sq ft, the temple is managed by the Vishwa Mangal Trust chaired by former MP and prominent industrialist Dr. Krishna Kumar Birla. The temple took almost 26 years to build and was inaugurated by former Union Minister Dr. Karan Singh on February 21, 1996. Rising to over 160 ft, the temple is an architectural marvel in itself. Forty-two *gavakshas* with carved images from ancient Hindu iconography form the facade.

Another temple is the Hare Krishna temple at 3C Albert Road. It has a nice and fairly priced guesthouse if you are just staying overnight while going to or coming from Mayapur. (You may have to book the room ahead of time.) The temple room has two altars, one with beautiful Radha-Krishna and Chaitanya deities, and the other with Jagannatha, Balarama, and Subhadra.

If you are a devotee interested in the sights where Srila A. C. Bhaktivedanta Swami Prabhupada grew up in Kolkata, there are several places you may want to see. But have a devotee from the temple show you around, or make sure your taxi driver knows how to get to these places. These include Prabhupada's birthplace, which is found underneath a jackfruit tree in a two room, mud walled house at Kataltala (Tallygunge). Iskcon owns a small house nearby there at P-63, Tollygunge Road, Kolkata 33. The property of the Mullicks where Prabhupada used to reside with his father Gour Mohan De and family in some rooms of a three-storied building is found at 151 M. G. Road. The Mullick's family Radha Govinda temple is at 142 M. G. Road. The entrance has two stone lions atop the walls that support a metal, arched gate.

Prabhupada's childhood school, the Mutty Lall Seal's Free College, is on M. G. Road at the corner of Harrison Road and Central Avenue. Scottish Church College is where Prabhupada graduated. Srila Prabhupada first met his spiritual master, Srila Bhaktisiddhanta Sarasvati Maharaja, at 1 Ultadanga in Kolkata. The first Gaudiya Math temple established by Srila Bhaktisiddhanta Sarasvati Maharaja is the Bagh Bazar Gaudiya Math temple. It is at 16-A Kali Prasada Chakrabarti Street in Bagh Bazar. It is still worth visiting and also displays Bhaktisiddhanta's room and bed where he left this world. And the "Bhakti Bhavan" at 181 Maniktala in Kolkata is where Bhaktivinoda Thakur left this world.

Once our brief stay and tour is accomplished, time to go.

MAYAPUR

We can easily get a taxi to our next stop, which is the holy *dhama* of Mayapur. North of Kolkata by about 90 miles or 125 kilometers is one of the holiest places in West Bengal. This place is known as Nabadvipa or Nadia and covers nine islands on the River Ganga. The nine islands are named Antardvipa, Simantadvipa, Madhyadvipa, Koladvipa, Modadrumadvipa, Rudradvipa, Godrumdvipa, Ritudvipa and Jahnudvipa. In the central island of Antardvipa is Mayapur, the birthplace of Sri Chaitanya Mahaprabhu. By understanding a little about Sri Chaitanya Mahaprabhu we can better appreciate the importance of Mayapur.

Sri Chaitanya was born on the 18th of February in 1486. His father, Jagannatha Mishra, and mother, Saci-devi, were both in the family line of Vedic brahmanas. He was called Nimai for having been born under a nima tree, and the local ladies called Him Gaurahari because of His golden complexion. As He grew up He performed many extraordinary pastimes that indicated exceptional qualities and character. In fact, it became understood that He was an incarnation of Krishna in the guise of His own devotee.

During Sri Chaitanya's tenth year He became a scholar in grammar, logic, and Vedic scripture. By the time He was 15 He was considered one of the best scholars of the area, and He defeated many of the most prominent pandits of the region. Scholars from other schools of thought were afraid to meet Him, fearing that they too might be defeated in their philosophy.

When He was 16 or 17 He went to Gaya where He was initiated by the great Vaishnava spiritual master Ishvara Puri, disciple of the renowned Madhavendra Puri. Thereafter, when Chaitanya returned to Mayapur, His disposition changed from that of an argumentative scholar to a religious Vaishnava preacher who was steeped in love for Krishna. It was at this time when He began the *sankirtana* movement, gathering friends and associates and engaging in congregational chanting of Lord Krishna's holy names for long hours through the night. He also showed many miracles of ecstasy, and all those who came in contact with Him were also infected with spiritual ecstasy.

When He was 24 years old He took sannyasa initiation from Keshava Bharati and renounced family life. He then went to live in Jagannatha Puri, where He did much preaching and performed many wondrous pastimes. He also went on a tour of South India which lasted 2 years. During His travels He talked with many Buddhists, Jains, and Mayavadi impersonalists, converting all of them to Vaishnavism. He also went to Vrindavana and began the rediscovery of many of the holy sites with the assistance of some of His renown followers, such as Rupa Gosvami and Sanatana Gosvami. Sri Chaitanya then traveled down to Prayag (Allahabad) where He used the Koran as the basis of His arguments to convert many Muslims to Vaishnavism. From there He went to Benares (Varanasi) where He gave spiritual instruction and turned many of the people and most learned scholars of the area into Vaishnavas.

From His 31st year, Sri Chaitanya lived in Puri where He was surrounded by His close associates and followers, and where the depths of His spiritual ecstasy increased without bounds. Thus, His life continued until His forty-eighth year when He left this world. Though this short description is most inadequate to understand Sri Chaitanya Mahaprabhu, His biographers have left us many details of His life to study in books such as the *Caitanya Bhagavaat*, or the *Caitanya-caritamrita*.

Mayapur is considered one of the special holy places, and no different in its spiritual nature than Vrindavana or Jagannatha Puri. Visiting Mayapur is considered exceptionally purifying and beneficial for one's spiritual progress. Staying in Mayapur for only a few days can give liberation from the material world through Krishna *bhakti*.

The Iskcon (Hare Krishna) center in Kolkata organizes bus trips to Mayapur a few times a week. Or you can just take a taxi from the train station or airport. But the best time to visit is during the celebration of the birth of Sri Chaitanya (the Gaura Purnima festival), which is on the full moon night of the month of Phalgun (February-March). Every year some 500,000 pilgrims come to visit Nadia from all parts of India. There are many simple guest houses for pilgrims, but the best place to stay is at the Iskcon center in Mayapur, the Sri Mayapur Chandrodaya Mandir. You will find many guest quarters there, which may fill rather quickly during or even months before the festival. There is a beautiful temple with the loveliest of deities of Radha-Krishna and the eight principal gopis, and the Pancha Tattva (Lord Chaitanya and His associates of Lord Nityananda, Advaita Acharya, Sri Gadadhara, and Srivasa), and a fierce form of Lord Narasimha. There are also stores, a restaurant, gorgeous flower gardens, exhibits, and excellent food for all who want to participate in the festival. And the sacred Ganga (Ganges) River is right across the road. Everything you need for staying at a holy place can be found here, plus nice saintly association with other pilgrims from all over the world. The large and impressive *pushpa* Samadhi of Srila Prabhupada is also here. Plus, the largest temple in Bengal is also planned to be built.

There are many sacred places to see while visiting Mayapur and the Navadvipa area. Many pilgrims go on a *parikrama* or foot journey to see all the significant places and temples of the area that are connected with the pastimes of Sri Chaitanya. In some cases this includes a route of up to 50 kilometers taken over the course of several days. The best way to see the most important places where spiritual events took place is to arrive in Mayapur a few weeks before the Gaura Purnima festival. The devotees of Iskcon organize a week long *parikrama* for all interested persons to go around in a large group and visit these places. They travel by foot and stay in tents at night. Food and facilities are brought to the participants. In 2007 there were 1900 pilgrims who participated in the *parikrama*. If one cannot do this, you can take a bus out to the places where they are visiting and just spend the day there, or pick which days you want to go. Of course, there are other places much closer to the Mayapur temple that you can see on your own, or just rent a taxi for a day to take you to the places that interest you most. Actually, a few complete guidebooks have been written about this holy place that describes all of the special locations and their importance, and directions on how to get to each one. These are listed in the back of this book. If you go to Mayapur, you can get them at the book shops you will find at the Iskcon temple so you can study them while you are there and get into the mood of the holy place and decide what spots you wish to visit. I cannot describe all of the places and their significance in this book, but I will try to describe a few of the most important places that are easy to find, and which should not be left out of your visit to Mayapur.

The area of Navadvipa *dhama* (including Navadvipa city, which has a population of around 150,000) covers nine islands which manifests in the form of an eight-petaled lotus flower, with the *dvipa* or island of Antardvipa being the whorl. Antardvipa has a perimeter of 10 miles. In the center of Antardvipa is Mayapur, where Lord Chaitanya was born in the small house of Jagannatha Mishra under a nima tree. This most important spot, called Yoga Pitha, is only a short walk or ricksha ride from the Iskcon temple. It is one of the tallest temples in the area, with its white tower protruding high over the trees.

As we walk down the road from the Iskcon temple, before arriving at the Yoga Pitha, we pass by a school on the right side of the road. This school was originally established by Bhaktivinoda Thakur. Even though he was so spiritually advanced, he also had the practicality to understand what the area needed for the well being of the people in general. So he established this school which has been expanded and used ever since.

As we enter the lovely gate to the Yoga Pitha, the impressive temple stands before us. To our right is a small temple to Bhaktivinoda Thakur, which has an image of him inside. The little lake that is nearby is the Gaura Kund, which was excavated by Srila Bhaktisiddhanta in 1920. Going back to the temple, we enter to get *darshan* of the deities. This temple has three altars. The altar on the left shows deities of Sri Sri Radha-Madhava and Lord Chaitanya. On the central altar is Lord Chaitanya as Gaura-Narayana with His two wives, Lakshmipriya on His right and Vishnupriya on His left. There is also a small deity of Adhokshaja Vishnu with four arms, standing about eight inches tall, which belonged to Lord Chaitanya's father, Jagannatha Mishra. His Shaktis of Bhu devi and Lakshmi devi are at His sides. The third altar shows the Pancha-tattva, Lord Chaitanya and His chief associates and expansions with a deity of Lord Jagannatha. Behind us or across from the altars is a large *kirtana* hall.

As we walk through the temple we will see in the yard a nima tree, which stands to the left side of the temple when facing it from the road. The nima tree which is there now is a cutting of the original tree under which Sri Chaitanya was born. This is how Lord Chaitanya acquired the name Nimai. Next to the tree is a re-construction of the little hut which belonged to Jagannatha Mishra, Sri Chaitanya's father, and in which Sri Chaitanya grew up. Inside the hut you can see deities of Jagannatha Mishra next to his wife Sachimata who is holding baby Nimai on her lap.

Next we go around the hut and come to a small shrine with two Shiva *lingas*. The smaller one is Gopisvara-Shiva who allows entrance into the Lord's service. The larger one is Vridha Shiva or Kshetrapala-Shiva, the protector of the holy *dhama*. It is advised that we pray to these forms of Shiva when we begin our stay in Mayapur to allow us to perceive the nature of the holy *dhama* and to attain *gaura-prema* or love of God within our hearts. There used to be a larger temple here for them during Sri Chaitanya's time, but it was later flooded by the Ganga River.

Turning south and at the end of the property behind the main temple is another small shrine with altars for the deities of Gaura-Gadadhara and Lakshmi-Narasimha. These were installed by Bhaktivinoda Thakura.

Back out on the road just a short ways down is the Mayapur Post Office which was also originally established by Bhaktivinoda Thakura. In the field nearby is a place that is called Ganga Nagara. It is now said to be covered by the Ganga River, but the legend is that when the Ganga was first called down from the heavenly region, once she arrived on earth it traveled across India toward the Bay of Bengal as King Bhagiratha went ahead. His plan was that the Ganga would travel to purify his family members that were at the place now known as Ganga Sagara. But when the Ganga arrived in Navadvipa, she stopped at the location that became known as Ganga Nagara. Only after King Bhagiratha performed austerities did Ganga Devi appear before him. She told him that she would stay for some time because this was the place where Lord Chaitanya Mahaprabhu would appear. "I am the water that emanates from His feet so I will perform austerities to please Him." She said that it was the month of Magh (January-February) and she will stay until the full moon of the Phalguna (February-March) month.

It is said that if anyone fasts and takes holy bath in the Ganga here and worships Lord Chaitanya, that person will attain Goloka Vrindavana after death, along with one thousand of his ancestors, regardless of where he dies. This place is also where Lord Chaitanya, from the age of eight to ten years old, went to the school of Ganga Dasa Pandita who was an incarnation of Sandipani Muni, the teacher of Krishna and Balarama.

Farther down the road is Srivasa Angan, the place that marks the spot where the house of Srivasa Thakura used to be. This is where Sri Chaitanya would perform ecstatic *sankirtana* with His close associates every night for a year. This is where the *sankirtana* movement originated. This is also where Lord Chaitanya showed Nityananda Prabhu His form with six arms that hold a bow and arrow, a flute, and water pot and *danda* (staff). This is the combined form of Rama, Krishna, and Chaitanya known as Sadbhuja. As we enter the temple for *darshan*, it has three altars. The one on the left has deities of Sri Sri Radha and Krishna with Lord Chaitanya. The central altar shows Lord Chaitanya sitting on a throne being fanned with a *chamara*, yak tail fan, by Gadadhara Pandit, and Lord Nityananda holding an umbrella over His head. This is the *maha-prakasha* pastime in which Lord Chaitanya reveals Himself to be the Supreme Personality of Godhead. A small 10-inch Narasimha deity is also there. The right altar shows Lord Nityananda and Lord Chaitanya leading the devotees in a *kirtana* on the way to the Chand Kazi's palace to protest his ban on *sankirtana*. Sometimes you can see a mridanga drum on this altar as well since this is the place called *"khol banga danga"* where the mridanga drum was broken when Chand Kazi, the local Muslim leader, demanded the stop of *sankirtana*, all congregational chanting of the holy names.

Across the yard there are two other little houses. The first one is called the Advaita Bhavan, which is a little place where Sri Advaita Acharya used to stay. It is here where such illustrious Vaishnavas as Srivasa, Haridasa Thakura, Chandashekhara, and Murari would listen to Sri Advaita's talks on Lord Krishna. Advaita stayed here until Sri Chaitanya took sannyasa, after which he moved back to his place in Shantipur. This shows a deity of Lord Chaitanya standing while Sri Advaita is sitting and offering some worship. Nearby is another little hut known as the Gadadhara Angam which marks the place where Sri Gadadhara grew up and associated with Lord Chaitanya. This has an altar which shows Lord Chaitanya on the left with His arm raised standing next to Sri Gadadhara on the right.

Going farther down the road we next come to the Sri Chaitanya Matha, a large temple complex which was originally established by Srila Bhaktisiddhanta Sarasvati Thakur in 1918. Entering the complex through the first gate we see a house called the Chandrashekara Bhavan. This was where Chandrashekara lived. He was the friend of Jagannatha Mishra and husband to the sister of Jagannatha Mishra's wife. Thus he was an uncle and close associate to Lord Chaitanya. Chandrashekhara took care of Sri Chaitanya when He was a child after His father left this world. Next, just past the little flower garden, we arrive at the *samadhi* tomb of Bhaktisiddhanta Sarasvati Thakura. He was the son of Bhaktivinoda Thakur and spiritual master of Srila A. C. Bhaktivedanta Swami Prabhupada. In essence, he was a most powerful preceptor of the teachings of Lord Chaitanya and the *sankirtana* movement. Inside is the life-size *murti* of him which is worshiped by the devotees here. Next, across from the building and towards the back we arrive at a pool of water known as Shyama Kund. This is a manifestation of the same Shyama Kund that we find in Vrindavana. Turning around and going back we now see the main temple building. The main deities here are Radha Krishna in the forms called Sri Sri Radha Gandharvika-Giridhari. These were the personal deities of Srila Bhaktisiddhanta. There are also two deities of Lord Chaitanya, one in front of the other, with His right hand raised. When we go around these deities to circumambulate the building, we also see separate altars with *murtis* of the *acharyas* of the four main Vaishnava lines of disciplic succession, or *sampradayas*. These are Sri Madhvacharya (of the Brahma *sampradaya*), Sri Vishnusvami (Rudra *sampradaya*), Sri Nimbarka (Kumara *sampradaya*), and Sri Ramanuja (Sri or Lakshmi *sampradaya*). Next we come to the *samadhi* of Gaura-Kishora Dasa Babji, the spiritual master of Srila Bhaktisiddhanta. He was considered to be renunciation personified. His *samadhi* was moved here by Srila Bhaktisiddhanta from another location in Kuliyagram at Mutanchada, known as Navadvipa, which was flooded by the Ganges River. Just across from this *samadhi* is another pool of water known as Radha Kunda, the manifestation of the same in Vrindavana. Next we come to a small hill of rocks called Giri-Govardhana. It was discovered by Srila Bhaktisiddhanta as being the same as the hill of Govardhana in the Vrindavana area, being made of large Govardhana *shila* stones from Govardhana Hill in Vrindavana. And if you look, you can see the rocks resemble the same kind that you will find at the larger Govardhana Hill. You can also see a little deity of a blue Krishna on top of this Govardhana mound.

Another place to see nearby is Murari Gupta's house. Next to the first gate we came to for the Sri Chaitanya Matha is a sign with an arrow for Murari Gupta's house. From here you follow the arrow and take a raised path over the rice field and to the road, whereupon you will see a big gate. Through the gate and up the short path is the place where Murari Gupta's house used to be. Now a temple, it houses the deities of Sita-Rama, Lakshmana and Hanuman. The ones you see now are the replacement deities for the older Sita-Rama and Hanuman deities that used to belong to Murari Gupta. There is also an ancient four-armed Narayana deity carved in bas-relief on stone that is next to Sita. This was found during the excavation for the temple, and said to date back to Satya-yuga. There were many pastimes with Lord Chaitanya at this location with Murari Gupta, such as when Sri Chaitanya showed His Varaha form to Murari.

Farther down the main road from the Sri Chaitanya Matha we are now on the island of Simantadvipa coming from Antardvipa. The way this place got its name is that one time in Satya-yuga many years ago Lord Shiva was dancing wildly while chanting the name of Gauranga. Parvati was affected with spiritual ecstasy by hearing the name and asked her husband, Shiva, "Who is this Gauranga? My heart is melting by hearing these names and seeing you dance." Shiva explained that it is Lord Krishna who will descend in the age of Kali in the area of Mayapur. He will distribute the highest jewel of love of God to everyone. I will live there in a hut along the Ganga and worship Him.

So Parvati went to Simantadvipa and also started to meditate on Lord Chaitanya and chant His name of Gauranga. After some time Lord Chaitanya appeared there with His associates to bless Parvati. She told Him that people say wherever there is Krishna, there can be no *maya*. "I am therefore forced to remain outside of your spiritual domain." When she asked to be allowed to see His pastimes, He allowed her to take the sacred dust from His holy feet and place it on her *simanta* (the parting in her hair). Thus, the name Simantadvipa was given.

Just around the bend on the road, going into the small village, is the *samadhi* tomb of Chand Kazi, who was the Muslim magistrate of Nadia during the time of Sri Chaitanya. The Kazi tried to stop the *sankirtana* movement, but Sri Chaitanya organized a large *sankirtana* party with many people singing the Lord's holy names to perform a demonstration in front of the Kazi's house. Chaitanya also talked to the Kazi in his house and defeated him in arguments based on scripture. Thus, the Kazi surrendered to Sri Chaitanya and promised never to interfere with the chanting of Krishna's holy name again. Actually, the Kazi was an incarnation of Krishna's wicked uncle King Kamsa, who was deservedly killed by Krishna. But this time Krishna, in the form of Sri Chaitanya, dealt with His uncle, the Kazi, in a much different way. At this stone *samadhi* where the body of the Kazi is buried, a nima tree, representing Sri Chaitanya, and a champa flower tree, representing the Kazi and which sprouted as soon as the Kazi had been buried, grew out of it intertwined showing the eternal relationship between the Kazi and Sri Chaitanya.

A short ride away from here by ricksha we turn down a dirt road and after a ten minute ride we arrive at the Jagannatha Mandir. The deities here are very special and have revealed Themselves to the surrounding devotees in many ways. A summary of the story about Them must be told. At the time of Lord Chaitanya, 500 years ago, there lived in Navadvipa a great Vaishnava named Jagadisha Ganguli. He would walk 600 miles to Puri each year to participate in the Ratha-Yatra festival. But he was an old man and was affected with a disease that left him blind. Thereafter, his friends advised him not to attempt the long trip to Puri since it would be too dangerous.

Feeling despondent he thought of committing suicide. But Lord Jagannatha spoke to him in a dream one night and told him that while bathing in the Ganges the next day a log floating down the river would bump his head at which time his sight would be restored. Then he should take the log to a particular devotee carpenter and ask him to carve the deity of Lord Jagannatha. When all this had happened, he took the log to the person to carve the deities, but the carver was very hesitant to take up the task since he was a leper. Not only did he feel unqualified to do it, but it would also be extremely painful since his hands were diseased. Jagadish insisted, however, explaining that Lord Jagannatha Himself had ordered this. So the carver began the work. To his surprise, as he worked he became cured of his leprosy.

Jagadish brought the Jagannatha deities to where They are now located and established Their worship. But after the disappearance of Jagadish, the worship of the deities decreased until They were forgotten. Over the years They became completely covered over by a termite mound. Centuries later the local villagers noticed a beautiful flower growing on the mound. When they went near it they could hear a voice saying, "Please bring me water, I'm thirsty."

Thus, some 50 years ago, the villagers cleared away the dirt and found the deities unharmed, even though They had been neglected for many years. In spite of the fact that the deities were carved from wood and covered by a termite mound, They were still intact. The villagers then established a simple temple for Lord Jagannatha, Lord Balarama, and Subhadra to resume worshiping Them.

Since that time the deities had been worshiped by Phatik Chaterjee. But in 1979 the aging priest realized he would soon die. After much consideration he decided to make sure the deities would continue being properly worshipped by giving Them to the care of the devotees of Iskcon. Phatik died shortly thereafter. Now the deities have a nice, new temple and are visited by many pilgrims from around the world. Many come here to try the *maha-prasada* (food preparations offered to the deities) and relish its spiritual taste. The scriptures state that Sri Ksetra, or Jagannatha Puri, is eternally manifest in this area of Mayapur. Thus, one gets the same benefits of visiting Jagannatha Puri by visiting this Jagannatha Mandir in Mayapur.

When we visit this Jagannatha temple we can see the deities in their nice new temple, which has an open *kirtana* hall in front of Them. In front of the *kirtana* hall is a series of diorama displays which relate the story of these deities. Behind the new temple is the old temple where the deities used to stay. This is still used when the deities play the part of getting colds and fever after Their bathing ceremony during Their annual Ratha Yatra celebration. Next to the road which is separated by a wall and in front of the old temple is the kalpavriksha tree. It is said that Shiva and Parvati came here to perform austerities and still come here. Under this tree you will also see a Shiva *lingam* known as Kshetrapala. This *lingam* has revealed itself as Lord Shiva to the devotees here in a number of ways. So devotees come here to pray to Shiva and Parvati for *krishna-prema*, ecstatic love for Radha and Krishna. Do not forget to try a little of the *maha-prasada* that has been offered to the deities while you are here.

The Sridhar Angam marks the place where the home of Kolavecha Sridhar was located. It is found past the mango grove behind the Jagannatha Mandir in a field. It is a small white building. Lord Chaitanya would take rest here after performing *kirtana*, thus, it is also called Vishrama Sthana, place of resting. Kolavecha Sridhar was a very simple but learned brahmana who sold banana leaf cups for his living. He lived on half of what he earned and used the other half to worship the Ganga. Sri Chaitanya would visit Kolavecha daily and take vegetables, flowers, or fruits. And after Sri Chaitanya took *sannyasa* and moved to Jagannatha Puri, Sridhar would go every year to visit Him. This is also where the huge *sankirtana* party went to take rest after Sri Chaitanya chastised Chand Kazi. It is accepted that Kolavecha Sridhar was the incarnation of the cowherd boy Kusumasava in the pastimes of Lord Krishna, and this place is no different than the forest of Madhuvana in Vrindavana.

Also in Simantadvipa, as we continue our pilgrimage to the holy places in the area, on the edge of Navadvipa on the south bank of the Ganges, is a place where Parvati, wife of Lord Shiva, meditated on Sri Chaitanya in the ecstasy of Krishna *prema*, love of God. When she saw Him she took the dust from His foot and placed it on her head. This showed how even the wife of Lord Shiva recognized the superior position of Sri Chaitanya. To the west of the Alakananda River is an area known as Kashi, called Mahakashi, where Lord Shiva resides and chants the name of Gauranga, another name of Chaitanya. Liberation is said to be easily achieved simply by chanting Gauranga at this spot.

The Simanti Devi temple has a deity of Parvati and Shiva as a *lingam*. This temple is associated with the pastime between Sri Chaitanya and Parvati when they met and she took the dust of His feet on her head.

Belpukur is farther north, about 9 km northeast of Mayapur. It is an expansion of Bilvavana in Vrajamandala. It was situated on the bank of the Ganga River, which is now about 6 km farther away. The father of Mother Sachidevi, Nilambara Chakravarti Thakura, worshiped and established the lovely Krishna deity here, Madana Gopal. The old temple is located behind and to the left of the Belpukur Library, which is a white building in a field.

There are many other places in Navadvipa *dhama* that should be visited. So starting back at the Iskcon temple and this time turning left as we exit the gate, we can go down the road about half a kilometer to one of the first temples on the left, yellow in color. This is the Sri Sri Gaura-Nityananda Mandir. It is where Nanda Acharya's house used to be, and where Their Lordships Nityananda and Sri Chaitanya met for the first time in Their most recent pastimes. When we go in through the gate, the temple is in the main hall on the left. There are three altars to view. The left altar has two deities of Lord Gauranga with right arms raised. The center altar has large nima wood deities of Lord Chaitanya and Lord Nityananda, along with Lord Narasimha. The right altar has beautiful Radha-Krishna deities known as Sri Sri Radha Vinoda Bihari. This temple also has painted terra cotta reliefs that display the pastimes of Lord Krishna and Lord Chaitanya. There are also moving diorama displays of Their pastimes up a flight of steps just inside the front gate.

If we keep going down the street there are many other temples that have been established along the road in this area known as Isodhyan. There is the Sri Gaura-Gadadhara Ashrama, the Sri Gaudiya Ashrama, Sri Chaitanya Gaudiya Math, Sri Chaitanya Bhagavad Math, Sri Krishna Chaitanya Math, Sri Gopinath Gaudiya Math, Sri Gauranga Gaudiya Math, and Sri Paramahamsa Gaudiya Math. You can take a morning walk here and visit each of them. Most were established by advanced devotees in the line of Srila Bhaktisiddhanta Maharaja in the Gaudiya tradition.

Going on to the Jalangi River, we will come to the boat dock where we can get a ride to the other side of the river. This is where we enter the island of Godrumdvipa. At the boat dock we can get a rickshaw to take us to a few places. Just down a ways at the first stop we can visit the Iskcon Bhaktivedanta Arogya Ashrama.

We now take a ricksha ride to Surabhi Kunj, the place where Bhaktivinoda Thakura started the head office of his Nama-hatta (giving of the holy names) preaching program.

There are some small deities to see here, and along the river is a newly built *ghat* where Bhaktivinoda would swim in the river. Long ago, Lord Indra came here with his carrier cow known as Surabhi and worshiped Lord Chaitanya to beg forgiveness for his offense to the Lord during His pastimes of Krishna. Thus, it is called Surabhi Kunj.

The house and *bhajan kutir* of Bhaktivinoda Thakur, called Svananda Sukhada Kunja, is farther down the road. He was the father of Bhaktisiddhanta Sarasvati who was the spiritual master of Srila A. C. Bhaktivedanta Swami Prabhupada who, under the orders of Srila Bhaktisiddhanta, came to America almost penniless and started the Iskcon movement. Here at this house Bhaktivinoda spent much time chanting, reading, and writing. It was also from here where he could see by transcendental vision that in the future many people from all over the world would come to Mayapur to engage in *sankirtana*, the congregational chanting of the holy names, which is now taking place. Everyone should come here to see the house from which the vision and inspiration for the spreading of *sankirtana* and the Hare Krishna movement began. At the end of the house is also the *samadhi* of Srila Bhaktivinoda Thakur as established by Srila Bhaktisiddhanta. Here you can also see Bhaktivinoda's Gaura Gadadhara deities next to his *samadhi*. There is also the *bhajan kutir* he had provided for Gaura Kishora dasa Babaji, and the *samadhi* of Krishna dasa Babaji.

If you go upstairs in the house you can also see his bedroom where he wrote numerous books. They still have the table upon which he wrote one of his famous books, *Jaiva Dharma*. In the corner is a closet room where he would sit to do his *japa* meditation and chant while being undisturbed. Also the room of Srila Bhaktisiddhanta is next to it where he would stay at times as well. From the Balcony, Bhaktivinoda could look over the Jalangi River and see the glow of what would be a temple where numerous devotees from all over the world would come to engage in huge *sankirtana* parties together. Now this vision has become a reality and is growing all the time.

Also in Godrumdvipa, farther away, is Suvarnavihara, the site of the capital of King Suvarna Sena, a most wealthy king who ruled during Satya-yuga, and who later appeared as Buddhimanta Khan, an associate of Sri Chaitanya. Srila Bhaktisiddhanta visited this place and arranged to buy it. Now there is a temple there, Suvarna Bihari Gaudiya Math, with the deities of Sri Chaitanya and Sri Sri Radha-Krishna.

Moving onward, we go through the small village of Amghata to visit the mango grove a little ways from the village where Lord Chaitanya planted a mango seed, which immediately grew into a full tree with ripened fruits. However, the exact spot or tree is not indicated. He had brought a number of devotees there, and they quickly picked around 200 mangoes from the tree to offer to Lord Krishna and then eat. The tree would provide fruits all year, which would be seedless and skinless. Lord Chaitanya and the devotees enjoyed these mangoes everyday for a year. Afterwards the tree disappeared. Visiting Amghata can be done while seeing Bhaktivinoda Thakura's house, or while using a taxi when visiting Narasimha Palli.

Narasimha Palli is our next stop, but since this is still some distance away, it can be visited by an hour long taxi ride from Mayapur, or by taking a boat from the *ghats* and going to Swarupa Ganj and then a half-hour cycle ricksha ride. This is where Lord

Narasimha came to rest after He had killed the demon Hiranyakasipu. Narasimha is the half-man and half-lion *avatara* or form of the Lord who appeared from a pillar in order to rescue His devotee Prahlada from his demoniac father, Hiranyakashipu. Mandakini Lake is where Lord Narasimha washed His hands and nails that had become tainted by Hiranyakashipu's blood. The Mandakini River used to flow past this place, which was also where Narasimha drank water to refresh Himself. The temple here has an ancient deity of Lord Narasimhadeva that is said to date back to Satya-yuga. It is carved in stone in bas-relief, and you can see Prahlada under the foot of Narasimha.

Devapally is where Prahlada Maharaja and numerous *devas* or demigods worshiped Lord Narasimha to try to calm His anger. Visvakarma, the architect of the gods, also came here and built many palaces for Lord Narasimha and other demigods. However, after time, the Mandakini River changed its course and the palaces deteriorated into hills in the area.

Hari-Hara Ksetra is not too far from Narasimha Polli and is where you can see the deity who is half Vishnu (Hari) and half Shiva (Hara). Other deities include those of Lakshmi, Shiva, Maha-Vishnu, Sitala Devi, and footprints of Gadadhara. The Lord manifested Himself in this form to show how Shiva, the best of devotees, is so dear to Him. It is also said that if one dies here, Lord Shiva himself will come to chant the name of Gauranga in the person's ear, thus transporting him to the spiritual realm.

Maha Kashi is not far from Hari-Hara Ksetra. Kashi is another name for Varanasi. But Maha Kashi is many times superior than ordinary Kashi because at this place Lord Shiva is said to be always dancing and chanting the names of Gauranga, Chaitanya, and requesting his followers to do the same.

Now we go to the town of Navadvipa which can be visited from Mayapur if we cross the Ganga River going west. There are several important places that can be visited. You may want to take a guide, or someone from the Iskcon temple to help show you around the city. Or if you know what you want to see, you can hire a cycle ricksha and make sure your driver knows where to go. Navadvipa is not a small town, and has a population of about 120,000 or more. But a cycle ricksha can take you wherever you want to go, unless you are in a hurry.

First, there is the *samadhi* and *bhajan kutir* of Srila Jagannatha dasa Babaji, the spiritual master of Srila Bhaktivinoda Thakur. This is located down a small lane. Here in a little temple we find beautiful Nitai-Gauranga, Radha-Krishna and Ladu Gopala deities. There is also a small residence for some of the few older devotees that stay here. You will find a small hall with a bedroom and the *samadhi* of Jagannatha dasa Babaji. Around the back is a small shrine that marks where his *bhajan-kutir* used to be. This was near banks of what used to be the flowing Ganga. Srila Jagannatha dasa Babaji was the person who found the exact location of Sri Chaitanya's birthplace for Bhaktivinoda Thakura.

The Dharmeshvara Mahaprabhu temple is another half-hour ride farther into town. This is a temple with its entrance along a crowded street. Once inside it opens into a nice *kirtana* hall, but you follow the path to the altar, where we can see the deity of Lord Chaitanya that belonged to Vishnupriya, the wife of Lord Chaitanya. He is a beautiful golden color, with arms stretched outward from the elbows, palms raised upward. The story is that Lord Chaitanya took *sannyasa* and left to travel and preach, at which time Vishnu-priya was given this deity when she was 16 years old. She worshiped this deity until she left this world at the age of 96.

Now we back track somewhat to see the Praudha Maya & Shiva temples. This is in an area called Parama Tala, and the temples are in the main bazaar of Navadvipa under a banyan tree. Praudha Maya is Yogamaya, the consort of Vriddha or Ksetrapala Shiva who is the protector of the holy *dhama*. She covers the holy place with her energy so that no demons can enter the area, or that they cannot understand the potency of the place. These deities used to be on the eastern bank of the Ganga between the Iskcon temple and the Yogapitha. However, when the Ganga flooded and shifted its course, many residents started to worship Praudha Maya at the present location, which is why they moved them here. Thus, it is now also called Praudhamatala.

The next place we can stop in and see is the Kuliya Dharamshala. This is the place behind which was an old toilet where Gaura Kishora dasa Babaji would stay in order to be left alone to do his worship, which was his *bhajan* and chanting of the Lord's holy names. That is why it is also called Srila Gaura Kishora dasa Babaji ka Bhajana Sthala. This is also where he left his body to enter *maha-samadhi*.

Going farther west we can visit the Sri Devananda Gaudiya Matha temple. This was established by Bhakti Prajnan Keshava Gosvami Maharaja, who had been a very active preacher of the Gaudiya tradition and also gave Srila A. C. Bhaktivedanta Swami *sannyasa* initiation in Mathura. This place is also where Sri Chaitanya forgave Devananda Pandita all his offenses. This was because the great devotee Srivasa Pandita had gone to one of his classes and was weeping, and then one of Devananda's disciples threw him out. There-fore, Devananda Pandita had committed a great offense, for which he had to be relieved. So whoever comes here becomes relieved of all offenses. On the central altar of this tem-ple are Radha-Krishna deities named Radha-Vinod Bihari with two deities of Lord Chai-tanya. On the left is a Varaha deity called Kola Varahadeva along with a Jagannatha deity. Sri Chaitanya also showed His form as Varaha in this area as well. On the right altar is a *murti* of Bhaktisiddhanta Sarasvati.

Farther west in Navadvipa is the Sri Chaitanya Sarasvat Gaudiya Math. This was established in 1941 by Srila Bhakti Raksaka Sridhar Maharaja, another important disciple of Srila Bhaktisiddhanta. His *samadhi* is also located here. The deities on the altar here are Sri Sri Guru-Gauranga, Gandharva-Govindasundarji, and Sri Sri Lakshmi Varahadeva.

Shantipur is another holy town to visit. This is where Sri Chaitanya distributed and took holy food, *prasada*, that was first offered to Krishna with many of His associates on the disappearance day of Madhavendra Puri. He proclaimed that anyone who partakes in this yearly festival in Shantipur achieves devotion to Lord Krishna. There is also a recon-struction of the house of Sri Advaita (a very important associate of Lord Chaitanya) and a temple commemorating the site where he resided. There is a *kirtana* hall in front of the temple, and the altar in the temple shows a golden deity of Advaita Acharya made of what looks like nima wood. Below are four *shalagrama shilas* of Narayana, Gopala, Madana Mohan, and Nara Gopala. The Narayana and Madana-Mohana *shilas* were worshiped by Advaita Acharya. In the back of the property to the left is a small shrine where it is said to be the place Lord Chaitanya, Lord Nityananda, and Advaita Acharya spoke together about the confidential pastimes of Lord Krishna.

These are only a few of the many places in the area that give spiritual merit when you visit them. It is also said that whoever fasts and worships Sri Chaitanya Mahaprabhu on Gaura Purnima, the full moon and appearance day of Sri Chaitanya in the month of Phalgun (February-March), and bathes in the Ganges, crosses over material existence along with 1000 of his ancestors and attains the spiritual abode of Goloka-Vrindavan after death. Thus, the importance of Mayapur can not be overlooked by any sincere pilgrim.

EKACHAKRA

Ekachakra is the birth place of Sri Sri Nityananda Mahaprabhu, the spiritual brother of Lord Sri Chaitanya Mahaprabhu, and incarnation of Lord Krishna's brother Balarama, according to the Gaudiya Vaishnavas. Ekachakra, combined with Birchandrapur, has a population of only about 4,000. It is an obscure village of Bengal, tucked away in a remote corner. It is located about 4 hours (165 km, or 100 miles) north of Mayapur, reached by bus or taxi. It is 11 miles north of the town of Rampur Hat, and 8 miles east of Mallarapura railway station. The village is about ten minutes walk from the Birchandrapur bus stop if you take a government bus. You can arrange the best means of going there with the help of the Mayapur temple offices.

Such people as Ishan Nagar in his book *Adwaita Prakasha*, Narahari Chakravarty in *Bhakti Ratnakara*, Nityananda Das in *Prema Vilasa*, Vrindavana Das in *Sri Chaitanya Bhagavata*, and others have glorified the place in their writings. But the significance of it is not widely known. It is a very simple town with few amenities to offer. There is hardly any place to buy even such things as cold drinks or bottled water. Of course, that could change in the future.

Sri Nityananda is the personification of the love that originated in Lord Sri Chaitanya. He was among the foremost of the league of illustrious men who had deepest sympathy and love for humanity. He helped people cross the barrier of color, creed, caste privilege, and united them with the knowledge that all are the children of the Divine. He had spontaneous love for each and everybody. He never discriminated while providing benevolence, even to thieves and dacoits. He never did demand from others, but inspired them through His generosity. The world will become a better place when we imbibe the spirit of Nityananda.

Sri Nityananda was born to a pious brahmana family. His father was Hadai Ojha and mother Padmavati. He also had a brother named Banka Raya. He appeared here in the second half of the 15th century, around 20 years before the appearance of Sri Chaitanya Mahaprabhu. Sri Nityananda was born on Shukia Trayodashi, in the month of Magha, in the year 1473, 12th of February (Shakabda—1395).

Just before the advent of Sri Nityananda a sage came to the home of Padmavati, mother of Nityananda. Upon seeing her, he started dancing and saying repeatedly "This is the womb". The stranger was Garga Muni in disguise. He predicted the arrival of Balarama on earth as Sri Nityananda. He emphasized that Padmavati was the reincarnation of Rohini (mother of Balarama), and that she cradled in her womb Balarama, the other self of Nityananda. He predicted the descent of Nityananda in the month of Magh, on Sukia Trayodashi. Saying this, Garga Muni disappeared. In this connection, one can remember that it was this Garga Muni who revealed the name of Balarama and Krishna in the Court of Nanda so many years before, as described in the *Srimad-Bhagavatam.*

To see the sites of Ekachakra, as you reach the central part of the village, or the road that divides Ekachakra and Birchandrapur, you will see an arch. This indicates the entrance to the road that leads to Nityananda Janmasthan, or the birthplace of Sri Nityananda, also called Garbhavasa. The village is very simple and has no facilities for travelers and pilgrims. That will change soon as the Iskcon temple is constructing a nice new temple and guesthouse. This will help support more pilgrims who do want to come for a visit, and allow them to stay in this peaceful village and absorb the spiritual atmosphere.

As we walk under the arch and down the road, we can see the simplicity of the homes and people here. We soon come to the small temple of Kadam Khandi on the left. This marks the place where Lord Nityananda recovered the Bankim Raya deity from the Yamuna River. The temple presently has a nice image of Sadbhuja, the form of the Lord in a combination of Rama, Krishna, and Sri Chaitanya. Further back is an altar that has small deities of Krishna and Balarama, and larger deities of Sri Nityananda and Sri Chaitanya (Gaura Nitai). Behind the temple is the Yamuna River, also called the Maudesvara River. This used to be much bigger, but is now like a little creek. On the bank is the Kadam Khandi Ghat where the Krishna deity of Bankim Raya was found.

As we make our way farther down the road, we come to the Iskcon temple, set in a very nice location. In front is the small and temporary temple with Gaura Nitai deities. Behind that is the guest house, and in the open field nearby is the place where the new and larger temple will be. The devotees here are working hard to make the new temple a reality. One of the devotees can also take you around the town to see the most important places.

As we take the road farther along, on the right we soon come to the Kundu Kund, a nice pond where Sri Nityananda used to bathe.

A little farther down the road we come to the Garbhavasa, or the Sri Nityananda Janmasthan, His birthplace. In front is the temple building with some offices. Then we see the *kirtana* hall in front of the main altars. The central and main altar has the middle deity of Sri Nityananda with Lord Chaitanya on the right with a raised arm, and Sri Advaita on the left. The altar on the right side has deities of Sri Sri Radha-Radhakanta and Radha-Srikanta, a larger dancing Gauranga in the center, and ten brass *sakhis*, girl servants, on the bottom step. It is wonderful to sit and engage in chanting *japa* or singing *kirtanas* in the hall. Behind the main temple you can see the new temple that they are building here, which should be done in a few years after the time of this writing. It will be several floors high and hold a beautiful temple and large *kirtana* hall.

As we leave the hall, across from it we see the Hadai Pandita Bhavan which marks the place where the house once stood of Nityananda's father, who is also called Mukunda

Bandyopadhyaya as well as Hadai Pandit. Nityananda was the first of six other sons of Hadai Pandit.

As we go to our left from the Hadai Pandita Bhavan, we see a very small white temple, which is the exact spot where Lord Nityananda was born. Inside is a deity of Lord Nityananda. This is also called a maternity temple, or "Sutika Mandir." Janhava Devi, wife of Lord Nityananda, Herself selected Madhab Bandyopadhyay and Raghav Pandit as the first and second custodian to look after the holy place. Close by on the left are two banyan trees that date back to the time of Lord Nityananda. Pilgrims always circumambulate the temple and trees. On the other side of the small temple is Nitai Kund, a pool where such things as the clothes, plates, etc., of Lord Nityananda were washed, and where He had also bathed. Embedded in its core and not visible to the naked eye is another tank named Ananga Kund. A beautiful Shiva *linga* and a lot of utensils were found while digging the tank.

Next to this *kund* is an old pippala tree surrounded by a cement platform. This is called Mala Tala (beads tree) for a number of reasons. First, just before Nityananda left home with the sannyasi who had requested His father that he let Nityananda travel with him, Hadai Pandita chanted there, but then also left his beads under the tree due to forgetfulness caused by anxiety when Nityananda was leaving. Many years later Sri Chaitanya also visited Ekachakra and left His flower garland on a branch of this tree. He was then in a transcendental stage of consciousness, quite oblivious of the mundane condition of the world. He came here with the earnest longing to meet Krishna. He removed His own garland and deposited it with the tree. This place is also called Sanyasitala. This is because Sri Ishwarapuri, who initiated Sri Chaitanya, once took rest under the same tree. According to *Prema Vilas*, Ishwarapuri begged to Nityananda's father to hand over his son to him. Then the place was named after the Sannyasi Ishwarapuri as Sanyasitala.

Behind the complex of the Garbhavasa is Padmavati Kund, also called Padamavati Pushkarini. This was dug by Sri Nityananda's grandfather for his daughter, Padmavati.

A little ways farther down the road we find a small deteriorated platform of bricks with a Bakula tree over it. The red blossoms fall all around it. This is where the original bakula tree once stood and where Nityananda and his friends would come to play, perform episodes of the *Ramayana*, or even have philosophical discussions. The original tree had branches that took the shape of cobra hoods due to the touch of Sri Nityananda. This area was once the estate of Hadai Pandita, and under the original tree was where Nityananda's umbilical cord was buried.

As we walk farther, on the right we see the place known as Hantugada, or Jahnu Kund. It is a small *kund* with a lone tree hanging over it. This is where Sri Nityananda would perform the Dadhi-cida festival and distribute chipped rice and yogurt. He would also kneel down while taking His own *prasada*. For the benefit of the residents, He also called all the sacred rivers into this *kund* so that they could all bathe here without the need to travel to all of the holy places, like the Ganga, to get a sacred bath.

Further in the fields, about 400 meters out, there is the place known as Pandava Tala. Keli-kadamba trees are around it. This is where the Pandavas once lived with their mother, Kunti, while they were exiled in the forest. This is in connection with another place called Sikhandabi, which was the residence of the Bakasura demon who terrorized the local residents by eating one person every day. This went on until Queen Kunti asked super strong Bhima to kill the demon, which he did after a fierce fight.

The Birchandrapur side of town can now be seen after seeing all of the above places. We make our way back down the road to the arch where we originally started. From there we go to the left and then make a quick right, and straight down the street through the houses we shortly arrive at the Bankim Raya temple. This temple was established by Nity-ananda's son, Virabhadra Gosai, to house Bankim Raya, the deity that Sri Nityananda had found when He returned to Ekachakra after being absent for 30 years. When you get up to the altar you will see the small Krishna deity in the center with Srimati Radharani on His left and Jahnava Devi on His right. It is said that Lord Nityananda left this world by entering into this Krishna deity. There is also a deity of Yogamaya on a separate throne to the right. The Radharani deity was also found in Bhaddhapur about ½ mile to the west in the region of Birchandrapur. After that She was installed with Bankim Raya and called Bhaddhapurera, the mistress of Bhaddhapura.

Outside the temple gate is another little temple for Lord Krishna as Madana Mohana, with Radha on His left and Chandravali on His right. Farther right are the deities of Sri Sri Radha-Vrindavana Chandra. The priest of this temple, who says his family has been worshiping these deities for 450 years, says he is a descendant of Nityananda.

Next is a nice little temple dedicated to Lord Jagannatha, Lord Balarama and Lady Subhadra along with Sakshi Gopal. After that we come to a small Shiva shrine for Ekachakra Mahadeva, Shiva or Bhandisvara, who was worshiped by Hadai Pandita.

The Sveta Ganga is a small *kund* near the Bankim Raya temple, and right across from the Jagannatha temple. This is said to have been dug by 1200 *shaktas* (worshipers of the Divine Mother) of the Nedadi sect who had approached the wife of Lord Nityananda, Jahnava Mata, to check her power.

A few other noted places include the Radha Kund (Raya Pukur) and Syama Kund (Syama Pukur) in the fields west of Birchandrapur, and a small mound known as Govard-hana Hill some distance south of the Bankim Raya temple. As you are walking around you will also see the occasional vendor of Nityananda and Chaitanya deities that are made from nima wood in the typical local fashion.

You can dive deeper into the history of Ekachakra and the pastimes that took place here by reading more about them. Another book that can help guide you around the vil-lage and elaborate its history can be purchased at the Garbhavasa temple.

RAMAKELI

Ramakeli is another place connected with Lord Chaitanya because it was the home to Rupa and Sanatana Gosvami. However, it is quite a ways north of Mayapur in West Ben-gal, near English Bazar, 15 kilometers from Malda. It is about half-way between Kolkata and Darjeeling, so if you want to visit this place you may want to plan a time when you are traveling north. It is a small village, not on the map, and has lush vegetation, and small thatched cottages, coconut trees, and pleasant lakes.

Here we can visit the Radha-Madana-Mohana temple founded by Rupa and Sana-tana, and later managed by Jiva Gosvami, their nephew. The temple had been closed for 300 years until Jitendranath Maitra, in the line of disciples from Jiva Gosvami, began worshiping the deities again. Then a new temple was built by Upendranath Maitra in 1930. This was after being requested by the local people to repair the temple, and then having a dream in which the deities Radha Madana-Mohana appeared and asked him to build a new temple.

Next to the temple are two lakes called Radha Kund and Shyama Kund built by Rupa and Sanatana in remembrance of Vrindavana. The area around these lakes is called Guptu or Hidden Vrindavana. Not far away is the sitting place of Lord Nityananda. It is next to a small temple with Lord Chaitanya's footprints, and faces two trees, the larger of which is supposed to be 600 years old. The other is said to have been started from a branch from the tree where Lord Chaitanya initiated Rupa, Sanatana, and their brother Vallabha, who became known as Anupama. Another temple nearby is one of Lord Chaitanya which was worshiped by Jiva Gosvami.

Outside the town along the road are the remains of Nawab Hussain Shah's government building. He was the Muslim ruler who had forced Rupa and Sanatana into his employment. Further down the road is the large prison house, with its tall arched brick ceiling. It was here where Sanatana Gosvami was held for 17 months and 19 days by the Shah when Sanatana refused to work for him.

Thousands of years ago this town was visited by Lord Ramachandra, which is how Ramakeli gets its name. There is also a lake where Lord Ramachandra's wife, Sita, per-formed the *pinda* or *sraddha* ritual for her mother. Every year thousands of people come here to perform *pinda* and pay respects to a large tree known as Bala Briksha, said to be 5,000 years old.

GANGA SAGAR

This little place is 105 km south of Kolkata and 64 km (40 miles) downstream on the Ganges from Diamond Harbor. Ganga Sagar or Sagardvipa is the last town along this branch of the Ganges, called the Hugli or Hooghly River.

Sagar Island is a little out of the way and most tourists avoid the trouble of going. But the best way to get there is to take a train from Sealdah station to Diamond Harbor, where the Ganges makes its last turn and heads to the ocean. Taking one of the over-crowded buses out of Kolkata can be a challenge and is not worth the trouble. After arriv-ing at Diamond Harbor you still must take a bus (one-and-a-half hours) or a taxi to Harwood Point, then a 30 minute ferry crossing to Kochuberia Ghat (Sagar), and then another bus to Ganga Sagar to where the Ganges meets the sea at the southern tip of the island (one-and-a-half hours). Then, of course, on your return trip it is another six hours of bus, ferry, bus, and train to get back to Kolkata after visiting the temple. But this tem-ple is one of the only ones you'll find dedicated to Kapila Muni.

This is also where the Ganges completes its journey across India and flows into the ocean. It is said that this place is so spiritually powerful that dying here brings salvation, or liberation. So this can be an important place for some spiritual pilgrims to visit. It is known for the three-day festival of Makara-sankranti, but especially popular is the mid-January Gangasagar Mela festival. At that time a half-million or more pilgrims gather from all over India to bathe at the confluence of the Ganges and the ocean to cleanse themselves of all sins. This can be austere because there are often few facilities to be found for all the people that visit. After their holy bath, people go to the small temple that is dedicated to Kapila Muni, the philosopher and incarnation of Sri Vishnu who performed austerities and died on the island, and also taught the sankhya-yoga system. The temple shows Him with Ganga Devi on His right and Raja Sagara on His left. It is said He still lives here in deep meditation in the spiritual dimension to deliver all souls. So that is why many people still undergo the austerity to visit this place.

REMUNA

When it is time to leave Kolkata or Mayapur, we go to the train station and book a ticket for Balasore. Some pilgrims will want to get off here in order to take an hour long bus or auto-ricksha ride to Remuna. In Remuna is the temple of Ksira-cora-gopinatha, which is an important place of pilgrimage. This is the deity who hid a pot of sweet rice (*ksira*) for His devotee Madhavendra Puri. The story is that once Madhavendra Puri, while visiting Vrindavan, was told in a dream by Krishna that the Gopala deity had been placed in a thick bush by a temple priest to keep Him hidden from the Muslim invaders. Gopala wanted Madhavendra Puri to find Him and establish a temple.

So Madhavendra Puri gathered the local residents, found the deity in the woods and built a temple. Then in another dream the deity told Madhavendra that He was still very hot from so many years of living outside and needed some sandalwood paste to help cool Him. So Madhavendra Puri traveled to Jagannatha Puri to get some nice sandalwood to bring back to Vrindavan.

On his way, he stopped at the Remuna Gopinatha temple, which is known for a special kind of sweet rice, called *amrita-keli* that they offer to the deity. He was attracted to the idea of learning how to make it the way the cooks prepare it there so he could make similar sweet rice for his own Gopala deity. But thinking that he was offensive for wanting to taste the preparation that was to be offered to the deity, he decided not to taste any at all. However, that night the deity Gopinatha told the temple priest in a dream to wake up and find a pot of sweet rice that the deity had hidden behind His dress and to give it to Madhavendra Puri. When the priest awoke and looked behind the deity's dress, there was the pot of sweetrice. Then the priest went out and after calling his name found Madhavendra Puri and gave him the sweet rice. From that time the Gopinatha deity at Remuna has been known as Ksira-cora-gopinatha, the deity who stole the pot of condensed milk for His devotee.

Furthermore, after Madhavendra Puri had secured a large amount of sandalwood and was on his way back to Vrindavan, he again stopped at Remuna. Then the Gopala deity in Vrindavan spoke to Madhavendra Puri in a dream telling him that he should simply turn the sandalwood into paste and offer it to the Gopinatha deity at Remuna. Since

Krishna as Gopinatha in Remuna or as Gopala in Vrindavan or wherever He might be are equally the same, offering the paste to Gopinatha would also cool Gopala in Vrindavan. Thus, Gopala relieved His devotee Madhavendra Puri from the task of bringing the heavy load such a great distance back to Vrindavan. In this way, we can see that the Krishna deities of this region, such as Jagannatha, Saksi-gopala, and Ksira-cora-gopinatha, are very active deities and display Their supernatural qualities in a way that attracts many pilgrims to the temples of this area.

The Ksira-cora-gopinatha temple is in good condition. Near the main entrance is a bakul tree, which is said to mark the place where the first temple was built by King Narasimhadeva. Near the entrance is also a manmade pond where pilgrims can bathe. And about 100 meters away is an old pond where the Bengali devotees would bathe while on their way to Jagannatha Puri to see Sri Chaitanya Mahaprabhu when He lived there.

As we go into the temple compound, to the left of the main entrance are footprints of Sri Chaitanya that were installed by Srila Bhaktisiddhanta years ago. When I visited the temple I was able to sit in the temple room and watch the priest dress the beautiful deity of Gopinatha. The main deity is flanked by two other three foot tall deities of Krishna. These are known as Govinda and Madana Mohana which were brought from Vrindavana by the devotee Caitanya dasa Babaji around 1938. After taking *darshan*, I went to the office area and purchased a clay pot of *ksira* (sweetrice) *prasada*, the kind Madhavendra Puri had tasted. It has a thick consistency and is very sweet, the likes of which I have tasted no where else. It is especially auspicious to take this *prasada* while thinking of the pastime of Gopinatha and Madhavendra Puri.

Also within the compound of the Ksira-cora-gopinatha temple is the *samadhi* tomb of the great Vaishnava devotee Rasikananda. Rasikananda was an important disciple of Syamananda. He had also helped bring numerous writings of the Vrindavana Goswamis to Bengal. Actually, it was Rasikananda who had found the Gopinatha deity in the nearby pond after Gopinatha had been placed there to keep Him hidden from the Muslim king. After that, Rasikananda renovated the temple after the previous one, which had been built by King Gajapati Maharaja Langula Deva, had been destroyed by Muslim invaders.

All this is elaborated by Sri Kaisoranandadeva Goswami, a disciple of Rasikananda. It all started in Treta-yuga while Lord Ramachandra and Sita were living at Chitrakoot. They had taken shelter of the ashrama of some sages during a rain storm. There were many cows in the ashrama. This reminded Lord Rama of His pastimes as Lord Krishna, for which He carved some figures of those pastimes on a black rock. Sita wanted to see these figures. So upon Her request, He showed Her the deity of Gopal He had made, along with figures of Krishna's eight main *gopis* and four other maid-servants. Other scenes included Lord Balarama wrestling Mustika, Lord Krishna wrestling Chanura, along with twelve cows and a few other scenes. Pleased by this, Sita began to worship the deity.

When Rama and Sita left Chitrakoot, Lord Brahma took up the worship of this deity, all the way through to the age of Kali-yuga.

Lord Ramachandra and Sita had previously visited Remuna when They were returning from Lanka after Lord Rama had killed the demon Ravana. They liked this place and

Sita wanted to bathe in the Ganga. So Lord Rama shot seven arrows into the ground to bring up the Ganga River. That is now called Saptashara (seven arrows) in Remuna. That is where the Shiva deity of Gadegadeshwara was installed. Durga Devi is in the nearby temple of Ramacandi. Because Lord Rama felt pleasure (*ramana*) here, it became known as Remuna.

It was in the thirteenth century when King Langula Narasimhadeva from Orissa stopped at Chitrakoot during his travels and happened to see the Gopala deity. He was amazed that no one seemed to be worshiping the lovely deity, not knowing that Lord Brahma was still arriving everyday to do the *puja*. But that night the king had a dream in which the deity of Gopala requested to be taken to a more inhabited place. So the king decided to take Him to Jagannatha Puri. However, while passing through Remuna, the deity again appeared to the king in a dream and asked to be installed there. So the king arranged it. The queen noticed the eight principal *gopis* on the stone of the deity, so she called Him Gopal.

Shortly after the time of Sri Chaitanya Mahaprabhu, there was a king who would go and smash the deities in temples. People of Remuna heard he was coming there, so they took the Gopala deity and hid Him in a pond three miles away. Being upset that he could not find the Gopala deity, the king assaulted and partially broke the Ramacandi Durga deity.

Later, the great devotee Rasikananda had a dream in which he was ordered to excavate the pond to recover the deity of Gopinatha. After doing so, he built a temple for the deity and established the worship. Later, when Rasikananda had made up his mind that it was time for him to leave this world, he entered the temple of Gopinatha and disappeared. Seven of his associates who had been performing *sankirtana* with Rasikananda also gave up their bodies to follow him into the spiritual realm when they became so spiritual distressed after hearing that Rasikananda had gone. Their *samadhi* tombs are also next to Rasikananda's in the temple courtyard.

An easy ten-minute walk from the Gopinatha temple is a Gaudiya Math temple. This had been the desire of Srila Bhaktisiddhanta Sarasvati Thakur when he had visited this place a few years before he left this world. Then shortly thereafter someone donated a 300-year-old temple of Lord Jagannatha to the Gaudiya Math. So the temple was started. Then, when Bengal was partitioned, the Radha-Krishna deities of Mymensingh were also brought to the temple.

Remuna is also known for being the birthplaces of Sri Baladeva Vidyabhushana, and of Shridhara Swami, the commentator of the *Bhagavata Purana* who is in the line of Sri Chaitanya Mahaprabhu.

After our visit to the temple, we ride three minutes farther down the road. In this area are the Ramacandi temple and the Gadegadeshwara Shiva temple, near the spot where Lord Ramachandra shot seven arrows into the ground to bring forth water from the Ganga River. This is also near the area where there was a market where Madhavendra Puri used to stay. There is a small temple that is Madhavendra Puri's *samadhi* tomb which has his sitting place. Also inside the room is a display case that shows Madhavendra Puri's shoes.

Seeing deities like Gopinatha and visiting the shrines of such powerful saints like Madhavendra Puri is not only spiritually enlivening, but also very purifying. It is because of saints like Madhavendra Puri that the mysteries of the Supreme become revealed to us. After this most auspicious visit we ride back to Balasore and then head down to Jagannatha Puri.

In this region of India there is also the Kutopokhari temple, which contains a two meter high granite image of Durga with 18 arms. Some distance away at Sajanagarh the Bhudhara Chandi temple contains a three-faced, eight-armed image of Shakti standing on seven boars. And on Devagiri Hill stands the Panchlingeswar temple that has five stone Shiva *lingas*.

JAGANNATHA PURI

Jagannatha Puri, a town of 160,000, is one of the most important pilgrimage centers and one of the four holiest cities in India, along with Badrinatha in the north, Dvaraka in the west, and Ramesvaram in the south. The deity of Badrinarayan in Badrinatha was especially worshiped in Satya-yuga, Rama in Ramesvaram in Treta-yuga, and Dvarakanatha in Dvaraka was especially worshiped in Dvapara-yuga. But Lord Jagannatha in Puri can be worshiped by everyone in Kali-yuga. In fact, the importance of Jagannatha Puri, sometimes called Purushottama-Ksetra, is explained in chapters 52 through 57 of the Uttarabhaga section of the *Narada Purana*. There we find it stated that simply by visiting Puri, which is rarely achieved except for those who have performed many pious acts, and by seeing the deity of Jagannatha (Krishna), one can easily attain freedom from future births and reach the spiritual abode.

In the middle of this city is the large temple dedicated to Lord Krishna as Jagannatha, meaning "Lord of the universe." It is in a huge complex where buildings house as many as 5,000 priests and assistants. The whole compound is surrounded by a thick stone wall 20 feet tall that encloses an area 665 feet by 640 feet. The wall has four large gates, one on each side. The main temple building, called Sri Mandir, was built in the 12th century by King Chodaganga Deva, though the site is said to go back at least 2000 years, if not much further. The additional smaller buildings were added after the 16th century. The main temple, which reaches 215 feet in height, is where we find the five foot tall deities of Jagannatha, His brother Balarama, and His sister Subhadra. They stand on a five foot high throne facing the pilgrims as they enter the temple room. Outside the main temple hall are over 100 smaller shrines dedicated to the various demigods and divine personalities. There is an *arati* ceremony six times a day from 4 A.M. to 9 P.M. when devotees come in for *darshan*, in which they sing, chant, or worship the deities in ecstasy. As many as 50,000 people come to the Jagannatha temple in a day. Unfortunately, foreigners are not allowed into the temple grounds, but you can get a look at the temple from the roof of the Raghunandan Library across the street for a donation. And everyone can see the deities when They come out during the annual Ratha-Yatra festival.

The temple compound also has a huge kitchen, employing over 650 cooks and helpers who make hundreds of vegetarian preparations for the 54 separate offerings that are given to the deities every day. The kitchen uses no electricity and everything is cooked on wood fires. After the food is given to the deities it becomes *prasada*, or the Lord's mercy. By taking such spiritually powerful food it is said that one becomes more and more spiritually surcharged and free from past karma. Much of the *prasada* is sold or given to people who depend on the temple. When I was in Puri I had my ricksha driver buy some for me. I got a basket with several clay pots filled with a variety of rice, vegetable, dahl, and sweet preparations. It was absolutely delicious and was enough for breakfast, lunch, and dinner. Taking this *prasada* at Puri is to partake in a tradition that goes back thousands of years and is considered especially purifying. It is said that only by Krishna's grace does one get the opportunity to receive the remnants of food offered to Him.

The significance of Jagannatha Puri and the story of how the deities first appeared goes back many hundreds of years to the time of King Indradyumna, who was a great devotee of Lord Vishnu. One time in his court the King heard from a devotee about an incarnation of Lord Vishnu, named Nila-madhava. (Nila-madhava is the deity form of Lord Vishnu.) The King very much wanted to see this form of the Supreme and sent many brahmanas to search for Nila-madhava. All came back unsuccessful except for Vidyapati, who did not come back at all. He had wandered to a distant town which was populated by a tribe of people known as Shabaras of non-Aryan heritage. He had stayed in the house of Visvasu, and later, at Visvasu's request, married his daughter, Lalita.

After some time Vidyapati noticed that Visvasu would leave the house every night and return at noon the next day. Vidyapati asked his wife about this. Though her father had ordered her not to tell anyone, she told Vidyapati that Visvasu would go in secret to worship Nila-madhava. After repeated requests, Vidyapati finally got permission to go see Nila-madhava, only if he went blindfolded. But Vidyapati's wife had bound some mustard seeds in his cloth so that a trail could be left to follow later. When they reached the shrine, Vidyapati saw the deity Nila-madhava after the Shabara took off the blindfold, and he felt great ecstasy.

The story continues to relate that while Visvasu was out collecting items for worship, Vidyapati saw a bird fall into the nearby lake and drown. The soul of the bird suddenly took a spiritual form and ascended back to the spiritual world. Vidyapati wanted to do the same and climbed the tree to jump in the lake. Then a voice from the sky declared that before he jumped he should tell Indradyumna that he had found Nila-madhava.

When Visvasu returned to worship the deity, Nila-madhava spoke and said that He had accepted the simple worship from him for so many days, but now He wanted to accept the opulent worship that would be offered by King Indradyumna. When Vidyapati went back to tell the King, Indradyumna immediately went to find Nila-madhava but could not locate Him. So the King arrested Visvasu, but a voice told him to release the Shabara and that he should build a temple on top of Nila Hill where the King would see the Lord as Daru-brahman, the wooden manifestation of the Absolute.

After great endeavor, King Indradyumna built the temple at Sri Kshetra, now known as Jagannatha Puri, and later prayed to Lord Brahma to consecrate it. However, Lord Brahma said that it was not within his power to consecrate the temple since Sri Kshetra is manifested by the Supreme's own internal potency and is where the Lord manifests Himself. So Brahma simply put a flag on top of the temple and blessed it, saying that anyone who from a distance saw the flag and offered obeisances would easily be liberated from the material world. So now, anyone who merely sees the flag on top of the present temple and in the mood of devotion offers obeisances to it can be freed from material existence. Nonetheless, after much waiting the King had become anxious since Nila-madhava had not manifested Himself. Thinking his life was useless, the King decided he should end his life by fasting. But in a dream the Lord said that He would appear floating in from the sea in His form as Daru-brahman.

The King went to the shore and found a huge piece of wood that had the markings of a conch, disc, club, and lotus. This was Daru-brahman. But try as they might, the men could not budge the wood. In a dream the Lord spoke to the King and instructed him to get Visvasu and put a golden chariot in front of Daru-brahman. After doing this and forming a *kirtana* party to chant the holy names, and praying for Daru-brahman to mount the chariot, Daru-brahman was easily moved. Lord Brahma then performed a sacrifice where the present temple now stands and installed a deity of Lord Narasimhadeva, the half-man and half-lion deity that is now on the western side of the temple.

From the wooden Daru-brahman, the King requested many expert carvers to carve the form of the deity, but none could do so for their chisels immediately broke when they touched the wood. Finally the architect of the demigods, Visvakarma, (some say the Lord Himself) arrived as an old artist, Ananta Maharana, and promised that he would carve the deity form of the Lord inside the temple in three weeks if the King would allow him to work behind closed doors. But after 14 days the King became very anxious because he could no longer hear the sounds of the carving. Finally, he could stand it no more. On the advice of the queen, he personally opened the doors of the temple to see what was happening. Then he saw the forms of Lord Jagannatha, Lord Balarama, and Lady Subhadra. But because the King had opened the doors sooner than he was supposed to, the deities were not completed: Their feet and hands had not yet been carved. Thus, the Supreme manifested Himself in this form.

The King felt he had committed a great offense for having opened the doors before the allotted three weeks had passed, so he decided to end his life. But in a dream Lord Jagannatha told the King that though he had broken his promise, this was just a part of the Supreme's pastimes to display this particular form. Occasionally, the King could decorate the deity with golden hands and feet. Yet, those devotees who were filled with love would always see the form of Lord Jagannatha as the threefold bending form of Syamasundara, Krishna, holding a flute. Thus, the Supreme appeared in this form so that people could approach and see Him, especially as He rides on the huge carts during the Ratha-Yatra festival.

In fact, during the Ratha-Yatra festival is the most popular time to go to Jagannatha Puri. This is usually in July when it is very hot. But thousands upon thousands of pilgrims flock to Puri to take part in this auspicious event, which is said to have been celebrated for thousands of years, making it one of the oldest and one of the biggest religious festivals in the world. This is the time when the deities come out of the temple for all to see. It is also the time when as many as a million people gather in this small city with one purpose: to show their faith and devotion to God in the form of Lord Jagannatha.

As big as this festival is, it can be quite expensive. The only festival in the world that is bigger than this is the Kumbha Mela festival that draws many millions of people. The Ratha-Yatra festival is financed primarily by the Orissan government with an annual budget of $50,000, which is a very large sum for India. But with the number of pilgrims that come to Puri each year, the temple and surrounding businesses also are benefited with the extra financial income.

The construction of the carts or chariots begins several weeks before the festival. In the main road in front of the temple huge stacks of wood are used to assemble the three chariots. These will reach up to three storeys tall and will roll on as many as 16 wheels, each eight feet high. The chariots are painted with bright colors and the tops are covered with red, black, yellow, or green canopies. The colors signify which chariot is for which deity.

About two weeks before the festival the deities of Jagannatha, Balarama, and Subhadra are given a ritual bath. This is done on a special platform near the front of the temple so that devotees outside the compound can still see what is taking place. Of course, many also try to use the nearby rooftops to get a better view. After this bath, the deities play the pastime of getting a cold. They are then taken to a designated area and given special treatments and offerings. They may also be repainted at this time. About every 12 or 19 years, the deities are replaced with new ones carved from a ritualistically selected Daru-Brahman in the form of a nima tree. During this time three huge carts are also built for the festival. You can watch their progress since the carts are assembled on the main street several blocks from the front of the temple.

As the festival draws near, thousands of pilgrims come to Jagannatha Puri, but as many as a million people may be in town on the day of the festival. Some are top officials in the Indian government. Many people begin arriving in front of the temple near the carts on the morning of the festival. At first it is very interesting to wander about looking at the nicely decorated carts and all the pilgrims who have attended. But then the police begin cordoning off the area around the carts. Then there are only certain areas where people can get between the carts and the buildings. This creates bottlenecks which can be very dangerous when too many people are pushing on each other trying to get through. I saw people begin to panic at times because of the pressure on them, and worried mothers had to hold their babies above the crowd to make sure they did not get crushed.

The Ratha-Yatra festival can be both spiritually ecstatic and physically exhausting. Though July is in the monsoon season, if the rains have not arrived yet, it gets very hot. When it is hot, you will be soaked with sweat a few hours after the sun comes up. In fact, from where I was, I saw dozens of Indian people who had collapsed from the heat and had to be carried away from the crowd on stretchers. Sometimes I would also hear the sound of conch shells blowing and then you would see a crew carrying a stretcher with someone on it who had passed out. The heat can take a lot out of you, especially when in a crowd of thousands. So it is best to have a bottle of water with you. There are also men who wander through the crowds with water tanks on their backs and who spray water on people to keep everyone a little cool. This can also greatly help those who are spending much time in the sun.

A good place to be during the festival, if you do not want to be on the street amongst the people, is on a rooftop so you can get a clear view of things. Being on the Raghunandan Library roof is a good place. But you usually have to make reservations and pay for your seats several days in advance. Even then there may not be any guarantee that you will get the seats you want because in the excitement everything goes up for grabs. And the sun can be quite hot while sitting on a rooftop.

Anyway, the road in front of the temple gets filled with people and groups of *kirtana* parties all singing the holy names and devotional songs. It becomes quite festive and spiritually blissful. Even television crews from Indian networks will be there to cover the event.

By 8 A.M. the temple priests come out to sanctify the carts. They walk up the gangplanks to the platform on the cart and sprinkle holy water around while circumambulating it three times and chanting specific mantras for purification. Then, after much waiting, the priests bring out the small deities that will also ride on the cart. [This description is as it happened in 2001. But when I observed it in 1990, everything took place much later in the day, and took much longer. I liked the way it happened in an earlier and more punctual and efficient manner. But things again happened much later and slower in 2007. So it may change from year to year.]

Then by 9:30 Lord Balarama is brought out. Suddenly excitement fills the air when many men blow conchshells and bang on drums and cymbals to announce the arrival of the deities at the main gate of the temple complex. Then the smiling face of Lord Balarama appears through the doorway and the crowd shouts and chants, "Jai Balarama. Baladeva ki jai!" Generally, however, unless you are situated on a tall building, you cannot see the faces of the deities as They are brought out because there are so many assistants that help move Them. But you can easily see the huge headdress They wear. Once the deity is on the cart, the headdress is torn off and distributed amongst the people as *prasada*.

Daityas, strongly built men who lift the deity, carry Lord Balarama from one large cotton pillow to another. Lord Balarama is five feet and five inches tall and has an arm span of 12 feet. When carried, there are five men on each arm, with up to 50 men pulling in front and 20 offering support in the back. All of these carriers are members of the Dayitapati family. Gradually, after about an hour, Lord Balarama moves to the chariot gangplank and slowly He is brought up to the cart and is placed on it so everyone in the crowd can see Him. Then Subhadra, who is less than five feet tall, is also taken from the temple to Her chariot. She is smaller and liter, so they carry Her and run out to the cart, up the gangplank, and place Her in the cart within minutes. And finally Lord Jagannatha is brought out. He is five feet and seven inches tall with an arm span of 12 feet, and also needs many assistants to be moved.

There are special names for the chariots. Jagannatha rides on the 14-wheeled Nandigosha, which means tumultuous and blissful sound. Balarama rides on the 16-wheeled Taladhvaja, meaning the sound of significantly powerful rhythm. And Subhadra rides on the 12-wheeled Darpadalana, which means destroyer of pride. When the chariots move, if you are walking near them, you can hear the thunderous sound they make. The chariots are also painted with certain colors to signify which chariot is meant for which deity. The deities are also painted with particular colors that mean something. Jagannatha's blackish color represents faultless qualities; Balarama's white color signifies enlightenment; and Subhadra's yellow color signifies goodness.

Shortly after the deities are in place, the King of Puri arrives in a procession, walks up the planks to the platform and sweeps the cart with a gold handled broom. He circumambulates the platform three times and is assisted by the priests. He does this to each of the carts. Only after this are the carts ready to go. It should be pointed out here that the way the King sweeps the carts is an example of how the festival has changed over the years. If you read accounts of the Ratha-Yatra festival as described in the *Caitanya-caritamrta*, there are some major differences in the festival we find today compared to 500 years ago. The King used to sweep the street in front of the carts as they paraded down through the town. The reason he no longer does this is related in a story I was told. It seems that at one time years ago a King of Puri was to marry a princess who was the daughter of a king from a local district. When the Ratha-Yatra festival was to take place, the father of the princess was invited. When he attended, the King of Puri performed the devotional tradition of sweeping the road in front of the carts. The visiting King, however, rather than being impressed with the devotion of the King for Lord Jagannatha, objected to the idea of his daughter marrying the King of Puri since he was merely a street sweeper. From then on the King of Puri discontinued sweeping the streets and now sweeps the carts.

The festival parade also used to start in the morning and stop at noon near the Jagannatha Vallabh Garden where the deities would get offerings of food, worship, etc., from the many devotees. Now this does not take place. There would also be many groups of people singing devotional songs, and though now you see people in large *kirtana* groups in the parade, as recently as 1990 there were very few. Once the carts got going, you mostly heard people simply shout out, "Jayo, Jai Jagannatha," and raise their hands in the air and watch the cart go by. And when it was gone, that's it: back to business. Then, when I saw it again in 2001, things were more devotional and like the way it was years ago.

When the deities are on the chariots, and as the King of Puri cleans each cart, the assistants immediately begin to take down the gangplanks and prepare the carts for movement. Many thousands of devotees surround the carts and the people in the front take up the long, thick ropes to prepare for pulling the chariots down the main road to the Gundicha temple, where the deities will stay for a few days. When everything was ready, it was about 1:30 P.M. when a whistle was blown by the chariot driver and a hundred people on each rope began to pull the chariot of Lord Balarama. Soon He was on His way. Many people begin to follow the cart as it goes to the Gundicha temple, yet many more wait for the other carts. Many police have to guard the chariot wheels to make sure no one gets too close and is crushed under them. Then about an hour later Lady Subhadra's cart begins to move and soon it pulls away and is rolling down the street. Then a little while after that Lord Jagannatha's cart is on its way.

The whole crowd and the *kirtana* groups all start moving in front of the cart, as many people pull the ropes. Sometimes the carts would stop and it would take a mighty effort to get them going again. Also, sometimes they start heading into the power lines. In that case, the city has to turn off the power to that section of the city to prevent problems or fires.

Lord Balarama's cart made it to the Gundicha temple that afternoon, but Lady Subhadra's and Lord Jagannatha's cart did not make it. The people pulled them about two-thirds of the way before Jagannatha's cart almost ran into some shops on the side of the road. So that is where it stayed until the next morning. The following morning the people redirected the cart and finished pulling it to the temple. The parade is a fascinating event in which to participate and see. But when the chariots get rolling, the crowd gets very intense. You either have to get out of the way to let them by, or struggle to move with the crowd as it goes with the cart. Many people try to pull the ropes and it is not always easy and can be dangerous to get a place near them.

Sometimes the chariots mysteriously stop, though everyone is pulling hard. In fact, it is not unusual, as in the case of the festivals I have attended, that a chariot may stop completely and stay there overnight and then continue the next day. Sometimes if there is difficulty, the local government minister will pray to Lord Jagannatha for forgiveness from whatever offenses the residents of the town may have committed. Then the chariots begin to move again as if they move only by the will of Jagannatha. The chariots continue to the Gundicha temple about two miles down the road from the main temple where the deities stay for a week before returning to the temple in a similar parade.

The deities may spend the first two nights on the carts outside the Gundicha temple. During this time, pilgrims can climb up on the carts and see the deities very closely and even embrace Them. But the priests are quick to charge everyone a certain number of rupees for this opportunity, which makes for a very good business. When I climbed a cart and was about to give a "donation," as many as five of the attendants grabbed the money at once before I let go of it. And when I did not let go of it right away, they started to get very angry. This was after I had been assured that I could climb the cart to see the deity of Lady Subhadra and there would be no charge, and I would also be allowed to take a photograph. I indeed was allowed to see Lady Subhadra and even embrace Her, which is a rare event for any pilgrim, what to speak of a Westerner. But after I had given my donation, I took out my camera to take a photograph and a guard immediately came over and objected and ordered me to get down off the cart. So that brought an abrupt end to that episode. Nonetheless, if one can overcome this business-like atmosphere, it can still be a very devotional and memorable event.

Some people simply stay on the ground and offer prayers and small ghee lamps to the deities. Thus, they exhibit their devotion from a distance rather than trying to be right next to the deities. Others climb all three carts to get the close and personal *darshan* of all three deities, though the carts of Lord Jagannatha and Lord Balarama are so crowded it can be difficult for anyone to get close to the deities. People continue to gather around the carts for the next few days until the deities are brought into the Gundicha Mandir in the evening. Thousands of people will be standing nearby to see how the deities are taken down from the carts and slowly carried into the temple. They again build large planks leading down from the carts where each of the deities are taken and brought into the Gundicha temple.

After the deities' stay at the Gundicha temple, They return several days later to the main temple in a similar parade that is attended by far fewer people. This can be a time when you can get much closer to the carts and walk more easily with the parade, providing you have time to stay in Puri until the next week. However, the road is still heavily crowded. Once they arrive back at the main temple, the deities will again stay on the carts for another couple of days. On the final evening They are dressed in Their gold outfits, called Sunavesha. They will have gold headdresses, gold necklaces, and gold hands and feet that are placed on Them. Many people come to view the deities at that time. Lines form blocks away and you have only a moving *darshan*. In other words, you keep walking in front of the carts as you look at the deities, and then go down the side lanes as other people follow. In this way, you see Lord Balarama and Lady Subhadra, then go down the street and come back around to get a similar *darshan* of Lord Jagannatha as you walk past His cart. But the deities look very powerful when They are dressed in this way, and it is indeed an amazing *darshan* to see Them like this. After most everyone sees Them, later that evening They are brought back into the main temple.

The meaning of the Ratha-Yatra parade is steeped in religious sentiment. The form that Lord Krishna takes as Jagannatha is the manifestation of His ecstasy that He feels when He leaves the opulence of His palaces in Dwaraka, represented by the Puri temple, to return to the town of Vrindavan and the simple and pure spontaneous love the residents there have for Him. Thus, there is no difference between Lord Krishna and Lord Jagannatha. So in the mood of separation from His loving devotees, Jagannatha mounts His chariot and returns to Vrindavan, which is represented by the Gundicha temple. In this way, the esoteric meaning of the Ratha-Yatra parade is that we pull the Lord back into our hearts and rekindle the loving relationship we have with Him. Many great poems and songs, such as Jagannatha-astakam, have been composed describing the event and the highly ecstatic devotional mood into which one can enter. Many verses are also written in the *Caitanya-caritamrta* that describe the pastimes Sri Chaitanya Mahaprabhu had during these Ratha-Yatra festivals 500 years ago.

It is also explained that by participating in this festival, chanting and dancing, or helping pull the ropes of the chariots, one becomes free of many lifetimes of karma. One can even become liberated due to the spiritual potency of Lord Jagannatha's presence. How this happens is explained as follows: at the very end of one's life when the memories of one's activities pass through the mind, when he remembers the amazing Ratha-Yatra festival his mind stops and focuses on that event. Thus, the person dies thinking of Lord Jagannatha and is liberated from material existence and returns to the spiritual world, just like a yogi is transferred to the spiritual strata when his mind is fixed on the Supersoul at the time of death. This is why thousands of pilgrims come to Jagannatha Puri every year for Ratha-Yatra. The experience of the event creates an impression that never goes away.

The Holy Places in and Around Jagannatha Puri. While in Jagannatha Puri, there are many other places of interest that pilgrims come to see, so I will describe a few of these. About a quarter mile from the Jagannatha temple, walking toward the beach, is the Siddha Bakula. This is where, 500 years ago, the great saint Haridas Thakur used to live and chant the Hare Krishna mantra 300,000 times a day, and where Sri Chaitanya would visit him. Haridas attained such an elevated position of ecstasy from chanting the Hare Krishna mantra that even though a beautiful prostitute came to tempt him with sex, he was not interested. Thus, he is called the *namacharya*: the master of chanting the holy names. Presently, a small temple is found here, along with the old and bent tree under which Haridas would chant. The tree is surrounded by a few walls and bars for protection. The tomb of Haridas Thakur is located next to Purusottama Gaudiya Math where you will also see beautiful Radha Krishna deities as well as an image of Haridas. This is an important place of pilgrimage.

A 15 minute walk from here is the temple of Tota-Gopinatha. The Radha Krishna deities here are very beautiful and it is accepted that Sri Chaitanya ended his life by entering into the deity of Tota-Gopinatha. Tota-Gopinatha is in the sitting position and next to Him is Radharani on one side and Lalita on the other. Two additional altars are also on either side of the main one. The deities of Radha and Tota-Gopinatha were installed 500 years ago by Sri Gadadhara. Tota-Gopinatha is a rather large deity and was first established in the standing position. Then as Sri Gadadhara was getting old, it became difficult for him to daily dress the deities and to stretch and reach up to put the garland on and other things. So Gadadhara asked Tota-Gopinatha if He could sit down, which would make it easier for him. So the deity moved into a sitting position. And this is why this is one of the few deities you will find of Krishna sitting down.

Just a short walk up the street we find the Purushottama Math. This is a Gaudiya Math temple established by Srila Bhaktisiddhanta Sarasvati. This has ashrama quarters and a central temple with Radha Krishna deities on one side of the main altar and Gaura-Nitai on the other side. In the back of the property is a hill called Govardhana and next to it is a house where Srila Bhaktisiddhanta would stay when he was in Puri. It has his bed where he would take rest and deities of Vyasadeva and Madhvacarya.

Also near this area is the old house of Kashi Mishra. It is now used as part of a temple and has nice diorama exhibits of Sri Chaitanya's life. It is here we find the Gambhira room, which is where Sri Chaitanya lived for 12 years. Through a small window you can see Sri Chaitanya's original wooden sandals, water pot, and bed.

A short walk to the east of the Jagannatha temple is the Jagannatha Vallabha Garden, which is almost across from the Balagandhi temple which used to be where Lord Jagannatha would stop during His Ratha-Yatra parade to accept food offerings from all the devotees. At this garden, Sri Chaitanya had many pastimes and is where He saw Lord Krishna manifest Himself. A little ways away from the garden is Narendra Sarovara, a small lake where many festivals have taken place with Sri Chaitanya and his associates. Even now many pilgrims will visit and take a holy bath in this lake. The Govinda deity from the Jagannatha temple is brought here for festivals. There used to be a little set of Lord Jagannatha deities here. So, if foreigners wanted to see Lord Jagannatha they could come here for *darshan*. But such deities are no longer there.

Further down the main road of town near the Gundicha Mandir is the very old temple dedicated to Lord Narasimha, which we can enter to view the deity of Narasimha from a distance. Foreigners cannot go all the way in. This is also where Sri Chaitanya engaged in many *kirtanas* with his close associates. Not far away is Indradyumna Lake where Sri Chaitanya once manifested His MahaVishnu form showing His associates His supernatural qualities as an incarnation of God.

A few other places to see include Jagadananda Pandit's house, and the house of Swarup Damodara.

About 14 miles from Jagannatha Puri is the Alalarnatha temple at Brahmagiri. Lord Alalarnatha is a four-handed form of Lord Vishnu. Whenever the Jagannatha deities in Puri would be removed from the altar before the Ratha-Yatra festival for two weeks, Sri Chaitanya would stay here. This is a temple where, at the end of the *kirtana* hall in front of a deity of Sadbhuja, there is a large stone slab with the imprint of Sri Chaitanya's body. Once when He fell onto the stone in an ecstatic trance, the stone melted leaving the imprint of Sri Chaitanya's body as we find it today.

Across from the Alalarnatha temple is another Gaudiya-Math temple that was established by Srila Bhaktisiddhanta. It is also here where we find the small Alalarnatha deity that was uncovered during excavations around the main Alalarnatha temple. However, once when Srila Bhaktisiddhanta was staying at his temple, the priest at the Alalarnatha shrine had a dream in which the Lord came to him and said that He wanted to accept the worship of Srila Bhaktisiddhanta. Then the priest brought the small Alalarnatha deity to Srila Bhaktisiddhanta who worshiped Him, and where the deity has remained since then. Also, in this town of Bentapur we can see the birthplace of Ramananda Raya, a close associate of Sri Chaitanya.

Nineteen miles north of Jagannatha Puri is Konarka, which has a most interesting temple to Surya, the sun-god. Although it is very old and no longer used for worship, many people come here every day. A Surya temple was here as long ago as the 9th century, but the present temple was built in the 13th century to resemble a huge chariot and has 24 gigantic stone wheels all around it. There are also carvings of seven strong horses that pull the chariot. The temple is covered with many panels of stone figures depicting many aspects of life, such as scenes with hunters, soldiers, ascetics, maidens, birds, elephants, erotica, etc. There are also three green chlorite deities of Surya in niches on the outside of the temple, reached by ascending flights of stairs. The interior has been filled in and blocked up to help support it. Outside the temple grounds are many shops along the walkway which sell food, devotional items, even Jagannatha deities, as well as the usual gamut of nick-nacks and souvenirs.

About six miles from Puri is the Saksi-gopala temple, located between the Jagannatha Puri and Khurda Road Junction railway stations. A new station called Saksi-gopala is there where people get off to visit the temple. The Saksi-gopala deity is the Gopala deity who walked from Vrindavan to Vidyanagara, a town located 20 to 25 miles from Rajahmundry on the banks of the Godavari River. How this happened was that two brahmanas were traveling and visiting the holy places. One was poor and young and was serving the older and richer brahmana. The older one was so satisfied with the charitable service of the younger brahmana that he vowed in front of the Gopala deity that he would give his daughter to the younger brahmana to be his wife. Later, when they returned home, the older brahmana hesitated to fulfill his promise due to pressure from his family who disagreed with the idea. There was some controversy about this between the two brahmanas and in a meeting with the townspeople it was agreed that if the deity Gopala came to testify as a witness, the older brahmana would give his daughter as promised.

The younger brahmana went back to Vrindavan and related the situation to Gopala who finally agreed to walk. He told the brahmana that He would follow him and that the sound of His ankle bells would indicate He was there, but if the brahmana turned around to look, He would walk no farther. So for 100 days they walked toward Vidyanagara, then the sound of the deity's ankle bells ceased to sound. The brahmana became worried and looked back, and the deity was standing there smiling. The brahmana went to gather the people of the town who were amazed to see the deity. Then the older brahmana agreed to give his daughter in marriage as promised and a temple was built for the deity.

Later the King of Orissa, Purusottama, was insulted by the King of Kataka (Cuttack). So Purusottama fought and defeated the King of Kataka and took charge of the city. He then brought the Gopalaji deity from Vidyanagara to Kataka and built a temple there. The deity also stayed in the Jagannatha temple for some time, but then was moved to a village about six miles from Puri, called Satyavadi. Some time after that a new temple was constructed where we find the Saksi-gopala deity today. Though the temple does not allow foreigners inside, many people visit this temple with the understanding that whether the Supreme is in the spiritual strata or expands Himself in the material realm in the form of a stone deity, He can change what is spiritual into material and vice versa whenever He wants. That is why a stone deity can do what is considered miraculous things, like walk, talk, etc. Thus, it is accepted that the bona fide deity of the Supreme is nondifferent from the Supreme Himself.

BHUBANESWAR

Bhubaneswar, 60 kilometers from Jagannatha Puri, is a busy town of 650,000, and has been the capital of Orissa since 1956. There are many government buildings and a variety of people who have government positions in this city. But as the city name implies, it is a city of Lord Shiva and is especially known for its numerous Shiva temples. Many years ago there used to be over 1000 temples. Most of them that still exist in varying degrees of preservation or decay can be found by walking or taking a ricksha around the area of the Bindusagar lake. I will mention several of these that can be easily found and are noteworthy for their Orissan architecture and the ornate carvings that cover the temple exteriors. Some of these temples are no longer used for worship and are locked up, so the interior is not possible to see. In most cases, the interior is not nearly as ornate as the exterior, so we would not be missing much.

First of all, Bindusagar is the water tank that is said to contain water from the Ganges, Yamuna, Sarasvati, and every other holy river and lake in India. Therefore, many pilgrims come to bathe in the spiritually purifying water. Once a year there is a festival when the deity from the Lingaraja temple is brought to the pavilion in the lake to be bathed.

The Lingaraja temple, just to the south of the Bindusagar lake, is the most important in Bhubaneswar and is known all over India. It is dedicated to Shiva as Bhubaneswar, or Tribhuvaneswar, "Lord of the Three Worlds," and dates back to 1090. The temple tower reaches 40 meters high and houses the Shiva *linga* which is bathed daily in milk, water, and *bhang*. The outside of the stone temple is covered with intricate Orissan designs. Non-Hindus are not allowed in the temple complex, but on the north side is a viewing platform near the wall that lets you see the temple and the numerous smaller shrines dedicated to other demigods in the courtyard. The only problem is that when you use the platform, you may be approached by men asking for a donation for either some local cause or helping maintain the platform, which gets little if any upkeep. Everybody knows that these guys are frauds, so we don't give them any money. A few men dressed as brahmanas approached me and gave me the hard sell when I was there. They said they had a food distribution program to feed many of the local poor people, but the smell of cigarettes was on their breath, and strict brahmanas don't smoke *bidis*. So that was enough to turn me off from giving them anything. And when it was time to leave I had to move quickly to get away from them.

North of the Bindusagar is a group of temples noted for their fine architecture and carved stonework. The small Muktesvara temple, reaching 11 meters high, the Kedareshvara temple across the path, the Siddeswar temple, and the well preserved Parashurameswar temple, built in the 7th century is one of the oldest. All are worth visiting and allow foreigners inside. The exteriors of these temples are exceptional for all the delicate carvings and sculpture work. There are images of important Vedic demigods, such as Ganesh, Kartikeya, Durga, Shiva, and figures of animals, birds, etc., or scenes from the *Puranas*.

There is also the Raj Rani temple about 100 metres down the road in a field. It has many carved stone figures decorating the exterior, but the door to the interior is locked. It is one of the finest examples of the Orissan style of temple architecture, and is profusely covered with many ornately carved images. Farther down the road is the Brahmeshwar temple, with four smaller shrines at each corner of the courtyard. This temple dates to the ninth century. Some of the carvings on the outside include the deities of the nine planets, demigods like Ganesh and Brahma, and different aspects of Shiva and Durga. We can also go inside to view the Shiva *lingam* which is worshiped in the morning. Not far away are the Bhaskareswar and Megheswar temples, though less interesting.

On the other side of Bindusagar is the Vaital Deul Shiva temple, built in the 8th century AD, which has an image of a fearsome form of Durga as an eight-armed Chamundi or Kapalini. She is the goddess who killed the buffalo-headed demon Mahishasura. A scene of this is carved on the northern wall of the temple. Near the Vaital is the Sisiresvara temple, which is worth seeing while you are here, but is not in as good of condition. The Markandesvara and Jambesvara temples are also in this area, but are not in the best of shape. The Rameshvar temple, some distance away from most of the others, is also an interesting and still functioning Shiva temple. Many other temples of less importance can also be found scattered throughout Bhubaneswar.

If you have seen enough Shiva temples, one of the few Vishnu temples in the area is the Ananta Vasudeva temple on the southeast side of the lake. This is an active temple that, unlike others in the area, allows everyone in to see the deities of Vishnu (Jagannatha), Balarama, and Subhadra. They also have a free food distribution program in which they take food that has been offered to the deities out to the poor in the nearby villages.

Located on the other side of town on Highway Number 5 is the beautiful Iskcon temple, with lovely deities of Krishna-Balarama, Sri Chaitanya and Nityananda, and Jagannatha, Balarama, and Lady Subhadra. This temple is open to everyone.

If you see Bhubaneswar on a bus tour you'll see a few of the nicest temples, but you may not have as much time to look them over as you would like. But by starting in the morning to walk or take a ricksha to these temples you will have enough time to easily wander around and look at each one. Remember that most of the active temples close between noon and four P.M.

If you have had enough of temple hunting, you can spend the afternoon visiting a museum or two. There is the nearby Orissa State Museum, which has displays of Hindu, Buddhist, and Jain sculptures. There is also the Tribal Research Bureau, and the Handicrafts Museum that has displays of local folk art.

Five kilometers outside of Bhubaneswar are the Udayagiri and Khandagiri hills. These hills have small caves or cells that were once occupied by Jain monks, the oldest of which date back to the second century B.C.E. Some of these have some nice stone carvings of Jain *tirthankaras* or Vedic images, but most of them are quite simple. At the top of the Khandagiri hill is an 18th century Jain temple where you can get some fine views over the area with the city of Bhubaneswar in the distance. Lots of people come here for picnics or short excursions, but unless you are on a tour bus that stops here and you just want to check it out, this place may not be interesting enough for you to make a special trip to see. The small caves are not really that significant.

Heading back towards Puri, eight km south of Bhubaneswar is Dhaulagiri. It is here that King Ashoka is believed to have been converted to Buddhism. Here we find a large new Peace Pagoda built on top of the hill by the Japanese Buddhists Biswa Buddha Nipon Sangha. It has four life-size images of Buddha facing each of the four directions. Behind the pagoda is a Shiva temple. At the base of the hill are the edicts of King Ashoka carved into the side of a rock that is five by three metres in dimension. The edicts describe the King's reasons for converting to Buddhism.

SRI KAKULAM to KURMAKSETRA

From Bhubanesvara we take a short train ride to Sri Kakulam to visit Kurmaksetra. The temple at Kurmaksetra is noteworthy because it is the only temple dedicated to Krishna's *avatara* in the form of Kurma, His tortoise incarnation, and many visitors come through to see it. Kurmaksetra is 22 miles south of Sri Kakulam and takes an hour to reach by bus or taxi. It is best to get a hotel at Sri Kakulam because there is not much to choose from at Kurmaksetra. Kurmaksetra is a small town and the temple is easy to find near a small lake called Kurma Lake. Anyone there can point the way. The temple is in the middle of a courtyard surrounded by a large wall and topped by a silver dome over the sanctum. There are as many as 500 carved and ornate columns and many other figures on the walls. Through a narrow and dimly lit corridor we enter the sanctum where the deity of Kurma is located. The temple is lit by torches and has paintings of Lord Vishnu's ten incarnations on the walls and ceiling. In the sanctum a few brahmana priests may be engaged in chanting hymns and making offerings. On the main altar is the deity of Kurma, which is a two-foot long mound with a tortoise head on one end. Another altar is for Lakshmi Devi and Bhu Devi, the consorts of Vishnu. The priests are friendly and glad to see Western pilgrims and will give you a few drops of *caranamrita* water and flowers and fruits that have been offered to the deity, so it is fitting to give a nice donation.

Just south of the temple along one of the exterior walls is a little shrine built by Srila Bhaktisiddhanta Sarasvati Thakur in 1930. Inside are the footprints he installed of Sri Chaitanya Mahaprabhu to commemorate Lord Chaitanya's visit here in 1512.

When we are finished visiting Kurmaksetra we return to Sri Kakulam, which has a few more Krishna temples we can search out while we have time. There is also a temple to Surya the sun-god with an exceptional deity of Surya, named Suryanarayanaswami, located in the suburb of Sri Kakulam known as Arasavalli. This image is believed to have been installed by Indra many years ago.

VISAKHAPATNAM

We arrive by train at our next stop at Visakhapatnam where we will visit the Jiyada Narasimha (Simhachalam) temple located about ten miles north of the city near Waltair. This is one of the 108 Divya Desams of Lord Vishnu. After leaving the train station, we book a room at a hotel and arrange that a taxi will pick us up at nine the next morning. The drive to the temple takes almost an hour, and we need to make sure we get there when the temple is open, usually between 8 and 11 A.M, otherwise we will not be able to get *darshan* of the deity. There are 1000 steps that go up the hill to the temple, unless you take a bus or taxi. Driving up the hill on which the temple is located provides some great views over the countryside. Buses take pilgrims up from the foot of the hill to the temple for two rupees. Most of what we see of this temple was built in the 13th century by one of the commanders of Narasimha I, who had also built the Surya temple at Konark.

Narasimha's devotee Prahlada is said to have built the original shrine when he was saved from his father Hiranyakashipu. The story is that the hill at Simhachalam is the one from which the demon Hiranyakashipu had his devotee son thrown in an attempt to kill him. The mountain was also placed over Prahalada, but the Lord saved him by jumping over the hill and lifting Prahlada from the sea. The hill may seem somewhat lopsided since it is also accepted that the Lord had lifted the hill enough for Prahlada to escape from underneath it. Thereafter, Prahlada asked the Lord to assume a deity form as both Lord Narasimha (the lion form) who would soon kill Hiranyakashipu, and Lord Varaha (the boar *avatara*) who had already killed Hiranyakshya, the brother of Hiranyakashipu. Thus, the deity is of Varaha Narasimha.

When Hiranyakashipu was later killed by Lord Narasimha, Prahlada built a temple around the deity where worship was conducted. In time, however, the temple was neglected and earth covered the deity. Much later, the king of the lunar dynasty, Puru-rava, was drawn to Simhachalam and rediscovered the deity under the earth. Hearing a voice, it instructed him to cover the deity with sandalwood paste and worship Him, and only uncover Him once a year. Pururava also rebuilt the temple and established the wor-ship of the deity again, which has continued to this day.

Along the streets in front of the temple are rows of shops offering all kinds of devo-tional paraphernalia. Other little shops offer snacks and drinks. Near the entrance are a set of footprints of Sri Chaitanya Mahaprabhu to commemorate His visit here 500 years ago, installed in 1930 by Srila Bhaktisiddhanta Sarasvati Goswami. We leave our shoes at the shoe stall and make our way around until we enter the temple compound through a side door. We climb a stairway and pass through long halls of the Kalyana *mandapa* with beautifully carved columns, walls with delicately carved figures, shrines with images of Lakshmi and Vishnu and the Alwars, and gateways that lead to the main temple.

Before entering the main hall we pass by an altar with beautiful deities of Radha and Krishna. Then we turn to go in the main sanctum where there is a silver throne with the deity of Narasimha, but He is covered with dried sandalwood paste. In fact, you cannot see any of the deity's features at all. There is simply a three foot mound of sandalwood. This deity is described as the form of Varaha Narasimha, standing in a three-fold bending form, with two hands, the head of a boar, tail of a lion, and a human torso. This is described in the local or *Sthala Purana*.

This Lord Narasimha is known as Ugra Devatha, or an angry form, and He gets very hot from anger when He sees the activities of the demons and materialists. The sandal-wood helps keep Him cool. Then, once a year, there is the festival of Chandan Yatra in April-May. This is when all of the sandalwood is removed and the deity, which is about two-and-a-half feet tall, gives *darshan* of His real form, *nija rupa*. This festival draws thousands of devotees from all over. It is very crowded at the temple at that time, and a quick view of the deity is all you get, while some of the priests have to push to keep peo-ple going in the line through the sanctum. But by evening the priests again begin cover-ing the deity with sandalwood paste. As He is worshiped every morning with more sandalwood, the layers get thicker and thicker until finally, after a year, they again observe the festival in which all of it is taken off.

As we circumambulate the main temple, which is covered with carved stone, in the back is a wonderful image of Narasimha bifurcating Hiranyakashipu who is lying across His knees. This Simhachalam temple is a very affluent temple with fine architecture, and is considered an important place of pilgrimage by many Hindus of the area. It has many residences for visiting pilgrims. The priests are members of the Ramanuja *sampradaya*.

Around on the left side of the temple, when facing it from the front, there is the Gan-gadhara spring that is said to have medicinal properties.

Visakhapatnam also has the Sri Venkatesvara Konda temple that you may want to visit. Also, the beautiful Borra Caves, discovered by William King in 1807, with its numerous stalagmites and stalactites and underground chambers, is located on the northern border of the city.

NAGPUR & RAMA GIRI

If we want to go west into central India, we can go to the pleasant city of Nagpur. This is northwest of Visakhapatnam, and is considered to be the very center of India. From the coast, it may be off the beaten track, but from Nagpur we can go to a place called Rama Giri hill, located 30 miles north near Ram Tek village. This is where the great ascetic Agastya Muni lived and received Lord Rama, Sita, and Lakshmana back in the age of Treta-yuga.

On top of the hill is Rama Giri fort, built by the Bhonsle clan of kings several centuries ago. The Bhonsle ruled until their defeat by the British at the Battle of Sitalbuldi in 1827. Outside the ashrama of Agastya Muni you will find a huge deity of Lord Varaha (Vishnu). He weighs several tons and overlooks the valley and fort.

The ashrama is nicely maintained by the *sadhus* there, and the *yajna-shala*, or ritual pavilion, is said to be the spot where Agastya Muni originally received Lord Rama. You can also see the deep cave, Hatiphor, where Agastya Muni meditated, although the iron door keeps all but a few serious sages outside.

Beyond the cave you will find a group of temples dedicated to Lakshmana, Lord Rama, Sita, and Hanuman. Lakshmana's temple is first because it is said that he led the way to Agastya's ashrama and voiced the approach of Rama and Sita to the nearby sages.

The deities here were reinstalled only in 1753 after King Raghu Bhonsle had a dream to search the River Sur a few miles to the north. When he did, he discovered the original deities. This was after he had visited Rama Giri in 1736 and found that only the wooden sandals of Lord Rama were being worshiped, and the deities were missing. The King arranged for new deities to be prepared in Jaipur for installation at Rama Giri. However, he had his dream just prior to the installation, and thus found the original deities.

On top of the fort you can get a good view of the surrounding area of farmland, lakes, and villages. Below the hill is the Ambala Kund, said to be named after King Amba who took bath there and was cured of a terrible disease. The water is said to come from an underground river, called Patala Ganges. The temples around the lake include those for Jagannatha, Pancamukhi Mahadeva (five-faced Shiva) and Surya Narayana (Vishnu's expansion as the sun).

If we have visited Nagpur from Visakhapatnam, we can move south to Hyderabad. But if we have not, then at this point we can keep going to Vijayawada.

VIJAYAWADA

If we arrive in the morning, then when we get off here we first make reservations for the next morning's train before leaving the station. We should be able to see everything in a day and be ready to hit the road again tomorrow. Otherwise we can always leave tomorrow afternoon. Luckily, a few hotels are located a couple blocks away, so the ricksha ride is a short one. I book a room and, the way I travel, I barely lock my things inside and I'm back on the streets looking for a motor ricksha to take me to a few temples.

The first temple we want to see is an ancient cave temple in Undavalil, a suburb south of Vijayawada. It is hardly used anymore and not maintained very well, and is visited only by a few local people. It does not attract many tourists and some ricksha drivers don't even know how to locate it. But we find a driver who not only knows where it is but also speaks English. So we head through Vijayawada and take the road south over the Krishna River. After a few minutes we turn off the highway and take a bumpy road that sees little use. After passing the homes of many villagers who look at us with wonder, we ask for directions from a few people and finally arrive at the deserted looking temple. The temple is not very large but is nonetheless an interesting place. It is a cave temple carved out of the solid rock hillside. It dates back to the sixth century and is dedicated to Lord Vishnu. It is four storeys tall and each level has many pillars that help support it. Scattered around inside are wall carvings of deities and scenes from the Puranic legends. The place still smells of the smoke that has passed through the halls over the years from ghee lamps, wood fires, or incense.

On the highest level of this simple but massive stone structure we reach an area that is secured by a wooden fence and has a locked gate. Fortunately, an old guard has followed us and unlocks the door to let us inside. Here we find the main deity of this temple, and it is quite a deity. Carved out of the stone is a 29-feet long image of Vishnu reclining on Sheshanaga, the largest we have ever seen in our travels so far. Carved on the walls nearby are demigods and other personalities that are offering prayers and obeisances. The deity is still well preserved and instills a feeling of reverence and wonder in us as we look on and think of how much worship and attention this deity must have been given by the local people many centuries ago. So we spend a few minutes here because, though we knew the temple might be interesting even if it was out of the way, we had no idea that such an awesome image of Lord Vishnu existed here. After our *darshan*, we come out onto the balcony of the top floor and can see Vijayawada in the distance. Our visit here has indeed been most fortunate. When we are finished, we climb back down, give the guard a tip for his assistance, get back in our ricksha and are ready to go.

After our privileged visit is over, we ride back to town where our ricksha driver takes us to see the famous Kanaka Durga temple on the hilltop that overlooks the town of Vijayawada. This deity is considered to be self-manifested. It is said that Adi Shankara had worshiped the goddess here, as well as Agastya Muni, Markandeya, and the Pandavas. Legend relates that she killed the powerful demon Durgama in this area, and is presently accepted as the protector of the city. This is an interesting temple and many people come to see it. You can see families arrive to see the deities and to perform their *puja* together.

There is also a hill in Vijayawada called Indrikiladri where Arjuna had performed penances in order to acquire the Pasupata weapon from Lord Shiva.

For those who wish to continue to explore the area, further upstream at Amaravathi are the excavated rock temples along the banks of the Krishna River. This used to be an important Buddhist center 2000 years ago with over 1000 monks and a large decorated marble *stupa*. But now ruins are all that's left. The Archeological Museum still has some fine pieces of sculpture work and large images of standing Buddhas that were found here. Anyone interested in ancient Buddhist relics will find this place interesting. And if you like this, much farther upstream (175 km west of Vijayawada) is the Nagarjunakonda site. This was one of the biggest of the Buddhist centers in southern India for about 500 years, starting in the 2ⁿᵈ century B.C.E. It was abandoned as the Vijayanagar Empire declined. It was rediscovered only between 1954 and 1961. Excavations have uncovered the ruins of *stupas*, temples, *chaityas*, etc., which have been moved to a museum for preservation before the Nagarjunasagar Dam caused the area to be submerged under water. Here you can see many of the rescued remains reassembled in new locations, and again the Archeological museum has some fine examples of Buddhist sculpture work.

Also in the area is the Mallesvara temple, said to have been originally established by the Pandava Yudhisthira to commemorate their victory in the southern area. The present structure was built by Tribhuvana Malla, the Chalukya king in the 10ᵗʰ century. The Vijayeshvara temple is said to have been originally established by the younger Pandava, Arjuna. Also in town is the Victoria Jubilee Museum on Bander Road that can be worth a visit if you have time.

MANGALAGIRI

Farther south of Undavalil on the hill known as Mangalagiri, which means auspicious hill, about 7 miles from Vijayawada, is the Panakal or Pana-Narasimha temple. Lord Narasimha is the half-man/half-lion form of Lord Vishnu. According to the local or *Sthala Purana*, in Krita-yuga a prince by the name of Hrisya Sringi performed penance in order to try to be free of his deformities. He perceived that his father was always displeased because of his oddities, so he secretly went to Pradita Ashrama, on the southern bank of the Krishna River, to do penance. When he learned that his father was coming for him, he prayed to the Lakshmi-Narayana deities to appear as Lakshmi-Narasimha. When Lord Vishnu awarded him with His presence, the prince wanted the Lord to stay forever to bless others. The prince transformed himself into an elephant and then into a hill. Thus, Mangalagiri resembles an elephant. The hill is also known as Stotradri since the Lord manifested here because of the prayers (*stotras*) of Hrisya Sringi.

The deity of Narasimha is worshiped only with offerings of water mixed with jaggery, which is a mixture of raw cane sugar, camphor, cardamom, and black pepper. He drinks only half of the offerings while the other half goes for the devotees. It is said that in times long ago other ingredients used to be offered. This is explained in a story. The sage Kashyapa Prajapati had one son, Namuchi, who was a cruel demon. To acquire powers, Namuchi underwent severe austerities which produced intense flames from his body. The fire became so powerful that they began to flow through the universe. The demigods could not withstand the heat that was spreading, so they went to Brahma about this matter. Brahma went to Namuchi to appease him by granting him a boon. Namuchi asked to never be killed by anything either wet or dry, which Brahma granted. After that he was overconfident and began harassing the demigods, who then had to go to Lord Vishnu. He assured them that Namuchi's end would come at the right time.

Later, during a battle which involved Indra killing the armies of Namuchi, Lord Vishnu in His form as Lord Narasimha took His disk and dipped it into some foam, which was neither wet nor dry, and then gave it to Indra who threw it at Namuchi. Namuchi fled and even went into a cave at Mangalagiri, hiding by giving up his physical form. But the disk followed and killed him there. The blood that began to flow turned into a stream called Raktakalya that spread into the area. Red soil surrounds the temple to this day. The Devas were fearful of the Lord as Narasimha, so they offered Him divine nectar to drink. He drank only half of it and said that in Satya-yuga he would drink only half of the nectar offered to Him. In Treta-yuga He would drink ghee. In Dvapara-yuga He would drink milk from a Kamadhenu cow, and in Kali-yuga He would drink half of the sweet jaggery water that was offered to Him. This is why He only accepts half of the offering, leaving the rest as *prasada* to be accepted by the devotees.

At the base of the hill are a few temples, one of which is to Lakshmi, the goddess of fortune and wife of Lord Vishnu, and Lord Narasimha. The deity is believed to have been installed by Yudhisthira, one of the five Pandava brothers, during their exile. You can notice this temple from the tall *gopuram* in front of it, which stands eleven stories high. This was built by Raja Vasireddy Venkatadri Naidu 200 years ago. This is a beautiful temple to visit. The central sanctum has the stone deity of Narasimha with Lakshmi. He is dressed in colorful clothes, sitting on a gold and ornate *simahasan* or throne. He has large brass eyes, a silver enhanced mouth that shows His teeth, and golden arms, weapons, and feet. He also wears a garland of 108 *shalagram shilas*. In this temple there is also a conch shell said to have been used by Lord Krishna Himself, which was given to the temple by the late King of Tanjore. There is an additional shrine for Lakshmi just to the right of the main sanctum. The deity therein is most beautiful, and is made from black stone. She is sitting on Her throne, covered with colorful clothes, lovely flower garlands, with gold crown and arms holding gold ornamanets. We visit this temple before climbing the hill to see Pana-Narasimha.

The Pana-Narasimha temple is at the top of a flight of 600 steps on the hillside. When we start to climb the steps, we also see a shrine on the right side of the stairway that displays within it a set of footprints and a deity of Lord Krishna. Srila Bhaktisiddhanta established this shrine in honor of when Lord Chaitanya visited this temple in 1512. It is said that He ecstatically offered many prayers to the deity of Narasimha.

Climbing the steps causes some fatigue, but after reaching the top we feel rewarded by entering the temple to see the deity of Lord Narasimha, the form of God who displays His lion-like anger to protect His devotees. However, in 2007 they established a road in which you can now drive all the way up to the temple. Before entering the sanctum we purchase some tickets for the cost of performing the *pana* (water) ritual. As we wait, we can hear the sounds of bells ringing and mantras being chanted as the Narasimha deity is being worshiped by the people ahead of us. After a few more minutes it is our turn to enter the sanctum. In the dim light of a ghee lamp, the deity of Lord Narasimha can be seen. The deity is a brass image or mask about a foot or so in height, set on the side of the rock wall on a little altar, and is shaped more like the face of a cat than a lion. The mouth of the deity is large and open, about four by six inches. Behind the mask or the deity of Narasimha, etched in the stone, you can see on both sides of the mouth the figures of a conch shell on the right and a disk on the left.

The priest guides us through the water ritual in which he offers prayers, flowers, incense, ghee lamp, and lots of the sweet water to the deity. In front of the deity is a bucket of sweetened water. The priest takes a conchshell and fills it with the water from the bucket and pours some of it into a bowl and the rest of it directly into the mouth of the deity. Try as I might, I cannot hear any sound of water hitting anything after the priest pours more and more water into the deity's mouth. It is as if there is no bottom.

When the ritual is over, we step out of the temple and an assistant gives us a cup of the water that was poured into the bowl. This is considered part of the offering to the deity and we drink the whole cup of refreshingly sweetened water, accepting it as deity *prasada*, sacred remnants from the offering. One noticeable thing is that in spite of so much sugar water here, there are not ants or flies to bother you.

This temple is also mentioned in such texts as the *Skanda Purana* and *Brahma Vaivarta Purana* as being one of the eight major holy places, which include Badrinatha, Naimisaranya, Srirangam, Pushkar, Srimushnam, Shalagram, and Venkatadri. It is said that the demigods still attend this temple to do their own worship here, and sometimes the priest who opens the temple in the morning finds evidence of this.

Mangalagiri is also a special abode of Hanuman. It is said that at the end of Lord Rama's pastimes He advised Hanuman to stay at Mangalagiri, and after obtaining blessings, stay in this world forever. So Hanuman is the Kshetrapalaka or maintainer of this shrine. Thus, this hill is also known as Mukthyadri, or the hill that grants *mukti* or salvation even to sinners. Even Indra has advised residents of heaven to do penance here in order to attain *mukti*.

Above the temple are caves that you can visit by climbing the stairways. There you will find the shrines to Lakshmi and Venkateshvara, and one shrine for Hanuman as well. To the west of the Lakshmi shrine is a cave that is said to reach the caves of Undavalil.

There is another interesting legend about this hill. It is said that this hill was once a volcano. It is also said that jaggery or sugar water, which is offered to the deity, can neutralise sulphur compounds found in a volcano. Thus such offerings may help prevent a volcanic eruption.

Another legend is in regard to a milk tree on the side of Mangalagiri Hill. The legend is that King Sasibindhu met the great sage Narada Muni while the king was doing pilgrimage to the Narasimha temple. The king explained that he was tired of worldly pleasures and pursuits and was on pilgrimage to the holy places. Narada advised him to do penance in Mangalagiri. However, the queen became furious and, because of his advice to her husband, cursed Narada Muni to become a Kshira Vruksham, or milk tree, on the hill within easy reach of the devotees. Thus, it would bless women at its sight with property, children, and purify them of sins committed by ignorance or oversight. Narada did not take this as a curse but as a blessing since it meant service to humanity. Therefore, he blessed the queen with a happy life with her husband and a thousand children. Nowadays, thousands of women visit and worship the tree for begetting children.

AGIRIPALLI

Agiripalli, easily reached by bus or taxi, is about 40 km north of Vijayawada and has the Vyaghra Narasimha temple, located on the hilltop. The deity's name is Sobhanachala Swami. A large *gopuram* at the base of the hill shows the beginning of the path up. It is said the Lord appeared in the cave on the hilltop. Also on the hill is the Malleswara Swami temple for Lord Shiva. Other shrines include those for Sri Venkatachala, Sri Venu Gopala, Rajya Lakshmi and the Alwars. The huge 100-acre water tank, Varahapushkarini, is said to have been dug by Lord Varaha, Lord Vishnu's boar *avatara*.

HYDERABAD & YADAGIRIGUTTA

On our tour of East India, we can take a bus from Vijayawada to Hyderabad, which is not too far away. Tours out of Hyderabad are also available and can be arranged to various places if we want to do that. While here, we can visit the Birla Venkateswara Balaji temple. It is a beautiful marble temple built on the highest point in Hyderabad and offers great views over the city.

Another place to see is the Salar Jang Museum, which has over 35,000 exhibits from all over the world. The Golconda Fort, 8 km west of Hyderabad, is interesting and can take a few hours to see. It certainly gives more depth into the history of the area, besides being a rare example of what a hilltop fort can be. You can get buses #119 and #80R from Nampally near the railway station in Hyderabad to the Fort, or just take a motor ricksha. You can wander through the passageways and rooms as you go up the hill to the top. There are also a few small temples along the way, and if you are into it, there is a light and sound show in the evening that explains more about the history of this fort.

The Iskcon temple in Hyderabad is also nice and not far from the railway station. It has lovely Radha Krishna, Gaura-Nitai, and Jagannatha deities.

Yadagiri-gutta is 60 kilometers northeast of Hyderabad, reached by bus (2 hours) from the new APSRIC bus station, Gowliguda, which leaves from platform 48 or 50 every half hour. Look for the big picture of Narasimha on the platform. Upon arrival at Yadagiri-gutta, you either walk a half-hour, or get an auto-rickshaw, or take another very crowded bus to the top of the hill.

Yadagiri was named after a sage named Yadava who performed heavy austerities to see Lord Vishnu as Narasimha. Being pleased with him, the Lord gave him *darshan* in three forms: Jwala Narasimha, Gandabheranda Narasimha, and Yogananda Narasimha. Yadava begged for the Lord to remain on the hill in these forms. Thus, you have the Lakshmi-Narasimhadeva temple on the hilltop with deities of the Lord in all three forms embedded in stone in the main cave. Actually, it is a cave about 12 feet high by 30 feet long, located in back of the temple hall, by the rear pillar. You take a stairway down into the chamber and then toward the back. Jwala Narasimha is in the shape of a serpent, while Yogananda Narasimha appears sitting in meditation in a yoga pose. You will also see silver deities of Lakshmi-Narasimha, which are quite striking in appearance and lends presence to the experience of seeing Them. To the right of the temple's main door is a Hanuman temple. You'll see a long horizontal gap in the rock just below Hanuman. This is said to be where Gandabheranda Narasimha manifested. This is a very popular temple. It is said that any wish of the sincere devotee visiting this temple will be fulfilled. On weekends the lines to see the deity can be very long. So it is best to go during the week. Plus, places to stay are few, therefore, consider taking a day trip from Hyderabad.

BASARA

From Hyderabad you can also take a day trip north of the city to the town of Basara, a small and quiet town near the Godavari River in the north corner of Andrah Pradesh. The Sri Gyana Saraswati temple is at Basara and is located on the banks of the Godavari. It is located about 40 km from Nizambad district headquarters and 70 kms from Nirmal town of Adilabad district. Situated at a distance of 205 kms (approx) from Hyderabad, the Saraswati temple at Basara is one of the two most famous Saraswati temples in India, the other being in Jammu and Kashmir.

According to the legend, Maharishi Vyasa and his disciples, and sage Sukadeva, decided to settle down in a cool and serene atmosphere after the Kurukshetra war. He reached the serene Dandaka forest in the Kumaranchala hills on the banks of River Godavari. In the quest for the peaceful abode, he came to and was pleased with the serenity of the region and selected this place. He meditated there and propitiated the Goddess who eventually appeared before him and granted her presence in the form of the divine trinity. The Goddess ordered the sage to place three handfuls of sand at three places everyday. Therefore, after his daily ablutions in the Godavari, Maharishi Vyasa used to bring three fistfuls of sand and place it in three small heaps. Then he made images of Sarasvati, Lakshmi, and Kali with his mystic power and later conducted worship to them. However, according to *Brahmanda Purana*, Adikavi Valmiki installed Saraswati and also wrote the *Ramayana* here. There is a marble image of Valmiki and his *samadhi* near the temple. It is believed that this temple is one of the three temples constructed near the confluence of the Manjira and Godavari rivers by Ashtrakutas.

According to another school of thought, Bijialudu, a Karnataka king who ruled the province of Nandagiri with Nanded as his capital in the sixth century, constructed the temple at Basara.

In the temple there is a life-size image of the Goddess holding a vina in one hand and books in another. The image of Lakshmi stands besides Goddess Saraswati in the sanctum. This image made of sand has its face smeared with turmeric. It is believed that eating a little bit of this turmeric paste will enhance one's wisdom and knowledge. Lakshmi is enshrined nearby, and an image of Durga is in a separate hall. Brahma is worshiped in a sacred tree near the sanctum. Due to the presence of Saraswati, Lakshmi, and Durga, Basara is considered the abode of the divine trinity. These are the presiding deities of Basara today. Despite the presence of the trinity, the temple is dedicated to Goddess Saraswathi.

The speciality of the temple is that the Rudra *abhishekam* (bathing ceremony of the image) is performed daily to the Devi in the morning and can be seen by the devotees, which is very rare. The deity of Sarasvati is really beautiful, attractive, and powerful. If one goes to the banks of Godavari near the temple, you can feel like you are in heaven. There you can get the water of the Godavari and perform *abhishekam* to the Shiva *lingams* on the bank, which some say is a wonderful experience.

Many people, in fact, take their children to Basara for doing *akshara abhyasam* before commencing formal school to start their education with the blessings of Saraswati, the Goddess of Knowledge. Special *pujas* and celebrations are held at the temple during Maha Sivaratri, beginning 15 days before (Vasantha Panchami) and continuing three days after the festival. Devi Navarathrulu is celebrated for ten days during Dashara. Since Maharishi Vyasa spent considerable time in prayers, the place was originally known as Vyasapuri, the place of Vyasa, and later called Vasara, which turned into Basara due to the influence of the Marathi language in the region. Goddess Sarasvati is also known as Vasara.

The Vedavathi Sila and the Ashtateerth are other places of interest around Basara. In South India, there are two temples devoted to Goddess Saraswati where Vasant Panchami is celebrated with great piety. At Koothanoor near Mayila-duthrai in Tamil Nadu, it is believed the Goddess has the power to make the mute speak and bestow writing and composing skills on the ordinary. Musicians come to the temple to have their first public performance in the presence of this Goddess of Art. Instrumentalists also have the *puja* performed and their instruments blessed at the altar of the Goddess.

If you do not wish to take a day trip to Basara but prefer to spend the night, there are a number of hotels or guest houses from which you can choose to stay. It is easily reached by train from Hyderabad, since Hyderabad is well connected from all cities of India. Basara has a Rail head between Secunderbad Jn and Mudkhed Jn (via Nizamabad). Also, regular bus services connect Basara with Hyderabad (201 kms), Nizamabad (40 kms), etc.

WARANGAL

Further northeast from Hyderabad and Yadagiriguta, by 150 km, is the city of Warangal. This was once the capital of the Kakatiyas who ruled from the 12th to 14th centuries through the greater part of Andhra Pradesh. They were great builders and patrons of the arts. Here you can see the Chalukyan temples that are related to those of Badami, Aihole, and Pattadakal. The ones here are not as nice, however, but if you are in the area you can see the 1000-Pillared temple, built in 1162. There are two temples here. The front one is still in use, and has three shrines connected by a central hall, only one of which is presently in use. They used to be for Shiva, Vishnu and Surya, but now only Shiva is worshiped. The lathe-cut columns and stone work here are quite nice and impressive. But no photography is allowed inside. Going toward the back, there is an image of Nandi, Lord Shiva's carrier, and then there is the 1000-Pillared temple. It is in a dilapidated state, but you can see the style of architecture from that period. However, upon visiting this temple again in 2008, the 1000-Pillared temple had been dismantled for renovation, with the parts scattered across a section of the lawn. Putting it back together seems a little more difficult than anticipated.

Further down the road is a well established Bhadrakali temple, and also a Shambu Lingeswara or Swayambhu temple. Inside, as you circumambulate the inner shrine, there are numerous brightly colored paintings of various aspects of Devi and other Vedic divinities. You can get in line for *darshan* and *puja*, with which the priest is ready to assist. The main image in the central sanctum is a large Badrakali deity, dressed in colorful clothes with Her crown and eight arms covered in gold and holding Her various weapons. Many people of the area visit this temple, which is nestled in between some little hills and a small lake. In the back is the lake, across which is another smaller temple of the sister of Badrakali.

There are several smaller temples along the main road to the Kali temple. The Siddhesvara temple is three km away. There is also the large fort, the old city that is one of Warangal's primary attractions. It has a circular plan, one mile in diameter, and was built during the reign of Queen Rudramadevi (1262-89). The fort used to have a water moat around it, and still has large walls made of cut stone that are put together with amazing accuracy. Four gates with winding entrances lead into it. The fort is large, and is now the residence of many people. The inner areas of the fort still have some small but functioning temples, and the remains of finely carved stone structures, a central Shiva temple, and arches that show the forms of various deities such as Ganesh, Vishnu, Shiva, Parvati, dancing girls, nagas, etc.

PALAMPET

Northeast of Warangal by about 60 km is the town of Palampet. Here we find the beautiful Ramappa temple, dedicated to Shiva. It was built in 1234 by Recherla Rudra, a general in the army of Ganapatideva (1199-1262). It remains an attractive example of the Kakatiya architecture, although with similarities to the Chalukya and Hoysala designs. The black basalt columns are especially nicely carved to show various forms and deities. The eaves also hold carved maidens in graceful dancing poses. It has a spacious *mandapa* hall which has carved panels that show scenes from the *Puranas*. In front of the temple is a separate pavilion with a beautifully carved Nandi. The temple tank, Ramappa Cheruva, is south by 1 km. Additional Kakatiya temples can be seen in the village of Ghanpur, 13 km northwest of Palampet.

VEMULAWADA

Vemulawada is a small village northwest of Warangal. First you go about 70 km northwest to Karimnagar, and then 40 km west to Vemulawada. This has the important Shiva temple of Sri Raja Rajeswara Swamy. It is located in the center of the village, on top of small hill. It has a gateway leading up the hill and a typical south India style *gopuram* to the left. This marks the entrance to the small temple complex. As you go in, you will see a number of bulls tied to a post. Pilgrims lead the bulls by rope around the temple, since it is a tradition that says that by doing so your wishes will be granted. The temple is also surrounded half-way by a colonnade under which are a variety of Shiva *lingams*. Circumambulating the temple, there is also a short pillar housed in a plastic covering, and decorated with writing which is no longer able to be interpreted. Thus, the age of this pillar cannot be determined.

There are a few temples within this complex. The central one is for the presiding deity (Shiva *lingam*) of Sri Raja Rajeswara Swamy, which is considered sacred by thousands of devotees because of the blessings they have received. To have *darshan*, you first go past Ganesh on the right. Nandi is in the hall in front of the sanctum. Following the line, you then make your way toward the sanctum where you can have *darshan* of Shiva. Doing *puja* consists of the priest offering prayers, flowers, ghee lamp and camphor, and then giving you the flowers as *prasada*. After doing *puja*, you then go past Durga, Sri Raja Rajeswari Devi, on the right. She looks similar to but smaller than the Badrakali deity in Warangal. Coming out of the temple, you circumambulate the temple again and then go to the next temple. This holds several small shrines, such as to Lord Vishnu in His form as Sri Anantha Padmanabha Swamy (reclining on Seshanaga), Lord Krishna in the center, and then another shrine to Sri Sita Ramaswamy on the left. In this way, this is one of the ancient places which embrace both Shaiva and Vaishnava cultures together. Additional shrines to Shiva and Durga are also present.

Behind the temple is the Dharma Gundam or "Pool of Righteousness," believed to be a perennial spring. Devotees take a holy dip in the waters and then visit the temple in wet clothes. Legend says that a king took a bath in this pool many years ago and was cured of leprosy. He also found the *lingam* in the water, which gave such purity to the place, and then installed it in the temple.

This has been a sacred place since ancient times, and is mentioned in various portions of the Vedic texts, such as the *Bhavishyothara Purana*. From the inscriptions in the area it is also learned that the Chalukya dynasty flourished in this region, and some 990 years ago this village was known as Lembula Vatika. It had been donated to the temples by King Arikesari II. Everyone is welcome to this temple, regardless of caste or creed.

About one kilometer away farther into town is the smaller Bhimeswara Swamy temple, also dedicated to Shiva. As you enter the gate, it is a white temple with a tower over the sanctum. In the left back corner of the complex is a small temple to Gayatri Devi. Continuing around the temple we come to a small pavilion structure which contains models of all the 12 *jyotirlinga* or self-manifesting Shiva *lingams* that are found throughout India. Next to that are two entwined peepul and banyan trees, under which is a small shrine to Hanuman. Another small temple is farther around before going into the main temple. Therein are four ancient carved pillars in the main hall, which also has a small shrine to Durga. In the main sanctum is a large *lingam*, Bhimesvara, covered in sandalwood paste. When doing *puja*, the priest will wipe his fingers on the *lingam* to take a little of the paste to give to you or smear on your forehead.

On our drive back toward Karimnagar, you can stop a short distance away at Namapalli to see the small hilltop Narasimha temple. On the side of the hill is a large image of Lord Krishna standing on a Kaliya serpent. You can see this from the main road as you drive by.

If we have more time, there is another place we can see called Dharmapuri, about 60 to 70 km north of Karimnagar, along the Godavari River, which is known for its significant temple to Lord Narasimha. After that, when we are ready to continue our journey to the holy places of India, we can go back to Hyderabad to head farther south.

SRISAILAM

The next place we can go to from Hyderbad is 200 kilometers farther south to Srisailam. This town is next to the Krishna River. It is found on Rishabhagiri Hill. It is mentioned in the *Mahabharata* and the *Puranas*. It has the Mallikarjuna (Shiva) temple, known as one of the 12 *jyotirlinga* (self-manifesting *linga*) temples in India. It is a large temple, built in 1404-5 by King Harihara Raya. There is a finely carved hall, beautiful silver doors, and a huge Nandi. The original Shiva *linga* is to the right of the main temple. This temple was visited by Adi Shankara and later by Lord Chaitanya, as well as by Prahlada and Lord Rama who is said to have installed the Sahasra *linga*, noticeable by the three-headed Naga which surrounds it. There are also the Panchapandavas, the five *lingas* installed by the five Pandava brothers found in the courtyard. The Parvati (Bhramarambika) temple, one of the 54 *shakti-peeths*, is up a flight of stairs behind the Shiva temple. Parvati took the form of a bee to kill the Mahisasura demon, the buzzing of which you can still hear by putting your ear to a small hole in the back wall of the sanctum. Other shrines around the temple are for Chandramamba, Rajarajeshwari, Virabhadra, and Annapoorni.

The legend of how this temple was established is that many hundreds of years ago a princess by the name of Chandravathi of the Chandragupta dynasty was residing on the hills worshiping Lord Shiva. One day she noticed a cow showering milk on a *lingam* in an isolated spot. Lord Shiva later appeared in a dream to her and asked that she build a temple there. Since the *linga* was entangled in jasmine plants, it was named Mallikarjuna. The temple is also known by different names such as Srigiri, Srimala, and Srinagara.

One nice thing about this temple is that anyone can go in and perform the *pujas*. The local tribals can go in the sanctum for worship because Shiva came to this place as a hunter and married a local Chenchu girl, who was Parvati herself. I experienced this openness as well. When I was there, before the *arati* started, a small shennai band started to play. I was listening near the temple when a man called me in. Later he said that if I would take my shirt off I could be close to the *linga* to watch the *puja*. So, thereafter, I helped do a *puja* to the big and beautiful Ganesh deity. Then soon was the time for the Shiva *puja*. I was the first in the growing line of people to see the *arati* with plenty of lit ghee wicks being offered, bells ringing, Sanskrit mantras being sung, and drums being played. It was quite awesome. Then we also rinsed the *linga* with water, took some of the water on our own head, and also touched our head to the *linga* itself. I also got personal blessings from the priest. It was all a rare experience, deep into the Vedic traditions, and rather invigorating and inspiring.

Part of the pilgrimage here is to bathe in the Pathalaganga (Krishna) River, which is about three kilometers east of the temple. It is located down a long flight of stairs from the south end of town. You can watch the pilgrims come here and wade into the river, do a little *puja* offering with the assistance of a local priest, or take a boat ride in one of the small round boats. Many *sadhus* live along this pathway, and some put pictures or postures up on the stairs as little shrines where a pilgrim can leave a few coins. On the way to the river, you'll see the Uma-Mahesvara temple, another very beautiful temple. The Shiva *linga* stones also can be found on the banks of the Krishna River. So, it is an interesting place to visit.

ALAMPUR

Alampur is about 125 km west of Srisailam, and 15 km northeast of Kurnool. So if we want, from Srisailam we can get a bus to Alampur to see the many temples in this village. You may want to stay in Kurnool where there are better facilities and take a day trip to Alampur. This town is on the north bank of the Tungabhadra River and has the earliest Hindu temples in Andhra Pradesh. There are nine red sanstone shrines known as the Nava Brahma temples, built by the Badami Chalukyas in the 7th and 8th centuries. They are all similar in that they face east and are dedicated to Shiva. They have a tower over the sanctum, topped with a circular stone, with a pillared hall in front of the sanctum. The Svarga Brahma temple has lovely sculptures of guardians, and various images of Shiva. You can also find elaborately carved stone columns, such as in the Padma Brahma temple. Bala Brahma temple is the only one wherein worship still goes on.

Nearby is the Archaeological Museum with a collection of sculptures from the area. And to the southwest of this complex are the Papanashanam temple from the 9th and 10th centuries. These temples have simpler exteriors, but display imposing multi-tiered pyramidal roofs. One has an impressive image of Durga and another exhibits Vishnu's *avataras* on a ceiling panel.

NANDYAL

From Srisailam, or from Kurnool, we take a bus ride to Nandyal, 280 kilometers south of Hyderabad. Nandyal is known for its Mahanandi temple, about 16 kilometers out of town. It is an ancient Shiva temple with a unique Shiva *linga*, Nandisvara, with two holes in the rough rock. The temple architecture is North Indian style, with a tower over the *lingam* and a huge Nandi in front. Many pilgrims visit this temple in their pilgrimage to Srisailam.

It is also said that Nandi the bull became Lord Shiva's mount because of doing penance here. Within a radius of 16 km, nine aspects of Nandi are enshrined in nine temples. These include Padma Nandi, Naga Nandi, Vinayaka Nandi, Garuda Nandi, Soma Nandi, and Shiva Nandi. Adi Shankara is said to have also worshiped Shiva here.

AHOVALAM

From Nandyal, or straight from Srisailam, we can easily take a bus to Allagada and then go on to Ahovalam. From the east, we can take a bus from either Tirupati or Nellore, or Vijayawada to Allagada, and then to Ahovalam.

This is said to be the place where Hiranyakasipu had his huge palace, which had a pillar from where Lord Narasimhadeva manifested to protect His devotee, Prahlada, and kill the demon Hiranyakasipu. When you arrive here, you will find only a tiny village and lots of jungle, which is the home of bears, tigers, and cobras. There are nine different temples of Lord Narasimhadeva scattered throughout the area, each for one of the nine forms of Lord Narasimha, but some are easier to find than others. However, it is dangerous to try to find them all without a guide, and rarely can a person see all nine temples in one day. Plus, they are meant to be seen in a certain order for those who are serious about it. So, it is necessary to use a guide if you expect to reach most of the temples quickly and safely.

The town of Ahovalam is quite small. The center is only about two blocks long with the bus stand at one end and the Lakshmi-Narasimha temple at the other. In between are only a few places to eat, one prominent guest house, a few shops to buy food and necessities, or what little they have to offer. A few more shops offer photos or posters of Lord Narasimha, or tape recordings of devotional songs and mantras in praise of Lord Narasimha. Some of this you will find no where else, so if you want to buy it you better get it here. The devotion for Lord Narasimha is infectious; you cannot help but feel it. This is also one of the 108 Divya Desams, or most holy places for Lord Vishnu. Garuda also did penance here to realize the Lord. Furthermore, the *Mahabharata, Kurma Purana, Padma Purana,* and *Vishnu Purana* all mention Ahovalam as a holy place for Lord Narasimha. The *Brahmananda Purana* also says that this was the place where Hiranyakasipu had his most opulent palace, at least before Lord Narasimha separated him from it.

When it is time to start our tour of Ahovalam, we begin at the lovely Lakshmi-Narasimha temple at the end of town. This temple is also called Prahlada-varada Narasimha because it shows the Lord blessing Prahlada. It has a tall *gopuram* and lovely carved stone work adorns the interior of the temple buildings. As you enter this temple on the right are eight ornately carved pillars, each displaying one of the forms of Lord Narasimha. There are many finely carved stone pillars in the halls. The deity of Narasimha is really beautiful, dressed in silver and jewels and colorful garments. There is also Lakshmi in a separate shrine, as well as shrines to Lord Rama and Balaji. When I was there, a large group of brahmanas was also sitting in the long hall chanting many mantras to Lord Narasimha. This certainly added to the impact of the place. Those who pray at this shrine with devotion would obtain the grace of the Lord and the Goddess who will ensure that their prayers are answered. This 800 year old temple is quite nice with regular worship going on. The other temples are more difficult to reach, being located in the jungles or a good drive away. So they get fewer visitors, and formal worship does not always go on at these, except at the Ugra or Ahovalam Narasimha temple which we will see when we visit Upper Ahovalam. When I visited these temples in the mid 1990s, hardly anyone was attending these temples. However, when I again visited these temples ten years later, some of them were becoming more developed, and priests from the central Lakshmi-Narasimha temple in town would take turns to go to these temples to do the *abhisheka* or bathing of the deity, or offer a few items once or twice a day. Sometimes the priest will remain at the temple throughout the day. At other times, you go to some of these temples and no one is around. So it used to be easy to get photos of the deities, but when the priests stayed there, they often put restrictions on such things.

We start our tour of the other temples around Ahovalam after we have met our guide. If you have not been here before, it is best to use a guide to show you around. The first temple of the nine sacred forms we will see is that of Bhargava Narasimha, located through a thick jungle. You are meant to walk to these temples, and this one is out through the fields and jungle, but you can also use a jeep in a few places to get you most of the way there more quickly.

First we reach Bhargava Kund, a small pond where Bhargava rishi would collect water to bathe the form of Ugra Narasimha which is up a steep flight of steps nearby. Bhargava did *tapasya*, austerities, to see the Lord in His most angry aspect. So the Lord granted him that blessing. When we go up the flight of steps and into the little temple, we see Bhargava Narasimha, which is one of the most ferocious of His forms. Narasimha is seen as He was just beginning to push His long fingernails into the abdomen of Hiranyakashipu. This is Ugra Narasimha, or angry Narasimha. It is also said that a dip in the sacred waters of the *kund* followed by sincere prayers addressed to Bhargava Narasimha would result in the Lord conferring His benevolence on the seeker and conferring success in life.

Then we go back into town and farther to the east side where we see Yoga Narasimha. He is in a little temple shrine, shown seated in a peaceful yogic posture. He is called Yogananda for having taught Prahlada some yogic exercises here, who meditated on the Lord at this place. Thus, anyone who meditates at this shrine would secure immense mental peace and tranquility.

The third form of the Lord we see is Chatravada Narasimha, found after a long two-kilometer walk away from the village. Again He is sitting in a yoga asana, giving blessings to all devotees. Here you can touch your head to the deity's feet, which is rare in most temples. Two Gandharvas, Haha and Huhu, sang the praises of the Lord at this place. It is said that anyone who offers prayers here would be able to obtain proficiency in music and fine arts.

To reach Upper Ahovalam, you go back to the bus stop and take the 20 minute bus ride through the rugged areas, and are let out near the Karanja or Karancha Narasimha temple, named after the fruit tree nearby. It is said that Rishi Kobila performed a penance at this shrine and rid himself of the curse of sage Durvasa. He regained all his past knowledge and wisdom. Thus, faithful prayers offered at this shrine will bestow spiritual knowledge and wisdom. However, sometimes the bus will stop at this shrine on the way down after the pilgrim has already seen the other temples in Upper Ahovalam making it the last place we see instead of the first.

The next form of the Lord to see is the fierce Ugra Narasimha, said to be self-manifested. The bus lets us out at the last stop and we walk up the hill and around one of the ashramas here, and then to the temple. The temple has a carved stone *mandapa* hall with a central tower. It appears on a ridge between two mountains in a lush jungle. It is said that at night this area may still tremble with noise from Lord Narasimha. Many pilgrims come to visit this deity, which was worshiped by Prahlada Maharaja himself. This is a main shrine for Ugra Narasimha who is inside a cave with small front *mandapams* or halls. He is so awe-inspiring while emerging from the pillar that if fear itself was to take human form and see Him, it would be frightened. Therefore, worshiping this Sri Ahobila Narasimha totally wipes out fear in the devotee and they are blessed by their ancestors for a harmonious life. Inside the cave we can see the deity as He is shown manifesting a bow and a chakra as Lord Rama with a single hood of Anantasesha over Him, again sitting calmly in a yoga posture. The deity is only about a foot or so tall. Nearby in a cave is the Guha Narasimha. Also here is a Sudarshan Yantra and a shrine for a beautiful Lakshmi called Chenchu Lakshmi.

Going outside and around the back of the Ugra Narasimha temple you can take a walk along the little Bhavanasin River and into the jungle, crawling over rocks and using the foot bridge to reach the little temple of Krodha Narasimha, also called Varaha Narasimha. The main temple is carved out of the mountain side, making a little cave that houses a Varaha Narasimha, the Lord's form as a boar. They have now extended the temple to include a stone *mandapa* hall in front of the two deities. It was Lord Varaha who killed Hiranyakasipu's brother, Hiranyaksha. So for thousands of years both forms of the Lord have been worshiped here. If you look closely, Varaha Narasimha has the head of Lord Varaha and holds Goddess Lakshmi in His lap. Worship at this shrine is said to bestow prowess and supremacy in the devotee's chosen path.

Coming back down the path we take a side route up onto the hill to the seventh form of the Lord, which is Mahalola Narasimha, another long walk away. He is in a small temple situated on the side of a mountain. Here the Lord is said to be always engaged in pastimes with Lakshmidevi, who did penance at this spot near a tree to attract the Lord to become her husband. There is a new and larger temple building here that has been built that houses both the new Narasimha deity and the older one. The old deity, made of black stone, had been worshiped so much that it was difficult to see all of His features. So now they have installed a new deity in which you can clearly distinguish His beauty and characteristics. This is the Lord's most merciful form just after He had married Lakshmi. When I was here I had the rare opportunity to witness the *pujari* bathing the old deity with various elements, such as milk, yogurt, honey, and water. It is impressive that they were able to bring all of the supplies here to construct this new temple. Goddess Lakshmi is seated on the lap of the deity and is depicted as embracing the Lord with her right hand. The divine couple showers all auspicious qualities on the devotees and bestows Their grace for a prosperous and happy life in this world and eternal bliss thereafter.

Across another part of this hill, and a climb up and down along the rocky hillside, we can reach the place where Prahlada went to school. It is a small cave up a stairway, not far from a small pool of water under a rock overhang. The cave is said to have had Sanskrit writing on the walls from the time when Prahlada studied his lessons here. Though this is not one of the main temples, in this cave there is also the deity of Yoga Narasimha. Though yoga means calm and peaceful, this deity still has a third eye in His forehead, which indicates anger.

The eighth of the main temples is quite out of the way. Few people go there. You have to cross the narrow river and then climb a steep stairway up the hill. Then it is about another eight kilometers farther over a mountain trail and through a jungle. Finally, we reach the small temple of Bhavana Narasimha where the deities of Lord Narasimha and Lakshmi reside. Again, you will need a guide to reach there safely and to keep from getting lost. No one stays here overnight because it is believed that the demigods come to worship the Lord in the evening. The deity is shown sitting with Lakshmi Devi on His knee after they have gotten married. So they are both very happy and give blessings to everyone. *Bhavana* means love or loving. This is the form that is especially recommended for householders to worship since Narasimha is more forgiving in this attitude. This is also known as Kshetra Ratna or the jewel among the Kshetras. Any devotee who is afflicted by his past and present sins (karma) would be able to get relief by worshiping the Lord here. Along the side of the sanctum wall is a Gopala Krishna deity shown playing His flute.

Coming back to the central area of Upper Ahovalam, we follow the river and walk into the jungle until we can see the Ugra Stambha. This *stambha* or pillar is where Lord Narasimha is said to have appeared. The ninth special form of the Lord is found after a half-hour's dangerous climb up the hill on the way to the Ugra Stambha. The first time I visited Ahovalam, you had to climb up the side of the hill and grab hold of trees and bushes to help pull yourself along. While I was climbing and working my way up, the humidity and heat made me sweat profusely, and I had to stop a couple times to catch my breath. Ten years later there was a long cement stairway, which made it much better, although it was still rather steep and I had to rest every 20 steps or so. Nonetheless, a visit to Ahovalam without visiting this next temple is said to leave your pilgrimage incomplete.

Finally, where the path levels out and after resting a bit and leaving my shoes behind, I walked the path that takes you along a cliff half way up the hill and under an overhang that drips cooling water. Continuing our way, we arrive at a cave with a shelter over the front near a steep cliff which is the Jwala Narasimha temple. This marks the exact spot where it is said Lord Narasimha killed the demon Hiranyakasipu. There are three forms or deities in this cave. They are all only about a foot or so tall, each one separately carved in stone as a bas relief. The first on the left shows Stanu Narasimha, or His form when He is emerging from the pillar. The deity on the far right shows Him fighting with Hiranyakashipu just before He tears the demon apart. Then in the center is Jwala Narasimha in His most angry form when He catches and tears the demon to pieces. He is shown in a sitting position holding Hiranyakasipu in His lap and tearing the demon's abdomen with His nails.

As we visit this temple that overlooks the valley below, we can take a few minutes to contemplate our good fortune to be here and see these deities and this special place of Lord Narasimha's pastimes.

Returning back over the path a short distance from the temple we see a tiny pond or *kund* of clear water in a hollowed out part of the cliff. Therein is also a tiny stream coming out of the rock called Rakta-kund which flows blood-red into this little pool. This is where Lord Narasimha washed His hands of the blood after killing Hiranyakasipu.

Continuing down the path, we pick up our shoes and then arrive at a fork in the path. Here it divides to go back down the hill, or turns upward for the steep one-and-a-half kilometer climb to reach the top of the Ugra Stambha, the 15 storey tall stone pillar from which Lord Narasimhadeva appeared. It is a tough climb up the side of this hill, and you may need a guide to reach it, but it is certainly a thrill to make it to the top and see the views over the area.

Other caves and temples are in the region, including the Girihari and Jyoti temples, the latter of which houses a most fierce deity. However, some of these are a long way off the beaten path, far away from Ahovalam village.

When our visit is over, we can now go south to Nellore, or on to Tirupati.

NELLORE

Nellore is another town that some of you may want to visit. It is between Vijayawada and Chennai, three-and-a-half hours north of Chennai by train. If you come straight down the coast from Vijayawada it is easy to reach and it will be on our way south. If not, you can always stop in if you head back up north from Chennai. If by chance you stop here, you can see the Ranganatha temple. This temple dates back from 1070 and sits on the bank of the Pennar (or Penarkini) River. You will first notice it by the 95 foot tall *gopuram* covered with hundreds of forms of Lord Vishnu. Inside the sanctum, you will see the Garbhodakashayi Vishnu reclining on Ananta Sesha. He is ten feet long. Lakshmi is sitting on a lotus on His chest, and Brahma sits on a lotus rising from His navel. Twenty-six inch deities of Sridevi and Bhudevi are at His feet. And nearby in front are the smaller festival deities, including a four-handed, seated Lakshmidevi called Ranga-nay-aki-devi.

GOING TO TIRUPATI

If you leave Ahovalam on the morning bus, you can be in Tirupati by around 2 P.M. You have to take the bus for the short distance to Allagada, then take another to Cuddapada, and transfer to the bus for Tirupati. If coming from Nellore and any points farther north along the coast, Tirupati can easily be reached by train. That is when we begin our tour of South India, which will be fully described in the next section.

*   *   *   *

Although we started this journey from Delhi in the north, we have gradually made our way through many of the most sacred towns not just of India but of the world. The history, traditions, and culture of these places go back thousands of years. We have seen the birth places of some of the most important spiritual personalities known to man, and have imbibed the atmosphere that exists in the renowned and famous temples and holy sites. We have also seen the appearance and pastime places of various *avataras* of God, according to the Vedic traditions. Now, with our arrival in Tirupati, we conclude our tour of the major pilgrimage places of the east and central parts of India. Naturally, there are many more temples and holy sites in this area that we could visit. But what we have seen has been more than an adventure in geographical or cultural terms. It has been a journey that allows us to look out over that vista that stretches back to the beginning of time and to the edge of eternity. A journey through India is also a journey into our spiritual self. And, for some of us, we may have delighted in what we have found. It may have been a journey that has let us better understand our position in this universe and our place in the scheme of things.

Of course, maybe not everyone can reach that feeling of inner exhilaration. After all, India does not so easily give its most valued treasures, especially when some of us are new to this sort of travel in countries that may be less than accommodating. We may find ourselves simply trying to survive the challenging circumstances that we encounter, rather than attempting to understand and absorb a different culture. Many people may be only too happy to get on that plane and head for home and return to the more familiar and comfortable surroundings. But for others, India may have provided an experience that will leave them with unforgettable memories, not only of what they saw and experienced, but also of what they realized from within about themselves, the world, and how they fit into all of it. Such realizations of what and who they are may change their whole view of life. Once they return home, their minds will continue to drift back to that memory of India.

One of the main ceremonies in the temples that the devoted come to see is the *arati* offering of lamps, as seen here with the deities Sri Sri Radha-Syamasundara, at the Krishna-Balarama temle in Vrindavana.

The interior of the Gurudwara Bangla Sahib Sikh temple, New Delhi.

Deities of Shiva and his wife Parvati holding their son Ganesh in their lap. This is in a small temple in Connaught Place in New Delhi. Many people stop in to say prayers or offerings on their way to or from work.

The ornately carved gate in front of *stupa* number one at Sanchi. The gate has many motifs and symbols that depict the life of Buddha. *Stupas* normally contain something sacred in connection with the Buddha or great lamas.

The large and ornately carved Lakshmana temple in Khajurao. Over a thousand years old and still being used as an active temple. It contains a large Shiva *lingam* inside, and has four smaller temples in the four corners of its platform.

People paying respects to Kal Bhairav, the Nepali form of the fearful manifestation of Shiva, in Durbar Square, Kathmandu.

This Maitreya, the Buddha of the future, is about two-and-a-half storeys tall at the Jamchen Lhakhang Monastery near the Bodnatha Stupa near Kathmandu.

The picturesque Svayambunatha *stupa*, one of the oldest in Nepal, has the
ever-watchful eyes of Buddha, and a large *dorje* or thunderbolt sitting in front.

The Mahabodhi temple in Bodhgaya, one of the most important places related to Lord Buddha, in front of the Bo tree where Buddha became enlightened.

As huge crowds wait, the temple priests bring the deities of Jagannatha, Baladeva and Subhadra out of the temple to the carts. Only the deity's headdress can be seen in the doorway, at Jagannatha Puri.

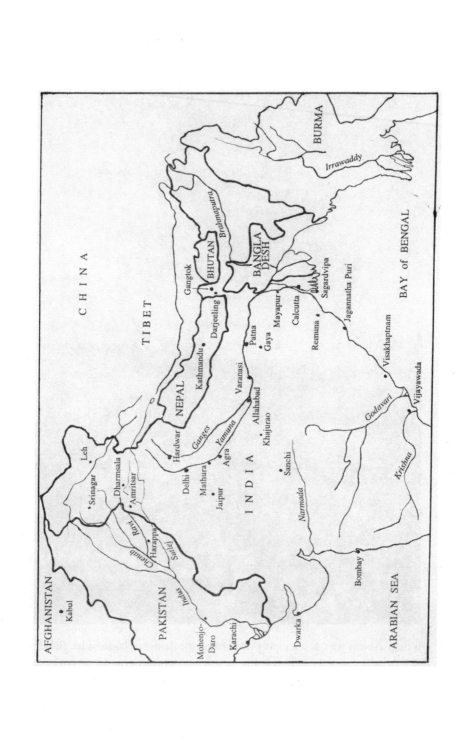

SPIRITUAL INDIA HANDBOOK (PART 2)

▼

The Historical Holy Sites
and
Temples of South India

As we begin our pilgrimage of south India, we should know and will soon see that it is the land of many temples. South India is especially the home of real Indian culture. The south was not as influenced by the Muslim invaders or the British Raj to the extent of northern or central India, so you will find that it still holds the traditional customs and religious views that it has had for hundreds of years. For example, it is the south that still remains primarily vegetarian, though that is changing because of losing the culture. And if you are interested in this kind of diet, there is no reason to eat any meat while you visit South India. Though the food is very different and spicier than that found in the north, there are still preparations that will be very tasty and easy to digest. It is a part of the experience of south India not to be missed. And the architecture is like nowhere else. The temples, which are generally in the center of town, have towering gates, called *gopurams*, that are amazingly ornate.

Fortunately, when we visit these temples we are not seeing relics of an ancient but extinct society, such as we find when visiting the Egyptian pyramids or ancient temples of the Mayan and Incas in Central and South America. But the temples of India present a living culture. In other words, the religious practice of the people, the festivals, and the rituals in the temples are the same as they were thousands of years ago. They still offer to the temple deities fruits and nicely cooked preparations, beautiful dresses, sandalwood paste, flowers and garlands, ghee and camphor lamps, incense and perfumes just as they have done throughout the ages.

One of the most unique temples to witness how important they can be is the temple near the town of Tirupati, which is a three-and-a-half hour bus ride northwest of Chennai (Madras). In the Tirumalla Hills above Tirupati town is the home of Lord Venkatesha (Vishnu), also known as Sri Balaji. Many people from all over India come to visit. No other temple in the world draws so many pilgrims, not even Mecca or Rome, which can number as many as 30,000 on an average day and many thousands more, even up to 500,000, on a festival day. It is here where we will begin our tour of South India.

TIRUPATI

Tirupati is a big town, so it is easy to find a place to stay. We may roll into Tirupati by bus or train. Across from either station are hotels you can choose. Or, you may stay at a temple guest house, which many pilgrims also do. Once we are ready, or the next morning, it is easy to get an auto-ricksha or taxi, or even take a bus, for a tour of the temples in this town. Of course, our main interest will be to see the temple of Venkateshwara at the hilltop complex of Tirumalla. But first we see Tirupati.

The Kapila Tirtham is near the base of the southern side of Tirumala hill close to town. It has the Kapilesvara Swami temple. This is also very beautiful, built around a pool next to the cliffs where there are lovely waterfalls flowing over the rocky hillside which fill the pools, after which the water flows into the valley. It is also called Kapila Tirtham because the sage Kapila had stayed here. He did meditation on Lord Shiva who was satisfied with his concentration and appeared to him here as a Swayambhu (self-manifested or *jyotir*) *lingam*. The *lingam* was originally underground but as the sage's prayers and meditations grew stronger, it emerged from the soil and Kapila was able to perform a milk *abhishekam* or bathing ceremony of the *lingam*. It is also said that Brahma himself came here as a cow to perform *abhisekham* (bathing) to this *lingam* with milk, and Maha Vishnu appeared as a cowherd man. The temple here has images of Brahma as a cow, Vishnu as a cowherd man, and Kapila as a saint. The Kapileshwara *jyotirlingam* is also found here.

One of the most important temples to see is the big Govindaraja Swami temple, established by the great spiritual leader Ramanujacharya. Many people stop in to see it and pay their respects to the deity. The temple is in the center of three enclosures, each entered through ornately carved gates. The first gate or *gopuram* is the most impressive and is seven storeys tall. Inside are two halls that are used for various festivals. The smaller second *gopuram* has many carved panels inside with scenes of Krishna from the stories in the *Puranas*, as well as scenes from the *Ramayana*. In the second enclosure we find the minor shrines to Garuda, Hanuman, and *avataras* of Vishnu. Through the third and smallest *gopuram* we reach the two main shrines. One has a large deity of Krishna holding a bow as Partha Sarathi, the charioteer of Arjuna, and the other has a deity of reclining Vishnu. This deity is a sleeping Vishnu lying on Seshanaga, Vishnu's serpentine bed, with Lakshmi and Bhudevi nearby. Vishnu's bird carrier, Garuda, and the devotee Narada Muni are in attendance as well. Brahma is also there on the lotus flower coming from Vishnu's navel. There is another temple room for Kothalakshmi who is connected to the Lakshmi deity in Kolhapur, and another shrine to Mahalakshmi. It is said that after visiting the

Lakshmi deity here, the pilgrim should visit Kolhapur where Lakshmi appeared to do penance and meditation.

On the way in on the left side is a shrine to Ramanujacharya. All the deities are beautifully adorned with silver hands, armlets, decorations, etc. They are made of black stone, typical of the south.

Two miles (or 6 km) from Tirupati, a motor ricksha ride away, is the temple of Goddess Padmavathi at Tiruchanur. Padmavathi is considered to be the wife of Lord Venkatesha, thus many pilgrims visit this temple. It is suggested that you have *darshan* of Padmavathi before going to see Balaji. Only after seeing Padmavathi will one's pilgrimage to Tirumala be complete. This is also the place where Lord Srinivasa did penance seeking reunion with Mahalakshmi, and also where the sage Sukhadeva did penance many years ago. Inside are also the deities of Lord Krishna and Venkatachalapati. Every year on the eve of the birthday of Padmavathi Ammavaru, Brahmotsavams are held here for nine days in a grand scale. The last day of the rituals, being Panchami, they perform 'Panchami Tirtham', which is known as Tiruchanoor Panchami. The same day the Chakrasnanam (holy bath) is held in the Pushkarini Lake. It is believed that anyone who takes bath there on this day will be freed from all sins.

Also in Tirupati is a temple of Lord Ramachandra called the Sri Kodhanda Ramaswamy temple. It has beautiful deities that had been visited by Lord Chaitanya on His south Indian tour. The temple is in an open and spacious courtyard, entered through a small but beautiful *gopuram*. There is a tall brass *stambha* or pole in the courtyard. This is a stone temple where you will find in the back a sanctum with black stone deities of Lord Rama, Sita, and Lakshmana that are beautifully dressed and have silver hands. They are large and lovely. According to legend, after killing Ravana, Lord Rama took rest at this place on his way to Ayodhya.

The Sri Varadaraja Swami temple is on Kapila Tirtham road. Varadraja Swami along with Chakrathalwar are the principal deities at this temple. The images of Chakrathalwar on one side and Sri Lakshmi Narayana Swami on the other side are installed here. It is said that Lord Venkatesvara in Kaliyuga was Sri Varadaraja Swami in Treta-yuga.

While in Tirupati you should also see the Iskcon Hare Krishna temple. It is a beautiful and large temple with much to be admired. Beautiful Radha Krishna deities and the eight main gopis are seen on the lovely altar. You will also find a few gift shops, and nice devotees make this a place worth visiting. You can easily see it as you return to town from Tirumala Hill and look out over the city. It also has a nice guesthouse.

The Sri Pedda Gangamma Ammavari temple is about 2 km from the railway station. The main shrine of this temple is to Goddess Gangamma. She is the local deity of Tirupati known as "Grama Devatha." Every year in the last week of the month of Chaitra, an Utsava ceremony is held here on a grand scale. In ancient times devotees who came to Tirupati for SriVari *darshan* would visit this temple first. It is said that Gangamma is the sister of Sri Venkatesvara. So every year during the Gangamma Jathara, turmeric, kumkum, and bangles are sent to this temple.

You can also get a bus at the Srinivas complex for a three-hour bus ride that takes you to all the major local temples, even the one outside of town where Balaji and Lakshmi are said to have been married. The time is limited, but it lets you have *darshan* of all the deities. Otherwise you can take a taxi or auto-ricksha to take you around town, which is what I prefer.

TIRUMALLA

The temple of Lord Venkatesha (Vishnu), also known as Sri Balaji, is perhaps the richest temple in the world. Money comes in from many different sources, but there is much that the administration of this temple does with it. They own and maintain their own bus system as well as the roads that take the pilgrims up and down the hills to see this temple. They also have several large universities that they manage, as well as banks, hospitals, and many programs for the poor and sick. They also give grants to writers of books on Eastern philosophy, and also freely send beautifully carved deities for installation in new temples in various parts of the world. In fact, to discuss in detail the many projects that this temple is involved in would take several pages. Besides, donations provide many blessings to those who give.

The legend behind the temple location is summarized as follows: Once Bhrigu insulted Mahavishnu, which annoyed Goddess Lakshmi. She then went to earth and did penance in Kolhapur, a location of another famous temple for Lakshmi. The Lord then came in search for the Goddess and arrived at these hills and stayed as Srinivasa. Here He met Padmavathi, an incarnation of Bhudevi and a princess of Narayanapuram, whom He had promised to marry when He appeared as Lord Rama. When He married Her, it was a huge wedding, and the pastime was that He needed extra funds. He borrowed it from Kubera, the treasurer of the demigods. Kubera insisted on repayment with interest. Hence, the devotees in Andhra Pradesh call the deity Vaddi Kasulaswamy (the Lord of interest), repaying Kubera's interest which never ends. The demigod Kubera is enshrined in the Govindaraja Swamy temple, believed to be there collecting the interest with a brass measure. Thus, somehow, many funds are always coming into the temple.

There are two ways to go to Tirupati, either by foot or by bus. Walking up the hill is a hefty climb, but it used to be the only way you could go. Some of the more determined pilgrims still prefer to walk up as a spiritual austerity and sign of their sincerity. The foot path starts at the Alipiri tower and continues to the Kali Gopuram at the half-way point, and then on up to the top. There are two temples along the path. The temple of Lord Narasimha, about four miles up, is a required visit. Otherwise, it is considered that your vows may not be fulfilled and the pilgrimage will not be complete. Of course, taking the bus means you by-pass this temple. The other temple is for Ramanuja and marks the place where he would stop to sleep on his way up the hill.

For the bus ride, you have to purchase a ticket in advance at one of the ticket booths in town. They say this is to plan or help control how many people crowd the temple at different times. So when you purchase your ticket, you decide at what times the next day you wish to go. Of course, this may change, since every time I have gone to Tirumalla the system is different. Of course, if you take a taxi, then you just go up when you want.

The bus ride is like taking a roller coaster that climbs steep and winding roads that overlook sheer cliffs that drop hundreds of feet down the hillside. You occasionally pass other vehicles on the narrow road, or even pilgrims who are walking up. Sometimes the bus comes precariously close to the edge of the road, and will make sharp turns that force you to hang onto your seat. While I was making the trip back down the hill, one old lady could not hang on tight enough and was thrown to the other side of the bus. Every time the bus turned, she would be thrown to the other side. Finally, she decided to simply sit on the floor in the aisle. And while I was hanging on for dear life, hoping the bus would not crash, a fat man who was sitting next to me was snoring away, oblivious to the whole thing. Sometimes the way the buses are driven during the ride up or down the hill will make you feel like you are risking your life. But thousands do it everyday.

Once we reach the top, we find many buildings and cottages that fill the area between the seven sacred hills. Many people stay here for days or weeks. It is indeed a complete city in itself and has all kinds of shops and stores offering whatever you might need, including free meals for pilgrims at certain halls.

As we get further into town, we see many people with shaved heads. Some men, women, and children perform the sacrifice of voluntary loss of hair as a way of signifying their surrender of vanity and ego for unity with God. By lessening one's concern for bodily beauty and distinction, it automatically becomes easier to focus the mind on higher goals. This is why pilgrims often shave their heads when they visit Tirupati. At Kalyana *ghat* many barbers are kept busy assisting people for this purpose. As you tour South India, you will often see individuals or complete families with shaved heads, evidence of their recent visit to Tirupati.

In the center of the town is the main temple where long lines of people are continually entering through the main gate for *darshan* of the Lord. *Darshan* is the devotional exchange of seeing and being seen by the deity. It is one of the most important devotional activities for a pilgrim to perform. The *darshans* begin at three in the morning and end at midnight. To enter the temple you have to go to a special gate some distance away from the temple entrance. (Anyone can tell you where it is.) However, as I mentioned, nowadays you get your ticket at one of the several booths in town at the base of the hill or at the bus station before ever going up to Tirumalla. There you can ask for a sixty-five rupee ticket for "special *darshan*." (Prices tend to increase with time.) This greatly reduces the waiting time of standing in line. Regular *darshan* may take three to four hours of standing in the queue, while "special *darshan*" takes only about an hour. Of course, on festival days the waiting time may take two to three hours for "special *darshan*" and up to twelve or more hours for regular *darshan*.

The nice thing about this temple is that they allow Westerners and non-Hindus inside to see the deity, whereas in some temples in the south you are not allowed to enter. Here, you simply have to sign a document stating that you are Hindu or respect the Hindu faith after you enter the queue gate. Then you proceed to the waiting rooms that can hold large numbers of people where you sit until your room is called. Then, along with everyone else, you stand in the queue that goes around the temple building. The lines are fenced off from the rest of the street and there is a roof to shade you from the sun.

When we finally enter the temple, we can see very opulent halls and pillars. The first hall has bright bronze statues of King Venkatapathi Raya and King Achyuta Raya and his wife and others, all of whom were great devotees of Lord Venkatesha. We make our way through other large halls and pass smaller shrines. As you enter the main temple sanctum, you can get a view of the gold roof and ornaments which look spectacular in the sunlight.

Finally, we pass through the golden gate of the sanctum, walking past the huge figures of the sentinels on either side. You are automatically pushed along in the queue to see the Lord. It is a walking *darshan*. In other words, you are walking the whole time as you are viewing the deity. As the deity comes into view, many people, with hands folded before them, exclaim, "Jaya Govinda, Jaya Sri Krishna," since Lord Venkatesha (Vishnu) is an expansion or incarnation of Lord Krishna. Some pilgrims have been dreaming of this moment for many years. The devotion they display as they come before the deity cannot go unnoticed. The feelings these people have for God leave the religious sentiments most Westerners have far behind.

The deity is very beautiful and from the time you first see Him, it takes maybe two or three short minutes to approach, walk up to the deity, bow slightly or say a short prayer if so inclined, and then turn away to walk back out. Lord Venkatesha, or Balaji, stands on a pedestal at a height of nine feet. He is richly decorated with jewels, crown, and colorful flower garlands. The *Purana* states that He stands here to forgive everyone of their sins and blesses them by granting whatever devotional requests they have. There are other deities in the temple room, such as Krishna with Bhumi and Rukmini, and Lord Rama with Lakshmana and Sita, but for lack of time They mostly go unnoticed.

As we exit the sanctum, priests may offer you a spoonful of *caranamritam*, the water that has been used to bathe the deity earlier that morning. This is considered especially powerful for one's spiritual merit. You hold out your right hand and take a few drops in your palm, sip it, and away you go toward the exit as hundreds of other pilgrims are waiting in the line behind you. Sometimes temple attendants have to push people in order for them to move on. Then we try to glance back to get one last view of the deity as you move among many others. All too quickly we exit the temple building and walk out and around the courtyard.

As you move around the central temple building, you can see in the back a separate area behind the glass where men are continually counting money that comes in through the *hundi*, or donation boxes. As you get ready to move back to the main street, you pass by an area where they provide everyone with a handful of *prasada*, sacred food offered to the deity. This is usually something like halava.

As we make our way out of the temple hallways and back out to the streets, we feel especially lucky for having gotten *darshan* of the Lord at this most popular and opulent temple. We also feel a little exalted for having been blessed by the Divinity, and maybe a little wiser after witnessing an ancient tradition of this culture in which thousands of people still participate everyday.

We can relax for a moment at the edge of Swamipushkarini Lake at the north side of the temple. This water tank is the most sacred water on the hill. The *Brahmananda Purana* explains that the goddess Sarasvati Devi herself has taken the form of this water tank to wash away the sins of all who bathe in it. Actually, it is said that pilgrims should bathe in this lake before going for *darshan* of Lord Venkatesha. The legend is that the great sage Markandeya asked Lord Brahma to put all the sacred waters into this kund. Instead, Brahma put samples of the waters of all the three planetary systems into the stream and decreed that bathing here would be equal to bathing in all the sacred waters of India. It is said that Lord Rama bathed here before going to Sri Lanka to regain Sita. On the western bank is the Swami Varaha temple, and on the southern bank is the Sri Venkateshwara temple.

There are other temples and places to see on the Tirumala hilltop, along with a small museum and a refreshing park at which we can walk and rest. The Sri Venkateswara Museum is near the Vaikuntam 'Q' complex and contains ancient pictures, deities, musical instruments, and other items connected with the temple, all dating from 8th to the 20th centuries. The pleasant park is located a short walk nearby. To see the additional sacred locations of the area one will have to use the TTD bus service, or will have to use a taxi to reach them all.

First, we can see the Bedi Anjaneyaswami temple opposite the Mahadwara Gopuram of the Srivari temple, near the main entrance. Anjaneyaswami in this temple is hand cuffed and standing in the position of making Namaskara or giving blessings. According to the old legends, it is told that Lord Vishnu had asked Anjaneya to remain before Him until the end of Kali-yuga, and thence he was hand cuffed.

Among the surrounding seven hills are more holy spots to visit. The seven hills of Tirumala represent the seven heads of Adisesha, the great serpent upon Whom Lord Vishnu reclines. The hills expand 250 miles with a width of 25 miles, and its tallest point is 3000 feet above sea level. There are a number of *tirthams* or holy places that can be seen in this area. Walking through these rolling hills to see the waterfalls and streams flowing through deep stone gorges is of the utmost beauty and another aspect of Tirumala you want to see, although you may need a guide to reach them. This is the beauty of nature at its best. So while visiting Tirupati, plan to stay several days to see everything.

The Chakra Thirtam, located 2 kilometers from the temple, is not far from the geological arch. This is where the image of Chakrathalvar is found. It is said the time when Lord Venkateswara turned Himself into a stone deity, Chakrathalvar took a bath in this tank and decorated Lord Venkatesvara. So this thirtam is called ChakraThirtham.

The Silathoranam or Geological Arch (1 km away) is situated near the road. This is a rare geological arch in the rock and few others can be found like it in Asia. They have made a small park around it.

Gogarbha Tirtham, two km from the temple and deeper in the hills, is on the way to Papavinasa Tirtham, and is where the Pandavas performed a *yajna* for attaining the *darshan* of Adi Varahaswami. As a mark of this, the images of the five Pandavas and their wife Draupadi are seen carved on the stones in the small cave or alcove. So it is also called Pandava Tirtham. The Pandavas are said to have spent a year here. While in meditation, Yudhisthira could see that they would win the war of Kuruksetra and regain the kingdom which was rightfully theirs. There is a beautiful stream and several small shrines here.

Japali Tirtham is said to have been where Anjaneya Swami appeared to a great saint called Japali. You will find a nice temple to Hanuman, Anjaneya. On the east side of the temple there is the Sri Rama Tirtham, and on the west side is Sita Tirtham. Agastya Muni also is said to have spent time here along with his disciples. There is a beautiful stream and small lake at this location. However you have to walk about 1 km off the road to reach this place.

Shesha Tirtham relates to Seshanaga. This takes a walk over the hill, allowing you to see the other seven hills in the distance. You can also find water flowing through the gorges which form deep caves.

Akasa Ganga, about 3.5 km (2 miles) away from the temple, is one of the prominent Tirthams in Tirumala. It is a lovely waterfall located a little walk down the side of the hill. According to the *Skanda Purana*, Sri Akasa Raju brought the Ganga and offered it during the marriage of Sri Padmavathi Devi to Sri Srinivasulu. Thus, it is called Akasa Ganga Tirtham. Also, the wife of sage Kesari went into deep meditation here. Her year long *tapasya* or austerity was rewarded by Vayu the wind god, who gave her a special fruit blessed as *prasada*. Upon eating it, a son was born to her, who was Anjaneya, according to the *Skanda Purana*.

Papavinasana Tirtham (about 6 km away from the temple) is where the water flows in seven small outlets over the ridge and down onto a flat area where the devotees can stand and take a holy bath in the flowing water. This is fairly easy to reach. According to the *Sri Venkatachala Puranam*, a holy bath in this Tirtham will purify the sins of the devotees who will be blessed with peace, prosperity, and progress. This is mentioned in the *Skanda Purana* as well. A small temple to Devi is also on the platform. This water is used for the *abhishekam*, or bathing ceremony, for Lord Venkateshwara. Those who can bathe here three days in a row are considered especially blessed.

Farther along this route is the small Venugopal Swamy temple with a small black stone deity of Gopal, Krishna. It is up a small hill with little shops that line the short foot lane to the temple.

There is also Narayanavam (5 km away), the holy place along the same route where Lord Venkateswara first set His feet. Even today the footprints of the Lord can be seen under a small dome that is situated up a short flight of steps.

The Ramakrishna Tirtham Sesham is six miles from Tirumala. This is another beautiful waterfall that cascades into a lovely, clear stream that flows through the deep ridges of the hills. This is where the sage of long ago had the direct *darshan* of Lord Vishnu Himself. Pilgrims take a holy dip in the waters for spiritual advancement and to be purified of sins. Other Tirthams in the hills also exist nearby, some of which are reached by more arduous paths through the hills, but the beauty can make it worth it.

Later, when we are finished visiting the hilltop complex, we can take a bus back down the hill to Tirupati town to continue our pilgrimage. There are more temples to see in the vicinity.

OTHER TEMPLES AROUND TIRUPATI

The Kalyana Venkateswara Swami temple is about 12 km away from Tirupati. According to legend, after His marriage with Goddess Padmavathi, Lord Venkateswara on his way to Tirumala reached the ashrama of the great saint Agastya Muni. On his advice Srinivasa stayed at his ashrama for six months. As Srinivasa started for Tirumala, Agastya Muni requested him to stay near the ashrama and accept their rituals. On this request Srinivasa appeared here as the deity Kalyana Venkatesvara.

The Agastheswara Swami temple near Thondavada Village is about 10 km away from Tirupati. Previously this place was the ashrama of Agastya Muni. The main diety here is Rudra (Shiva) and was installed by Agastya Muni. At the time of installation it is said that all three crore (Mukkoti) gods appeared in this ashrama. So this place is also named "Mukkti". Rudra here is known as Sri Agasteswara Swami along with his consort Anandavalli. Within the Swarnamuki River that flows around the temple is a *mandapa* (temple hall) wherein the image of HariHara is carved out of a single piece of stone seven feet tall. Images of Ayyappa, Ganapati, and Muruga are also here.

The temple of Sri Prasanna Venkateswara Swamy is found in Appalayaguunta, a small village about 18 km from Tirupati. The main deity is in the position of giving blessings. According to tradition, after marrying Padmavathi Devi at Narayanavaram, on His way to Tirumala Lord Venkateswara appeared to Siddeswara Swami who was doing meditation on the hill of Vemula near Appalayaguunta.

The Sri Kalyana Venkateswara Swami temple is in a small town about 25 km from Tirupati and 4 km from Puttur. It was Akasa Raju of the Chandravamsa dynasty who ruled Narayanavaram as the capital when Srinivasa came here from Venkatadri and married Padmavathi, daughter of Akasa Raju. From that time He has been offered *pujas*, worship, as Kalyana Venkateswara. The main deity of Kalyana Venkateswara has Lakshmidevi on his breast.

The Parasurameswara Swamy temple is found in Gudimallam 22 km away from Tirupati. This is an ancient site marked by this temple that was built during the Vikrama Chola dynasty, around 1126. In ancient times the *linga* found within was offered prayers by the Vishnu *avatara* of Parasurama, from where this temple gets its name. In the main shrine you will see Brahma, Vishnu, and Shiva carved on a single stone. This is located about 7 feet underground, which is opened by rock plates under the main shrine from which comes the name Gudipallam. The name has changed to Gudimallam, the present name of the town. To the south of this temple is a temple to Surya and another to Murugan.

The temple of Sri Venugopalaswami, with Rukmini and Satyabhama at the sides of the main deity, is about 58 km from Tirupati via Puttur at Karvetinagaram. This temple was built by King Sri Venkataperumal of the Venkataraja dynasty who brought and installed deities of Sri Venugopal here from the Narayanavaram temple.

The Sri Lakshmi Narayana Swamy temple is located in the small village of Vepanjeri, about 65 km away from Tirupati, 15 km from Chittoor. Vepanjeri is the short version of "Vem Panch Hari" which means the Lord who removes the five grave sins of His devotees. A significant aspect in this village is the 21-foot tall image of Lord Vishnu depicting His Dasavataras (ten main incarnations) in one deity. There is also a new Asta Lakshmi (Lakshmi in Her eight forms) temple in the village as well. The central shrine has Lakshmi-Narayana and Kubera Lakshmi, while Her forms of Adi Lakshmi, Dhanya Lakshmi, Veera Lakshmi, Gaja Lakshmi, Santhana Lakshmi, Vijaya Lakshmi, Aiswarya Lakshmi, and Dhana Lakshmi are in surrounding temples.

The Varada Siddi Vinayaka Swamy temple is about 72 km away from Tirupati in a small village of Kanipakam, on the banks of the Bahuda River near Chittoor. This is a nice temple in typical South Indian style. The main image is Ganesh covered with vermillion as a self-manifested or Swayambhu form.

The Sri Veda Narayanswamy temple is at Nagalapuram, about 65 km from Tirupati on the way to Satyavedu. Here He is shown as Matsya *avatara*. It is said that the emperor of Vijayanagara, Sri Krishnadevaraya constructed this temple in the 14th century on the wish of his mother, Nagamambha Devi. Previously the town was known as NamambhaPuram. One unique feature of this temple is that it faces east in a way that every year on March 25, 26, and 27, the sun comes or shines in to worship the deity. On the 25th the light touches His feet, on the 26th his naval, and on the 27th on his head when Surya Mahotsavam *puja* is celebrated.

The Sri Pallikondeswara Swamy temple, dedicated to Lord Shiva, is an ancient temple on the banks of the Arani River in the town of SuruttaPalli, 77 km from Tirupati, and 12 km from Nagalapuram. In most Shiva temples of South India he is represented in the *linga* form. But here in this temple he is manifested in a majestic human form, one of the few temples that exhibit Shiva in this way. Goddess Parvati and other deities are also seen in the sanctum. The legend is that after he consumed a large amount of poision during the churning of the milk ocean to produce the amrita nectar, he rested here briefly. Thus, the temple marks this ancient legend.

The Sri Valleswara Swamy temple is found in Ramagiri, 65 km away from Tirupati and 5 km from Nagalapuram and Pitchattoor, enroute from Chenai. Surrounded by picturesque mountains, there are two temples here, one at the foot of the hill and one on top of the scenic hillock. The lower temple is dedicated to Shiva as Kal Bhairava in the form of a *linga*, while the upper temple is dedicated to Murugan. The water tank here is said to possess curative powers and is fed by a spring in the mountains. The water flows into the tank through the mouth of the bull Nandi which is mounted on the side wall.

When we are ready to leave Tirupati, instead of going straight to Chennai, we can take a bus to another temple at Kalahasthi.

KALAHASTHI

The Sri Vayulingeswara Swamy temple, a famous Shiva temple, is on the bus route out of Tirupati, 22 kilometres away to the northeast in Kalahasthi. Kalahasthi is an important place of pilgrimage in this region. It is one of the Pancha Bhutha Sthalams, or holy places dedicated to Vayu, the wind god. Kalahasthi is also a Navagraha Sthalam, one of the holy places dedicated to the nine planets, in this case Rahu and Kethu.

It is also here that the hunter devotee Kannappa attained salvation by offering his eyes to Lord Shiva. One day when he saw that the eyes of the deity were bleeding, he offered his own eyes to Shiva, and was thus offered blessings from Lord Shiva. A small sanctuary with his image is on the summit of the hill above the temple, which is reached by following the path from the temple's south *gopuram*. The temple is surrounded by high walls and is entered from the south. The temple's main *gopuram* is six storeys tall and faces the Svarnamukhi River. Inside the enclosure you will find the usual assortment of columned pavilions and smaller structures and shrines. It has four main shrines, the principal one to the west houses the main object of worship: the Vayu (air) Linga which appears as an ant-hill. Proof that it is the Vayu Linga, or wind *linga*, is that the nearby lamp keeps flickering in spite of the fact that there is no air circulating in the temple.

The other shrines are for Jnanaprasumbha to the east, Dakshinamurti to the south, and Ganesh to the north. Adi Shankara also visited this place many years ago.

CHENNAI

Our next stop is in Chennai, a pleasant city that is important for business, politics, and culture. Chennai was founded only 350 years ago in 1640 when Francis Day and Andrew Gogan built a fortified structure on a piece of land that was given by the local Vijayanagara governor. They called the place Fort St. George. From that British bastion evolved the city of Chennai. Inside the Fort are a variety of buildings that are used by the Tamil Nadu Government. There is also St. Mary's Church, built in 1680, which is the oldest Protestant church in Asia, and one of the oldest British buildings in India. There are also a few temples worth visiting in Chennai.

The Parathasarathy temple is probably the most important and is popular with many Hindus. It is dedicated to Lord Krishna as Parathasarathy, the chariot driver of Arjuna, as described in the *Mahabharata*. The deity of Parathasarathy is made of black metal and has a very powerful appearance. The temple has some very nice deities of Krishna, His consort Rukmini, His brother Balarama, and others. No other temple worships Krishna's entire family as they do here. There is also a separate shrine for Sri Ranganatha, the reclining form of Vishnu resting on Adisesha. The incarnations of Vishnu as Narasimha and Varaha are also seen here. Unfortunately, they do not usually allow Westerners into the temple. So, if you are a Western tourist or pilgrim, going to this temple may not be very fruitful. But I gained entrance by being dressed in devotional clothes, meaning a *dhoti* and *kurta*, and explaining that I was a member of the Hare Krishna movement.

The Kapaleeshvara temple complex is another important temple, devoted to Shiva. This is in Mylapore in the south part of Chennai. Within a courtyard and through the ornate and colorful *gopuram*, the principal shrine houses a large Shiva *linga* and an image of Subramanya, Shiva's son, also known as Murugan. A smaller shrine to goddess Parvati is nearby. Legend has it that Parvati, Shiva's wife, once incarnated as a peahen and worshiped Lord Shiva here to obtain deliverance. Actually the story is that Shiva was once imparting knowledge to Parvati, but she became distracted by a beautiful peacock and was not listening to her husband. Thus, Shiva cursed her to become a peahen to experience that life, but told her by worshiping him in the form of a Shiva *lingam* under a Punnai tree, he would again join her. After years of searching, the peahen finally found such a *lingam* in this area known as Mylapore.

There are many sculptures depicting a number of the local legends. However, they usually do not allow Westerners into the sanctum. Nonetheless, it is an interesting temple, and when I was visiting with a friend of mine, while wearing a *dhoti* and *kurta*, I simply went into the sanctum like anyone else and was able to see the Shiva *lingam*. Nonetheless, it was some distance away from where people stand, so the view was not that good. There were many devotees offering respects, and I was glad to have been able to have *darshan*.

When I was there a wedding ceremony was going on with nearly a hundred people in attendance. The ceremony included a simple ritual as the bride and groom sat in the middle of the crowd in one of the outside halls. The groom was dressed in a silk *dhoti* and shirt, while the bride had a beautiful red sari and gold bangles and hair pieces. After the short ritual, there was an exchange of flower garlands between the bride and groom, and the groom marked the bride's forehead with the red dot that means she is a chaste and married lady. The senior ladies, all dressed in their most opulent and colorful saris, came forward to bestow their blessings on the bride by placing their hands on her head and saying some prayers or offering her some advice. Soon the ceremony was over. Then everyone very happily gathered around to congratulate each other. The people at the wedding received me very nicely and were glad I was interested in watching it. They gave me some fruits that had been offered in the ceremony, as well as some other *prasada* that was being passed around to everyone. They also wanted me to meet the bride and groom. It was as if I had become a part of the celebration. Afterwards, I made my way through the courtyard and out the temple gate feeling quite satisfied by this chance encounter.

One word of caution: if you leave your shoes at the shoe minder's stall near the temple entrance, pay only a rupee or so at the most when you pick up your shoes. This is the standard price at any temple. Don't allow yourself to be cheated by paying up to 10 rupees if they ask for that. Many times shoe minders, guides, *ricksha* drivers, or even shop keepers will automatically charge Westerners considerably more than local people. For a *richsha* it is best to find out what the going rate is from someone who is impartial and then stick with that. However, *ricksha* and taxi rates do change a little according to the region. So be aware of what it is.

The Adikeshava Perumal temple in Mylapore is located only one furlong from the Kapeeleshvara temple. The temple sits on 1½ acres and contains two main sanctums with numerous other shrines. It has a seven-tiered *gopuram* over the main entrance, which is vacant of any sculptures. The present temple was built during 1955-58. This temple is steeped in ancient tradition that explains that Lord Vishnu lived at this spot for a time many years ago.

In the sanctum, the presiding deity of Adikeshava gives *darshan* in a standing position and faces east. The divine consort Mayuravalli Thayar is on the right side and ever offers blessings to all who visit. A separate shrine has the deities of Rama, Lakshmana, and Sita. On the other side is the shrine for Andal.

Ramanujacharya also had connections with this holy place. The *Ramanuja Divya Charita*, composed by Pillai Logam Jeeyar, explains that Asurikesava Perumal who came from Sriperumbudur, visited the shrine of Adikeshava Perumal and conducted a Vedic ritual to invoke the Lord to favor him with a son. The son was Ramanuja who was destined to continue the line of the Vaishnava faith. The book explains that Ramanuja went to the Parthasarathy temple at Triplicane and offered devotional hymns to the deity. Then he came to the Adikeshava Perumal temple and dedicated hymns that became the Sanskrit text known as *Ramanujasamboo*.

In the 18th century the adherents of the Vadakalai *sampradaya* asked to place a shrine of their preceptor there, Vedanta Desikar. Since then other shrines have appeared for the great saints and divine personalities that include those of the Alwars, Alamalu Mangai, Lakshmi Narasimha, Andal, Sudarshan, and Ramanuja.

While visiting this Adikeshava temple, the priests were especially nice and provided special *prasada* in the form of morning halava. We got up close to the deity and watched the arati, and also received plenty of tulasi leaves and *caranamrita* water as well. So it was a really nice spiritual experience.

A few minutes drive from the Kapaleeshvara temple is an important church for local Christians. This is the San Thome Basilica which was originally built in 1504 and rebuilt in 1898 on the ruins of the original Portuguese church which is said to house the remains of the Apostle "Doubting" Thomas Didymus who used to preach every day in this area after he had arrived in India. He was supposed to have originally been buried on the nearby beach, but then was moved to a crypt where the Basilica was built. However, evidence has been discovered that this may be a fabricated history of the place. Near the airport is St. Thomas' Mount where it is believed he died. A small Portuguese church is there with relics of the saint. It has a tranquil atmosphere and a great view of Chennai.

South of the San Thome Basilica is the Adyar River estuary where the Theosophical Society has its world headquarters, founded in 1882 by Madame H. P. Blavatsky. This place has hundreds of acres of gardens with magnificent buildings, shrines, and a world-class library. In the gardens is a 200 year old banyan tree, one of the biggest in India.

On the way to Elliot's Beach is the Ashtalakshmi temple, dedicated to goddess Mahalakshmi, one of the few shore temples in the country. Chennai also has the very interesting Government Museum and Art Gallery on Pantheon Road. It has excellent displays of a variety of deities, bronzes, and artwork from different regions and historical periods. This will give you some insight into the spiritual heritage and culture of India.

TEMPLES IN THE CHENNAI AREA

Tiruneermalai

There are hundreds of temples in this area, from various schools of thought and sects, but here are some of the more important ones. Tiruneermalai (10 km from Chennai) has the Divya Desam temple known as the Sri Ranganatha Perumal temple. The *Brahmanda Purana* says it is one of the eight places where Lord Vishnu manifested Himself. The Lord is seen in four postures here; Neervannan—standing, Lord Narasimha—sitting, Lord Ranganatha—lying, and Lord Trivikrama—walking. The temple with the last three deities is at the top of the hill, 250 steps up. The Neervannan Perumal temple, with the standing Neevannan is at the foot of the hill. A Valmiki shrine is on the hillside.

Mangadu

Mangadu (23 km from Chennai) has the Kamakshi Amman temple. The goddess in this temple is depicted as doing penance by standing in the midst of fire (Panchaagni) in a mango field in order to marry Lord Shiva.

Tiruninravar

Tiruninravar (30 km from Chennai towards Arkonam) has the Sri Bhaktavatsala Perumal temple.

Tiruvallur

Tiruvallur (42 km from Chennai on the railway line toward Arkonam) has the Sri Veeraraghava Swami temple with Lord Vishnu lying on Adi Sesa, with Brahma coming from His navel. There is a huge intricately carved *gopuram*. It is located 5 km north of the railway station. Lord Vishnu is said to have killed Madhu and Kaitabha here at Veeksharanya Ksetram. The Hridaya-tapa-nasini-tirtham is a tank said to cure one's illnesses.

Tiruthani

Eighty-six km from Chennai and north of Arkonam, this is one of the six holy sites of Lord Murugan, Arupadai Vidu. The temple is on top of the Thangai Hill, 365 steps up. It has a large *gopuram*. There are several shrines in this complex. The deity is worshiped here as Jnana Shaktidharar, or one who gives his devotees knowledge, *jnana*. His consorts Valli and Deivayanni are also enshrined here.

Sholingar

Ninety-one km from Chennai are the shrines of Lord YogaNarasimha and Yoga Anjaneya on two hills. Anjaneya has a Shanku and a Chakra in His hands that are said to have been given by Sri Narasimha. People circumambulate the hills, and visiting these shrines is said to cure mental afflictions.

Thiruvidaventhal

Thiruvidaventhal (40 km south of Chennai and 10 km north of Mamallapuram) has the Sri Nitya Kalyana Perumal temple with the nine feet tall deity of Sri Lakshmi Adi Varaha. Bhumidevi is on the Lord's thigh, and the Lord wears a garland made of 108 *shala-gram-shilas*.

MAMALLAPURAM

Mamallapuram (officially renamed from Mahabalipuram) is situated on the coast 59 kilo-metres south of Chennai. It can be reached by a bus ride from either Chennai or Kan-chipuram. This small town is known for its rock-cut cave temples, stone carvings, and the shore temple on the beach. The shore temple, one of Mamallapuram's most noted land-marks, is dedicated to Shiva and has a 16 sided *lingam* and a relief of Somaskanda. The steep pyramidal tower above the temple is capped by an octagonal dome. The temple has been in a state of renovation for some time due the deterioration from the salty air, but is interesting to see.

From here we go up the road toward the hill that dominates the town. On our right as we walk along we can see the main temple of the town which we can visit if it is open. (One thing to remember is that most temples are closed from noon until 4 P.M.) The temple, dedicated to Sri Vishnu, is still active and receives many visitors. The sanctum sanctorium is rather dark, so the priest will take a ghee lamp to provide a little light so you can make out the features of the reclining Vishnu. This form of Vishnu is popular in the South, so take a good look since there may be other temples with a similar deity that may not allow Westerners to enter.

As we leave the temple and reach the hill, we see a huge boulder 90 feet long by 30 feet high with 153 different figures of deities, humans, and various animals carved on it. This is a most fascinating composition of Indian art. It has a large assortment of animals, beings, gods, and goddesses that are included in it. It depicts the story of Arjuna doing penance in order to attain a boon from Lord Shiva. It also shows the story of the Ganges descent from the Himalayas.

From here you can continue up the hill to follow the path and read the signs and see the rock-cut temples and halls that are scattered around the hill. These include the Krishna Mandapa with its stone carving depicting Krishna protecting the residents of Vrindavan from the heavy rains by lifting Govardhana Hill to use as a huge umbrella. Heading south and going clockwise around the hill, there is the Dharmaraja Cave temple, and then the Adivaraha Cave temple, with an image of Varaha and panels depicting Lak-shmi and Durga. Next is the Mahishamardini Cave temple, which has a carving of Vishnu reclining on Seshanaga surrounded by the demigods.

Further along the path is the Trimurti Cave temple that has three shrines in a row with stone carvings of Brahma (left), Vishnu (middle), and Shiva (right), and a niche for

Durga. The Varaha Cave temple has a large carving on the wall showing Varaha lifting Bhudevi (left) and Trivikrama (right), and Lakshmi and Durga are on the rear wall. The Ganesha Ratha is after that. Most of the carvings and halls were completed by the 7th and 8th century. Just south of the hill are the Five Rathas, which are small temples said to have been used as prototypes for Dravidian architecture. Each is dedicated to one of the Pandavas, namely Draupadi, Arjuna, Bhima, Dharmaraja, and one for Nakula and Sahadeva.

Mamallapuram has always been known for its stone work, which you can still find plenty of today. There are many shops around to sell you little deities or souvenirs, or even take custom orders for works of carved stone. There is also a school here that teaches sculpture work as well. Furthermore, the tsunami of 2003 uncovered the remains of another ancient temple near the shore.

TIRUKKALIKUNDRAM

Fourteen kilometers west from Mamallapuram is Tirukkalikundram. This place is known for its hilltop temple on Vedagiri Hill, which is a tough climb up 565 steps. The temple is dedicated to Shiva as Sri Vedagiriswara. It is built on three huge blocks of stone, which form its inner walls. On the walls are sculptures of Shiva and Parvati and Subramanya, and the main deity in the central room is a Shiva *lingam*. The priests are friendly and gladly show you around, so be sure to leave a little donation, which is customary at any temple. But I have a rule that if I don't get *darshan* of the deity, I give no donation. At this temple the priests will also give you some deity remnants.

This temple is also called Pakshi Tirtha, holy place of the birds, and is famous for the two eagles that arrive every day at noon and are fed by the temple priests. After being fed, the eagles fly to the other side of the hill to clean their beaks where there are large indentations in the hillside from this being done for so many years. Legend has it that they were once two sages who had sinned and were cursed by Lord Shiva to repeatedly take birth as eagles. They come to the temple to offer respects to Shiva for their salvation. This daily event has been going on for hundreds of years. It is even mentioned in the *Puranas*. No one is sure where the eagles come from, but some say that they fly from Varanasi. Five hundred years ago Sri Chaitanya Mahaprabhu also visited this hilltop temple to offer respects to Lord Shiva and saw the eagles being fed.

From the hilltop are excellent views of the area, especially of the temple below. This temple at the base of the hill is also very interesting with tall *gopurams*, through which you enter the complex. It has many carved pillars and hallways, and when I visited there were a number of students sitting about studying textbooks. This temple is also dedicated to Shiva and the priests allow you to see the deities here, one of a Shiva *linga*, the other of Subramanya. It is a large temple complex and worth the visit.

To visit these temples, it's good to take a short day trip by bus from Mamallapuram. But go in the morning because if you arrive after the temples open in the afternoon, you'll miss the feeding of the eagles and it may start getting dark before you are ready to return. After dark is not a good time to be trying to get a bus. Buses can be full and will drive past without stopping. And some of the local people who live along this road are not the kind with whom you will want to be alone after dark. Especially if they are poor and intoxicated peasants who look at you as a person who has money.

KANCHIPURAM

When we are done visiting Mamallapuram, we can go to Kanchipuram. This is a bus ride several hours away, or 72 kilometers from Chennai. Kanchipuram is also easily reached from Tirupati. It is another important and interesting temple town. It is one of the seven most sacred cities of India, which include Kanchipuram, Varanasi, Haridwar, Ujjain, Mathura, Ayodhya, and Dwaraka. As you approach Kanchipuram by bus, you will see the tall temple *gopurams* from miles away. There are many temples in this town. Although Kanchipuram has as many as 125 recognized shrines, some of the noteworthy temples include the Chitragupta temple, the Iravataneshvara, Matangeshvara, Mukteshvara, and Jvarahareshvara Shiva temples. The 21 major temples listed are the Sri Kumarakottam temple dedicated to Subramaniya, the Sri Katchapeswara Shiva temple, the Ekambaranathar, Pandava Thuthar, Kailasa Nathar, Kamakshiamman, Pachai Vannar, Pavala Vannar, Ulagalandhar, Vaikunda Nathar, Vilakkoli Perumal, Ashtabujam Perumal, Yathothakari Perumal, Varasharaja Perumal, SivaSthanam Sri Brumma Purisar, Sri Punniakotesar, Vyasa Santhalesar, Onakantheesar, Thirukkalimedu Sri Sathyanatheesar, the Sri Chandr Praba Nathar (Jain temple), and the Sri Kayarokaneesar—Thayar Kulam.

Kanchipuram also has a number of the 108 Divya Desams, or holiest sites for Lord Vishnu for the followers of Ramanujacharya. Fourteen of these temples in Kanchipuram are in this category. To explain further about these temples, the Divya Desams revered by the Alwars in Vishnu Kanchi (the part of Kanchipuram with the Vishnu temples) are Attigiri (the vast Varadaraja Perumal temple), Ashtabuyakaram, Tiruttankaa, Tiruvelukkai, and Tiruvegkaa, while those in Shiva Kanchi are Tiru Oorakam (Ulagalanda Perumaal Koyil), Tiru Neeragam, Tiruppaatakam, Nilaattingal Tundam, Tirukkaaragam, Tirukkaarvaanam, Tirukkalvanur, Tiruppavalavannam, and Parameswara Vinnagaram. The vast Ekambeswara temple (Prithvi Stalam) revered by the Tevaram hymns, is located in Periya (Shiva) Kanchi, as are the Kamakshi Amman and the Kanda Kottam temples. The Alwars were prominent and influential Vaishnavas, worshipers of Lord Vishnu, who were present from 4200 to 2700 B.C.E. So this may help provide insight into the importance of Kanchipuram.

Out of all these temples, there are five main ones that pilgrims and tourists visit. Starting on the west side of town we first visit the old Kailasanatha temple, dedicated to Shiva. For a while it was no longer a functioning temple and the only person there was the guard who would show you around and explain some of the more interesting aspects of the temple, if you could understand his English. But now renovation work has been done on it and it is again used for worship, if on a small scale. There is now often a tour guide that can explain things to you for a small donation. It was built around 700 C.E. by Rayasimha, a Pallava king. It is enclosed by a wall that has numerous carved figures and small shrines in it. The outside of the temple has many sculptures of various aspects of Shiva, and there is a fine sculpture of Ardhanaresvara, the half-male and half-female form of Shiva/Parvati. Other sculptures of various *avataras* of the Lord, such as Narasimha, are also found. The top of the temple is a pyramidal structure that rises a few storeys high, and inside the sanctum is a Shiva *lingam*. It is a quiet place, although the local children will follow you while asking for a pen.

The Ekambareshvara temple is our next stop. This is still a functioning temple dedicated to Shiva and many visitors are continuously coming and going. It is also one of Kanchipuram's newest and largest temples, built in 1509 by the Vijayanagar king Krishna Devaraja. It covers nine hectares and has a *gopuram* that stands 192 feet tall. There is a large water tank on the north side of the temple next to the long columned *mandapa* hall in front of the main entrance to the temple. You can walk around and get a feel for the place, visit many of the shrines and see the deities therein, but you will not be able to go directly into the main temple room if you are a Westerner. In the main sanctuary is the Prithvi Lingam, a Shiva *lingam* representing the element of earth. This principal shrine is surrounded by a corridor that has many stone carvings of animals and lotus flowers. However, one of the more important parts of the temple is the small central courtyard where you will find the sacred mango tree under which is the place where Shiva and Parvati were married. Several varieties of mangoes are produced from this one tree. However, when I later visited this temple in 2005, I found that the mango tree had dried up and fallen, and now another had been planted in its place. Near the doorway leading to it is an altar with the deities of Shiva and Parvati. The priest will gladly do a *puja* for you at this shrine, even if you are a Westerner. After walking around the halls and seeing the other smaller shrines, including one of the *avataras*, and the sacred water tank, we can go on to the next major temple.

From here we go to the Kamakshiamman temple, dedicated to the goddess Parvati, Shiva's wife. This temple is also enclosed by a wall with a gateway in each direction. Within the enclosure is an ornate columned hall and a water tank with stepped sides. In one corner of the enclosure is a shelter where they keep a couple of elephants for temple functions. All of the visitors briefly stop here to see them. This is another temple complex you can walk around in, but if you are a Westerner you will not be allowed into the main temple, which has a beautiful golden sculpted dome above it. Inside the temple, the goddess is worshiped as a *chakra*, which is placed before the deity of Kamakshiamam. Kamakshi is worshipped as Durga, but is said to be Lakshmi in the *Brahmananda Purana* in the description given by Lord Hayagriva in His talk with the sage Agastya. It is also related that it was here where Dasaratha, Lord Rama's father, prayed to Kamakshi for children. There is also an image of Shankaracharya, the spiritual teacher who advocated monism. The Shankaracharya Mutt here in Kanchipuram is also quite prominent.

Now we go to the Vaikunthaperumal temple, which was built around 700 C.E. Inside the surrounding wall you will see many pillars with sculpted lions on them, a forerunner of the later 1000 pillared halls that we find in temples farther south. There are also sculptures on the walls depicting some of the Pallava history, such as coronation scenes, as well as images of Vishnu and His *avataras* in scenes from the *Puranas*. This temple is dedicated to Lord Vishnu and is worth visiting if you are in Kanchipuram. It is still a functioning temple, and if you visit in the morning when the priest is there, he will show you the main deity. The deity is a beautiful black stone Vishnu, standing with four hands and nicely decorated with shiny brass ornaments. Smaller deities are in front. I was quite impressed and upon leaving a small donation, the priest gave me *caranamrita* water, tulasi leaves (an important plant whose leaves are used in the worship of Vishnu or Krishna), and *prasada* (food that has been offered to the deity and is considered to be spiritually very powerful) in the form of little sweets. The temple consists of three sanctuaries, one above the other on the different floors reached by climbing through narrow stairways, the lower one being the main one. The shrine on the third and top floor, which is often locked, has a small (maybe three feet long) but lovely reclining Vishnu on a Seshanaga. The guide also took me to a few parts of the temple that were usually kept locked. This allowed me a look at other stairways that have carved images on the walls as well as a much closer look at the carvings on the central dome over the temple. This is another temple undergoing renovation work in my later visits to this place, and is certainly worth seeing.

Another important Vishnu temple in Kanchipuram is for Varadaraja. It is one of the 108 Divya Desams, or holiest sites for Lord Vishnu. The Varadaraja temple is said to be on the site where Lord Brahma performed a fire (*yajna*) ritual to invoke Lord Vishnu. The central enclosure of the temple is supposed to conform to the raised altar that Brahma had used for the ritual. The temple is built on a small hill and has two high *gopurams* on the east and west sides of the temple compound that lead into the first enclosure, and a smaller gate leads into the inner enclosures. As you enter through the main gate, you will first see a separate *mandapa* hall which houses 96 elaborately carved columns that show many figures, such as dancers, animal riders, and scenes of the Vaishnava iconography. Some of them also produce musical tones when struck. There is some excellent sculptor work here. In the back of the hall is a *kund* or pond, called Ananta Thirtam. This is because Lord Ananta is said to have created it so He could recline in it and observe the pastimes of Lord Varadaraja. There is also a story that once during the summer's intense heat, the original deity of Lord Varadaraja felt overly hot and appeared to a priest in a dream requesting to be put into the water. So they keep the deity in a silver chest in a shrine inside this pond. Every forty years the deity is taken out and worshiped in a grand way for forty-eight days. Around the pond are several shrines, among which include a temple in which the main deity is Lord Narasimha on one side, and a deity of the Sudarshan chakra on the back. A shrine to Ramanujacharya is also nearby.

The temple complex has beautiful examples of stone workmanship. One such example is a huge chain carved from one piece of stone hanging near the mandapa hall. Other shrines and pavilions are also found, such as the shrines for Perundevi, the consort of Varadaraja. Along the water tank is a temple with a deity of Vishnu on one side and Lord Narasimha on the back. From here we can walk to enter the smaller gate to get to the main temple. Here again they almost did not allow me inside because of being a Westerner, but after some talking they could understand I was qualified, being a member of Iskcon.

I went into the temple to first see a beautiful deity of goddess Lakshmi. She is located in a separate temple building in which devotees line up to see Her beautiful form.

One time I was there on the day of Ekadashi, so they were doing a special bathing ceremony of the small deities, which was quite interesting. They brought the smaller *utsava* deities in on a palanquin to a central stage and began the bathing process. There were about two dozen brahmana priests chanting appropriate mantras while others were doing the bathing. Later I went around the back, as someone had told me to do, and I saw inside the main temple building a wonderful shrine to Lord Narasimha, which had three deities of Narasimha, each one consecutively larger than the other. The priest did a special *puja* for me and gave me tulasi leaves and sweets. Lord Narasimha has a special place here because it was He who granted Lord Brahma permission to perform the fire ritual from which Lord Varadaraja emerged.

I then went half-way around the building and found an entrance that lead upstairs to another hall that circumambulated a central shrine. Other shrines and paintings of Vaishnava divinities are located in the corridor that surrounds the central sanctuary. In the central area was the shrine for the main deity of Varadaraja. This deity of Varadaraja (Vishnu) is beautiful and large (maybe five or six feet tall) and made of black stone. He holds a large club in one hand, and disc and conchshell in two others, and has gold or brass ornaments and crown. His forth hand is raised in blessings, with the Sanskrit words *ma suchaha* (Do not worry) inscribed. He was dressed very nicely with fine cloth and beautiful jewelry. One gold necklace had the thousand names of Vishnu carved on it. He was most impressive. If you look closely, He also has pink spots on His face that is said to have been acquired when He sprang forth from the flames in Lord Brahma's fire ritual. I really liked this *darshan* and was again given *caranamritam*, tulasi leaves, and sweets as I stood in meditation in front of the deity.

There is also a hall next door where one can have the *darshan* of an image of the sacred green lizard that is located on the ceiling in a corner room, for a small donation. I then went back to the stage area to watch the priests finish dressing the smaller deities. They bathed and dried Them, and then offered Them new cloth to wear, and new flower and tulasi garlands. Afterwards, the crowd was allowed to get on the stage and get close to the deities, and to receive handouts of *prasada*. I also got a fresh tulasi garland and had the shoes of the deity placed on my head. It was quite impressive and most transcendental. I was walking on air after that. This was a real experience in Indian Vedic culture, the likes of which many Westerners do not get the chance to receive. In other areas in this temple complex you can find shrines to Lord Rama and a mirrored hall.

Tiruvelukkai is another Divya Desam temple located in Kanchipuram, 1 km south west of Ashtabhuyakaram, which is a mile west of the Varadaraja Perumal temple. The Moolavar deity here is Azhagiyasingar or Mukunda Nayakar, who is in a standing posture facing east, while the Taayaar here is Velukkaivalli or Amritavalli.

Legend has it that Narasimha, while in his Hastisaila cave (the Attigiri hill sanctum in the Varadaraja Perumal temple, with the cave shrine to Narasimha), manifested himself yet again as Narasimha, and proceeded westward to banish the *asura* demons from the vicinity, where he stood in the posture of Yoga Narasimha, in what is known now as Tiruvelukkai. The word Vel means desire; since Narasimha, out of desire for this place, resided here, this shrine is known as Tiruvelukkai.

Kanchipuram is a place where many *sadhus* and saints have visitied. Sri Chaitanya, Sri Nityananda, and Madhvacharya have all visited. And Chanakya Pandit as well as Vedanta Deshika, the important Vaishnava *acharya* after Ramanuja, were both born here. It is also here, it is said, that Ramanujacharya received the *vashishtadvaita* philosophy from Kanchipurna, one of his gurus. On the birth celebration of Vedanta Deshika, the small deities of Vishnu and His consorts of Lakshmi, Sri and Bhudevi are brought out for a procession around the temple and to the shrine of Vedanta Deshika to give him Their blessings. It is a grand festival. Priests chant mantras from the *Taitiriya Upanishad, Purusha-sukta* and *Tirupavai,* and distribute *prasada,* sandalwood paste, and tulasi garlands after offering them to the deities.

Many other temples can be viewed here in Kanchipuram if you have the time, as previously listed. You can also see a thirty-five foot high deity of Lord Trivikrama (Vamanadeva), as He lifts His leg to the shell of the universe. There is another Krishna deity called Pandava Dootha, or "Messenger of the Pandavas", which stands twenty feet tall. Ask around to find these and other temples you may be interested to see. Most any motor ricksha or taxi driver will know of these.

Another point of interest in Kanchipuram is the highly regarded and valued silk saris that are made here. The weavers use vibrant colors and rich designs, and sometimes use gold thread in the borders. These saris are often sold by the weight of the material. There are numerous shops that sell silk and cotton saris and your *ricksha* driver will want to take you to see a shop or factory where they make them. This is because if you buy any, he is likely to get a commission for bringing you there. Nonetheless, if you need any saris, Kanchipuram is a good place to purchase a few. However, as for me, I feel there are just too many living beings that are killed in the process, namely silk worms, and there are places in the world that use child labor in making silk cloth. So I do not buy any silk products. Cotton is good enough for me. There are also some nice lodges where you can stay, such as the M. M. Hotels, which also have the Sravanama Bhavan pure vegetarian restaurants.

Tiruputkuli is a nearby place you may want to see. It is located outside of Kanchipuram by about seven kilometers and has the Vijaya Raghava temple, another of the Divya Desams of Lord Vishnu. You can reach it by bus, or just take an auto-ricksha or taxi. The *Vamana Purana* also describes that this is where Lord Rama is said to have performed the funeral rites for Jatayu, the special large bird who tried to save Sita from the clutches of the demon Ravana. The pond opposite the temple hall is also where Ramanuja had studied under Yadhava Prakasha. However, Yadhava taught the impersonalistic *advaita* philosophy, which Ramanuja continued to refute, thus earning Ramanuja expulsion from the school. Yadava also once tried to kill Ramanuja but failed. Thereafter, he finally understood Ramanuja's saintly qualities and accepted him as his own spiritual master.

When we have seen all we need to see in Kanchipuram, we can go on to our next stop, which is Tiruvannamalai.

TIRUVANNAMALAI

Leaving Kanchipuram we board a bus and head south to Tiruvannamalai. This is another temple town, said to have over 100 temples. But the town is dominated by the central Shiva-Parvati temple, one of the largest in India. The main *gopuram* reaches 66 meters (217 feet) in height, and there are massive walls all the way around the complex. Other *gopuram* gates are situated in the four directions around the complex, nine altogether. The thousand-pillared hall has many intricate carvings and enshrines Pathala Lingeswara. There are several smaller shrines and temples within, such as to Murugan, known as Kambathu Ilayanar. But the main temple is dedicated to Shiva in the form of the *jyotirlingam*, representing fire. Inside the inner sanctum, it is a small room with little air circulation that can become oppressingly stuffy after they have done numerous fire *arati* ceremonies for the guests that arrive for worship. Yet, seeing the image of Shiva is extremely auspicious. Next to that temple is one for Parvati. The management here is quite organized and for a yearly donation they will send you deity *prasada* and remnants every month to wherever you live. During the month of Keshava, November-December, there is a big festival during which a huge bonfire is lit on top of Arunachalla Hill, behind the temple. The fire can be seen for miles and devotees offer obeisances to it, considering it to be the manifestation of Shiva's fiery form.

Arunachala Hill is where several Hindu seers and saints have perfected their lives. Many pilgrims circumambulate the hill (14 km) before worshiping the *jyotirlingam*, Sri Arunachaleswara. One can also climb the hill by taking the stone path behind the Ramana Maharshi Ashrama. Everyone climbs the hill barefoot and it's a hefty walk up. I had to stop and rest several times. At the end of the path, half way up the hill, is Skandashrama, the place where Ramana Maharshi lived and attained enlightenment. This place is like a little heaven on earth. Amidst the barren rock of the hill, there are trees for shade, refreshing breezes, a pleasant house, and a well with very nice water that tastes exceptionally good after the hard climb up. It is a great place for solitary meditation. You can look out over the city and get great views of the temple below as you sit and relax until you are ready for the walk back down. But do not wait too long. I went up in the morning and by the time I came back down at 11 A.M., the rocks on the path had already soaked up so much heat from the sun that I felt like they were burning my feet. And this was in March. So you must plan accordingly. The best time to visit South India is between the months of October and March. After that it starts getting very hot and is not a good time to visit if you are not used to the kind of heat that you will experience here. By the time I got back down the hill at 11:30, they were serving lunch at the Ramana Maharshi Ashrama, and for a small donation it was well worth it.

Tiruvannamalai is not a town that seems to cater to Westerners. There are not many signs in English or English speaking people. But when lunch was served at the *ashrama*, I was surprised to see all kinds of Westerners show up. Obviously, many people come here to study yoga and the Shaivite form of Hinduism at the Ramana Maharshi Ashrama. The *ashrama* also has a temple dedicated to Shiva in the form of a *lingam*, and the rooms where Ramana Maharshi lived are kept as a memorial. They also have living quarters for guests and students.

My own visit to Tiruvannamalai was quite interesting. I had never been there before and did not even know where to get off the train when we arrived. But I became friends with a monk in saffron who was riding on the train and he showed me where to get off. He was getting off the train here as well. However, he did not speak a word of English, and I not a word of Tamil. Nonetheless, we walked the streets into town from the train station, he leading the way, where I found a hotel for the night. I then went to the main temple in the morning. There we met again, and he actually showed me the way through the streets to Ramana Maharshi's ashrama, some of the shrines around the ashrama, and the way up to Arunachala Hill, all the while communicating without language. Somehow we simply knew how to let each other know what was on our mind. This kind of thing has happened to me so often while traveling in India. Somehow, I am given the means to find my way around with the proper assistance at the right time.

Once we have finished seeing Tiruvannamalai, we can move on to our next place of interest.

THE STORY OF THE SHIVA LINGAM

One thing you may be questioning is why Lord Shiva is almost always represented as a *lingam*. According to the *Puranas*, there was a great sacrificial ceremony that was going to take place many hundreds of years ago. The great sage Narada Muni was invited to it and asked who would receive the effects of the sacrifice. No one could answer, so the sages who were present asked him who should receive it. Narada said that Sri Vishnu, Brahma, and Shiva were all eligible, but they would have to find out which one had the most patience and purity to be the receiver of the sacrifice. So he chose the great sage Brighu to learn the answer.

Brighu had many mystic powers and was able to travel to the domain of the demigods. So first he went to see Lord Brahma, but Brahma was preoccupied and did not notice Brighu's presence. Feeling insulted, Brighu cursed Brahma, "You are so proud of your power of creation, you did not notice my arrival. For this you shall have no temples on earth." Thus, there are very few temples of Brahma on earth. Next, Brighu went to see Shiva in Kailash, but Shiva also did not notice Brighu's arrival. Brighu, again feeling offended, cursed Shiva to be worshiped only as a *lingam* on earth. This is the reason why Lord Shiva is primarily worshiped as a *lingam,* which is the shapeless representation

Then, to continue the story, Brighu went to see Lord Vishnu, who also did not recognize Brighu's presence when he first arrived. Brighu was so angered that he went forward and kicked Vishnu's chest. Lord Vishnu apologized if He had hurt Brighu's foot and began praising Brighu. Brighu immediately felt pleased and could understand that Vishnu was actually the most qualified to receive the offerings from the sacrifice. However, Lakshmidevi, the goddess of fortune and Lord Vishnu's wife, was very displeased by Brighu's action and, therefore, does not bestow much mercy on the brahmanas who, as a result, are often without much money.

Linga basically means a sign or symbol. So the *lingam* is essentially a symbol of the shapeless universal consciousness of Lord Shiva. "Shiva" also means that in which the creation lies dormant after the annihilation. So, one explanation is that the *lingam* is a representative of the dormant universal consciousness in which all created things rest after the cosmic annihilation. It also represents the *pradhana*, the potential but unmanifest ingredients of the material world. Another explanation is that Shiva means auspicious. So the *linga* is the shapeless symbol for the great god of auspiciousness. It is intended to bring the shapeless unknown into our attention.

The *yoni* upon which the *lingam* often sits represents the manifest universal energy. From the unmanifest comes the manifest energy, through which all other things are created. The *yoni*, which is a symbol of Shakti, combined with the *lingam*, is a symbol of the eternal union of the paternal and maternal principles, or the positive and negative, or the static and dynamic energies of the Absolute Reality. It is the communion of the eternal consciousness and dynamic power of the Shakti, the source of all actions and changes. It is also the symbol for the creation of the universe through the combination of the active energy of Lord Shiva and his Shakti. This is how Lord Shiva and Durga are considered the parents of the universe. The symbolism of the *lingam* and *yoni* also represents the base of the spine, meaning the Muladhara *chakra*, upon which the *kundalini* is resting, waiting for awakening.

The *lingas* in the temples are often formed in three parts. The lowest part is the base square called the Brahmabhaga or Brahma-pitha, which represents the creator Brahma. The next part in the middle is the octagonal Vishnubhaga or Vishnu-pitha, which signifies Lord Vishnu the sustainer. Both of these parts form the pedestal. The top cylindrical portion is the Rudrabhaga or Shiva-pitha, which is also called the Pujabhaga since this is the worshipable part. The top portion is also meant to symbolize the projecting flame or fire. This flame also represents the destructive aspects as well as the preserving power of God.

There are twelve important *jyotirlinga* (self-manifested *linga*) temples scattered across India. They are found at Kedarnatha, Kashi Visvanatha, Somnatha, Baijnath, Ramesvare, Ghrisnesvar, Bhimasankar, Mahakala, Mallikarjuna, Amalesvar, Nagesvar, and Tryambakesvar. The five Pancha Bhuta *lingas* in India are located at Kalahastisvar, Jambukesvar, Arunachalesvar at Tiruvannamalai, Ekambesvara at Kanchipuram, and Nataraja at Chidambaram. The temple of Lord Mahalinga at Tiruvidaimarudur (Madhyarjuna) is also a great temple in South India.

The reason Lord Shiva is often worshiped by pouring Ganges water over the *lingam* is that it represents the Ganges or Ganga descending from heaven on to Shiva's head. The legend is that when the Ganges first began to flow to the earthly planet from the heavenly region, the force of it would have destroyed the earth. To prevent this, Lord Shiva agreed to let the river first fall on his head before it formed into a river. It is also explained that when worshipers pour milk or Ganga water on the *linga*, it represents the pouring of ghee on the sacred fire in the fire ceremony, or *yajna*. This is the symbolic offering of ourselves to God.

This further helps to show how the *lingam* is not formless nor really a form, but a symbol for the divinity of Lord Shiva. In Sanskrit, *linga* also means "mark." It is a mark or symbol of Lord Shiva in the same way that large puddles of water is an indication of heavy rains. It is an inference for something else, like the form of that which is formless and omnipotent.

THIRUKKOVILUR (or TIRUKOILUR)

Thirukkovilur is our next stop located about 35 kilometers south of Tiruvannamali and 40 km west of Villupuram. Its history makes it occupy a distinct place in Vaishnava history. It is one of the 108 Divya Desams of Lord Vishnu. The Kshetra Khanda section in the *Padma Purana* discusses some of the glories of this holy place. It is associated with the Trivikrama *avatara* of Lord Vishnu. After Trivikrama or Lord Vamana had taken the whole universe with three steps from Bali Maharaja, ablution to Trivikrama's feet was performed by Brahma with the sacred waters of the Ganges. That water trickled off His feet and took the form of the sacred tank called the Chakra Tirtha. Indra is said to have had a dip in that water tank, and regained his lost possessions that had been taken by Bali. That same water was the source of the river Pennar (Pannaiyar) that flows nearby. Ganga Tirtha, Akasa Tirtha, Varaha Tirtha, and Kalava Tirtha are other holy points that are believed to exist in this spot.

The Trivikrama temple occupies an area of five acres. It has two huge towers on the east and west sides. A majestic eleven-tiered *gopuram* located a few yards from the main entrance compares with some of the tallest temple towers found in India. The pilgrim enters the main shrine after passing the Garuda *stambha* and the main tower on the east side. This is said to have been constructed under the direction of Tirumangai Alwar.

In the sanctum, the deity of Trivikrama is enormous and must be about 15 feet tall from top to bottom. He is very beautiful, black in color with gold hands and feet and ornaments. He wears a garland of *salagram shilas* and another of gold coins, and is dressed in fine cloth. You can see His huge gold foot under the altar. It is a great experience to have *darshan* of this diety of Trivikram, one of the few and one of the largest standing Vishnu deities I have seen. He has one leg raised to measure the heavens, and the second one is placed upon Bali Maharaja's head, which brings out the devotion and reverence in the devotee. Trivikrama's right hand holds the conch shell. The deity is made of wood and faces east. You can also see Brahma and Namuchi, the son of Bali, offering obeisances at Trivikrama's foot. The priest will use the ghee lamp to show you Brahma on the wall and the other images of personalities in the sanctum. Nearby you can see Sukra, the sage Mrikanda and his wife Sridevi and the three Alwars—Poigai, Bhuthatha, and Pei Alwar.

There is also a shrine to Durga at this temple. It is said that she was performing spiritual austerities at the foot of the Vindhya mountains. Trivikrama requested her to take up the position as a guardian of the temple, which she did. Thus, she has her own shrine here.

Another large shrine has the consorts known as Pushpavalli Thayar or Poongoval Nachiar who blesses the devotees. Other shrines in the temple complex are to Lord

Vishnu's *avataras* as well as to deities of Lakshmi Narayana, Lakshmi Narasimha, Andal, Rama, Varadaraja, Viswaksena, Ramanuja, and other devotees.

In the days of the Alwars, this temple was a major pilgrimage center. The Pandava brother Arjuna is also believed to have visited this holy place during his tour of South India. According to "15 Vaishnava Temples of Tamil Nadu" (p. 44) by M. Rajagopalam, the main shrines were originally built of bricks. In the days of Vira Rajendra Chola (1057-58), Narasimha Varma reconstructed the central shrines with granite. Munificent grants of land, gold, and paddy executed by Chola rulers like Kulothunga, Udayar Rajendra, Rajendra II, and Chola Keraladeva, Vikramapandya, Koperunjinga, and Vijayanagara rulers Saluva Narasimha and Sadasiva Raya, are gleaned from the many inscriptions found in the temple. The temple was expanded with elaborate *mandapa* halls in the days of the Vijayanagara and Nayak rulers. The temple even served as a fortress for the British during the Carnatic wars. It was even attacked during the days of Hyder Ali.

In the township of Thirukkovilur you can also find the Veerattaneswara Swamy temple of Kilur and the Oppilamaneeswara temple of Arankandanallur, both of which are known to have ancient histories.

AUROVILLE

Another *ashrama* that's popular with Westerners is the Sri Aurobindo Ashram, located along the coast in Pondicherry, southeast of Tiruvannamalai. This was founded in 1926 and has many programs in the evening that are open to all visitors. Auroville, a project of the Aurobindo Ashram, 10 kilometers north of Pondicherry, was to be an example of how all people could live in peace and harmony above the distinctions of race and creed. It was started in 1968 and at first attracted many people, particularly Europeans, and many organizations donated lots of money for its growth. But a power struggle followed for control of Auroville when "The Mother" died in 1973. She was Mirra Alfassa who joined Aurobindo's household in 1920. Mirra and Aurobindo together launched a spiritual movement that was to show the world that India had the means to raise the human race to a higher consciousness. It was actually under her management that the original small group of students became a community of over 1200 participants, later to be called the Sri Aurobindo Society. And it was also Mirra who envisioned the Auroville project. But at one point after her death, things got so bad that construction on many buildings was stopped and help was needed to prevent many of the residents from going hungry. Later, the Indian government had to step in to make some managerial decisions for its continued operation. Nonetheless, some construction has gone on and there are now new forests where there was once only dry land, and there were over 700 residents again.

There is, however, some controversy surrounding the *ashrama* and it tends to be somewhat unpopular with local people due to the way it has managed the society. Its spiritual philosophy is based on a combination of yoga and modern science. Whether this is effective or not for you is something you would have to find out for yourself, opinions tend to sway either way. Sri Aurobindo, however, has written many books and provided many insights into the practicality of Hinduism and the direction of India.

There are still a number of projects going on at Auroville, and a couple thousand residents, mostly from the West. But if you are looking for the traditional Eastern or spiritual culture, you may need to look elsewhere. Of course, if you are in the area you can always drop by to check it out.

TIRUVANDHIPURAM

Tiruvandhipuram is a small town located on the banks of the Kedilam (or Gadilam) River about five kilometers from Cuddalore. It is best to stay at Cuddalore and then take local transportation to the temple at Tiruvandhipuram when visiting. It is the only Vaishnava holy place located along this river, which provides a nice backdrop for the temple. On the northern banks are the Shaivite places of Tiruppadiripuliyur, Tirunavalur, and Tiruamur. Tirumanikuli and Sendamangalam are found on the southern banks.

The temple's main entrance is to the east, although without any tower. The west side has a simple five-tiered *gopuram* that faces the river. The main deity is known as Devanarayan or Devanatha, and is in a standing posture facing east. The *utsava* or smaller festival deity is known by other names such as Muvaragghia, Achyuta, Dvishatnatha, Devanatha, Vibhuthanatha, and Dasasathya. His divine consort is also located in a spacious sanctum where she is seen in a sitting pose, and is known by many names, including Senkamalavalli Thayar, Hemambujavalli Thayar, Vaikunthanayagi, and Amritavasini. The temple interior also has shrines for several other deities as well, such as the most beautiful deities of Sita-Rama, Lakshmana and Hanuman.

Worship or *pujas* are conducted in the temple four times a day. There are major festivals throughout the year, among which is the 10-day festival in Chithari (April-May) and the Margazhi festival that lasts 21 days. During the Masi Magam festival, the deity is taken in a grand procession to the Cuddalore coast where He has a dip in the sea.

The nearby "Oushada Giri" hill is said to be a fragment of the Sanjeevi Hill that was carried by Hanuman to cure Lakshmana of his wounds, as described in the *Ramayana*. A small shrine at the top accommodates the deities of Hayagriva, Lakshmi, Venugopala, Adisesha, and Garudalwar. This Hayagriva (horse-headed *avatara* of the Lord) is one of the only of its kind in South India. Hayagriva is propitiated as the one who gives *jnana* (knowledge) which repulses ignorance.

A longstanding custom is that the presiding deity of Devanatha is the elder brother to Lord Venkatachalapathi, the deity at Tirupati. So, according to this tradition, the devotees who cannot visit Tirupati can make offerings and fulfill their vows for Tirupati here at Thiruvandhipuram.

A number of *tirthas* exist at this holy place. One of which is a lake known as Vraja Tirtha. A holy bath in it is said to be equal to bathing in all the holy places of heaven. The Garuda Tirtha is also said to be the origin of the Kedilam River, after MahaVishnu allowed Garuda to take a ceremonial bath there during the *rathotsavam* festival. A place called the Sesha Tirtha has now taken the shape of a well, the wall of which is embellished with the image of a serpent. Devotees pour many offerings into it that range from milk, pepper, jaggery, camphor, etc. The water is used for cooking food in the temple to offer to the Lord.

This holy place is described in five chapters of the *Brahmananda Purana*, the *Brahma Naradiya Purana*, and four chapters of the *Kantha Purana*. The history of this place is that a group of sages went to Tirupatkadal to have *darshan* of MahaVishnu. But Narayana could not be found there, so they moved on to Sri Vaikuntam. However, they were also disappointed there at the time, so they were directed to a serene spot that was in between Kanchipuram to the north, Kumbakonam to the south, and Thiruvenkatam to the northwest. At this place there was Bhudevi and the sage Markandeya engaged in austerities to invoke the vision of MahaVishnu. So when the sages arrived, they had a beautiful *darshan* of the lovely form of MahaVishnu as He wore His Kaustuba gem, armbands, and crown. His Sudarshana chakra weapon and the Panchajanya conch shell were also in attendance. His nails glowed like the moon, His eyes twinkled like gems, His white teeth were like pearls, and His muscular arms resembled elephant trunks. This was the form that made the devotees feel the delight of transcendental ecstasy. The atmosphere also vibrated with musical instruments that accompanied devotional hymns. Others were also there to offer salutations to the Lord, such as Garuda, Bhudevi, Markandeya, Sanatkumara, and so on.

Mahalakshmi was happy to see the penance shown by the sage Markandeya. So she blessed him with her presence as a child that appeared on a fragrant lotus. The sage gladly took her as his own child. He named her Tarangamukha Nandini, since she was found on a lotus on the gentle waves of the river. She fully bloomed into a paragon of beauty, talented in all the arts under his care. At the appropriate time MahaVishnu appeared and took her as His wife.

Another history of this temple explains its origin. This *kshetra* was named Tiruvahindrapuram in honor of Adisesha (Ahindra) who called for Devanatha (Vishnu). It was once a Shiva temple and later converted to a Vishnu temple. The local Chola ruler was such a Shiva fanatic that he would demolish any Vaishnava temple that he saw. Then he came to Tiruvandhipuram and marched up to the temple gates. He then saw the images of Vinayaka and Dakshinamurthy, who are usually associated with Shiva temples, and he became perplexed. As he came near the sanctum, Lord Devanatha showed His form as the combined features of the Trimurti or Vishnu, Brahma, and Shiva. Even today one can see the *utsavar* deity bearing the marks of the lotus of Brahma, the conch and disc of Vishnu, and the third eye of Shiva. Thus, He shows the unity of the three deities.

CHIDAMBARAM

The Chidambaram temple is dedicated to Nataraja, dancing Shiva. It is also one of the five important places of pilgrimage that represents one of the five elements. Chidambaram represents space. This is why when we enter the inner temple for *darshan* we can see that to the right of the image of Nataraja in the sanctum is a circular arch under which there is no image but from which hangs a string of golden vilva leaves which represents Shiva as *akasha*, or the element of air or ether.

The temple complex is large and located in the center of town. It covers 13 hectares of land and its *gopurams* reach up to 49 meters high on the north and south sides. It also has a hall of 1000 pillars, which is open only at certain times of the year. The temple employs 300 families to help with its operation. In this temple, the *puja* (worship) is performed strictly according to the Vedic rites and the brahmanas receive no salary for doing the worship. There are three *pujas* in the morning and three in the evening. There are also several festivals held each year, but one of the most important is, of course, Shiva Ratri, which is a big 10-day celebration.

According to the *Puranas*, this temple is where Lord Shiva exhibited his cosmic (Paramanantha, very joyful) dance to many demigods and sages thousands of years ago. After the dance, the sages Patanjali and Vyagrapada requested him to accept worship and exhibit his dance forever in this place for the good of his devotees. Thus, Shiva granted their request for the benefit of the world. Though the present temple was built in the 10th century C.E., the history of this place dates back much further.

The history of the temple building is said to go back to the Chola king, Simhavarman, who, before being crowned king, was suffering a prolonged disease. While wandering around the country, he was told by a hunter about the self-manifesting Shiva *linga* in the Tillai forest, Chidambaram. Simhavarman reached the forest and met Vyagrapada and Patanjali and requested that they cure his disease. They instructed him to bathe in the water of the sacred tank Shivagangai (presently the large pool on the north side of the temple) and to worship the Shiva *linga*. Having done so, he was at once cured of his disease and his body turned golden in color, for which he was named Himayavarman or Hiranyavarman. After being crowned king, he returned to the Tillai forest with great wealth and built a big temple for Lord Shiva and the many Gods and demigods who had witnessed Lord Shiva's dance many hundreds of years earlier. In the days of later Chola kings, they also served this temple and through the years added many structural additions. The central hall was covered with gold by the Chola king Paranthaka I at the beginning of the 10th century.

There is a large *gopuram* (gate tower) in each of the four directions in the outer walls. The west and south *gopurams* date back to the time of Maravarman Kulashekhar in the 13th century. The east *gopuram* also dates back to that time. The north *gopuram* was built by the Vijayanagara king Krishnadevaraya. You can see all of the 108 postures (*mudras*) of the Bharatnatyam dance depicted as sculptures on both sides of the *gopurams*. Other beautiful sculptures on the *gopurams* include Durga in combat, Vishnu on Garuda, Shanmukha fighting Taraka, Shiva dancing, and many other pastimes from the Puranic legends.

When we enter on the south side, we can first go around the temple courtyard and visit the many outer shrines and temples. We first see a small shrine for Lord Ganesh, one of Shiva's sons. As we circumambulate to the left, we can also visit the shrine to Lord Murugan, the other son of Shiva. Going further around, we can visit more shrines, such as those to Vishnu, Lakshmi, and others. There is also the sacred water tank nearby, and then the hall of 1000 pillars, which is not used anymore and rarely open. But there is also another outer hall with many beautifully carved pillars with horse figures on the east side of the temple building.

We enter the very large temple building from its east or west entrance. The east side has 21 steps to the inner hallways. It has halls all the way around it with many carved columns, interspersed with shrines and priests doing worship. Throughout the complex are smaller temples and shrines for personalities such as Shivakumasundari (Shiva's consort whose name means the beautiful girl who invoked Shiva's love), Durga, Ganesh, Nandi, Subramanya, and many other aspects of Shiva. We can walk around the building to see the many aspects of this place, the halls and lamps. As we work our way through, we arrive at the inner courtyard where the main temple is located, noted for its golden roof. It is said that it has 21,600 golden tiles (which represent the average number of time a man breathes in a day) held on by 72,000 nails (the average number of heartbeats in a day). The roof is crested by nine golden *tealasas* (pots). These represent the three actors (time, space, and causation), the three *gunas* or modes of action (*sattva*, *rajas*, and *tamas*, or goodness, passion, and ignorance), and the three functions of creation, preservation, and destruction. It is here where everyone gathers for the main worship of Lord Shiva in the morning and evenings.

The sanctum has an image of Shiva as Nataraja in his dancing pose, but also as the Akash Linga, the *lingam* of space or ether. This is why when we enter the inner temple, to the right of the image of Nataraja in the sanctum is a circular arch under which there is no image but from which hangs a string of golden vilva leaves which represents Shiva as *akasha*, or the element of ether. This wisdom (*chit*) or space or atmosphere (*ambaram*) is the basis of the name of Chidambaram. Also used in worship on special occasions is a small crystal or ruby which represents the Shiva *lingam*.

When I was there they had a special bathing ceremony in which the priests bathed the crystal *lingam* of Shiva in a variety of elements. Many people came to see it. I stood near the right side of the temple platform, just outside the silver doors. Directly in front of me was a spout where the water and milk used in the bathing drained down from the platform. Many people came to collect this *caranamritam* water in their hands and sip it or pour some over their heads. Others had containers to collect larger quantities. But everyone treated it with special regard. After the bathing, they set the Shiva deity up on the altar again and then performed the *arati*, the ceremony in which they offer the deity of Nataraja (dancing Shiva) sweet incense and large flames in the ghee lamps. It was a most interesting experience.

The reason Lord Shiva is often worshiped by pouring Ganges water over the *lingam* is that it represents the Ganges descending from heaven on to Shiva's head. The legend is that when the Ganges first began to flow to the earthly planet from the heavenly region, the force of it would have destroyed the earth. To prevent this, Lord Shiva agreed to let the river first fall on his head before forming into a river.

Close to the main Shiva temple is also a Vishnu temple with a reclining Vishnu and Parathasarthi deities. In fact, a unique and rarely seen thing about this place is that from one position in the sanctum you can have *darshan* of both Shiva (by looking straight ahead) and Lord Vishnu (by looking to your left). There is another Vishnu temple in the complex with Lakshmi-Narayana deities. And in the Nritta Sabha court, which is carved to resemble a large chariot with horses and wheels, there is a temple of Shiva in his angry form.

The months of June and December are when they hold the main festivals, each ten days long. On the ninth day the deities are taken around the town on a *rath* cart. The wooden cart is pulled by thousands of people to its destination. The tenth day is for the special *darshan*.

In the early morning you can also witness the way they wake the deities. They take Lord Shiva from his room with Parvati, which is across the courtyard from the temple, and bring him to the main temple when they start the main *pujas*. Many people attend and then circumambulate the temple afterwards. In the evening they also bring Lord Shiva back to his evening room. .

Chidambaram is a great temple. If you are in South India, be sure to stop in to see this place. Visitors come from all over India. Group tours of Westerners regularly come through, but being able to visit on your own or with a few friends and take some time to absorb the atmosphere is the best way to see it. The nice thing about it is that you are allowed to see as much as anyone else. You can watch all the ceremonies and deity worship along with the Indian visitors. Thus, the temple is a great place to study and learn Eastern philosophy and watch how real Vedic brahmanas live and perform their rituals.

The one unfortunate thing is that unlike in 1990 when I first visited, now (in 2001) they are charging entrance fees to visit, at least among the foreigners. They say it is to help maintain the temple, which is all right but you never know. They told me if I did not give a certain amount that I should leave. That is not exactly real hospitable, and I have never experienced that before. If they had been friendlier about it I may have complied. I new better than to think I would be forced to leave, so I gave a small portion of what they wanted. I also noticed that this was only on the western entrance. People entering by other doors were not faced with this sort of thing. Also, you used to be able to take photographs of the interior of the temple but just not of the deities, but now that is also restricted to only the outer courtyard. This is probably for security reasons, which is a new concern for many temples after some have been attacked and people have been killed by Islamic fundamentalists.

Nonetheless, you can spend plenty of time wandering around the grounds and hallways of this complex, finding the different temples and getting *darshan* of the deities. If you are not sure where to look, just ask. Temple assistants can guide you. Although some travel books say not to bother with taking on a guide, it really depends on the temple, how big it is, and how much time you have. If your time is limited and you want to see a lot of the temple quickly, then it may be best to have a guide give you a quick tour and then continue on your own. In many cases, however, a guide may be nothing more than a useless waste of time and money, telling you things that you already know, or not telling you much at all if his accent is too thick and you do not know Hindi.

At Chidambaram I had a guide who had been at this temple for 20 years and spoke fairly good English. He had also helped work on Mike Wood's video on Chidambaram for the B.B.C. He helped show me where the many temples were and after he saw that I was also an initiated brahmana, he arranged for me to get *darshans* of the deities of Vishnu and Shiva, and get closer than some of the regular Indian visitors were allowed. He also arranged for me to receive deity remnants like flower garlands and sweets that had been offered to the deities. He also told me what times the special ceremonies took place so I could be sure to attend, and he was also there to meet me and explain what was taking place. This can be important since some temples may do things differently than others. And you will want to know exactly what is happening if you have never seen it before so you can understand it, even if you are already familiar with most of the customs.

This temple has played a great part in the lives of many saints and poets of the past. Sri Chaitanya also visited this temple nearly 500 years ago. Chidambaram is where you can see how the people of India find harmony and peace in a world full of changes. The people are usually friendly and enthusiastic for sharing what they get in their abandonment for the soul. Here, or in any holy city of India, the people know why they are in this world, how they fit into it, and who they are. They may have much less than most Westerners have, materially speaking, but they have much less to worry about as well and are often happier. I actually felt quite at home here. So it was with some regret when I said farewell and took a motor *ricksha* to the train station to reach my train for my next stop. For some travelers, the next destination may be Kumbakonam. But I wanted to go to Vaithisvarankoil for an astrological Bhrigu reading.

SIRKAZHI

Sirkazhi (Shiyall), which is just south of Chidambaram and about 50 km northeast of Kumbakonam, is a place that a few people may want to stop and see. There are several temples here that can be visited in a day or two. There is the Taadaalan temple of Trivikrama one km from the railway station. Five km east is the Senganmal temple and Manikkooda temple. Ten km east is the Gopala Krishna temple at Thirukkavallambadi. Elevan km southeast is the Kannan Narayana temple at Tiruvellakkulam (Annankoil). Ten km southeast is the Vayalali Manavalam temple at Thiruvasli. Fifteen km away is the Taamaraiyaal Kelwan temple. Eight km east is the Narayana Koil temple, with the Kudamaadu Kootham temple nearby. The Vaikunthanatha temple is also eight km east, and the Perarulaalar temple at Tiruvanpurodottam is eight km southeast of town. The Daivanaayaka Perumal temple is also eight km from town at Tiruttevanarthogai.

VAIDESVARANKOIL (or VAITHISVARANKOIL)

This is a small village about 25 to 30 miles south from Chidambaram, and just south of Sirkazhi. It is about an hour bus ride south from Chidambarama. It has an important Shiva temple here and is where many people come for getting an astrological Bhrigu reading. It has horoscopes on leaves for everyone. It is said that it can take up to seven days for a complete astrological history. But for that you have to go to the Bhrigu readers who are the most knowledgeable.

After departing from the bus at the corner of town and checking into a hotel on the main road, I first went to the Shiva temple where I knew I could find information about local Bhrigu readers. The thing was that in the front of the temple near the main road, there were so many young men asking if I wanted a reading. They were all representing one person. This through up a red flag to me because I knew that if everyone wants you to go to a certain person, that means they are getting a commission for bringing you. I do not want to go to a person who is paying others for clients. So I went to the other side of the temple and no one approached me. I actually had to ask about it. Then an older person reluctantly advised me and called over someone to take me to a reader. I had never had such a reading before, so I was mostly doing it for the fun and experience.

I was taken down the road to a reader, a jolly pot-bellied man who was not far away in a little hut. He worked as the translator and his son-in-law was the astrologer. He also had others waiting to see him. During my turn he took my thumb print and I was asked various questions about my date of birth and my life. From this they were able to pick out a leaf that held the information that most closely matched my situation. It was quite interesting. It had my parents and sister on it, and other things about me. Then I was asked to wait. After an hour or so I was called into the next room to have a reading. This lasted for about 45 minutes, and through the translator my basic future was foretold. I found it quite fascinating and powerful. They also recorded the session on tape. All of this took a few hours, and I left with the tape and some basic notes that I had gathered while there. After that I walked back down the road to visit the temple.

The Shiva temple here is quite larger than I had expected, almost as big as Chidambaram, but the *gopurams* are not as prominent. It is a long temple, and no one here bothers you about money. There are few beggars in this town. The temple also has numerous columns, and long halls in which there was a wedding taking place in one. At the sanctum, I easily entered and the guard there was kind enough to show me around and explain a few things. I was able to get *darshan* of the main temple sanctum of Sri Vaidyanathaswamy, as well as the other smaller shrines for the other divinities. The shrine for Murugan is said to be where he received his trident. And the Jatayu Kundam found from the southern hallway is where Jatayu, the great devotee bird of Lord Rama, had his last rites performed by Lord Rama.

After having visited the temple and my Bhrigu reading, I was quite satisfied with my visit to this town, though it is a little out of the way. Once we are finished here, we take a bus onward to Mayuram and then on to Kumbakonam.

MAYURAM

This town is a bus ride a couple hours southwest from Vaidesvarankoil. Mostly we are just stopping here because we need to connect with another bus. We get off at one bus stop, walk down several blocks to another bus station, where we wait for our bus to arrive. The trick is to make sure we get on the right bus. Fortunately, we find some others who are also waiting for the same bus. And once it comes in, we are on our way to Kumbakonam.

However, if you want to see the Shiva temple here, the presiding deity here is the Swayambhu Lingam, which is called Sri Mayuranathaswamy, along with his consort

Abhayapradhambika. Tradition is that Parvati Devi assumed the form of a mayura (peahen) and worshiped Shiva here, and, thus, attained reunion with him. Many others are also said to have visited this place to worship Lord Shiva, such as Brahma, Lakshmi, Brihaspati, Indra, and sages like Agastya Muni.

KUMBAKONAM

Kumbakonam is an interesting town with many shops, bazaars, people wandering through the streets engaged in all kind of activities, and, of course, many temples. The temples are of all sizes, from quite large to no bigger than a closet. But there are several significant temples to see in this city. Plus, if we have time, this place is a good stopping off point from which we can take day trips by bus to many other temples in the region, which we will also describe.

First, we will see the Sarangapani Vishnu temple which ranks third with the Sri Rangam and Tirupati temples in importance, and is the largest Vaishnava temple in town. It covers 3 acres of land and the main *gopuram* is 147 feet tall with 12 storeys and is covered with sculptures. The sanctum and large front *mandapam* (hallway) enclosed in the building are built to resemble a huge chariot with large wheels and horses. Legend is that the sage Himarishi invoked the aid of Lord Vishnu from this place, who then descended to earth in a chariot. By the side of the temple is the Golden Lotus Tank, also known as Lakshmi Thirtham. It is related that Goddess Lakshmi performed penance here to attract Vishnu, who came down as Aravamudhan and married Her. Sri Sarangapani, Aravamudhan, and Komalavalli are the deities here. The reclining Vishnu is really beautiful in black stone and with silver feet and ornaments. The small *utsava* deities stand in front. Another shrine is nearby with goddess Lakshmi.

The Adi Kumbhesvara is the temple after which the town is named. It is in the heart of the city and has a *gopuram* that is 128 feet tall and beautifully carved and painted. It is dedicated to Shiva and the *linga* in the main shrine is in the shape of a *kumbha* (pot), beneath which stands Nataraja, dancing Shiva. The legendary basis of this temple is that Shiva once gave a pot that held the seed of creation to Lord Brahma. During the great deluge the pot was carried to this place where the pot was broken and the contents drained out and spread over an area of 10 miles. This nectar settled in two places: one was the Mahamaham tank on the other side of town, and the other place was the Portamarai tank of the Sarangapani temple. Out of the broken pieces of the pot and the wet sand, Shiva made a *lingam* which he installed here at the Kumbhesvara temple and called it Sri Adi Kumbeswara. In the Navaratri Mandapam (hall of the planets), all the 27 stars and 12 Rasis (zodiac signs) have been carved from one block of stone. The temple also has many painted pillars and fine sculptures, and Westerners are allowed inside.

The next temple is the Chakrapani temple, which is dedicated to Lakshmi, the goddess of fortune and wife of Lord Vishnu. One has to climb a flight of stairs to see the colorful eight-armed image in the sanctum of the main building. Another shrine is across from it in which you must climb some stairs to reach its sanctum. Many women attend this temple.

From here we go to the Sri Ramaswami temple, which is dedicated to Lord Ram-achandra, another incarnation of Lord Vishnu or Krishna. This temple has deities of Ramachandra and Sita (His wife) sitting on the same seat. Hanuman (His great monkey servant) is portrayed as singing praises to the Lord with vina, and Lakshman and Satrughna (Lord Rama's two brothers) are nearby, one holding a chamara fan and the other an umbrella. They are made out of black stone and decorated with silver jewelry and paraphernalia. All the way around the inside of the walls that enclose the courtyard are many paintings depicting the story of the *Ramayana*.

Another important temple is the Nageshvara with shrines to Shiva and different expansions of Parvati. This is one of the oldest temples in town. It is said that Adisesha and Surya, the sun god, worshiped Sri Nageshvara in this place. The temple is built in such a way that on the 11th, 12th, and 13th of the month of Chitra (March-April) the sun lights the *lingam* in the sanctum. This temple is known for the fine sculptures of the Chola period.

From here we go to a temple that I really liked. It is a good place to sit and relax away from the heat outside and talk with the temple priests. This temple is dedicated to Lord Brahma, which is rare to find. It has no large *gopurams* to show the way. You just have to know where it is or ask your auto-ricksha driver to take you there. But once you enter and go through the hall of carved pillars, you reach the sanctum where there are three altars with beautiful deities. One altar has a big image of Brahma with four heads and four hands, made of black stone and holding silver items in his hands. At his sides are god-desses Sarasvati and Bhumi. The central altar has Lord Vishnu, Lakshmi, and Bhumi. And the third altar has a big Lord Narasimha and Lakshmi. I wish I could have taken photos, but they tend to be quite fussy about that. Some of the blessings of visiting this temple include being successful in your business.

If one wishes, you can go to the big Mahamaham water tank, which covers 20 acres. There are 16 different shrines in the shape of small pavilions along the banks which are dedicated to a variety of Vedic divinities. Once every 12 years on the full moon day of Magha (January-February) there is a festival attended by thousands of pilgrims who bathe here. At that time it is considered that all the holy rivers of India enter this tank. Taking a dip in this tank on that day is believed to give the person the merit of bathing in all the holy rivers. The last festival was in 1992 and 2004. Next to the Mahamaham water tank is also the local Kashi Visvanatha temple which has the personified forms of some of the main sacred rivers of India, such as the Cauvery, Ganga, and others whose shrines are located around the central sanctum that holds a Shiva *lingam* known as Visvanatha.

Other temples in Kumbakonam include the Banapurishvara, the Gautameshvara, the Somesvara, Somanatha, and Vedaranya Perumal temples.

GANGAKONDACHOLAPURAM

This temple is 35 kilometers north of Kumbakonam. Not many people come here to visit and it is no longer a functioning temple, so it is now only a grand reflection of the past. This place can be visited as a day trip from Kumbakonam or on your way from Chidambaram. It has an enormous temple, also built smaller but similar to the temple in Tanjore in the 11th century by King Rajendra Chola to commemorate his northern conquests. Dedicated to Shiva, it has many beautiful sculptures and a large water tank said to have received many large pots of Ganges water. In the sanctum, the *lingam* is more than four meters high and the *peetam* (seat) is 18.5 meters in circumference. In the interior of the temple is a huge representation of the nine planets (Navagrahas) installed on the shape of a chariot. Surya (the sun) occupies the prominent position in the chariot and Saturn is the driver, while the other planets are on the sides.

DHARASURAM

This town is only four kilometers west of Kumbakonam, a small town with two old but well preserved temples, easily reached by auto-ricksha. They are built side by side, separated by their huge outer walls. The first temple, the Daivanayaki Ammoan goddess temple, is interesting and built much like the second temple next to it. It keeps intact the atmosphere of the old ways and traditions. The second temple, the Airateshvara, is in much better shape and is a good example of Chola architecture. The legend is that Airavata, Indra's white elephant, and Yama, the god of death, had worshiped Shiva here. Thus, the name Airateshvara. The temple was built in the 12th century and is little used but is still a functioning temple in the morning. Otherwise, the sanctum is locked. The temple is in a rectangular court surrounded by a colonnade, which is entered through two gateways. The exterior of the temple building has rows of stone sculptures and images of demigods, goddesses, saints, folk art, etc. Inside the temple, which has a large *mandapa* hall in front of the sanctum, there are many more stone images on the walls and columns, especially different aspects of Shiva. Lotus designs and musicians are carved on the ceilings. The entrance hall is built to resemble a chariot. You can go into the sanctum, which is topped by a structure that reaches 85 feet high, and see the Shiva *linga*. The old priest or the temple guide will show you around and tell you all about this place. He is remembered with fondness by all who visit. This temple is definitely worth visiting.

There is also the Shakti Thazhuviya Nathar temple at Thirushaktimutham 3 km from Darasuram, as well as the Sri Somanathaswamy temple at Kizhapazhayarai 5 km from Darasuram.

SWAMIMILAI

Swamimilai is another four kilometers farther west of Dharasuram with its Swaminathaswamy temple. This colorful temple with various sculptures outside along the walls is dedicated to Murugan, who appears in the form of teaching his father, Lord Shiva, the Pranava (Om) mantra which Shiva had forgotten. The temple is very active with many people who stand in line for *darshan*. The temple is reached by climbing 60 stairs up to the main shrine dedicated to Murugan. First, as you enter the line, on the left you go pay for special *darshan* tickets and then get in line for a chance to have a close *darshan* of the main image of Murugan much more quickly. This allows you to take a side entrance into the sanctum when you reach it, thus avoiding the longer line of people. Thirty steps up you will see the life-like image of Murugan teaching Shiva the mantra. The presiding deity in the sanctum, Sri Swaminathaswamy, is a six foot tall granite image of Murugan in a standing position. You can stand there for a little while watching the worship before making way for others to get a view.

Back on the ground floor are other shrines for Sri Sundareshwarar, goddess Meenakshi, and Vinayaga. In front of the temple are many shops selling devotional items. This town also features artists who still make bronzes by hand in the traditional way of their Chola ancestors.

TIRUVALAMJULI

If you are going to be staying in Kumbakonam for a while and want to see more of the spiritual culture of India in this area, there are more temples short distances away. Ten kilometers from Kumbakonam near Swamimilai is Tiruvalamjuli with its temple of Sri Vinayaka. It is noted for its architectural grandeur, intricate stone windows, and fine sculptures. The sanctum that houses a white deity of Sri Vinayaka is full of architectural splendor, but it is an old temple and in need of much renovation. Smaller shrines are also found in the complex. The legendary basis of this temple is that when the demigods churned the ocean of milk for the special nectar for immortality, they had ignored the worship of Sri Vinayaka and, thus, first produced poison from the ocean, which was swallowed by Shiva. When they realized their mistake, the demigods took the white foam from the ocean and fashioned an image of Vinayaka; therefore the deity in the temple is white. Some temple rooms had little light to see the interior of the central images. So be sure to bring your own flashlight or torch as they call them here while visiting this temple.

SURYANARCOIL

This town is 15 kilometers east of Kumbakonam. It is said to be the only temple in the south dedicated to Surya, the sun god. The navagrahas (nine planets) are believed to influence the destinies of people. Thus, they are worshiped to acquire peace, prosperity, longevity, and other good results. The central shrine of this temple complex faces west and is dedicated to the sun. The other eight planets, namely Brihspati, Rahu, Sukra, Ketu, Chandra, Angaraka, Budha, and Sani, also have shrines in the courtyard. In the sanctum, Brihaspati is shown worshiping Lord Shiva as Suryanarayana.

TRIBHUVANAM (THIRUBHUVANAM or TIRUBHUVANAM)

This town is eight kilometers east from Kumbakonam, a village with its temple dedicated to Shiva as Sri Kampaharesvara. It is an impressive and colorful temple, built in the 13th century by the Chola King Tribhuvana Chakravarti. It is similar to the temple in Tanjore. The tower and sides of the temple are full of sculpted figures depicting scenes from the *Puranas*. The unique point of this temple is the shrine to Sarabha, the form Shiva took as a bird-man to subdue the divine fury of Vishnu when He appeared as Lord

Narasimha. This is an interesting place, but mostly if you have not already seen many of the temples already described.

OTHER TEMPLES IN THE AREA OF KUMBHAKONAM

Other temples in the area of Kumbhakonam include the Sri Ramalingaswamy temple at Papanasam 14 km from Kumbhakonam, the Sri Kalyanasundareswarar temple at Nallur 5 km from Papanasam, the Sri Mullaivananathaswami temple at Thirukkarugavur 5 km from Papanasam, and the Madhyarjuna temple at Tiruvidaimarudur 8 km from Kumbhakonam, The Venkatachalapathi Vishnu temple at Uppiliappancoil 6 km from Kumbhakonam is one of Divya Desams, or 108 most holy places of Lord Vishnu.

If you really want to see more temples in the area, you can take some of the bus lines out of Kumbhakonam to reach temples of varying importance, all of which provide blessings for various purposes. So here are a few more temples you can see:

Taking the Tanjore bus route we can see the Pattishwaram temple, to Goddess Durgambigai (10 kms), Thiruskathimutram temple to Sivasakthi Ambigai (10 kms), Oothukadukrishnan (18 kms), Nathankoil to Lord Jagannatha Perumal (15 kms), Udayalur temple for Mahakali (15 kms), Swamimalai (10 kms), Papasanam to 108 Shiva *lingas* (18 kms), Thirukarukavur to Rakshambigai (22 kms).

Taking the bus route to Thiruvaiyar we can see the Ganapathigraharam temple to Maha Ganapathi (25 kms), Thirupurampiyam to Vinayaka (15 kms), Thinagallur as the seat of the moon god Chandra (30 kms), and Thiruvaiyur to Saint Thyagaraja (35 kms).

Taking the bus route to Mayiladuthurai we can see Thirubuvanam for the temple previously described (8 kms), Thiruvidaimarthur temple to Mahalinga Swami (11 kms), Suryanarcoil as described above (15 kms), Kanchanoor temple for Sukra (21 kms), Thirumanacheri for Kalyanasundareshwarar (28 kms), Thiruvenkadu for Budhan (60 kms), Kizhaperumpalam temple dedicated to Kethu (57 kms), and Thirukadaiyur to Ambal Abirami (59 kms).

Taking the bus route to Karaikal we can see the OppiliyappanKoil temple dedicated to Thirumala Venkateshwara (10 kms), Thirunageswaram to Rahu (10 kms), Ayyavadi to Prethayanga Devi (12 kms), Koothanoor to Sarasvati (45 kms), and Thirunallar to Saniswara (57 kms).

Taking the bus route to Nagapattinam we can reach the place of Azhagaputhur to Sri Shanmuganathan or Murugan (6 kms), Nachiyarkoil as described below (10 kms), Thiruvarur as will be described below (30 kms), Sri Vanjiyam to Eman (28 kms), Nagur to Nagore Darga (65 kms), and Vellankanni to Annai Arogya Matha's temple on the seashore (65 kms).

NACHIYARCOIL

Nachiyarcoil, 10 km from Kumbhakonam, has the Srinivasa Perumal Vishnu temple. This temple can be seen on the way to Tirucherai. You will pass right by it. So it is easy to stop and see it and have *darshan* of the deities here. You enter the compound in a hall with a recently constructed roof with huge black stone columns. You climb a short stairway into the front hall. It has nicely carved columns and shrines to other divinities. Then you climb a second stairway. There on the right side you will see a lovely deity of Garuda, Lord Vishnu's bird carrier, again adorned in silver with wings of silver as well. Then, after climbing the third stairway, you arrive at the main sanctum with a beautiful deity of a tall standing Vishnu, Srinivasa, who must be 10 feet tall or so. He is made of black stone and adorned with silver while dressed in yellow cloth. He is quite impressive and lovely. In front you will see the smaller *utsava* deities.

This place also has an ancient history and is considered the birth place of Nachiyar (Sri Devi). On Thursday the deity gives *darshan* with His family seated on the throne of Garuda. It is said that all desires are fulfilled if one participates in the *puja* here.

TIRUCHERAI

Tirucherai is a small village located 15 kilometers southeast from Kumbakonam on the main road to Tiruvarur, which is on our list of the next places to visit. So now we leave the area of Kumbakonam and again head south. Tirucherai, which like many villages may not be on the map, is one of the 108 Divya Desams of Lord Vishnu. It is here at the Saranatha Perumal temple where MahaVishnu resides.

The temple compound occupies 1½ acres of land (116 meters in length, 72 meters wide). In front of the temple is the large Sara Pushkarini water tank, which also occupies the same dimensions. The front gate of the temple complex has a fine looking nine-tiered *gopuram* that rises 120 feet tall. Inside the front gate is an additional but smaller *gopuram* of two tiers that leads into the temple. The sanctum is guarded by two sculpted *dwarapalas* or guards. Inside the sanctum, Saranatha Perumal, the presiding MahaVishnu deity, appears in a standing pose that is twelve feet tall while facing east. He is carved from black stone but is adorned with silver hands and chest plate. It is very auspicious to have *darshan* of this deity. On the left side is the personification of the Cauvery River, Cauvery Devi, and on the right is the sage Markandeya. In front is the smaller *utsavar* festival deity of Saranatha, accompanied by Bhudevi, Sridevi, and Neeladevi. Actually, the presence of all five consorts of Vishnu, namely Sridevi, Neeladevi, Bhudevi, Saranayaki Amman, and Mahalakshmi within the same temple is a unique feature that is not found in other Vaishnava temples.

Many other shrines also exist within the temple, so there are numerous blessings we can receive by visiting each of them. First, another deity of Vishnu as Sri Rajagopalaswamy occupies a separate shrine, and is accompanied by His consorts Rukmini and Satyabhama. Another shrine has Lord Venkatesha as Thiruvenkatamudayan. The metal deities of Sri Rama, Sita, and Lakshmana are in another shrine, as well as Lakshmi-Narasimha. Other shrines are for Kaliyamardhana, Balasaranatha, Senai Mudaliar, Manavala Munigal, Ramanuja, and the twelve Alwars. At the southwestern corner of the Sara Pushkarini lake is a separate shrine for Cauvery who is seen embracing the child form of Vishnu. Images of Brahma and MahaVishnu are also there. This represents the austerity Cauvery Devi performed in order to gain the favor of the Lord.

Texts such as *Brahmanda Purana*, the *Bhavishya Purana* (Chapters 68-72), and the *Maheswara Narada Samvardha* offer descriptions of the importance of this *tirtha* and pastimes related to it. One of the pastimes is described how Lord Shiva explained the significance of Tirucherai to the sage Narada Muni. On the eve of the universal deluge MahaVishnu ordered Brahma to safely keep the sacred Vedic texts, like the *Vedas, Agamas, Sashtras,* and *Puranas* in an enormous earthen pot. But with every attempt the pot would brake. He felt discouraged and prayed to MahaVishnu about this. Vishnu then told him that there are twelve Vaishnava holy places that are the most sacred. These included Sri Rangam, Tirupati, Kanchipuram, Tirunarayanapuram, SriMushnam, Naimisaranya, Kumbakonam, Vrishabathri, Ayodhya, Badarikashrama, and Sara Kshetram (Tirucherai). Out of all of these, He regarded Sara Kshetra as the most sacred. The hallowed center is graced with nine sacred *tirthas* of which the Sara Pushkarini Lake is the highest. So he instructed Brahma to journey to that place and take a dip in the Sara Pushkarini Lake and form a pot from the clay found in the lake. This would be successful. This lake is located across the street in front of the temple.

So Brahma went there and he felt greatly satisfied. He then had a dip into the sacred lake and formed a pot from its clay. The earthen pot stood firm, much to his surprise. Brahma then stored all the major Vedic texts within it and kept them safe. Thus, his mission was complete. It is also believed that the seven great *rishis*, namely Bhrigu, Sowraga, Vyasa, Markandeya, Parasara, Vamadeva, and Baninthrathiya, continue to perform penances there to preserve the holy sanctity of the place.

The Senneriappa Iswara temple, a noted Shiva temple, can also be found in this town along the southern bank of the Cauvery River. This is not far from the Vishnu temple. It is smaller but no less sacred, and the priests are glad to see visitors. In front of the temple is a lake that is said to have been formed by a drop of ambrosia. It is called Jnanavavi or Bindhusuda. It has a small three-tiered *gopuram* over the second entrance into the temple. Passing through a few hallways one can reach the place of the presiding deity. This is the Shiva *linga* known as Senneriappar or Sara Parameswara. The sage Markandeya installed a *linga* in this temple, which is now in the inner sanctum. The sage worshipped it everyday. Surya also is said to have atoned for his participation in Daksha's ritual here. Every year the rays of the sun grace the presiding *linga* for three days in the month of Masi (Feb-Mar). In the inner hallway are other shrines for various Shaivite saints. There are also three images of Durga and two of Chandeswara that are also in this temple. The outer walls of the main shrine have lovely sculptures.

THIRUVARUR

Thiruvarur is a town 50 km east of Tanjore, south of Sirkazhi, about 30 km southeast of Kumbakonam, and is easily reached by bus. It is famous for its temple of Shiva as Sri Thyagaraja. The original structure of this temple, built in the 10th century, was the shrine to Vanmikanatha (Shiva), a Swayambhu *lingam*. The adjacent Thyagaraja temple has divinities of Shiva with Uma (Parvati) and Skanda (son of Shiva and Parvati, also known as Karttikeya, Kumara, and Subrahmanya), and was built in the 13th century. A *sphatika* (crystal) *lingam* is kept in a box inside the shrine. The Nandi here, Shiva's bull carrier, is in a standing position. The grounds have other shrines around the central temple, all with various meanings. These include a shrine to the Goddess as Nilothpalambika in a standing posture, blessing the child Murugan. Another shrine is to Sri Kamalambal, the virgin form of Parvati, doing penances to marry Lord Shiva. Others are for various forms of Shiva, one of which is in the middle for Sri Naganathaswamy.

In a different part of the complex is a temple to Achaleshvara, another aspect of Shiva, also built in the 10th century. Additions to this complex continued up to the 17th century, which include several columned halls, *gopurams*, and ceilings that are adorned with many fine sculptures and paintings.

NAGAPPATTINAM

If you have stayed at Thiruvarur, then it is easy to take a morning bus for a short day trip east to Nagappattinam. It is on the seashore 24 km east of Thiruvarur, or 70 km east of Tanjore. This town has a Vishnu temple with three full sized Vishnu deities that are standing, sitting, and lying on Ananta Sesha. It is a Divya Desam, one of the 108 most important Vishnu temples in India. You go in the front entrance, down a hallway and into the main temple hall and then into the sanctum. This is surrounded by a courtyard wherein we find a few other shrines, such as to Lakshmi. Once inside the sanctum you can see the smaller brass standing Vishnu deity with Sridevi and Bhudevi at His sides. Behind Them is the main deity, Sundaryarajan, who stands over 15 feet tall. He is spectacular, made of shiny black stone, but He and His ornaments and weapons are covered with solid silver, with a gold Lakshmi on His chest. He is really something to see and I was in awe. This was the whole reason for coming here, and was glad to do so. After the crowd moved on, I was able to get a close up view. Afterwards I was able to circumambulate the temple and view the other shrines.

The *Brahmananda Purana* explains that this temple, or the Soundarvaraja Perumal temple, has existed in all four yugas. The legend is that Nagappattinam was originally called Soundaranyam. The name Nagappattinam, which means City of the Serpent, is derived from the fact that Adisesha, in Satya-yuga, performed austerities here to get the blessing to be able to stay forever in the presence of his Lord, Vishnu. The *Purana* also relates how Dhruva also performed austerities in this place. Dhruva's intention was to get the Lord to appear before him and then ask for the blessing of becoming ruler of the entire world. However, when Dhruva saw Lord Vishnu, he was so overwhelmed by the Lord's beauty that he was entirely content and forgot his materialistic wish. He then simply requested the Lord to remain in Nagappattinam as Soundarya Rajan, "The King of Beauty," and bless the devotees. This is how the temple was manifested.

A smaller Vishnu temple is also located here in this town, where I got *darshan* and had fun taking photographs of the children who came to see a white person visit their temple.

The Nilayadvaja Shiva temple in town is dedicated to Karayoganaswami and Neelayadakshi. The place is one of the Shakti Peethams. Shiva as Thyagaraja is also called Sundara Vidangar here. It is a fairly good sized temple with large and old hallways. The people here were having a holiday with a special bathing ceremony of the image and wanted me to stay for it. One family was showing their daughters' expertise in singing Vedic *slokas* and was very friendly, but for lack of time I had to move on.

There is also a temple for the Goddess Miriaman that has large black stone deities of Devi with silver ornaments behind smaller brass deities. It had several other smaller shrines within the complex.

Now as you are traveling in this area, practically every town has a noteworthy temple in it. But if your time is limited, then you have to decide which temples you want to see, which ones are the most important to you and which to leave out. Otherwise, you could be in this region for months just going from one temple town to another.

THIRUKANNAPURAM

Thirukannapuram is the place of the Sowriraja Perumal temple, another form of Vishnu. This town is but a small farming village next to the Mudikondan River, a tributary of the Kaveri. This is not an easy town to find on the map, so it is best to take it as a day trip if you want. The town can be reached by bus from Nagapattinam, Tiruvarur, Kumbakonam, or Mayiladuthurai.

The temple is located in the heart of the village. It has a large seven-tiered *gopuram* that rises up to 100 feet over the eastern entrance. The temple is in a compound of 1½ acres that is surrounded by massive walls covering an area of 316 feet by 210 feet. By passing under the main *gopuram*, you walk to a second smaller three-tiered *gopuram* that is 60 feet tall.

In the inner sanctum, the main deity of Neelamegha Perumal gives *darshan* in a standing position with Sridevi and Bhudevi on either side. On the sides farther away there are the images of Dandaka Maharishi and Garuda.

The main deity holds His discus as if ready to throw it. There is an interesting story that describes that one time the temple was insurmountable with huge walls extending for nearly 13 miles up to the seacoast. One Chola ruler who was a stout Shaivite was determined to crush the temple walls. His minister tried to dissuade him and said that as long as the Tiruvoimozhi and *Ramayana* exist, Vaishnavism cannot be exterminated. But the ruler did not listen. Thus, an ardent devotee fervently prayed to the deity for protection, but there was no reaction. Exasperated, the devotee threw a hand cymbal at the Lord that struck His head. The deity then threw His discus that acted to drive away the Chola forces. It is considered that the deity still bears the mark of the injury.

In the center of the altar is the beautiful *utsavar* or smaller festival deity, known as Sowriraja Perumal. At His sides are Sridevi, Bhudevi, Padmini, and Andal. The festival deity is taken out on a procession around the temple each Friday evening. There is a story of how the deity got the name. A few centuries back, Rangabhattar who was the priest that performed the daily rituals had a courtesan to whom he was greatly attracted. He used to offer the flower garlands first to her before offering them to the deity. This is most offensive in worshiping the deity, who should receive everything fresh and unused by anyone else. One day the Chola ruler noticed a hair in the garland worn by the Lord.

When questioned, the priest said the hair belonged to the deity. In order to save the priest, the Lord himself appeared with a wig. From then onwards He was given the name Sowri (wig) Rajan.

The main *mandap* hall is beautifully set with marble and mirrors. It is in this hall where the festival bathing of the *utsavar* deity takes place. Other nearby shrines includes one for Senai Mudaliar who is considered the general of the Lord's forces and keeper of His weapons. There are also shrines for Sita-Rama and Lakshmana, Nardhana Krishna (another form of the Lord) and the twelve Alwar devotees in separate chambers.

The temple also has four sacred water tanks. The large one is in front of the temple and known as Nitya Pushkarini. It is believed that all the sacred *tirthas* are collected here, and that a dip in it confers prosperity. On the western side of the temple is the Anantapila tank. It is through this tank that Adisesha came to worship the Lord here. On the northern side of the temple is the Muthakaram tank, and another tank is the Boothavadan.

The history of this place is related in the *Sthala* or local *Purana*. It is said that Lord Krishna, also known as Kanna, chose this place as His abode many years ago. It is also considered that Thirukannapuram provides a place wherein the devotee who worships here derives all the benefits of having chanted the Ashtatshara or eight-lettered (in Sanskrit) mantra, which is *Hari Om Narayana*. It is also considered to be Bhuloka Vaikuntham, or the spiritual realm of Vaikuntha on earth. Other centers that offer moksha or liberation to the devoted who worship there include Tirupati, Sri Rangam, Sri Mushnam, Nanguneri, Salagramam, Pushkar, and Badarikashram (Badrinatha).

Pujas are performed six times a day according to the Vaikanasa Agamas. Devotees can have *darshan* of the Lord from 6 A.M. to 12 P.M., and from 4 P.M. to 9 P.M.

MANNARGUDI

Mannargudi is known for the Rajagopalaswamy temple. Mannargudi is a large city located southeast of Tanjore, and only about 26 kilometers southwest of Thiruvarur, easily reached by bus, and almost two hours from Kumbhakonam.

You will notice the tall *gopuram* as you ride into town from the north. It is covered with sculptures only near the top and the rest of it shows architectural designs. You walk through the *gopuram* and into the halls that have numerous carved columns. Going farther in there are various shrines, but inside the sanctum Para Vasudeva is the main deity, which gives the name of the place as Vasudevapuri. He is a beautiful black stone image and gives *darshan* in a standing pose with Sridevi and Bhudevi at His sides. He holds the disc Sudarshan and the conch shell Panchajanya, and is bedecked with golden hands and ornaments, and a garland of gold coins hangs from His neck. His presence is quite powerful. The small festival or *utsavar* deity of Vishnu presents Himself as Rajamannar and Rajagopalan, which thus also gives the name of Rajamannargudi to the town. He rests His left hand on His consort Satyabhama while His right hand holds a golden rod. In the sanctum the pillars are nicely embellished with copper plates. Images of Durga and Ganapati are situated beneath the main altar. As you exit the sanctum, you turn right and circumambulate the exterior of it to see the outer walls covered with paintings depicting scenes from pastimes of Lord Krishna.

The massive temple complex occupies six square acres with as many as sixteen towers, seven major halls, and 24 different shrines within it. The main entrances in the four directions all have towering *gopurams*. However, the eastern *gopuram* that rises to a height of 154 feet is the only one in fairly good condition. It was renovated in 1966. In front of the eastern entrance is the Garuda Stamba that stands 54 feet tall. Garuda, the carrier of Lord Vishnu, sits on top with his hands held in supplication.

In the western part of the temple there are smaller shrines to Venugopala, Lakshmi-Narayana, Lakshmi-Narasimha, Anantha Padmanabha, and Gajendravarada. MahaVishnu as Lakshmi-Narayana also reside in a small shrine on the banks of the Tirupatkadal water tank.

The history of this holy place goes back thousands of years. It is said that near the end of Dvapara-yuga, the two sages of Gopila and Gopralaya embarked upon a journey to Dvaraka in order to acquire the *darshan* of Lord Krishna. However, after meeting Narada Muni, he told them that the end of Dvapara-yuga had arrived, and Lord Krishna had gone back to His own spiritual abode. The two sages were extremely disappointed, so Narada asked them to go to the Shenbaga forest on the banks of the Harithra River. There they should perform penance to invoke the appearance of Lord Krishna by chanting the Dwathashatsara mantra for one year. The place was once a dense forest comprised of many sweet smelling Shenbaga trees, thereby giving the name of the area as Shenbagaranyam.

Their endeavors bore results and Lord Krishna appeared before them. Upon their request, He related thirty-two pastimes that occurred during His stay on earth. Before He was finished, Lord Krishna again performed His Rasa-lila pastime in the company of the other cowherd friends near the Harithra River. When the pastime was over, the residents of the spiritual world went back, leaving only Krishna who presented Himself to the two sages. He assured them that He would reside eternally at that place under the name of Vidya Rajagopalan. This is the origin of this temple.

The Harithra River also acquired its name because to assist Lord Krishna, it turned into a water tank to enable Him to perform the Rasa-lila dance with His friends, the cowherd girls or *gopis* of Vrindavana. The *gopis* had applied layers of turmeric and spices on themselves, which dissolved in the water, thereby changing the color and odor of the water. Therefore, the river got the name Harithra.

An interesting part of the history of this temple is that once Swarnasikhamani, the son of the successor of King Rajasekhara, felt bad that he had not been blessed with a son. Thus, after praying to the Lord, the Supreme appeared in his lap as Santhanagopalakrishna and blessed him with a child. So even today it is a custom that couples who long for a child will hold the deity of Santhanagopalakrishna in their lap for a brief period in hopes of getting blessed with a child.

The temple we see today originated in the days of Kulothunga Chola I (1072-1122) who conferred the name of Kulothunga Vinnagar on it. He was a faithful devotee of Lord Vishnu. The sanctum, central hall, and the third tower were created under his administration. The Nayak ruler of Tanjore, Achyutappa (1580-1600), along with his minister Govind Dikshitar, also gave their personal attention to the temple. Raghunatha Nayakar (1600-1634) constructed a hall for the main deity. And Vijayaraghava Nayakar (1633-73) accepted the deity of Rajagopalaswamy as his family deity. He directed that five grand towers and halls were made from granite stone taken from Mamalai (50 km away), which were embellished with beautiful sculptures. He also made the steps that lead to the Harithra River. His dedication to the deity was so great that he also made the Rajagopalaswamy temple in Tanjore.

Pujas are offered seven times a day according to the principles in the *Agamas*. There are also a large number of festivals that are celebrated throughout the year.

There are a numerous variety of additional temples and holy water tanks in this city. It is one of the eight holy places known as "Swayam Vijaktha Kshetras" where MahaVishnu manifested Himself of His own will. One kilometer from the temple is the Durvasa Tirtha on the banks of a water tank named after the sage who obtained benediction from MahaVishnu. It is more popularly known as Gajendra Moksha Tirtha or elephant tank after the elephant named Gajendra received the blessings of *moksha* or liberation from Lord Vishnu, the pastime of which is found in the *Bhagavata* and other *Puranas*. Other *tirthas* near this town include Tirupatkadal Tirtha, Gopika Tirtha, Rukmini Tirtha, Agnikunda Tirtha, Krishna Tirtha, Sangu Tirtha, and Chandra Tirtha. Plus, additional temples in this town include those of Naganathaswamy, Gopinatha, Meenakshi Sundarar, Kailasanathar, Anjaneya (Hanuman), Vinayaga (Ganesh) and Mariamman.

VEDARANYAM (DAKSHINA KAILASAM)

Vedaranyam, also called Dakshina Kailasam, is another one of those towns that is off the main route but has some spiritual merit to it. It is about 60 km southeast of Mannargudi or Tiruvarur along the coast. This is a sacred place for Hindus because Lord Rama was supposed to have stopped here when He was returning from Lanka. Nearby is a mound where one can find the preserved footprints of Lord Rama.

Furthermore, the four main *Vedas* in their personified forms were supposed to have worshiped Shiva here. The Shiva temple is for Thyagesar with an adjacent shrine to Vedaranyeswara, the lord worshiped by the *Vedas*. It is said that the main door to the temple remained closed for years and only opened after the saints Appar and Sundarar sang in praise of this deity.

TANJORE (or THANJAVUR)

When we are ready to move on from Thiruvarur, Mannargudi or Kumbhakonam, our next stop is at Tanjore (or Tanjavur). This is said to have over 40 temples. The main attraction here is the Brihadeshvara temple fort. If you did not see the other temples outside of Kumbakonam, this is the temple after which many of them were styled. It was built a thousand years ago by Raja Raja I (985-1013), the Chola king who was also a pious devotee. Entering the courtyard through *gopurams* that are 90 feet high and that have sculpted figures with clubs that guard the doorway, we see a large pavilion under which is a monolithic Nandi deity (12 feet tall by 19 feet high), considered the second largest in India after the one at Lepakshi.

The main temple has a huge tower (217 feet high) over the sanctum covered with carved figures. It is topped by a dome cut from a single piece of granite (81 tons). It is estimated that the dome was put into position by using an inclined plane starting at the village Sarapallam four miles away, but still it is only a theory. Westerners are allowed inside the temple to see the large cave-like hall and the biggest Shiva *linga* I saw anywhere in India. It must be about seven or eight feet in diameter and over 8 meters high, and is noted as being the largest in India. There are tall platforms around it so that priests can climb up to pour liquid offerings (usually Ganges water) over it in worship, which then drain through a spout and into a small tank outside the temple. If you arrive early in the morning, you can see the priests bathe the image in gallons of milk during its worship.

In the northwest corner of the grounds is a small shrine to Subramanya, built in the 17th century, which is a real gem of decorative stone work. There are other small shrines in the complex, including one for Chandeshvara near the temple entrance, and a small museum is on the south side. The huge walls surrounding the courtyard have open rooms filled with rows of Shiva *lingas* and small shrines. On His South Indian tour Sri Chaitanya also visited this temple 500 years ago.

As I was traveling through this town 18 years later from when I first visited this temple, I was very surprised at how much the town had expanded around the temple. The first time I saw it, the temple was out away from everything. Now houses and shops are all around it, and even the buses drive right by it. Quite a difference.

On the other side of town there is also the museum and art gallery that has displays of many deities that one can see and photograph, including many figures in granite and bronze of Shiva, as well as Brahma, Buddha, Vishnu, Krishna, etc. There is also a 190 feet tall lookout, built like a *gopuram* that provides a good view over the city if you climb through the narrow stairways to reach the top. But the Shiva temple is the main reason people come to this city.

TIRUCHIRAPPALI (TRICHY)

After spending a day or two wandering around Tanjore and the area, we get our things together and take the 7 P.M. train to Tiruchirappali, otherwise called Trichy. Or we can take the bus anytime, and there are many that make the 1 ½ hour journey.

When we arrive, it is dark but the streets and shops are busy with people shopping, socializing, or whatever. After making our way out of the noisy train station, we get a ricksha ride to a nearby hotel to get a room and settle in for the night, knowing full well that tomorrow will be a busy day.

It is said the town was originally known as Tirusirappally, named after the three-headed asura Tirusiras who got a blessing from Lord Shiva after worshiping him here. Trichy has three major attractions. One is the Rock Fort temple in the heart of the old city. To get there we board the number 1 bus near our hotel and ride to a place several blocks away from the hilltop temple. We walk past the Teppakulam water tank and find the entrance to the Rock Fort temple in the Chinna Bazaar. We leave our shoes at the shoe minder's stall and proceed up more than 400 steps that are cut through the rock of the hill. It is a steep and laborious climb to the summit 273 feet up where the views are great. If it is not too hazy, you can see the Sri Rangam temple to the north. Westerners are, unfortunately, not allowed inside the hilltop temple to see the image of Vinayaka, known here as Uchi Pillayar.

The legend of this deity, as explained in the *Sri Ranga Mahatmya*, is that when Brahma was in a state of deep meditation, Lord Vishnu, being pleased with him, gave him a deity of Himself, known as Ranga Vimana, a form of Vishnu reclining on Adisesha. As time went on, Brahma later gave the deity to Viraja, who later gave it to Manu, who passed it along to his son Ikshvaku, and finally to Lord Rama. Lord Rama, in gratitude to Vibhishan, the brother of the demon king Ravana of the *Ramayana* epic, gave him the deity. Vibhishan was returning to Sri Lanka from Ayodhya with the Vishnu deity that had been presented to him by Lord Rama. However, he had been told that if he should set the deity down on the ground, he would not be able to move it again.

The gods were not pleased that the deity would be taken away from India and devised a plan to keep the deity in Bharat. Thus, when Vibhashan stopped at Sri Rangam to take bath and perform his worship on the banks of the Kaveri River, he gave the deity to a brahmana boy with instructions not to place it on the ground. But the boy, who was Lord Ganesh in disguise, placed it on the earth anyway. Then the deity became firmly fixed to the ground and could not be moved from the spot where it remains to this day. Vibhishan became angry and chased the boy who ran to the summit of the hill that is the Rock Fort today. There Vibhishan caught and struck the boy, who then revealed his real form and stood transformed as Vinayaka. Even though Vibhishan begged to apologize before going on to Sri Lanka, the image of Vinayaka still has a depression on his face where he had been struck.

The area where the deity was set down gradually became covered by a thick forest. The deity was only discovered thousands of years later by a Chola king who accidently found it while chasing a parrot. It was the king who established the Sri Rangam temple, which is presently one of the largest temples in India.

As we climb the stairway up the hill, the shrine to Thayumanavar, Shiva, is located half way up, but is also closed to non-Hindus. Legend explains that when a pious mother could not cross the Kaveri River to tend to her daughter who was in labor with child, Shiva appeared to help the daughter as a midwife to avoid her being disappointed. When the real mother arrived, Shiva disappeared, and the mother was surprised that her daughter had already given birth. Thus, Shiva is called Thayumanavar, the one who became the mother. This temple was excavated in the 8th century and belongs to the Pandya era. It is a columned *mandapa* hall with two side shrines with wall carvings of Vishnu and Shiva. In niches in the rear wall are images of Ganesh, Subrahmanya, Brahma, Surya, and Durga.

Sri Rangam is our next place of pilgrimage. From the Rock Fort temple we walk back to the bus stop to catch a bus to the Sri Ranganathaswamy temple on the north side of town. This is another very large temple complex, a town in itself, and one of the most important Vishnu temples in the South. It has 21 *gopurams* marking the gateways through seven walls that surround the main temple. The largest *gopuram* is the south entrance which was completed in 1987 and reaches a height of 236 feet, one of the tallest in India. The outer walls contain an area of 3000 feet by 2400 feet. The temple complex covers an area of about 190 acres. It is situated on the island of Sri Rangam which is between two branches of the Kaveri River. Thousands of pilgrims, especially Vaishnavas, visit this temple all year long. The legend is that the deity of Sri Ranganatha was once worshiped by Lord Rama thousands of years ago. He gave the deity to Vibhishan who unwittingly allowed it to be placed on the ground. When the deity could not be moved, a temple was built at the spot.

Unfortunately, once again, they do not let most Westerners into the main temple or a few of the many smaller shrines, some of which are for Sri Krishna, Narasimhadeva, Ganesh, Garuda, etc. My guide told me that not even some Hindus are allowed inside, depending on what school of thought they subscribe to. But there are plenty of other things to see, including a variety of shops and commercial enterprises. Nonetheless, some Westerners who have accepted the path of *sanatana-dharma* (bhakti-yoga) and dress accordingly are allowed into the sanctum to have *darshan* of the deity and see the worship. I have been able to get wonderful *darshans* of the deity whenever I have visited, such as when the priest shows us all aspects of the large reclining Vishnu and the *utsavar* deities, forcing others to wait in line behind us. In fact, Iskcon devotees are welcomed by the head *pandita*, Sri Rangaraja Bhatta, who is a descendant of Sri Gopala Bhatta Gosvami's father, Vyenkata Bhatta. His house is located in the temple complex and is called "Mahaprabhu Sadan" for being the place where Sri Chaitanya Mahaprabhu had stayed for four months with Vyenkata Bhatta while He visited Sri Rangam in 1510. He lives on North Chitrai Street. It is a temple of Jagannatha, Baladeva, and Subhadra. You can take the central boulevard north from the temple to North Chitrai Street and then turn left until you find a small temple with locked gates, hanging from which are signs that indicate it as Mahaprabhu Sadan. The deities are said to have been hand carved by Sri Chaitanya Himself in a feeling of intense separation from Lord Jagannatha in Puri. Sri Rangam is another temple visited by Sri Chaitanya Mahaprabhu where He danced in ecstasy many years ago. Ranga Raj Bhatta is the last of the Vyenkata Bhatta family and is the head priest at Sri Rangam.

The temple complex contains many shrines that take time to view. You can easily go around to see the outside shrines and take photographs. But you have to buy a photo ticket and leave any bags at the cloak room. After the guide that I accepted who spoke fairly good English took me around to the smaller shrines. I took a guide because it had been long time since I had been here, and he was friendly and aware of my spiritual connections and was quite favorable. So I knew he would help me enter all the areas without a problem, even if someone else may object. A good guide can explain many things about this temple as you go through it.

After seeing all the outside temples, we went into the main building. It has cavernous halls and various rooms and walkways that you make your way through to the main sanctum. Finally, approaching the main temple, there is a line of people which you follow until you are in front to see the deity. The priests are doing *pujas* for the people, but when you can step forward, they often help you get a good view of the full length of the deity. The main deity is an 18-feet long reclining black Vishnu lying on His serpentine couch of Seshanaga. He has silver feet and near them are His consorts Bhu Devi and Nila Devi. Just in front is the beautiful standing Vishnu deity, adorned with flowers and jewelry. Images of Nathamuni, Yamunacharya, and Ramanujacharya are also found in the sanctum. The priest may explain various aspects and stories in connection with the temple and deity before you continue on your way and allow others to step forward. Of course, a nice donation to the priest for the extra attention is always in order, and also paves the way for other Westerners to be treated with similar respect when they arrive.

After seeing the main deities, we can go around the back of the main building to see the Lakshmi temple. The Lakshmi deity is called Sri Ranganayaki Nachiyat. This was a great experience because few people were there when I visited, which is most unusual, so I could get a close-up view of the deity. Often it is packed and people are pushing one another to get or maintain a good view. As we exit the Lakshmi temple we can see the "doors of paradise" that are in the back of the main temple building. These are opened during a special festival once a year and anyone that comes through them is said to reach Vaikuntha, Lord Vishnu's abode. Now we continue to wander through the complex and see the other shrines if we have not already seen them.

After wandering the halls a little more, I walked back outside and went to see Sri Ramanujacharya's *samadhi* (burial place). You can see this little temple where he is located. There is a small *murti* or image of him in front of a larger one. After spending some time there in respect of the accomplishments of Ramanujacharya, I also went to the viewing area on the rooftop where you can get a better look over the temple and higher levels of the *gopuram* towers. These are very beautiful and colorful, so it is great to see them from that height and take some photos. Many tourists also go up to view them there. So in this way, our visit to Sri Rangam to have *darshan* of the deities and get association with other spiritually oriented people can be very uplifting. This is the reason for our pilgrimage to such temples.

The traditional and Puranic history of Sri Rangam is quite interesting and goes back to the beginning of time. After Lord Brahma had done penance to help in the creation of the universe, Lord Vishnu was pleased with him. So Lord Vishnu manifested Himself as Lord Ranganatha, a form of Vishnu reclining on Seshanaga, the Lord's great serpent servant. Brahma worshiped Lord Ranganatha for many years and later gave the deity to Vivasvan, the sun-god, who later handed the deity over to Svayambhuva Manu. Manu passed on the deity to King Ikshvaku, the great leader of the solar dynasty in which Lord Krishna would later appear as Lord Ramachandra.

Lord Ramachandra gave the deity to Vibhishana, who was a great devotee and brother of the demon Ravana. However, when Vibhishana was traveling with the deity, he stopped and put the deity down briefly at a holy place called Chandra Pushkarini, near the Kaveri River. However, the deity would no longer move. It turned out that a king, Dharma Varma, had seen Lord Ranganatha in Ayodhya and prayed to worship Him. So the Lord blessed the king to stay at Sri Rangam. Nonetheless, the deity blessed Vibhishana by promising to always look toward his kingdom. This is why the deity reclines with His head toward the west, looking toward the south in the direction of Sri Lanka, Vibhishana's kingdom.

King Dharma Varma and his dynasty of the Chola kings built a large temple around Lord Ranganatha. The worship was quite opulent. But, unfortunately, things declined and gradually the temple was forgotten and covered over by sand. One day a king was resting under a tree when a parrot explained that Lord Ranganatha was buried in the sand. So the king excavated the temple and restored it. Over time, many other Chola kings again expanded the temple.

However, the 14th century saw the invading Moghuls plunder most of the Lord's treasures from this temple. The Vijayanagar and Nayak rulers again revived it in the 15th and 16th centuries. Then in the 17th and 18th centuries, the Muslims, French, and then the British used the fortress in furthering their domination over the area. Only after India gained independence in 1947 did the Indian government and the Ramanujas or Sri Vaishnavas finally gain control to oversee the temple properly.

Back outside the main gates of the temple complex, we catch the bus to the other side of the main road and walk down the lane to the Sri Jambukesvara temple, dedicated to Shiva. It is not as big as the Sri Ranganatha temple, but is nearby and quite interesting. It has massive carved pillars in its huge hallways, along with outside courtyards, water pool, etc. And for ten rupees you can photograph most any part of it. Here, as at the previous temple, you may be approached by a guide or temple assistant who will want to show you around, for a nice tip, of course.

There are two main temples in this complex, one to Parvati (Akilandesvari), and one to Lord Shiva. The main deity is a small Shiva *linga*, Sri Jambhukeshvara or Appulingam, which is half submerged under the water of a natural spring next to it. The room is somewhat little, but the *lingam* is on an altar where a natural spring brings water up to the surface. Thus, the *lingam* is sitting in a little pool of water. They do not allow non-Hindus into this main temple, but upon seeing that I was an initiated brahmana, I was allowed in to see the sanctum. Of course, that also means that the priests will do a special *puja* ceremony for you, offering lamps and mantras to the deity, and then expecting some nice donations for it. But this is an aspect of worship that many pilgrims perform and is spiritually beneficial and fascinating to observe and partake in. Thus, for our own spiritual merit, we also participate.

From here we can go through the halls and around to the left where we find the shrine to Parvati. Here we buy our ticket, get in line, and when we get close to the altar we get a view of the almost lifesize and lovely image of Parvati as Akilandesvari. After this we wander onward through the halls and *gopurams* and go back out front. There we can wait for the next bus or our waiting auto-rickshaha to take us to the next temple.

The Lakshmi-Narasimha temple is another noteworthy place to visit while we are here. It is not so popular, so some people may not know where it is. But most priests at the Sri Rangam temple can give directions, such as to your auto-riksha driver if you have taken one. It is east of the Sri Rangam temple not far from the local train station. Once you reach it, it does not have any imposing architecture, but as you enter it you will see some halls and a temple building that is entered through a side door. You then climb up the short stairway and down the hall where you can see the deity of Narasimha with Lakshmi sitting on His lap. As you enter the sanctum you can also see how impressive this deity is, practically as tall as the priest though in a sitting position. He is the largest Narasimha deity I have seen in the form of Lakshmi-Narasimha. He is made of black stone and is adorned with silver crown, hands, and ornaments. The priests will use the ghee lamp to show you His form and give you *caranamritam* water and tulasi leaves during your *darshan*. It is quite an experience.

Coming out of the sanctum, the walls in the hall have beautiful paintings depicting the pastimes of Lord Narasimha bifurcating Hiranyakashipu and later being pacified by Lakshmi. So this is a temple not to be missed while you are here.

Remember, the temples here close around 12:30 for the afternoon, so you will want to get an early start to see everything in one morning. The temples, of course, open again in the afternoon for *darshans* and *pujas*, but you can spend all morning wandering around seeing everything you need to see here, unless you want more time to view the architecture and sculptures. So plan accordingly and do not cut yourself short of time.

THADICOMBU

On our way south to Madurai, if we want we can stop at Dindigul to see Thadicombu. This is a small village eight kilometers from Dindigul, reached by bus. It has the Sundararaja Perumal temple. The temple sits on 1½ acres of land with a five-tiered *gopuram* over the eastern entrance. The temple is surrounded by massive walls, outside of which are roads to facilitate pilgrims and the *ratha* cart festival. There are several shrines in the complex, including those for Lakshmi-Narasimha, Venugopala, and others. But in the main sanctum you will find Lord Vishnu as Sundararaja Perumal standing five feet tall with Sridevi and Bhudevi on either side. In a separate shrine Goddess Sundaravalli Thayar also offers Her blessings. The shrine for Sudarshana in the southwest corner is quite spacious. Some of the halls in the temple are filled with lovely sculptures. A few worth noting include the large standing Ganesha, and Anjaneya on some of the pillars. This temple is closely connected with the Alagar temple in Madurai.

Five hundred or so years ago, a most pious and wise man named Vidyaranya lived in South India. It is said that Goddess Mahalakshmi was quite pleased with his devotion and showered gold on him. He realized that something special was meant for him to do. During that time, numerous invading Muslims were threatening to put an end to the native religion of Hinduism. Vidyaranya wanted to use his fortune to establish a new empire that could protect the native religion as well as the ethical principles of the faith. With that intent manifested the city of Vidyanagar that was ruled by Harihara and Bukka, and later developed into the Vijayanagar Empire. Under the auspices of such rulers like Krishnadevaraya, the empire not only shielded Hinduism or Vedic culture from the Muslim invaders, but also revitalized it. Temples sprang up in many areas, and the rise of the Vedic tradition spread throughout Tamil Nadu. One of those temples was this Sundararaja Perumal temple here at Thadicombu.

PALNI (PALANI)

After returning to our hotel and relaxing a while, we can now prepare to catch the evening train for the short ride to our next stop, which is Madurai, one of the most interesting temples in the South and a big attraction for tourists and pilgrims alike. However, if you are a devotee of Murugan, you might want to get a train or bus to go a little farther west to Palni.

Lord Murugan, one of the sons of Shiva, is very popular in Tamil Nadu and Kerala. The main temple at Palni is the most renown of the six temples of Murugan. It is located on the hilltop and reached by climbing 659 steps, or by taking an electric winch. The Murugan deity is in the form of an ascetic who has renounced the world, standing with a staff in his right hand and rudraksha beads around his neck. The deity is said to be made from nine different kinds of poison which, mixed together, resembles wax. The exact proportions, calculated by a sage named Bhoga, is unknown. But substances that touch the deity are believed to acquire healing powers. The deity is bathed daily with different liquids, such as milk, rose water, sandal paste, etc., all of which becomes prasadam with strong healing potencies. There are a series of festivals through the year at this hilltop temple that draw thousands of pilgrims from Tamil Nadu. At the foot of the hill in Palni is another temple dedicated to Subramanya (Murugan) with his consorts Valli and Devayanai.

The legend behind the deity of the main temple is that Lord Shiva once showed his sons, Ganesh and Murugan, a rare fruit and said it would be the prize for the one who first returned from circumambulating the world. Murugan immediately started out, riding on his peacock carrier. Ganesh, however, simply walked around his parents and said that since the universe rests in them this was equal to traveling around the world. So Shiva gave the fruit to him. When Murugan returned and found out what had happened, he became angry and renounced all worldly connections.

MADURAI

Madurai is a very interesting city. If you travel through the south, this is a place you should not miss. It leaves an indelible impression on all visitors and enriches their knowledge of South Indian art, architecture, and spiritual culture. Madurai has a population of over 1,000,000, but it is not as big as you would expect. If you get a hotel that is centrally located, you can walk to most of the places you'd be interested to see. Of course, if you stay at a larger hotel across the river, you may have to take a taxi or ricksha to get around. It is not far from the train station to the central hotels, or from the hotels to decent restaurants. The fruit vendors and shops that sell most anything you might need are also nearby. There are lots of little stores and small industries. The city stays busy all day and into the evening. Lots of people wander the streets, shopping or selling, all adding to the variety this place has to offer. You will see people from all over India as well as from any part of the world. Tour companies bring large groups of tourists here, especially to visit the Meenakshi temple. It is said that as many as 10,000 pilgrims a day may visit this temple, and you can see the tourist buses out front, sometimes lined up along the road.

The Meenakshi temple is one of the 51 Shakti Peetams. It is located in the center of the old town. It is a huge complex (covering 847 feet by 729 feet) with 12 *gopurams*, four of which are towering that dominate the landscape and mark the entrances through the outer walls. The *gopurams* are some of the most famous in India since they are tall and covered from top to bottom with colorful and intricate images of gods, goddesses, scenes from the *Puranas* and Vedic epics, guardians, animals, and so on. The south tower is the tallest at 169 feet, and covered with over 1500 sculptures. At the top on each side is a yali, which is a creature that is a combined form of an elephant and a lion. The eyes are each 2 ½ feet across. The west tower is also most decorative, stretching up over 154 feet tall, with 1124 sculptures. The north tower is 152 feet tall with 404 sculptures.

The main entrance to the temple complex is on the east side. Over the doorway you will see the sculpted representation of the wedding of Meenakshi. This shows Lord Vishnu giving Meenakshi to Shiva. On each side you will also see sculptures of Ganesh and Subrahmanya. As you enter the large cavernous hall, you will soon be greeted by the temple elephant and its attendant. A little crowd of people, especially children, is usually gathered around it and are fascinated by the way it takes an offering of money from their hands and then gently blesses them with a tap on their head with its trunk.

Further into the temple you will find a long hallway with many little shops selling everything from bangles, spices, and miniature deities and pictures, as well as toys for children. It is quite interesting to stand back for a bit and watch the incredible variety of people who walk through. There are the expected Indian tourists, pilgrims, and holy men dressed in saffron, as well as Westerners from America or different parts of Europe, some not knowing what to make of it all, or others who are living and studying the ways of the East and familiar with what it is all about. It is a most fascinating mixture. It is also the area of the Ashta Shakti Mandapa, or hall of the eight goddesses that are carved on the pillars.

This is the area where you buy your ticket to the Temple Art Gallery. Then you enter the impressive Hall of 1000 Pillars, at the end of which is a large deity of Nataraja, dancing Shiva. Each stone column is beautifully carved. From this hallway you can wander through the museum, which has a good selection of wood, stone, and metal deities of all sizes from different eras. Some of the displays need maintenance, but it is worthwhile nonetheless.

After seeing the museum, you can continue into the temple and explore its many shrines, sculptures, the long cave-like hallways, and almost get lost in it for hours. The halls are filled with columns and sculptures of the many *avataras* of Vishnu, demigods, goddesses, and forms of their varied personalities. There are also many images of animals and statues of kings and rulers who either helped build the temple or were devoted to the deities. To understand them all would take much time and you would have to have a very knowledgeable guide to explain them. From here we can go through the Chitrai *gopuram*, which is seven storeys tall and covered with 700 sculptures. Then we find the Mudali Pillai Mandapa, a hall with Puranic scenes on the walls.

The walls around the Golden Lotus tank have murals which depict the 64 miracles that were performed by Lord Sundaresvara in and around Madurai. Across from the tank is the sanctuary for Meenakshi, the Divine Mother, where she stands with a parrot and a bouquet in her right hand. They do not let Westerners in, but if you are dressed in something like *dhoti* and *kurta*, just go in anyway. It may be all right, and at the worst they will tell you to leave. However, if you have a certificate saying you are a Hindu, you can be allowed in. I was told you can get such a certificate from the local Iskcon (Hare Krishna) temple there in Madurai. I had a letter from Swami Dayananda Sarasvati of Coimbatore saying I am a devout Hindu and that I should be allowed in the temple. He is fairly well-known in India, so he carries some influence. So you go to the administrative office on the south side of the temple and request to show your certificate or letter. If they accept it, they will give you permission for *darshan*. So then if you show one of the priests, or if you have a guide who can assist you, then you can be taken in for *darshan*.

When I went in the priest led me past the rows of people for special *darshan* and did a *puja* for me, first to Meenakshi. Then we went to the Sundaresvara *lingam*, past lines of people who were waiting to do the same, looking at me wondering who I was to get special treatment, and then the priest again did a small ritual for me. You still need entrance tickets to get up close. Near the sanctums there are numerous people and it is a little hectic, so I was glad I had someone leading me through it and not have to stand in line for a long time.

As we leave the inner sanctums and continue wandering through the temple, we can see that next to the entrance to the Meenakshi shrine is the Oonjal Mandapa, the hall where there is a swing where the two main deities are worshiped every Friday evening at six. Across the hall and to the north we reach the Sundaresvara shrine.

In front of the Sundaresvara shrine on the east side of it is the Kambathadi *mandapa* hall. This has many fine sculpted pillars, among which is one that depicts the wedding of Meenakshi to Shiva, and shows Lord Vishnu giving away His sister, Meenakshi, to Shiva. This is a famous column. Nearby at the end of the hall is the shrine to the Navagrahas, or nine planets. The nearby Kambathadi Mandapa has carvings of Lord Vishnu's ten *avataras*.

As we enter the temple room for Sundaresvara, by the door is an eight-foot tall image of Ganesh. This is said to have been uncovered during the excavation of the Mariamman Teppakkulam tank. In the north end of the shrine are the images of Durga, Siddhi, and Lakshmi. The image of Kashi Visvanatha is in the northeast corner. Then there is a small shrine to Shiva as Nataraja just before you go into the inner sanctum. In the main temple room, Sundaresvara is the Shiva *linga*.

When we exit this shrine and head north, we can see the five musical pillars that produce sounds when they are struck. From here we can cross the inner courtyard and exit the compound through the north *gopuram*.

The legends concerning this temple go back thousands of years. It begins with Indra, the king of heaven, who was wandering through the universe looking for a means to purify himself from the sin of killing a brahmana. While near the Kadamba forest of Madurai, he discovered that he had become purified. He realized the cause of it was due to the presence of a Shiva *lingam* under a tree. So he bathed in what is now the temple's Golden Lotus tank. Using golden lotus flowers, he worshiped the *lingam*. Afterwards, he built a little shrine for it and then returned to his heavenly abode.

Much later, King Kulashekara Pandyan learned of this incident and went to the forest to see and worship the *lingam*. He cleared the forest and started building the temple at the site, and developed the city of Madurai into greater prominence. When the consecration of the temple took place, it is said that Lord Shiva himself appeared to give his blessings. Droplets of nectar, or *maduram* in Tamil, flew from Shiva's locks and fell on the surrounding town, which was called Maduraipuri, or the land of nectar. Later the name was shortened to Madurai.

Malayadwaja Pandyan succeeded the throne and, since he and his wife were childless, performed a sacrifice to beget a child. From the sacrificial fire appeared a three-year-old girl who had three breasts. They were told that the third breast would disappear when she met the person she would marry.

Malayadwaja was a little disappointed that he did not get a son, and heard a voise that told him to raise the girl like a boy. Thus, the child, Thadathagati, an incarnation of Shiva's wife Parvati, was raised and trained like a prince and mastered all the arts of war. She succeeded the king and in her warrior spirit conquered all the nearby countries up to the Himalayas, even reaching the abode of Lord Shiva, Mount Kailash. But when she met the gaze of Lord Shiva on the battlefield, her third breast disappeared and she knew he was her husband. On the order of Lord Shiva, she returned to Madurai and eight days later Shiva came to marry her. They ruled Madurai together for some time and after making their son, Ugra Pandyan (an incarnation of Muruga), the King, they assumed the divine forms as Sundaresvara and Meenakshi.

The temple of Sundaresvara was still a shrine in the 7th century C.E. and the temple of Meenakshi was built in the 12th century. Most of the complex as we see it today was designed by Vishwanatha Nayak in 1560 and built during the 200 year reign of the Nayaka rulers, especially Tirumalai Nayak (1623-55). And it was almost 500 years ago that Sri Chaitanya Mahaprabhu also visited this temple to see Sundaresvara and Meenakshi.

The Kudalalagar (Kudal Alagir) Devasthanam Vishnu temple on South Masi Street is another temple in Madurai to see. It has a long history. Presently, the nice temple building sits on 2 acres of land with a five-tiered, 125 feet tall *gopuram* over the east entrance. Once entering the temple, the main shrine is reached by climbing up a flight of steps. Therein we find the beautiful black, six-foot tall deity of Koodal Alagar (Vishnu) in a sitting pose with gold colored hands and ornaments. He is sitting with Sri Lakshmi (Sridevi) on His right and Sri Andal or Bhumi on His left. The *utsavar* or festival deity is smaller, four feet tall, but with similar grace as the larger deity.

If the stairway is unlocked you can go to the second floor where there is another Vishnu deity. This is Suryanarayana who is in a standing pose along with His Devis, Lakshmi and Andal. If you go up to the third floor you can see the small temple room for MahaVishnu, known as Kshiraptinatha, who is in a reclining position. There are also images of Lord Vishnu's Dasavataras, or ten incarnations. Also in the temple you can find smaller shrines for Lakshmi-Narasimha, Rama, Lakshmi-Narayana, and Krishna. There are also a few shrines for Garuda, Anjaneya, and of some of the great devotees, such as Ramanuja, Vedanta Desikar, and the Alwars. There is also a shrine for the Navagrahas, the nine planets. The beautiful paintings and sculptures that grace the temple are an additional attraction.

On the south side of the temple is a separate temple for Sri Lakshmi and on the north side there is one for Sri Andal or Bhumi. There will be guides at this temple who will want to show you around and then ask for large tips. They may also take you "for free" to the temple sari shop to show you how they make and dye saris to sell and help support the temple. It is interesting to watch, but they really want you to buy something. I easily went into the temple several years earlier and saw all the dieties, but in 2005 they almost did not let me in. The guards were all right about it, but the man selling the tickets said no, I was not a Hindu because of my skin color. Then I put up a fuss saying I have been a bhakta for a long time and I should go in. So after a few minutes, and with the help of one of the guards, he gave us the proper tickets and we went in for a very nice *darshan* of Lord Vishnu.

There is also another smaller temple a few blocks away. Around the corner to the right from the Kudalalagar Vishnu temple is another smaller temple dedicated to Krishna. There is a nice *gopuram* on the east side. The central shrine has a lovely black stone diety of Krishna with Satyabhama on His right and another on His left. There are other smaller shrines in the complex that surround the central shrine. It is a very nice place and easy to visit this temple.

From here, turning left from the main *gopuram*, we walk to another temple to Shiva and Parvati called the Everail Nanmai Eharuvar Kovil. The main deities are again Meenakshi Devi in one shrine and a Sundaresvara *lingam* in another. It is a simple temple complex, but if you cannot see the main deity in the Meenakshi temple, you can see them here.

If you are staying for a while in Madurai and want a change from seeing temples, you can visit the Tirumalai Nayak Palace about a kilometer from the Meenakshi temple. This has a museum on the history of Madurai, and the Gandhi Museum is across the river. Several kilometers east of the city is the large (1000 feet by 950 feet) and tranquil pool called Mariamman Theppakulam with a temple structure on the island in the middle of it. Not much happens here except when, in late January or early February on Thai Poosam day, they bring the deities of Meenakshi and Sundaresvara here for the Teppam (float) festival. They place the deities on boats to give them rides across the water. People from all over India attend, so the city can be rather crowded at this time.

Another festival in late August or early September takes place when they bring the deities out on big carts that are drawn through the streets of Madurai. Another important festival is the Chitra festival in late April or early May when the wedding of Meenakshi and Shiva is celebrated. For this festival, the deity of Lord Vishnu from the Alagarcoil temple also attends in a procession that goes to the Vaigai River. This festival draws up to 100,000 devotees from all over India. Other festivals go on around the year that commemorate the 64 *lilas* (pastimes) of the Lord.

ALAGARCOIL

Alagarcoil is 12 miles (19 kilometers) north of Madurai where a beautiful Vishnu temple is found on the side of a hill. This is an important place and was visited many years ago by King Yudhisthira, Arjuna, plus the twelve Alwars. It also once had an ancient fort. The large Vishnu deity in the main sanctum is Sri Sundararajan. He is made of black stone with gold plate covering His body and paraphernalia, like His disc, club, etc. He is also called Kallalagar, or the deity of the Kallas tribe. Sundararaja is also known as Alagar, the brother of Meenakshi. He is the form of Vishnu who gave Meenakshi away in marriage to Shiva, or Sundaresvara. Large deities of Sridevi and Bhudevi are at His sides. The *utsava* or smaller processional deity of Sundararaja is made of very valuable gold called *aparanji*. It is interesting that water for the bathing of the Vishnu deity is brought only from Nupura Ganga, since any other water will discolor the deity. This is a sacred *thirtam*, or site, three km up in the hills.

Not many people were visiting this temple when I came to see it, so I had a nice long *darshan* of the deities and talked to the priest about various aspects of Vishnu. They usually do not allow Westerners into the temple, but they easily allowed me in while dressed in *dhoti* and *kurta*, and knowing that I was a member of Iskcon.

Walking through the halls you will see many beautiful sculptures depicting various incarnations of Vishnu as well as paintings of the *Ramayana*. You will also find the other shrines in the temple for such deities as Parthasarathi, Ashtabhuja Krishna, Garuda, a most beautiful Lakshmi, Kalyana Sundaravalli Nachiyar, Andal, the Lord's Sudarshan disc which is said to be over 2000 years old, and Saraswati. There is also a shrine for Jwala Narasimha, or the angry form of Narasimha. This deity is bathed daily in milk, curd, and other items to cool His anger. An opening in the ceiling above His head allows a space for His anger to leave the temple.

The important event for this temple is the Chitra festival. On the fourth day, the deity is brought in a procession to Madurai to attend His sister's (Meenakshi's) marriage to Shiva. They also celebrate the marriage of Alagar (Vishnu) to Sri Andal with great pomp. At the top of the Alagar hill are temples dedicated to Shiva, Shiva as Bhairava, Murugan (Subrahmanya), and Ganesh. While you are here, watch out for the monkeys who are always waiting to be fed. To reach this temple you can easily catch a bus from the main bus stand in Madurai.

THIRUPPARANKUNDRAM

There are many other temples around the area of Madurai, one of which is the Thiruppa-rankundram, 7 miles (10 kilometers) southwest of Madurai. This is one of the six famous temples to Lord Murugan. This is a 6th century rock-cut cave temple on the northern side of a hill that marks the place where Murugan married Devayani, daughter of Lord Indra, after he defeated Surapadma. The sanctum is carved out of the rock and Murugan's wedding with Devayani is depicted here. The front of the temple has 48 large pillars carved very artistically. It has a beautiful *gopuram* seven storeys tall over the Kalyana Mandapam.

The sanctum has five separate cells with a deity in each. In the central area we see Muruga, Durga, and Vinayaka, who is portrayed holding fruits and sugarcane. Muruga is seen in the sitting posture with Daivayani. On her right is the sage Narada Muni. Above them are Brahma, Indra, Surya, and Chandra. There are also images of Vishnu flanked by Sridevi and Bhudevi, and a Shiva *lingam*. Further up at the top of the hill there is also a shrine to Kashi Vishwanatha with the Tamil poet Nakkeerar standing nearby.

TIRUMOHUR

Tirumohur is the village that has the Kalamegha Perumal temple. This temple is located around 15 kilometers from Madurai. It is one of the eighteen major Vaishnava holy places in this area of Madurai, Tirunelveli, and Ramanathapuram.

The temple has a large and beautiful *gopuram* that rises over the eastern entrance. It leads to a large hallway that is supported by massive pillars. A smaller three-tiered *gopuram* leads to an inner hallway which has columns that display many stone carvings of figures from the Vedic epics and *Puranas*.

The deity of Lord Kalamegha (Vishnu) is in the inner sanctum, with Sridevi and Bhudevi at His sides. The impressive form of the Lord is also dressed in opulent outfits and beautiful ornaments. Other shrines for the usual assortment of deities also can be found in the temple.

SRIVILLIPUTTUR

This town, 70 km southwest of Madurai by rail, has two major temples and some minor ones. The Valapatrasayee temple has a large Vishnu deity, viewed through three doors, reclining on Adi Sesha. There is also the Sri Andal temple nearby. This temple has a 12-storey, 192 foot tall *gopuram*. In the southwest part of town there is a temple of Krishna, Rukmini, and Satyabhama. Southwest of town is a large Shiva temple. And four km north of town is the Tirupati Srinivas temple.

TIRUTHANGAL (TIRUTTANGAL)

If we decided to visit Srivilliputtur, then Tiruthangal is not far away. This town is located two kilometers north of Sivakasi, which is about 18 km east from Srivilliputtur. It is reached by bus from places like Madurai, Srivilliputhur, Sankarankoil, and Virudhunagar. It has the Ninra Narayana Perumal temple.

The temple faces south on a small 100-foot tall hill in the northern part of town. Climbing the stairs, one reaches the spacious entranceway. A sculpture of Narayana Ramanuja, who was the person who spent much of his money to build this hallway, adorns one of the pillars. In the back and to the west is the cave temple wherein we find the deity of Pallikonda Perumal, Lord Vishnu in His reclining pose. Sridevi and Bhudevi are at His feet while sages like Markandeya and Bhrigu are on either side. The history of this place is that once Lord Ranganatha journeyed to Srivilliputhur to seek Sri Andal for marriage and spent the night here.

A second floor of this temple accommodates another hallway, a lovely mirror room, and another room. In a separate shrine, Arunakamalamahadevi offers *darshan* in a standing pose while facing east.

Another flight of stairs leads the pilgrim to the main sanctum. Therein we see Garuda, Lord Vishnu's carrier, grasping a pot in one hand, the Amrita Kalasha, and a serpent in the other hand, while two more hands are in a pose of reverence. The entrance is guarded by two huge *dwarapalakas*, or guardians, with imposing features. The main deity is Ninra Narayana Perumal, or Vishnu who is in a standing pose facing east. The sanctum has eleven other large and colorful images in it. There is Markandeya in a submissive pose, along with Garuda, Aruna, Viswakarma, Bhudevi, and Sridevi all standing around the central deity. Then there is Appan, Neeladevi, Usha, Aniruddha, and then Bhrigu on the far left.

The history of this place goes back to a time when the three main Devis, namely Sridevi, Bhudevi, and Neeladevi, wondered who was most favored by Lord Vishnu. Sridevi (Lakshmi) wanted to prove her supremacy and retreated to a secluded spot in order to engage in deep meditation. Many devotees and sages came to that spot to have *darshan* of this Goddess of Wealth. In response to their devotional requests, she agreed to reside there eternally as Arunakamalamahadevi. Realizing that living there in isolation would be improper, she prayed for the appearance of Lord Vishnu. The Lord was pleased and agreed to also reside there. Bhudevi and Neeladevi followed in His footsteps and reconciled with Sridevi. It was actually the desire of Lord Vishnu to bless His devotees at this spot, along with His Devis. Thus, this drama was enacted only to accomplish His desire.

Another piece of history of this place deals with Banasura. Many years ago he was the ruler of Mahishmathi and a zealous devotee of Lord Shiva. He had the strength of 1000 arms that adorned his shoulders. His daughter Usha was a devotee of Parvati, who prayed to the goddess for a suitable husband. That night after praying, she dreamed she met a prince of unparalleled charm, but after awaking, she did not know who he was. Her good friend Chitralekha knew the art of painting the images of all the eligible princes. When Usha saw the portrait of Aniruddha, the grandson of Lord Krishna, she greatly blushed. Chitralekha then used her skills of conjuration to transport Aniruddha to the palace of Usha. There they merrily spent a few days together.

Banasura soon detected something was amiss and was infuriated to learn what was going on. Banasura took his army to find and crush Aniruddha, but Lord Krishna also brought His army to find His grandson. Then, due to the entreaties of Banasura, even Lord Shiva appeared to offer assistance. It looked as if Shiva and Krishna would engage in battle. But by Lord Krishna's power, Banasura lost his 1000 arms and was left with only two. After realizing his mistake in the matter, the marriage of Usha and Aniruddha was allowed to take place in grand style. The *Sthala* (or local) *Purana* relates that it was here at Tiruthangal where the extraordinary wedding took place. Thus, the images of Usha and Aniruddha are also found in the main shrine.

The Karunellinathar temple is found on the other side of the hill. It is also a rock-cut cave temple dedicated to Lord Shiva. The main deity is a Shiva *linga*. His consort Meenakshi is in a separate shrine. Inside the temple are separate shrines for Vinayaka,

Dakshinamurthi, Chandra, and Surya. There are also life-size stone images of Nataraja and Shivakami.

RAMESVARAM

After seeing Madurai and the surrounding area, it is easy we catch the early morning train for Ramesvaram. It is a relaxing ride (about six hours) as we head toward the coast. Ramesvaram is a tropical island surrounded by coral reefs and sandy beaches with coconut palms and tamarind trees. It is a major center of pilgrimage for both Vaishnavas and Shaivites. The Sri Ramanathaswamy temple is one of the most important in India. It is a massive complex with a number of shrines, holy wells, *gopurams*, and several long hallways, one reaching 4000 feet in length, the longest in the country. The halls are adorned with many large pillars, some of which are covered with scroll work, lotus designs, animals, and other figures, and colorful painted medallions are on the ceilings.

According to legends, this temple was originally started by Lord Rama. Lord Rama had gone to Sri Lanka to rescue His wife, Sita, and engaged in a great battle during which He killed the demon Ravana. Afterward, He wanted to absolve Himself of the sin by installing a *lingam* at Ramesvaram. He sent His most trustworthy servant Hanuman to get a Shiva *lingam* from Mount Kailash, but Hanuman was delayed in his return. Since Shiva had to be worshiped by a certain time, Sita made a *lingam* (Sri Ramanatha) out of sand. When Hanuman returned with a *linga*, he was disappointed and angry to find another *linga* already installed. To pacify Hanuman, Rama had the Hanumath *lingam* (Visvalingam) installed next to the Ramanatha *lingam.* Then He ordered that all worship should first go to the Visvalingam. So, in this complex the main shrines are for Visvalingam and the Sri Ramanatha *lingam.* It is now the seat of one of the 12 *jyotirlingas.*

The Ramesvaram temple is also where Sri Chaitanya Mahaprabhu found the *Kurma Purana.* Within it He found a verse stating that Ravana kidnapped an illusory Sita, and the real Sita was safely hidden by Agni. This information has greatly relieved many devotees of Sri Sri Sita-Rama.

When we arrive at the train station, it is not unlikely to be greeted by a guide who wants your business. Actually, the first time I visited Ramesvaram I stayed for three days and saw everything on my own, taking buses instead of rickshas, etc. But the second time I took a guide and actually with his help I did more in one day than I did during the previous visit in three days. So it all depends on how you want to do things.

So we first set out to find a room in a hotel. If there is enough time left in the day, we can do the whole pilgrimage to the main temple. This begins with a holy dip in the waters of the ocean at Agni Thirtam, which is just on the east side of the temple. It is actually quite beautiful here, and you will see many *sadhus* who stay in the nearby ashramas, or who are begging for the maintenance from the pilgrims who are visiting.

After that we go to the main temple, wearing devotional clothes like *dhoti* and *kurta*, and with the help of a temple assistant we go to take a holy bath in the 22 spring-fed wells within the temple complex. The temple is quite beautiful, and I loved wandering through the halls. It takes a little while to get to know your way around since it is quite large. Anyway, with the help of an assistant, he shows us where each well is and the order in which to visit each one. Then he drops a bucket into the water and pulls it up by the rope and pours the water over you, or at least over your feet and some on your head. Some of the wells are right next to each other, but the water from each is different, some sweet while others may be more salty. Each well has a certain significance and offers particular blessings, and each bath purifies and frees us from so much karma. So, as we make our way around the temple bathing in the wells, we are purified of lifetimes of karma and become purified enough to enter the inner sanctum and make an offering to the main deity.

When our guide gives us a bag full of *puja* items, we later give it to the priest when it is our turn. These include incense, a flower garland, coconut, incense, etc. We first get in line for *darshan* of the Ramanath *lingam*. There is a special *darshan* line for 50 rupees that goes much quicker. When our turn comes, we are called forward and sit on the steps at the entrance to the sanctum and give our offering to the priest. These are offered and you can see the priest put the garland over the *linga*. Then after offering flowers and the other items, he brings some back for you as *prasada*. If no offering was provided for the priest, we still get to watch his prayers and *puja*, and he brings back the flame for us to touch and sacred ash to accept.

Then we move on to the Hanuman *lingam* (Visvalingam) which Hanuman had brought for Rama and Sita to use but was a little late.

Then we circle around to the shrine for Parvati (Parvathavardhani), the companion of Shiva, where we get in line to have *darshan* of her image while the priest does a *puja* for us. The deity is a little distance away from us and lit by ghee lamps, so the finer details are a little difficult to see. There's also a separate shrine to Lord Vishnu with a deity made of white marble, known as Sethu Madhava. There are additional shrines and small temples for Ganesh, Murugan, etc. within the temple complex. Performing this bathing and *puja* gives us immense spiritual merit and is the height of our visit to Ramesvaram. I felt very good upon doing this. Thereafter, we can continue to wander the halls of the temple for a while if we want to see whatever else there is to view, and there is, indeed, still more.

The original shrine that housed the *lingams* many years ago was but a simple thatched shed. But the temple as we see it today was begun in the 12th century and expanded over the centuries by the rulers of the area. Only Hindus or those of us willing to bathe in the 22 wells are allowed into the inner sanctum, but fortunately while I was there they also brought some of the deities out for a little parade through the streets around the temple, enabling me to see them quite clearly in the daylight as well as take photos of them.

Our next visit at Ramesvaram is to see Dhanuskodi, which is the long peninsula that extends into the sea. There's not much to see here but the small fishing village where the curious children follow you asking for rupees. But three kilometers further out on this thin stretch of sand is the confluence of the Bay of Bengal and the Indian Ocean that is considered to be Sethu Bhandan. This is said to be where Lord Rama and His devotees built the bridge from floating stones that reached Lanka in order to rescue Sita, as fully described in the *Ramayana*. At the request of Vibhishan, after having used the bridge, Rama broke it with the end of his bow, causing it to sink. Hence the name Dhanuskodi, which means "bow end." Some people say that the many rocks below the surface of the sea that leads out to Sri Lanka is evidence that such a bridge actually existed.

It is at the tip of Dhanuskodi where sincere pilgrims bathe either before or after their pilgrimage to the Ramesvaram temple. And a pilgrimage to Ramesvaram is recommended before one makes a pilgrimage to Varanasi in the eastern part of India. It is said that by taking a holy bath at Dhanuskodi one gets all the fruitive results of performing the *agnistoma* ritual, and simply by visiting Dhanuskodi one is liberated from the cycle of repeated birth and death. So, this area has many important historical connections dating back to the time of Lord Ramachandra as related in the *Ramayana*.

So, once we arrive at the fishing village, we get a ride in a truck with other pilgrims out to the sea. While there we walk over the sand to the water where we take a little holy bath in the sea for further freedom from past karma.

Heading back from the fishing village, and five miles east of Ramesvaram, is the Kothandaraman temple. It is said that Vibhishana, Ravana's brother, surrendered to Lord Rama at this place. We make a short stop here to get *darshan* of the deities and then go to see other points of interest.

About a mile and a half north of the temple is Gandhamadana Parvatham, a temple that houses the footprints of Lord Rama. It is on a hilltop from where Hanuman is believed to have leapt across the sea to Lanka. It is also from this spot that Lord Rama looked out to see where the closest place was to Sri Lanka to start building the bridge. From the top of the temple one can get a beautiful view of the town. Just at the base of the hill is a Hanuman temple that marks where Lord Rama gave His ring to Hanuman when he was to jump over the water in order to find Sita. It was this ring which he gave to Sita to prove that he was a friend of Lord Rama.

About eight kilometers west of town is Valundi Thirtam. This is where Rama and Sita got fresh water after Rama rescued Sita. Rama made a well here by shooting His arrow into the ground when Sita was thirsty and requested water to drink. There is a narrow and deteriorating bridge that takes you over the sea waves out about 30 yards to the well that is located in the salty water.

Jata Thirtam, two and a quarter miles or eight kilometers east from Ramesvaram, in a forest off the road that leads to Dhanuskodi, is a place glorified in Chapter 20 of the *Sanat Kumara Samhita* of the *Skanda Purana*. This place is said to be where Lord Rama first took His bath after killing Ravana and before worshiping the Ramanatha *lingam*. This place is also called Sidai Thirtam or Jatayu Thirtam and is where Jatayu fell after his wings had been cut by Ravana.

If we have time and interest, after we leave the Ramesvaram temple from the west entrance, then walk 25 minutes north along the road to a small Kali temple. This is maintained by a family who takes pride in their duties of devotion to the Goddess.

Ten miles northeast of Ramesvaram is the coastal village of Devipatnam or Navapashanam. Here is a temple to the nine planets, said to have been originally installed by Lord Rama for worship. The nine stone columns in the sea are said to be all that is left of the original temple.

Sixty kilometers from the Ramanathaswamy temple is a Vishnu temple known as Thiruppullani or Darbhasayanam. This marks the place where Lord Rama lay on a bed of Darbha grass before proceeding to Lanka. Inside are deities of Sri Rama lying on His grass bed. In this way, there are many points of interest that are connected to the pastimes and history of Lord Rama.

When we have completed our tour and pilgrimage to Ramesvaram, we can take leave to go toward Kannya Kumari. The best way to do this is to secure your bus ticket the day before you leave. Either your guide or using help from your hotel can make this possible. Then we go to the bus station early enough to catch the 7:30 A.M. bus out of town. The bus straight to Kannya Kumari takes about eight hours, but it has become an extremely bumpy road, and even the bus has to take it slow in parts so it is not damaged by the deep potholes that are encountered along the way. I have taken the bus straight to Kanyakumari before, but now I look forward to a break on this route.

TIRUCHENDUR

On our way from Ramesvaram we can stop to see the coastal town of Tiruchendur, 100 km northeast of Kanyakumari. Here there is a temple that many people stop to see. It is a popular place and one of the six principal temples of Muruga. The legend about it goes back to Puranic times. The architect of the demigods, Maya, built a temple for Murugan's worship of Shiva. Muruga (Subramanya) came here with the demigods to launch his attack in the last part of the war against the demon Surapadma from this location, who was camped nearby on the mid-ocean fortress. After his victory, he returned in the form of a young child and worshiped Shiva at this spot, which the temple commemerates. The other demigods and the sage Brihaspati also accompanied him.

To commemorate the victory, the celebration of Skanda Shashti is observed for six days here as well as at the other main Murugan temples. Thousands attend to especially witness the re-enactment of Surasamhara on the concluding day.

The Tiruchendur Murugan temple, also called Arupadai Veedu, is a massive structure with a typical South Indian style *gopuram* (tower gate). It is the only Murugan temple built on level ground, whereas others are on hills or elevated places. It is near the sea shore. The *gopuram* is 137 feet in height and can be seen from the main road. The beach is only about 200 yards east of the temple. About 200 yards south of the temple is a well which is 14 feet across and at the bottom of a flight of 14 steps. It is called the Nazhi Kinaru. The water smells sulphurous and is brakish. But inside this well is a smaller well, which covers an area of only one foot and is seven feet deep with sweet and crystal clear water. Bathing in the sea as well as the Nazhi Kinaru is considered spiritually auspicious.

The main temple sanctum is in a cave. The main deity is Balasubramanya, which is Subramanya or Murugan as a saintly child. He is carved from granite and is portrayed as a young child, facing east, in deep thought of Lord Shiva while holding some flowers for worship in one hand and a *japamala*, or string of beads, in the other. Shrines for Murugan's consorts of Valli and Deivayani are also here, along with shrines for Vishnu and Lakshmi in a rock cut niche. Another few images of Valli and Dattatreya are located 60 meters north of the temple along the seashore inside a natural rock facing east. Adi Shankara also visited this temple many years ago.

Five Shiva *lingams* are reached through a small tunnel behind the sanctum. It is said that Murugan still attends to offer prayers to these *lingams* through a little opening at the top of the tunnel. There is also a shrine to Lord Vishnu as Sri Venkatesha. Lord Murugan in his form as Shanmuganatha can also be seen in another major shrine here. In this form he has six faces and 12 arms.

THE PILGRIMAGE TO SIX MURUGAN TEMPLES

There are six main temples to Lord Murugan, the son of Lord Shiva. Those who are especially devoted to him may want to do such a pilgrimage. The Tiruchendur Murugan temple is one of the six main temples of Lord Murugan, and a few others we have already described. These temples are supposed to be visited in a particular order, which begins at the Tiruparankundram temple, a 30,000 year old site near Madurai. From there the route goes to Tiruchendur, Palni, Swamimalai, Tirutani, and then Palamutirsolai.

SRI VAIKUNTHAM

From Tiruchendur we can take a bus about 23 kilometers west to Sri Vaikunthum. It is about 80 km northeast of Kanyakumari between Tirunelveli and Tiruchendur. It has a train station about 2 kilometers from town. Or you can take a bus from Rameswaram to Tuticorin and then over to Palayankotai or Tirunelveli, which have better hotel facilities than what you will find at Sri Vaikuntham. Then just take a bus to Sri Vaikuntham and use an auto-ricksha to see the temples.

Sri Vaikuntham is another temple town that may interest you. There are a number of temples here that are scattered in the area called the "Nava Tirupatis" on the banks of the Tamraparni River. Once we arrive in town, we can visit all of these temples in one day if we start early enough, by 7 or 8 A.M.

We start at the nearby **Sri Vaikuntanatha temple**. This is about 1½ km from the train station, or also not far from the bus stand. The temple at Vaikuntham is regarded as Vaikuntha (the spiritual domain) on earth. This is one of the 108 Divya Desams (most holy places) of Lord Vishnu. It has a lofty, nine-tiered tower rising to a height of 110 feet over the east entrance. It is one of the tallest of the Vaishnava temples. The temple complex occupies 5 acres of land and is surrounded by a wall that stretches 580 feet long and 396 feet wide. In the typical south India fashion, there are pillars with wonderful sculptures near the entrance. Inside the temple, the deity is in the standing position with a huge mace in one of His hands. Adi Sesha is seen nearby in a position of reverence. The image of the deity is made of *shalagramas* and is bathed in milk, thereby giving the name of Pal Pandian. Though the sanctum is deep inside the temple, the sun shines its light on the deity twice a year, once during the month of Chithra (April-May) and in Aippasi or Kartika (Oct-Nov). In the temple there are also separate shrines for Senai Mudaliyar, Gurudalwar, Venugopal, Manavalamuni, and Yoga Narasimha. Another shrine has lovely deities of the ten *avataras* of Vishnu.

The hall near the main *gopuram*, facing south, is a treasure of architecture. It has the shrine of Venkatesha, called Thiruvenkatamudaiyan. This was built by Vadamalayappa Pillai, an official of the Nayak ruler of Madurai. Extremely ornate figures of Krishna's *avataras* and more adorn the pillars, some of which are 5 feet wide. There are also exquisite sculptures depicting scenes from the *Ramayana*. Other halls contain sculptures of animals, scenes from the *Bhagavata Purana*, and even paintings of the 108 Divya Desams.

The legend behind this temple is related to Lord Brahma. A demon named Somuka took the four *Vedas* from Brahma who was helpless to the force of the demon. Thus, he went to Vaikunta Vana forest on the banks of the Tamraparni River and engaged in austerities. MahaVishnu, seeing the sincere efforts of Lord Brahma, appeared before him and promised to retrieve the *Vedas*. Indeed, Lord Vishnu did overpower the demon, acquired the *Vedas*, and returned them to Brahma. He also consented to reside at Vaikunta Vana as the deity of Vaikuntanatha.

The image of Vaikunthanatha had no patron to care for it, so in time, He became neglected. Both the shrine and the image lay buried under the earth. The area became one of the grazing areas for the cows when it was under the rule of the Pandya kings. One of the king's cows never gave any milk, and after watching, the king's officials reported back that the cow always poured her milk onto a specific site in Vaikunta Vana. The ruler sensed the presence of a divine element and then dug the spot with caution and respect. The deity of Lord Vishnu was recovered, making the king exhilarant. He constructed the temple at that spot and reinstated the deity in the temple.

Later on there was a gang of robbers that roamed the area that would rob the wealthy of their ill-gotten riches. One-half of the booty was always given to the deity of Vaikuntanatha, and the other part was given for the poor. In this way, the poor very much liked the head of the gang. The Pandya ruler, however, tried most seriously to catch him. He caught everyone in the gang but the leader, Kaladushana. Then MahaVishnu, masquerading as Kaladushana, surrendered himself to the Pandya king. But later, MahaVishnu revealed His true form to the ruler and said that he had created Kaladushana only to teach the world that large accumulation of ill-gotten wealth and possessions without utilizing them for charitable purposes would result in ultimate loss. The ruler was greatly enlightened by these words and built a huge temple to accommodate the Lord, who came to be known as Kallapiran (Lord of Thieves).

As we visit the following temples that are also in the area of Sri Vaikuntham, they are all similar in design. They all have *gopurams* of varying sizes, some are larger and more embellished than others, with halls containing sculpted pillars, and sanctums deep in the temple with Lord Vishnu in one of His forms. Each of these temples has Puranic lore that is associated with them, and are known as places where Lord Vishnu had descended or shown Himself to persons for various reasons.

Riding the auto-rickshaw to see these eight temples is a rather enjoyable ride through small villages and farms, seeing the simple life of the people here. These temples are not near populated areas, so they are rather quiet and peaceful as we visit them and walk through the halls and get *darshan* of the lovely Vishnu deities.

The next place we go to is the **Adinatha Swami temple** at Alwar Tirunagari, which is about 33 km east of Tirunelveli and 28 km west of Tiruchendur. The pillars in the temple can make musical notes when they are tapped. This is also the birthplace of Manavalamuni and Namm Alwar, one of the most eminent of the Vaishnava Tamil saints. The tamarind tree called Toongapuli next to the shrine of Namm Alwar marks his birthplace. The deity here is beautifully adorned with gold and has five devis, sincluding Sri, Bhu, and Neela.

Three km further east is **Tirukkolur**, the third place we visit. The temple here houses the Vishnu deity known as Vaitthama Nidhi. He is a very impressive reclining Vishnu.

Also three km east of Alwar Tirunagari is **Tholaivillimangalam**, our fourth and fifth temples to visit. This is called Iratti Tirupati since the two shrines here are considered as one in the list of Divya Desams. These are dedicated to Srinavasa, a sitting Vishnu in silver adornments, and also called Aravind Lokshana. The other is for Senthamarai Kannan, a standing Vishnu.

The **Makaranedugulaikkaadan Vishnu temple** is the sixth place to see, and is located in Tirupperai, five km southeast of Alwar Tirunagari.

Tirukkulandai is our seventh stop at 11 km northeast of Sri Vaikuntham. The temple to see here belongs to the Vishnu deity of Sri Mayakuthan.

Our eighth stop is at **Thiruppulingudi**, three km from the train station at Sri Vaikuntham, to see the temple of Kaisina Vendan, a lovely reclining Vishnu.

Our ninth and last stop here is at the town of **Varagunamangai**, only a half km east of Sri Vaikuntham, to see the temple of Vijayasanar Vishnu, another reclining Vishnu deity.

The **NavaKailasams**, the nine holy temples for Lord Shiva, are also found in this area. They are similar to the NavaThirupatis, and are also located along the banks of the Tamraparni River. They are in various locations known as Papanasam, Ariyanayakipuram, Cherkadevi, Tirunelveli, Murappanadu, Sri Vaikuntham, Thenthiruperai, Rajapathy, and Serndapoomangalam. The presiding deity in all of these nine temples is known as Kailasanatha.

The Kailasanatha temple of Sri Vaikuntam is located only one kilometer from the Vaikuntanatha temple. The main deity here is in the form of a *swayambhu linga* or self-manifesting *linga*. The consort is named Sivagami. The hall contains many artistic sculptures on the elegant pillars. Chandrakula Pandya, the ruler of Madurai, is said to have constructed the sanctums and hallways. Veerappa Nayak (1609-23) further embellished the temple.

TIRUNELVELI

Tirunelveli is fifty or so kilometers northwest from Tiruchendur, or about 25 km from Sri Vaikuntham, and 90 km northeast of Kanyakumari. It has the large Kanthimathi Nellayappar temple complex which occupies 14 acres, dedicated to Shiva-Parvati in two temples, one for each. This is a very active place with many *pujas* happening and numerous pilgrims stopping by. It is filled with long and ornately carved multi-pillared halls with numerous shrines. So it takes some time to go through it. In front of the main sanctum is a hall with musical pillars. There is also a golden lily tank, and a beautiful 1000 pillared hall where they perform the Shiva-Parvati marriage in Oct-Nov. The temple was built by a Pandya king in the 7th century. This is one of the five places where Shiva is known to have performed His cosmic dance.

Another temple in this town is **the Sri Sanjeevi Varadha Anjaneyar Swamy temple**, more popularly called the Getwell Anjaneyar Hanuman temple. This is dedicated to Hanuman wherein there is a most beautiful deity of Hanuman. It is very small but quite active with a steady flow of pilgrims that engage the priests in regular *pujas*.

Other temples in the area of Tirunelveli include **Papanasam**, 42 kilometers away. This holy place on the western *ghat* of Pothigai Hills is close to the Papanasam Falls, on the banks of the Thamiraparani River where Shiva and Parvathi appeared before the great saint Agasthiya. Hence the falls is popularly called the Agasthiya Falls. To commemorate the visit of the divine couple, the Agasthiya temple was built here.

Tenkasi is 53 kilometers from Tirunelveli and as the name implies is the Kashi (Varanasi) of the south with more temples to see.

The Kutralanathar temple, 50 kilometers away, is dedicated to Lord Thirukutralanathar (Shiva). This temple contains many inscriptions about Chola and Pandya kings. Less than a furlong from here is a small temple called the Chitra Sabha (Hall of Pictures) dedicated to Lord Nataraja, Shiva as king of the dancers. This temple is decorated with paintings of rural deities and devotees, Puranic stories, and religious events. This *sabha* is one of five where Lord Nataraja is said to have performed his cosmic dance.

KRISHNAPURAM

Krishnapuram is a tiny village about 10 kilometers from Tirunelveli. It has the temple of Sri Venkatachalapathy, which provides fine examples of the art of Nayak sculpture. The town was originally known as Thiruvenkatapuram, or the place of Lord Venkatapa, Vishnu, after the presiding deity, but was later named Krishnapuram by Krishnappa Nayakar.

The temple complex occupies an area of 18 acres and is located about two furlongs from the highway. A five-tiered *gopuram* over the eastern entrance shows the way. Panels on it and pillars in the halls show sculptures of Mahavishnu, Adisesha, Narasimha, Trivikrama, and Subramanya on a peacock. The temple has three inner *prakaras* or courtyards, each surrounded by sturdy walls. The temple is not very active nor in a very popular area, so not as many devotees visit this temple.

In the central sanctum the main deity of Sri Venkatachalapathy greets the devotees in a standing position with Sridevi and Bhudevi at his sides. The deity is made of granite and stands about four feet tall. Two of His hands hold the conch and disc, the other two are in poses of greeting and blessing. The smaller *utsavar* deity, Srinivasa Perumal, is identically formed. Additional shrines in the temple accommodate other associates of the Lord, or other prominent devotees.

The temple has several halls, and the complex has numerous examples of excellent stone carving work in various forms. The magnificent images and the ingenious workmanship, descriptions of which could go on for several pages, have won the appreciation of numerous art lovers who have visited this temple. More people should be made aware of the unique artwork that exists here, although photography is not allowed.

KANYAKUMARI

To reach Kanyakumari, we can either take a direct bus from Ramesvaram, Tiruchendur, or Tirunelveli, depending on where we are coming from. The direct bus from Ramesvaram to Kanyakumari is the best way to take this trip if you do not want to stop and see anything along the way. It used to take about 9 hours. However, the road has gotten so bad over the years with pot holes and deterioration that the ride now takes almost 12 hours. It has become a tortuous ride until they fix and maintain the road again. However, the ride from Tirunelveli is much smoother and quick. On this ride to Kanyakumari, you will pass by many agricultural areas, lots of rice fields, and groves of coconut and banana trees. Along the coast you can see places where they produce salt from sea water. You often pass through little villages with small and simple shops. Huts with thatched roofs nestled in the shade of lots of palm trees are often found on the outskirts of town. It can be very exotic. You will see the local people going about their business, stopping long enough to watch the bus go by. The bus from Tirunelveli or Palayankotai first goes to Nagercoil, where you then switch to a bus to Kanyakumari.

At Kanyakumari, the southernmost tip of India (Land's End), we find a small but busy tourist town hosting people from all over the world. It has a resort feel to it with numerous hotels and guest houses in various price ranges. There are many souvenir shops and lots of vendors selling all kinds of sea shells. This town takes pride in the fact that it is the only place where, during a full moon, you can simultaneously watch the sun set into the sea in the west and the moon rise from the sea in the east. The Bay of Bengal is to the east, the Indian Ocean to the south, and the Arabian Sea to the west. Many people gather at the open monument near this confluence of seas to watch the sunrise and sunset, which are most beautiful to see. There is also a bathing *ghat* here, and to bathe in the confluence of these three seas is considered sacred and has the means to purify one from sins. It is said that only after bathing here and worshiping goddess Kanyakumari is one's pilgrimage to Varanasi in the north considered to be complete.

This town is a holy place of pilgrimage. The temple here is dedicated to Devi Parashakthi's (Parvati's) incarnation as goddess Kanyakumari. The legend and the reason for the sanctity of this place is that goddess Kanyakumari did penance here in order to secure Shiva's hand in marriage, and gave a blessing for all who bathe in the waters here. The legend is that once there was a time when the demons (*asuras*) gained supremacy over the demigods (*devas*) and unrighteousness (*adharma*) began to abound. Banasura in particular was the demon who threatened the *devas*, creating havoc amongst them, having gained a boon by which he could only be killed by a virgin girl.

Lord Vishnu advised the *devas* to worship Parashakti because only she would be able to vanquish Banasura. So the *devas* performed the Vedic fire rituals and Parashakti appeared as a small girl and promised to annihilate the evil forces. She traveled to the southern tip of India and meditated on Lord Shiva. As time went on, she grew into a teenager. Seeing her in this way, Lord Shiva became attracted and agreed to marry her, and arrangements were made. However, the great sage Narada Muni, seeing this development and realizing that the marriage would destroy the potential for Parashakti to kill Banasura, stepped in to change things.

Narada told Parashakti that maybe it was not Shiva but Banasura in disguise who wanted to marry her. So he told her that a test was in order, and that she should ask Shiva to deliver her a coconut without eyes, a stalk of sugarcane without stump-joints, and a betel leaf without veins. Of course, Shiva did all that easily, and the marriage plans went on accordingly.

So on the day of the wedding, which was to take place at midnight on a certain auspicious day, Lord Shiva began his journey from Suchindram to Kanyakumari. But when he was in the town of Vazhukhamparai, 5 km away, Narada took the form of a rooster and crowed, falsely heralding the new dawn. Thinking that he had missed the appointed hour of his marriage, Shiva returned to Suchindram. In Kanyakumari's anger over Shiva not arriving, she scattered all the food that had been gathered for the wedding, which then turned into the small pebbles and different colored sands that remain on the shore of the town. Though heart broken because she could not get Lord Shiva as her husband in that lifetime, the goddess vowed to remain a virgin (Kanya) and continue her austerities. It was on the rock island (where Vivekananda's memorial is now located and which may have been part of the mainland at one time) that the goddess Kanya did her penance. There is a small shrine, the Shripada Mandapam that houses a stone with the goddess Kanya's footprint on it. Many pilgrims take the ferry for the short ride to the island to see this stone.

The demon Banasura heard about the beauty of Kanyakumari and decided to try asking for her hand in marriage, but she rejected him. The demon tried to take her by force and drew his sword, but she was also armed with her weapon. A fierce battle ensued and Kanyakumari fatally struck Banasura with her chakra in the place of Mahadana Puram, about 4 km north of the town of Kanyakumari.

However, at the moment of his death, Banasura repented for his wicked deeds and prayed to Parashakti for compassion and absolve him and anyone else who bathed in the waters off Kanyakumari of their sins. The goddess granted Banasura the blessing. This is why people who come to Kanyakumari bathe in the holy confluence of the waters off the tip of Kanyakumari, which include the Bay of Bengal, the Indian Ocean, and Arabian Sea.

As we enter the Parashakthi temple complex through the *gopuram* at the southern tip of town, we first leave our shoes at the shoe stall, which can be quite crowded and disorderly with people leaving or getting their shoes. Many people will be mingling in the area either entering or moving on. We make our way into the temple and may have to get in the line with other pilgrimis. The deity in the Kanyakumari temple is in the form of a young girl holding a rosary in her right hand, still performing austerities as she waits for Lord Shiva to arrive. It is said that the deity, made of blue stone, was installed by Sri Parashurama many hundreds of years ago. The temple also has shrines to Indra Vinayak and Thyagasundari. Westerners can also go in to see the beautiful deity. When I went to the temple, a priest at the gate objected to my carrying a camera bag into the temple, but my guide, an old man who spoke no English, argued with the priest and got me in. He also took me through the east door by-passing the queue of people. The deity was very nice to see, though poorly lit with only several ghee lamps hanging from the ceiling, as it is with many South Indian temples. Plus, you could only view her from a distance of 10 to 15 feet, adjusting yourself as people move about. As you walk through the temple, you can also view the deities in the other shrines, which include Ganesh, Surya, Bala Sundari, and Lord Ayyappa. There is also a special well inside the courtyard that supplies water for worshiping the deity.

There is also a memorial to Gandhi on the beach across from the temple where his ashes were displayed before being immersed into the sea. It is three storeys tall and is shaped with elements of Hindu, Christian and Islamic architecture. You get a nice view over the beach area from the top. There is a hole in the ceiling that allows the sun's rays to enter, which shine on the memorial stone where Gandhi's ashes were once displayed. Along the most southern end of the beach are also smaller shrines, such as one to Adi Shankaracharya.

The memorial to Swami Vivekananda is on the rock island 200 meters off the shore. Vivekananda came to this place to meditate for three days in 1892 before traveling to America and around the world as one of India's most renowned spiritual crusaders. A ferry service takes you out to it, if you are willing to wait in the lines for a while. It also takes you to the second island next to the Vivekananda rock on which there is the large, 133 feet tall statue of the great Tamil poet Thiruvalluvar, which was erected in 2000. The islands offer a good view of Kanyakumari. When I went there back in 1990, you had to check in your camera upon arrival at the island because no photography was allowed. Now they have relaxed that and you can take photos everywhere but in the temples.

The Guhanantheswara temple dedicated to Shiva is another small but noteworthy temple in Kanyakumari. It is just around the corner to the south from the railway station. It is of legendary and historical importance. The *Sthala Purana* (local Puranic history) of Kanyakumari says that Lord Muruga Guha selected Kanyakumari as the best place for worshiping his father Lord Shiva and erected a Shiva *linga* for worship. So the presiding deity of the temple came to be known as Guhanandeswara (the Easwara or Ishwara who blessed Guha). According to inscriptions it is learned that Raja Raja Chola renovated the temple in the Chola style of art and architecture in the year 1000 C.E., and Kanyakumari was then called Rajarajeswaram, and the deity was called Thirupenthuswarar.

SUCHINDRAM

At Suchindram, 13 kilometers to the northwest of Kanyakumari, a pleasant taxi ride away, there is the Stanumalayam (Trimurti) temple, an interesting place to visit. The original construction of the temple was in the ninth century, but it was greatly expanded in the 17th century. The *gopuram* is 134 feet tall and can be seen from a long distance away. Once again we find a temple filled with large hallways, temple art, painted ceilings, and beautifully sculpted pillars, some of which are musical and produce different tones when you knock on them. The outside of the temple is covered with carved designs and friezes that depict legends from the *Ramayana* and *Puranas*. Westerners can enter this temple and see all the divinities as well as the *arati* ceremonies, the offering of lamps. However, photography is not allowed inside. Plus, when going in, you used to have to wear a special *dhoti* or wrap one over your clothes, but that practice seems to have ended. It is also best to take a guide for a few rupees if you want to quickly find your way around. The temple has several shrines to various Divinities but is dedicated to Trimurti, the three main personalities of Vishnu, Shiva, and Brahma, all on a single *lingam* in the main sanctum. Many legends are connected with this place. One tradition is that Indra, the King of Heaven, worships the *lingam* here every night, as he has done for many years. In one of the halls, there is an impressive image of Hanuman that stands 18 feet tall opposite Lord Rama's shrine. Around the main sanctum are several other shrines to Ganesh, Murugan, Parvati, etc.

When our visit to Kanyakumari is finished, we board the early morning train to start traveling north along the coast. From Kanyakumari through Kerala and Karnataka, there are a number of interesting and spectacular temples that you should not miss if you are in the area. To go to these various temples, many of which are in small towns, you will have to take a bus or combination of train and bus. Buses in this area give horrendous rides, either driving full speed on the bumpy roads through the countryside and villages, or braking hard to avoid hitting something, or slowing just enough to let passengers get on or off. This tends to bounce you up and down and throw you back and forth continuously until you feel like you are getting blisters from your seat. Sitting in the back of the bus gives a rougher ride but allows for some relief from the constant shrill noise of the horn which is worse in the front and used every few seconds. It is adventure at its finest.

THIRUATTUR (or THIRUVATTUR or THIRUVATTAR)

Thiruattur, about 50 kilometers south of Trivandrum, is the Adi Keshava temple located near the banks of the Payasvini River. Thiruattur is a small town, but many pilgrims stop in to see the temple. The easiest way to visit Thiruattur and Suchindram is to take a taxi from Kanyakumari for about 700 rupees. It is 46 kilometers from Kanyakumari, or a 1 ½ hour taxi ride. You can also reach it by getting a bus from Trivandrum going to Nagarcoil or Kanyakumari, and stopping at Marthandum, and then get another bus to Thiruattur. Thiruattur is on the Thoduvetti Kulasekharam Road. The temple is only about ten minutes from the bus stop in a calm and isolated area. A bus from Trivandrum, or by taking a tour for Kanyakumari, will stop at Padmanabhapuram to see the palace there. You can also stop to see it when traveling from Kanyakumari for Trivandrum. This is a lovely palace with parts dating back to the 14th and 16th century.

The Adi Keshava temple has beautiful architecture but is not as large as the one in Trivandrum, though the style is similar. The architecture here, as with several other temples in Kanyakumari district, resembles that of the temples of Kerala, using a combination of wood and stone. This temple has been glorified by a decad of 11 verses composed by Nammalwar in the first millennium C.E. It is an important center of worship and is also referred to as Adi Anantam and Dakshina Vaikuntham.

The legend behind this temple involves Lord Brahma. It is described that once when Brahma wanted to have *darshan* of MahaVishnu, he performed a penance, but he failed to perform it properly in regard to the rules in the Agamas. Thus, from the sacrificial fire came a demon named Kesha, along with his sister, Keshi. They immediately had one thing in mind, and that was to mitigate their enormous appetites. Brahma granted them the blessing of long life and that they could go anywhere in the universe in search of prey. Then the demons went everywhere, subjecting even the virtuous and pious to fear and suffering. The great sages could no longer cope with the atrocities that were being committed and prayed to MahaVishnu to save the world from this terror. Upon hearing the prayers of the devout sages, MahaVishnu and Adisesha both descended to the Earth planet. A battle ensued and the demon was soon forced to give up his pride and surrender to the Lord. MahaVishnu ordered Adisesha to coil himself over the body of the Kesha demon. Then MahaVishnu reclined on Adisesha and, in this way, keeps the demon bound up, otherwise he would escape and again wreak havoc over the planet.

However, the demon's sister, Keshi, vowed vengeance for her brother. She is said to have taken the form of the Tampraparni River, and then made the Tamraparni River flood the land. MahaVishnu, however, directed Bhudevi, the deity of the Earth planet, to raise the level of the land, thus ending the attempts of the river to immerse the area. Humbled by this course of events, the Tamraparni offered obeisances to the Lord and went around His abode, like a garland that wrapped the temple with water. The place where the river divided itself to form a circle is called "Moonattu Mugam" and "Kothai Pirali." And the place where the river circles around it is called Thiruattur.

Shiva is believed to have taken on 12 forms to witness the battle that went on between Vishnu and Kesi, and to worship Vishnu. A pilgrimage to all of the 12 main Shiva temples is considered complete only after visiting this temple at Tiruvattaar.

The temple at Thiruattur is situated on a platform in a compound of 1 ½ acres. It is surrounded by a massive 30-foot tall wall. Nearby on three sides is the Tamraparni River and its tributaries. On the western side is the *ghat* where a dip is considered to relieve one of numerous sinful reactions.

The temple still maintains the old traditions and male members must wear a *dhoti*. Entrance with pants or trousers is not allowed. You enter the temple through the eastern doorway after climbing about 25 steps. The gate is a lovely structure of tiles and wood, typical of the Kerala style of architecture, but similar to the South Indian temple *gopurams*. From the entrance, one goes south to the shrine of Sri Butanatha. Next is a room in the southwest corner where we find deities of Adikeshava, Devi, and Venkatachalapathi. Walking along the outer hallway, we reach the place of the copper flagstaff, the *dwajasthamba*. This was installed by Maharaja Mulam Tirunal of Travancore in 1895. Next we come to the Nalambalam, the circumambulatory passage around the sanctum (Sri Balippuram), which is a hall with 224 ornately carved granite pillars. These have lovely images of Deepalakshmis, which are the Lakshmis (the goddess of fortune) that carry the lamps. No two images are the same, each one differing in hairstyles or in positions.

In front of the sanctum is the Mukhamantap hall, which is shaped out of a single piece of black granite. This is three feet thick and 17 ½ by 15 feet long. It certainly shows the skill of which the stone carvers had during the day when this temple was built. The pillars nearby in the Balipeeta Mantap have life-size images that include Vishnu, Lakshmana, Indrajit, Venugopal, Nataraja, and Parvati, and even Brahma playing the veena, as well as others. There is also a shrine to Tiruvambadi Krishna. Additional shrines to Adi Kesava, Venkatachalapati, and Taayaar are also found. And the flag staff of copper was built by the Travancore royal family.

The sanctum faces west, although the main temple entrance is to the east. In this inner sanctum is the deity of MahaVishnu who is 18 feet long and lies on Seshanaga. The deity faces west as it is said that He is looking toward the Sri Padmanabhaswamy temple in Trivandrum. For a full *darshan*, the deity must be viewed through three doors. The sanctum has been designed so that the rays of the setting sun illuminate the face of the deity. MahaVishnu lets His left hand hang down. The hoods of Adisesha rising over the head of MahaVishnu can also be seen. The deity is beautifully made out of a combination of ingredients that is known as Katusarkara yogam. This requires that the deity is not washed with water, but the smaller or festival deity is regularly worshiped, anointed, and dressed in ornaments and flowers. One man there told me the deity was made of 16,108 *shalagram shilas*. This deity is also accompanied by Lakshmi and Bhudevi on either side. A separate shrine is found in which the deity of Alambadi Krishna is located.

The *Padma Purana* describes the original temple at this location as having been built in Treta-yuga many thousands of years ago, originating before the Sri Padmanabhaswamy temple in Trivandrum. This temple is also one of the 108 Divya Desams (most holy places of Lord Vishnu) of the Vaishnavas. This is also the Krishna temple which Sri Chaitanya Mahaprabhu visited on His tour of South India and found a copy of the ancient *Brahma-samhita*. This has become an important text for all Vaishnavas.

According to the descriptions in "15 Vaishnava Temples of Tamil Nadu" by M. Rajagopalam, this temple is noted for particular miracles that have taken place here. One example is that in 1674, the Muslim vandals chose Thiruattur as one of their targets of attack. Queen Rani Umai Ammai Nachair, the ruler of this area, found herself unequal to the task of thwarting the attack. She went to the warrior-king Kerala Varma of Kottayam for support, but he was not hopeful for his chances at victory. He went to the Adikeshava temple and chanted fourteen verses to invoke the Lord to grant success for his endeavor. These verses are known as the *Bhakta Sangeerthanam* and are recited even today by the devotees. After chanting them, the ruler felt that a soldier clad in green armor had left the sanctum of the Lord. As the Muslim army approached, they were attacked by hoards of wasps. Their commander was stung to death. Thereafter, the demoralized forces ran for their lives and the attack was thwarted.

Another example is that in 1741 Marthanda Varma, the king of Travancore, was engaged in a bitter struggle with the Dutch at Colachel. Before embarking on the venture, he placed his sword at the feet of Adikeshava and sought His blessings. He emerged triumphant in the battle. Dilanoi, the Generalissimo of the Dutch forces, became his captive. Later, Dilanoi became an admirer of Marthanda Varma and was appointed the commander of the Travancore army.

In the eighteenth century the temple was again the target of the Muslim invaders. The army of the Nawab of Arcot desecrated the temple and defaced it of its ornaments. The Utsava deity was also captured and stored in a lumber room along with other articles. The deity would appear on top of the pile everyday, pushing aside all the weights that were put on it. The perplexed Nawab had it chained down, boring two holes in the pedestal. At that time the Begum of the Nawab was afflicted with a disease. She was unable to withstand the excruciating pain. The physicians could do nothing about it. Then the deity appeared to the Azhathi or guard of the temple, and told him to recover the small festival or *utsava* deity. Explaining the greatness of the Lord, the Azhathi convinced the Nawab that the disease would be cured once the deity was restored to its original place in the temple. The Nawab complied and was surprised that the disease in his Begum had disappeared. The Nawab repented for his blasphemous deeds and as a token of gratitude, he offered a pillow, crown, and a plate of gold. A special *puja* or worship was performed wherein a cap that is used to crown the deity is fashioned like the Muslim head-dress. This was instituted by the Nawab and is still performed during the two annual Utsavams.

During the original *puja*, the Azhathi carrying the deity placed it alongside the Shiva temple at a place called Thali and had a bath. On return he was dismayed to find the deity could not be moved. The Maharaja came to know of this strange phenomenon and decided to take the deity of Adikeshava to Thali every year for performing an *arati* worship. Only after this decision was made could the deity be moved. This incident is commemorated every year during the Aippasi festival performed at Thali.

TRIVANDRUM (TIRUVANANDAPURAM)

Here we find the Sri Padmanabhaswamy temple, a large ornate structure built about 400 years ago. It is popular and busy. It is dedicated to Sri Vishnu as He reclines on His servant, Ananta or Adisesha. In fact, the name Trivandrum is short for Tiruvanandapuram, which means the abode of the serpent Anantha (Sesha). The temple is a Divya Desam, or one of the 108 most important temples to Lord Vishnu. The deity of reclining Vishnu in the sanctum is flanked on all sides by Sri Devi, Bhudevi, Niladevi, and different sages. From His navel sprouts a lotus on which is Lord Brahma. The deity, made from 12,000 *shalagramas*, always had a black complexion. He does display gold feet, hands, and crown. This place is mentioned in five of the *Puranas*, namely the *Padma, Skanda, Vayu, Varaha,* and *Brahmanda Puranas.*

The deity is 20 feet long and in a compartment that has three doors in the front: one for His upper body, one showing His midsection, and another for His legs and feet. To get a full view, one has to do obeisances at all three doors. There are other shrines throughout the temple for Krishna, Narasimha, Subramanya, Ganesh, etc. It is open only to Hindus who must wear or rent a *dhoti* to go in. Men must remove their shirts as well. However, Westerners or white-skinned Hindus are forbidden to enter. Nonetheless, they can go in if they sign a form stating their respect for Hinduism. You can do this at the management office across from the north entrance to the temple. It is well worth it. The first time I went, this was a fairly easy procedure. I simply signed a form while with some Indian friends and then went in. The second time a few years later, the management said that I needed to first get a certificate from the local Iskcon temple, which is not too far away, that said I was a Hindu. Then you have to go to the palace and get it signed by the local prince's personal secretary. Then you come back to the temple and submit it to the security department on the eastern side of the temple who will then let you in. However, if you want to return to the temple at a later date, make sure you retain the certificate and not lose it. This whole prcodure seems to be a filtering system based on prejudice to keep out anyone who is not Indian. But if you are serious, plan ahead and accept that it is a process that may take a day of your time. So plan accordingly.

Once in the temple, the halls are cavernous and there are beautifully carved columns and stone and woodwork. The hall that leads to the sanctum has 324 carved pillars. The Kulashekara Mandapam hall has 24 columns of excellent quality, four of which give musical sounds when tapped. It would be a photographer's delight if only you could take photos. But no cameras are allowed inside.

The origin of this temple is prehistoric. There is no clear evidence of when this temple was established or who had installed the deity. However, according to the late Dr. L. A. Ravi Varma, a great historian, the original temple was built on the first day of Kali-yuga and is at least 5000 years old. From records such as *Grandahavali* and the *Ananthasayana Mahatmya*, it appears that the temple was constructed on the 950th day of Kali-yuga by the saint Divakar Muni from Tuludesh (Mangalore). The story in brief is that the sage was doing penance offering prayers to his favorite deity. Suddenly, Lord MahaVishnu appeared before him as a little child. The saint became so fascinated and affectionate to the child that he could hardly think of anything else. He pleaded to the child not to leave him and it was agreed that the child would stay under certain conditions that there could be no misconduct by the sage. But one time the child began to chew on the sage's *shalagrama shilas* and acted in a most mischievous manner, and the sage got angry. Then the child said "If you want to see me, you must go to Ananthankadu," and immediately diappeared. Then the sage understood who the child was. The sage became so remorseful and began searching for the child. Finally, he saw the child disappear into the hollow of a big Alappa tree near the sea coast. The tree fell to the ground and assumed the shape of a huge reclining Vishnu, extending as much as 13 kilometers. His head was at the town of Tiruvallam (about 5 km from the present temple) and His feet at Trippapur (8 km in the opposite direction). Elated with joy, the sage prayed to the Lord to shorten His huge form so that it could be seen within the view of one's eyes. So the Lord shortened His form to equal three times the length of the sage's staff or dunda. The sage then began to happily worship this wooden form of the Lord.

Much later, after 1731 during some of the renovation of the temple, the deity was replaced with a bed of 12,000 *shalagrama shilas* molded into the shape of the deity with the help of kadukusarkara, which is a kind of mortar. This is the deity that is worshiped to this day.

Thiruvananthapuram was mentioned in the *Bhagavata Purana* as Syanandoorapuram in descriptions of the pilgrimage of Lord Balarama. The temple has undergone various stages of renovation and reconstruction over the years.

Festivals are naturally a part of this temple. Ten-day festivals are held in the months of Meenam (March-April) and Thulan (Sept-Oct). These are noted for their colorful flag hoisting on the first day, and then on the ninth is a grand procession, and on the tenth they observe taking the processional deity to the sea to give Him a sacred dip in the ocean. Thousands of devotees come to watch this event. Navaratri is also a big festival here with the worship of goddess Sarasvati. Beautiful *pujas* (rituals) and musical concerts are arranged for the event. Also, twice a year they have Bhadra Deepams, the lighting of many lamps, and at the end of 12 such festivals, or once every six years during Makara Sankranti, they have Laksha Deepam, the lighting of one *lakh* (100,000) of lamps.

For a change of pace, while in Trivandrum, you may also want to visit the Napier Museum to see its collection of bronzes, costumes, old deities, etc., or the Sri Chitra Art Gallery which has works of art from many Asian countries. There is also a zoo, Botanical Gardens, and an aquarium. There is also the Kerala Kalaripaytta demonstration, which is a form of martial arts that is famous all over the world and said to pre-date other forms of Far Eastern martial arts. The Kathakali form of dancing in Kerala, using colorful masks and costumes, is also world famous.

There are numerous temples near Trivandrum and many others throughout Kerala. Most of them are smaller, made of wooden and styled in a conical form or even rectangular with multiple storeyed roofs. For example, the Neyyattinkara Sri Krishna Swamy temple is 18 kilometers from Trivandrum on the route toward Kanyakumari. The Thiruvallam Sri Parasuramaswamy temple is 5 kms from Trivandrum on the route to Kovalam. The Pazhavangady Ganapathy temple is in the heart of the city and is visited by thousands of devotees daily. The Srikanteswaram (Shiva) temple is also not far from Trivandrum.

VARKALA

As we continue to head north from Trivandrum, there are drastic changes in the architecture of the temples. No more do we find large pyramid-like stone *gopurams* at the gates of huge complexes with many buildings. Instead, we find carved woodwork and much smaller temples.

Varkala, 35 kilometers north of Trivandrum, has a very ancient temple (said to be over 2000 years old) dedicated to Lord Vishnu as Janardhana. This temple is in a beautiful location not far from the sea and is a fine example of Kerala architecture. There are some smaller shrines to Shiva and Ganesh, but the main deity is a standing Vishnu, believed to have been found in the sea by fishermen who installed Him in a temple. This temple has a circular sanctum topped with a conical dome made with sheets of copper. The deity is four-armed and stands four feet tall. It is said that Brahma worshiped Vishnu here and did penance. Numerous temple festivals go on throughout the area at particular times of the year.

Besides this temple, there are other small temples scattered throughout the communities here. You can ask your hotel or any local ricksha driver about them. The beach here is also becoming well known by Westerners who are looking for a place to hang out, since places like Kovalam are filling up and becoming too congested with people. Varkala has great beaches and cliffs above which there are numerous restaurants, cottages, guest houses, and places to stay. It is also a place where you can see examples of the Kathakali style of dancing. Exhibitions of the local dancing go on regularly.

KOLLAM TO AMRITAPURI

On your way north you may want to stop at Kollam, which is a nearby stopping point and railway station from where you can take a bus or taxi to Amritapuri, the ashrama of Mother Ammachi, otherwise known as Amritanandamayi. But if we stop at Kollam, there are a few temples we can see while we are here.

The Sri Uma Mahesvara Swamy temple is in the heart of Kollam, just a few minutes walk from Chinnakkada Junction. So if you do stop in Kollam, this is a temple that you can see. It is open to all irrespective of cast and creed. Uma and Mahesvara are on the same pedestal in the Srikoil. This is rare and worship here is good for fulfilling desires.

The Sri Ramesvaram temple in the outskirts of town has a main deity of Shiva. It is one of the 108 Shivalayas. This 12th century temple has archeological importance in its design.

The Thirumallavaram MahaVishnu temple is five kms from Kollam situated near the beach. It is famous for Karkataka Vavu Bali or doing oblations to the ancestors. The Meenam Aarattu festival is famous for its procession of 40 caparisoned elephants.

To reach Amritapuri, you can easily take a bus or taxi, or book the train to Karunagapally (10 km south of Amritapuri) or to Kayamkulam (12 km north). Anyone is welcome here, but you may want to make arrangements at least ten days in advance to make sure there will be rooms in which to stay if that is your intention.

The place which takes up several acreas of land is very busy with numerous foreigners as well as Indian pilgrims who come to see Mother Ammachi. They say there are about 2500 people there at most times. There are tall apartment buildings for guests, and there is a central great hall where they serve food at certain times for the pilgrims at breakfast, lunch, and dinner. There are also a few cafes that provide a small menu of items. There is also a regulated schedule for worship, chanting, meditation, bhajans, and personal study. There are also classes offered in yoga, Sanskrit, Vedanta, and meditation. So it is easy for someone to plug into a regulated scheme of study and practice here. However, there are also many foreigners and tourists who mostly wander around and hang out, spending time talking to friends, etc. In the temple building on the second floor are the information centers to help visitors find their way around, as well as laundry service, internet café, mail service, etc. Tapes of Ammachi's talks and bhajans are also played most of the time over the loudspeakers throughout the area of the ashrama.

In the midst of the buildings is Kilari, the little house where Amma was born and the addition to it where she first started giving *darshans* and talks. So for many, this is a place of pilgrimage. You will always find several or more people here doing prayers or doing meditation. Next to that is a three-storey structure where Amma now lives.

In the great hall Mother Ammachi, when she is not traveling abroad, gives lectures, bhajans, and also her *darshans* on a daily basis in which hundreds and thousands of people line up to receive her hugs. Sometimes there can be as many as eight or nine thousand or more people in a day who seek her blessings. And she will stay there giving hugs and guidance for as long as it takes, which can be until the early morning hours the next day if necessary, only to start over again with the new day. Foreigners who are not staying long or who are new can get a priority ticket at the Seva desk in which you are given a certain time slot around noon in which to get in line for easier *darshan* with her. However, absolutely no cameras, lenses, or cell phones are allowed when you go up for *darshan* due to security precautions. You have to leave these at the security desk. While in the line, you can watch as she hugs numerous people, some with illnesses and physical disabilities or other problems. Others are perfectly healthy and just want the experience of her hug. When you reach her, she is surrounded by assistants who help her and guide the guests in to receive their hug. You must take your shoes and glasses off and then you are received in her arms. She takes your head and chants some words into your ear, then hugs you for a few moments and then it is time to go.

There are some devotees who have been here for years, others who spend months out of each year here, and, of course, others who just come to pay a visit out of curiosity, hang out, and see what is happening. Many people come to try to find inner peace, or to release themselves from various problems, or who genuinely seek spiritual wisdom and upliftment. But the overall mood of the place seems quite positive and peaceful and well organized.

HARIPAD

The Subramanya Swamy temple is a centuries old temple with marvelous wood carvings and architectural excellence. This is a place, north of Kayankulam on the main road along the coast, known for being where Parashurama established a deity of Subramaniya (Murugan) in the temple here.

Also in the area is the Mannarasala Nagaraja temple 1 ½ km north of the Haripad Subramanya temple. Chettikulangara Devi temple dedicated to Bhadrakali is two kms west of Mavelikhara and six kms east of Nangyarkulangara. Everyone is allowed in this temple. There are huge and elegantly decorated chariots inside and are used for bringing images of Bhima, Panchali, and Hanuman in front of the temple by the local villagers.

CHANGANNUR

This city is east of Haripad on the banks of the Pampa (or Pamba) River, easily reached by train from Trivandrum. Located here is the Bhagavathi Shrine, dedicated to Shiva and Parvati. The legend is that once the sage Agastya had his ashrama here on the hillside. After Shiva and Parvati had been married at Mount Kailash, they came to pay the rishi a visit here since he could not attend the wedding. Since the Devi had her period at the time, the couple had to wait for her to take the purificatory bath.

It is with this tradition that the image at the temple here also has regular periods, at which time the temple is closed for those three days. Then on the fourth day the temple is open and the worship starts again after the Aaraattu and Thiruputtu festivals when the deity is taken to the river Pampa for the ritual. The devoted consider it especially auspicious to witness this. Changannur is also considered to be another one of the 51 Shakti Peethas, where a part of Devi's body fell after her body expired at the Daksha Yajna.

ARANMULA

This is a very small place eight km from Changannur, which can be reached by auto-ricksha or bus. The Parthasarathi temple here depicts Lord Krishna as Parthasarathi, the chariot driver of Arjuna. It is related that the deity was installed by Arjuna at Nilakkal on the banks of the Pampa River when the Pandavas were on pilgrimage thousands of years ago. The deity was later taken to this place in a shaft made of six (aru) bamboos (mula).

This temple is considered to be one of the 108 Divya Desams for Lord Vishnu (Krishna). It is also one of the five major Krishna temples in Kerala, along with Guruvayur, Trichambaram, Thiruvarpu, and Ambalapuzha. The main festivals here are performed with boat races. The Uthirattathi festival is held on the last day of the Onam celebrations (Aug-Sept) with a boat race in honor of the installation of Lord Parthasarathi that is attended by thousands. The Vallasadya feast is held during the Onam festivities with the Vallomkali boat race. This honors the time when the Lord once appeared before a pious Nambudri. A boatload of food is still taken to the village of Aranmula from the village of Kattoor.

SABARIMALA

Sabarimala is in the Sabari Hills about 30 km due east of Changannur, 47 miles southeast of Kottayam, and 185 km north from Trivandrum. Sabarimala, otherwise known as Dharma Sastha and Harihara Puthran, is the abode of Lord Ayyappa. During the main festival season in the month of Narayana (December-January), numerous pilgrims come to this place while observing strict vows. During this time, many men wearing black can be seen in the nearby cities converging on Sabarimala and singing the chants of Lord Ayyappa.

Reaching the temple is not easy. You have to take the road going south from Kottayam and then up to the Pamba River. The traditional route is through Erumeli. Pilgrims then trek some 15 miles for two days barefoot through the forests to Pamba. From Pamba you wade across the Pamba River where pilgrims bathe or wash clothes. Thereafter, you go to the Pamba Ganapati temple to receive blessings there. Then it is an additional three miles of walking through thick forest to this wilderness hill temple at Sabarimalai. Another route is from Tamil Nadu through Vandiperiyar. An easier route allows the pilgrims to drive directly to Pamba and then trek the three miles to Sabarimalai.

You finally go up the stairs to the temple complex where you can offer prayers to the Divinities in the secondary shrines. There is an altar where you can offer prayers and lit camphor. Further on by several hundred feet is the sacred banyan tree (*saramkuti*) where it is said Lord Ayyappan directed his troops to throw down their weapons to prepare for worship. There is a long narrow path through dense jungle to a valley between the Neelimala and Sabarimala mountains. You then begin the mile-long climb up Neelimala, the temple mountain. It can be tough making your way up the uneven steps and it gets steeper as you go, so it is not unusual to take rests along the way. Some people have to be carried up. This takes a few more hours before you reach the final 18-step stairway to the main temple itself where the Sri Ayyappa deity is enshrined in a little sanctuary on a raised area. The 18 steps represent the gods on the 18 hills that surround the temple. At the first step, the pilgrim breaks the coconut he has been carrying. Then you climb the 18 steps. In the rush during the main pilgrimage season, it is so crowded that this alone can take up to an hour to reach the sanctum where the pilgrim can finally attain the vision of the deity of Ayyappan. Then you move forward. A small shrine to Lord Ganesh is on the right where you offer respects. Then you go to see the main deity, called Panchaloha, which is an image of Ayyappan made of five metals. Now you perform the main *puja* or worship, the Neyyabhishekam, in which you anoint the deity with some of the ghee that you have brought with you. It is only a small portion of the vast amounts of ghee that has been brought by the pilgrims, which number in the thousands. You offer the ghee that you have brought to the priest at the main shrine. He pours it over the deity. Thereafter the pilgrimage has been completed and you can begin the journey back.

The legend behind Ayyappa is that he is said to be the son of Shiva and the incarnation of Vishnu known as Mohini Murti, Lord Vishnu's form as a most beautiful woman. This is why Ayyappa is also called Hariharaputra, meaning the son of both Hari, or Vishnu, and Hara, Shiva.

The reason for this is described in the *Srimad-Bhagavatam* (Canto Eight, Chapter Twelve). Therein it is related that once when Lord Shiva had heard about the pastimes of the Lord in the form of an attractive woman, Mohini, during the churning of the milk ocean, Shiva went to see the Lord. After offering descriptive prayers, he asked to see this beautiful feminine form of the Lord. Being merciful to His devotee, the Lord expanded His energy and manifested Himself as a most attractive woman. Lord Shiva, upon seeing this form, was immediately captivated. Shiva lost his sense and began to follow Her. While chasing Her through the woods for some time, he passed semen. Only after discharging semen did Lord Shiva realize how he had been dragged by the illusory energy and then ceased to follow the beautiful form. However, in the version in the *Bhagavatam*, Shiva's semen did not produce the child Ayyappa, but fell on the earth where mines of gold and silver later formed. So those who follow the *Bhagavata Purana* and similar Vedic texts, they do not put much emphasis, if any, on Ayyappa.

Ayyappa is often portrayed with four arms, three eyes, and seated peacefully in the lotus position, *padmasana*. Two of his hands carry a sword and a shield, while the other two exhibit the *mudras* or positions of assurance of fearlessness and giving blessings. Other views of him present an image with only two arms and two eyes. He wears gold ornaments and crown. Ayyappa is also called Shasta, which means the controller of the world.

How the location of Sabarimala came to be is also explained. The story is that after Durga killed the demon Mahishasura, his spouse undertook the endeavor of intense austerities to gain the favor of Lord Brahma that she would not be killed by Shiva or Vishnu. She became increasingly powerful, much to the consternation of the gods. Then Shiva and Vishnu together formed an idea in which she could be destroyed by creating a person fit for the job. This child was discovered by King Rajashekara who reigned in Panthalam in Kerala. He had no children so he named the child Manikanthan and raised him as a son. The child killed Mahisha when he was only twelve years old. He had also brought female leopards back from the forests since the milk was supposed to cure the queen's headache. The king, however, had realized the divine nature of Manikantham. The king had been told to build a temple to Manikantham at the spot where his arrow landed, after Manikantham disappeared. The king then shot the arrow, which found its mark at the top of Sabarimalai hill. This is where the temple was supposed to have been built originally by Lord Visvakarma, the demigod architect. Parashurama is said to have made and installed the image. Now there are millions of pilgrims who make the trip to the hill to see this temple of Lord Ayyappa.

ALAPPUZHA

Getting back on the main road from Haripad, another 45 km north we arrive at Alappuzha. This has a temple to Lord Krishna that had been established by Bilvamangalam Swami and King Puradam Thirunal of Champakasseri. The story, which took place back in 1613, is that they were once sailing in a boat and heard the melodious tunes from a flute coming from an Ashwatha tree. The Swami knew that it had to be the music of Balagopala, Lord Krishna. So they decided to build a temple at that spot. Then, when they were ready to install a deity, they discovered that there was a slight flaw on the deity. The king and the devotees were quite disappointed. However, following the Swami's advice, they secretly brought a new deity of Parthasaratha from the village of Kuruchi and installed Him in the new temple. This event is celebrated with a boat race during the month of Onam. The deity in the temple is seen holding a whip in one hand and a conch in the other.

ETTUMANOOR

Now we head farther north to Ettumanoor, 13 kilometers from Vaikom. Here is one of the richest temples in Kerala, the Sri Mahadevar temple, dedicated to Shiva in the form of a *linga*. There is also an Aghora Murti, or fierce form of Shiva that was installed by a demon named Khara. It has some amazing murals inside depicting scenes from the great Vedic texts. It is a large circular building inside a rectangular enclosure. Though non-Hindus or Western, white-skinned Hindus are prohibited at the time of this writing, as you enter the temple you will see a large oil lamp, said to have been brought there and lit by Lord Shiva himself. As people enter the temple, they show honor to the lamp by pouring oil into it. Inside the temple is a circular columned hall where a square sanctuary enshrines the Shiva *linga*. To the east of the sanctum, Parvati is worshiped, but there is no image. In the hall, there are separate shrines to Ganesh, Sastha, and Dakshinamurthi. It is said that anyone suffering from witchcraft or mental diseases can be relieved by praying for a Mandalam (41 days).

On the route south of the city there are a few other temples that you may want to see. These include the Pallipurathu Kavu Bhagavathy temple at Kodimatha (south side of Kottayam). Further south is the Mariappally Mahadevar temple, 3 kms south of Kottayam with deities of both Shiva and Vishnu. The Pakkil Sri Dharmasastha temple is in Pallom. The Panachikkad Saraswathy temple is five kms northeast of Chingavanam, with a main temple to MahaVishnu. Thousands of devotees gather here to worship the goddess of wisdom, Sarasvati, during the Navaratri festival. The Neelamperoor Palli Bhagavathy (Durga) temple is 12 kms south of Kottayam, and two kms west of Kurichi is where there is a noteworthy deity of MahaVishnu.

VAIKOM

The Sri Mahadevar Shiva temple at Vaikom, about 15 miles northwest of Ettumanoor, is a large temple with bright murals between the doorways and windows that depict scenes of dancing Shiva, Parvati, Vishnu, etc. It is one of the oldest and largest of the local temples. It has a flagstaff 64 feet tall. There is a simple square sanctuary that houses a huge *linga*, called Sri Vaikkathappam, a benign form of Shiva. It is a five-foot tall *lingam*. It's said that Parashurama installed this *lingam* and established the system of worship for the temple. It is worshiped as Dakshinamurthi in the morning, at noon as Kirata the hunter as he appeared before Arjuna, and as Sachidananda or Uma-Mahesvaran in the evening.

The temple feeds many people here every day, but again only Hindus are allowed inside, and this usually means that you have to be born in an Indian family to be considered a real Hindu.

There is also the Vadayar Elamkavu Devi (Bhadrakali) temple five kms east of Vaikom between the main road and river. The Thirumani Venkitapuram temple, five kms south of Vaikom on the eastern bank of Vembanad Lake, has a main deity of Lord Rama. It is famous for its intricate wood carvings.

KALADI

Kaladi is a small town north of Vaikom, just east of Angamaly by 10 kilometers along the banks of the Periyar River, 23 km from Alwaye, 48 kilometers northeast of Cochin, and 42 km south from Trichur. Though this town is not on the map, if you are taking the train on this line, you will see a sign at a nearby town that will tell you where to get off to reach Kaladi. It is easy to get off the train from Trivandrum or Kollam at Angamaly (pronounced as Angamadi) and get a room, and then simply get an auto-ricksha to tour Kaladi. At the train station you can have an auto-ricksha take you a few blocks, or walk if you have little luggage, to Hotel Providence, a decent place to stay while near the train station.

Kaladi is a major pilgrimage center where Sri Shankaracarya, the great proponent of Advaita impersonalism, was born in the eighth century. He helped defeat Buddhism by his arguments and was considered to be an incarnation of Lord Shiva. Sri·Abhinava Vidya Thirtha Narasimha Bharati of the Sringeri Math helped bring Kaladi to the pilgrim's attention. He built shrines for Sharada Devi, Adi Shankara, and Dakshinamurthi.

You can take a bus to Kaladi or an auto-ricksha so you can go directly to each important place, and then stay as long as you want, and then return directly to your hotel. Going over the bumpy road into Kaladi, we first see the Sri Adi Sankara Keerthi Stambha Mandapam. This is a nine-storey octogonal tower, 150 feet tall in height. Each floor has illustrations commemorating a period of Shankaracarya's life. Each floor also has a temple room, one to Ganesh, Murugan, Shakti, Krishna, a Shiva *lingam*, and, finally at the top, an imposing image of Shankara with his four disciples.

The main attraction in town is the Shankara Janmasthan, or Shankara birthplace. This is enclosed in a complex with several shrines. As you enter the gate and go through the well kept grounds, you enter a pavilion with the major shrines in it. One is for Sharada Devi. Not far from there, toward the back of the building, is a small lamp post, about four feet tall, that marks where Shankara was born. It is also this area where Shankara's mother was cremated and where her *samadhi* is found. On the other side of the pavilion is another temple shrine for Dakshinamurthi.

As you exit the pavilion, directly to your left is the temple of Lord Krishna that has a deity of Krishna that was installed by Shankara himself, proving that in spite of his impersonalistic preaching he was actually a devotee of Krishna. It is said that Shankara established this deity especially for his mother. But go in the morning so you can be sure of getting *darshan* in this temple before it closes in the afternoon. However, no *langis* (typical cloth dress for men of the region) or shirts are allowed for men who want entrance. It has simple architecture in the wooden keralite style.

In the back of the main complex you will find the banks of the Periyar River. This *ghat* is called the Crocodile Ghat because when Shankara was still young, a crocodile grabbed his leg with his jaws and would not let go. Shankara pleaded with his mother that if she allowed him to take *sannyasa*, the crocodile would release him. So she gave her permission for him to take the renounced order and he was released from the grip of the crocodile. Thus, many people take a holy bath at this spot.

It really only takes a few hours to see everything here, and then once we are finished we can make arrangements to take the next train out of town to our next stop. Generally, from here there is no need to make reservations for a particular seat, but getting a ticket ahead of time is recommended.

CRANGANORE

Cranganore, 35 kilometres north of Cochin, has a temple to Kodungallur Bhagavathi Devi. It is one of the most important Devi temples in Kerala. It has beautiful carvings on the granite pillars and wooden ceiling, though the exterior of the building is rather simple.

GURUVAYOOR

We next take a train farther north to Trichur, where we get a bus to take the 29 km trip on over to Guruvayoor, where there is the famous temple dedicated to Lord Krishna. The first time I went to Guruvayoor was back in 1990. At the time, there was only about one hotel in the town, not much to choose from, and anybody who came there was only interested in visiting the temple. However, when I visited this town the next time in 2001, there were numerous hotels and lots more being built. It was turning into a real tourist resort as opposed to being merely a pilgrimage center. Sometimes the resort atmosphere in these small pilgrimage centers begins to outweigh the spiritual importance. When that happens, the temple begins to become less and less significant and then some tourists go to the temple only as a sideline.

Nonetheless, at this temple the devotees wishing to perform the special Udayasthamana Puja have increased so much that it is booked ahead for the next 42 years, at least at the time of this writing. This *puja* is only performed 130 days out of the year, so people must join the long waiting list to do it. Plus, on auspicious days, the number of devotees visiting the temple can be over 100,000, which opens at 3:30 A.M.

In any case, this temple does not let non-Hindus, or white people, inside. I know of some who have gone in, but not many. And today was not my turn to go in. However, there have been some discussions in the management about changing that, but I have not heard the conclusions. So maybe one day this temple will be open to all devotees, regardless of their skin color.

When I visited this temple, I checked in my shoes and camera bag at the cloak room, then took off my shirt to enter the temple, dressed in *dhoti* and *kurta*, but I was stopped. Then I was told that if I wanted to get in I could, but I would need a certificate from the Arya Samaj saying that it was all right. Unfortunately, the office was in Calicut, which was quite a ways away, and not something I could do unless I had a few extra days on my hands. So I walked away disappointed. However, the deity is within sight by standing in front of the door, which many people do without entering the temple. So, you can join many other people who merely stand in front of the doorway by the large oil lamp and offer your obeisances and prayers from there. The temple interior is somewhat dark, however, and the deity is poorly lit, so you can hardly see Him because of the lack of light.

The deity is a four-armed standing Vishnu with a chakra in the right hand, conchshell in the left, and mace and lotus flower in the other two. Sri Krishna showed this form of His only twice during His appearance on earth: once to Arjuna just before the battle of Kurukshetra while speaking the *Bhagavad-gita*, and once to His parents, Vasudeva and Devaki, at the time of His birth. The deity is said to have been worshiped by Lord Krishna Himself at Dwaraka thousands of years ago. The legend is that when Krishna left this world, He gave the deity to His devotee Uddhava to look after it. He then ordered Brihaspati, the guru or spiritual teacher of the demigods, and Vayu, demigod of the wind, to take care of this Vishnu deity and to install it somewhere for the benefit of humanity. When they arrived at Dwaraka to get the deity, the city of Dwaraka had already sunk into the sea. After searching in the water, they found the deity and went south. Not knowing where to go, they sat down by the side of a lake and began to meditate. Soon, Shiva appeared and after some discussion they decided to start a new temple for the deity of Vishnu near the Rudratirtha Lake. Since that time 5,000 years ago, the place has been known as Guruvayoor (*guru* for Brihaspati and *vayoor* for Vayu).

As in most temples, the deity here is served from three or four in the morning until nine at night. The service includes bathing, dressing, offering food, and receiving the many hundreds of devotees in the temple for *darshan*. Shrines to Sastha, Vinayaka, and Durga are also in the halls. Marriages are also often performed here in front of the temple.

The temple manages a large elephant yard and the elephants play a major role during the annual 10-day Ulsavom festival in February-March. There is an elephant race at the start of the festival. Then every evening is the main event, which is a grand procession with the temple elephants bedecked with gold and jewels, one of which carries a miniature of the temple deity. Then, with instruments playing and people joining, the procession circumambulates the temple complex three times. Afterwards, there are performances of Krishnattom style dancing and other festivities, all based on ecstatic love for Lord Vishnu.

When we have finished our visit to Guruvayoor, we can easily go to the train station and get tickets for the 1:25 P.M. train to Trichur. Also, if we are ready to end our trip through the south, we can also book our tickets for an overnight train from Trichur to Bangalore.

TRICHUR (or THRISSUR)

In Trichur we find the Vadakkunnatham temple, which is one of Kerala's largest temples on a little hill. The temple is typical Kerala-style wood architecture in the center of a rectangular court surrounded by a colonade. There are three main shrines or buildings facing west: one for Vadakkunnatha (Paramashiva) in the form of a ten-foot-tall mound of a ghee *ligam* (which can be hard to see since there is little light except for a few lamps), one for Shankara Narayana, and another for Lord Rama. Each has an open pavilion in front of it. There are smaller shrines for Ganesh, Krishna, and Parvati. The walls of the shrines, especially in the passageways, are beautifully painted with scenes of Nataraja, Vishnu, and depictions from the *Mahabharata*, etc. The temple also has exquisitely carved wood in its architectural designs.

The legend is that the temple was originally established by Lord Parashurama many hundreds of years ago. The temple is known for its Pooram festival in April. They have a parade of some 30 to 40 grandly ornamented elephants accompanied by the fanfare of traditional Keralite musical instruments. Afterwards, there is one of the best fireworks displays you will find in India that goes on until dawn.

When I visited this temple I went in without any trouble. I was able to see all the temples, even though men take their shirts off to enter. Then after I had done everything I needed for my spiritual curiosity and to get *darshan*, I put my shirt back on and took the outer path around the temple grounds to circumambulate the temple. After three-quarters of the way around, some security man came and was talking to some of the maintenance men, and then ordered me, in his Kerala language, to follow him. He then escorted me to the main door and out of the grounds. So whether foreigners are allowed in or not I don't know. But I took my chances and saw what I wanted before I got kicked out. So, mission accomplished.

Other temples around Trichur include the Paramekkavu Devi temple, with the biggest Devi deity in Kerala. It is on the eastern side of Trichur. The Thiruvampady Sri Krishna temple is two km west of Trichur. The Thiruvullakkavu Dharma Sastha temple is 11 kms southwest of Trichur. The Oorakathamma Thiruvadikal Durga temple is 12 kms southwest of Trichur, and is a centuries old mandir. The Koodalmanikkam Sri Bharathar Swamy temple is 20 kms southwest of Trichur, and is one of the biggest temples in Kerala and famous for its wood carvings and murals. The image is six feet tall with four hands of Chathur Bahu.

KARAMADAI

If we do not want to keep going straight up the coast, then from Trichur we can go northeast to Coimbatore and then to Karamadai, which has a significant Ranganatha temple. Karamadai is on the Coimbatore Mettupalayam highway about 23 kilometers from Coimbatore and just south of Mettupalayam, a good stop on our way to Mysore or Bangalore. The temple itself is not far from the bus station.

The temple is not the largest but occupies about one acre of land. The main eastern entrance has no tower, but the 40-feet tall *gopuram* rises over the northern entrance. However, they are building a new *gopuram* for the east entrance, which is probably finished now. This temple is rather modern, being constructed by Mr. Thiruvenkatavan Chettiar of Udagamandalam in 1944. Usually Vishnu is shown in detail only in standing, sitting, or reclining poses. However, the unique point about this temple is that the main deity of Vishnu here shows Himself as a *linga* but wears the Vaishnava *tilak*. This is seen nowhere else. It is said that Bhrihaspati performed an arduous penance and gained the favor of the Lord, who appeared in this way according to the sage's wishes. In other parts of the temple, there is the deity of a two-armed form of Vishnu, Ranganayaki Thayar, whose charms attract numerous devotees. Also, the smaller *utsavar* or festival deity shows Himself in a sitting posture. Other shrines are found in the temple and the outer walls of the sanctum have three niches with lovely images. Sculptures of the Dasavatars of Vishnu also adorn the pillars of the main hallway, all of which reveal extraordinary craftsmanship.

In historic times, the area used to be dense forest that was filled with Karai trees. So the region was called Karaivana. Settlements of the Thottiar tribe were here, and their livelihood was raising cattle. One of them owned a cow that hardly gave any milk. So after watching it for a time, they found that it emptied its utter on a particular anthill. Thus, with utensils the tribesman tried to dig up the anthill but found that blood gushed forward. The main instigator of the dig also lost his eyesight and collapsed to the ground. His kinsmen sought advice from the spiritual preceptor, Vedavyasabhattar. Under his instruction, they built a temple to accommodate the deity of the Lord that they found who appeared at this place of his own accord.

However, they could not understand who exactly this Svayambhumurti (self-manifesting deity) was. Some felt that He was Lord Shiva, while others felt He was MahaVishnu. Then MahaVishnu appeared in the dream of a devotee named Pitchu Mandradiar and requested him to cover the deity with sandal paste before dawn. While the sandal paste was being applied, Lord Vishnu gave *darshan* with the conch and disc in His hands, showing that He was certainly Vishnu.

One interesting story is that during the time of the British rule, there was one man who was in charge of mapping the route for the railroad tracks. He prepared the tracks in such a way that it would be damaging for the temple and the water tank. Then in a dream, Lord Vishnu mounted on a horse appeared to him and hit him with a cane. The man then lost his eyesight. He repented for his irreverence to the Lord's temple and rearranged the route of the train tracks. Thereafter he regained his eyesight. As a token of gratitude, he gifted the temple with a horse *vahana* and arranged to re-lay the floor of the main shrines.

The Nanjundeswara temple of Shiva is also nearby the Ranganatha temple. The main image is a reddish stone Shiva *linga*. There are also sculptures of Virabhadra, Vinayaka, Mahishasuramardhini, Subramanya, Anjaneya, and Nataraja that adorn the walls of the sanctum, and additional images are also found in other places in the temple.

There is also a lively and modern temple for Venkateshwara to the east of Karamadai by a few kilometers. It is small, built so that you climb a flight of stairs to see the lovely Vishnu deity. You circumambulate the temple to see another shrine to Lakshmi. On your way out they give everyone a little *prasada* that you can eat in a park-like setting next to the *prasada* booth.

From Karmadai or Coimbatore, we can head back to the coast to go on to Udupi, or if we are running out of time, we can go to Mysore, or straight to Bangalore.

UDUPI

Our next stop of the major holy places in South India is Udupi (sometimes spelled Udipi), the coastal town north of Mangalore. This is the place where the great spiritual teacher Madhvacharya was born and lived. Udupi is a small but pleasant town where the famous 13th century Krishna temple is located. This is an important temple, and inside we will see several altars, but the main one is for Madhvacharya's deity of Lord Krishna, said to have been originally worshiped by Krishna's wife Rukmini in Dwaraka in the Dvapara-yuga. Another alter is for a four-armed standing Vishnu deity. When Sri Chaitanya visited this temple, He became completely ecstatic when He saw Madhvacharya's Krishna deity. Westerners are also allowed in to see the deities and watch the *puja* rituals that are performed each day as they have been for centuries.

How the deity came to this land is quite a story. It started when Sri Madhvacharya was meditating near the beach about 5 km from Udupi. Then he saw a ship in danger due to a severe storm. By his own yogic strength he saved the ship from sinking. He could see that the ship carried the deities of Krishna and Balarama. Upon retrieving Them, he installed the Balarama deity in the Vada Pandeshwara village near the beach, and then the Krishna deity at Udupi near the Chandramoulisvara shrine.

The deity of Krishna shows Him holding the churning rod in one hand and a rope in the other, with a little smile on His face, reminiscent of the childhood activities He performed in His days in Gokul. It is said that Lord Krishna asked Visvakarma to make the deity for Rukmini, who worshiped it till the end of Krishna's pastimes. Arjuna later hid the deity in the gardens of Dwaraka, and reached Udupi in the course of time. The shrine of Sri Madhvacharya is situated next to the sanctum. The silver *simhasana*, or seat, used by Sri Madhva, is held most sacred.

This temple has a unique festival twice a month on Ekadasi. On these days, they bring the deities out to ride the tall ornate carts that are pulled through the streets. The temple elephants are also in the procession and on their backs stand temple priests who wave big whisk fans, one in each hand, to fan the deities in the nearby carts. It's a fascinating festival to see and many people join the parade. This is the best time to come to Udupi for a visit.

There is also the holy town of Pajakaksetra (or BhajagaKshetra) 12 km southeast of Udupi. This is the birthplace of Sri Madhvacharya who is also considered an incarnation of Hanuman. Here there are also shrines to Bheema, the five Pandavas, and Vayu.

SRINGERI

From Udupi we can go to Sringeri if we would like. It is a small place about 80 km due east from Udupi. You can go from Udupi to Karkal by bus, and then up to Sringeri.

Sringeri is most connected with Sri Adi Shankara. He once visited this place and as he was appreciating the peaceful atmosphere, one summer noon he witnessed a frog in labor being sheltered by the hood of a cobra raised over it. This prompted him to establish one of his now famous Shankara Maths to teach Advaita philosophy. He also installed in a small shrine a sandalwood image of Sharada Devi, the goddess of learning.

So what we can find in Sringeri includes the Devi Sharada shrine. Here in the front hall the images of Rajarajeshwari and Mahishasuramardhini Devis are quite beautiful. In the sanctum, the sandalwood image of the goddess was replaced by a golden deity about 700 years ago by Sri Vidyaranya. The deity is seated on a Sri Chakra Peetham. She has a *japa mala* in her upper right hand with a parrot perched on it. Her lower right hand exhibits the *mudra* or posture of blessings, and her lower left hand holds a book. The processional deity is also enshrined in the southern side of the temple. You can find Ganesh with ten hands on the western side. Near the sanctum is an image of Bhuvaneshvari.

The Adi Shankara shrine is on the left side of the Sharada shrine. Inside, there is the image of Adi Shankara seen sitting in the yoga posture on a two foot tall seat with a *lingam* in front of him. Images of four of his disciples are nearby. It is in the front hall of this temple where philosophical lectures by the local swami are given to the devotees who attend.

One of the most noteworthy temples in Sringeri is the Vidya Shankar shrine. It is shaped like a Sri Chakra, constructed in the style of the Vijayanagara, Hoysala, and Dravidian architecture, and built by Bharati Krishna Thirtha. He was a disciple of Sri Vidya Shankara Thirtha over 700 years ago. The sanctum has a *lingam* dedicated to Sri Vidya Shankara who entered his *mahasamadhi* at this place. He had ordered his disciples to open his *samadhi* only after 12 years, and they would discover an image of Chaturmurthi Vidyeswara like the one in the Sringeri shrine. But they opened it early and only found the *lingam*.

Other temples and shrines also can be found here, and many people do come to this place for learning about the teachings of Adi Shankara as they are passed down by the local swamis who live here and represent those teachings.

KOLLUR

Kollur is farther north of Udupi, east of the coastal town of Bhatkal. This town is a little off the beaten path and may not be of interest to everyone. But it is here that we find the temple of Mukambika at the foot of the hill known as Kudashatri. The Sowparnika River that originates on the hill flows past the temple. Many yogis and sages have performed austerities here. The *Skanda Purana* describes the glory of this holy place and how a sage named Kola did penance here. Devi Adi Shakti, who vanquished the demon Mukasura, was praised by the Devas as Mukambika. Devi Shakti is said to have also appeared before Adi Shankara in these Kudashatri hills.

The temple houses a Svayambhu *lingam* worshiped as the form of Shiva-Shakti. The devoted accept that all three forms of Shakti, namely Mahakali, Mahasarasvati, and Mahalakshmi, are housed in this sacred image of Mukambika. It is also said that the Panchaloha image of the Devi as well as the Sri Chakra was installed by Adi Shankara himself, who also set up the methods for the various rituals and worship. The image of the Devi holds a conch and chakra, and shows the hand gesture of blessings and freedom from fear. Images of Kali and Sarasvati are enshrined nearby.

The stone seat called the Shankara Simhasana is revered by devotees who meditate near it to receive the blessings of the guru. Adi Shankara is said to have meditated here. Also in this temple are enshrined images of Vinayaka with ten hands, Anjaneya, Virabhadra, and Subramaniyam. The Kudashatri hill can be explored by pilgrims who want to look for the cave called Ambavanam and Chitramulam where Adi Shankara did penance.

GOKARNA

Going back to the main road to travel up along the coast, we can visit Gokarna. This small town is 170 km north of Mangalore, and 50 km from Karwar. Gokarna has the Mahaballeswara Shiva temple, which is very powerful, second only to Vishwanatha in Varanasi. Legend is that Ravana brought the Atma *lingam* here from Mount Kailash. When he was carrying it to Lanka, the *devas* or demigods tried to stop him. Vinayaka, a form of Ganesh, came to their rescue and appeared before Ravana as a simple *brahmachari* boy (celibate student). When Ravana gave the *lingam* to Vinayaka, he set it down where it became grounded. Even Ravana could not move it after that. So the *devas* named the *lingam* Mahabaleshvara. Another legend from the *Puranas* is that at the time of the creation of the world, Lord Shiva emerged from the ear of Bhumidevi at this spot. Thus, the *lingam* is called Adi Gokarna since *go* means earth and *karna* means ear.

The sanctum of the temple reveals only a three-foot square *peetam* or seat. A small hole is in the middle through which one can have a glimpse of the Atma *lingam*. The six foot tall *lingam* inside can be seen only once in 40 years when they perform the festive bathing ritual for the *lingam* known as the Ashta Bhandana Kumbabhishekam. Other shrines in and around the temple are for Chandikesvara, Vinayaka, Adi Gokarneswara, Dattatreya, Parvati, and Ganesh, which has a small dent on his head said to have been caused when Ravana hit him for placing the *lingam* on the ground. The sacred water tank is Koti Thirtam Kund, said to have been created by Garuda. There is also a Krishna temple where it is said that Krishna performed penance, and a temple to Sri Venkateswara.

Many of the devoted take a bath in the sea, then make a *lingam* out of wet sand and worship it before going on to the main temple. Many of the devoted also perform the *sraddha* or funeral rites for their relatives here. Sri Chaitanya also visited this temple. It is said that by entering this *ksetra* one loses the karma of hundreds of sins.

Other Shiva temples around Gokarna include those to Sejjasvara, Gunavanteshvara, Murudeshvara, Dharesvara, and Mahabalesvara. These five temples together are called the Pancha Maha Kshetras. On the hill is also a shrine for Rama, Sita, and Lakshmana, as well as Manikesvara and Siddesvara. The Pandavas are also said to have visited this place, which is why it is also called Pandavakudi.

MYSORE

From Gokarna or Udupi we go to back Mangalore and catch a bus to Mysore. It is a journey that takes several hours, but you go through some beautiful and hilly country. You will see small communities and houses on the hillsides that have been terraced for rice farming, some of which are many miles away from anywhere. You will also pass through the town of Hunsur where you will see Buddhist monks walking about. The reason is that near this place are a Tibetan refugee settlement and two monasteries. They also have factories that produce Tibetan carpets that you can buy, or they will gladly take your custom orders if you care to stop here to do some business. But it is a small town with little facility for travelers and most people continue on their way.

Mysore is a clean, friendly city with many local attractions, and it's easy to get around. It is a great place, so if you are in South India, do not miss it. And if you are looking for a place to buy souvenirs, this town has many shops offering much from which to choose. Mysore is particularly known for its sandalwood. There is sandalwood oil, sandalwood incense, sandalwood soap, and so many sandalwood, rosewood, and teak carvings and furniture, that you are bound to find something you will like. There's also plenty of brassware and paintings. Street vendors also try to get your attention. If you buy something rather large and don't want to carry it while you travel, you can go to the post office and send it home. Don't depend on the store to send it for you unless it is the Cauvery Arts & Crafts Emporium. Many times tourists rely on a store to ship their merchandise back to the West, only to never receive it. There are also decent restaurants that offer something for whatever taste you have. But for a variety of fresh produce, go to the local Devaraja Fruit and Vegetable Market. This is an interesting place to watch people do business whether you buy anything or not.

The most interesting time to be in Mysore is for the Dussera celebration in October. The city and the palace are resplendent with lights and festivities that last for ten days. This is when the town celebrates the slaying of the Mahishasura demon by the goddess Chamundeswari, a form of Parvati. The tenth day is the peak of the festivities with a parade a mile long. People come from all over to watch the procession of soldiers, dancers, brass bands, floats, the Camels Corps, and decorated horses and elephants. Near the end of the parade, one gold bedecked elephant carries an image of the city's patron goddess, Chamundeswari. Then there is a grand fireworks display.

The legend is that goddess Chamundeswari protected the people of this area from the demon Mahishasura by killing him, and then made her residence on the hill just south of the city. The city or Mysore was named after the demon, Mahish Asura, and is even mentioned in the *Mahabharata* as Mahishmati. The top of the Chamundi Hill is where Devi slew the demon. The demon's statue can be seen at the top of Chamundi Hill with a sword in one hand and cobra in the other. Nearby this is the main temple of the city. The Chamundi temple, 3489 feet above sea level, is entered through a tall outer *gopuram* gateway (built by Krishnaraja Wodeyar 1794-1868) and a smaller inner *gopuram*. The doors are of embossed silver that depict scenes of the goddess. The temple itself is not so elaborate, and the sanctuary is entered through a small *mandapa* hall. The small deity of Sri Chamundesvari is adorned with rich attire, but you are not allowed to get very close and must view the deity from a short distance. In fact, you are likely to get a better view from the photos they sell outside the temple. She has eight arms holding various weapons and is in the act of killing the demon Mahisha.

To reach this temple, you can either take a bus, auto-ricksha, taxi, or walk up the over 1000 steps on the hillside. Three-quarters of the way up is a huge Nandi (Shiva's bull carrier) carved out of solid rock. It is one of the biggest in India (5 meters high and 7.6 meters long) and was established by Dodda Devaraja (1659-1672). It is always visited by pilgrims. Once you reach the hilltop, there are plenty of little shops for refreshments and great views over the city. Near the temple are other shrines dedicated to Shiva as Mahabaleshvara and to Vishnu as Lakshmi Narayana.

Mysore has a lot of history, too. It has some very beautiful palaces and museums, especially the Mysore Palace, completed in 1912, which I found to be one of the most beautiful places I have seen, incredibly ornate and elegant. It has huge halls, stained glass windows, carved wooden and ivory inlaid doors, mosaic marble floors, some solid silver doors, paintings of the life in Mysore years ago, and displays of silver chairs, a golden throne, musical instruments, fabulous ceiling murals, and much more. Outside of the festival times, the palace is lit up with the many exterior lights every Sunday eveing. The palace also has several temples on or near the grounds that you can visit.

The Kodi Bhairavasvami temple is just outside the fort and is dedicated to Shiva in the form of Bhairava. This is a historically significant temple since this is where Yaduraya and Krishnaraya met the royal priest that caused the founding of the Mysore Kingdom in

1399. The image of Bhairava is less than a meter high and has four hands in which he holds a trident, a drum, a skull, and a sword. To the left of the deity is Bhadrakali holding a sickle in her upraised right hand.

There is also the Sri Lakshmiramana Swami temple in the western part of the fort with a beautiful Vishnu deity adorned in gold. This is one of the oldest temples in the city and has much history and some miracles associated with its existence.

There is the Sri Shveta Varahasvami temple dedicated to Varaha, an *avatara* of Lord Vishnu, near the main entrance in the south side. It is built in the Hoysala style of architecture. The main image of Shveta Varahaswami in the sanctum was brought from Sri Mushna in Tamil Nadu by Chikka Devaraja Wadiyar and installed in a new temple at Srirangapatnam which was the capital at that time. That temple was destroyed by Tipu Sultan and the deity was brought to Mysore in 1809 and installed in the present temple, which was constructed by Dewan Purnaiah according to the wishes of Krishnaraja Wadiyar III. The smaller *utsavar* deity has an inscription saying that it was a gift of King Chikka Devaraja Wadiyar (1673-1704). The temple also has mural paintings that were done in 1875 on the walls of the pillared hall next to the sanctum. These depict the stories of the *Ramayana* and *Bhagavata Purana.*

The Sri Prasanna Krishnasvami temple is dedicated to Lord Krishna. This has many shrines around the central sanctum with various images of Krishna and Vishnu, many of which are covered in silver. The central deity is made of chlorite and is a lovely image of Lord Krishna as a child in a crawling posture. He has a butter ball in his hand with a child-like expression. The temple is also known for its paintings in the central hall. This temple was built because the Mysore dynasty claims its descent is from the Yadu race, which was founded by Lord Krishna. For this reason Krishnaraja Wadiyar III felt sad that there was no temple for Krishna at that time. So he started the construction of this temple in 1825, finishing it in 1829.

On the northern side of the fort is the Sri Bhuvanesvari temple, corresponding to the Varahaswami temple in the south side. It is a more recently built temple, constructed by Sri Jayachamarajendra Wadiyar in 1951. The main deity of Bhuvaneshvari was carved by Sri Siddalingaswamy, the famous sculptor of Mysore. Other images in the temple include Surya, MahaVishnu, Maheshvara, Rajarajeshvari, Ganapati, and Chamundeshvari, also all carved by the sculptor.

The Sri Gayatri temple, dedicated to Gayatri and Lakshmi, is in the southeast corner, corresponding to the Trinayaneshvara Swami temple, dedicated to Shiva. Within the compound are the three main shrines to Savitri, Gayatri, and Lakshmi. There are also sculptures in the pillared hall of Ganesha, Shiva, Surya, and MahaVishnu. This temple was built in 1953 by Jayachamarajendra.

Nearby is the Venkataramana Svami temple. This was established by Queen Lakshanammanni, wife of Krishnaraja Wadiyar II, after the deity who was in Balamuri at the time, Lord Venkataramana, appeared to her in a dream and instructed that He should be installed in a temple in Mysore. So she proceeded to Balamuri and brought the deity to Mysore where she consecrated and worshiped Him. For this pious act, the kingdom was restored to the Wadiyar dynasty after the death of Tipu Sultan in 1799.

The temple of Sri Trinayaneshvara Swami is located on the bank of the Devaraya Sagara. It existed before the time of Raja Wadiyar before it was enclosed in the palace complex. Only after the fort was expanded did the temple come to be within it. The temple was then also enlarged and a verandah was constructed. Therein Kanthirava Narasaraja Wadiyar consecrated five *lingas* and several deities, including Dakshinamurthy, Kshetrapala, Kumara, and Surya. The sage Trinabindu is said to have performed penance toward Shiva at this place. Shiva was pleased and appeared before the sage, who then installed the *linga* here. Therefore, the *linga* is called Trineshvara in connection with the sage. The temple used to have a tall *gopuram*, but it was destroyed during the late 18th century.

All these temples are very nice to visit. Aside from the fort temples, Mysore is also known for many other unusually attractive temples in the area. The easiest way to see these other temples around Mysore is to simply take a tour. Check with your hotel or local tourist office and book a tour for the temples or places you would like to see. They usually stop long enough at each place for you to get a good look around and it saves you the trouble of trying to arrange all the transportation yourself.

SRIRANGAPATNAM

This is 16 kilometers from Mysore, situated on an island made by the Cauvery River. It is believed to be where the sage Gautama had his ashrama on the banks of the river, and who founded the shrine of Lord Ranganatha many hundreds of years ago. This was also Tipu Sultan's capital in the 18th century when he ruled this part of India. Many people come here to see the historical remnants, such as Tipu's summer palace at Daria Daulet Bagh. There is not much left of the fort at Srirangapatnam, but there is the Sri Ranganathaswamy temple, the largest in Karnataka. It is a rather plain temple from the outside with a medium size *gopuram* in front, but very popular amongst Hindu pilgrims. It is dedicated to Sri Ranganatha, Vishnu reclining on Adisesha. Images of Gautama and Goddess Cauvery are enshrined at the feet of the deity. In its cave-like interior, you will find several shrines to other aspects of Vishnu, such as Lord Venkatesvara, Narasimha, and Lakshmi, the goddess of fortune, and so on. As you go to each altar, the priest will give you a few drops of *caranamrita* (water that bathed the deity) and deity remnants, like tulasi leaves, etc. All the deities are very nice looking and They are worshiped and well cared for. Two pillars in front of the inner entrance are called Chathurvimsati, and has the 24 main forms of Vishnu and their names inscribed thereon. On the way out, there are stalls with *prasada* sweets you can purchase. Personally, I felt quite enlivened after visiting this temple. Nearby are shrines to Gangadharesvara and Lakshminarayana, which have rare images of Hamsa Gayatri, Dkashinamurthi, and Sri Adi Shankara.

SRAVANABELAGOLA

This town is a little further out from Mysore (82 km). The name means the "white pond of the ascetic," which no doubt refers to a pond that used to be where the large water tank is presently located at the base of the hill. It is a small town but is the single most important Jain holy site in Southern India, and attracts thousands of them from all over the country. At the top of Vindhyagiri Hill, over 500 steps up, is the Jain temple with an image of Lord Bahubali, Gomateshvara, that stands 58 feet tall, said to be the tallest in the world. He is considered the son of the first Jain *tirthankara*, Vrishaba Deva (Rishabadeva) or Adinatha, who was a ruler of a kingdom in northern India until he renounced his throne to become a saint. The image is from the Digambara or "sky-clad" sect. It was built in the 10th century by Chamundaraya, minister to Rachamalla of the Ganga dynasty.

Once every 12 years the Maha Masthaka Abhishesha ceremony takes place in which they pour milk, honey, water, coconut milk, turmeric, vermilion, flower petals, and other items over the head of the image. Hundreds of thousands of people attended the last festival in 1981, the 1000th year anniversary of the image. The hill also has the Odegal Basti, which is a plain temple that houses images of Adinatha (south), Neminatha (east), and Shantinatha (west) on the way up near the temple. You will also pass the Brahmadeva Mandapa, a small pavilion that contains an intricately carved column.

There are a few more temples in town that are worth seeing. The Bhandari Basti enshrines 24 images of *tirthankaras* arranged in a row in the sanctuary. You will need someone to explain which one is which if you are interested. And the Jain Matha has several altars with bronze images around a courtyard, some of which date back to the 10th century, along with fascinating wall murals. The paintings depict some scenes of the life of Parsvanatha and Nagakumara. Even if no one is at this Matha, you can still see the images through the large glass windows that protect them. Smaller shrines are scattered around the town.

On Chandragiri Hill, there are a few other Jain temples, including the Parsvanatha Basti from the 12th century that has an image of Parsvanatha that reaches over 16 feet high. The Chamundaraya Basti has images of Neminatha and Parsvanatha, and the Chandragupta Basti, which is the tomb of Chandragupta Maurya, has interesting carved stone work that depicts scenes from the lives of Bhadrabahu and King Chandragupta.

The town has a long history going back to the 3rd century B.C.E. At that time Chandragupta Maurya, having given up his kingdom, came here with Bhagwan Bhadrabahu, his guru. As Bhadrabahu's disciples spread the Jain teachings throughout the region, Jainism became established in the South. The Ganga dynasty took to Jainism, and between the 4th and 10th centuries it was an important part of the culture of this area.

BELUR, HALEBID, and SOMNATHPUR

Belur, Halebid, and Somnathpur are the Hoysala temples in this area which are some of the most amazingly ornate temples you can see near Mysore. They are not as large as many of the other South Indian temples, but they are certainly some of the most beautiful, having the most intricate carvings and designs that you can imagine. You will find sculptures of a variety of deities, dancing girls, scenes from the *Mahabharata* and Vedic texts, images of the Hoysala rulers, animals, daily life activities, and so on.

The Hoysalas did not really become prominent in their rule of this area until the 11th through 13th centuries when Tinayaditya (1047-78) began utilizing the fact that the Gangas and Rashtrakutas were losing power. It was Ramanuja who converted Vishnuvardhana, formerly known as Bittiga, from Jainism to Vaishnavism, the worship of Vishnu. Ramanuja also defeated the Jain texts in public, which took away much of its credibility. Jainism began a rapid decline after this. After Vishnuvardhana's conversion, he began erecting temples devoted to Vishnu and Shiva. The temples at Belur and Halebid were built during the reign of Vishnuvardhana (1108-42). Other temples that he built include Melkote, Thonnur, Talakkad, and Gadag.

The Channekeshvara temple at Belur (155 km from Mysore) is the only one that is still a functioning temple. This temple is over 800 years old, started in 1117, and was built entirely of green chlorite by Vishnuvardhana after his victory over the Chola armies. It is said to have taken nearly 103 years to complete it. The temple enshrines the beautiful, four-armed deity of Keshava, which is said to have been worshiped by Lord Brahma at Satyaloka. Later, King Indradyumna is said to have brought the deity here and worshipped Him until he left this world, after which the *devas* continued the worship until King Vishnuvardhana began the worship. The king discovered the deity when he was traveling through the area and one of his servants took a bath and was cured of leprosy while bathing in the lake known as Vishnu Samudra, which is situated on the outskirts of town. Legend says that the lake appeared from a drop of nectar that fell from Garuda's pot. The king understood that this was a special place, which was confirmed when the deity of Keshava appeared in the dreams of both King Vishnuvardhana and Ramanujacharya, telling them to build a temple for Him. Thereafter, as instructed, the king discovered the deity at Chandra Drona Hill, from where he took the deity to Sri Narayanapura and then on to Velapura, now known as Belur.

The deity of Chenna Keshava is four-armed, holding the disc and conch shell in the upper hands, and lotus and club in the lower. The temple has remarkably intricate carvings around the doors and over the interior and exterior walls. These consist of guardian figures, many images of Vishnu, dancing girls, musicians, elephants, and other animals, numerous unique geometric designs, and many depictions from the *Puranas*. This collection easily represents some of the finest of Hoysala art.

There are five buildings in this complex, but the main structure is shaped like a 16-pointed star, erected on a raised platform. The central hall in the temple is a pavilion with perforated walls that allows outside air to come through. There are a total of forty-six pillars of various shapes and designs. The Narasimha pillar once rotated on stone ball-bearings. The middle of the pillar shows Lord Narasimha, surrounded by smaller images of the incarnations of Vishnu, Shiva, Ganesh, and dancing goddesses. The ceiling has an octogonal base with an amazing, intricately carved dome. There is a search light that can be used to light the detailed craftsmanship, otherwise the temple interior is rather dark. But use of the light costs two rupees (at the time).

The temple also has a *gopuram* several stories tall at the entrance to the courtyard that surrounds the temple, and a well-sculpted image of Garuda stands nearby facing the main temple. There are a few other temples in the complex you can also see. Around the main temple are also small shrines dedicated to the deities of Shanti-Narayana (built by Vish-nuvardhana's queen, Shantala Devi), Sudevi (Saumyanayaki), Vira Narayana, and God-dess Bhudevi (Ranganayaki). Other shrines in the temple compound include those of Ramanujacharya, Lord Nrisimha, Krishna, and Sita-Rama-Lakshmana and Hanuman. In the right corner of the compound is the small pond known as Vasudeva Tirtha. Along the wall is a pillared veranda with many sculptures, with inscriptions that describe the con-struction of the temple.

One interesting thing is that there is a large pair of chappals in a glass case in the front *mandapam* hall. The local cobblers believe the Lord walks to Bababudangiri hill daily to visit Lakshmi who resides there. It is said that the Lord appears in the dreams of the cob-blers when the chappals need replacing. They spread red kumkum on the ground so that His footprints appear when He walks through it. Then they prepare new chappals according to the size.

Outside the temple is a sculpture of a man fighting a lion. This is considered to be Sala, the leader of the Hoysala dynasty. The name Hoysala is interpreted as "Strike Sala," meaning that Sala should strike. The men shouted this at the king while he was fighting the beast, which is now depicted in this sculpture of the king fighting the lion, which he killed single-handedly.

The temple at Halebid (16 km from Belur), which was built in the mid-12th century, is dedicated to Shiva and has two Shiva *lingas* in two separate rooms. They are known as Sri Hoysalesvara and Kedaresvara. Construction started in 1121 by Ketamalla, a general of King Vishnuvardhana. It is actually two identical temples linked together. In front of each hallway is a detached pavilion with a large Nandi image in each. This temple has extensive carvings inside and out that show the expertise of the chisel work. The outside walls are decorated with exquisite friezes with rows of elephants, lions, scrollwork, and scenes from the *Ramayana* and *Mahabharata*. There are exceptional carvings of Vishnu and Lakshmi, Vishnu's *avataras*, Rama and Sita, one of Bishma dying on a bed of arrows, and others. The nearby Archeological Museum has additional stone deities and panels depicting a variety of scenes and divinities of the Vedic pantheon.

The temple at Somnathpur (40 km east from Mysore), which is dedicated to Lord Vishnu, is one of the best preserved of the Hoysala temples. It was erected by a Hoysala general, Somnatha, in 1268, and was created by the artist Janakachari, who had a part in the construction of other Hoysala temples. It was said that this temple was so perfect that even the demigods thought of stealing it. This temple is shaped like a star in the center of the courtyard. In the temple are three shrines: the stone deity of Keshava is in the center, Janardhana is to the north, and Gopala is to the south. All around the temple exterior are carvings of the various incarnations of Vishnu, such as Narasimha, Varaha, Venu Gopala, etc., as well as demigods like Brahma, Shiva, Ganesh, Surya, Lakshmi, and so on. This is another small but beautiful temple that clearly exemplifies how much regard the Vaish-nava Hindus gave to the worship of Sri Vishnu and to the construction of the temples they built for Him. Even though it is no longer a functioning temple, many people still visit it as a sign of their devotion and pay their respects to the three deities of Vishnu within.

MELKOTE (or MALAKOTE or MAILKOTE)

Melkote is a small town 48 km north of Mysore. It has little in the way of accommodation, so it is best to be visited as a day trip from Mysore or Srirangapatnam. It is a sacred hill shrine with a temple of Madhvacharya, which has a deity of Vishnu made of pure gold, standing 1 foot tall. Tiru Narayana is the name of the main temple. The Puranic names for Melkote are Vedadri (which means Veda Hill from which the *avatara* Dattatreya instructed his disciples), Narayanadri (the hill of Narayana), Yadavagiri (Yadu Hill where the Krishna and Balarama of the Yadu dynasty worshiped the Lord in Dvapara-yuga), Tirunarayanapura (abode of Lord Vishnu), Bhulokavaikuntha (the realm of Vaikuntha on earth), Doddagarudanahalli (place of elite warriors), Doddagurugalahalli (place of great teachers, Ramanuja), Jnanamantapa (house of knowledge), Vaikunthavardhana Kshetra (the place which increases the population of Lord Vishnu's abode), Dakshina Badrikachalam (the southern Badrinatha), and Yathisailam.

The main deities are said to have been given to Brahma by Lord Vishnu Himself. Tradition, as the *Naradiya Purana* explains, is that Lord Brahma once performed penance here, and Lord Narayana responded by coming to Melkote and assumed the form of a divine temple. Also, many thousands of years ago, Brahma gave one deity to Sanatkumara. Lord Vishnu ordered Seshanaga to take the form of a hill at Melkote and wait for His arrival. Sanatkumara then installed the deity and the temple complex in Bhuloka, planet Earth, at Melkote for the benefit of mankind. He later gave the deity to Lord Rama, and Rama worshiped this deity and later gave it to His son Kusha. Kusha also gave the deity as his daughter's dowry when she married a prince of the Yadu dynasty.

When Lord Krishna appeared in the Yadu dynasty, He also worshiped this deity. It was during this time that, while residing in the milk ocean, Lord Vishnu's diamond crown was stolen by Virocana, the son of Prahlada. Garuda killed Virocana and recovered the crown. However, while returning he saw Lord Krishna playing in Vrindavana with His friends. Garuda gave Lord Krishna the crown, known as Vajramukti. Krishna then gave the crown to the deity Ramapriya.

When Lord Balarama, Krishna's brother, returned to Dwarka from one of His pilgrimages, he related to Lord Krishna that the deity in Melkote was the same as their own family deity. So they took the deity to Melkote and found no difference between the two deities. So Krishna installed the deity of Ramapriya in Melkote and the Yadu family regularly came there to worship that deity.

Later, the story goes that in the 11th century, the Jain King Bittideva embraced Vaishnavism with the training and influence of Sri Ramanuja, and changed his name to Vishnuvardhana. However, at that time, because of the Muslim invaders, Narayanapuram was in ruins. Both the main deity of Narayana and the smaller deity of Ramapriya were lost. But Ramanuja had a vision in which Lord Vishnu showed him where the deity could be found. Thus, he located the larger deity among some Tulasi trees in an ant-hill in Yadavagiri, and then installed the deity in the temple. As a service to his guru, Bittideva renovated the Tiru Narayana temple and built five shrines to Lord Vishnu known as the PanchaNarayana temples.

The smaller Vishnu deity or Ramapriya had been given to a king who gave it to his daughter who became very attached to it as one of her dolls. Then later, when the sages wanted to install it in the temple, Ramanuja came to ask for it back. The king laughed and said, "I have so many dolls. You call it and if it comes, then you can have it." So he called it by name and the deity practically flew into his arms. So then he took the deity and it was also installed in the temple. The king's daughter, however, was so attached to it, but she was a Muslim and could not be allowed into the temple. Nonetheless, she also came to Melkote and there attained *mukti*, liberation. She is known as Beebu Nachiyar and is one of the saints of the temple. Her image is shown near the deity.

The main deity of Lord Vishnu is black stone and shows Him holding a shanku (conch), chakra, and gadha (club). These are all covered in gold as are the deity's hands, feet, chest, and crown. He also wears a colorful outfit, gold bead necklaces, bright garlands, and a large string of *shalagrama shilas* hang from the altar to His feet. So He is quite lovely to see. He is directly in front of you as you enter the temple and stands nearly five feet tall. The deity of Ramapriya is in the Ranga Mandapam hall in front of the sanctum, on the right side of the entrance. This deity was worshiped with great love by Lord Ramachandra. Shrines for the deities of Vaikunthanatha, Chakrathu Alwar, and Anjaneya are on the *parakramas*, walkways of the temple. And the Goddess Yadugiri Nachiyar (Lakshmi) and Kalyani Nachiyar have separate shrines in a *mandapam* hall of beautifully carved stone pillars in the back right corner of the complex.

Around the temple are the maths of various Vaishnava sects, and there is also an image of Ramanuja here, which was installed before he went back to Sri Rangam. He spent twelve years here. Thus, it is one of the four most holy sites for Sri Vaishnavas, followers of Sri Ramanuja. There is also a spectacular festival of Vairamudi (the festival of the diamond crown) which lasts for 10 days and attracts thousands of pilgrims. This diamond crown is held so sacred that the deity wears it only during the time of the festival. This is the crown that was said to have been given to Lord Krishna by Garuda when he was taking it to Vaikuntha from Patala Loka. Krishna decorated the deity Ramapriya with this crown, and it came to Melkote with Ramapriya.

The main holy pond is the Kalyani Pond. It is said in the *Isvara Samhita* that when Lord Varaha lifted the earth from the universal ocean, some of the drops of water from His body fell at Melkote which created the pond. The *Matsya Purana* explains that Garuda, Lord Vishnu's eagle carrier, brought some white clay here from Lord Vishnu's planet of Svetadvipa.

On the hilltop at the other end of town, many steps up, is a temple to Lord Narasimha sitting in the Yoga position, so He is called Yoga Narasimha. He is nearly three feet tall and beautifully dressed and adorned in gold, with gold hands, feet, and crown with large flower garlands covering His chest. This deity, according to the *Naradiya Purana*, is said to have been installed here thousands of years ago by Prahlada Maharaja, Narasimha's devotee and son of Hiranyakashipu. Beneath the temple is a small cave, just under the deity, where Prahlada is said to have meditated. If you would like, you can also arrange to sponsor a bathing ceremony of the deity of Lord Narasimha, in which case you can watch the priests do the bathing of the deity. From this temple you can get a great view over Melkote. The town also has the Academy of Sanskrit Research, which has a large library of old Sanskrit manuscripts and palm leaves.

SUBRAMANYA

This is a small temple town some 180 kilometers northwest of Mysore and north of Madikeri. It has one temple to Subramanya, or Karttikeya, and another to Lord Narasimha, which also has a Narasimha *shila* that was given by Madhvacharya to his brother. It is a nice and friendly place.

BRINDABAN GARDENS

This place is 19 kilometers from Mysore, below the Krishnarajasagar dam on the Cauvery River. It is a pleasant place to relax and reflect on our experiences during this pilgrimage tour. It is known for its beautiful flowers, many water fountains, and evening illumination from its many lights. Numerous Indians and tourists come here to relax with families and friends. It is easily reached by bus or taxi, or as one of the stops on the Mysore tour bus.

Here we can casually walk around the fountains or simply sit back and reflect on our tour of South India. After all, we have just completed a pilgrimage that many people can only dream of doing. Now we have actually seen and been a part of some of the most important aspects of Eastern spiritual culture. We have seen the temples that were built many hundreds of years ago, as well as the devotional activity that still goes on in them today. We have heard many legends of antiquity that are associated with some of these famous holy places. And, depending on our consciousness, maybe we were able to enter into the spiritual atmosphere for which these holy places are known. Maybe in our meditations we attained a glimpse of the spiritual vision that the great sages have, and then returned to our external awareness with a new view and deeper understanding of ourselves and the world. Maybe we realized the importance of the path taken by the spiritual masters who have left their teachings for us to ponder. Maybe, if we were fortunate, we realized the essence of the spiritual truths that are explained in the Vedic texts, and will leave South India with memories of a most unforgettable experience.

Certainly, this is a culture that dates back farther than most others and is still very much alive. The customs and traditions we see today are quite the same as they were when they were performed thousands of years ago. And the philosophical reasonings and spiritual insights found in the ancient Vedic texts often challenge today's most mature Western theologians. We also see many Westerners studying and accepting yoga and the Vedic philosophy in their search for experiences and answers not attainable in conventional Western philosophy and religion. Surely, the East and West have many things to learn from each other, and a beneficial balance can be reached.

For now, however, as we sit in the park, the sun has gone down, the air has become cool, the many lights have been turned on, the musical water fountains with their colorful illuminations will start up, and it will not be long before we board our bus for the ride back to our hotel in Mysore. At the hotel, we will pack our bags so we can be ready to catch the early morning train for our journey to our next point of interest.

BANGALORE (BENGALURU)

If we get into Bangalore by train, we can walk to a hotel that is just around the corner from the station. I prefer this because when it is time to leave and start traveling again, we are right next to the train station. We can check on getting tickets anytime, and not have to worry about getting a ricksha or taxi when it is time to go. As we leave the train station, just turn right when we get to the street. Just walking along the sidewalk we can find several to choose from, depending on the standard we want. Restaurants and tour companies are all nearby, and auto-rickshas are easy to get at the train station.

Bangalore has a little of everything and anything in which we may be interested, no matter whether it is temples, museums, nice gardens, or pleasant accommodations in which to relax and get ourselves together for further travels. Or maybe we just want to contemplate what else we want to do with the rest of our life. If you like shopping, there are plenty of stores from which to choose. Bangalore is a good place to shop for saris or cloth items, books, or whatever else you may want. But in recent years the automobile traffic around Bangalore has increased tremendously.

Bangalore is known especially for its beautiful parks, wide avenues, busy bazaars, and pleasant climate. It's a thousand meters above sea level and usually feels somewhat cooler than most South Indian cities, even in midsummer. Most of the city is rather modern, especially around Kumpegowda Circle and along Gandhi Nagar and Chickpet streets. In fact, it's the second most westernized city in India, next to Mumbai, with a population of more than 4,000,000. But not far away is the old part of town around Sri Narsimharaja Road, and farther south is where you can get a feel for the earlier culture of the area. The streets there are narrow and winding, and the older temples and cottage industries and historical landmarks are also there.

Bangalore is also the capital of Karnataka state and you will find the very distinguishable buildings that house the government offices and some museums around the Cubbon Park area. The Vidhana Soudha is in this district and houses the legislature and Secretariat, and is styled in neo-Dravidian architecture. It opens for guests at 5:30 P.M. The Government Museum is also worth a visit and, started in 1886, is one of the oldest in India.

In the southern part of town is Lal Bagh Botanical Gardens, one of the nicest parks in the city with a wide variety of trees, flowers, ponds, and tropical plants, although I was besieged by begging children here while trying to eat a little ice cream. Going up Lalbagh Fort Road you will reach Tipu Sultan's Summer Palace. This was completed in 1791. This is a small but interesting structure made from wood, and architecturally designed to catch any cool breezes that come through. Nearby is an interesting temple, although it's closed in the afternoon like most temples. This is a temple dedicated to Vishnu called Srinivasa Prasanna Venkataramanaswamy temple. Up Avenue Road is Tipu's fort, but it is mostly in ruins and not so interesting, but all right if you have got the time to see it.

Going farther south to Bugle Hill is Bull temple. It is one of the oldest temples in the city and is dedicated to Nandi, Shiva's bull carrier. It has a huge image of Nandi 4.6 meters tall, similar in size to the one in Mysore. The original plan was to simply build the huge Nandi image, but when it was completed the image miraculously began to grow and stopped only after the temple was built over it. After it was completed, an angry bull that had been devouring the peanut crop in the area ceased disturbing the local farmers. Since that time the farmers hold a little peanut festival every year in thanksgiving of their peanut crop. Near the Bull temple (400 meters west) is one of the four watchtowers of Kempegowda.

To the northwest of Bangalore is the Gavi Gangadheswara shrine, near the Kempambudhi Tank. This cave temple is dedicated to Shiva and Parvati and houses 33 deities, including Agni the demigod of fire. The main shrine houses a Shiva *linga*. The sanctum faces south and has shrines to Devi Parvati and Durga. Sage Gautama had worshiped Lord Shiva in this cave. There is an image of him in the cave, along with other deities that you see as you circumambulate the main shrine, but keep your head down since the ceiling is low. An interesting point is that during the Makara Sakranti festival in January, the last rays of the evening sun shine through an archway to lighten the image of Shiva.

A few kilometers from here is the small Viranjaneya temple in a neighborhood opposite the Iskcon temple. It is on a small hill and up a flight of steps. A stage and meditation area is on the left. A large image of Lakshmi is in the main sanctum, sitting about 18 feet tall, with hands, feet, and crown adorned in silver. There are a few other shrines to Ganesh, Sita-Rama, and Lakshmana. Then on top under a golden dome is a huge stone image of Hanuman holding the mountain in one hand and a club in the other. His feet are adorned in silver.

Not far away, another place that is very impressive and is now a major spiritual attraction and source of inspiration in Bangalore is the Iskcon Hare Krishna temple. The temple is about a half-hour out of town, along Chord Road. As you come around the final corner on the highway, you look over and see this huge temple building that covers seven acres of the hillside. It was officially opened in May of 1997, and is drawing as many as 2,000 visitors a day. The President of India at the time, Dr. Shankar Dayal Sharma, headed the inaugural ceremonies at the temple, which is named the Sri Chaitanya Mahaprabhu Center for Advancement of Culture.

This new temple is a massive and tall building. The team of architects designed it with a blend of traditional styles with modern applications and materials. It has five temples on different floors within the complex as you walk up to the main part of the building, starting with the deities of Lord Narasimhadeva, then Lord Venkateshvara, and then up to the main temple room with Gour-Nitai, Sri Sri Radha-Krishnachandra, and Krishna-Balarama. You will also find a large vegetarian restaurant inside with a dining hall that can seat 1500. It also has a multi-media cultural presentation in the air-conditioned theater, which includes digital surround sound, special effects, and animated dioramas or doll exhibits. The complex also contains an open amphitheater, conference rooms, a Vedic museum, a recording studio, guest facilities, offices, a room with demonstrations on the life of Srila A. C. Bhaktivedanta Swami Prabhupada (the founder of the movement), and much more, such as the beautiful gardens that surround it.

In the suburb Banashankari II Stage is this famous Balaji or Devagiri Varaprada Sri Venkateshwara temple. An attractive *gopuram* shows the entrance, and the main deity inside is like the deity at Tirupati.

The Banashankari temple on the southern boundaries of Bangalore is also popular. The deity of the Goddess is seated on a lion, and hundreds of people come here for special worship on Sundays, Tuesdays, and Fridays.

Many other shrines and temples exist in Bangalore, but you may not be interested to see them all. Besides these places that have been mentioned, there are two others that I saw in Bangalore that I really liked. One was the Vishwa Shanti Ashrama that is more than 24 kilometers north of town. This was established by Sant Keshavadasa, a Vaishnava teacher and a well-known devotional singer who believes that the future world religion will be Sanatana Dharma or, as he calls it, the Cosmic Religion in which all the world's religions will become united and their essence practiced.

Vishwa Shanti Ashrama is a very peaceful place and has several interesting temples on the property, with more construction underway. Near the front of the property are little temples and shrines, which include black stone Radha-Krishna deities, a black stone Ganesh, an outdoor altar for the nine planets, a small temple of a three-headed image of Dattatreya, and an outdoor altar with a black stone Hanuman. Nearby is a larger temple with an altar that had a Shiva *lingam*, a couple sets of Sita-Rama and Lakshmana deities, white marble Radha-Krishna deities, Hanuman, and other smaller deities.

As you go down the path, you will stop at the shoe-minder's stall where you will leave your shoes, pass by a large hall for meetings and meditations, and then find yourself near a large tulasi tree stand which is in front of a very impressively large, 36 feet tall, black granite image of Vishwa Vijaya Vitthala. The top of the deity reaches the treetops. He stands behind a small pavilion with an altar with more deities. On either side of the pavilion you will see two buildings that contain four different images of Lakshmidevi in each, eight in all.

Then you follow the path back through the trees to the Bhagavad-gita Darshan Mandir. It is a large round structure with the interior of the walls covered in black granite plates, each having a verse from the *Bhagavad-gita* in four languages: Sanskrit, English, Hindi, and Kannada. In the center of the building are the images of Krishna speaking the *Bhagavad-gita* to Arjuna, behind which is a huge image in white granite of Visvarupa, Krishna's universal form, with numerous heads and many arms holding various weapons. This is very awe inspiring to see. I had to spend a good half-hour just meditating on this huge form of Krishna as He stood before me in this way. Then I walked around the building reading the verses from the *Bhagavad-gita* and realized I should slowly read and meditate on this book again. It is certainly the essence of the most elevated spiritual knowledge. Below this floor is another hall with a deity of Gayatri Devi. In front of the building will be a large rose garden with fountains, and more plans for cottages for guests, a separate kitchen, etc.

We can also visit Mother Karunamayi's ashram in the southern suburb of Bangalore, Ashok Nagar. The address is: Karunamayi Santhi Dhama, 14/5, 6th Cross, Ashok Nagar, Banashankari 1st Stage, Bangalore. If she is in town, she will give *darshan* and a talk in the evenings about 6:30 or 7 P.M. Otherwise, she may be at her retreat in the forests outside of Bangalore, or doing a tour in another country.

If you are in need of getting your health together after so much traveling, there is the Jindal health resort some distance out of Bangalore on Bombay road where you can rejuvenate yourself in a natural way.

DENKANIKOTA

Denkanikota is the place of the Betrayaswamy temple. It is roughly 20 kilometers from Hosur, which is 40 km southeast of Bangalore and reached by bus from Hosur or other towns besides Bangalore. It can easily be visited as a day trip from Bangalore. From the nearest bus stand, the temple is a two-kilometer walk or ricksha ride.

A five-tiered *gopuram* of the ornate Hoysala style of architecture rises over the eastern entrance. The temple itself sits on one acre of land. A wall that surrounds it is 244 feet long by 204 feet wide. In front of the temple is the Swamy Pushkarini Lake that is 220 feet square. Inside the sanctum is the main deity of Sri Betrayaswamy who is in a standing pose. He is in the exact formation as the Lord Venkateswara deity of Tirumalai Hills. He wears beautiful ornaments and is accompanied by Sridevi and Bhudevi at His sides. Like other temples of the south, there are additional shrines in the hallways to various Divinities and personalities. These include Venugopala with Rukmini and Satyabhama, and Sita-Rama and Lakshmana and Anjaneya (Hanuman).

There are eight chapters of the *Skanda Purana* that describe the glories of this place. The history of it started when the Yaksha brother of Kubera's maternal grandfather, Maharnavan, underwent a rugged penance for achieving the blessings of Brahma. Brahma was impressed enough that he gave Maharnavan the boon of deathlessness to him. However, excited by this new strength, he went berserk with harassing the celestials and turning their abodes into rubble. He did this with such determination that he was given the nickname "Deva Gandakan", the Harrier of the *devas*.

Then, once when Kanva Rishi was engaged in austerities, Deva Gandakan chose to harass him as well. But Kanva then beseeched the Lord to intercede. Thereupon, the Lord appeared in the guise of a hunter and engaged in a battle with the Deva Gandakan. After some time, Deva Gandakan charged the hunter, but the Lord pommelled the Yaksha, severely wounding him. The Yaksha then achieved not only redemption but also realization. He then asked the Lord that the place be named Denkanipuram in memory of this incident. Kanva was also blessed with the *darshan* of Lord Venkateswara (Vishnu), who accepted the name of Betrayaswamy, which means Lord as the hunter.

ENDING OUR TOUR BACK AT BANGALORE

Naturally, not all of the holy spots have been described. Only the larger or more significant places were included. Numerous smaller ones are also there that you can visit if you wish. Nonetheless, after seeing these projects in Bangalore and so many other holy places on our tour of South India, I felt so satisfied, enlivened, enthused, and determined, that I did not feel any need to see anything else. In fact, I could have left India right then and felt perfectly happy with all that I had seen and experienced. On this particular journey, I can sincerely say that I was spiritually touched on a very deep level. Not only did I see the way others display their devotion, but I also was caught up into it. Plus, coming in contact with spiritually potent places where significant historical episodes have taken place, and where powerful temples are found and where holy men visit, can make a pivotal change in your consciousness and spiritual perception. Having this sort of energy charge your consciousness is a most profound and, practically, indescribable experience. This sacred journey has been a complete adventure on every level. And now, in this small way of providing descriptions and photos, I can share it with others.

After our visit in Bangalore, we can either continue our journey through India, or prepare for returning home. We can fly back to Delhi or, if we wish to travel by train, we can take a train to Chennai, which is the best place for booking the faster connecting trains for going north. If that is what we want to do, then once we reach Chennai, we go straight to the Indrail Pass Office (for foreigners only) and book a place on the evening train to Delhi, which takes about 32 hours. It is a long but interesting ride. However, if we are ready for more, we can start our tour of East and Central India, or head westward where we can continue our spiritual journey and visit many more temples and holy places. There is so much opportunity to increase our spiritual experiences in this land.

The front *gopuram* or gate and lines of people waiting to go into the Balaji temple at Tirumalla up the hill from Tirupati, to get *darshan* of the deity. *Darshan* lasts only a minute or two because of the continuous lines of people coming through.

People coming into the large Vishnu temple complex at Sri Rangam, the most important Vishnu temple in the south. This is the first of its seven gates.

One of the huge pillars inside the Jambukeshvara Shiva temple, which is a short ride across the road from the Sri Rangam temple. It has a Shiva *lingam* that is supplied water from a spring right next to it.

The sculpture of Lord Vishnu's and Krishna's universal form, located on the south *gopuram* of the Meenakshi temple in Madurai.

The longest temple hall in India is this one in the huge temple complex at
Ramesvaram.

The image of Bahubali (Gomateshvara) at the Jain hilltop temple at Shravanabelagola, one of the most important holy places of the Jains.

One of the tall gopurams on the north side of the Meenakshi temple in Madurai.
Buses line up with hundreds of pilgrims to visit the temple.

A happy bride and groom and family members after their Vedic wedding at the Kapeeleshvara temple near Chennai.

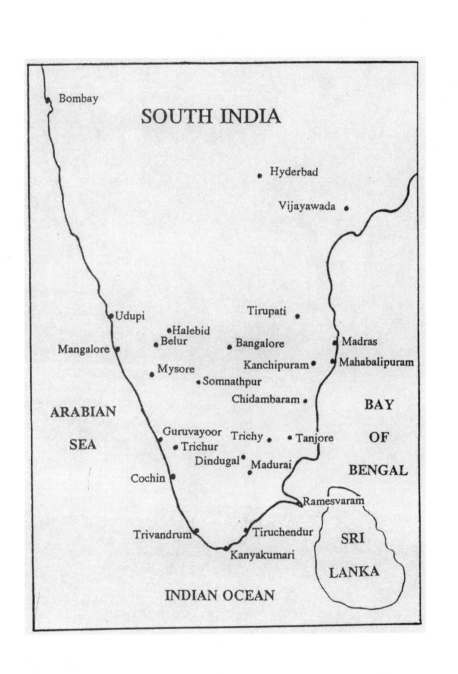

SOUTH INDIA

Bombay

Hyderbad

Vijayawada

Tirupati

Udupi

Halebid
Belur
Mangalore
Bangalore
Madras
Mysore
Kanchipuram
Mahabalipuram
Somnathpur
Chidambaram

ARABIAN

SEA
Guruvayoor
Trichy
Tanjore
Trichur
Dindugal
Madurai

Cochin

BAY

OF

BENGAL

Ramesvaram

Trivandrum
Tiruchendur
SRI
Kanyakumari
LANKA

INDIAN OCEAN

▼

The Major Holy Places of Western India

STARTING IN NEW DELHI

We will be starting our pilgrim's journey of West India from New Delhi. After our arrival in Delhi we may want to spend a day or two making whatever final arrangements we need for our travels. I usually always stay a day here just to get used to being in India again if I have just flown in from the West, and to see whatever sites in the Delhi area that I have not already visited. Also, I never travel through Delhi without visiting the most holy places of Mathura and Vrindavana, the land of Krishna. I usually go there at the end of my journey when I'm getting ready to go back to Delhi to get my flight. There are so many holy sites and places to see in this area, and it is so spiritually powerful and enlivening, that you should make a point to visit this area at every opportunity. I have already described the major sites of this region in a previous chapter.

When we are ready to leave Delhi or Vrindavana and begin traveling west, we will take a train into Rajasthan, which has many interesting cities and towns. Rajasthan, for the most part, is quite dry but the people are very colorful in the way they dress and decorate themselves. The men are known for the large turbans and the women for their fancy dresses and heavy jewelry. It is a style unique in India.

If you don't want to visit Karauli, we can reach Jaipur by flying or taking the train or bus from Delhi, which is about a six-hour ride. There are several trains from which to choose. Simply pick up a train schedule book from the New Delhi train station, if they are not out of stock, and you can choose whichever train best suits your travel needs. I often do that because in many situations I never know how long I will be in each city. On this trip we will also go to Karauli first.

KARAULI

Karauli is our first stop. There are several trains we can take from either New Delhi or Mathura (100 km away), depending on where we are. We will first travel to Gangapur, from where we will take a very bumpy, one-hour bus ride to Karauli. If you take a late train from New Delhi, you may have to spend the night in Gangapur, which has minimal choices for hotels. From there we continue by bus the next morning. If you first go to Jaipur from New Delhi, you can also get to Karauli by bus from Jaipur (182 km). If such is the case, you may have to spend the night in Karauli and return to Jaipur the next day, unless you are going back toward Agra or Delhi.

Once we get to Karauli, the bus station is on the edge of town and is very crowded and confusing. It is a good idea to travel light since there are no rickshas here and the temple is a two-kilometer walk away from the bus station. If we spend the night here, it means we have a small choice of a few *dharmashalas* to stay at: A few next to the temple and a few farther away. There is one place near the bus station and, if you plan to leave Karauli before the day's end, you can store your luggage in a small, locked cabinet for a few rupees. These places only provide the most basic accommodations, and one of them doesn't have water. So be prepared. But we can handle it for a night.

Karauli is a small town, but the major temple we want to see is the home of Sri Madan Mohana, a most significant deity. The name "Madana Mohana" means "one who can enchant Cupid." Sri Madan Mohana was Sanatana Gosvami's deity in Vrindavana from whom Krishnadasa Kaviraja got blessings and the inspiration to write his classic work, the *Sri Caitanya-caritamrita*. In 1670 the deities were brought to Jaipur due to fear of the Muslim Aurangzeb. Later, the deities were taken to Karauli when Maharaja Gopal Singh, king of Karauli, convinced his brother-in-law, Jai Singh, that he should take them after having a dream in which Madan Mohana expressed His desire to return to the area of Vraja. Karauli is considered to be a part of greater Vrajamandala, which is the expanded holy area around Vrindavana. The royal family built a very nice temple for the deities where many devotees worship them every day.

The temple is on a small hill and is reached by walking through many narrow and winding streets. The buildings are very close to each other, making it impossible to see the temple from a distance. So you may have to have someone show you the way. I was lucky enough that when I arrived, a little boy came up and readily asked if I wanted to see the temple, and he lead the way. The temple building is surrounded by a big courtyard within the Karauli city palace. The interior is beautiful with high arches and Krishna-lila paintings on them. There is a silver door in front of each of the three altars. The central altar is for Madan Mohana, who stands about five feet tall, taller than I expected. Then there are smaller deities of Radharani on His left and Lalita Devi on His right. Next to the main altar is one of Radha-Krishna. There are eight *aratis* and food offerings a day, beginning at 4:30 A.M. when over 300 people attend, with a midday offering of over 54 preparations. You can buy some *prasadam* (which means the Lord's mercy, or food that has been offered to the deities) at nearby stalls. Spending the night allows us to have *darshan* of the deities in the evening and the next morning before getting a bus back to Jaipur.

Near the temple is the City Palace which has a nice assortment of sculptures and paintings, which you may also like to see.

When I visited this town, I felt like something special was happening. When I saw the deities, I simply stood there for several minutes, praying to be blessed similar to the way Madan Mohana blessed Krishnadasa Kaviraja. When I completed my circumambulation of the temple, I sat in the back of the courtyard to rest and look at the deities from a distance. I had not eaten in almost two days and was feeling a little tired and weak from the endeavor of traveling. Just then a girl who happened to be there came up and started talking to me. Her name was Leena and was from a Brahmin family. After the deity curtains closed, she was kind enough to make arrangements for me to get some *prasada* at a stall across from the main temple. I greatly relished the sweet *prasada*. She also took me to her aunt's house where I had a nice meal of rice, *dal*, *chapatis*, vegetable, and sweets. I felt that this was all the mercy of Sri Madan Mohana, like the story of when Krishna came with milk for Madhavendra Puri who was fasting, and Krishna told him that no one fasts in His land. So I was very refreshed after such a nice meal, and greatly appreciated the hospitality.

Leena also took me to her house, and I had a chance to see the way her family lived. She also showed me her personal altar which had pictures and small deities of Lord Krishna, Whom she worships every morning and evening. This was all more than I ever expected to happen in Karauli, and when it was time to leave, she sent her family servant to help me make sure I got on the right bus for Jaipur. This was a special blessing because even the locals seem to have a hard time knowing which of the many buses is the right one to take.

JAIPUR

Jaipur is our next stop. The bus from Karauli, if that is where we are arriving from, is often very crowded with many people standing and competing for seats. As with most buses in India, the seats offer little comfort and you get banged with every bump in the road. The ride is about eight hours long and will take you past many small villages, areas of deserts, farms that grow crops only with the help of irrigation, plus herds of cows, goats, camels, etc. And like most country roads in India, this one is only one lane in width. Any time there is oncoming traffic, the bus driver swerves at the last minute to avoid crashing. And the shoulder of the road is soft sand so the bus will lean to the side making you wonder if it might fall over. If the bus comes up behind slower traffic, like a truck or ox cart, the bus driver will have to honk many times before the vehicle ahead will finally move over enough to pass. If the bus makes a stop at one of the small villages and you get off to buy some fruit or something, a small crowd of people will soon gather simply out of curiosity to watch a foreigner.

Jaipur is one of the most interesting cities in all of India and one of the most visited. It is known as the "pink city" due to the buildings in the old section of town being made from pink sandstone. Jaipur used to be light gray but was ordered to be painted pink, the color of welcome, when Prince Albert visited in 1883. Then it stayed that color. Though

Jaipur has a population of 1,500,000, it is spread out and the streets have a lot of room compared to other cities in India. However, it can be quite a hair-raising experience when you are riding in a motor-ricksha on a street packed with cars, bicycles, motorbikes, motor-rickshas, pedestrians, camels, goats, cows, ox carts, buses, trucks, etc., and the driver is taking you from one side of the street to the other in his attempt to get through the traffic. It can be especially thrilling, or should I say nerve racking, when you are riding on the wrong side of the street facing a mass of oncoming traffic just after the light has changed from red to green. Whoopee! Watch out folks, anything can happen.

The name "Jaipur" literally means "City (Pur) of Victory (Jai)". This is in relation to Jai Singh's (1699-1744) victory over Aurangzeb's planned attack against Vrindavana to destroy temples and deities. Jai Singh had heard of the planned attack and quickly went to Vrindavana to warn the people and save as many temples as possible. Many of the Vrindavana deities were brought to the area of Jaipur. When Aurangzeb arrived in Vrindavana, he found that numerous people had vacated the town and many temples were without deities. He was furious and tore down the upper storeys of the Govindaji temple until there was a loud and frightening noise that shook the ground and made Aurangzeb stop his attack and retreat. Meanwhile, Jai Singh had already taken the deities of Radha-Govindaji to Jaipur and was worshiping them in a place near Amber, called the "Palace of Clouds". Later, as the threat of Mughal attacks decreased, Jai Singh brought the deities down into Jaipur. After this the city was further developed. Presently, Jaipur has 106 main temples and numerous other minor ones.

The story is that as the town of Jaipur expanded, Jai Singh made his quarters in the middle of town and established the deities of Radha-Govinda in a shrine in a prominent location. Although Jai Singh was providing nice service for the deities, Jai Singh had a dream in which Lord Krishna appeared and kicked him out of bed. Jai Singh awoke on the floor and was startled by the implications of the dream. So he gathered his brahmanas to discuss the incident. They interpreted it to mean that Jai Singh's quarters should not be in the center of town, but the deity should be there instead. So that day Jai Singh relocated his quarters and made it the temple of Govinda. The City Palace, overlooking the temple, was thus constructed and became Jai Singh's new home.

This temple of Sri Sri Radha-Govindaji, located on the north side of the City Palace, is one of the most important of all temples in Jaipur. The deity of Sri Govinda was originally installed in Vrindavana nearly 5000 years ago by the great grandson of Lord Krishna. The deity had somehow become lost for many years but revealed where He was buried to Rupa Gosvami in a dream. Rupa Gosvami found the deity and installed Him in the Radha-Govindaji temple in Vrindavana 450 years ago. Then He was brought to Jaipur around 1728, as related above. The temple is very opulent and the deities are very beautiful. There is also a small Krishna deity, Gaura-Govinda, that was worshiped by Kasiswara Pandit. This temple is extremely popular and is visited both morning and evening by hundreds of devotees. People will crowd around the altar to see the deities, and after the *arati* the priests will hand out *maha-prasada* to the guests who try to scramble to get some from the booth on the left side of the deities. Devotees can purchase offered food, *prasadam*, from the nearby stalls after the noon *arati*. In the early morning or evening there may be a lecture given by one of the local holy men, and afterward there will be the final *arati* for the day. Worship times are 5:00, 7:45 and 11:30 A.M., and then 5:45, 6:30, and 8:30 P.M. The temple is closed in the afternoon.

There are many other temples in Jaipur, some of which are easy to find and others that I did not find so quickly. On occasion you can be walking along and see a small temple where you least expect, sometimes privately owned. And other times you can go looking for a specific temple and not find it. So you have to have some idea where it is and ask around until you locate it, at least if it's one that is important to you.

Another significant temple is the Radha-Damodara temple near the Tripolia Gate, which is less than a half kilometer from the Radha-Govinda temple. It is located up a stairway from the street, and there is little to mark its location, nor does it look like a temple. The deities were originally installed in Vrindavan by Rupa Gosvami in 1542, and then cared for by Jiva Gosvami, and later taken to Jaipur to escape the Moghuls. There is also a small deity of Lord Narasimha here and a Govardhana *shila* that was worshiped by Sanatana Gosvami. The temple is small but opulently decorated, and has nice marble columns, mirrored panels on the walls, paintings on the small ceiling beams, and the very beautiful deities are about two-and-a-half feet tall. In the courtyard are a few cows that are kept for offering milk to the deities. This adds to the devotional mood and Vrindavan-like atmosphere of the temple.

Across the street from the Radha-Damodara temple is a Shiva temple that houses the *lingas* of Vishveshvara and Tarkeshvara, and has a large standing Nandi (Shiva's bull), a large Ganesh, some deities of Krishna, and several other images. If you are in this area, this temple is easy to find and worth visiting.

Going back to Tripolia Bazaar Road by foot from the Radha-Damodara temple, and then around the corner to the left, behind the Hindu Hotel, through a small door to the left of shop number 295, and up a flight of stairs, is the Radha-Vinoda temple, which houses the deities of Lokanatha Gosvami of Vrindavan. These were originally worshiped in Vrindavan at the Radha-Gokulananda temple. Lokanatha Gosvami was a great Vaishnava poet and disciple of Narottama dasa Thakura. The beautiful deity is about 12 inches tall. Be sure to visit in the morning while the temple is open. If you're foreign, the priest will be glad to see you. I found this temple the first time I was in Jaipur, however, the second time I just could not find the stairway that leads to it for some reason. So it can take some determination to locate it.

Some distance away, about four blocks north of the Chandpol Bazaar district is the temple of Radha-Gopinatha. This deity of Gopinatha (Krishna) first appeared to Paramananda Bhattacarya at Vamsivata in Vrindavan. His disciple Madhu Pandita founded the temple at Vamsivata, one of the seven original temples of Vrindavan. This is another of the deities that were moved to Jaipur during the raids of the Muslims. It was Rae Shilji of Jaipur who constructed the present Jaipur temple and arranged to bring the deity here. This temple is worth seeing and has artistic frescoes on all the walls displaying pastimes of Krishna. When I was there, I stayed for the *arati* and the people were very glad to see me and gave me garlands, *tulasi* leaves, and *prasadam* that had been offered to the deities. In temples like this you can feel very spiritually charged. Of course, after having received so many blessings from the priests and people, it is always nice to show your appreciation by leaving a donation in front of the deities.

Five minutes from this temple to the west is the large, castle-like temple for Balanandaji, built by Jai Singh for his guru.

Five minutes walk east of the Radha-Govindaji temple in the Moti Katta Bazaar is a temple of Lord Kalki, the incarnation of Krishna who is to descend at the end of Kali-yuga in another 426,000 years. I have to admit that try as I might, I could not locate this temple, but I know it was around there somewhere.

Down the street about four or five blocks from the Radha-Damodar temple is a small Madana Mohana temple. However, the most important temple of the original Madan Mohana deities of Vrindavana is in the town of Karauli.

On the east side of Jaipur is the Surya temple in Galta. This is on the road to Agra, National Highway 11, reached by taking a bus from the Hawa Mahal, Palace of Winds, to the far end of Ramganj Bazaar. Or you can simply take a motor-richsha there. It's on a hill about three miles from the city. You get dropped off at the Suraja Pol gate and continue on foot for about 20 minutes. By climbing up the road you reach the Surya temple. This temple was built during the time of Jai Singh II by the Kachawaha Rajputs. Their dynasty is said to come through Kusha, the son of Lord Ramachandra, and is traced back to Lord Surya, the sun-god. The temple is small and there is not much to see, other than the view over Jaipur, which is especially nice in the morning. The altar in the temple had nothing but a small plastic image of Surya, which is a gold face on a sun disk.

As we cross over the hill we can find some Sita-Ram temples, and up over the hill and down the other side to the east you will find a very simple temple to Galtiji, the main temple of Galta. The sage Galtiji had kicked his foot into the side of the hill after calling the Ganga River to appear there when the people complained that the previous water had become salty. Further down the hill you will reach Surya Kund where clear mountain water pours from the mouth of a marble cow. The water arrives at this place by no man-made arrangement. The water pours into the kund where pilgrims take their purification bath, and you may see many people splashing around in the water. Nearby are two Shiva cave temples; one for Galteshvara, and the other for Yogeshvara. If we continue down the hill, we will see additional and charming temples with Radha-Krishna deities set in a row in a lovely garden setting around a pond below Galta Tirtha.

A lovely new temple in Jaipur, about 30 or so minutes south of the city, is the Laxmi-Narayan temple that's been built by the Birla family. It is made out of beautiful white marble. The deities of Sri Sri Laxmi-Narayan are large, about six or seven feet tall. The temple has some lovely stained glass windows depicting various demigods and incarnations of Lord Krishna. There is also a museum that displays the history of G. P. Birla and his industrial enterprises. He has built temples in many other holy places and towns as well.

Twenty kilometers south of Jaipur is a very old Jain temple dating back hundreds of years. The marble work is very fine and it has a large collection of Jain images, some of which they will tell you date back more than 2000 years, and one of Adinatha that is said to be 5000 years old. The ride to reach this temple is a long one and unless you are a serious Jain pilgrim, you may prefer to stick with seeing other things.

Near the City Palace is the Jantar Mantar observatory built by Jai Singh, which dates back to 1728. This is the largest of the five observatories that he built including others in Delhi, Varanasi, Ujjain, and one in Mathura which no longer exists. Though the instruments are very large, they are still quite accurate for their purpose.

The Palace of Winds, built in 1799, is a very decorative, narrow, five-storey building in the east wall of the old city. It was built so the royal ladies could look down on the activities of the people outside. This seems to be a major landmark in Jaipur, and there are many photos of this place.

There is another museum in the Albert Hall of the Ram Niwas Gardens. The building is very impressive with marble columns and a palace setting, and the museum contains portraits, costumes, woodwork, brassware, jewelry, and pottery of Rajasthan. It is worth the visit but it really didn't take me long to go through it.

The most interesting part of Jaipur is the old, walled city, which becomes even more pink in the glow of the evening twilight. It is also fun to shop here since the stores of all kinds stay open until 9:00 P.M. and the city remains very busy. You can buy jewels, metal crafts, Rajasthani style clothes, hand bags, jackets, miniature paintings, artwork, etc. But be careful if you are buying high priced items, like jewels, if you are not experienced at it. It is easy to get cheated.

If you are looking for temple deities, the best place to go is Khajanewalon ka Rasta— The Lane of Treasures. There are many shops here where they offer beautiful carved and painted marble deities, or they can custom carve the deity of your choice. Many shops also pack and ship deities to any part of the world. Carpets are also a big item in Jaipur and there are many carpet weavers who can specially make any pattern or design you want. Otherwise, there are many standard eastern or oriental designs from which to choose.

The main tourist stops include the City Palace, built by Jai Singh, which has buildings that blend Rajasthani and Moghul architecture. Inside is the seven-storey Chandra Mahal, which has the Maharaja Sawai Man Singh II Museum on the first floor with a collection of art, carpets, and a large section on old weapons, some of which date back to the 15th century.

There is also the very interesting Amber Palace 11 kilometers north of Jaipur on Jaipur-Delhi Road. This dates back to 1592 and was built by Raja Man Singh (1589-1614), although some feel it dates back much earlier than that. There are some imposing stairways to be climbed to reach the palace, but you will find interior gardens, lovely mosaics, and many apartments where the royal family used to live. And if you don't want to climb the stairs, there is usually an elephant available that you can ride. The palace has got some great examples of Rajput architecture, including the usual assortment of buildings like the Hall of Public Audiences where the king would greet the public or hold meetings. This hall has some beautiful rows of ornate columns, and is open to the cool hilltop breezes. The Jai Mandir has a ceiling with numerous small inlaid mirrors. When it's dark inside when the doors are closed, the mirrors look like stars in the sky if there's a lit candle in the room. Other rooms lead out to balconies, or have windows over-looking the hills and lake below. It can be fun just to wander around the place to see where you end up. Buses to the Amber Palace leave every few minutes from near the front of the Palace of Winds and take about a half-hour to get there.

Not far from Amber Palace is the Jaigarh Fort, which overlooks the Amber Palace. The fort is surrounded by massive walls with watch towers and gateways. It shows very little deterioration and has palaces with dining areas and women's quarters and meeting areas in the residential buildings. Elsewhere it also has gardens, open and covered water reservoirs, an armory, a cannon foundry, a few temples, and a giant mounted cannon, the Jai Ban, which has a barrel that is 20 feet long. However, it was only used once. Exploring this fort is a real visit into the area's past.

If you are into forts, check out the Nahargarh Fort, or Tiger Fort, which sits on the north ridge overlooking Jaipur. You can reach this by taking a long winding road up by motor-ricksha or taxi. At the top are great views of Jaipur below. The fort walls still exist but the main point of interest is the King's House. This has ten apartments built around a small central courtyard. One apartment is for the king and the other nine are for his queens. There is also a secret passageway that enabled the king to visit any one of his queens without anyone else knowing of it. Each apartment had an upstairs and a down-stairs, with fireplaces, bedrooms, kitchens, dressing rooms, etc.

Not far from the road to Tiger Fort is the Kanak Gardens (or Kanak Vrindavan), which has a temple of Sri Sri Radha Govinda on the right as you drive in. The four-foot tall deities look very similar to those of the main temple of Sri Sri Radha Govinda in the center of the city. Krishna is made of black marble with a brass Radharani. The smaller deities here were worshiped by Jayadeva Gosvami and brought to Jaipur in 1560. Across from this is a temple called the Natwarji temple, established in the 18th century that has some small Radha-Krishna deities. These belonged to Jai Singh's sister, Amarkuar. The gardens themselves have some nice fountains but little else.

Driving back to the city, you'll pass Jal Mahal, the Water Palace, which sits in the middle of a small and shallow lake that was created by a nearby dam. The palace and the reflections in the water look quite lovely.

On the north side of town, down from the Tiger Fort, are the exquisitely carved mar-ble tombs of Ram Singh, Jai Singh, and various family members. The columns and domes are adorned with figures of damsels, animal motifs, pastimes of Krishna, etc. It's worth a short visit to see it.

From this area is the steep stairway up the hill to the Gat-Ganesha Mandir. This tem-ple of Ganesh is located on the top of Moti Doongri hill about a mile and a half from the well-known Radha-Govindaji Mandir. Once you reach the hill, a 30 minute climb to the top is required. The climb up provides some nice views over Jaipur. When I made the climb up, there was a large, intimidating dog that looked out over the temple wall and barked at all visitors. At first I was not sure how to enter the huge door, but another visi-tor let me in through a smaller opening in the door. Once inside the temple building, the altar has a small vermilion-covered mound with garlands, which is the main deity, and a few other figures. Mice, sacred to Ganesh since he has one as his carrier, would sometimes crawl around eating some of the sweets that remained on the altar. After a simple *darshan* and sampling some of the sweets that had been offered to Ganesh, the long climb back down the hill awaited me.

After we have finished seeing whatever else we want to see in Jaipur, we can make arrangements to go to our next stop on this pilgrimage tour, which is Pushkar. To reach Pushkar, we first go to the city of Ajmer.

AJMER & PUSHKAR

We reach Ajmer by taking a train or a tour bus from Jaipur. The train leaves near 12:20 P.M. and arrives around 3:15. Tour buses leave at various times and usually take longer than they say. A bus leaving at 1:30 arrived in Ajmer around 5:30 after all the stops.

Ajmer, which is about 80 miles or 135 kilometers southwest of Jaipur, is one of the most holy places of pilgrimage for Muslims in India. It was founded in 1100 by Aijpal. Then in 1193 Sultan Mohammad of Ghori took over Ajmer from Prithviraj Chauhan. At that time the Persian saint Khwaja Moinuddin Chisti settled in Ajmer and spent time preaching until he died and was buried there. Akbar took Ajmer in 1556 and visited Chisti's tomb where he prayed for a son. When Akbar's prayer was granted, the fame of Ajmer was greatly enhanced.

Ajmer had been an important city before the Muslim invasions. The full name of Ajmer was Ajeya-Meru, a Sanskrit related name. This shows that Ajmer once was a busy Aryan or Vedic city. In fact, many of the buildings credited to Muslim design and construction show elements, such as motifs and brackets, that are pre-Muslim or Vedic in origin. The buildings were merely captured and then converted for Muslim use. Such conversion sometimes incorporated covering the ornate building exteriors with plaster and camouflaging it with Arabic lettering.

Pushkar is only a short bus ride, 11 kilometers, through the hills from Ajmer. The bus stand for Pushkar is across the street from the train station. You can book a room in Ajmer, where the hotels are better, and then visit Pushkar by bus on a day trip, or just take a bus and stay in Pushkar, which has many small hotels from which to choose. Most are quite simple and offer various degrees of comfort. When going to Pushkar on the bus, it's easy to get a seat in the evening, but difficult in the morning when so many other pilgrims are also going. Returning to Ajmer in the afternoon is also a time when getting a seat can be difficult, especially if you have got luggage. However, it's an interesting ride up through the winding hills, and a night ride is especially nice when you can see the lights of the surrounding towns.

Pushkar is a fascinating little village of about 12,000 residents and many Indian pilgrims. Children here are really fond of American pens, so if they think you have one they will keep after you until they get it or you disappear. There are restaurants in town that often play copies of western rock music, often outdated and terribly worn. The Roof Top Restaurant is nice and the breeze on a hot day and the view of the lake is quite refreshing. English is a common language here and there's lots of western tourists and hippies of all kinds. In some ways it reminded me of Kathmandu.

The most popular time to visit is during the camel fair on the full moon of the month of Kartick (Oct-Nov). This draws as many as 200,000 people with herds of camels, horses, and cows. To accommodate the mass of people in this village, they erect a tent city, one of which you can expect to stay in if you arrive at that time. At any other time, you simply have to try the various hotels or guest houses until you find one with a vacant room, which usually is not difficult.

Pushkar is an important place for Hindus and has one of the major temples of Lord Brahma in India. Other Brahma temples are found here and there, but they are rare. Brahma is part of the trilogy of Lord Vishnu (the maintainer), Brahma (the creator), and Lord Shiva (the destroyer). The legend goes that Brahma himself chose Pushkar for his temple. It is said that Brahma threw a flower down on earth, and water appeared where the three petals landed, thus the name *pushpa* (flower) and *kar* (hand) or Pushkar. It is related that the flower fell and hit three separate places, namely Senior Pushkar first, where all the activity is found; then Middle Pushkar about three km down the road where a Hanuman temple and 200 year old banyan tree is found; and then Junior Pushkar, three km north, which has a small Krishna temple. It is considered particularly auspicious to do *parikrama* (16 km) around all three Pushkars during the full moon of the Kartika month.

Pushkar is said to have more than 550 temples, which include temples of Raghunatha, Varaha, Savitri, Gayatri, etc., although most of these temples are fairly small and I could only find a few of these. However, most of them are open to foreigners. The main place of pilgrimage is Lake Pushkar where many visitors go to bathe or perform *shraddha* ceremonies in honor of their deceased relatives. The *Mahabharata* states that billions of *tirthas* (holy places) gather at Pushkar at sunrise and sunset, and that one's sins are cleansed just by thinking of Pushkar. Furthermore, men and women are relieved of many sins by bathing at Pushkar. This is why bathing in the lake is a priority for pilgrims, especially during the Kartika Purnima (full moon of Oct/Nov.) which is said to be the time when it gives liberation from *samsara*. It is also said that Lord Varaha appeared here at Varaha Ghat, and that Lord Rama bathed here. Also, the Sarasvati River is said to restart here after disappearing at Vinasanna in the area of Kuruksetra.

The main temple is the Brahma temple on the west side of town, which is topped by its red spire. It is customary to buy some sweets and flowers at the nearby shops in front of the temple to offer to the deity of Brahma. When you go into the temple and reach the altar, which is usually crowded with visitors, you give your offering to the priest and in return he gives you *prasada* in the form of sweets and flowers that have already been offered. You get *darshan* of the old, four-faced Brahma deity which has a small image of Sarasvati at his side. Surprisingly, this temple does allow you to take photographs.

In the temple courtyard are other altars and shrines to Sarasvati, the goddess of learning, a few of Shiva, Durga, one beautiful marble four-faced *lingam*, and others of Indra, Kubera, and sages such as Dattatreya, Narada Muni, etc. So you can spend a little time here getting *darshan* of Lord Brahma and then looking around at the other shrines. After this temple, we can wander around and visit some of the other temples.

There is a Varaha temple in town in commemoration of Varaha's appearance in Push-kar, at Varaha Ghat specifically. Inside is a white marble deity of Lord Varaha that stands two feet tall. Along the *parikrama marg* or footpath near the lake is a small temple to Parashurama. Not far from there is a small temple to Badi Ganeshji.

There is a newer Raghunatha temple (Rama-Vaikuntha) that has the deities of Lakshmi-Vaikunthanatha and is on the east side of town.

The Old Raghunatha or Ranganatha temple has deities of a beautiful six-foot tall Venu Gopala, or Krishna with a flute, Radharani, Rukmini, Narasimha, and Lakshmi. However, I did not go inside because of the signs at the gate that said "Foreigners not Allowed." This happens more often in South India, but I was not expecting this in a place like Pushkar. So we move on.

The small temple on top of the big Savitri hill to the southwest of town offers great views over the town. But it takes about an hour to climb, so it is best to go in the early and cooler part of the day. The temple dates back 2000 years. The legend of this temple is that after Brahma had established this place of Pushkar, he wanted to do a Vedic ritual, but was required to perform it with his wife, Savitri, also known as Sarasvati, who was late. He asked the great sage Narada Muni to go bring her, but she was not ready to leave. So after asking Indra to arrange a marriage for him, a priest produced a daughter. She was of low rank, but was purified when the sages provided the means of passing her through a cow. Thus, she took on the name of Gayatri and Brahma married and performed the ritual. However, when Savitri, Brahma's original wife arrived, she was most upset to see that he had married again without her consent. So she cursed him to be worshiped only at Pushkar, which is one reason why few temples are found for Brahma anywhere else. In her anger, she then went and established this temple for herself on the hilltop.

On the northern side of town is the Gayatri temple. Near the Marwar bus stand you will find a path that leads to the stairs that go up the hill.

When our visit in Pushkar is over, we take a bus back to Ajmer. On the way back, you will pass near Nag Hill, which is about 2 km from Pushkar. It is said that a visit to Nag Hill is auspicious. The hill used to be huge during Satya-yuga, but has decreased in size with every yuga that followed, until it will disappear by the end of Kali-yuga. The tradition is that during the ritual that Brahma performed, on the second day Rishi Chyavan cursed the grandson of Brahma, Vatu, to become a snake. This was because Vatu was mischievous and released a snake that curled around the the great sage Bhrigu Muni, the father of Chyavan. Vatu begged for forgiveness, and Brahma granted that he could live near the natural pond that exists on Nag Hill. Agastya Muni was also supposed to have lived here in a cave for a time.

From here, if we decide to go farther north, we can catch an early morning train through Beawar to Marwar June and then off to Jodhpur, or simply take an express bus from Ajmer to Jodhpur, which takes about four-and-a-half hours. A bus is also available straight from Pushkar, but it can take up to eight hours to get there. Just five miles or eight kilometers north of Jodhpur is Mandore, the main temples of which are for black Bhairav and white Bhairav, the destructive and protective aspects of Lord Shiva. The deities are covered with layers of silver leaf.

OSIAN

Osian is farther north, 40 miles or 65 kilometers north from Jodhpur, and is where we find a collection of both Hindu and Jain temples. These date back to the 8th to 12th centuries. These 16 temples are in good shape and very interesting, built by wealthy traders when Osian was an important stop on the trade route to Central Asia. The town has the largest number of the earliest temples in Rajasthan. The majority of them are clustered in several groups south and west of town. A smaller group lies to the north with the Sachiya Mata temple in the center, which is still used for worship.

The 8th century Mahavira temple is most impressive with a lovely ceiling and 20 carved pillars holding up the main portico. The 10th century Sun temple and the profusely sculpted Vishnu and Harihara temples from the 8th and 9th centuries are also amazing examples. Most of the temples have some excellent stone carving work with images of Krishna and His *avataras* on the walls, along with sculptured panels, lotus ornamentation, or images of Durga, Surya, Ganesh, and so on. On the east side of town there is the 12th century Sachiya Mata temple, a form of Durga, that is approached through a series of beautifully crafted arches. Women come to this temple for the blessings to have children. The town also has many peacocks. Buses to Osian from Jodhpur are about six a day for the two-hour journey. Osian is a ways off the general tourist path, so you may not want to come out this way. If you have gone to Osian, then once your visit is over you can take a bus or a train back to Ajmer and then travel down to the impressive hilltop fort at Chittorgarh.

If you want to go directly south from Pushkar, we can get up early to catch the first bus back to Ajmer, when seats are easy to get, to make it to the 8:45 train to Chittorgarh. And if you don't care for massive forts, you can take the bus or train directly from Ajmer to Udaipur.

CHITTORGARH

At Chittorgarh we can get a decent room at the Panna Tourist Bungalow. As soon as I checked in I was off to see the fort. Hiring a motor-ricksha can make it easy to see the fort and all the main points of interest, which easily drives you up the steep roads to the hilltop.

The Chittorgarh hilltop fortress is very impressive and takes up a huge area. It is a deserted ruin now, but dates back to earlier than 1300 C.E. The original construction is said to be credited to Bhima, one of the Pandava brothers described in the *Mahabharata*. It sits on a 180-meter high hill and takes up 280 hectares of land. You pass through seven gates to see the various buildings, palaces, a nine storey tall Tower of Victory, temples, etc. The Tower of Victory is covered with religious symbols and carvings, both inside and out, and was built by Rana Kumbha in 1448 for his victory over the Muslims in Delhi. The tower is dedicated to Vishnu and you can climb up inside it to get a good view of the surrounding area. The passageway is very small and can get completely dark in parts. In fact, people going up and down can run into each other because it is so dark. It is almost like a tower within a tower. Nearby is a temple of Shiva with a very unusual deity with large faces of Vishnu, Brahma, and Shiva. Other sights include Rana Kumbha's Palace, the small but elegant Padmini's Palace, the Kalika Mata temple, and so on.

For me, the most important was the Krishna temple that was built for Mira Bai (1498-1547) by her husband Prince Bhoj Raj. She was the great devotee poet and singer who, as a young girl, had given her heart to her lord and master, Sri Krishna, and was in love with no one else. To walk the halls and stones where she had worshiped her little deity of Krishna with all her heart was very moving and wondrous for me.

Archeological digs at Chittorgarh have found Buddhist relics in the area, some that date back centuries before Christianity. Most of the buildings are deserted, but there are still Jain and Hindu temples that are used in worship. After seeing this fortress, we can take the early morning Chetak Express to Udaipur. On the three-hour train ride, you will go past fields of opium poppies, all legal and quite organized, grown for medicinal purposes.

UDAIPUR

Udaipur is a large city of near 400,000, and is based around two large lakes, both man-made. It is a very beautiful and exotic city known for its gardens, parks, temples, museums, and palaces. It is so beautiful that Rudyard Kipling said, "No tour of India is complete without seeing Udaipur." The Lake Palace, or Jag Niwas, in Lake Pichola is now converted into a luxury hotel. If you can't afford the rates to stay there, catch a boat from Bhansi Ghat near the Palace Museum and have dinner and look around the place. It is extremely beautiful with courtyards, gardens, and fountains.

The City Palace and Museum are the largest in Rajasthan with towers and balconies that offer great views over the city. It is an assortment of buildings, patios, inner courtyards, and balconies that were constructed over the years, but originally started by Udai Singh. A museum is kept in the main part of the palace, which has collections of mosaics, miniature paintings, porcelain figures, and some Rolls Royces. The palace itself is quite something to see and worth the visit. It is open 9:30 A.M. to 4:00 P.M. In one part of the Palace is also an important temple called Sri Pitamber Raiji. This houses the original Krishna deity, Sri Giridharilalji, to whom Saint Mirabai gave her heart in her youth. However, the deity is in the private part of the palace and generally cannot be seen unless you know someone who can get permission to take you inside.

One temple that is worth seeing is the beautiful Jagdish temple, located just north of the City Palace. It is opulently built and stands 80 feet tall. It was originally constructed by Maharana Jagat Singh I in 1651. It houses a black stone deity of Lord Vishnu as Lord of the Universe. You will also find a brass image of Garuda, Lord Vishnu's bird carrier, in front of the temple facing Lord Vishnu. Three other temples of the Vallabha *sampradaya* are located to the side of the temple. The nearby shops offer visitors many types of excellent crafts and paintings on paper, cloth, or, now that ivory is banned, on thin pieces of marble. The temple of Navanitaraya is also an important one, located on the banks of Bhaijiraya Kund.

One of the easiest ways of seeing Udaipur is to go on a sightseeing tour. You can also just hire a motor-ricksha to take you around so you can spend as much time as you like anywhere you want. But some places will only turn the fountains or garden lights on for the government operated tours. So there is an advantage at some of the places to be in a tour group.

There are plenty of sights to see as you wander around the city, such as the memorial to Maharana Pratap, one of the Rajputs who courageously helped defend this region from the Muslims. There are also beautiful gardens and fountains such as Saheliyon Ki Bari, or the folk art museum of Bharatiya Lok Kala Mandal, or the park and simple zoo at Gulab Bagh, among other places.

NATHDWARA

By taking short excursions away from Udaipur we can reach several other places we want to visit, such as Nathdwara, which is a very holy town. You can easily reach it by bus 48 kilometers northeast of Udaipur. It is the home of the famous deity, Sri Nathji. Sri Nathji is Lord Krishna as He is depicted at the age of seven while He was in the act of lifting Govardhan Hill. Actually, Sri Nathji used to be called Gopalaji and had been worshiped near Vrindavan before being moved to Nathdwara. The story of how Gopalaji was dis-covered is described in the *Caitanya-caritamrita*. It was Srila Madhavendra Puri who came to Govardhan Hill and, after he went around the hill and began preparing for evening rest near Govinda Kund, a local cowherd boy visited him with a pot of milk. The beautiful boy made Srila Madhavendra Puri forget his hunger and thirst. Madhavendra asked the boy how he knew he was fasting, and the boy replied that he resided in this vil-lage and in his village no one fasts.

That night in a dream the boy lead Madhavendra to a bush and explained that he was in the bush and suffered from severe cold, heat, rain, and wind. So Madhavendra was thus instructed to find the deity with the help of the local villagers. Gopalaji had been hidden in the bushes and was discovered by Madhavendra. After the deity's installation, a structure was made for Him on top of Govardhan Hill. The deity of Gopalaji stands with His left arm raised in the air in the pose Krishna took when He lifted Govardhan Hill as an umbrella to protect the local residents from the fierce rains sent by the demigod Indra.

Many people came to the place, named Jatipura (meaning "the home of the saint" in reference to Madhavendra Puri), to see and worship Gopalaji. Then a member of the royal family constructed a temple for the deity. After a few years, the deity appeared in a dream and ordered Madhavendra to go to Jagannatha Puri to get sandalwood, which could be used to cool the deity who was still feeling feverish from being in the ground for so many years. So Madhavendra left Jatipura to perform this service. When he arrived in Shantipur, Sri Advaitacharya, an associate of Sri Chaitanya, asked him for initiation.

When Madhavendra arrived in Remuna, north of Jagannatha Puri, he stopped at the temple of Gopinatha. Here the priests offer a thick sweet milk preparation to the deity. Madhavendra wanted to try some to understand how to prepare it so he could make it to offer his own deity in Vrindavan. Because of his desire to taste the food that was offered to the deity, he felt that he was a great offender and left the temple. That night the deity spoke to the temple priest in a dream and explained that He had hidden a cup of sweet rice behind His dress, and the priest should get it and find Madhavendra Puri to give it to him. The priest than went and found the cup of sweet rice behind the deity's dress. Taking the cup, the priest went and called out for Madhavendra until he found him. Madhavendra became spiritually ecstatic to receive the *prasadam*. After that, the deity in Remuna became known as Ksira-cora-Gopinatha, or Gopinatha who stole the sweet rice.

After this Madhavendra went to Jagannatha Puri and got about eight pounds of sandalwood and some camphor for his deity in Jatipura. On his way back, he again stopped to see Gopinatha at Remuna. That night his deity, Gopalaji, appeared to him in a dream and explained that there was no difference between His body and the body of Gopinatha in Remuna. Therefore, smearing the sandalwood on the body of Gopinatha would be the same as smearing it on the body of Gopalaji and His body would be cooled. So Madhavendra did this every day until all the sandalwood and camphor were gone. A few months later Madhavendra Puri left this world and his *samadhi* tomb is located in Remuna a few minutes away from the Ksira-cora-Gopinatha temple.

All pilgrims traveling through Orissa should stop to see the temple of Ksira-cora-Gopinatha at Remuna, who stands with deities of Govinda on His right and Lord Madana-Mohana on His left. Also, see the *samadhi* of Madhavendra Puri. [This has been described more thoroughly in the section on East India.]

After the disappearance of Madhavendra Puri from this world, the worship of Lord Gopalaji at Jatipura was taken over by Srila Vallabhacarya, who had been initiated in the disciplic succession coming from Sri Vishnuswami. It was during this time that Gopalaji started being called Sri Nathji by the devotees.

As with other deities who were moved from Vrindavana to escape the fanatic Muslim Aurangzeb's destruction of Hindu temples, Lord Sri Nathji was moved to the land of Mewar from Jatipura. The deity was first moved to Agra where the devotees kept Him in secret for six months, and then moved Him farther west. As the deity was being moved, He reached a place where He could be moved no farther. The Maharana Sri Raj Singh accepted it as a sign from the deity, so he made arrangements to build a temple there. This is the place that later developed into the village of Nathdwara, which means the doorway to the Supreme Lord. This city has become one of the important pilgrimage places for the worshipers of Lord Krishna, especially for the followers of Vallabhacarya.

Nathdwara was established around 1675. The region of Nathdwara is very dry and barren. By midday the hot sun is scorching the land. The town is filled with low, whitewashed houses, some with interesting paintings of elephants, tigers, peacocks, or people flanking the doorways. The temple is the center of town to which the narrow roads lead. As you pass by various shops, you reach an impressive gateway which is the entrance to the temple of Sri Nathji. The gateway looks like that of a large fortress with thick doors that have metal spikes protruding from them. Beyond the gate is a large courtyard and the entrance to the shrine which has big paintings of elephants on each side.

The temple is more like a large royal palace, fashioned in the traditional Rajasthan style. Once you enter, you can wander and get lost in it. There are many rooms for different purposes. There are also numerous passages and halls and small gardens and court-yards. Most of the rooms that are used by the public are on the ground floor, and you will see armed guards at various places where the public is not permitted to enter. Some of the rooms in the temple are for specific purposes, such as for flowers, clothes and clothes-making, vegetables, milk, grains, for keeping *prasadam* (food that's been offered to the deity), and a treasury office. The building is white, but has colorful paintings around its doors and windows. The marble and stone floors contain a variety of colorful patterns.

The worship of Sri Nathji in the temple goes on throughout the day and is adjusted according to the daily activities in which Krishna engages, from getting up in the morning, getting dressed, eating different preparations at different times, going off to play with His friends, taking afternoon rest, and so on. He is dressed in different types of clothes according to the hot or cold seasons. These arrangements are especially noted during the festivals that take place throughout the year in which devotees celebrate a variety of events, including Krishna's birthday for which so many food preparations are made for His pleasure. All such arrangements are offered to Sri Nathji.

The holy town of Nathdwara evolves around the deity of Sri Nathji. Many people's lives and businesses are connected with the temple. They may be priests or temple assistants, or those who work outside as vendors who sell flowers or fruits and vegetables for offering to the deity. Others may operate stores and sell devotional paraphernalia such as pictures, books, tapes of devotional songs, or operate hotels for pilgrims, or any number of other things. People even greet each other in reference to Krishna, saying "Jai Sri Krishna" or "Hare Krishna". You will not easily forget Krishna in this town.

Even the daily habits of the residents of this town evolve around the deity. For example, a little after five in the morning a *shenai* band begins playing over the loudspeakers, and people know it is time to go to the temple. So people get ready and attend the 5:30 A.M. *arati*. They simply crowd into the temple any way they can get in. The temple assistants have been known to exclude foreigners, but this was not the case for any of the foreign tourists when I visited, and if you are a member of ISKCON, you can easily enter the temple.

To go into the temple, you stand with the crowd just outside the temple doors and wait for the temple assistants to allow people to enter. This happens after the conch is blown, but a few minutes may pass before the doors open. This is because once the Lord left the temple and tore His garment in a rush to get back for *darshan*. So, now the tradition is to wait a few minutes after the conch is blown before opening the doors.

Everyone rushes in to get to a good position to see the deity. The women are allowed in the front section and the men in the back. As soon as you are inside, many people are pushing you from behind to see the deity while others are pushing back in order to keep from losing sight of Sri Nathji. So you may feel like you are getting crushed. I thought it was all great fun. As you are pushed through by the crowd as well as by the temple assistants, your *darshan* of the deity may last only a few minutes. However, if you are good at holding your place it may last longer. In any case, it is indeed an honor to see the special and famous Sri Nathji deity.

As you see the deity, He appears as a bas-relief emerging out of stone. His left hand is raised in the pose of lifting Govardhan Hill, and His right hand is in a fist resting on His hip. The stone has several markings around the deity, such as two cows, a snake, a lion, two peacocks, a parrot near the Lord's head, two seated sages on His right side with a snake under them, and a third sage on His left. After the *arati* ends and the curtain closes, the people shout out for more. So the priests may raise the curtains to allow for *darshan* a few more times. When the curtain is closed for good, some people offer obeisances and go on their way while others take up brooms and, as a service to the deity, begin cleaning the temple area. And lots of people come to the temple and feel very happy doing some menial service for the deity. This may include helping cut vegetables, making flower garlands, carrying and chopping wood for the temple kitchen, etc. So everyone helps create a very blissful and spiritual atmosphere by performing service to Lord Krishna.

As you leave the main temple you can also visit the smaller temples which are connected to it. These have a few deities to see, including Naveet Priya (Krishna as the butter lover), and another of Madana Mohana. An additional small temple opposite the entrance to Sri Nathji is that of Vitthalnath which used to be in Gokula near Mathura, and another deity is that of Vanamali.

If you can't perform service, people also give things to the deity, such as fruits, vegetables, flowers, and ghee (clarified butter). In fact, people give lots of ghee, many cans of ghee, sometimes even train car loads. And, of course, people also give money. You can see how so much is given to the temple as you walk around. In fact, this temple is considered to be the second richest in India.

You can easily buy some of the deity *prasadam* from numerous shops. You can also see temple assistants selling little clay pots of it near the temple, or small vendors with push carts in the bazaar. You can purchase it at anytime and in varieties, such as sweets, vegetable preparations, salads, *chapatis*, rice, huge *samosas* and more, depending on the time of day. This is an especially spiritually charging place to visit.

KANKROLI

At Kankroli, our next stop 18 kilometers north of Nathdwara, there is the temple of Lord Dwarkadisha, managed by the Vallabhacarya *sampradaya*. The legend is that the deity came from Mathura where He was worshiped thousands of years ago by the great devotee King Amburisha. The temple is located on the banks of the man-made lake of Raja Samand. I feel I must say here that it is indeed incredible that we can see deities that have been a part of such histories which are described in the Vedic texts as the *Srimad-Bhagavatam*, or that were once worshiped by the likes of such spiritually powerful devotees as King Amburish, who was favored by the Supreme Being Himself. Being able to see such deities is not only extremely beneficial, but it is also a way of participating in the great pastimes of the Supreme and His devotees that have taken place thousands of years ago and continue into the present. Not everyone can fathom the depths of how powerful this experience can be.

CHARBUJAJI

From Kankroli you can go 36 kilometers to the Charbhujaji temple, which has a deity of Krishna in His four-handed form. In this area, the four temples of Nathdwara, Kankroli, Charbuja, and Ekalingji represent the four major holy *dhamas* of India, namely Jagannatha Puri, Dwarka, Badrinatha, and Ramesvaram respectively.

EKALINGJI

Ekalingji, or Kailashapuri, is 22 kilometers away from Udaipur, 30 kilometers south of Nathdwara. The Ekalingji temple is a small but especially popular temple complex of Lord Shiva. The temple is marble and houses a four-faced, black marble image of Lord Shiva, which has been the object of worship for years by many powerful local kings. Though the temple has been renovated many times over the years, the original part of the temple dates back to the 8th century. The present building dates to 1473. Enshrined within the Ekalingji temple compound is an earlier Lakulisha temple and other shrines with deities of Ganesh, Durga, Lakshmi, Kali, etc., and surrounded by small individual shrines, each with a Shiva *lingam*. The town also has a few other ancient temples.

The story of this temple goes back to the time of Bappa Rawal, one of the kings of Mewar who reigned from 714-767. His capital was the huge fort at Chittor, which remained the capital of Mewar until 1567. When he was a boy, Bappa worked as a cowherd. One of his cows would always come back from the fields without any milk, and Bappa was accused of stealing the milk. Feeling hurt by this accusation, Bappa watched out for this cow and discovered what was happening. There was a hermit sitting in deep trance amidst the bushes. The cow would go there and milk would spontaneously drain from its udder onto the area where the sage was sitting to nourish the sage. When Bappa saw this, the sage came out of his trance and was friendly toward him. Bappa would bring him milk every day and the sage educated Bappa with spiritual knowledge from the Shaivite school of thought. His teacher was quite pleased with Bappa's progress and called him the "Regent of Eklinga." To pay his respects to his teacher, Bappa constructed the Eklingji Shiva temple where he had first met the sage.

NAGDA

Nagda is a couple of kilometers away from Eklingji with more ancient temples that have very ornate stone carvings and architecture. Regular bus service is available for these places that can be visited in a day trip out of Udaipur.

RANAKPUR

Ranakpur, 98 kilometers northeast of Udaipur, has one of the largest and most prestigious of all Jain temple complexes in India. It has an entrance in each of the four directions, with a stairway that takes you into each of the four walls topped with spires and into the forest of pillars and halls inside. The image of Adinatha is housed in the main temple, which was made in 1439 and is huge with exceptionally beautiful white marble architecture. There are 29 halls in the temple with 1444 beautifully and elaborately carved pillars that support it, each one different. The filigree carving on the concentric ceiling patterns and the grace of the goddesses who form the support brackets is amazing. There are many carved motifs in the marble walls and ceilings. You cannot look anywhere without seeing some extraordinary artwork. A photographer can shoot lots of film here, there are so many things to view. Let's hope they do not change the freedom to take photos here, of everything but the deities. I know the Jain temple at Mount Abu gets a lot of attention, but I think Ranakpur is much better. Besides, you can not even take a camera into the temple at Mount Abu. The Ranakpur temple is also made to look like a lotus flower if seen from the top. There are also temples to Neminath and Parsvanath within the complex. The temple is open from noon to 5:00 P.M. for non-Jains. A little distance away, across the field, is a sun temple with a nice little image of Surya, the sun-god, and further away is an Amba Mata temple.

You can spend the night here or get a good meal at the Shilpi Tourist Bungalow. For a donation, you can also get meals in the temple complex dining hall which is on the left just inside the main entrance. If you do not feel like making a special trip out here to Ranakpur, you can see it as part of a package bus tour from Udaipur.

RIKHABDEO

Traveling south, 65 kilometers from Udaipur, you will find Rikhabdeo where there is another 14th century Jain temple with graceful architecture, dedicated to Adinath. You can also visit this if you like, otherwise we will be going from Udaipur directly to our next stop, which is Mount Abu.

MOUNT ABU

Mount Abu can be reached by bus from Udaipur, seven hours away. The tour bus that I rode was not too crowded, but the ride was one of the roughest and bumpiest I had ever taken. The last hour was the long 27-kilometer ascent up the mountain, which really provided some amazing views. Once we get to town, Mount Abu is a slow-going hill station retreat on a 1200-meter high plateau. The higher elevation definitely makes the climate much cooler, which provides a break from the heat of the plains. But in the off season it can be quite chilly. The town is located mainly along Abu Road near Nakki Lake. It is in this area that you will find most of the hotels, restaurants, shops, and enterprises cashing in on the trendy nature of the place. Few Westerners but lots of Indians come here, such as families, newlyweds, etc. There are no bikes or auto-rickshas, but horse and camel riding are available, and you can go boating on the lake. The higher elevation definitely makes it cooler here.

Nakki Lake is said to have been dug out by the demigods, and while walking around it you can see some of the rock caves that were occupied by ascetics that used to live here. It is one of the few lakes that you'll find at this altitude.

Not far from here you can take the road eight kilometers to Agni Kund, which is formed by a stream that starts 700 steps up at Gaumukh, with water pouring from the mouth of a marble cow. This is said to be the place where the sage Vashistha performed a great sacrificial fire from which four of the main Rajput families started. You will find an image of Vashistha next to deities of Rama and Krishna. The story is that when Parashurama killed all of the nefarious kshatriya warriors, the demigods came to Mount Abu to ask Vashistha to restore the class of kshatriyas on the planet. So Vashistha performed a fire ritual and out of the flames came the four mighty Rajput clans. The present ashrama of Vashistha Muni is said to mark the place where this happened. The teacher of Lord Rama also lived at Mount Abu. Also in the Nakki Lake area is a Raghunatha temple, founded in 14th century.

Near the town is the Om Shanti Bhawan (Universal Peace Hall) built by the Brahma Kumari order who teach raja-yoga. Guides will usher you in and will be glad to give you a short discourse on their teachings.

Farther out are temples to Ganesh and Durga (Adhar Devi), which is in a small cave three kilometers out of town. You have to climb the hill on foot up 360 steps to the temple, which is chiseled out of a huge rock in a natural cliff. Inside is dark and stuffy and can be crowded since it is small. There are a number of bells you can ring, if you wish, and then see the image of Durga.

According to tradition, Mahavir, the last of the 24 Jain *tirthankaras*, also lived here at Mount Abu for a year, which brings us to the most important points of interest, which are the Dilwara Jain temples located about 5 kilometers out of town. You can walk there in an hour or so or take a taxi, or just book yourself on a tour bus at the stand across from the bus station to see most of the important places. The oldest of the five Jain temples is dedicated to Adinatha, the first of the Jain *tirthankaras*, whose image is in the shrine, installed in 1322. The temple was built in 1031 and is called Vimal Vasahi. It is said that it took 1500 sculptors and 1200 laborers 14 years to complete it. You enter the courtyard through 48 beautifully carved pillars, each one different. The niches in the walls house images of the other 52 Jain *tirthankaras*. As you enter the doorway leading to the inner chamber, you'll see elaborately carved guardian figures. The columns in the chamber and the ceilings all have ornate carvings of figures, including dancers, musicians, soldiers, and animals. The large central dome is more than 23 feet in diameter. The main figure of Adinatha is bronze and wears a gem necklace and eyes of jewels. A beautiful sculpture of Krishna is also in the temple in His form of subduing the serpent Kaliya. The unfortunate thing is that they no longer allow cameras inside, so if you have one you have to drop it off at the front ticket office "at your own risk", and pick it up later.

The Tejpal temple, or Luna Vasahi temple, built by Tejpal and Vastupal in 1230, is dedicated to Neminath, the 22nd *tirthankara*. This temple has extremely intricate and fine marble work, especially the filigree of the lotus which hangs from the center of the dome. The main hall has a magnificent lotus-shaped, tiered pendant carved from a single block of marble in its domed ceiling. The other three temples of the complex are not nearly so beautiful. But the Chaumuka temple is the tallest, and the Sri Risha Deoji has an image of a *tirthankara* made of a combination of five metals weighing 4.3 tons. The complex is open from noon to 6:00 P.M.

Farther out by 11 kilometers is the Shiva temple of Achaleshvara at Achalgarh. A gold image of Nandi, Shiva's bull carrier, is located in front of the temple and is said to have been made from five metals. This temple does not have a Shiva *linga*, but where it would normally be is a deep hole that is said to reach the underworld. The hole is said to be an imprint of Lord Shiva's toe when he stood on Mount Abu to steady it. If you look deep into the hole you will see an imprint of what looks like a toe. Nearby is also a Lakshmi-Narayana temple which contains images of the ten main *avataras* of Vishnu. Up the hillside is a path that leads to several Jain temples with pleasant views over the area.

The Guru Shikhar, 15 km outside of town, is at the end of the plateau and is said to be the tallest point in Rajasthan 5650 feet above sea level. You take a winding bus ride to the parking area. Then you walk up to the temple of Dattatreya that has a small altar and a two-foot tall, three-headed deity of Dattatreya and His footprints. Then you go on up another several flights of stairs, 300 steps, to the peak where inside a huge rock at the top is the small temple of Atri Rishi. It is big enough only for one person at a time to squeeze into it, and you'll find a very small altar which has images of Shiva and Atri Rishi. Outside you will get tremendous views over hundreds of miles around, but the wind can be so strong it could almost blow you off the hilltop. Even while wearing my winter coat, I was still freezing, and this was in March.

AHMEDABAD

Once I was finished seeing all the sites in Mount Abu, I booked a bus for the long and bumpy ride to Abu Road. Just as I arrived, someone asked me where I was going, I said Ahmedabad, and he said the train (The Ranakpur Express) was just leaving. I ran down to the platform and the train was already moving. So I threw my bag on the train, grabbed the ladder and pulled myself up and away I went for the four-hour ride to Ahmedabad.

Although Gujarat is not known for a large number of tourist attractions, it does have some interesting spots of spiritual value that we will want to see. The distinct Gujarat culture and diet are also worth experiencing. It is easy for vegetarians to find places to eat here. Gujarat is also known for its textile industry, especially in regard to silk saris and the zari (gold thread) products. Ahmedabad can be an interesting place to stop and look around. It provides an unusual blend of Hindu and Muslim architecture amongst both religious and secular buildings. However, there are large numbers of both Hindus and Muslims, which can cause periods of unrest.

Ahmedabad, which was once known as Karnavati in the old Vedic tradition, is said to have 1000 mosques. However, historical research has provided evidence that many of these mosques were Muslim-captured Hindu temples that were defaced and converted to mosques. Especially the main mosque of the town, the Jama Masjid, has been proved to be an ancient Bhadrakali temple before its capture and conversion by Muslims. A story that confirms this is most interesting.

Around 1964 the K. C. Brothers, a rich hosiery firm, demolished its decades old building and built a towering mansion in its place. Unfortunately, this was near the Jama Masjid. The Muslim trustees of the mosque were quick to find a new reason to quarrel with the Hindus and filed a suit in a court of law demanding that K. C. Bros. demolish their mansion since it dwarfed the mosque, and thus was an insult to Allah. The Hindu K. C. Brothers were worried about what to do. However, thanks to Allah, no by-laws required that any building must be smaller than the local mosque. After considering the situation, they contacted Mr. P. N. Oak, a great advocate of rewriting Indian history.

Mr. Oak arranged with their lawyer to file a countersuit that the Muslims should surrender the mosque since it was actually a captured Hindu temple. The Muslims were shocked by this retort, having never been rebuffed in such a way before. After consultations with mullahs, archeologists, and historians, it became clear that the mosque was indeed a captured Hindu temple. They also realized that Mr. Cunningham, who had been in charge of the Archeological Survey of India in 1861, was a liar. Due to his faulty and political motivations, he had put a sign in front of the building saying that the mosque was built in 1414 by Ahmedshah. The truth is that the mosque was once the main temple that housed the guardian deity of the city, which was originally known as Rajnagar, which became known as Ahmedabad after being captured by Ahmedshah.

This shows that many buildings, forts, Muslim tombs, mosques, Rajput palaces and temples, and landmarks throughout India that have been credited to Muslim construction were originally built by Hindus, Vedic Aryans, and were merely captured by Muslims and converted for their use, and then claimed as their own. British historians helped pervert Indian history and hide these facts in a further attempt to demean Indian culture and maintain control over it.

The new and smaller Bhadrakali temple is across from the old Bhadrakali temple, which is now the main mosque. Many of the devout go here and offer their prayers to the deity of Kali in this temple.

Ahmedabad also has a prominent Jain temple built as a smaller version of the Ranakpur temple. It is extremely ornate, as most Jain temples are, and is surrounded by an outer wall that is full of niches and shrines, each containing an image of a Jain *thirtankara*.

One place in Ahmedabad that has an ancient tradition is the place on the banks of the Sabarmati River called Dudheshwara. This is said to have been the ashrama of the great sage Dadhichi. His story is described in a few different places, including the *Rig-veda*, *Srimad-Bhagavatam*, *Srimad Devi Bhagavatam*, and the *Mahabharata*. According to the legend, he was a master of the Vedic ritual known as Madhu Vidya, wherein a person could obtain the long life in Brahmaloka, the planet of Lord Brahma. Thus, his body was spiritually surcharged with much power. However, Indira, the king of heaven, was always insecure about anyone knowing this art of Madhu Vidya, because they could become strong enough to usurp Indra's position. So Indra cursed the science and stated that he would cut off the head of anyone who taught it.

The Ashwini twins, however, wanted to learn this science from Dadhichi, but knew of the curse placed on it by Indra. So they devised a plan to circumvent Indra's anger. They would cut off Dadhichi's head and preserve it, while replacing it with the head of a horse.

Thus, when Indra displayed his wrath and cut off Dadhichi's horse head, the Ashwini twins replaced it with Dadhichi's original head. Thus, everything went on as before, and the twins learned the Madhu Vidya science.

Nonetheless, another problem arose when there was a great demon named Vritrasura who terrorized all of the *devas* and sages. Indra went to Lord Brahma for a solution, and was told that Vritrasura could not be killed by normal weapons, but only with a spear fashioned from the spine of Dadhichi Rishi. So Indra went to the banks of the Sabarmati and approached Dadhichi. Amazingly, Dadhichi agreed to give his life and body for the benefit of the *devas*, even though Indra had already cut off his head due to Indra's selfish anger. Dadhichi figured that the body would wither and die away one day, so if can be used for the benefit of others, so be it. So he withdrew his life breath, *prana*, and vacated his body. After animals had eaten away the flesh, Indra used Dadhichi's spine to make the thunderbolt known as the Vraja Ayudha. After a battle that lasted 360 days between Indra and Vritrasura, Indra finally killed the demon and regained his throne.

While we are visiting Ahmedabad, another place worth seeing is the new Iskcon Krishna temple on Sattelite Road. It is one of the largest and most ornate temples in India. The grand opening in April, 1997, was attended by over 10,000 Gujarati devotees. Three altars have beautiful deities of Lord Chaitanya and Nityananda, Sri Sri Radha-Govinda and Sri Nathji, and Sri Sita-Rama-Lakshmana and Hanuman.

Not far from the Iskcon temple, further down the highway, is the Divine Life Society center. They teach yoga here every morning and have a few small temples on the property. But what I appreciated most was a temple dedicated to Lakshmi. It is quite lovely and has a central image to Lakshmi on the altar, surrounded by Her eight other forms, four on either side. Such a temple is quite uncommon to see with all the forms of Lakshmi. So I recommend it to anyone who is interested.

The Sabarmati Ashram, which was founded in 1918 on the west bank of the Sabarmati River, was the second home for Mahatma Gandhi. This was his headquarters while he fought for his ideals of Indian independence. It was from here that he devised his plan for the final struggle for India's freedom. His cottage, Hriday Kunj, is still fairly intact and is now a small museum that contains some of his personal items such as his round eyeglasses, wooden slippers, books, and letters. They still make handicrafts at the *ashrama*.

You can also visit the textiles museum in the morning, which also opens its sculpture and religious paintings section in the afternoon. Also the Eldi Institute of Indology near the Gujarat University is a good museum.

AKSHARDAM

In the nearby town of Gandhinagar is the headquarters of the Swami Narayana group, called Akshardam. This was attacked by Islamic terrorists only a few months before I had visited this place, which was in December of 2002. They came into the temple with guns hidden underneath their coats and then opened fired on anyone. A number of innocent pilgrims had been killed and others wounded. The temple needed repairs from being hit with bullets. But it was now re-opening under heightened security measures. A large fence had been set up, and no one was allowed to bring in coats or hand bags. But we could still bring in cameras to photograph the grounds.

The temple complex is large and quite beautiful. There are fountains in front of the main temple. The surrounding buildings have offices and a research center on the left side, and large diorama displays of the life of Swami Narayana on the right. In the middle is the large and most ornate temple dedicated only to Swami Narayana. He was a great devotee and sage who was accepted as an incarnation of Narayana. So for those who follow this path, he is called Swami Narayana. You can enter the temple after taking off your shoes and climbing the stairway. In the center of the temple is an image of Swami Narayana sitting on a throne, surrounded by beautifully carved columns and ornate panels and ceilings.

MODHERA

Modhera is 106 kilometers northwest of Ahmedabad. We can take a direct bus to Modhera from Ahmedabad, or if we want we can simply take a taxi directly to the Surya temple. With the new modern roads around Ahmedabad the ride is smooth and goes fairly quickly. This is the home of a ruined and ancient Sun temple that dates back to the time of King Bhimdev who built it around 1026. This is one of the finest examples of Vedic temple architecture in Gujarat.

I always wanted to see it, but quite honestly I did not know that it was quite so beautiful and ornately designed. It overlooks a deep water tank, though it was dry at the time, which has small shrines to various divinities all around it. It is similar to the Sun temple at Konarka, and the rising sun shines on the image of the sun-god, Surya, during the equinoxes. However, at Konarka you cannot enter the temple because it is sealed shut. The outside of this temple at Modhera is finely carved all over it and, as you would expect, it was the Muslim Mahmoud of Ghazni who tried defacing it. Nonetheless, the rich designs and ornamentations are easily visible. It has a marriage and dance hall in front of the main temple building. This is still used on occasion for festivals. It has amazing stone columns inside that are covered with carvings of designs and images. It has 12 images of Surya that depict the phases of the sun in each month through the year. The temple itself is a little bigger and the walls and pillars are richly covered with carved panels of the Vedic personalities, dancers, and other designs. Unfortunately, there is no deity of Surya inside the temple. In a yard next to the temple is the ongoing collection of parts of the temple, images, and maintenance work on the temple buildings. This is certainly worth a visit for anyone interested in this kind of architecture and Vedic design.

PATAN

Patan is about 120 kilometers northwest of Ahmedabad and can be reached by bus or on the same taxi ride that we take to Modhera. This city was a great capital until Mahmoud of Ghazni reached it and caused much destruction in 1024. Any Jain will want to stop in to see any of the 100 Jain temples found here.

A more recent discovery is the Rani ni Vav, or Queen's Well, said to date back to the 11th century. This is a step well that was used for collecting water many years ago. This is no ordinary well, but is quite large and was buried for several hundred years under the threat of the Muslim attacks in the area. Having been buried is what protected the large number of carvings that adorn the walls of the well, making them one of the most well preserved examples of stone carvings you can see. It has a long flight of steps descending 11 storeys that gradually reach the deep circular water well itself. The walls and support-ing pillars and beams of the multi-storeyed structure are covered with exquisite stone carvings of many Vedic deities and personalities, alluring maidens, as well as other flower-ing motifs and designs. It is truly magnificent.

Also in Patan is the Sahasra (Thousand) Linga tank. It is what remains of a long but shallow water tank in which are set two rows of short columns, which are *lingas*. These would make the water more holy in that it was used to worship the *lingas* or shapeless forms of Shiva. It is located in a park-like setting surrounded by trees, which can give some indication of the luxury in the intent of the tank.

DAKOR

Dakor is popular for the temple of Lord Krishna in His form known as Ranchor Raya. Ranchor means, "The one who deserted the battle field," and Raya comes from Raja, or a king or person of respect. The legend is that Lord Krishna left the battlefield when deal-ing with the soldiers of Kalayavana and Jarasandha. But this was not because He was afraid, but because He was renounced from concern over it and more interested in a dif-ferent matter. That was to attend to the issue of a letter sent by Rukmini who wanted Him to become her husband. Thus, Krishna preferred to give His attention to His loving devotee rather than the soldiers who wanted to challenge Him.

The present temple was built in 1772 and is near the town of Nadiad, easily reached by a 1 ½ hour bus or taxi ride from Baroda or Ahmedabad. It is best to take a day trip to visit it. Only simple accommodations are available in Dakor. Devotees at the Iskcon cen-ter in Baroda can help you get there. It is a town of only 30,000 but they must attend to the swells of devotees and pilgrims that come to see the temple and deity of Ranchor Raya. This is especially the case on Purnima or full moon days when you may see as many as 100,000 pilgrims coming to town. Many groups of devotees walk from their villages on important days, all singing *bhajans*, dancing or walking many kilometers to reach the temple. You can watch them as they offer flags to the priest, who hoist them to the top of the temple spire. On the auspicious Sharad Purnima day of Kartika (October/November) huge crowds arrive to commemorate the day when the deity of Ranchor Raya was installed years ago.

During the festivals and on important days, although there are closed-circuit televi-sions that show the deity, people want to go in to see Ranchor Raya personally. Pilgrims who come for the festival often bring flags as an offering to the deity. They give their flag to the priests who raise it atop the temple, until another group brings their flag. This can continue throughtout the day. The pilgrims are allowed into the temple in groups, men and women entering separate doors, women in front of the men and divided by a barricade. It is quite crowded with people rushing to see the deity and then pushing and shoving each other in order to try and maintain their position as long as possible, while calling out His name. Some come just for *darshan*, while others also bring purchased boxes of sweets which they offer to the deity by raising them above their heads for the deity to see. Once a group of devotees have viewed the deity, after their allotted time they pass through the temple and exit.

Regular offerings of food go to the deity seven times a day, so the temple kitchen is always busy. In the evening there is an offering called the *chapan-bhog*, meaning that it has 56 preparations. Only silver pots are used, and on Diwali they are gold. After 6 P.M. everyone can watch as the deity is dressed for the night. The priest removes the ornaments and day clothes of Ranchor Raya and dresses Him in the simple night dress. While watching, pilgrims will call out the name of Ranchor-Raya in jubilation and enthusiastic devotion.

When it is not so crowded, getting *darshan* of the deity is fairly easy. You can go into the temple room and wait for the next *arati* when the priest opens the silver doors to reveal the deity of Ranchor Raya. When the doors open, there is only a simple *simhasan* or altar in gold, under which is the deity of Keshava with four hands, large conch shell eyes, and playing His flute. Everyone moves forward and you can look without much pushing. The deity is a beautiful four-handed form of Lord Krishna, similar to the way He looks as Dwarakanathji in Dwaraka. He is dressed in colorful outfits, jewelry, and turban with a peacock feather. As we exit the temple building, there are rooms for pilgrims to stand and wait that are in the surrounding buildings. As we go around the temple, there is a room where you can buy some *prasada*, and another with a smaller deity of Ranchor Raya and His footprints where a devotee can do more personal worship.

Legend is that the deity appeared here because of the desire of a devotee named Boudanath about 1500 years ago. It is also said that this Deity was worshiped in Dwaraka as late as 800 years ago. The temple is an interesting structure with a central tower upon which is the flag pole. It has plain gates on four sides of the courtyard. Inside the temple is only a small hall, decorated with lots of art, scenes of Krishna's pastimes, with lights and a painted, domed roof.

DWARAKA

From Ahmedabad we are going to go to the far end of Gujarat and will start our tour of this state in the holy town of Dwaraka. So we will take an early morning train (the Saurashtra Mail) to Dwaraka. The train doesn't get into Dwaraka until about 5:00 P.M., so it can be nice relaxing and visiting with some of the other travelers, most of whom seem to get off as the train gets closer to Dwaraka. On this ride I met a group of school boys who were going to Dwaraka for a weekend outing with their teachers. The boys were very curious and a few spoke English. They asked me all kinds of questions. Later, after our arrival in Dwaraka, I met them again on a tour, and they brought me to meet their teachers and took photos of me as well. They were all very happy to meet a Westerner who was on a Dwaraka pilgrimage.

As we get closer to Dwaraka, seeing the large flag atop the Dwarkadish temple from quite a distance away is the sign that the long journey has reached its end. Many pilgrims offer prayers or obeisances when they first see the flag on the temple. The tradition is that people either bring or subsidize a new flag for the temple, which is then put up on top of the pole 235 feet high, and also sponsor feeding a group of brahmanas.

Along with Badrinatha, Jagannatha Puri, and Ramesvaram, Dwaraka is one of India's four main holy places where, it is said, the spiritual realm overlaps into this material world. It is also said to be one of the Saptapuris, or seven holy places, which also includes Ayodhya, Mathura, Haridwara, Kashi (Varanasi), Ujjain, and Kanchipuram. Shankaracharya established one of his four *mutts* or centers here, and even Ramanujacharya and Madhavacharya came here on pilgrimage. Dwaraka is the remains of Krishna's capital city, which He established around 3000 B.C.E. It was one of the most developed and advanced cities anywhere. Descriptions of it are found in many Vedic texts, including the *Mahabharata, Bhagavat Purana, Vishnu Purana, Vayu Purana, Harivamsha,* and in 44 chapters of the *Skanda Purana.* It is described as having been full of flower gardens and fruit trees, along with beautiful singing birds and peacocks. The lakes were full of swans and lilies and lotus flowers. The buildings were also beautiful and bedecked with jewels. There were temples, assembly halls, residential homes, and as many as 900,000 palaces. While Lord Krishna lived here, the people of the town would often see Him. By local tradition, the present people of Dwaraka are considered to be family descendants of Lord Krishna, or members of the Yadu dynasty.

Dwaraka existed for nearly 100 years while Krishna lived here. This is where He appeared with 16,108 palaces for 16,108 queens. Although the city came under attack from local warlords, they could never conquer Dwaraka. When Lord Krishna was making final arrangements to depart from this world, when He left His capital the island fortress was covered by the sea, as Krishna said it would be. Presently, major excavations and archeological digs have uncovered varieties of artifacts that give evidence for the location and advanced nature of the city. On shore digs, conducted by the Deccan College of Pune, they found evidence of a settlement dating back to the first century. Further findings brought forth evidence that a city certainly could have been existing there from as long ago as 5000 years.

Offshore excavations, started in 1981 by the National Institute of Oceanography, brought forth evidence of a number of things. The sea level at Dwaraka was 60 yards lower 5000 years ago. A large fortification was found under the water. Other findings include pottery, bronze statues, terra cotta beads, and so on. The dates of some of the finds go back to the Harrapan Age.

The Times of India News Service also released an article on April 7, 1997, called *Krishna's Dwarka May Not be a Myth.* In the article, Mr. S. R. Rao, who heads the Dwaraka underwater excavation project and is a consultant to the Marine Archaeology Centre of the National Institute of Oceanography in Goa, remarked on some of the findings. The remains of three temples and a township on the seashore near today's Dwaraka compare well with descriptions of Dwaraka found in the *Mahabharata* and the *Harivamsha*. Another major township was also found nearly 30 kilometers away at a depth of 30 feet, spread over a four-kilometer area near the island of Beyt Dwaraka during underwater excavation. Mr. Rao identified Beyt Dwaraka as Kusasthali where the first town of Dwaraka was built under the direction of Lord Krishna as described in the *Mahabharata*. Excavations on the island reveal that civilization was active here as far back as the Harappan culture in the 2nd millennium B.C.E.

The findings they have made concerning ancient Dwaraka make it clear that the stories in the ancient Vedic texts, such as the *Mahabharata* and the *Puranas*, are not mere myths or fables. Dwaraka was a highly sophisticated and well organized city. Remnants of the wealth of the old town still affects life in Dwaraka today since gold fragments wash up on shore. More excavations are scheduled to begin at the end of 1997.

Presently, Dwaraka's climate is similar to a resort town, located on India's west coast, and has a comfortable temperature year round. It's a very small town with a population of 34,000, so it is easy to find your way around. It is a 24-hour train ride from Bombay, if you do not reach it from the east as from Ahmedabad. Even though this town is out of the way for most tourists, there are hotels that offer pilgrims nice facilities at reasonable rates, and vegetarian meals are easy to find.

After we've checked into our hotel room (I stayed at Hotel Meera not far from the train station) and are ready to see the main temple of Lord Dwarakadish, we'll make our way into town and under the arch that was constructed to commemorate the visit of the *padayatra* (the assembly of pilgrims traveling by foot) of Iskcon, the Hare Krishna Movement. The archway is dedicated to Srila Prabhupada, the founder of Iskcon, and the Hare Krishna *mantra*. Iskcon also has a nice temple here that was established since I have visited. Going under the arch is a pleasant way to remember the significance of this town. As we go through the narrow streets, we pass by a wide assortment of shops that sell vegetables, fruits, devotional paraphernalia, and other items. In the morning you will see many vendors sitting in the shade of the buildings selling many types of vegetables.

When we find the temple, we will make our way through a high archway and into the temple courtyard. The main temple is said to be 5,000 years old and built in one day by Visvakarma, architect of the demigods. However, most of the present day temple is said to have been built in the 16th century, but there are parts of the sanctuary walls that date from the 12th century, and the temple sanctum is said to date back at least 2500 years. It is supported by 72 pillars and reaches up to 235 feet tall. The temple is covered by ornate stone carvings, columns, and ornamentation. Like many temples in India, no photography is allowed inside. But once seeing it, the beauty of the place will stay with you for a long time. It is certainly a temple you will remember.

The temple is visited by many hundreds of pilgrims, local as well as from all over India. As you enter it, you first notice the smell of incense and the hum of the pilgrims chanting *mantras* and prayers. As you look around, the ceilings have many beautiful paintings of the pastimes of the Lord based on the descriptions in the *Puranas*. The floor is made of pink and black marble that is set in lovely patterns. The deity of Dwarakadish is in the central shrine and has four hands. He represents the four-armed form of Vishnu called Trivikrama. This deity is very old and is mentioned in the *Varaha Purana,* and He is worshiped with much opulence and reverence.

To see Lord Dwarakadish, you can stand in the central viewing area with the growing crowd of devotees. One side is for men, the other side for women, and the back is for everyone. When the curtain opens behind a silver doorway, the Lord is revealed in His beautiful four-armed form and the *arati* begins. Lord Dwarakadish stands five feet tall and is dressed in colorful clothes and beautiful gold, silver, and jewels. Around the deity are priests who sing Sanskrit verses that relate the glories, characteristics, and pastimes of the Supreme Being. Above the altar are two-winged angels or Gandharvas who help protect the deity. The priest then begins to offer such articles as ghee lamps, incense, and chamara fan. Everyone gazes at the deity with the utmost respect. Some chant prayers and sing while others are very quiet.

As you go around the complex, you will see other shrines, all of which contain a myriad of deities of demigods and goddesses, and various forms of Lord Vishnu and Krishna and Their consorts. All of Them are said to be very old. To the right of the main deity is a small temple of Lord Balarama, Krishna's elder brother. To the left of the main temple is a smaller temple with a large deity of Pradyumna and a small deity of Anirudha, Krishna's son and grandson. Across from this is another temple of Purushottama (Vishnu). Another temple dedicated to Shiva as Kuseswara Mahadeva is next to this. Directly across from the main temple is a small temple for Devaki, Krishna's mother. And next to that is another for Veni-madhava (Vishnu). Once you visit these temples you can go behind the main temple to a rectangular building that has several altars around the sides with the deities of Radhika, Jambavati, Satyabhama, Lakshmi, Sarasvati, and Lakshmi-Narayana. Seeing the temple at night is also very beautiful because it is lit up very brightly with many spotlights. Many people visit at this time as an uplifting way to end the day.

One evening *arati* that I attended was not so crowded and I was able to get to the very front to watch the ceremony. The temple assistant saw me and gave me lots of offered sugar sweets and *tulasi* leaves. I was very surprised at this and felt that this was special mercy from the Lord. As I stood there and watched, I became very ecstatic. Soon it was as if I was seeing nothing else but the deity. My whole consciousness was focused strictly on the deity of Lord Dwarakadish. In fact, I could not take my eyes off Him. It became a very powerful *darshan* in which I felt I was not only looking at Lord Dwarakadish, but He was also looking at me. I had not experienced such an exchange in a long time. It was very moving and the feeling and energy I got from it lasted for days.

As in many holy places, the temple is the center for much spiritual activity, including devotional music, dance, lectures on spiritual topics, plays, as well as meditation and service to the deity. If you are a devotee and dressed like one, you will have no difficulty being allowed inside to see the deity. Otherwise, the guards may ask you to fill out a form stating that you believe in Hinduism.

Other nice temples to visit include the Chakra Narayana, also called Samudra Narayana, temple near the mouth of the Gomati River in the south end of the beach. Where the Gomati River meets the ocean is called Chakra-tirtha Ghat, where it is especially auspicious to bathe in the water and said to give liberation. A small island in the river is also where a Lakshmi Narayana temple can be found. A walk along the beach is also quite nice, and you can see the Gayatri temple while you are there. The Gomatiji temple has an image of the Gomati River, which is said to have been brought to earth by Vasistha Muni.

The Gita Mandir is not far away and has a deity of Lord Krishna teaching the *Bhagavad-gita* to Arjuna. Verses from the *Bhagavad-gita* cover the walls. There is the small and old Bhadkeshwar temple by the sea that has a small Shiva *lingam*. And the Sidheswara Mahadev temple along with other assorted temples and ashramas of various sizes are scattered throughout the town. You will also find many *sadhus* wandering around, some of which live in Dwaraka, and others simply traveling through. Many of them, as well as old ladies, rely on begging as a means of support. I was surprised by the number of them. And children too will follow you, asking for rupees or pens. While visiting I saw no other Westerners there.

To get a bus tour of some of the surrounding temples around Dwaraka, you can book a tour in the tour office which is located in the main vegetable market building on the west side of town. The temples you will see include the Nageshwar Mahadev temple, which contains one of the 12 Shiva *jyotirlingas* (self-manifesting *lingas*) in an underground chamber. It is on the route from Dwarka to the Beyt Dwarka island. The *Shiva Purana* explains that the Nageshwar temple is in a place called Darukavan.

One legend connected with this temple is that a devotee named Supriya was attacked by the demon Daruka who imprisoned him and several others at his capital Darukavan, where he resided with his wife, Daruki. But Lord Shiva appeared as the *jyotirlingam* and destroyed the demon with the weapon known as the Pasupatastram.

Another legend is that Shiva, being sad over the death of his wife Sati, lived at Darukavan for some time in the guise of a sage. Darukavan was a land of snakes, and they cursed him to become a *linga* when their wives were enchanted by him. They were not aware of who he was. From the curse of the nagas, the *linga* was cast into the *kund* (water pool) and came to be known as the Nageshwara *jyotirlinga*.

This *linga* was installed here in Dvapara-yuga when the Pandavas found this unique form of Shiva. Lord Krishna told them it was Bholenath (Shiva's) *jyotirlinga*, and that its worship will benefit the world. To diminish the brilliance that emanated from the *linga*, Lord Krishna instructed the Pandavas to bring sand from Ramesvaram to cover it. They removed the *linga* from the *kund* and installed it as Nageshwara *jyotirlinga*.

In this *linga* dwells both Vishnu and Shiva, so it is also called Hari/Hareshwar. This temple's main door is to the west, unlike other temples. This is because once Shiva's devotee Namdev was in the eastern doorway and the priest asked him to move. So he went to the back of the temple on the west side and worshiped there. Then Shiva turned and faced west to accept his devotee's worship.

The assorted temples around the Gopi Talav area is where Krishna met the *gopis* (cowherd girls) of Vrindavana when they came to see Him. From the banks of the small pond comes the *gopi-chandana*, the clay that many devotees use as *tilok* to mark their foreheads signifying that their bodies are temples devoted to Krishna or Vishnu. This area is located about 25 kilometers north of Dwaraka.

Closer to Dwaraka (1.5 kilometers north of town) is the Rukshmani temple, dedicated to Rukmini who is the most important of Krishna's 16,108 queens. This temple dates to the 12th century. Some of the wall panels of the Rukshmani temple sanctuary are badly eroded, but the columns, balcony, and high basement are all nicely carved. The deity of Rukmini is very beautiful. The architecture outside is quite lovely, but you can see where the salty air is causing the stone to erode.

The reason why the Rukshmani temple is located away from the Dwarakadisha temple is that once Krishna and Rukmini were invited to dinner by Durvasa Muni. It was customary that guests do not eat or drink anything until offered by the host. But Rukmini got very thirsty and could not wait to be served by Durvasa. She asked Krishna for help and He placed His foot on the ground and brought up the waters of the Ganges from which she drank. But Durvasa saw her drinking before being served dinner and he became angry and cursed her to live separate from Krishna.

BEYT DWARAKA

You should also visit the Island of Bet (Beyt Dwaraka), 30 km north of Dwaraka, just off the northwest tip of the peninsula, which is reached by ferry from Okha. This is where Lord Vishnu killed a demon and where Sudama Brahmana, Krishna's childhood school mate, is supposed to have met Krishna when he came for a visit. A pilgrimage to Dwaraka is considered incomplete without a visit to this island. The Krishna temple here is, basically, a large house with a series of shrines for Krishna and 56 of His consorts, all of which are said to be very old deities. The deities here include Radha-Krishna, Saksi Gopala, Radhika, Ambika, Ganesh, etc. None of Them are more than two feet tall and all are made of black stone. Deity *prasada* is also available at a stall inside.

After spending as much time as we feel necessary to experience and see this holy place of Dwaraka, the best way to get to our next destination is to take a five-hour bus ride to Veraval and then bus or ricksha to Somnath.

The Mul Dwarakadish temple or Visavada is a small place 25 km north of Porbander. It is a place where Lord Krishna is said to have stopped on His way to Dwaraka. It has a lovely deity of Lord Krishna. There is also the Ranachodji temple across from a Shiva temple.

PORBANDER

On our way to Veraval we will pass through Porbander, which is southeast of Dwaraka along the coast, although we won't be staying at this place. This town was known as Sudamapuri after Sudama Brahmana. The story is that Sudama was a very poor brahmana who had hardly enough to eat. He had been a childhood friend of Lord Krishna when they were schoolboys. When Lord Krishna moved to Dwaraka, Sudama wanted to visit Him but was hesitant because he had nothing to offer and was not sure if Krishna would want to see him. His wife convinced him that he should go and packed a little chipped rice for him to take to offer to Lord Krishna. When Sudama visited Sri Krishna, Krishna was very happy to receive him and remember their childhood activities. Seeing that Sudama had a parcel but was hesitant to offer it, Krishna snatched the little bag of rice from Sudama and greatly relished it. After their visit was over, Sudama returned home and could not recognize his residence. It had turned into a great and opulently beautiful palace. Thus, the town became known as Sudamapuri. There are a few temples in town that commemorate the incident. Aside from this, Porbander is also known as Mahatma Gandhi's birthplace. The Kirti Mahal, in a small alley in the western part of the city, marks the place where he was born in 1869. A swastika marks the location where he took birth. Next door is a building with a photo exhibit on Gandhi's life, along with extracts from his writings and speeches. A small bookshop is also found here.

VERAVAL & SOMNATH

The bus continues for a few more hours to Veraval. There we can get a room at a local hotel, especially if it is late, and take rest. In the morning we can take an auto-ricksha six kilometers to Somnath. The temple that Somnath is most noted for houses one of the 12 *jyotirlinga* Shiva temples in India. References to the presiding deity of the temple, Someshvara, is found in the *Rig Veda*. It was also mentioned as a sacred place in the *Mahabharata*. The *Prabhas Khanda* in the *Skanda Purana* describes the *linga* of Somnath as a Swayambhu *linga* of great power, surrounded by a serpent, of the size of a hen's egg, called Sparalinga and situated underground. It was called Bhairaveshwara in Satya-yuga, Shravanikeshwara in Treta-yuga, and Shrigaleshvara in Dvapara-yuga.

Legend has it that it was built and destroyed many times but was originally built out of gold by the moon-god, Somaraja, many years ago to atone for a curse that Daksha had put on him. The curse was that Somaraja, also called Chandra, would suffer from tuberculosis and lose his beauty and radiance until he waned to nothing. This was because Somaraja showed preference to Rohini over his other 26 wives who were all Daksha's daughters. The curse also disturbed the tides and growth of the vegetation, and the sages asked Daksha to remove the curse. Daksha said he did not have the power to do so, thus Daksha told Somaraja to go to the place of Somnath and get rid of the curse by worshiping Lord Shiva. So he found the *jyotirlinga* and began the worship, and Lord Shiva blessed Chandra with the forthnightly phases of waxing and waning, thus he regained his light. This is why it is called Somnatha which means the "lord of the moon." It is also called Prabhas (to shine) since the moon regained light here.

After this the temple was built by Ravana in silver, then by Krishna in wood, then by Bhimdev in stone. Then it was destroyed in 1024 by Mahmoud of Ghazni. The temple was so rich at the time that it was supposed to have had 300 musicians and 500 dancing girls. And so many pilgrims visited that there were 300 barbers to shave their heads.

It is also related that when Ghazni attacked it, the temple finally succumbed when Muslim soldiers scaled the walls with ladders. All they found inside were defenseless worshipers. Fifty thousand devotees praying and weeping with hands clasped were massacred in cold blood. The Shiva *linga*, adorned with gems and precious stones, was broken and the temple was burnt. After the battle, Ghazni and his troops are said to have taken 6.5 tons of gold with them across the desert. The temple gates were also taken and set up at Ghazni.

The temple was rebuilt and again torn down in 1297, 1394, 1469, and in 1701 by the orders of the fanatical Muslim Aurangzeb. The temple we see today was rebuilt in 1950. Somnath, then, has withstood the tests of time and the attacks of destroyers. Yet it has risen each time again, just as Vedic culture itself has kept standing regardless of oppressors who have tried to annihilate it. Many pilgrims visit this temple. Westerners are allowed in as well.

Near Somnath is the holy place of Prabhasa, where the Yadavas drank a beverage and became intoxicated and engaged in a mutual fight in which they killed each other with hard stalks of cane. It was in this way that the Yadavas left this world as Lord Krishna began to wrap up His pastimes in this material universe. Also at Prabhasa-ksetra is the holy place of Bhrigu-tirtha, which was manifested by Lord Parashurama. This is where the Rivers Sarasvati and Hiranya flow together into the ocean, and where the hunter who shot Lord Krishna cast his arrow. Nearby, 5 minutes down the road to the right of the temple, is a small museum with an assortment of relics from the old Somnath temples. Benefits of visiting Prabhasa-ksetra are described in the *Srimad-Bhagavatam* (starting at 11.6.36). By bathing at this holy place, or making offerings to the forefathers or demigods, or feeding the local brahmanas or giving gifts, we can cross over all terrible dangers as one crosses an ocean in a suitable boat.

Not far away is the Pandava-gupha, the cave linked to the Pandavas and where the Pandavas are said to have performed penance at Prabhas. There is also the Sada Mai temple of Shankaracarya, which has a deity of Lord Narasimha and a Shiva temple. One kilometer farther down the road is a small temple complex that has a Gita temple with a Krishna deity, a Lakshmi-Narayana temple, and in between a small cave temple which marks the spot where Lord Balarama, Krishna's brother, left this world by turning into a snake and entering into the earth region known as Patal. These are near the confluence of three rivers, called Triveni Tirtha. This marked Balarama's final earthly pastime. In the courtyard is also a room that was used by Vallabhacarya, the founder of the Pushti Marga spiritual line. The most noteworthy spot, however, is on the river banks where you will find a small pillared shrine with Lord Krishna's footprints. This marks the place where Lord Krishna walked or was taken after He had been shot by the hunter Jara, which is about four kilometers from Bhalka Tirtha. This is the place where His last rites were performed and from where He left this planet, and where His illusory body was cremated, although He left this world in His spiritual body.

A little drive away is the holy place of Bhalka Tirtha, the place where the hunter mistook Krishna or Krishna's foot for a deer. Then he shot an arrow into Krishna's foot as He sat on or slept in a deerskin. The story is that Lord Krishna, in His four-armed form, sat down under a pippala tree, and placed His left foot with its red heel upon His right thigh. Jara the hunter was watching from the shore of the ocean at Prabhasa, and mistook the Lord's red-colored foot to be the face of a deer and shot his arrow at it. This was Krishna's arrangement so He could perform the pastime of leaving this world after all of

His affairs were finished. It has also been at this spot where Lord Krishna gave His final instructions to Uddhava, as explained in the *Srimad-Bhagavatam*.

At this location is a small temple. Within it is a tree said to be the one under which Lord Krishna was sitting when Jara shot His arrow. The temple is built around the tree, which comes up through the roof of the temple. On an altar, under the tree, you will see a deity of Krishna reclining on a seat. Nearby is an image of the hunter, Jara, with bow and arrows, paying respects to Krishna, begging pardon for his offense. To take a few minutes to sit and meditate on the significance of this is a must for all devotees of Lord Krishna. One mile from the tree on the seashore, where Jara is said to have shot his arrow, is the Vira-prabhanjana Matha temple. Dusk, the time when Krishna was shot, is marked by the rhythmic playing of cymbals so all pilgrims know that it is time for special meditations or prayers.

JUNAGADH & GIRNAR HILL

After our visit to Somnath, we travel by bus to Junagadh, which is a stop for a day or two, depending on your interest. Jains and pilgrims will want to see the temples on top of Girnar Hill. Girnar Hill is actually a cone of an extinct volcano. The best way to get to the base of Girnar Hill is to take a bus, No. 3 or 4, from the Junagadh bus stand. A bus leaves for Girnar Hill every hour. Or just take a motor-ricksha. On our way to Girnar Hill not far from the base of it we will pass a building on the right that houses a rock which has 14 edicts inscribed on it by Emperor Ashoka around 250 B.C.E.

In the foothills of Girnar Hill is the Radha-Damodara temple with beautiful deities of Krishna's four-armed form. As Lakshmi-Narayana, the deities are formed of the typical black and brown stone, and are described in the *Skanda Purana* as being self-manifested over 12,000 years ago. Next to the main temple is another for Lord Balarama and Revati, His consort. The original temple at this site is said to have been built 4500 years ago by Vajranath, Lord Krishna's grandson. Not far away is a place where lived Vallabha, the 16th century Vaishnava acharya.

Along the Swarnarekha River near the temple is Revati Kund, named to indicate that Revati Devi lived in the area. Only about 20 meters away from Revati Kund is the cave of Muchukunda, who was awoken by Lord Krishna, and who then burnt to ashes the demon Kalalayavana by his angry glance, as related in the *Bhagavata* and other *Puranas*. The cave is found in a temple to Lord Shiva. The forests in the area are known to support numerous leopards. As you pass over Suvarnarekha River by crossing the bridge there is Damodar Kund where many pilgrims take a holy dip.

Many *devas* or demigods are said to live around this mountain. Lord Shiva especially liked it. The *Skanda Purana* describes that Lord Shiva came here from his home in Mount Kailash and found this place to meditate. He declared it to be one of the holiest places and stayed here in the form of the Bhavanatha deity. Other *devas* live in the nearby mountains. The festival of Shiva Ratri is celebrated here, especially near the Mrug Kund behind the Bhavanatha temple.

The top of Girnar Hill is reached by climbing up 10,000 stone steps that rise 600 meters, to a height of 3666 feet. This was the mountain formerly called Raivataka as mentioned in the *Puranas* and *Mahabharata*. As you climb up the mountain, it is not unlikely to see many grey monkeys. The climb can take you more than a couple of hours, so be ready for it and start early before it gets hot. But you can rest occasionally by any of the refreshment stands along the way. The climb up will take you through jungles and then over rocky terrain and under stone overhangs. Along the principal path are a number of gates, shrines, and water tanks. After some time you will reach a group of Jain temples behind a large gate. They are a group of 16 Jain sanctuaries on a large rocky ledge, the largest of which is dedicated to Neminatha, the 22nd *tirthankara*, built in 1128. In the shrine is a large black image of Neminatha.

Several other Hindu temples are along the path. A few significant temples include the temple of Mallinatha, the 19th Jain *tirthankara*, built by two brothers in 1177, along with the temple of Samprati Raja (1453), and the Melak Vasahi temple (15th century). The Gauramukhi Ganga temple has a spring of the Ganges that flows out of a spout shaped like a cow's mouth. Farther up is the stone temple of Parvati in the form of Amba Devi, who resides there to fulfill her promise to Lord Shiva. This was built in the 12th century and offers a great view of the Jain temples and the surrounding area of Junagadha.

As we move on we finally reach the mountain's peak where we find a small shrine which houses an image of Gorakhnath, a sage who is considered an empowered incarnation of Shiva. Around the shrine are white marble tiles. Here we can take in the scene for a while before next heading toward Lord Dattatreya's ashrama. This is said to be where he engaged in austerities for 12,000 years. Inside the ashrama is a fire that is in the middle of a pile of wood. It is always kept burning to indicate the soul which is covered by darkness.

Our last stop on the summit is another 200 steps above the ashrama which is the new temple to Vishnu as the three-headed form of Lord Dattatreya, which represents Brahma, Vishnu, and Shiva. Images of four dogs surround the deity which indicates the four principal *Vedas*.

Besides this, Junagadh has the Uparkot Fort, built in the 4th century on a plateau at the eastern edge of town, which I thought was of little interest. There is also the Nawab mausoleums, Durbar Hall Museum, and a surprisingly nice zoo about three kilometers out of town in the Sakar Bagh, which also has a little museum. There are also Buddhist and Jain rock cut monuments and caves in Uparkot that date back to the 2nd century. These include numerous cells and columned verandahs. Not far away are the Khapra Kodia Caves from the 3rd-4th centuries. This contains five square cisterns approached by descending staircases.

After our visit to Junagadh, we will take a five-hour bus ride to Bhavnagar and then a train to the sacred Jain city of Palitana.

BHAVNAGAR & PALITANA

When we pull into Bhavnagar, we can find a hotel to stay here. Again this is because the facilities in Palitana are much fewer. The hotels seemed to be rather expensive for my taste, and then someone suggested staying at a place called the "Mini Guest House." Even though the place is not as clean as it could be, I got a room there for a reasonable price. They also have dinners in the evening for the guests when you order it, but there are also dinner cafes down the street that offer nice vegetarian meals for very reasonable prices. However, one added benefit is that the train station is only a block away. For me, being close to the train station is a real convenience and makes a bad hotel better. Especially since the next morning we take the 6:25 train straight to Palitana, which gets into town one-and-a-half hours later. When we arrive, we have to take a horse drawn *tonga* through town because they do not allow motor-rickshas here.

Palitana, 56 kilometers southwest of Bhavnagar, is a major holy place for Jains because of the Shatrunjaya hilltop a mile out of town. This is where we will find a total of 863 Jain temples on the twin peaks. It is the largest and most sacred Jain temple city in India. As you climb the 2500 steps up the hill, you will ascend 600 meters. It's not a steep climb but it can take about one-and-a-half to two hours, and it can take a lot of energy out of you. You just keep walking and walking, thinking that it's not much farther to the top, and then you realize there's still a long way to go. You have to be pretty determined to make the climb, yet you will see Jain nuns that seem to run right past you and you wonder how they do it. If you can't make the climb on your own, there are plenty of men who will carry you up in a *dooli* swing chair carried by one man at each end of the poll. It is not all that expensive, but the ride itself can be rather uncomfortable.

On top of the hill you will find that it is covered with temples, many of them are small but some are big and quite popular with the pilgrims. Within the temples are thousands of images of Jain *tirthankaras*. These temples were built over a 900-year span. The earliest of which were constructed in the 11th century but were torn down when the Muslims came through around the 14th century. So most of the present temples date back no further than the 1500s. Nine enclosures separate the temple groups, each of which consists of a number of small temples surrounding a central temple. The main temple on the hill is dedicated to Sri Adinath, who is the first of the Jain *tirthankaras*. This temple is the most popular and lots of activity goes on continuously. On the tallest hilltop is the Chomuka temple which is very big and impressive. It has a very large sanctum with four central images of Adinatha, each facing one of the four directions. The images must be about ten feet tall in sitting postures, decorated with silver on their hands, feet and chest, with large crystal eyes. The southern ridge is dominated by the 16th century Adishwara temple. Inside, the main image is of Rishabadeva who has crystal eyes, a gold crown and necklaces.

The importance of the place lies in the tradition that Adinatha, the first Jain *tirthankara*, visited the hill several times and the original temple was built by his son, Bharata. Furthermore, the chief disciple of Adinatha, Pundarika, is said to have obtained enlightenment here.

As with many Jain temples, you will find much beautiful and very intricate stone carving work. You can visit the temples from 7 A.M. to 7 P.M. The hill is dedicated to the gods and everyone, even the priests, leaves the hill at night. You will need a permit to take a camera, which is available for Rs. 20 at an office near the shoe minder's stand. After walking around and seeing all of the temples, you may start getting hungry, but little food or drink is found up here, except for the yogurt (here it is called curd) sold by the entrance. Otherwise, all food stalls are located at the base of the hill. So bring your own water.

Even while walking back down the hill I had to stop for rest a few times. The views are tremendous, but coming down I realized how far up I had gone. After stopping to get some drinks at the base of the hill, and trying to deal with all of the beggars who are mostly women and young girls, we take a horse drawn *tonga* to the bus stand to get the next bus back to Bhavnagar. Trains are also available, but only at certain times.

At Bhavnagar, we will take an early morning train back to Ahmedabad. Once again, the train station being nearby is very helpful. From Bhavnagar, trains take a couple hours and busses, although crowded, take about 45 minutes. After we arrive at Ahmedabad, we get a nice hotel room and get cleaned up and refreshed, and then do whatever business is required. Ahmedabad is a good place to cash travelers' checks at the State Bank of India in the International Department. Many towns in Gujarat do not have banks big enough to cash travelers' checks, so take plenty of cash with you just in case, because they can always convert the major foreign currencies into Indian rupees. When we are finished in Ahmedabad, there are a few places just short excursions away that we can check out if we are interested.

LOTHAL

Lothal is south of Ahmedabad by 80 kilometers, an easy day trip from Ahmedabad by bus, and is 16 kilometers or 10 miles from the sea. It is 6 km west of the confluence of the Sabarmati and Bhogavo Rivers. This town was related to Harappa and Mohenjodara of the Indus Valley when it was in its prime 4500 years ago. Anyone interested in archeology can see this city that was similarly laid out and used the same sort of brickwork and drainage system in the houses as those of the ancient Indus region. You will find the remains of brick houses, channels, and wells, with many additional artifacts of the Harappan culture, such as stone weights, clay impressions of seals, terra-cotta plaques, clay figurines, pottery with painted animal motifs, etc. Evidence of sea travel to and from Lothal is the brick-lined rectangular dock, measuring 715 feet by 121 feet. Thus, it was once a flourishing port that traded with Egypt, Persia, and Mesopotamia. Further evidence of the Indus relationship is the discovery of a seal from Bahrain depicting a double-headed dragon. The city is suspected of falling into ruin by the perennial floods that destroyed it around 1900 B.C.E.

In 2001, Indian oceanographers found the remnants of two submerged cities in the nearby Gulf of Cambay, complete with streets, houses, staircases, temples, and carved wooden logs that were carbon-dated back to 7500 B.C.E. This indicates that civilization may have started 5000 years earlier than previously believed. There is some thought that the city may have been submerged around 8000 B.C.E.

BARODA & MORE

Baroda (Vadodara) is 112 kilometers south of Ahmedabad. The town itself is not what we'll spend much time seeing, but there are a few places nearby that are worth mentioning. Nonetheless, while you are here you can see the Laxmi Vilas Palace, a grand Indo-Saraceni structure, which is still the residence of the ruling family. But the Maharaja Fateh Singh Museum in the palace grounds offers a collection of paintings by Raja Ravi Varma (1848-1906). The central park called Sayaji Bagh offers a zoo. And you can see a collection of Mughal miniatures, European oil paintings, examples of textiles and royal artifacts in the Vadodara Museum and Picture Gallery.

Champaner is northeast of Baroda. This place has an interesting history, and was once the seat of the Rajput Chauhan dynasty, until it was conquered by the Muslim ruler Mahmud Begada in 1484. He spent 23 years rebuilding the place, adding mosques, palaces, and tombs. It was a capital until it was conquered by the Muslim emperor Humayun, after which it fell into ruins. That is why much of the town is still in a deteriorated condition. The Jami Masjid has a richly ornamental exterior, with 172 pillars, and minarets that rise 30 meters tall. It is considered one of the finer Islamic monuments in Western India.

From a more spiritual perspective, there is the Pavagadh Hill that is said to have been a part that fell off the mountain that Hanuman carried to Sri Lanka as described in the *Ramayana*. It has a grouping of Hindu, Jain, and Islamic shrines, and the ruins of ancient fortifications. On the way up the hill is the Sat Mahal, a seven-storeyed palace of the Chauhan kings who were slain by the Muslim invaders for having refused to convert to Islam, while their women and children committed *jauhar*.

Broach (Bharuch) is south of Baroda (Vadodara). Here you can find a temple of Bhrigu Rishi on the bank of the river east of town. Bhrigu was the great astrologer who is given credit for the astrological treatise called the *Bhrigu Samhita*. Followers of Bhrigu are usually very good astrologers.

Navsari is twenty-nine kilometers south of Surat. It is the town of which the people of the Parsi faith will want to visit. This town is an ancient base of the Parsi community dating back to the time when the Parsis first started settling in India. And the town of Udvada, 10 kilometers north of Vapi, is said to have the oldest sacred fire in India that the Parsis originally brought over from Persia to Diu, a town on the southern Gujarat coast.

If we have taken this route south, we will now backtrack up to Baroda (Vadodara) where we will take a long overnight train ride into Madhya Pradesh to the holy town of Ujjain. Otherwise, we can go straight from Ahmedabad directly to Ujjain on an early morning train.

UJJAIN

Ujjain is not a tourist town, but is a major pilgrimage center, and pilgrims of all kinds come through. But most are Indians and not many Westerners visit here, except those like me. So there are not a lot of people who speak English here. Plus, if you visit, keep in mind that the State Bank of India can change foreign currency, and it also has an ATM machine, but if you have traveler's checks, you must take the one-and-a-half hour bus ride to Indore to cash them. There are also various hotels and ashramas where you can stay located throughout the town, but several are also across from the train station. However, check them to see what prices and standards of clealiness are best for you.

Ujjain, which used to be called Avantipura in the Sanskrit tradition, is located on the banks of the Shipra River. The Shipra flows into the Chambal River, which goes on into the Yamuna which flows into the Ganges. The most popular part of the Shipra River in Ujjain is along Ram Ghat where there are more small temples and shrines, mostly to Shiva, and is where many thousands of people gather during the Kumbha Mela festival to bathe in the river which is especially purifying at that time. Bathing in it is said to give liberation. Ram Ghat is also said to be where Lord Rama, Sita, and Lakshmana did *pinda*, or the funeral rites for Lord Rama's father, Dasaratha. Ujjain is sacred for Shaivites due to the Mahakal temple. It is sacred for Shaktas due to the Siddhi Devi temple, and it is special for Vaishnavas because Lord Krishna went to school here at the Sandipani Ashrama.

Ujjain becomes the sight of the huge Kumbha Mela festival every 12 years, starting on the full moon day in Chaitra (May-June) and lasts for a month. During the festival as many as three million pilgrims, and as of 2004 possibly 30 million, come from all over India to associate with other holy men and to bathe in the holy waters at the most auspicious time for spiritual purification. Besides this, there are a number of temples in this town that are worth visiting. Most of them are dedicated to Lord Shiva. One of the best ways to see the major temples is to simply hire an auto-ricksha for the day and let the driver take you around. Your hotel can help you arrange this.

There are six major temples outside the city and six in the city, with many more of various sizes throughout the town. Starting with those that are outside, we can first go to the Sandipani Muni Ashrama in the Ankpaat area. This is an ashrama and temple which marks the place where Lord Krishna, His brother Balarama, and Their friend Sudama Brahmana went to school and was taught by Sandipani Muni. It is still a place of study, and in the small temple room you will find a central altar with an image of Sandipani Muni. By the wall are small deities of Krishna, Balarama, and Sudama in the mood of students. Outside and nearby is the Gomati Kund where Krishna called all of the holy rivers, thus saving His teacher from having to go on pilgrimage to reach these rivers. There is also the place where Krishna washed His writing tablets. Parents with children that have difficulty learning come here to observe the *patti puja*, the worship of the slate upon which they learn to read. The priestly family that takes care of the ashrama here can trace their line back 2000 years and are descendants of Sandipani Muni. This ashrama has been greatly upgraded and improved over the last several years, with new sidewalks, an arch at the entry of the place, and also a separate and new temple room and a display of many paintings showing the history and stories of the ashrama.

Another temple which is quite popular is the Mangalnath temple on a hillock near the Shipra River. This is only a short distance from the Sandipani Muni Ashrama. Many people come here to see the images of Shiva and Durga. Where the temple is now is the result of a battle between Shiva and a demon Andhkasur. The battle also concerned Mangal, the planet Mars, making this place the only location where Lord Mangal appeared. People with an inauspicious Mars in their astrological chart come here to do a special worship with curd and rice. Couples who wish for a child also come here to offer worship to a left-handed swastika.

There is also the Siddhavat temple at another location along the Shipra River. This has a vermilion-covered face of Shiva near a special tree. Several Shiva *lingas* are also in the room. It is said that Parvati performed penance here. Just in front of the sanctum at Siddhavat is a banyan tree that is sacred, some say it was planted by Parvati herself. It is said that once a Muslim ruler cut the tree down and covered the roots with iron plate to prevent it from growing back. He did this to show his authority and to belittle the Vedic customs. But the tree pierced the iron sheets and grew back within a short time. Thus, even today many people pay homage to this tree and the area. Many people also come here to observe the *pinda* ceremony or funeral rites of a relative 10 days after they have died, and then take a dip in the waters of the Shipra for purification. Thus, this place is often busy with spiritual activity.

The Kalbhairav temple is next, located several kilometers to the north of town along the Shipra River, and built by King Bhadrasena. This temple is visited before going to the Mahakaleshwar (Shiva) temple because Kalbhairav is the chief of Lord Shiva's army, whose permission you need before seeing Shiva. Worship of Kalbhairava is believed to have been a part of the Kapalika and Aghora sects. Ujjain was a prominent center of these sects. The temple has an image in the form of a large face of Kalbhairav (Shiva) that is built up with many layers of vermilion, which creates deep eyes and mouth, surrounded by a small layer of silver leaf. This deity drinks offerings of wine. When such an offering is made, the priest pours part of a bottle of wine onto a plate which is tilted to allow the wine to run into the mouth of the deity. Where it goes, I don't know, but half a bottle of wine is poured into the mouth of the deity, and the rest is kept aside as remnants. Such liquor offerings have been made here for the past 5600 years in the *tamasic* form of worship. The image is also offered *sattvic* worship in the mode of goodness with flowers and fruits. *Rajasic* worship in the mode of passion consists of offerings with ornaments of gold. It all depends on the desire of the worshiper. On normal days when *tamasic* worship is conducted, as many as 250 bottles of liquor may be offered. A smaller shrine to Devi is also located nearby on the temple grounds.

The fifth temple we will go to see is the Gaurakalika (Gadhalika) temple, which is a nice building architecturally, situated about 2 miles from the city. Emperor Harshavardhana had this temple renovated in the 7th century C.E. It has been rebuilt by the Gwalior State in recent times. In the sanctum is a big face of Kali covered with vermilion showing her tongue. Kalidasa is said to have worshipped this image many years ago. He is said to have been very dim-witted but later became a great literary genius due to his devotion to Kali. This temple is one of the 51 Shakti-peethas, where a part of the body of Durga dropped when it was being carried by Shiva after Durga had immolated herself at Daksha's sacrifice in Haridwar thousands of years ago. So this temple is a center for tantra, too.

Not far from here above the banks of the Shipra River are the Bhartihari Caves. Bhartrihari was the step-brother of King Vikramaditya, and the caves are where he stayed and meditated after giving up worldly life when he learned that his beautiful wife had been unfaithful to him. He was also a disciple of Guru Gorakshanatha, who was a disciple of Guru Matsyendranatha whose resting place is nearby. Bhartrihari was also a scholar and poet and composed a few books in Sanskrit, including *Shringarshatak*, *Vairagyashatak*, and *Nitishatak*. Be careful around the pavement near the caves as the sun can make it burning hot.

The Bhartihari Caves are within a very simple brick building with a series of underground chambers. There is a small Shiva shrine in one cave and a section where a great sage had performed austerities, and where Lord Vishnu was supposed to have appeared to give *darshan*. Another section was supposed to be 15,000 years old and held a doorway to an underground passage that could take you in any of the four directions, even all the way up to Badrinatha or Kedarnath in the Himalayas. It also could be a link to a major cave or underground system of tunnels that could lead elsewhere in the world. But Nehru and the Indian government came and permanently closed it off some time ago, I guess because they did not want people getting lost in there.

Pir Matsyendranath is a pleasant place along the way between the Gadhalika temple and the Bhartihari Caves. It is a small shrine that you will likely see along the way. It is dedicated to the memory of Matsyendranath, one of the great leaders of the Natha sect of Shaivism. Excavations near this site have yielded antiquities which date back to the 6th and 7th centuries B.C.E.

To see the major temples in the city, we can start with the modern Yoga Mata (Durga) temple which is very colorful and has a central deity of a very beautiful and life-like Durga. The higher floors also had shrines, one of which had a nice Shiva deity.

Next, the Harsiddhi temple has a famous image of goddess Annapurna, covered with dark vermillion, between the images of Mahalakshmi and Mahasarasvati. There are lots of paintings of the different forms of Devi around the circular ceiling of the temple room, and a large Sri Yantra painting is in the top center. It also has a rock in the middle of the court which is covered with turmeric paste. It is believed to be the head of Vikramaditya and is offered to Durga during the Dussera festival. King Vikramaditya is said to have worshiped the image of Durga here daily. Out front there are two large lamp posts covered with places for ghee wicks that are used during Shivaratri. Another shrine in the back on the right side contains a Shiva *lingam*. To the right upon first entering the complex is a small shrine to Ganesh who is thickly covered with vermillion. Across from that are openings in a structure to view the underground shrine to Devi.

According to the *Shiva Purana*, the significance of this temple is that it marks the place where Durga's elbow dropped when Shiva was carrying her body when she had committed Sati. This was after having been strongly insulted by her father, Daksha, at his sacrificial ritual in Haridwar. Thus, it is one of the 51 Shaktipeeths. Another legend from the *Skanda Purana* relates that once when Shiva and Parvati were alone on Mount Kailash, two demons called Chand and Prachand tried to force their way in and disturb the peace. Shiva called upon Chandi, Parvati, to destroy them. Pleased, Shiva bestowed the name Harsiddhi upon her, meaning one who vanquishes all.

Not far away is a colorful temple to Lord Rama. It has a small temple room and very beautiful white marble deities of Sita-Rama and Lakshmana, all who were wearing lovely outfits. On either side of the central altar are two other altars, one for Durga and one for Shiva.

Another prominent temple of Ujjain is the Gopal Mandir. This was built in the 19th century by the queen of Maharaja Daulat Rao Scindia. It is a very nice temple for all Krishna worshipers. Because of its location, in the middle of a bazaar, it is not easily seen. The marble-spired temple is in the middle of a small courtyard and the altar has a beautiful, two-foot tall, silver deity of Gopal, Sri Krishna. The beautiful silver doors in front of the altar were from the Somnath temple and taken by Ghazni to Afghanistan and on to Lahore by Mahmud Shah Abdali. They were later retrieved from Lahore by Mahadji Scindia before being installed in the present temple.

The most famous Shiva temple in Ujjain is the Mahakala, in the central part of town. This houses one of India's 12 *jyotirlingams*, the self-manifesting and internally most powerful type of *linga* that derive currents of power from within itself. You enter the temple grounds through a hallway and walk to the back, passing several shrines along the way, including those to Lord Krishna, Sita-Rama, and Devi. At the end of it you reach an open water tank with a nice fountain in the center. Around the fountain and in the large courtyard are several shrines for many personalities, such as Hanuman, Sita-Rama and Lakshmana, Shiva, and others. One large Shiva temple is in the middle with three floors which looks quite majestic with its shikhara rising in the air. The main entrance is to the underground shrine to Lord Shiva with the main Shiva *lingam* of Mahakaleshvara. You walk underground and in the central portion is an area where people pay respects to the main *jyotirlingam*, Mahakal. They have now greatly expanded this area from what was once a small hallway to what is now a small auditorium. It now has a large side room where people can sit, with stepped levels going higher in the back so that everyone can wait and watch the services that take place. There is also a closed circuit television that also shows the *lingam* and the ceremonies that take place. This is also broadcast on the local television so you can have *darshan* even while at home or in your hotel. This *lingam* faces the south, the only one that does.

Several impressive ceremonies are held here during each day. For tantriks especially the first ceremony of the day is the most important. This is the *bhasma-arati*, said to be the only one of its kind wherein the *lingam* is bathed with special substances, including *bhasma* or ashes. Many pilgrims come to watch the early *bhasma-arati*. It is said that the worship once used the ashes of cremated God-realized sages who had willingly left their bodies through their special powers. Today the ash is only from cow dung burnt in the sacred fire. Worship here is said to have gone on since previous yugas. The family of priests has a lineage that goes back 5000 years. Sixteen brahmana families are engaged in the temple service, with 80 priests serving in shifts.

On the second floor of this temple, entered from upstairs and the outside, is the Omkareshwara Shiva *linga*. Images of Ganesh, Parvati, and Karttikeya are installed in the west, north, and east of the sanctum. To the south is the image of Nandi, Shiva's carrier. On the third or upper storey of the temple is the image of Nag Chandereshwar, the snake god. Only the sages from the Mahanirvani Akhara do the worship on that day.

Around the corner and down the street from the Mahakala temple is the Bade Ganesh Ka Mandir, which is a small temple with a large image of Ganesh in the front temple room. Such a large image of Ganesh is rarely found. In the back are three more shrines to Shiva and to Radha-Krishna and Krishna's mother, Yasoda. There is also an image of a five-faced Hanuman in the middle of the temple. When making their rounds to the various shrines, most people also stop here to ask for the blessings of Lord Ganesh who is the son of Lord Shiva and who takes away obstacles and gives good luck.

Several kilometers south of town is another important temple for Ganesh. It is about a 20 minute auto-ricksha ride away from the city, and is the temple known as Chintamani Ganesh, or the Ganesh who assures freedom from worldly anxieties. The image is considered a *svayambhu* or self-manifesting image, and the origins go back to ancient antiquity. The image is small, about two feet tall in the largest part, and appears nearly like a mound covered with vermillion. The consorts of Ganesh, Riddhi and Siddhi, are seated on either side of him and make up part of the mound of the image.

Along Indore Road, about 10 very bumpy kilometers from town, is the temple of Nine Planets, the Navagraha Mandir. It's located at the *sangam* (confluence) of the Gambir River to the north and the Shipra River which join together and flow past Ujjain. This temple has no special architectural features and is hard to see from the highway. The temple has nine very plain and small rooms with small *lingas* in the center of each, along with a framed poster of each planetary deity above it. Unless you are really interested, it is hardly worth the extra trouble to see this temple, at least in my opinion.

Another place to mention is about six kilometers north of town where excavations have revealed pottery and iron objects that date to the 8th century B.C.E., showing the ancient history of this town. A couple other places you may find of interest is the small Vedh Shala Observatory built by Jai Singh near town which has five large astronomical instruments used for identifying and locating celestial objects. You can spend an hour or so here looking over the instruments. Also, the Kaliadeh Palace is on an island eight kilometers north of town in the Shipra River. You may also like to visit the Vikram Kirti Mandir which has the Scindia Oriental Research Institute, an art gallery with old Rajput and Moghul style paintings, an archeological museum, and a collection of some 18,000 old manuscripts. But call first to make sure they are open.

The Siddha Ashram is also a noteworthy place to see since it has completed the construction of a small temple that holds a Shiva *linga* consisting of 1500 kilograms of Parad (mercury), making it the largest of its kind in the world. It is considered that only the great good deeds from previous lives make it possible for a person to touch or worship such a *linga*. The Siddha Ashram is along the Shipra River between Narsimha and Ram Ghats.

Ujjain also has the new Iskcon temple, which is a large and beautiful white marble structure dedicated to Sri Sri Radha-Krishna. It has lovely paintings throughout, and there is also an altar for Sri Sri Krishna and Balarama with Their teacher Sandipani Muni nearby. It also has a vegetarian restaurant and 28-room guesthouse. Thousands of people visit this temple on a regular basis.

FROM BHOPAL TO SANCHI AND VIDISHA

From Ujjain we can take a side trip and go farther east to Bhopal, which is also easily reached from Indore. It is known most for the gas leak at the Dow Chemical Company that killed 20,000 people and injured more than 150,000. This happened on December 3, 1984 when more than 27 tons of poisonous gas leaked from a storage tank at a Union Carbide pesticide factory. However, Bhopal is not where our interest lies.

From Bhopal we take a short excursion to Vidisha and Sanchi. Most trains stop at Vidisha, but not all of them stop at smaller Sanchi, so we have to check the schedule to see where we need to get off. In our case, the train stops at Sanchi, so we'll get off there and stay at the Ashok Travelers Lodge, which is one of the better of the few hotels in the area, unless they have built more since I have been there. But rickshas are hard to find in this town, so we have to walk several blocks from the train station to the hotel. Rickshas and taxis are not waiting at the train station as you find in many places. So it's a good thing we have traveled with little luggage.

SANCHI

Sanchi is a very small and simple town. The significance of it is that on the hilltop that overlooks the town is a Buddhist place of pilgrimage. Buddha never spent any time here, but it had been an important and thriving center while Buddhism flourished. Gradually Buddhism declined and the site became neglected and forgotten until it was rediscovered in 1818 by a British officer, General Taylor of the Bengal Cavalry. It has a wide variety of high quality sculptures and monuments. The hilltop is surrounded by a stone wall, and in the center of the site is a huge *stupa* that was constructed by Ashoka, said to cover some relics of Lord Buddha. It is 120 feet in diameter and encases an earlier *stupa* of the 3rd century B.C.E. It has four finely carved gateways, built in the first century B.C.E. The panels are in very good condition and illustrate pastimes from Buddha's life, the worship of the Bodhi tree, as well as scenes of sports, animals, and designs. *Stupa* three, built in the 2nd century and though somewhat inferior in quality, contains relics of two of Buddha's foremost disciples, Shariputra and Maudgalyayana. Around the site are many other ancient and interesting Buddhist structures that have been restored and are well preserved, including monasteries with small cells for the monks. Some of the oldest of these antiquities date back to the third century B.C.E. and belong to the Maurya and Gupta periods. You will find *stupas*, columns, gateways, etc., most of which have excellent carvings with many designs and scenes of Buddha's life. There are also the remains and foundations of temples, monasteries, and other ancient ruins. The best way to see Sanchi is to buy a guidebook, pay your admission fee, and simply wander around the site for a few hours. More artifacts are found in the Archeological Museum a short distance from the base of the hill. This has a good collection of artifacts from the area, an Ashoka pillar, and sculptures of Vedic divinities, such as Vishnu, Lakshmi, Ganesh, etc.

VIDISHA

Vidisha is next to visit. After our tour of the Buddhist site, we walk back down the hill and are fortunate to find a motor ricksha. So we take a 45-minute ride (10 km) on the very bumpy road to Vidisha or Besnagar where we find the Heliodorus column, locally known as the Khamb Baba pillar. This was erected by Heliodorus, the Greek ambassador to India in 113 B.C.E. He writes on the stone pillar the time it was erected and the fact that he had converted to Vaishnavism, or the worship of Vishnu. The inscription on the column, as published in the Journal of the Royal Asiatic Society, says:

> This Garuda column of Vasudeva (Vishnu), the god of gods, was erected here by Heliodorus, a worshiper of Vishnu, the son of Dion, and an inhabitant of Taxila, who came as Greek ambassador from the Great King Antialkidas to King Kasiputra Bhagabhadra, the Savior, then reigning prosperously in the fourteenth year of his kingship. Three important precepts when practiced lead to heaven: self-restraint, charity, conscientiousness.

This shows that Heliodorus had become a worshiper of Vishnu and was well versed in the texts and ways pertaining to this religion. It can only be guessed how many other Greeks became converted to Vaishnava Hinduism if such a notable ambassador did. This conclusively shows the Greek appreciation for India and its philosophy.

The British Sanskritists were developing the idea that much of the Vedic traditions and stories of Lord Krishna had to have been incorporated from the Bible and the stories of Jesus. However, this column was the archeological discovery that proved to the disappointed British that knowledge of Krishna and the Vaishnava tradition predated Christianity by at least 200 years. It also disproved claims of the Christians and British that the stories of Krishna in the *Puranas* were merely modern and merely taken as adaptations from the stories of Jesus.

This column also signified that the Indians did not adopt legends of Christ to put in their *Puranas* to be used for the stories of Krishna as the British had hypothesized. One point to consider is that if a Greek official was so impressed with the philosophy of Vaishnavism that he converted to it in 200 B.C.E., then it means that Vaishnavism and the element of spiritual devotion to God, as found in the bhakti tradition, had to have been developed several hundred years if not several thousand years earlier. So this is a serious historical site to see.

Seven more very bumpy kilometers north of Vidisha is Udayagiri, which is known for the sandstone ridge that has 20 cave temples that date back from 320 to 600 C.E. Two of the caves are Jain and the others are Vedic. Half of these are merely little niches. Of the others, only a few are worth mentioning. Cave five has a sculpture of Lord Varaha rescuing the earth, represented as goddess Bhudevi. Brahma and Agni are also in the illustration, along with musicians and sages. A few caves, such as caves four and nineteen, have Shiva *lingas*, and others have images of Varaha and Durga, or Puranic legends on the walls or doorways, but most of these are well worn.

Personally, I could easily find only four of the caves and some of the others after exploring the ridge. Though they were a little interesting, I thought they were not worth the endeavor. So after looking around for a while, we take another very bumpy hour long ride back to our hotel in Sanchi. Once we are back at the hotel we make arrangements with our ricksha driver to pick us up at five the next morning to get the early train at Vidisha since it does not stop at Sanchi. If he picks us up, then we will pay him for both today and tomorrow. If he sleeps in, then our ride today is free. This is the way to be sure he will show up on time. And now we can spend the rest of the day relaxing, catching up on our writing, or whatever, while sitting in the garden-like setting of the hotel. After doing so much traveling over the past several weeks, it's good to take some time and reflect on all we have and experienced in this amazing country. I have to admit, there is some satisfaction to be felt when thinking of all we have encountered, both good and bad, that we would have missed had we not come to India.

When our visit to Sanchi is finished, we take a train back to Bhopal and then on to Indore.

BHIMBEKTA

Bhimbetka, which is 40 kilometers south of Bhopal, is a village you might want to see if you are interested in the more than 500 caves or rock shelters in a sandstone ridge that were found containing neolithic rock paintings. Some of these date back 12,000 years, or to the prehistoric Paleolithic period. The earliest paintings from the Upper Paleolithic times show scenes of life during that period, including bison and rhino done in red pigment, whereas humans are shown in green. The paintings from the Mesolithic period (8000 to 5000 B.C.E.) show scenes of hunting, dancing, ceremonies, animals, and more. Later caves from the 1st century C.E. include scenes of battles and some Vedic deities. Although the caves are fairly easy to find, remember that this is a small village and little else is here, so plan on making a quick day trip from Bhopal.

INDORE & MANDU

From Bhopal, or from Ujjain, we can go to Indore mainly to stay a couple of days and take some day trips to nearby points of interest. However, although Indore is not a city known for being a place of pilgrimage, there are a few things that you might like to check out. The Old Rajwada Palace is worth seeing, and is entered through a seven-storey gateway. It is an interesting range of buildings. To the right of the gateway is the Gopal temple, built in 1832, which has a large central hall with supporting granite pillars and decorated roof. There is also the Mahatma Gandhi Hall, which is a fine example of Indo-Saracenic architecture, designed by Charles Frederick Stevens of Mumbai, and is known for its central domed clock tower. It is still used for conferences and lectures. The Lal Bagh Palace may also provide some interest and is a quaint three-storey built between 1886 and 1921, set in a beautiful garden and is quite luxurious on the inside. It is not like a real palace, but more like a big house, yet the interior is quite lush with marble columns, large rooms, a few stuffed tigers, and hanging chandeliers. The Bada Ganapati temple is worth a quick stop to have *darshan* of the image of Ganesh that is eight meters high, one of the tallest you will find anywhere. The Krishnapur Chhatris also offer some charm in their temple structures found in town. They are no longer used much in any official worship, so you can mostly wander around them as you like. There is one shrine in the main *chhatri*. They are not too big, so this will not take long. The Kanch Mandir is also an interesting temple. It is a Jain temple which looks quite plain from the outside, but is covered with multi-colored mirrors inside. There are also the Annapurna and Shiva temples north of town with numerous deities and displays, one of which has a 12-15 feet tall image of Shiva, which is quite impressive.

MANDU FORT

Mandu Fort is one place that is interesting, if you like looking at historical buildings. It is a hilltop fort which is about 98 kilometers or 61 miles from Indore. It is best reached by a private tour bus, but you have to reserve your seat a few days in advance or you may not be able to get a seat. You can also take a taxi to the fort, which your hotel can help arrange for you. Otherwise, you can take a local bus from Indore to Dhar, and then another bus from Dhar to Mandu. Buses from Indore to Mandu take a while, so you may want to stay overnight. If this is the case, be sure to reserve your room early, the best places are usually fully booked. Indore has many tourist offices that can take care of these things for you. However, the fort is so large that there are several small villages and communities on these hills. So you will need transportation at Mandu to reach the various ancient buildings if you want to see everything in a day, unless you are going to stay there and do a lot of walking. Even with transportation it will take at least three hours to see everything. Thus, a taxi to the fort and back, and to use during your tour of it, is not as bad a deal as it may sound, which for me was 850 rupees at that time.

The Mandu Fort was captured by Raja Bhoj in the 10th century. Some historians give credit to Raja Bhoj for the construction of some of the buildings there. But most of them, such as the mosques and harem houses, were pre-Muslim constructions and only captured and converted for Muslim use. Mandu is another one of those places that you will find in India that earmarks the history and many changes that have taken place in this country. It also provides your adventure in India with another place to roam around and look at all the interesting buildings and architecture while imagining what life must have been like 1000 years ago. Many of the later buildings were constructed from early remains of Hindu buildings. This is why you will see so many Vedic elements in the ornate details of the architecture. In fact, the fort is littered with many such remains. So many remnants of Hindu buildings are a sure sign that this was originally built by great Hindu kings. You will also see palaces, harem houses, mosques, and other quite impressive buildings. You can get some great views from the hilltop over the southern ridge. If you really want a good understanding of the historical significance of the place while visiting, tour guides can assist you or you can get a copy of *Mandu* from the Taveli Mahal in the area known as the Royal Enclave. [The only thing about mentioning this is that sometimes such books are available and then a few years later they are no longer around.] Some people say that a tour of the Malwa region is not complete without seeing Mandu. Indeed, it is the largest fortified city anywhere. If you visit Mandu, be ready for a lot of walking, or rent a bike, or hire a motor-ricksha if you can get one. Or just use your taxi.

OMKESHVARA

From Indore we can easily take a bus to Omkeshvara as a day trip and return to Indore in the late afternoon, unless you want to stay at Indore for a couple days. And some people, including Westerners, will find a simple place on the island or nearby and just hang out. It is a very peaceful and quaint place to be if you want to get away from everything for a while and don't need any exotic beaches or anything like that.

Omkeshvara is located on Mandhata Island at the confluence of the Kaveri and Narmada Rivers, not far from Sanawad or Barwaha. Once you get to the town, you wander down the streets toward the bridge or the boats that take you to the island. You will pass many little cafes or shops that sell devotional items. Then you can reach the island by taking a boat or crossing the bridge. It is a little town on the island, with an assortment of buildings, the center of which is the main temple. There are a few very ornate Shiva temples, and the main temple houses one of the 12 *jyotirlingas* of India. One temple has an 18-foot long image of Chamundi with 10 arms holding clubs and skulls.

The priests there are all too willing to help you do a *puja* to the *linga* of Shiva. And being there for what may be my first and only time, I thought I would allow myself to go along with it. So they take you to get the paraphernalia at one of the little shops and then go into the main temple and then sit you down right next to the Shiva *lingam*. They will chant all the mantras for you, tell you when to chant or repeat along with them and to say your name at the appropriate times. Then you offer flowers to the *linga*, along with the five ingredients in the specific order that they will direct, and you actually touch the *linga* as you do this, putting some of the water on your head. The *linga* is small, only about 10-12 inches, but perfectly formed, which is interesting since it is a *jyotirlinga*, or naturally manifested. After the *puja*, you give a little donation to the priests who also wanted to be photographed with me. They were a friendly bunch which I appreciate, not like some places where they want your money more than they want to help you. Walking back through the buildings, there are numerous shops selling all kinds of devotional and spiritual paraphernalia, from beads, books, incense, to video CDs of tours to other holy places, all in Hindi. Many other pilgrims are also here looking around.

In the evening, in front of the main temple room, there is a bed that is arranged for Lord Shiva and Parvati. Every night a backgammon game is also set up, and the temple doors are closed leaving Shiva in solitude until the next morning. But every morning it is in disarray. So it is considered that Shiva and Parvati play the game at night.

After having been relieved of a portion of our karma by doing our *puja* and feeling all the lighter for it, we can take a walk around the island, which has a circular *parikrama* route which begins below the Mandhata temple. Some people also take boat rides around the island, which dock at particular temples along the way. The path takes a couple hours to walk so you can visit a few extra places, such as the Gauri-Somnatha temple. In front of it is a huge Nandi carved out of green stone. Inside is a large Shiva *linga*. You keep going around the path on the ridge with a cool breeze under a warm sun and the sound of the Narmada River rapids below you. It is quite peaceful watching the boats go upstream. You can sit in the shade for a bit, have a cold drink, and then move on. We can go to the Surajkund Gate with nine feet tall sculptures of Arjuna and Bhima. Then there is the Siddhanath temple which has elaborate carvings and dates back to the 10th century. You also pass small shrines to Ganesh, Shiva, Parvati, etc.

At the west end is the *sangam* or the joining point of the Narmada and the local Kaveri Rivers. People take a dip at the *sangam* as a holy bath. There is a small temple here with the female image of the Narmada personified. People often pay homage to her before taking their dip. As you start back on the northern side of the island, you take a stairway up to a walkway that is along the top. You will walk to a nice small temple of Sri Sri Radha-Krishna, and then past small huts of Vaishnava *sadhus* and Shaivite *babas*, and what looked like a few ashramas with numerous deities along the way out in the open. Then you go back toward the main temple after passing another ruined shrine and an old Shiva temple with a large black *lingam* inside. Across from it is an outdoor museum of old deities and Vedic personalities. Other ruins included stone archways, and what is left of the Maharaja's palace. A few more old ruined temples on the river bank are dedicated to Vishnu and the Jain religion. It was all great fun for me, exploring in this way.

One other temple is there at Omkeshvara for Mamleshvara, also a *jyotirlingam*. It is said that without visiting the Mamleshvara temple, one's pilgrimage to Omkeshvara is incomplete. Though it is also a *jyotirlingam*, together with Omkeshvara they are counted as one.

At night many pilgrims gather along the banks of the Narmada and worship it by offering *arati* and ghee wicks in leaf cups that float down the river. The area is well lit with street lamps and decorative lights.

Once we are finished with our visit to Omkeshvara we can take the two-hour bus ride back to Indore and make arrangements to go on to Ajanta or Aurangabad. Or if we are staying at one of the local *dharamshalas* or guest houses for a night, we can catch a bus there as well.

AURANGABAD TO AJANTA & ELLORA CAVES

The next place we want to visit is Ajanta to see the famous caves that are filled with either elaborate stone carvings or wonderful murals. The best way to go to Ajanta is to take a train to Khandwa, then to Jalgaon, and then take a bus to Ajanta. We can stay there at a hotel, or we can go on to Aurangabad since it has many more facilities. From Aurangabad we can visit both the Ajanta and Ellora caves by taking a tour bus through the Maharashtra Tourist Development Corporation.

While we are in Aurangabad, it has a few places of interest. There are 10 caves a few kilometers to the north of town, reached by auto-ricksha. They are in two groups separated by a kilometer and were made near the 6th and 7th centuries. There are five caves in the western group which are monasteries. Cave four has a ridged roof which is similar to the Karla caves, which we will see later. Cave three has 12 columns that are highly ornate. Cave two has many pillars and detailed work, while in a central shrine are the large figures of Avalokiteshvara on each side of the doorway. In the shrine is a large seated Buddha in a teaching posture, and the side walls are covered with little Buddhas in contemplation. The shrine is too dark to see much so the guide, if he is there, will use what little light he can get from the outside and reflect it with a silver board into the cave and onto the figures.

The eastern group has another five caves, some of which have exotic sculptures of women, along with a figure of Buddha, Ganesh, and a Bodhisattva. In all, some of the caves are small cells while a few are temples with a central shrine to Buddha around which you can find a passage with many meditation cells carved out of the wall.

From the caves we can go see the Bibi-ka-Maqbara, which is the smaller and wooden version of the Taj Mahal. It is said that this was built for Rabia-ud-Darani, Aurangzeb's wife, by his son in 1679. It is no where near being like the real Taj Mahal, but since we are in the area it's worth a few minutes of our time.

Next is the Panchakki water mill, powered by water and was used for free by the pilgrims and local people when it used to work. It has a series of water pools with fish that create a cool and relaxing place, especially on a hot day. This is the memorial of the Sufi saint and spiritual guide to Aurangzeb who was buried here in 1624. Men can go in to the mosque and visit the saint's burial place, but women must wait outside.

AJANTA

The Ajanta caves (103 kilometers away from Aurangabad) were made earlier than the Ellora caves and are known for their mural paintings. Thirty caves, carved into the face of a rock gorge along the Waghora River around 200 B.C.E. to 650 C.E., make up this group of Buddhist caves. The caves were occupied only for a short time, and the jungle grew to conceal them. At the time of their discovery in 1819 by John Smith while he was on a hunting expedition, the area was very much overgrown, but he was still able to spot the unusual entranceway of cave ten. After that the other caves were also discovered.

Amongst the caves are five temples and 24 monasteries, and vary in size and in intricacy of design. Caves one, two, 16, and 17 have the best paintings which are on the walls, pillars, and ceilings. These are not simply large paintings but often a series of small and detailed portraits and motifs, which make them even more impressive. The wall murals often tell stories of the Buddha, or his brother, or many other topics. After years of neglect the caves show various stages of water damage to the paintings and stonework. Patches of the paintings have simply fallen off the walls. In some caves little of the paintings are left to be seen. Many of the decorative motifs in the paintings have been incorporated into the designs of the Indian carpets that are made today. Most of the caves follow a plan of having a columned porch entranceway that leads into a large hall with columns around it. At the far end is the sanctum in which sits an image of Buddha, usually in contemplation, sometimes flanked by assistants. In the monastery caves there are meditation cells around the wall. Cave 26 has a huge sculpture of a reclining Buddha, similar to the one at Kushinagar, showing him preparing to leave his body and enter Mahanirvana. Other paintings in this cave show Mara's attack on tempting Buddha with sensual delights. The caves are rather dark, so you should plan to pay for lighting if you expect to see the paintings. Of course, if you are with a tour group the lighting will be included. Having your own flashlight is also a good idea. The paintings include subjects such as beautiful women, Bodhisattvas, many scenes from the life of Buddha, elephants, etc. They are well worth the time to see. To reach the view point where you can see the cave entrances from across the gorge, there is a path along the river from the garden.

In brief, they are divided into three groups, the early Mahayana group (caves 1-7), the Hinayana group (caves 8-10, 12, 13, & 15), and the later Mahayana group (caves 16-29), numbered from right to left as you face them. To get a detailed tour, it is best to purchase the book on Ajanta at the ticket booth.

ELLORA

The Ellora caves (29 kilometers from Aurangabad) are most easily seen by taking a bus tour, but it only gives you a certain length of time at each place. Once you are booked, you get on at the Holiday Resort or India Tourist Office. The Ellora tour will also include a few sights around Aurangabad and the Daulatabad hilltop fortress, which you may not find so impressive, especially in comparison to some of the forts we have already seen by this time in our tour. It was built by Bhilama Raja of the Yadava dynasty in the 12th century, but was captured by the siege of Mohammed Tughlaq, the Sultan of Delhi, in 1327. It is especially known for the 640-foot long underground passageway to reach the top. This was to prevent raiders from being able to attack and instead keep them under duress from things like hot coals being thrown at them, or filling the tunnel with poisonous gas to prevent their progress. The last few meters you have to crawl through a tight space. If you come to see this fort, the tour guides have good torches to help you through.

The bus tours can save you a lot of time rather than using the local bus system to get to and from these places. However, to see the Ellora Caves, there is really no reason to take a bus tour unless you simply want to see the other stops. You can easily take a local bus to get to Ellora, and most of the other local tour places as well, which allows you to take all the time you want to view everything, which is what I strongly suggest. I used the local bus system to go to the Ellora caves, and it is quite easy. Just take the first bus to Ellora in the morning, about 6 A.M. (check the local bus schedule) and you will be there in about 45 minutes. I found it to be best this way since you can be at the caves before anyone else arrives, and it can be so quiet and mystical to be there when no one else is around. It is just you and the old spirits of the caves, and maybe one of the sweepers cleaning the place. After 10 A.M. is when the other busloads of tourists and classes of children start showing up.

After Daulatabad on our way to Ellora is the walled town of Rauza, where a number of important Muslim personalities are buried in the Alamgir Dargah, including Aurangzeb, the fanatic known for destroying many important and beautiful Hindu temples. Also located in the building is supposed to be a robe that was worn by the Prophet Mohammed, but it is only shown once a year. A few hairs from the Prophet's beard is said to be in a shrine across the road.

Ellora includes 34 caves in a line extending about two kilometers or one-and-a-half miles on the west face of a basalt escarpment. Twelve of the earliest, on the southern end, are Buddhist that date back to 600 to 800 C.E. Seventeen of the caves are Hindu, and the northernmost five are Jain, completed in 1000 C.E. These caves are especially known for their sculpture work.

These caves were developed over a period when there was a decline in Buddhism and a renaissance in Vedic culture lead by the Chalukya and Rashtrakuta dynasties (7th to 9th centuries). As the older Ajanta caves became abandoned, the Ellora caves were developed due to the revenue from being on the trade route between Ujjain and the west coast.

The Buddhist caves (1 through 12), however, are monasteries, not temples, and are, thus, not so ornate or architecturally as interesting as the Hindu caves. These were developed during the 7th and 8th centuries. They are, nonetheless, quite fascinating to see. Some of the Buddhist caves have three levels, each with many pillars and central shrines with large and impressive images of Buddha and seated Bodhisattvas, a goddess (probably Mahamayuri, the Buddhist Goddess of Learning) and guardians. Other caves are simple halls. The Jain caves (30 to 34 from the 9th century) at the far northern end have some excellent detail in the carved stone.

The Hindu caves (13 to 29) are more impressive and quite fascinating, and contain many other carvings depicting scenes with Shiva, Parvati, Vishnu, etc. These were developed between the 7th and 9th centuries. Some of these caves (14 and 15) have impressive sculptures of the Vedic pantheon, such as of Durga slaying the buffalo demon, and Varaha, etc. However, the most outstanding is cave 16, the Kailasha temple. This is a huge temple, a cathedral is more like it, cut out of solid rock. It is estimated that it took thousands of craftsmen 150 years to remove 200,000 tons of stone to make this temple. The courtyard is 881 meters by 47 meters and as much as 33 meters high. You will see many exquisitely carved panels with scenes of Shiva and the Vedic legends at this cave, especially in the halls which surround the temple. Inside the temple, a couple flights of stairs up, is the central temple room with 16 massive pillars and a sanctuary with a Shiva *linga* inside. There are also two large stone elephants toward the front and a hall with Nandi, Shiva's bull carrier, across from the main shrine. Cut into the hillsides on either side of the temple are additional halls and shrines with rooms for various purposes. It is actually quite an astounding work. I have never seen anything quite like it, and I have seen many, but not all, of the rock cut temples and caves that are found in India.

VERUL

The **Grishneshwar Shiva temple** is in the town of Verul, located just a two-kilometer walk down the road from the Kailasha cave temple. It has one of the 12 *jyotirlingas* (self-manifesting *lingas*) of Shiva in India and is important to all Hindu pilgrims. So while visiting Ellora we also take the time to pay our respects to Shiva in this 18th century temple, built by Rani Ahilyabai of Indore. As you enter the sanctum, the *linga* is in the center of the *yoni* on the floor in the middle of the room. Everyone gathers around it to do their *puja*. Worship and ceremonies still go on here in ways that are very much in line with the old Vedic customs. No photography is allowed in the sanctum, or so the sign says, but I have seen videos taken within the sanctum of the worship. It is an old style temple surrounded by walls, with a central tower over the sanctum. You will see it from the road as you walk down from the Kailash cave at Ellora.

The legend is that the reason for the installation of this *lingam* is because of the devotion of Grishma. She used to make 101 Shiva *lingas* everyday. Out of jealousy, Sudeha killed her son, and threw his body in the same *kund* where Grishma used to worship Shiva. That still did not deter her devotion to Shiva. Pleased with her faith, Shiva revived her son and appeared before her. So on her ardent prayer, Shiva stayed here as the Grishneshwar *jyotirlinga*.

There is a *kund* near the side of the temple that is said to have arisen by the power of Shiva. The story is that once when Shiva and Parvati were wandering in the jungle nearby, Parvati became thirsty. Shiva pierced the ground with his trident and made the Patal Ganga (underground Ganges water) rise to the surface and quench Parvati's thirst. That is worshiped as Shivalaya Tirtha today. Lord Brahma also appeared here and said the mere touch of this water will absolve all of life's troubles. It is also called Brahma Tirtha because Brahma is said to have installed the Astha (eight directional) Tirthas here. These eight tirthas, represented as *lingams*, are each enclosed in little shrines around the *kund*. These include Kashi on the north, Gaya on the northeast, Ganga *sangam* on the east, Varaj on the southeast, Vishal Tirtha on the south, Trimbak on the southwest, Dwaravati on the west side, and Reva Thirtha on the northwest side.

When our visit to Ellora is over, we can get a bite to eat at the local MTDC restaurant and then flag down a bus for the ride back to Aurangabad. Yes, another traveler and I had to flag down the bus to get it to pause since the buses were not stopping to pick us up. The bus was full, but we managed to find some standing space. It is all part of the adventure in India. Then, back at Aurangabad, we will get ready and take a train the next day to our next place of importance: The holy city of Nasik.

NASIK

When we arrive at Nasik, the train stops at the Nasik Road station, which requires us to take an auto-ricksha ride into town. When I arrived everyone was celebrating the *holi* festival that marks winter's end. The town celebrates it five days later than the rest of the country, and there were parties of people at different street corners seriously making sure everyone was covered with colored dyes. Some of these guys were going nuts, banging on metal drums, chasing their friends around, splashing dyes on each other and on vehicles, and leaving large puddles of colored water in the streets. So I stayed in my hotel for the rest of the evening.

The name *Nasik* means "nose", and the city gets its name because it is considered to be the place where the nose of the ugly she-demon Surpanakha fell when Lakshmana cut it off when he became tired of her trying to convince him to marry her, as related in the

Ramayana. The Godavari River goes through Nasik and as many as 2000 temples, *ghats*, and shrines are scattered along the river banks. So part of the adventure of Nasik is to find our way around some of these many *ghats* and temples of significance. Across the Godavari River from Nasik is the place called Panchavati, which is especially noted for being where Lord Rama spent two years of His exile from Ayodhya with Lakshmana and Sita.

To start our tour of Nasik we first go to the city bus stand and book a bus "Darshan Tour" which is the easiest way to see the main sites. However, it is not unusual that the guides will not be speaking in English. Nasik is not oriented to the English speaking audience. But if the guide is kind enough and does speak English, he might give a separate summary for you later of each site. Another option is that we can negotiate with the auto-ricksha drivers on a price for taking us to all of the major holy places in Nasik, and then be able to take all the time we want. As I mentioned, English is limited here, so you may have to use the help of a local English-speaking person to help finalize the deal. And then we are on our way.

Our first stop is the Sundara Narayana temple (built in 1756) which is very nice architecturally, but is rather simple inside. It is near the bridge across from Rama Kund. Here we find three black stone deities that consist of Vishnu with two consorts in the sanctuary. From here we cross the Godavari River and go to the very popular and holy Rama Kund, where Sita and Rama used to bathe, and is also the water pool where it is believed Lord Rama performed the funeral rites in memory of His father. This is one of the most important places in Nasik, especially during the Kumbha Mela festival every 12 years. This place draws many hundreds and thousands of pilgrims from all over India who bathe in the river to spiritually purify themselves. At the height of the festival there may be as many as a million-and-a-half pilgrims who bathe in the Godavari at Rama Kunda. However, this count seems to be on the increase. The last Kumbha Mela was in 1991. Even now this place is full of people bathing in the holy water, or washing clothes, and many wandering *sadhus* are seen near the river or visiting the local temples. It's a very festive and vibrant atmosphere. If we walk down the river a ways, you'll see many vendors and selling all kinds of things from holy paraphernalia, shoes, bottles, watches, etc. There is also a large fruit and vegetable market where many people come to purchase goods for the day. This area is the center of activity in Nasik.

This area also has many temples, all with varying degrees of importance. Across from the Rama Kund is the Kapaleshvara temple, one of the oldest in Nasik. It is dedicated to Lord Shiva and located through a gateway and up a flight of 80 steps. You will find a main altar or sanctum area with a *lingam*, and around the temple are smaller shrines, but there is no Nandi, Shiva's bull carrier. The reason is explained that Shiva bathed here in the river to purify himself of the sin of *Brahma Hatya*, at which time the representation of the karma of that sin, which was the skull (Kapal) that was pursuing him, fell to the ground. That is why Shiva stayed here and Bhagavan Vishnu named the place "Kapaleshvara". Here Shivaji took Nandi to be his Guru and accepted instructions from him, so there is no image of Nandi at this temple.

On the north side of the Rama Kund is the Chatur-sampradaya Akhada, which is a temple with a grand deity of Vyankatesh Balaji. You may have to ask around a bit to find it.

The Rameshvara temple (18th century), also known as the Naro-Sankara Mandira, was built by the Marathas and houses a Shiva *lingam*.

From here we go to the Kala Rama Mandir (1782), one of the oldest temples in the area. You enter this temple through a gate and behind a large hall is the nice, blackish, but not ornate, temple of Kala (black) Rama. It has three black stone deities of Sita-Rama and Lakshmana, and various pictures of Rama or Krishna in the central temple room.

Nearby is the Sita Gupha Cave where Sita hid when Rama and Lakshmana fought with Khar and Dushana and 14,000 *rakshasa* demon agents of the wicked Ravana. To visit this cave, you go into the specially marked building and then down a little stairway. Then you go in a little room and bend down to crawl through a small entry into the cave where there is a little altar of Sita-Rama and Lakshmana who is served by a little old priest. Then you crawl through another doorway that leads to a small room with a Shiva-*lingam*, and then go out through another very tight entryway and then up the stairs and you're out. Across the street is a small cottage with a diorama of Ravana, disguised as a *sadhu* begging from Sita. Some people agree that this is the place from which Ravana kidnapped Sita while he was disguised as a begging brahmana. It is at Lakshmana Rekha where Lakshmana drew a magical line in the sand to prevent Ravana from crossing it and kidnapping Sita. Part of that line is said to still be there. Only after Sita crossed the line did Ravana have the opportunity to take Sita.

At Parn Kuti, Lord Rama prepared a cottage of leaves and lived with Sita and Lakshmana where He had the best days of His life during Their exile.

We next go to the Sita-Haran Mandir, which is a very old and very small temple of Sita. Here in the little temple room is a small deity of Sita in the pose of giving alms, as when she was giving alms to the demon Ravana who was posing as a *sadhu*. At the other end of the small dirt courtyard is an image of Ravana. I was told that this was where Ravana kidnapped Sita when he took her to his kingdom in Sri Lanka.

Across the street you will find the Sri Katya Maruti (Lamba Hanuman) temple. In the sanctum is an eleven-and-one-half-foot tall deity of Hanuman, covered with vermilion. It is said that this deity was originally found under a big thorny tree. It is also said that one's pilgrimage to Panchavati is not complete if one does not stop here, after which all of the desires of the *yatri* (pilgrim) become fulfilled.

About six kilometers away outside of town you will find Tapovana where sages used to engage in meditation and penance. This is near the confluence of the Godavari and Kapila rivers. At one small shrine here you will find diorama displays that depict Lakshmana cutting off the nose of the demoness Surpanakha, as described in the *Ramayana*. There are many nice temples in this area, reached by auto-ricksha, which include the Swami Narayan Mandir that has altars of Lakshmi-Narayan, Radha-Krishna, and Ranchor Rai Vikramji. You can ask your driver to take you to other temples in this area if you wish.

Farther out is the *sangam* or place where the Godavari River joins the Kapila Ganga. This is one of the areas that become part of the city of tents when thousands of pilgrims come for the Kumbha Mela festival. As you approach the area by road, not far from Tapovan, there is a large banyan tree. Under it is a small shrine where an image of Lakshmana is worshiped. Nearby is a little exhibit that shows a sculpture of Lakshmana cutting off the nose of the demon Surpanakha, Ravana's sister. Legend says this was the spot where it happened.

Kapila Tirtha is also at this *sangam* and is where the Supreme Being appeared as Kapila Muni and taught His mother, Devahuti, the science of bhakti-yoga, devotional service, as recorded in the *Bhagavata Purana*. When I first visited this place a number of years ago, it was very simple. But now (in 2004) there are cement walkways, a few holy huts, and a bridge that crosses the small but rapidly moving river. It is quite lovely. If you cross the bridge, you will come to an area where you will see the cave hermitages of a few of the *sadhus* and holy men who live in them. These are quite old and carved right out of the rock on the hillside. Some of the men are quite friendly and will want you to come in to see them. So you climb up a bit on the rocky hill and enter their cave. A few have their own deities of Durga or others. They will be glad to talk to you, maybe give you some sweets *prasada*, or ask for a little donation. You can also take photos of them. The significance is that they are here living the ancient lifestyle of the *sadhus* in the caves that have been used for such purposes for many years. In a sense, it is like stepping back through time. Just don't get so involved that you miss getting back on your tour bus on time.

PANDU LENA

Pandu Lena is eight kilometers southwest of Nasik and has 24 Hinayana Buddhist monastic caves that may interest you if you are in the mood for exploring. They are on a hillside up a short but steep climb, and date to around the first century B.C.E. to the 2nd century C.E. Some of the caves have very interesting stone sculptures, while the others are not that outstanding. Caves 3, 10, and 18 are the most developed with outside carvings, large interior halls and a central shrine surrounded by cells for living or meditation. You can see all of the caves in about an hour. The hillside gives a good view over the area. You can easily reach these by taking a motor-ricksha, or this stop will be included if you take a local bus tour of the area. Our next stop is a little farther west to Trimbak.

TRYAMBAKESHVARA

Trimbak or Tryambakeshvara means the lord (Ishvara) with three (tri) eyes (ambaka). Shiva appeared here because he was pleased by the austerities of sage Gautama. This town regularly draws hundreds of pilgrims each day who want to come for *darshan* and purificatory baths. This is a very historical place, and was also visited by Sri Chaitanya 500 years ago.

This town is near the source of the Godavari River (30 kilometers west of Nasik). It is easily reached by bus and is good for a day trip out of Nasik. It is only about a 45-minute ride to the bus stop, and then a short walk down the streets and through the shops to the most noteworthy temple in the town, which is the large Tryambakeshvara temple. This is another of the 12 *jyotirlinga* Shiva shrines found in India, and has some excellent stone carving work. There is a tall tower topped with a flag and *trishul* over the inner sanctum. To go inside, you get in line and it leads to the altar where you will see into the sanctum where there is a hole in the *yoni* where the *lingam* would be. In the *lingam* dwells the three divinities of Brahma, Vishnu, and Shiva. This is where the primary worship is conducted. Oddly enough, they do allow people to take only one photo of the altar, which I'm always happy about. So make it a good one.

The interior hall is rather dark and cavernous. Many people come in and sit for a bit to absorb the holy atmosphere and observe the other sculptures and figures in the temple, and then proceed outside. There is also an outdoor shrine to Nandi and along the interior of the south wall are other small shrines. Numerous shrines and ponds are found in this town, such as the Kushawartha Tirtha bathing tank on the west side of town, where many people also take a holy dip in the waters. It used to be surrounded by Kusha grass, from which it gets its name. Now it is surrounded by a pillared hall and a few small shrines. It was originally established by the sage Gautama, whose image can be found here. A small deity of Narasimha is also nearby.

Our next place to visit is the Godavari River, which is considered as sacred as the Ganga. It springs up from the Brahmagiri Hill to the west of town and trickles into a tank where people can bathe for spiritual merit. To reach it takes a hard climb of a couple hours up the hill. So you will need to start early and carry drinking water. During your climb up you will see such things as a temple to Ganga Devi, a cave shrine with 108 Shiva *lingas*, a temple of Gautama Rishi who had an ashrama here, and the ruins of Anjeri Fort. You will continue to walk up the hill for over five kilometers, past an image of Hanuman carved in the rock along the walkway where many monkeys also hang out. The path continues through solid rock and finally onto the dusty trails to the hill top. You simply follow the path up, and will also pass other pilgrims along the way. There are a few stops for refreshments if you need any. At the top the breeze is refreshing after the long climb up, and the views are spectacular. From here we can look over to the other side of the hill. The thing is, I thought the Godavari source was on the side of the hill. I didn't know that actually you had to climb the steep hill to the top and then go over it to reach the other side where the source was located. If I had known there was so much steep walking involved, I don't know if I would have gone. Which is a good thing I didn't know too much.

The Vedic texts, such as the *Shiva Purana*, explain that the Godavari River was created when the sage Gautama wanted to bathe in the sacred river to atone for accidentally killing a cow. How this happened is that once Gautama, who was living in the area, did a penance to bring rain. Then the *deva* Varuna appeared before him as a result. Gautama asked him to produce rain to benefit the area, but Varuna told him that he could attain his desire by pleasing Lord Shiva. Under Varuna's instructions, Gautama dug a well that was filled with water by Varuna, who told Gautama that it would never go dry. But then the sages who had abandoned that place because of the lack of water returned.

338 SPIRITUAL INDIA HANDBOOK

The sages and their wives began using the well and would not let Gautama or his disciples fetch water from it. So Gautama's wife, Ahalya, agreed that she would go get water everyday. However, once she encountered the sages wives who tried to prevent her from using the pond. The wives went back to their husbands and explained what happened. The sages became angry and worshiped Ganesha to acquire his blessings to drive Gautama away from the area. Ganesha was not interested but finally complied and took the disguise as a cow and entered Gautama's barley field and started eating the grains. Gautama tred to drive the cow away by hitting it with a simple bundle of grass, but the cow died when it was struck. Gautama was extremely sorry for this. Then the wicked sages drove Gautama away from the area.

When Gautama enquired about how to atone for this sin, the sages recommended a few ways to do so, including bathing in the waters of the Ganga, if he could help make her manifest in the area. Or he could worship 30 million Shiva *lingas*. When Gautama started worshiping so many Shiva *lingas*, Shiva himself appeared, pleased by his devotion. That is when Gautama asked Shiva to free him from the sin of killing a cow. So Lord Shiva dashed his hair against the Brahmagiri Hill and some of the Ganges water, which he always carries on his head, fell from Shiva's hair.

So as we stand on the Brahmagiri hilltop facing west, we can see to our right that there is also a small temple down the path which marks the location where Shiva is said to have done this. When you go to this temple you can see some lines on the ground where Shiva's hair is said to have struck the earth. The water began to trickle down the hill and formed what became the Godavari River. The Godavari is thus known as the Ganges of the south. Later, when the Ganga asked to leave, Shiva requested that she stay. Ganga agreed as long as Shiva also remain on earth. So Shiva became the *jyotirlinga* at Tryambakeshvara while Ganga stayed as the Godavari, or Gautami Ganga.

As we stand on the hilltop, further to our right is another trail that leads up a ways to the highest summit of the hill, from where you can get the best views over the area and the town of Tryambakeshvara.

To our left is another trail that leads to a cluster of buildings, one of which is a small temple. This is where we go first. Walking down the hill, we approach the temple, then take our shoes off to go inside. There within the temple we see a small water tank from which water is draining into it from an altar. On our left is the altar to the Godavari, or Gangadevi, where water drips out of a small spout, and then goes to the tank. We can take some water and place it on our heads. Or another bigger tank exists outside where we can take a holy bath in the source of the Godavari. Many people also collect small bottles of water here to take with them for later. Bottles outside the temple are also for sale. By the door, there is a small shrine to Shiva located down a few steps.

Then we go farther through the buildings to the well where the water of the Godavari is situated. The source of the Godavari in the Gaumukha temple is where it begins its flow, and the well is where the water itself originates. From here the water forms a stream and then a river which goes 1000 kilometers all the way across India to the Bay of Bengal. The well is next to a tree, and an image of Gautama Rishi is sitting next to the well. While I visited, there was a 92-year old man watching guard over it, sitting on a cushion next to the well. He would use a bucket to bring some water up from the well for everyone to sip. He would walk up from the city below every day to this well to attend to his service here. And another man told me that the old man had no heart trouble at all. I could not imagine walking up this hill, and then back down again, everyday to sit here. It would, however, certainly help you stay in good shape, even if it was physically exerting.

So this had been a most interesting visit and I was glad to have made it. Once we have seen everything, we can make our way back down the hill and return to the town of Trimbak and catch our bus back to Nasik.

PARALI

Going farther west from Nasik, about 100 kilometers north east of Mumbai and west of Igatpuri is the small town of Parali. This town is a little out of the way and not along any route in between important places, so the only way you can reach it is by bus. Nonetheless, some people will want to stop and see this town because it has the Vaidyanath or Baijnath Shiva temple. Some people feel that this has one of the 12 important Shiva *jyotirlingas*, called Vaidyanath. However, this shares the same legend as the temple in Deoghar, so you can read the legend under the description of that town.

This temple has a Shiva *linga* that is nicely worshiped and decorated with sandalwood everyday. The courtyard also has the representations of the other 12 *jyotirlingams*. Every Monday the priests take Baijnath in the form of a metal mask out on a palanquin in a grand procession so that everyone can see him. If you have stopped in to see this temple, then when we are finished we can go on to Mumbai.

MUMBAI

Mumbai is 14 miles in length and three miles at its widest, with a population of around nine million people. Mumbai is a big commercial center. The Indian stock market is located here, and, being a natural harbor, it handles more than 40% of India's sea trade. Most of the Indian movies are produced here as well. Socially, there is a wide mixture of religious faiths, but sometimes there is serious friction between the Hindus and Muslims. While being the most modern city in India, Mumbai also has some of the worst slums and urban areas. Even across from the Taj Mahal Inter-Continental Hotel, one of the most prestigious hotels in downtown Mumbai, you will see homeless beggars trying to make their way through life. And one traveler I met said that while staying in one downtown hotel, prostitutes were busy trying to attract prospective clients as he walked through the lobby.

As you approach Mumbai from Nasik by train, you'll pass many areas of slums and small shacks built by the railroad tracks. In some parts, this seems to go on forever, all the way into Mumbai. However, Mumbai is a big city and has lots of things a tourist or pilgrim may want to see.

When you first get into Mumbai, finding a place to stay may be difficult, especially in the downtown area since lots of travelers are always coming into the city. Also, the prices are high compared to other cities in India. Your best bet is to look around for a room early in the morning, otherwise hotels get booked up quickly.

Mumbai has some very hot and humid summers, but the sea breeze helps keep things cool. The weather also can bring strong monsoons that can flood the streets.

Mumbai has some very nice sandy beaches. Chowpatti is a beach along the northern part of Marine Drive which becomes a gathering place in the evening for families. This is also where the processions meet during the Ganesh Chaturthi festival when they bring the many images of Ganesh to be immersed into the sea. You will also find the Tarapore-vala Aquarium along Marine Drive if you are interested in tropical fish. It is one of the best in India. And while on Marine Drive, you can take it on up to Malabar Hill where you will get some nice views of the Chowpatty Beach and Back Bay area. The formal Hanging Gardens are also on top of Malabar Hill and across the street from the Hanging Gardens is Kamala Nehru Park where you get some more great views over Mumbai.

The Gateway of India on the waterfront at Apollo Bunder is worth a visit. This was built as an Arch of Triumph to commemorate the time when George V and Queen Mary visited India in 1911. The last of the British troops also left India through this arch.

The Prince of Wales Museum has fine collections of art, miniature paintings, images and stone carvings from the Elephanta caves and other areas of India, along with sections on archeology and natural history. The museum is near the Colaba Causeway and was built for King George V's visit to India in 1905. It was opened in 1914. The museum is open from 10:15 to 5:30, closed Mondays and free on Tuesdays. You will also find the Jehangir Art Gallery within the museum's compound, which is one of the main art galleries of Mumbai and is a good place for buying paintings by local artists. Another interesting museum is the Victoria and Albert Museum in Victoria's Gardens, now known as Veermata Jijabai Bhonsle Udyan, in which you'll also find a zoo.

The Victoria Terminus Railway Station is probably the most impressive example of Victorian Gothic architecture in India. It is a rich collection of domes, spires, arches, motifs, stained glass, and more. It was designed by Frederick William Stevens and completed in 1888 and named to commemorate Queen Victoria's Golden Jubilee.

Mumbai also offers shoppers a large variety of items and places to shop. Chor Bazaar, near Grant Road, is good for all sorts of jewelry, antiques, and other nicknacks. A large fruit, vegetable, and fish market is the Mahatma Phule Market and can provide a few interesting shots for any photographer. And the Colaba area has shops for lots of handicrafts, art, and antiques.

There are also places of spiritual importance that Mumbai offers for pilgrims of any faith. Starting at Malabar Hill, at the end of the peninsula, is the temple of Walkesvara, an important place for Hindu pilgrims. According to legend, as described in the *Ramayana*, when Lord Rama went off from Ayodhya to rescue Sita from Ravana in Sri Lanka, He rested here. It was here where Rama constructed a Shiva *lingam* out of sand for His worship. The present temple, built in 1715, is a reconstruction of the original temple that was built over 1000 years ago. It used to be very popular but is fairly quiet now.

There is also a Jain temple dedicated to Adinath not far away. It is built with lots of mirrors and paintings in the interior. Next to the Hanging Gardens is the Parsi Towers of

Silence where the Parsis put their dead so they can be eaten by birds and vultures. Parsis do this rather than cremating or burying their dead because they believe fire and earth are sacred. However, they keep the towers from being easily seen since they do not appreciate tourists snooping about.

The Mahalakshmi temple, dedicated to Lord Vishnu's wife, the goddess of fortune, is located a short drive away from Malabar Hill. It is one of the oldest temples in Mumbai, and it is said that the deities of Lakshmi and her two sisters were found in the sea. The deities on the altar are three brass faces.

A little farther back into the city is a Lakshmi-Narayana temple. And not too far away is the Mani Bhavan. Closer to the Aquarium is the Parsi Banaji Fire temple, and a little farther down the road is the Wadiaji Fire temple and the Anjuman Fire temple. Some of these are not so historically significant, and if you have got a full schedule, they may not be worth your time.

The Iskcon Hare Krishna temple is a large and popular complex in the Juhu Beach area. It has lodging, a restaurant, and a beautiful temple room with lovely Radha-Krishna, Gour-Nitai, and Sita-Rama, Lakshmana and Hanuman deities. People are always coming through to see this temple, especially in the evenings for the worship and a stop at the *prasadam* [sacred food] stall. When there are important festivals here, the nearby streets will be completely shut off due to the number of people that attend. This is a great place to stay if you do not want to lodge in downtown Mumbai. Everything you may need is here or nearby. No matter whether you want banks to change money, a local post office, fruit stands, travel agents, a bus stand for local city buses, taxis and auto-rickshas, not to mention the beautiful temple and deities, and great morning *prasadam* breakfasts for the devotees and guests, everything is here or close by. And nice morning or evening walks along Juhu Beach, which is only five minutes away, are also quite pleasant.

The name of Mumbai is also connected in the spiritual tradition of the city. In the Sanskrit *Sthala-Purana* or local history, as related by city historian K. Raghunath in his book *Hindu Temples of Bombay*, published in 1900, it is explained that there was once an island in the city's vicinity where lived a powerful giant named Mumbarak. The island was named after him. After engaging in great austerities, Mumbarak pleased Lord Brahma who gave him a blessing that he would be free from death at anyone's hands, and would be successful in his undertakings. Upon receiving such a blessing, Mumbarak became a source of trouble to the people and the *devas* or gods. Therefore, the gods and people went to Lord Vishnu for a solution, that they be protected and the demon destroyed. Thereafter, both Vishnu and Shiva extracted a portion of their luster and made it into the Goddess Devi to destroy the giant. The Goddess beat the demon almost to death, and threw him on the ground and told him to ask for one last blessing. He begged that she join his name with hers and perpetuate that name on earth. The Goddess agreed and named herself Mumbadevi. In this way, the name Mumbai is connected with that tradition. "Mumbai" is the invocation of the Goddess for protection of the city.

The history also explains that the city of Mumbai was once a series of islands, which the British started connecting in 1782. This was gradually completed in the early 1900s. One of the islands was known as Mumba Devi. Today a Mumba Devi temple exists in the Kalba Devi area of Mumbai, built in 1830. The original temple is said to have been built in the late 14th century at the Phansi Talao (Gibbet Tank) along the Esplanade, near the Chhatrapati Shivaji Terminus.

The Elephanta Island Caves, located ten kilometers away in the middle of the harbor, are also interesting. These are reached by getting the launch from the kiosk at Apollo Bunder. Get there early in the morning to be sure you get tickets. The ride is about an hour or so over the water each way. The caves are four temples that were cut out of the rock sometime around 450 to 750. The island used to be called Gharapuri and was renamed by the Portuguese after they found the big stone elephant near the landing. The elephant, which later collapsed, was removed in 1864 and is now on display at the Victoria Gardens. The Portuguese, however, did their best to damage many of the sculptures of this "different" religion, but the size and beauty of what is left is still quite impressive. Although some people say it doesn't come up to the quality of the rock-cut temples at Ellora, they are still quite interesting. However, you may not be all that impressed if you have already seen all the caves I have described so far.

Once the boat arrives at the island, you reach the caves by climbing up a long stairway on the hillside from the boat landing. Along the stairs are many vendors selling an assortment of all kinds of items. At the top of the stairs is one main cave temple dedicated to Lord Shiva. In it you will find a large hallway supported by many columns. There is one small room sanctum with a Shiva *linga* in it. But in the innermost area of the hall, you will see a panel of Trimurti (a three-headed image of Shiva, Brahma, and Vishnu) which is world famous. Many photos of this have circulated in books. Next to one of the entrances is another panel of Arddhanarisvara (Shiva as half-male and half-female). Other carved panels relating to the pastimes of Shiva are also found. Another three main cave temples are also here on the hill and worth visiting. A little museum can also show you pieces of the area and give further insight to the region. To better understand the temples, consider taking a guide. I don't often do this, but at some places it is simply more helpful. But get an official guide at the top of the hill who speaks good English, not the freelancers you see as soon as you get off the boat. Once we are finished here, we go back down the stairs and out to the boat dock to catch the next boat back to the mainland.

The Kanheri Caves are about 42 kilometers north of Mumbai. They are, basically, 109 small Buddhist caves that date from the 2nd to 9th centuries. Not many are all that fascinating and it takes a special trip to reach them. So how much appeal they may have for you remains to be seen. But cave number three, the great Chaitya Cave, has two figures of Buddha that are 21 feet tall, richly carved pillars, and a hemispherical *stupa*. And several caves do offer some interesting aspects, such as 1, 2, 10, 11, 14, 21, 34, 35, 66, and 67, and you can see the coastline from cave 35. It is best to approach the caves from the northern entrance.

Tours of Mumbai are available through the ITDC and the Travel Corporation of India, and the Maharashtra Tourist Development Council. These can take you to a number of places without the usual inconvenience of trying to get around on your own. Or if you know where you want to go and want to take your time, it may be best to simply hire a taxi for the day. But traveling in Mumbai is not cheap. It's a big and congested city and getting around like this will take time and money. Many people use the electric trains, but if you are not familiar with them, they can be confusing. You have to know where you want to go and which train to take and at which stop you need to get on or off. Plus, the number of people that use these in the morning and afternoon rush hours can make them a great place for pickpockets, so you have to be careful with your wallets and things.

Actually, although I was glad to visit Mumbai to see some of the important places and to experience what Mumbai is like, I did not stay more than about four or five days. I simply found the city to be too big, too congested with people, and too expensive compared to other places that I've visited that offer as much if not more with less expense, less congestion, and, in some cases, less trouble. So after I had seen everything I had wanted to see, I was looking forward to our next place of interest, which can be reached by bus or train.

KARLA & BHAJA CAVES

The Karla and Bhaja Caves are about 130 kilometers or a three-hour train ride southeast of Mumbai. Although some people may feel a little disinterested in seeing any more caves at this point in our journey, the rock-cut caves at Bhaja are some of the earliest examples of Buddhist art in this region. Although we have certainly seen the most spectacular of all the rock-cut cave temples in India by now, since our train is traveling right past them, these caves at Karla and Bhaja are certainly worth a day's stop to see them.

We can stop at the Lonavla train station and get settled in a hotel room. Then we hire an auto-ricksha to take us the 12 kilometers to the Karla Cave, which is a couple of kilometers off the main road. The Karla Caves are on a hill which forces us to make a steep, winding and tiring 500 meter climb up to see it. It is a Hinayana Buddhist cave temple made around 80 B.C.E. and is the largest in India. There are a number of smaller monastery caves around the hill, but the largest is the temple, Cave Eight. It has an excavated court in front of the entrance and a tall column on the left side topped with four lions. A modern and less complimentary Hindu Devi shrine is on the right. The front of the hall entrance is a large horseshoe-shaped window. There are images of Buddha that were placed here around the 5th century. The interior has three aisles and rows of carved columns topped with elephants being ridden by embracing couples. At the end of the hall, about 150 feet into the hillside, is a large *stupa* with the usual hemispherical dome, topped by a wooden umbrella with delicately carved patterns. The roof of the cave is ribbed by teakwood beams. This cave is similar in ways to a few of the caves we have seen at Ajanta.

The Bhaja Caves, which are south of the railway tracks by about three kilometers, are a group of 20 caves made around 200 B.C.E. Again you have to take a climb up the hillside to reach them. Most of these are small and designed with a verandah and hall with small cells. One small area has 14 rock-cut *stupas* for various Buddhist teachers. Cave 12 is the most noteworthy and is divided into aisles divided by octagonal columns. The roof is curved and had teak beams. There is also a large, hemispherical *stupa* inside. Cave 19 is a monastery with a verandah and guardian figures on each side of the doors. The verandah has a half-vault roof with wood ribbing. Inside are carved stone panels, one of which shows Surya the sun-god, served by two ladies while riding a chariot, and another panel showing Indra riding an elephant. These are considered some of the earliest of figural art in India that still exists.

Lonavla is considered a hill station where residents of Mumbai go for a break from the city, at which time they also visit the caves. So try to avoid stopping here on the weekends when it can be especially crowded. After our visit here we take a train or bus to Pune if we want to stop there, or we simply keep going by bus to Pandharpur.

PUNE

For those who want to stop at Pune, it is not a holy place in the traditional sense, but there are a few things we can see. It is also a place where we can stay if we want and take a day trip by bus to the Bhaja and Karla caves, rather than staying there. This is a pleasant town, and has the Shanwarwada Palace of the Peshwas built in 1736. However, even though it is a large fortress, it was burnt down in 1828 and now the interior lies mostly in ruins. So there is not much to see, but you can get a good idea of the opulence that this place once had.

If you are traveling by train, staying a night or two, there are hotels right across from the train station of various standards, inexpensive as well as more costly. So just walk across the street and check them out. If traveling by bus, the same holds true for hotels right across from the bus stand. Otherwise, most hotels in Pune can be rather expensive.

A quick trip to the Raja Kelkur Museum can be interesting. It is a four-storey building with a nice and large collection of artistic pieces from the area. It is the personal collection of Shri Dinkar Kelkar. These include large carved wooden doors, musical instruments including both the usual as well as the unconventional, strange locks, miniature paintings, styles of clothing, and other items.

The hilltop Parvati temple, built in 1749, is worth a stop. The hill is not so big, so the climb is not difficult. But it does have a nice shrine to Durga, and offers great views over the city, and also has a small museum of more items of the area. It is said that the last of the Peshwa rulers watched his troops being defeated by the British from this spot. There is also another Panchaleshwar temple that is a rock-cut cave shrine from the 5th century, similar to the Ellora temples. Legend is that it was excavated in one night.

The Gandhi National Memorial is the building where Mahatma Gandhi and his wife Kasturba, along with other members of the India Independence movement were imprisoned. Kasturba died here. Some of the scenes from the move "Gandhi" were filmed in this building. Around the back of the grounds is a place called the *samadhi*, where some of Mahatma Gandhi's ashes have been enshrined.

There is also the Empress Botanical Gardens, which had a few tigers amongst the animals it keeps, one of which was white. And there is the Bund Gardens, which many people use for an evening stroll, but I was not so impressed with either of these places. There is a better Tribal museum not far from the railway station and south of the rail line.

Many people also know Pune to be the location of the commune of the controversial Rajneesh or Osho. Rajneesh was known for preaching in rather unconventional ways, but not directly of any particular traditional persuasion, and was rather uninhibited in sexual norms. This, of course, is hardly any kind of genuine spiritual path, and some people seem to think that it is what lead to the untimely demise of Rajneesh who is said to have died of AIDS in 1990. Rajneesh was notorious for his fleet of 93 Rolls Royces which he had at his commune in Oregon, before the U. S. government deported him on grounds of immigration fraud. The Oregon commune was controversial by itself with all kinds of questionable activities going on as well as power struggles from within the ranks of its leaders.

At the Pune Osho Commune International, only 100 or so disciples remain to operate the 31-acre site. Most of the people there are visitors on holiday, spending a few days engaging in meditation. Up to 8,000 daily visitors pay 40 rupees a day to enjoy the many shade trees and walkways, nice grounds, modern buildings, vegetarian restaurants, the meditation courses, numerous alternative educational programs, and the bookstore that contains all the books and tapes of every lecture that Rajneesh ever gave. However, things are changing. The large Buddha Hall Dhyan Mandir is gone, and numerous lecture tapes and books from the collection have disappeared, and many of his pictures that used to hang throughout the commune have been removed. In fact, it is said that the management of the place is making it more of a tourist resort instead of a shrine to Osho's teachings. There has been some resistance to these changes, but what happens remains to be seen.

The majority of visitors are from such countries as Germany, Italy, England, and America. They average from 35 to 45 years of age and stay in hotels around Pune. You'll notice them by the maroon robes they wear while in the commune, or maroon swimwear and shorts for those engaged in swimming or sports. As usual in India, directly outside any popular place are many vendors hawking all kinds of items to newcomers, of which the maroon robes are a popular item. So if this is the sort of thing you're looking for, Pune is your place. As for me, I'll be traveling on to Pandharpur.

THE ASHTAVINAYAKA YATRA

One thing to mention while we are in Pune is that from Pune a devotee of Lord Ganesh can take the Ashtavinayaka Yatra. This holy pilgrimage is to the eight prominent temples of the self-manifesting forms of Vinayaka or Ganesh that are nearby. All of these images were self-manifested, found already formed without the need of a sculptor. The pilgrimage will take a few days, even by car. They are located in the towns of Morgaon, Siddhatek, Theur, Lenyadri, Ozar, Ranjangoan, Mahad, and Pali. This is the typical order in which most pilgrims visit the towns, but there is a more traditional order in which a pilgrim is meant to see these deities. It goes like this: 1. Morgaon to see Lord Ganesh as Sri Moreshwar, 2. Siddhatek to see Sri Siddhivinayaka, 3. Pali to see Sri Ballaleswar, 4. Mahad to see Sri Varadvinayaka, 5. Theur to see Sri Chintamani, 6. Lenyadri to see Sri

Girijatmaj, 7. Ozar to see Sri Vighneshwar, and 8. Ranjangaon to see the Sri Mahaganapati temple.

When you have *darshan* of these deities, you will see them all covered with thick coats of red sandalwood paste. This builds up with time, sometimes over years, and often obscures the finer details of the smaller deity inside the coatings.

BHIMASHANKAR

Pune is also a good base from which we can travel 110 kilometers north, 50 km northwest of Khed in the village of Bhavagiri, to see the Bhimashankar temple, which is one of the 12 Shiva *jyotirlingams* in India. This is also where we find the source of the Bhima River in the Sahyadri hills, which flows east to the Krishna River. Dakini Bhimashankar *jyotirlinga* is the only *linga* in which dwells Shiva along with his consort Parvati in the form of Ardhaneshwara.

One legend is that Shiva fought and slayed the demon Tripurasura, after which Shiva began to feel tired and, upon the request of the gods, sat on the Sahyadri Mountain. Mother Ganga, who resides in his hair, emerged from his body as sweat and began to flow as a stream. This is the origin of the river Bhima, which is a part of Shiva himself and the same as the Ganga River.

The temple is built in the nagara style, partly bright orange and the other part dark stone. This dates back to the 18th century, with the temple shikara built by Nana Phadnavis. The main *lingam* is in the lower and central sanctum. Other shrines to see here include one to Kamalaja, an incarnation of Parvati who helped in the battle wth Tripurasura, and who is said to have been worshiped by Brahma with lotus flowers. The *ganas* of Shaakini and Daakini who helped in the battle are also honored. Behind the temple is the Mokshakund Tirtha, a pond associated with the rishi Kaushika. A few other points of interest include the Kusharanya Tirtha where the Bhima River starts its flow eastward, and the Sarvatirtha and Jyanakund.

SHIVPUR

South of Pune is the small mosque dedicated to the Sufi saint Qamar Ali Dervish. On the lawn in front of a one story building is a large granite boulder weighing about 120 lbs. Sometimes when visitors come to see the stone, the *mula* of the mosque will ask eleven of them to circle the stone while each one places their right index finger on the stone. While chanting "Qamar Ali Dervish" loudly, the stone rises about six feet off the ground, defying gravity for a second or two. Then it heavily falls to the ground. The same thing happens with a smaller (41 kilograms) stone which requires nine people.

MAHABALESHWAR

This town is 115 km south of Pune or 250 southeast of Mumbai. This is known for two reasons: one, as the largest hill station in Maharashtra with an altitude of 1370 meters (4000 feet) in the Sahyadri range of mountains, and two, as the home of Mahabaleshwar temple, where we find one of the 12 *jyotirlingas* of Lord Shiva. There are a number of other temples in this town that date back to 13th century. These include the temples of Atibaleswara, Hanuman, Rama, and the Krishna temple that is built on the site of the Panchganaga, or the origin of the five rivers known as the Koyna, Savitri, Venna, Gayatri, and Krishna River, which stretches from this place all the way to the east coast and Bay of Bengal.

PANDHARPUR

Pandharpur can be reached by bus from Pune, 250 km (155 miles) Southeast of Pune, or 156 km east of Satara, after visiting Mahabaleshwar. It has been called the spiritual capital of Maharashtra and is where the deity of the Supreme Being is worshiped in His form named Vithobha, Panduranga, or Sri Vitthala. This place is called Bhu-Vaikuntha, the manifestation of the spiritual world on earth. The town is located along the Bhima River, which is considered as sacred as the Ganges and locally known as the Chandrabhaga. There is a short road with many shops on it that connects the temple of Sri Vitthala to the river. There are 14 bathing *ghats* along the river, but the main one is Maha Dvara Ghata.

How Lord Krishna came to Pandharpur many years ago is explained in the *Skanda* and *Padma Purana*. It was while He was living in Dwaraka when Srimati Radharani, His consort from the village of Vrindavan, came to visit Him. But when Krishna's queen, Rukmini, saw how Krishna was dealing more intimately with Radharani than He had with her, Rukmini left Dwaraka and went to Dindirvana, a forest near Pandharpur. So Krishna went to find her, but His apology had no effect. So Krishna went to see one of His devotees at Pandharpur.

This most fortunate devotee was Pundarika, or Pundalika as he is known in Maharashtra. When Krishna saw him, he was engaged in taking care of his elderly parents. Pundarika, being a simple devotee, gave Krishna a brick to sit on and asked that He wait until he was finished serving his parents. So Krishna stood there waiting. In the mean time, Rukmini also joined Krishna and They both decided to stay in Pandharpur and accepted the forms of deities. Now devotees from all over can come to Pandharpur and see Krishna as He stands on the same brick that was given to Him by Pundarika.

When I first arrived in Pandharpur by bus, I asked around for a nearby hotel and found one a few blocks away from the bus stand. Of course, being near the bus station means it's convenient when it's time to leave, but it is in a noisy area. The hotel was simple, cheap, and rather dirty, but tolerable for a short stay. It was late afternoon and I had not eaten much that day, so I got a small meal from a restaurant across the street, after which I went to the Vitthala temple which, when you are not in a hurry, is an easy walk away.

The present Vitthala temple complex faces east toward the river in the center of town. When you approach it from the west, you have to go around it to reach the entrance. There you find many flower vendors and little shops selling the usual assortment of holy paraphernalia, such as photos of the deities, incense, beads, etc. In the very front of the temple on the steps is a brass bust of Namdev, the 13th century poet. People do not place their feet on the step on which the bust is located. It is stated that Namdev wanted to be on these steps in order to receive the dust of the feet of Vitthala's devotees. Out of respect, people come and worship the bust of Namdev, and you can watch as they offer incense, coconut, flowers, or place their heads on the base of the shrine.

Namdeva was a famous saint and devotee poet of Lord Vitthala. The most famous story about Namdeva is when he was a child and was instructed to care for the family deity at home while his father was away. When it came time to offer a plate of food to the Lord on the altar, he expected the deity literally to eat the offering. Namdeva waited to see if the deity would eat, but after a while when the deity still had not eaten, Namdeva went into the deity room and insisted that if the Lord did not eat, he would smash his own head against the wall. Then the deity ate the food, using His own hands to feed Himself. Of course, when his family returned, they expected to see the remnants from the Lord's offerings, so they did not believe Namdev when he told them that the deity ate the offering. Only after they witnessed the deity directly eating the offering were they convinced.

To enter the temple you must go through a gate on the left side to reach the doorway. Inside, you pass by a shrine to Lord Ganesh where you stop and pray that he removes any obstacles in your devotional service. The temple's courtyard is surrounded by a colonnade and in the middle are several altars and a pavilion for Garuda. Crossing the courtyard you will see the aisles where the queue of people line up to enter the temple's main hall. In the morning and on festival days the line of pilgrims can be very long. But in the evening of this ordinary day I was able to go right in with no waiting.

You enter the temple's sanctuary through two columned hallways. Embossed silver plates cover many of the 16 columns and doorways. Although most of the temple dates from the 17th century, parts of it date back to the 12th and 13th century. On either side of the door to the sanctuary are huge images of Jaya and Vijaya who guard the entrance to Vaikuntha, the spiritual world. I had prearranged to get some deity *prasada*, so the temple assistants gave me some deity flower garlands, *tulasi* leaves, a coconut and sugar sweets, which they instructed me to take home and distribute to my whole family. Then I went inside the sanctum to see the deity of Lord Vitthala.

The deity of Sri Vitthala is said to be 5,000 years old and self-manifested, without being carved or installed, as previously related. In the sanctuary you can see Lord Vitthala as He stands on a brick, slightly smiling, and dressed in fine, colorful garments, and wearing a *vaijayanti* garland. His hands are on His hips, His right holding a lotus flower and His left clutching a conchshell. He is a deity of black stone, about three feet tall, and always attended by two or three priests. When you see Him, you grasp His ankles and place your head right on His feet. This is very special because in most temples you can only see the deity from a distance, never being allowed on the altar or touching the deity.

The temple priests take elaborate care of Lord Vitthala starting with *mangala-arati* at four A.M., and then a bathing ceremony using milk, yogurt, ghee, honey, and sugar water. The deity is also given a lump of butter mixed with sugar candy, then another quick *arati* is performed, and then the deity is finished being dressed. Unlike most temples, you can watch the bathing from the queue in the hall. Afterwards, the people are let into the sanctum and you can go up and touch the deity's feet or put your head to His feet. However, in the morning hundreds and even thousands of pilgrims want to see Lord Vitthala, so you have to get there early, move fast, and put up with the crowd.

As everyone exits the hall, the devotees pray to the Lord to forgive any offenses they may have committed. They may also embrace the Garuda Stambha pillar and pray that Garuda will carry them back to the spiritual world at the end of their life. Also in the hall are additional shrines to Rama and Lakshmana, Kashi Viswanatha, and Kal Bhairava. Hanging from the ceiling near the hall's exit is the *Pandurangastakam*, the eight prayers composed by Shankaracarya that he wrote that glorify the qualities and devotees of the Lord when he visited Pandharpur. After we've seen Lord Vitthala, we circle around the main temple to the shrine of Srimati Rukmini, wife of Lord Vitthala, to offer our respects to her. As you wind your way through the halls and carved stone pillars of the temple, you see a few other shrines, such as one to Mahalakshmi, one to Vishnu or Balaji, another for Radha and Satyabhama, and so forth. Then you go out the back door facing town, which means you have to go around the temple and back to the entrance to get your shoes.

Arati ceremonies continue at various times throughout the day, so if your thirst to see the Lord is not quenched, you can go back through the lines again. The lines on a normal day are not long in the afternoon. The deity is given a short rest in the afternoon before there are more *aratis*. Later in the evening after eleven o'clock He is put to rest for the night when the priests chant special hymns for Him to go to sleep.

Anyone who visits Pandharpur will find a spiritual atmosphere very much like Vrindavana or Nathdwara. The whole town is centered around serving Krishna. Everyone helps out, regardless of anyone's background. Being in such an environment can have a lasting affect on one's consciousness and can provide deep realizations of the power of such all-inclusive devotional service.

To get to the river from the temple of Lord Vitthala is quite easy. On your way you will see a grand temple to Lord Dwarakadish on the right. In the sanctum He stands about a foot tall on a small but ornate altar. At the river, which is quite dry during the winter, you will see the temple for Pundalika, which is a Shiva temple. Pundalika's temple, built in the 18th century, is about 500 meters directly east of the Vitthala temple. It is, basically, a funerary shrine that stands in the middle of the Bhima River. It marks the spot where Pundalika spent his final years.

The Vishnupada temple is also in the middle of the river bed connected by a causeway about 1 km south of the Pundalika temple. Within the sanctuary is a square about five feet wide with three boulders that are said to have the footprints of Vishnu or Krishna carved on them. One set is of Krishna standing on both feet, while another set shows Him standing on His left and balancing on the toes of His right foot. This temple is where many pilgrims perform the funeral rites for their relatives. The shoes of Lord Vitthala are brought here on the first day of the Margashirsha month, and on the last day the Lord's chariot is also brought here in a stately procession.

Pandharpur is also a place where several other noteworthy devotees had lived and spread their devotional influence. The famous saint Tukarama lived here during the 17th century and wrote more than 4,500 verses of poetry about the Lord and devotional service. Even now many people read or sing his verses in *bhajans* or *kirtanas*. You will see the *samadhi* tomb of Tukaram near the river not far from Pundalika's temple, which has his image inside. Saint Tukarama is said to have met Sri Chaitanya Mahaprabhu when He was traveling through Pandharpur. Sri Chaitanya stayed for eleven days and saw the Sri Vitthala deity. He also met Sri Ranga Puri, a Godbrother of Isvara Puri, Sri Chaitanya's spiritual master, and had endless talks about Krishna for five to seven days. It was also through Ranga Puri the He learned that His brother, Visvarupa, had left this world in Pandharpur.

Another influential devotee of Sri Vitthala was Jnanesvara who lived here in the 13th century. He translated the *Bhagavad-gita* into Marathi at the age of 16, and made purports so simple that anyone could understand them.

Festivals are held often in Pandharpur. The festival of Sukla Ekadasi (the 11th day of the waxing moon) is held every month. But on the Asadhi (July) Ekadasi day the Dindi (procession) Yatra festival attracts several hundred thousand people. This annual festival draws people from all over the area, many of whom walk on foot to Pandharpur to see Lord Vitthala. The *Padma Purana* explains that on this day the Lord goes to sleep for four months during the rainy season, and awakens at the end of Kartika (in October) when there is another festival. The processions are often organized in groups made up of those who follow different spiritual teachers. They may travel for days, and each evening they gather to perform *kirtanas* and enliven the villages through which they pass. Each group will also have a crew to cook food and distribute *prasadam* to the pilgrims. Finally, the groups converge on Pandharpur which overflows with traveling devotees, and all want to see Lord Vitthala on the special Ekadasi day. During such festival times, the lines for *darshan* at the temple can reach up to 5 km long.

There are many other temples in Pandharpur, which include the Jnaneshvara temple on the north side of town, the Namdeva temple a little way away from the main bathing *ghat*, and the Mallikarjuna temple on the southwest side of town, amongst others. There is also a small Jain temple. It is said that there are more than 1000 temples in the area of Pandharpur of varying sizes, and if you want to see all of them you can go to the local museum in town and get a guide to take you. But many of them are small.

There is also an Iskcon Hare Krishna temple across the river on the bank. The devotees there take care of their own land and cows, and help serve pilgrims on the Ekadasi days. So, all in all, Pandharpur is not to be missed when traveling through this area.

After this visit, we will next take a bus for the very bumpy four-and-a-half hour ride to Kolhapur to see the famous temple of Lakshmi. If we don't want to visit Kolhapur, we can simply take the rough ride to Bijapur.

KOLHAPUR

Kolhapur is another major pilgrimage center in Maharashtra, 225 km south of Pune. It has a number of temples, both Hindu and Jain, from the Yadava period in the 10th and 13th centuries. Nonetheless, it was a Shakti center for the worship of the Shakti or the

Mother Goddess from ancient times. There are also bathing *ghats* along the Panchaganga River. Some people have called this town the Banares of the South, or Dakshina Kashi. However, some of the temples along the river seemed to have sunk into the water and are unusable.

The most prominent temple is the Mahalakshmi (Amba Bhai) temple, which was built in the 7th century by the Chalukya king Karnadeva. This temple has an exuberance of sculptured detail of late Chalukya art. The columned hall has a magnificently carved ceiling divided into eight panels with a standing Vishnu in the middle. You will find a number of different shrines for Ganesh, Balaji, etc, before you enter the central hall. On the main altar is the deity of Lakshmi. She is of black stone, is nicely dressed, stands about two feet tall, and has a beautiful silver altar. She is said to be self-manifested. This temple also was visited by Sri Chaitanya Mahaprabhu during His tour of South India, so we want to have *darshan* and get the blessings of Mahalakshmi.

The Kotitirtha temple, dedicated to Mahadeva, to the east of town and by the side of a lake, is very small but is said to be an important temple. I personally found it to be of little inspiration.

There are other interesting palaces to see in Kolhapur since it used to be the capital of the area years ago. There is the Shahaji Chhatrapati Museum, which is the old maharaja's palace with its clock tower and museum, and the Shalini Palace Hotel. After this we will take a bus 175 km east to Bijapur.

BIJAPUR

It was a long hot ride to Bijapur, after which I was ready for locating a hotel and cleaning up. There are a lot of hotels from which to choose, but most of them are small and dirty. Hotel Mysore, however, does offer a good menu and cold drinks if you need that. The tourist books may recommend a few, like the nearby Hotel Tourist as a decent place to stay, but it was just too dirty for me. Although I spent a night there, the next day I went to Hotel Sanman, across from the Golgumbaz, where I got a double room which was much cleaner, and the restaurant was quite nice. Also, it is a ten minute walk from the train station, which is convenient because I needed to get times of the departing trains, and also because I would be taking an early morning train to Badami when I would be leaving the next morning.

While you are visiting this town, hire an auto-ricksha and have the driver take you to all of the most interesting sights. You can probably see everything of interest in an afternoon. This includes elaborately designed mosques, forts, palaces, and, of course, the usual Islamic mausoleums.

Bijapur is a prominent Muslim town and, thus, is filled with Muslim architecture dating from the 15th to 17th centuries. At least that is what is said. However, the name *Bijapur* is a Sanskrit name, which means that it was once an ancient and flourishing Aryan or Hindu town. Therefore, although much architecture is credited to the Muslims, there is other evidence that indicates that many of these were originally Vedic Aryan designs and structures.

The most famous of all of Bijapur's landmarks is Asia's largest dome, the Gol Gumbaz mausoleum, the tomb of Mohammad Adil Shah (1627-57) and two of his wives, a daughter, and grandson. It covers 1704 square meters and the corner towers are seven storeys tall. You'll see this structure from miles away. If you climb up the stairs to the top of the building, you will be able to get a grand view of the area from the outside, and on the inside you will be in the "Hall of Whispers" located at the top of the dome. The acoustics in the dome make any sound echo ten times for about 15 seconds. The morning is the best time to see the place when few people are there, but after the tours and the children start arriving, it can get really noisy because you can hear every sound ten times. It opens around 6 A.M.

Although the Gol Gumbaz is presently recognized as the tomb of Adil Shah, it appears to be a building of pre-Muslim origin, that it was captured and converted for Muslim use. Evidence has shown that it was an ancient Shiva shrine of the Lingayats, the local Hindu community known for being Shiva worshipers.

For example, the ornamental stone dressing had apparently been peeled off. And the echo effect in the dome had been designed to emphasize the *Nada-Brahma*, the phonetic ecstasy during the great Shivaratri celebrations. Mr. G. G. Joshi, an architect from Nagpur, inspected the Gol Gumbaz and stated that he was convinced that it is of pre-Muslim design built to the specifications of the ancient, Vedic *Shilpa Shastras*, typical of Vedic temple designs. Around the shrine there have been numerous Vedic images and deities that have been uncovered, many of which had been buried in the ground. This was a typical way Muslims tried to rid areas and cities of all signs of previous cultures. Fake graves also would be set up during the Muslim invasions to give a somber religious tone to the captured Hindu buildings to prevent recapture by Hindus and to resist any revived claims to the buildings, and to create support among the local Muslim population. Thus, when the Muslims captured the city they engaged in massive destruction and desolation of Hindu shrines, and converted the remaining buildings for their own use. Muslims used to credit themselves with building such structures to add to their own glory, and in the early days of the Archeological Survey of India, the foolish English accepted whatever history of the building was given to them by the Muslim occupants.

In *The Intelligent Tourist's Guide to the Glory that is Bijapur*, the author, S. Padmarj, observes, "There is no evidence at Bijapur (which is the city with the famous Whispering Gallery and many so-called Muslim tombs, mosques, etc.) of any foreign influence, but very strong evidence of Hindu tradition adopting itself to the Muslim requirements. There is not a detail in the splendid buildings at Bijapur that cannot be explained as the logical sequence of India's living building craft. To understand the buildings of the Muslim Bijapur, the student must first turn to the Hindu Vijayanagara (famous capital of the medieval Hindu empire)."

Herein, we must remember as we tour cities like Bijapur that the historical information we hear may be quite inaccurate, and more than slightly slanted in favor of the Muslim version. The Muslims were invaders. They came to destroy all that was Vedic or Hindu, to enslave and massacre. The Aryans constructed while the Muslims destroyed. Islam spread its faith and religion mostly through force. Therefore, not only were many

Muslim towns and cities, like Bijapur, originally Vedic, but almost all families in India can be traced to a Vedic heritage before they had been forced into Islam over the course of the last several generations or more ago.

Another place in town to see is the Jami-e-Masjid Mosque, said to have been started by Ali Adil Shah I (1557-80) and finished in 1686. It is quite large, the interior has many lovely arches, and it is made to accommodate 2250 worshipers.

The Methar Mahal is down the road and is a little gem with exquisite sculptural work. It is an entranceway for a small mosque. From here we will continue to the Asar Mahal, which once served as a Hall of Justice and used to house two hairs from the Prophet's beard. The rooms on the top floor are covered with flower motif oriented fresco paintings. The central fort, called the Citadel, used to be where you'd find the palaces, gardens, and public halls of the Adil Shahi kings. Most of them are in ruins now, but there are some that will still allow you to get a good idea of how big and elaborate the standard of these buildings were.

Next we can see the huge Malik-e-Maidon cannon. It is over four meters long and nearly 1.5 meters in diameter and weighs about 55 tons. It took as many as 10 elephants, 400 oxen, and many men to bring it to Bijapur and put it into place. It was cast in 1549 using an alloy of copper, iron, and tin by a Turkish officer.

At the far end of town is the Ibrahim Rauza, an elegant building that Ibrahim Adil Shah II (1580-1626) is said to have built for his queen. It has some fine decorative stone carvings and filigree, unlike most of the other buildings in town that are impressive primarily because of size. This is a tomb that houses the graves of Ibrahim, his queen, daughter, two sons, and mother.

There is also the Upli Buruj watchtower which reaches 24 meters high and provides a good view over the area by climbing the steps around the outside.

After my tour was over, I went back to my hotel and had a lite meal, after which I went over to the Gol Gumbaz and sat on a bench to relax, look at the big monument and watch the people. As I sat there, so many people, especially children, had to come up and shake my hand, ask my name, or sit and chat. Some of it was amusing, and some of their antics were a botheration. At one point as I sat there, I was surrounded by a couple dozen children who were sitting around me, staring and making comments. Maybe I was more of a spectacle than the building. But there were a few people, medical students attending the medical college in Bijapur, with whom I had nice conversations. It was quite interesting to hear their views on what it is like living in Bijapur (which they considered quite a boring town), or what they thought of the Indian government, politics, American movies, etc. One boy had a brother who joined the Hare Krishna Movement and was living at the Washington, D.C. temple. What I noticed most was that everyone seemed to be interested in coming to America. But sitting there and meeting so many people was a most educational part of my visit to Bijapur.

The next morning at about 3:45 A.M., after cleaning up and getting ready to leave, I tried to check out of the hotel, but the hotel workers were all sleeping in the lobby and wouldn't wake up, even as I was trying to make noise at the front desk. So I left my room key on the counter and made my way out of the hotel. This is why it is sometimes wise to pay the exact amount for your room instead of expecting change when you checkout. Sometimes the cash register may be locked up at that time and no one has the key, or there is simply no one around to take care of you. As I left the hotel, it was obvious that the whole town was still asleep and no *rickshas* would be available for a ride to the train station. Fortunately, the station was only a ten minute walk away, so I simply walked down the street to get on the 4:10 A.M. train to Badami. It was also fortunate that I travel with only my camera bag and a shoulder bag of belongings. Otherwise, I would have had too much weight to carry. At the train station, there was only one train to board and I had a whole car to myself. Shortly after I got on, I was standing in the train car doorway looking into the night, watching the city lights of Bijapur go by as the train slowly got started and headed to Badami.

As the train continued, we stopped at all the little villages as night turned into day. We passed by many small towns and train crossings where people in trucks, buses, or on scooters, bullock carts, and pedestrians were waiting for the train. You could see school children going to school, and men and ladies going to work, along with tribal women with their heavy silver jewelry and colorful clothes. It was all quite interesting, sitting in the train watching it all go by.

BADAMI

I got into the Badami train station around 8:00 A.M. The train station is located several kilometers away from the town, and you can take a 30-minute ride on a horse drawn *tonga* to reach Badami. The Tourist Bungalow, now called the Challukya Mayura Hotel, is one of the better places to stay, but a more centrally located place is the Shree Laxmi Vilas Hotel. Once I got a bite to eat at my hotel's small cafe, with a very limited menu, I hit the streets to see the temples and sights.

Badami is famous for its five caves, four of which are carved out of the cliff while one is natural. These are located along the south side of the Agastya Tirtha Lake. The natural cave is Buddhist, and of the four man-made caves, one is a Jain temple, another is dedicated to Shiva, and two are dedicated to Vishnu. Cave One (6th century) contains a small square sanctuary with a Shiva *linga* in the rear wall of a columned hall. There are also large sculptured panels at each end of the porch, and outside are small shrines to Durga, Karttikeya, and Ganesh. An 18-armed dancing Shiva is carved on the nearby rock. Cave Two is similar but dedicated to Vishnu with different panel sculptures and motifs, including those of Varaha, Vamana, Krishna, and Vishnu. Cave Three is the nicest because of its elaborate and exceptional sculptures and ornamentation. The columns have medallions on the shafts with amorous couples and lotus ornaments, and the brackets are also quite involved, fashioned as embracing couples or maidens under trees. Around the porch are carved compositions of reclining Vishnu on Seshanaga, Varaha, standing Vishnu, Narasimha, Trivikrama, Harihara, and scenes from the Vedic epics. Cave Four is a smaller and less elaborate Jain temple from the 6th century. Cave Five is a small natural cave with an image of Buddha carved out of the rock in the back. The cave itself is really not so special. It is located on the far side of the lake near one group of Bhutanatha temples.

Besides these caves, there are numerous small temples scattered throughout the village, along with stone inscriptions and buildings left behind by the various people who have occupied this town. These include the Pallava King Narasimhavarman, the Chalukyans, Rashtrakutas, the Kalachuryas, the Yadavas, the Vijayanagara rulers, the Adil Shahi kings from Bijapur, and the Marathas.

Some interesting temples, although small and rather simple, are the two groups of Bhutanatha (Shiva) temples near the lake. This man-made lake, called Agastya Tirtha, is named so because the sage Agastya Muni is said to have meditated by a pool on the hill above. The lake is supposed to have curative powers because Agastya Muni once cured a king's leprosy. During the monsoon season the waters come down from the hill and pour into the lake.

There is also the Lower Shivalaya temple and the Upper Shivalaya (Vaishnava) temple from the 7th century that are reached through rugged steps on the north cliff of town, which exhibits scenes of Lord Krishna and Narasimha on some of its stone panels. The interesting Malegitti Shivalaya temple sits on a lone boulder near the main road north of town and has images of Shiva and Vishnu on the outer walls. The Jambulinga temple dates to 699 and has three shrines, one each to Brahma, Vishnu, and Shiva. The Yellama temple has a multi-storeyed tower and dates to the 11th century. Taking a stone path behind the hill on the northern side of the lake will bring you to a small shrine dedicated to Hanuman. The Archeological Museum is also worth a visit and has sculptures from the area around Badami, Aihole, and Pattadakal. Don't expect to see large temples at Badami. All of them are rather small and lack much in the way of ornate carvings, especially compared to the caves. But plan to spend a whole day to see the main points of interest.

Other temples and shrines can be seen in Mahakuta, 5 km away, which has two dozen Chalukyan shrines to Lord Shiva from the 7th century. Two km away is the noteworthy Naganatha temple.

In Bijapur we had to tolerate the problem of infrequent flow of electricity, but it was even worse in Badami. Sometimes you want to go into a shop for a cold drink, but the coolers have not been working because there has been no electricity. And no electricity also means no fan in your hotel room. And by now, as we head farther south in India, it is getting quite hot, so a working fan and some cold drinks can mean a lot.

PATTADAKAL

While staying at Badami, we can also take a day trip to Pattadakal (29 km away) and Aihole (46 km away). These are both reached by bus, which can be tricky. It is not so easy to make sure you are on the right bus or where you are going once the ride starts when visiting these small towns. Nothing is in English and you practically have to keep asking which bus to take. Then once you find your bus, you are going into the countryside through very small villages, and there are few signs that will indicate where you are or which village you are going through. So you have to depend on someone letting you know where to get off. A better yet more expensive way to go is to hire a car or taxi to take you. Check with your hotel to do this.

Pattadakal was another capital of the Chalukyans in the 7th and 8th centuries. It has seven Hindu temples grouped close together in a large fenced yard to provide a view of the different building styles derived from different regions. Many minor shrines are also located in the vicinity.

The Virupaksha and Mallikarjuna temples (8th century) are the largest and most prominent temples in this town. Both are dedicated to Shiva and have *lingams* in the sanctuaries. They were built by two queens of Vikramaditya II for the victory of the early Chalukyas over the Pallavas at Kanchipuram. They have porch entrances leading into decorative columned hallways. The outer walls have many carved panels depicting such scenes as Shiva's and Vishnu's different forms, as well as Bhairava, Durga, etc. There are also scenes from the *Ramayana* and the *Mahabharata*. Many of the ceiling panels are also beautifully sculpted. The Mallikarjuna temple has sculptures that tell the story of Krishna from the *Bhagavad-gita* and the *Panchatantra*, and the Virupaksha temple has a pillar that displays the story of Ganga Devi killing the Vasus. East of the temples are open pavilions with large images of Nandi. A smaller shrine north of the Virupaksha temple has an exceptional three-dimensional image of Durga.

North of these temples is the Kashivishvanatha temple and the incomplete Sangameshvara temple (both 8th century). Next is the Galaganatha temple which is similar in design to the temples at Alampur. After this are the Kadasiddheshvara and Jambulinga Shiva temples, which have dancing Shiva (Nataraja) images carved on the front panels. There is also a Jain temple in the vicinity dating to the 9th century.

The path from the Virupaksha temple gate along the river leads past the village to the Papanatha temple. This has two halls in front of the sanctum, and carved stone panels show scenes from the *Ramayana*, along with floral motifs and ornate brackets and beams.

Seeing the temples at Pattadakal took me about an hour or so, and though the temples were interesting, I wasn't that impressed with the architecture, and most of the carvings are not all that detailed. I had planned to go back to the Pattadakal bus stand and wait for the next bus to Aihole as a local guide had informed me to do. However, it turned out that even the local residents could not agree on when or if there was any such bus. So I had to take a small van that was acting as a bus and filled with people back to Badami. This was a most cramped and bumpy ride, but in this case I was glad to get it. The only thing to do was to get back to Badami and then take the next bus out to Aihole (pronounced ai-o-lay).

AIHOLE

Aihole (Ai-o-lay) has as many as 100 different Hindu and Jain buildings, some of which are rather fascinating, but most quite small and not so impressive. And as it gets hotter in this part of India, seeing these temples can become rather strenuous. However, these temples show some of the many styles and earliest designs in Chalukyan temple architecture, spanning the 6th-12th centuries. You will see curved towers with elaborately carved motifs and doorways, not to mention the usual carved panels of deities, personalities, and scenes from the Vedic epics. The town is enclosed by a circle of walls with gateways, while both inside and outside the town are temples of different periods.

The most impressive of the monuments include the Durga temple in town, which is the largest at Aihole. It is elevated on a high porch and surrounded by a colonnade. It has a semicircular sanctuary and a tower over it and is entered through a columned hall. However, there is no deity. The sculpture work is some of the best of the early Chalukyan style. The columns are adorned with amorous couples or garlands and jewels. The ceiling panels are also carved beautifully. The outer colonnade has niches in which are deities of Shiva, Narasimha, Vishnu on Garuda, Varaha, Durga slaying the buffalo demon, Harhara, etc.

South of this temple, amongst many others in town, are the Surya Narayan and the Gaudor Gudi temples from the 7th century. And the nearby Lad Khan temple is one of the earliest (5th century) which is named after a Muslim noble who once lived in it. It is a simple, low, flat building which has a porch on the east side, and carved panels and pillars show deities, amorous couples, and the goddesses Ganga and Yamuna are on each side of the entrance.

Farther south is the Kunti Group of four Hindu temples dating from the 7th to 9th centuries. These offer open columned halls and interior sanctuaries. You can find stone panels showing Brahma, Shiva, and Vishnu. South of these is the Hucchappayya Matha, and on the west side of town is the Hallibasappa Gudi from the 9th century.

Taking a path to the top of the hill to the southeast overlooking the town, past a two-storeyed Buddhist temple, brings us to the Meguti temple, from 634 C.E., one of the earliest dated structures in Karnataka. It shows South Indian style architecture, with a Jain image in the sanctuary. It has figures of Parsvanatha, Bahubali, and Mahavira sculpted on the walls. Going back down the hill following the fortifications will take us past the Jyotirlinga Group and back to the Durga temple.

Outside of town in the northeast area are other noteworthy temples, including the Chikki Gudi with exquisitely carved columns, beams and ceiling panels, the Huchimalli Gudi, the Mallikarjuna Group of temples, and the excavated 6th century Ravalphadi Shiva cave temple. The stone work, especially the depictions of Vishnu and Shiva, and Varaha and Durga in this temple are more detailed than some of the others you will find. Farther south of town is the Hucchappayya Gudi temple and the Galaganatha Group of Hindu temples from the 9th-10th centuries.

After we have seen the various temples at Aihole, we'll take a bus back to Badami. Make sure you're at the bus station on time, unless you want to spend the night here if you miss the last bus.

Remember, places like Badami, Pattadakal, Aihole, and Bijapur, are not places of pilgrimage. They have some ancient temples, or what's left of them, but you will not see any wandering *sadhus* or many pilgrims coming to see these places. You may see a few priests and local people at the temples that are still used for worship, but that's about all. These temples usually do not represent the locations of ancient holy pastimes, but mostly show the architectural styles and forms of worship used by the various kingdoms that once inhabited these areas. Therefore, such ruined temples may be of some historical interest, but offer little else in the way of spiritual merit. If you want to see large and fantastic temples, then you should go right into South India, as described in the South India section. There you will find some of the most amazing temples anywhere, most of which are still functioning and often represent or mark the locations of spiritual or historical incidents. In the area of India I am presently describing, you will find that Hampi has a far wider range of temples and historical and spiritual significance than those of the Badami area. So after we are finished seeing Badami and the neighboring towns, we will continue south.

When we are ready to leave, we take a horse drawn *tonga* back to the train station and then wait for the 8:00 A.M. train to Gadag.

Gadag is a place where we can stop if we are interested, which has a few noteworthy temples such as the Trimbakesvara Shiva temple with an ornately carved exterior, three shrines that face the common hall, and a temple of Sarasvati in the rear of the compound. In town is the Someshvara temple. Though no longer used, the ornate carvings are still well preserved. Then from Gadag we can take a bus to Lakkandi, where we can visit and then head toward Hospet and Hampi.

LAKKANDI

Lakkandi is a small village and, again, not necessarily a place of pilgrimage, nor is it a place you may want to stop and see. But I do mention it because we are traveling so close to it and it does have 17 Hindu and Jain temples from the 11th–12th centuries. So if you have time and the curiosity, you may want to stop for a visit. The temples are scattered throughout the town, some down small and narrow streets. But all of them have elaborately sculpted details on the multi-storied and pyramidal structures. The porches and halls have either lathe-turned or multifaceted columns. The doorways are also richly covered with figures and motifs. The Jain temple (11th century) is the largest of the temples, with a pyramidal tower reaching up five storeys. The Kashivishveshvara temple (12th century) is also quite interesting, although incomplete and collapsed in parts. Other temples to see include the Manikeshvara (Krishna) temple, the Kumbhareshvara, Nageshvara, Nauneshvara, the Nandeshvara, and Iswara temples. There's also a museum.

DAMBAL

The village of Dambal is not far away, if you want to check it out, and is reached by a short bus ride. Dambal has the Dodda Basappa (Great Nandi) temple of the 12th century. A multi-storied structure rises above the sanctuary. The building has numerous angled projections that continue up with each storey. The very large polished stone image of Nandi is in an attached *mandapa* hall to the east of the temple. This temple is somewhat similar in design to the exquisite Hoysala temples of South India near Mysore. So if you are going to Mysore be sure to check them out when you get there.

HOSPET & HAMPI

Now we take a bus back to Gadag and a train to Hospet. However, when I went through Gadag, there was much construction at the railroad station and no trains were going from Gadag to Hospet. So I had to take a bus. The bus was full by the time I got to the station but they still made a seat for me by setting a plank in the aisle supported by two seats on either side. So there I sat on a wooden board in the middle of the aisle until a few seats opened up. At least it was better than standing, which I've had to do plenty of times before. Of course, you can easily get to Hospet from Bangalore by taking the daily overnight Hampi Express. It starts in Bangalore and goes to Hubli and will have you in Hospet by around 8 A.M.

Hospet is the best place to stay while visiting Hampi, 13 kilometers away, if you want nice accommodations. Try to get a room at the Malligi Tourist home or the Hotel Priyadarshini, both of which have good vegetarian restaurants. Hotel Nagarjuna is also good. There's not much to see in Hospet, which has a large number of Muslim residents. But the Muslim festival of Moharam brings everyone out to watch the firewalkers who walk barefoot over the hot coals that have been burning for a couple days. When you are ready to see Hampi, you can easily take one of the regular buses from Hospet to the Hampi village bus stop. There is one about every half-hour from early morning to 7:50 at night. The ride takes about 30 minutes or so. However, taking a jeep or car into Hampi means that you also must pay 10 rupees for a vehicle entrance fee on all private vehicles. So add that to whatever price the ricksha driver tells you when going by that means. Only the government buses do not pay such fees, so it is always cheaper to go by bus, which as of this writing is 9 rupees.

If you want to stay in Hampi, there are plenty of small places available, especially if you want to become a part of the simple village life, or if you are on a tight budget. Local residents also rent out rooms, but accommodations are limited and simple. It's a very interesting town and it can be quite an experience to live with the local people for a time.

As you would expect, as the world finds out about a nice place, more people visit Hampi and it has become increasingly commercialized over the years, and everything becomes more expensive. There is still plenty of room so that you can have your own experience here without being too encroached by other tourists, or hawkers trying to sell you something, but that is also changing. However, they have done a good job at keeping the area fairly clean, and new signs now show you how to reach certain temples and destinations, especially if you are going by foot or bicycle. The sites and monuments have also been kept up well.

Hampi was previously known as Pampa Kshetra in the *Puranas* and *Mahabharata*, as well as Kishkinda in the *Ramayana* where Lord Rama met Hanuman and Sugriva and his tribes, with whom Lord Rama planned the rescue of Sita from Ravana. So there is much history here and it is certainly a spiritual power place wherein you can feel the spiritual potency of the area. Hampi (Vijayanagara) was the strongest and largest Hindu capital of the Deccan region from 1336 to 1565. During this time the city was transformed into a fortified capital. It once had a population of more than a million people. Not much of the defense system has survived, but some of the 20 foot high granite walls still remain. Historians and travelers who visited Vijayanagara in its prime agree that it was one of the largest and most powerful and flourishing capitals of the world, larger than Rome. The kings were Hindus but allowed the practice of other religions. In fact, Krishnadeva Raya was a disciple of Vyasa Tirtha who was also a disciple of Madhvacharya. The kings also promoted culture, the arts, and developed new ways of agriculture and city planning. Vijayanagara has quite a history, which we will not detail here, but when it was the capital the kings sponsored the building of many new temples, and that is why there is a wide variety of them. Most of the city was destroyed when the combined Muslim kingdoms of the Deccan invaded the city in 1565. The emperor fled and more than 100,000 remained to be massacred.

There is a lot to see here. If you want to see everything on foot, start early and expect to walk as much as seven kilometers (about five miles). A bicycle rented in Hospet may make things easier for most places. There are footpaths between the sights, and if it's overgrown with plants, just follow the goat trails. Or do what I do, which is to see what you can by hiring an auto-ricksha and then walk to the other places that can be reached only by footpath.

The best place to start our tour of the area is in what is called the Sacred Center near the village of Hampi. The Hemakuta Hill region is first. After you get off the bus, you will see the small temples on the hill facing the south side of the village. Nearby, at one end of town, is the temple of Virupaksha, an aspect of Shiva and his consort, goddess Pampa. The temple has a self-manifested stone Shiva *linga*. Pampa is the goddess that symbolizes the nearby Tungabhadra River. This is the only temple used for regular worship here. Thousands of pilgrims attend the annual chariot festival that celebrates the marriage of Virupaksha and Pampa. Just before the festival you can see the big carts in front of the temple as they are being built. The temple complex is entered through tall *gopuras* or gates, the largest of which rises 170 feet. To me, these tall *gopuras* are a sure sign that we are entering the southern portion of India where they are most common. The outer court contains some smaller shrines, and the inner court is surrounded by a colonnade that has many sculptures along its top. The temple is in the center. Paintings of Shiva adorn the temple ceiling, and the inner sanctuary has a Shiva *lingam* with the face of Shiva on it, and there's a brass Nandi across from it. Watch out for the monkeys that roam in the courtyard because they can be temperamental and may grab your camera or something else if you get too close. Inside the temple are other altars for Pampa, Bhuvaneshvari, and a small altar for the nine planets. All of the priests that attend to the altars are ready to give you *caranamrita* (a few drops of water used for bathing the deities) but also want some coins in return. In the basement of the Virupaksha temple is a shrine with a deity of Lord Vishnu holding a scale, said to be for weighing the merits between the holy places of Kashi and Pampa Kshetra, which wins out.

From the entrance of the Virupaksha temple we turn right and climb up Hemakuta Hill. Soon we can see over the town and can view some of the other shrines, *mantapas*, nearby temples, and the many boulders that make the landscape of Hampi so unique. A little farther up the hill near the road is a simple temple building. As we enter, we can see the monolithic Kadalai Kallu Ganesh deity in a seated posture rising 4.5 meters high. From here as we face south we can go over to the right and find another shrine, a smaller open hall, with another monolithic Sasivikalu Ganesh deity, 2.4 meters high, also sitting. Both of these are striking for the size and detail.

Down the hill, continuing our way to the south is a temple of Lord Krishna built in 1513 by Krishnadeva Raya who reigned from 1509 to 1529. He built it for a deity of child Krishna holding butter. That deity is now placed in a government museum in Chennai. Unfortunately, the temple is a little delapidated and no deity is found in the sanctuary, although you can wander around what is left and view the nice carved stone work on the temple walls, domes, and colonnade, some of which is exceptional. After wandering around the Krishna temple complex, we get back on the road and across from the temple is another area where they are excavating what was an area that was a bazaar in the old town.

From here we simply follow the road to the south until it reaches a field. Then by taking a small road to the right into the field you will find the huge (22 feet tall) monolithic image of seated Lord Narasimha. This is said to have been cut out of a single boulder in 1528, although it could be much older. Though damaged, the deity has four arms and is seated under a canopy of the seven hoods of Seshanaga. Originally, goddess Lakshmi was seated on His lap. Nearby is a shrine with a huge three-meter high Shiva *linga* called Badavilinga. It is permanently surrounded by water that comes through an ancient channel.

All of this can easily be covered by foot, but if it is really hot in Hampi, which it can be from April until late October, then it is not a bad idea to merely hire an auto-ricksha to take you around to those places accessible by road.

I next went to the Sister Stones, which are two huge boulders that lean together. The next stop is the (underground) Virupaksha temple. This is on the west side of the Royal Center. This was dedicated to the guardian deities and served as the king's private temple. It has a number of sanctuaries, colonnades, and courts. This is a low built temple that now gets flooded by water in parts.

South of the Matanga Hill is the Royal Center. Here we find a few palaces where the Vijayanagara rulers lived, and buildings that functioned as administrative and military quarters. It's quite interesting to go through these historic monuments. As you look around the remains of the Vijayanagara capital, viewing the old temples, palaces, and other buildings in the barren landscape, there is a mystical feeling to the area, a reminder of the power and spiritual orientation of the people who resided here so long ago. We can only wonder how much more it may have continued to develop if not for the invading Muslims who forced the residents of the town to flee, giving up this capital forever.

The next stop was the Lotus Mahal, an interesting building where the queen would relax and catch some breezes. It is a graceful two-storied pavilion built with a combination of the Hindu and Islamic styles of architecture. It is called the Lotus Mahal for its recessed archways opening to the sun and the wind like lotus petals.

Not far away are the elephant stables, a huge long building that once housed eleven elephants. There was also a temple nearby. All of this was surrounded by a stone fence that had intermittent watchtowers. Nowadays, this Royal Enclave of the Lotus Mahal, elephant stables and watchtowers cost 250 rupees as an entrance fee for foreigners. But this ticket will also include the Vitthalanath temple, which is where they will also ask for the entrance fee of 250 rupees if you do not already have a ticket. However, the ticket to see both of these places must be used in one day.

Next we come to the Ramachandra temple, known as the Hazara Rama, or temple of 1000 Ramas. This is in the middle of the Royal Center. On the outside of the compound walls are reliefs depicting processions of elephants, horses, militia, dancing girls, etc. On the inside of the walls are many panels depicting scenes from the *Ramayana*. No deity is found in the sanctuary, but you can imagine how the many Vijayanagara rulers used to come to this temple and offer respects to the deity when it was active. Nearby is another smaller double-shrined temple, possibly for Krishna and Narasimha.

Not far away is the large Mahanavami platform on which temporary superstructures were built for the kings of Vijayanagara to view the Dussera festivals. Nearby there are also excavations of what's left of old palaces. A walk away from this is the Pushkarini tank with multi-tiered sides going down to a central pool that was once fed by a water system that collected water from other areas around it.

The next stop down the road is the Queen's Bath, a nice pool house where the queen would bathe. It appeared very plain on the outside but has ornate ceilings and arched corridors with projecting balconies surrounding a central pool inside.

A short ride away is the village of Kamalapuram, and one kilometer away is the Pattibhirama temple, an impressive 16th century complex. It has a towering *gopura* and a large rectangular courtyard, within which is the main shrine in a long elevated *mandapa* hall. Other temples are also in the area. From here we can also wander to the Archeological Museum which has a collection of sculptures from all over the site and is worth a visit.

Another temple is on the road toward Kampli, the Raghunatha temple built on Malyavanta Hill, which is related to the *Ramayana* epic. It was here where Lord Rama and Lakshmana stayed for the rainy season after Sugriva had been installed on the throne. It was also here where Rama and Lakshmana stayed while Hanuman went to search for Sita. You enter the courtyard through two towered *gopuras*. Inside are a few temples, the main one of which has a sanctuary with images in black stone Rama and Lakshmana who are in sitting positions, with a standing Sita, and Hanuman kneeling near Them carved from a boulder. The scene is said to depict how Rama and Lakshmana were dismayed and discussing the means to save kidnapped Sita. Behind the temple complex is a cave temple to Shiva made from enclosing the space in which a large boulder sits on top of several other smaller boulders. So you walk into the white building and then under the big boulder there is just enough overhead room for sitting next to a small Shiva *linga* in the center of the room. It is on the hilltop, which offers great views of the surrounding area.

Down the hill from here heading west is Madhuvan, which has a little temple of Hanuman. It was here where the monkeys stopped to enjoy the gardens of fruit after Sita had been found. From here you can take the road toward the Tungabhadra River by about 2 kilometers, and then go left to the Vishnu Vitthala temple. However, approaching Hampi from this direction also requires that you pay another 10 rupees for the entrance fee, even though you may have already paid the fee for the main entrance.

Going this way back toward Hampi we pass by several smaller temples and coconut groves until we take a left and arrive at the Vitthala temple. This temple complex is considered one of the most splendid of the monuments at Hampi. It has a variety of architectural styles and very fine stone carvings. Though parts of it are in ruins, it is nonetheless quite impressive. Tradition has it that it was built for a deity that was brought from Pandharpur. The temple is in the middle of the courtyard, which includes smaller shrines as well. The temple is not a tall building and the tower over the sanctuary has a hemispherical roof. The sanctuary holds no deity, though its outer walls are full of carvings. There are 56 pillars in the dancing hall, each of which has been carved out of a single granite block with a cluster of granite columns which give various musical tones when tapped. Within the temple, on the columns, walls, and ceilings, are remarkable stone carvings of animals, motifs, foliage, etc. In front of the temple is the well-known and delicately designed stone chariot with an image of Garuda. Three elaborately carved *gopurams* give access to the complex, and a colonnaded street runs from the entrance to another impressive temple with carved reliefs of scenes from the *Ramayana* on the gates. Besides the central temple, there is also a meeting hall and a lovely marriage hall which have very beautifully and ornately carved columns. These are all quite fascinating and worth the visit.

Not far from here is what's left of the King's balance in which there once was a scale where the King would weigh himself against food to give to people or brahmana priests.

Our final stop is a small temple near the picturesque Tungabhadra River where people have picnics with friends and relatives, bathe in the river, or simply relax after seeing the sights. This is near a spot that also overlooks the ruined bridge that crosses the river that is said to have been built by Lord Rama, Lakshmana, and Hanuman when they started on their way to rescue Sita. All that's left now are the numerous stone supports.

I then paid my auto-ricksha driver and took the footpath back toward Hampi. Now we can walk back toward Mantanga Hill. The path was hot but very interesting. It took me past trees, rocky hillsides, piles of boulders, more ancient temples, and so on. There was an old and deserted, multi-storey temple to Lord Narasimha, the half-man and half-lion incarnation of Krishna. Across from this was the natural and ancient cave where Sugriva hid Sita's jewels after she dropped them while being kidnapped by the demon Ravana. This is the area called Kishkinda in the *Ramayana*, where Rama connected with Sugriva and his tribe to rescue Sita. Remember, in Nasik we saw where Sita had been abducted. Now we see where she dropped her jewelry.

When I found the cave, there was an old *sadhu* talking to a Westerner inside. The *sadhu* had lived in the cave for over 30 years. It was very interesting talking with him. He told me of a time when the river flooded and the whole cave was covered by water. At one point I began explaining the spiritual significance of the cave and the area to the Westerner, since my English was better than the *sadhu's*. The old sage liked the way I was explaining things so nicely that when I thought I should stop, he would say, "Go on, go on talking."

After some time the sage had to go somewhere so I continued down the path and found the ancient Acyutaraya or Tiruvengalanatha temple. This is to the east of Matanga Hill which is called Rishyamukha Mountain in the *Ramayana*. This temple was built under the authority of Achyutadeva Raya. Though much of it is ruined, some of the sculptures are still in good shape. To the north of the hill is the Kodandarama temple, which is said to mark the spot where Lord Rama crowned Sugriva, as described in the *Ramayana*. A large deity of Lord Rama is inside the temple. After looking around this large and deserted place, there are two ways you can go. You can keep going along the river, which is a pleasant route by the rocks near the river and then through the trees to make your way back to the central bazaar area of Hampi. Or you can go to the western side of the Acyutaraya temple, which is the east side of Matanga Hill. There you will see a path where you can make the climb up to the top of Matanga Hill.

Matanga Hill requires a steep climb up along the rocks, some of which have been cut into steps, but it offers great views around the area. Once you reach the top of the hill, there is the small Virabadra temple. It is painted white with a small hall of pillars and a shrine room with a few images in it, one of Virabadra. There is also a small stairway that leads to the roof, upon which you reach one of the highest points in the area. You can spend some time here looking over the whole area of Hampi and the Tungabadra River to the north. Some people like to be up here for the sunset or sunrise. However, if you climb up in the afternoon and wait until night, you must be cautious for the climb down to make sure you do not fall, so a flashlight in the darkness can be helpful.

I took the climb down fairly slowly to enjoy the views over the area and the Acyutaraya temple. Once I reached the bottom, I continued around the path on the north side of Matanga Hill and found a small old Hanuman temple. It was built like a cave against the rock and had a nice life-size image of Hanuman on the wall carved as a bas-relief and painted. This is called the Yantrodara Anjaneya temple, which is the location where Hanuman first saw Lord Rama and Lakshmana.

Then I kept wandering until I found the path to the main street of town. I stayed on top of the hill in a large stone shelter and reflected on how a person can feel the vibrations of ancient activity in this now tiny village. It's a most mysterious place, yet simple and small. It has interested and attracted many people to come and see what is left of the ancient Vijayanagara kingdom. Today, many young foreigners from around the world visit this old town.

As I stood there a young man from Scotland walked up and I talked with him for a bit. This is one of the pleasures of traveling: meeting other travelers from other parts of the world and sharing in their experiences of India and wherever they come from. He said he was staying in Hampi, but the heat was getting to him. He also related how the spiders and scorpions, some of them quite large, were starting to come out of their rock shelters, and soon the snakes would be coming out as well. He felt it was about time for him to travel on, maybe toward the north.

After talking with the man, I started walking down the hill and then between the long stone corridors on each side of the street. I walked toward town and got to the bus stop just minutes before the bus left for Hospet. The bus generally fills up for the evening ride back to Hospet, so you want to be there on time so you can get a seat if you are getting tired after a long day of lots of walking. Then we will be back tomorrow to see more of Hampi and go to Anegundi village.

ANEGUNDI

While we are still visiting Hampi, Anegundi is another place we can visit. From the Raghunatha temple on the outskirts of Hampi we keep going straight along the road to the Tungabhadra River. There you can cross the the river in small round boats to the other side to reach Anegundi village, the original Kishkinda. This is next to the construction of the new bridge. You can take the boats for 10 rupees (5 for locals) to reach Anegundi village, where there are several points of interest to see. You can also reach this by going past the Vitthalanatha temple a ways and then taking a left at the crossroads. After a short walk or ride, you will come to the river crossing.

A visit to Anegundi may best be done as a separate day's project since getting there and walking around can take some time. After exploring Hampi for a day or two, you can visit Anegundi the next day.

As we get off the boats and then make our way into the village, after about 20 to 30 minutes we come to the old Ranganatha temple where worship still continues. It is a small temple complex with a lovely little temple in the middle. Through the hall we enter the sanctum where we see a small Vishnu deity about three feet long reclining on Seshanaga. There are some lovely paintings of Vedic divinities on the walls in the hallway. In the back of the temple on the right side is a separate shrine to Lakshmi. While I was there, absolutely no one was around, so it was very quiet except for the children's school nearby.

Not far from the temple is the samadhi tomb of Madhvacharya's disciple Narahari Tirtha. However, you may have to ask around for directions.

As you keep walking through town you will pass under an old stone structure with a road going to the left. You can take this road by foot, or you can walk a little farther and see some benches in front of a small Lakshmi temple. This is the bus stop where you can get a small bus that comes by for the 3 kilometers to be dropped off at the road that leads to Pampa Sarovara. Or you can take it another one-half kilometer to the base of the hill that has the white Hanuman (Anjenaya) temple on top.

For Pampa Sarovara, as the road curves to the left, there is another road that turns off to the left that takes you around the rock hills where Pampa Sarovara is located. You cannot see this from the road since it is surrounded by rocky hills on three sides. Once you walk around the last bend, you see two *kunds* or ponds and a temple building on the side. One *kund* is quite lovely and filled with water lilies. It is a very refreshing place to sit and relax for a time. It was here at Pampa Sarovara where Rama and Lakshmana met the old woman ascetic Sharbari. She had offered fruits to Them and pointed the way to Rishyamukha Mountain. Five hundred years ago on His tour of the south, Sri Chaitanya also bathed in this lake while visiting Hampi. Above Pampa Lake is a hill upon which is a cave where Shabari had lived. Indian pilgrims, especially families, often have a picnic next to the lovely water kund. In fact, while I was there one friendly Indian family came to picnic and insisted on sharing their food with me. It was quite refreshing, and I was getting hungry at the time anyway. So it was a very pleasant experience.

The Pampa Ambika temple next to the *kund* is small and dark inside. In the sanctum of one room, the priest said that the deity is of Lakshmi. In another room there are two shrines, one had a Shiva *linga* and another had the image that looked like Ambika, another name of Durga.

When we are finished visiting, we can head back toward the road and easily see the highest hill in the area not far away. If walking, you can take a shortcut to the road rather than backtracking down the lane. Just follow the road around the rocky hill to the first left and take that. It is actually part of a driveway to a farmhouse, but do not take it that far. Then just take the next right to the path that follows the small irrigation canal and that takes you through the field and to the road where you will be much closer to the entrance of Hanuman hill, which is now in sight.

This hill is the place of Hanuman's birth, the Hanuman Janmasthan, noted by a white temple on top, locally called the Anjaneya temple. You must climb 600 steps to reach the summit, which will also take you past Kesharitirtha, the cave where Hanuman's father, Keshari, had lived. This cave is about half-way up and a marker along the stairway will show where it is. Then just off the stairway to the right on the hillside you can see it. This is a large cave-like area underneath a ledge in the rockside of the hill, which creates a shelter.

As you continue to climb up the hill, you will pass many monkeys that hope you have some food for them. They will not bother you much, but they will take your bag or shoes if you give them a chance. Small local boys may also try to attach themselves to you to be your guide and later ask for rupees for their assistance. Once you reach the top, there are great views over the area. In the main sanctum of the temple, a red-colored deity of Hanuman is carved on a huge boulder. A priest takes care of the worship here. In the opposite shrine is Hanuman's mother, Anjana.

When we are finished here, we make our way back down the hill and keep going west along the road to the little village. There are a few quaint places to stay here if you are interested. It is a pleasant walk, though you may have to ask once in a while for the proper road to take to reach the boat crossing at the river. It will take you past banana trees and a little ancient but ruined temple, and the stone supports for what was an ancient bridge that crossed the river. When you reach the boats, they may ask for a large fee at this place if you are a Westerner, such as 20 or 30 rupees, and even more if you want a ride to the Kodanda Ram temple which is a little further upstream though in sight. Just ask for a basic or short ride across and stick with the 10-rupee cost. If there are a few other people who need a ride across, then that price should not be a problem. You can then easily cross the river here and walk back to Hampi along the path. When going to Anegundi, you can also cross the river from this place as well, but you have to be careful, especially by the Kodanda Ram temple where the boatmen ask foreigners for absurd prices, even as much as 300 to 500 rupees for one person. It is not even worth talking to them at that price.

In any case, we can go back to Hampi for the next bus back to Hospet where we will now plan where to go for our next destination. If we get back in time, we can also make reservations for the Hampi Express toward Bangalore.

HARIHARA

If, however, you have the time and desire, before leaving Hospet you can take a short day trip to the town of Harihara, which is easily reached by bus south of Hospet. Harihara has the Sri Hariharesvara Hoysala temple, built in 1223. More was added to it in 1268 by Soma, who built the Somnathpur temple near Mysore. The deity in the sanctum is the very unique Harihara, half-Shiva and half-Vishnu. When we are finished here, we can continue south.

TADPATRI

From Hospet we can go to Guntakal and over to Tadpatri. Tadpatri can be reached by bus if going to Nandyal or Allagada to Ahovalam, from which it is 120 km southwest. It has two interesting temples: the Venkataramana temple (16th century) dedicated to Lord Vishnu (1 km north of the bus station), and the Ramalingeswara temple for Lord Shiva (1 km north of the previous temple). Both temples have outstanding sculptures and impressive *gopurams*. The stand of the Shiva *linga* is filled with water.

PUTTAPARTHI

On the way to Bangalore some people may be interested to stop at the town of Puttaparthi, where you can visit the residence and ashrama of Sri Sathya Sai Baba. To get there you exit the train, if not taking a bus, at Dharmavaram or Anantapur, or even a closer town of Penukonda, and then ride to his nice and large estate. Puttaparthi is about 110 miles from Bangalore, which offers a special train (the Prasanthi Nilayam Express) to go to the nearest station for Puttaparthi.

The town lies in a valley surrounded by mountains which reflect the hot Indian sun like an oven. So temperatures can go up to 110 or 120 degrees Fahrenheit in the shade during summer. The town is a very small and quaint village with a few of the usual stray dogs and wandering cows. The main street is lined with shops and small shacks. Photos of Sai Baba are displayed in the storefronts. Along the way, particularly as you approach Prasanthi Nilayam, Sathya Sai Baba's ashrama, there can be a heavy traffic jam of people and vehicles all going to his place. So you should try to get there early. From the main street you will turn left through an old gate in the stone wall which surrounds Prasanthi Nilayam, and then you'll be within the ashrama grounds.

Many people stay in the ashrama, which has separate quarters for men, women, and guests. However, there is generally no specific program for engaging the majority of guests, so many people bide their time sitting around waiting for the next time Sai Baba gives *darshan* or they go wandering into town. The conditions of the ashrama are simple for some of the Westerners who visit and who often are used to the comforts of Western culture. So some guests may stay for some time while others leave shortly after arriving.

You'll hear the chanting of *bhajans* as people await Sai Baba's appearance when he gives *darshan*, which he does twice a day around eleven A.M and five or six P.M. He comes out to greet the crowd, holds up his hand to bless everyone, and then goes back up to his quarters. Sometimes, especially at festive or significant occasions, he will give a talk. There is no altar, only an image of Lord Krishna in the center of the *darshan* hall. There may also be an *arati* ceremony. After these *darshans* the people can do as they like. Often hundreds or thousands of people wait to see him in front of the temple in which he lives, so it is likely you will not get very close to him. So you may appreciate that at times they have used video monitors to project his image onto big screens. Sometimes he will pick out a few people with whom he will give an interview. Otherwise, he may wait a few days before granting interviews with guests or he may see them at least before they leave, especially if they are staying in the ashrama for some time. But the continuous stream of people who wish to see him can make this rather difficult.

During such interviews it is not unlikely that he will manifest something with a wave of his hand, such as a medallion, a ring, *japamala* beads of wood or crystal, or photos of himself, candy, and *vibhutti*—sacred ash. Regarding these manifestations, or miracles as some people call them, Sai Baba says they are not magic or mystic *siddhis*, but they are the power of God, and his will brings the object in a moment. Many people agree with this and feel that Sai Baba is an incarnation of the Divine, and that these manifestations are proof of that. The stories and witnesses of Sai Baba's manifestations are quite varied. It has also been said that he is able to read minds, see the past and future, manifest himself many miles from where he is, be at many places at once, assume different forms, stop rainstorms, create winds, cure illness, etc., all of which are common in powerful mystics or *yogis*.

However, not everyone agrees with this. Some people feel that this is all trickery, like a magician doing magic for fame and fortune, or that he hides the things he manifests up his sleeve. Others say that these manifestations serve no real purpose in connection with spreading spirituality for the benefit of humanity. And there have been those who have become completely disillusioned with him. So it seems that everyone has their own opinion.

For the faithful, Sathya Sai Baba (born November 23, 1926) is accepted as the incarnation of Shirdi Sai Baba, a Muslim saint who also distributed sacred ash to his devotees, but from a lit fireplace, not from his open hand. Sathya Sai Baba is also said to be the manifestation of both Shiva and Shakti. As Shirdi Sai Baba is said to have been Shiva alone, Sathya Sai Baba is both Shiva and Shakti. And he has said that in the future he will incarnate again as Prema Sai Baba and will then be Shakti alone.

One of the main controversies surrounding Sathya Sai Baba is his claim to be God, or Krishna, Rama, etc. In this case, Sai Baba says that people should just meditate on him. In *Sathya Sai Speaks* (Volume II, page 219), he says that we are all the God of the universe, and our identity as body, mind, and soul is but a dream. He also claims that we are all God and are meant to realize this, but he is a special soul because he has already realized that he is God and he is just playing a *lila* or pastime in his role as Sathya Sai Baba. Sai Baba has also referred to himself as the Lord amongst all Lords and that he has complete mastery over every aspect of the universe. He has also stated in a discourse given on Christmas Day, 1972, that he is God the father who sent Jesus into this world, and that Jesus declared that God would come again and His name would be "Truth" (Sathya).

Some people accept all of this, and some people don't accept any of it and claim that he is misleading people with his mystic performances and his talks of being God. There certainly is much debate over these premises amongst the various schools of thought. But his other teachings about the need for vegetarianism, spiritual practice, *bhakti* (love and devotion for God), cleanliness, austerity, the need for *kirtans* and *bhajans* (the hearing and chanting of the Lord's names), helping the poor, protecting women, etc., are all good and very much in line with the general Vedic view. Therefore, some people accept him as a genuine spiritual teacher while others argue otherwise.

LEPAKSHI

While we are heading south toward Bangalore, or by taking a day trip from Bangalore, there is one more temple town that we can visit, which is Lepakshi. It is only 29 kilometers south of Penukonda and about 85 miles north of Bangalore and 17 kilometers east of Hindupur. We can stop at Hindupur and get a room for a couple hours to store our things, visit Lepakshi and then continue to Bangalore. Or we can see it while staying in Bangalore because it is easy to get a morning train to Hindupur. We just get up early, check the train schedule, and get a ticket for Lepakshi. The train is at 6:45 A.M. and arrives in Hindupur at 9:10. From Hindupur we get a motor ricksha to the bus station and get on the next bus to Lepakshi. There's one about every half-hour or less. The bus stops in the center of Lepakshi town, which is only several blocks from the Virabhadra Shiva temple.

Lepakshi is said to be where Jatayu fell after having fought with Ravana, as described in the *Ramayana*. The *Skanda Purana* describes this place as one of the 108 important pilgrimage sites for Lord Shiva. Here we find the Virabhadra temple that is located on a little hill called Kurma Sailam because of its shape like a turtle.

It was Virupanna, a Vijayanagara governor of Penukonda, who used state funds to build it in 1530. Though externally it is rather plain, this temple complex is in a walled enclosure, entered through a *gopuram* gate on the north side, and contains many well preserved sculptures and beautiful frescoed ceilings. The paintings, for which this temple is especially known, depict the popular stories of Lord Krishna and Lord Rama from the *Mahabharata*, *Ramayana*, and *Puranas*. The detail and vibrant colors of the dress and facial characteristics are outstanding. The stone carvings display deities, sages, animals, guardians, musicians, dancers, plus 14 forms of Shiva. On the sides of the temple entrance are carved figures of the goddesses Ganga and Yamuna. A boulder on the east side is carved into a coiled serpent with multi-hoods sheltering a granite *linga*.

The principal deity is a life-size Virabhadra carrying weapons and bedecked with skulls, and is housed in the main sanctuary. Another shrine for Maheshvara and Uma is partly cut out of a boulder on the east side of the main temple. A shrine to Lord Vishnu is also found here. The sage Agasthya is said to have installed the *linga* and stayed for sometime. From the sanctum there is part of the cave that is said to be where he lived.

A distance of 200 meters east from the temple is an image of Nandi, Shiva's bull carrier, which has been carved out of a single granite boulder and is said to be the biggest in India, at 20 feet tall and 30 feet long. It faces west, looking back toward the temple.

The name Lepa-akshi means the "village of the blinded eye." The story is that the treasurer of the King of Vijayanagar used the King's collected taxes to build the temple. When the king returned to an empty treasury, he ordered his treasurer to be blinded as punishment. The treasurer blinded himself and smashed his eyes on the wall, leaving two dark stains, said to remain there near the Kalyana-mandapa. Thus, the name of the village.

I was very happy to have visited this temple and took numerous photos of the carvings, pillars, paintings, etc. You can take photos of most everything but the deities, which is normal. When we are ready to go, we just go back to the bus stop, get on the bus back to Hindupur, and from Hindupur, get another bus back to Bangalore. Make sure you inquire as to where in Bangalore to get off as the bus keeps going to the south side of town, while the train station is on the north side.

TUMKUR, SHIVAGANGA

From Hindupur we can get a train into Bangalore, but if we want, we can travel by bus to Tumkur to visit Shivaganga, which is northwest of Bangalore by about 40 miles. Or, once again, we can just take a day trip out of Bangalore by train to Tumkur. Just on the way there from Bangalore, or southeast of Tumkur is the village of Shivaganga. The bus stops 10 miles from Tumkur, then you walk 6 or 7 miles to the hill of Shivaganga, which may be a bit much for some pilgrims, especially if you have done most of the pilgrimage described so far. Anyway, this holy hill (5000 feet in height) has been a popular pilgrimage place. Depending on which angle you view the hill, a person can see it as a huge Nandi bull, or Ganesh, or a *lingam*. The temple of Sri Gangadhisvara is situated in a cave-like structure. Here the Shiva deity is sunk 30% in the earth inside the cave. When ghee is offered to it and poured over it during *abhisheka*, it turns to butter, which is a rare phenomenon. It is then said to possess medicinal qualities.

Other shrines in this temple include those to Chandikesvara, Dikbalakas and the Navagrahas (nine plants), and a Sri Chakra that was established by Adi Shankara. On top of the hill inside a cave is a shrine to Sri Virupakshesvara with a natural spring known as Patala Ganga (underground Ganga). There is also has a prominent Narasimha temple.

From Tumkur we can easily get a train or a bus back to Bangalore.

BANGALORE

Bangalore is our next and last stop on our tour of the holy places of West India, and now we are entering South India. Seeing South India is a whole separate tour in itself with many amazing places to visit and appreciate, which I have already described in the section on South India. Bangalore is not necessarily a place of spiritual pilgrimage, but it is a most fitting place to end this tour. If we have taken this tour as described herein, or even part of it, we can reflect on how fortunate we have been to experience this part of India and enter into its spiritual traditions and legends.

We get into Bangalore by train and walk to a hotel that is just around the corner from the station. Once our visit in Bangalore is complete, we can either continue our journey through the south, or prepare for returning home. We can fly back to Delhi or, if we wish to travel by train, we can take a train to Chennai, which is the best place for booking the faster connecting trains. Once we reach Chennai, we go straight to the Indrail Pass Office (for foreigners only) and book a place on the evening train to Delhi, which takes about 32 hours. It's a long but interesting ride. Or if we still have time to stay in India, we can take a tour of the Eastern portion of India, which is also described in the section on East and Central India. India has much to offer. You merely need to decide on how much of it you want to experience.

The Hawa Mahal, or Palace of Winds. A famous landmark of Jaipur, originally built so the queens could overlook the activities of the day below.

Some of the beautifully carved marble columns leading to the sanctum of the Jain temple, Ranakpur.

The tall and ornately carved Tower of Victory at the Chittorgarh hilltop fort that displays many of the pastimes of Krishna. Even in the interior you will find elaborate carvings as the stairways twists and turns to the top.

Interior of Cave 19 with an image of Buddha at Ajanta.

The monolithic image of Narasimha at Hampi.

Another of the mural paintings of the life of Buddha in the Ajanta caves, especially in caves 1 and 2. Other caves have images of Buddha or cells where the Buddhist monks lived and studied or meditated.

The great temple of Lord Dwarakadish (Krishna) at Dwaraka. This site goes back over 5000 years.

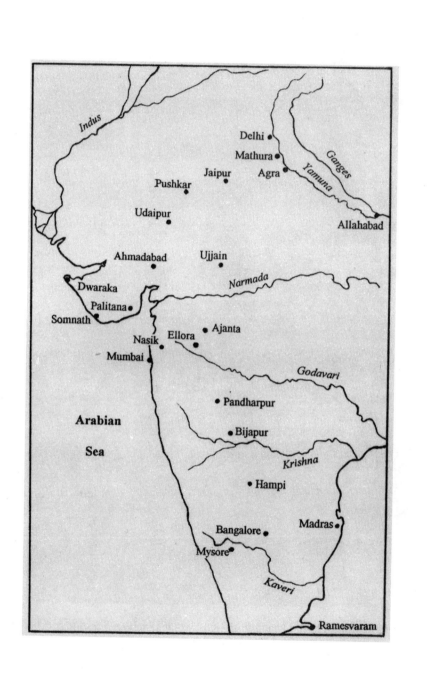

▼

The Major Historical and Holy Places of Northern India

Seeing spiritual India is like a pilgrimage into spiritual dimensions. And Northern India has some of the most important holy places in India. This includes the mountains of the Himalayas, which are known all over the world for being an area of sages and ancient sites, many of which are described in the *Mahabharata*, *Bhagavata Purana*, and other classic texts. This has been where many people have ascended into lofty levels of consciousness and spiritual experience. Specific places include the holy site of Kuruksetra. This is where Lord Krishna sang the sacred *Bhagavad-gita* just before the start of the Mahabharata War, along with other places relating to the Vedic legends of the universal creation. Also in Northern India is the sacred site of the Sikhs at the Golden Temple in Amritsar. Or you can visit the holy place of the Tibetan Buddhists at Dharamsala where we find the residence of the Dalai Lama. These and other important places that carry spiritual significance we'll describe on our tour of Northern India.

Even if you do not see all of these places, it can be fascinating to learn about and know the locations where many of these legends originate. And we are only describing the most important of the holy places found in this region. There are many more smaller ones that are not included in this tour, especially in the area of Himachal Pradesh. Most of these sites and temples are small in size, especially when compared to the large temple complexes we have seen in the south. Yet, many of them are nonetheless quite exquisite in craftsmanship, artwork, or in the wood or stone sculptures that we find.

We will first start our travels in Shukratal going north from Delhi, and then journey on up into the Himalayan Mountains. Traveling into this part of the mountainous region allows us to go back into history as well as experience the reason so many spiritual seekers have come here for thousands of years. This area abounds with legends. The unique beauty, peace, and high energy of the land also help us to further our spiritual development and insights into the purpose of life. This is where various higher dimensions intermingle with the earthly plane. You will see many *sadhus*, yogis, and sages, some of whom are very powerful and who are in tune with these higher realities. So if the opportunity arises, get a little of their association.

The grand views of the tremendous mountains will inspire as well as humble us before this awesome display of God's energy. This area is full of lush forests, flowering meadows, significant temples, and points of spiritual importance, as well as the tallest mountains in the world. Some of the mountains you will see include Nanda Devi (25,645 feet), Dhaulagiri (26,810 feet), Annapurna (26,504 feet), and farther south you might see Everest (29,028 feet). These alone are quite breathtaking. Simply by traveling through this area you may feel extremely fortunate and a sense of wonder and achievement. For some, this pilgrimage is but a dream, and for others it is but a once in a lifetime experience. So while you are in this region, remember to take some time in the solitude of the mountains, or in a quiet cave, or a peaceful meadow or forest, to meditate and contemplate your place in the universe and the meaning of your life. Sometimes you have to get away from things to get closer to your self.

The name "Himalayas" means the "land of the snows." But its nickname is "the playground of the *devas*." And those who are advanced sages can, indeed, perceive the divine dimensions in which the demigods exist. So we will make our way first toward this area of lofty heights in both geographical considerations as well as our inner consciousness.

SHUKRATAL (SUKARA-TALA & SHUKTEERTH)

From Delhi, the first important holy place we can see is about two-thirds of the way between Delhi and Haridwar. It is a four to five hour drive, and about 86 kilometers before you get to Haridwar. The little town sits on the banks of a branch of the holy Ganga (Ganges) River, where it has cut a swathe through the rocky region. This is a special place where Shukadeva Gosvami spoke the *Srimad-Bhagavatam* (*Bhaguvata Purana*) to Maharaja Pariksit 5000 years ago.

First of all, the village and the road to get to it are so small that they do not show up on most maps, so it is not easy to find unless you know how to get to it. But it is about an hour east of the city of Muzaffarnagar, where you can get a bus from the local bus stand that will take you there. One leaves about every hour. Or hire a car to drive you. The ride takes you over a bumpy and narrow road where it can become so congested that traffic can come to a halt in the three small villages that you go through along the way. The first village along the road is Morna, which is part of the legend of Pariksit that we will describe shortly. Then after some time there is a fork in the road and an arch over the way to the left that leads to Shukratal. A short drive later you enter the town itself. The bus will take you to the local bus stand or drop off point. But as you enter the town, the first place you reach is Shukteerth and the Bhagavata Peeth Shukdev Ashrama. If you stop here, you walk or drive up the hill to the ashrama's parking area and see the large Akshay Vriksha tree that is 5100 years old. This is the exact place where Shukadeva Goswami spoke the *Srimad-Bhagavatam* to Maharaja Pariksit. The ashrama is built around the tree.

To comprehend the importance of this place, you must understand the history. The *Srimad-Bhagavatam* is considered the most important literary work of Srila Vyasadeva, who was the author and compiler of most of the important Vedic texts, such as the *Vedas*, *Upanisads*, and *Mahabharata*. The *Bhagavatam* is said to be Vyasadeva's own commentary on all of his own writings. At one point, Mahamuni Ved Vyasa was dissatisfied with all of his writings. At that time the great sage Narada Muni arrived and encouraged him to explain the Vedic truths by elaborating on the pastimes, character, qualities, and names of the Supreme Being, Sri Krishna, for the benefit of humanity. Thus, Vyasadeva accepted this instruction and composed the 18,000 verses of the *Bhagavatam*, which included all of the wonderful pastimes of the Supreme Lord.

These ultimate spiritual truths revealed in *Bhagavatam* were first revealed by the Supreme Lord to Brahma. Brahma passed them along to the great sage Narada Muni, who then gave it to Krishna Dvaipayana Vyasa (Vyasadeva). And Vyasa wrote the *Srimad-Bhagavatam* and also passed it along to Shukadeva Goswami, who also spoke it to Maharaja Pariksit.

How the narration between Shukadeva Goswami and King Pariksit happened is a story in itself, which shows the importance of not only the *Bhagavatam* but of the holy place of Shukratal. King Pariksit is the son of Abhimanyu and the grandson of the great warrior Arjuna who was Lord Krishna's friend and the person who heard the *Bhagavad-gita* from Lord Krishna. One day while King Pariksit was hunting, which many kshatriya kings did in that era, he became thirsty and tired. He was about 60 years old at the time and while looking for water came across the hermitage of the sage Shamik. However, the sage was in deep meditation and was completely unaware of the King's presence. When the sage did not respond to the King, the King did not know the reason for the sage's silence and felt insulted. The King, feeling his importance was being neglected, responded by taking a dead snake with the end of his bow and garlanding the sage with it. This was certainly an insulting and sinful act by the King toward the sage.

At that time, the corruption and confusion of the age of Kali-yuga was beginning, and the effect was felt by the actions of all involved. What happened next indicated all the more that the influence of Kali-yuga was spreading. Shringi, the young son of the sage Shamik, was playing with his friends, the children of other sages. But when he heard about the incident with his father, he became angry at King Pariksit. Shringi then took some holy water from the Kaushaki in his hands and cursed the King, saying that within seven days the poisonous snake Takshaka would bite the man who had insulted his father, thus killing him.

When Shringi returned to his father's hermitage and saw the dead snake on his father's shoulders, he began to weep loudly. On hearing the sobbing of his son, Shamik finally came out of his trance. He opened his eyes and saw the dead snake around his shoulders, but like an elevated sage, he did not consider it important and merely threw it away. He then asked his son why he was crying. However, on hearing the entire story, the sage Shamik felt remorse at what his son had done. He knew that the King had done a shameful act, but in a moment of weakness. Then he chastised his son, telling him that he had committed a great sin, giving such a grave punishment for a small mistake, and that he was very immature to consider the King an ordinary person.

At that time the King returned to his palace. Putting his crown aside, he realized his mistake and felt saddened by treating the innocent sage like a wicked person. He wondered how he could be absolved of this sin. As he thought in this manner, a disciple of the sage Shamik came to Maharaja Pariksit to warn him of the curse that was put on him by the sage's son. The King, accepting his fate as a blessing, handed over his kingdom to his son, Janamejaya and went to the banks of the Ganga to fast for the seven days before he was to be bitten by the snake. The news of this traveled rapidly and brought many sages along with their disciples to where he was fasting. On the pretext of making a pilgrimage to a holy place, these saintly men actually purify the places they visit.

The King was glad to see all the holy men assemble near him and worshiped them by bowing his head as they arrived. Then the King asked them, "O great sages, what is the most important duty of one who is about to die? Please consider this."

All the sages who had gathered around King Pariksit deliberated on this question and also decided to remain there until he left this world.

The great sage Shukadeva, the 16 year old son of Vyasadeva, was wandering nearby, free from all cares and completely content within himself. Wearing the garb of an *avadhuta*, one who is completely carefree from all rules and social standards, and as though others had neglected him, he was being followed by children. At that time he appeared on the scene in the presence of the sages and King Pariksit.

Even though Vyasadeva and Narada Muni, Shukadeva's guru and grand guru, were also present in the assembly of great sages called *brahmarsis*, *rajarsis*, and *sadhus*, they all rose from their seats to pay their respects to him. King Pariksit also addressed Shukadeva: "You are the supreme among saints, therefore I would like to ask what should a man do who is about to die? What should he hear, chant, remember and worship?"

Shukadeva at first responded, "The question you have asked is glorious because it is beneficial to everyone. The answer to this question is the prime subject for life and is approved by all transcendentalists. At the last stage of life, one should be bold enough to not be afraid of death. But one must cut off all attachment to the material body and everything pertaining to it and all such desires."

In this way, to answer the request of Maharaja Pariksit, the nectar of the *Bhagavata* flowed from the lips of Shukadeva Goswami in a way that seemed to them that they had never heard it before. This question and answer format, the discussion of all of the most important of spiritual topics, became the *Srimad-Bhagavatam* as we know it today.

After the whole *Bhagavatam* had been discussed, Shukadeva concluded that for a person who is suffering in the fire of countless miseries and who desires to cross the insurmountable ocean of material existence, there is no vehicle more suitable than cultivating a transcendental taste for the narrations of the pastimes of the Supreme Personality of Godhead.

This was the second time the whole *Bhagavatam* had been recited. The first time was when Srila Vyasadeva had recited it at his ashrama at Badrinatha. [Vyasadeva recited it once to his son Shukadeva, and also recited it to Ganesh who had written it down.] The second time it was recited was at Shukratal. The third time was when Suta Goswami recited it to the many sages at Naimisaranya.

After the week long recitation of the *Bhagavatam*, King Pariksit thanked Shukadeva Goswami for his merciful instructions, and said: "Now I have achieved the purpose of life. You have personally related to me the narration of the Supreme Lord and have revealed to me what is most auspicious—the knowledge of the supreme personal feature of God. I am now full of transcendental knowledge and self-realization, and my ignorance has been eradicated. I no longer have any fear of Takshaka or any other living being, because I have absorbed myself in the purely spiritual Absolute Truth. Kindly allow me to absorb my mind, purified of all lusty desires, within Him and to thus give up my life."

Then Shukadeva, along with the other sages, departed after blessing the King. Pariksit then laid the *darbha* grass on the bank of the Ganga so that the tip of its stalks faced east and he turned himself toward the north. The King settled his mind within his spiritual Self, and he became as stationary as a tree. As the time came when the curse was to take effect, the snake bird Takshaka, who could shift into any shape he wanted, approached Shukratal in the guise of a brahmana to bite the King.

As Takshaka went, he met the brahmana Kashyapa Muni who was traveling in a hurry. Takshaka asked where he was going. Kashyapa Muni, who knew the science of counteracting poisons, said he was going to meet King Pariksit because he could neutralize the affect of the snake bite. To test the sage, Takshaka exposed his fangs and bit a green tree which turned to ashes in seconds. Then Kashyapa chanted some mantras and the tree was restored and as green as before. So Takshaka asked whether the sage was going in order to receive rewards for his knowledge, and the sage replied to the affirmative. Takshaka said that he could reward Kashyapa more then the King, if he would only go back home. So the brahmana Kashyapa took much wealth from Takshaka and returned home.

The place where this incident occurred is known as Bheraheri, which is five miles away from Shukratal. The place where Takshaka asked Kashyapa to return home is called Modna which later became known as Morna, the village on the road four miles from Shukratal as we come from Muzaffarnagar.

Legend continues to explain that when Takshaka got to the area of King Pariksit, he was not allowed to enter. So he changed himself into a caterpillar and entered one of the fruit baskets being taken to the King's area. On reaching the King, Takshaka came out of the fruit, and assumed the form of a brahmana and easily approached the King, and while the King was in devotional meditation, bit him. As everyone looked on in horror, the King's body was immediately turned to ashes by the fire of the snake's poison. Thus, Maharaja Pariksit left his body and, immersed in the Absolute Truth of the Supreme

Being, felt no pain as he entered the spiritual world. This is why the whole area of Shukratal is full with the sweetness of *bhakti* or devotion for Lord Sri Krishna. This is also the importance of hearing the powerful and fully transcendental literature of the *Srimad-Bhagavatam*. It can deliver one from the pangs of material existence and into the absorption of the spiritual pastimes of the Lord.

It is said that only after many lifetimes of performing pious acts does one achieve the opportunity of being able to hear the *Srimad-Bhagavatam*. Also, wherever the *Bhagavatam* is read, Lord Krishna will manifest. It is also said that all of the holy rivers, *kundas* or ponds and lakes, all sacrifices, and the seven holy cities of Ayodhya, Mathura, Haridwar, Kashi (Varanasi), Kanchipuram, Avanti (Ujjain), and Dwaraka, and all the holy mountains are present where *Srimad-Bhagavatam* is discussed. This is only a small portion of descriptions on the power found within the vibrations of the *Srimad-Bhagavatam*. Thus, the holy place of Shukratal gives importance to the sacred text of the *Srimad-Bhagavatam*.

What you will find at Shukratal is first the Bhagavata Peeth Shukdev Ashrama. This is built around the 5100 year old Akshay Vriksha tree which sits on top of the hill where 80,000 sages of all ranks gathered to hear Shukadeva speak the *Bhagavatam* to Maharaja Pariksit 5000 years ago. It was under the branches of this tree where Shukadeva and King Pariksit sat. The tree is quite large, towering up to 150 feet, with branches spreading in all directions, even coming out of the sides of the hill just below the tree. One branch has a nub coming out of it that is in the shape similar to Lord Ganesh. The ashrama includes a number of shrines and deities within its complex, including one close to the tree that has the images of Shukadeva sitting and speaking to King Pariksit. Others include those for Hanuman, Shiva, Devi, Rama, along with a *yajnashala* or hall for Vedic rituals, a Sanskrit Vidyalaya or center for teaching Sanskrit, a reading room, and a dispensary. The lecture hall, the Srimad Bhagavata Bhavan, is for holding continuous discourses and week-long *kathas* or recitations on the *Bhagavata Purana*. Many pilgrims come here from all over India to participate and can also stay the night in the ashrama. Across from the tree is also the Samadhi tomb of Swami Kalyandevji Maharaja, who established the Shukdev Ashrama and worked to bring back the significance of Shukratal. He also helped bring the sacred Akshay Vriksha tree back to good health. Therefore, much of the present day condition and recognition of Shukratal can be credited to him. He entered Mahasamadhi on July 14, 2004, having been born in Kotana village in Uttar Pradesh in 1876. The Bhagavata Peeth Shukdev Ashrama is now under the guidance of Swami Omanand Brahmachari.

From the top of the hill near the tree you can see over the town and the other temples that are here. Going down the hill along the street you can easily find the Hanuman temple, which has the world's tallest image of Hanuman at 75 feet high, standing outdoors over the main shrine, and built in 1687. This is presently managed by Swami Naistika Brahmachari Sri Keshwananda Ji Maharaja. To the right of this temple going down the street are shrines for Lord Rama, and another of Sri Sri Radha-Krishna, plus two more for Shiva and Durga.

If we go back to the street and around the corner in the direction we came from we will see the Ganesh temple which has a tall outdoor image of Ganesh, which stands 35 feet tall.

As we continue to explore the town, there are many more temples and ashramas of various sizes, mostly small but quite devotional. There is the Pracheen Ganga Mandir, a Ram Krishna Mandir, the Gayatri Teerth, and others. As we make our way through the central part of this small town and to the east we come to the Ganga, which is a quiet and peaceful river here compared to the swift and powerful river we find at Haridwar and Rishikesh. Many pilgrims take a holy bath here. However, this is a branch of the Ganga that flows next to the village, while the main branch of the Ganga is 3 to 4 kilometers away. It is in this area where King Pariksit gave up his body.

As we make our way back, there are other temples we can visit, and you can see the tall outdoor images of the 101 feet tall Shiva in one place and Parvati in another that stands 51 feet tall. In another area is the Maheshwar ashrama, a *goshala* that takes care of several dozen cows which sells and distributes milk to a number of the temples. Many sannyasis or renunciant monks wander the streets here and visit this place in the evening. Farther out of town there are small temples and ashramas where swamis may stay for the peace and quiet that is found here, which is especially nice for meditation and pondering the spiritual significance of this place and the importance of the *Srimad-Bhagavatam*. There is a long list of other ashramas and *dharmshalas*, along with a tourist rest house, that are located here. My visit to this sacred village was short, but I could see where a person could easily stay for days and experience the peaceful but spiritually powerful nature of this holy place. One word of caution: A local tradition, in line with the way Maharaja Pariksit died after being bitten by the snake, is that anyone who receives a snake bite in Shukratal is sure to meet with death.

HARIDWAR

Haridwar, population 190,000, 225 kilometers northeast of Delhi, is easily reached by bus from New Delhi or Shukratal. Or, if visiting Vrindavana, you can get an overnight bus straight from Vrindavana to Haridwar.

"Haridwar" means the door to Hari, the Supreme Lord Sri Vishnu. It is also known as Hardwar for its relation to Lord Shiva. It sits on the banks of the Ganges River, known as Mother Ganga. Many years ago it used to be called Kapilsthan because Kapila Muni had lived, meditated, and performed penance here. Haridwar is also known for being where the Ganges leaves the mountains and enters the plains. This is the reason Haridwar also has the name of Ganga-dwara. It is one of the seven major holy places of India and has plenty of spiritual significance. This is where Vidura was instructed by Maitreya. Daksha performed his great sacrifice nearby at Kankhal, which was attended by all the great demigods. It is about four kilometers south of the railway station. The Dakseswara (or Dakshaprajapati) Mahadeva Shiva temple at Kankhal, the oldest temple in Haridwar, marks the place and commemorates Lord Shiva coming to help his wife, Sati. The contemporary temple was built in 1962. The central image in the temple is a Shiva *lingam*. The little pit in the Daksha Mahadeva Mandir is said to be where Daksha had his original sacrificial fire.

Sati Kund, on Kankhal Jwalapur Road, is one of the oldest of the significant places in Haridwar and marks the spot where Sati (Durga) left her body and where she burned herself after being insulted by her father, all of which is described in the *Srimad-Bhagavatam*. Lord Nityananda also stopped here on His tour 500 years ago. However, the *kund* is in the middle of nowhere on the road and not developed in any way. It is overgrown with greenery and water lilies and can easily be overlooked.

To explain the legend in brief, Durga's father Daksha, son of Brahma, did not like Durga's husband, Shiva. So when Daksha had his huge ritual, he did not want Shiva to be there. When Daksha had entered the arena, all sages stood in respect except Brahma and Shiva, which offended Daksha. So Daksha cursed Shiva to not partake in the rituals. Thereafter, Daksha and Shiva both left the arena.

Afterwards, Daksha did not invite Shiva to the ritual, but Durga still wanted to go, even against the advice of Shiva. After arriving, she underwent insults by her father, Daksha, toward her because of being married to Shiva. So she self-immolated herself in fire, thus committing Sati. After Shiva heard about this, he became extremely angry and created and sent a huge black demon, Virabhadra, and his followers to fight and destroy Daksha's ritual. He also cut off Daksha's head and threw it into the fire. When Shiva came and gathered Sati's body, he was grief stricken and carried her body wherever he went. To relieve Shiva's grief, Lord Vishnu cut Sati's body into pieces with His chakra and wherever they dropped became Shakti-peeths, or places of power where people go to worship Shakti, or Durga. The Daksha Mahadeva Mandir is said to mark the place where the fire of Daksha's Vedic ritual was located.

Haridwar is known for its many temples, more of which are always being built. One popular temple is the Mansa Devi temple, another form of Durga, located on the hill above the city. You can walk up the hill or take a cable car which gives you a way to get a great view of the city and the mountains and plains that surround it. The deity in the temple is small, but the temple is organized and often crowded.

Other holy temples in Haridwar include the Chandi Devi, Hanuman, and a temple to Hanuman's mother, Anjani Devi, on top of the Siwalik Hills about four-and-a-half kilometers away, and south of the river. You can easily see it from the Ganga. You can also reach this hill top temple by means of a cable car. Also, the Narayana-shila, Bhairava, and the Mayadevi temple is one of the oldest in Haridwar. The Mayadevi deity is a three-headed, four-armed female in the act of killing a prostrated demon. Other temples in Haridwar include the Shravannath Mahadeva, Neeleshwar, Navagraha, Bharaha Khamba, and Bolagiri. The Bilvakeshwar Mahadeva temple is where Parvati performed austerities to get Lord Shiva as her husband. She ate only leaves of the Bilva trees, which are still respected here for the part they played in this pastime. Not far away is a temple marking the place where the Ganges originally appeared in order to supply water for Parvati to drink.

Another more modern temple in Haridwar is the Bharata Mata (Mother India) Mandir. It was consecrated in 1983 and stands eight stories tall. The first floor contains a standing image of Bharata Mata and a map of India on a raised platform. The second floor contains the Shrine of Heroes, dedicated to those who were active in India's independence movement, such as Bhagat Singh and Shivaji. The third floor is dedicated to great women of India's legends and recent history. The fourth floor is the shrine of Indian saints from various religions. The fifth floor is the assembly hall. The sixth floor contains the Shakti Shrine with various images of the goddess. The seventh floor is dedicated to Lord Vishnu with many examples of His forms. And the eighth floor is the Shiva Shrine with many images of Shiva and various gods and goddesses associated with him.

This temple is located along a road in the eastern part of Haridwar. The road has numerous temples that one can visit, several of which have diorama displays which are quite popular with the pilgrims. There is one that is a replica of the Vaishno Devi temple, and has a route that you take in which you must cross water, crawl through caves and narrow passages before you finally reach the sanctum. Visiting it is said to equal the same merit as going to the real Vaishno Devi temple in Jammu. There is also a temple of mirrors nearby which has many deities with mirror thrones and Krishna and Arjuna on a chariot with horses, all made of colored mirrors.

One of the holiest places in Haridwar is Har-ki-Pauri, where all pilgrims come to bathe in the water of the Ganga River. Some people believe that this is the location where the celestial waters of the Ganga flow into the river. Therefore, the river is known as the Ganga from this spot onward. As the pilgrims bathe, they may hang onto chains or rails in the wall to stable themselves in the swift current. If they get carried away by the water, there are also chains hanging from the bridge which they can try to grasp. Otherwise, the water, especially if it is high, can take them downstream a ways before they can reach a point of getting out of the river. The pilgrims come here first to bathe before going on the northern pilgrim tour of Char Dhama, the four major places farther north.

The Ganga at Har-ki-Pauri is actually a canal that channels the water to the side of the city. The main branch of the river is a little ways away. Imprints of Lord Vishnu's footprints are found on a wall under the water here at Har-ki-Pauri. One of the priests can help you find them. There are many little shrines and temples here for Ganga Devi, Haricharan, Vishnu, Shiva, Parvati, and others. Every evening around 6:30 P.M. you can see the *arati* ceremony to the Ganga as the priests offer large ghee lamps to the river while *kirtan* music goes on with banging hand cymbals and gongs. This is a major event and lots of people turn out to see it. It creates a very festive atmosphere every night. Many pilgrims and *sadhus* or holy men attend this. So get your seat at least a couple hours before it starts, or they may also close the bridge to pedestrians so you can't cross. You may also pay a priest a small sum to assist you in doing your own *puja* or worship to Mother Ganga. He will gather the items and then conduct the ritual while telling you what parts of the prayers and mantras to repeat, as you offer flowers and a ghee lamp or a small leaf boat with flowers and lamp to the Ganga. You can see many pilgrims do this, and some of these small leaf boats can be quite fancy. It is considered most beneficial to do this, especially if you are continuing up into the mountains to see other holy places along the Ganga. The southern end of this *ghat* is where people pour the ashes of their deceased ancestors into the Ganges so their existence becomes purified.

The most auspicious days to bathe here are the full and new moon days, plus Ekadasis, all solar and lunar eclipses, and the full moon during Kartika (Oct/Nov). The first day of Vaisaka (April/May) is also important because this is said to be the date when the Ganges first appeared here, and it also marks the beginning of the Hindu solar year.

The Kumbha Mela is a month-long festival that is very important and marks one of the most auspicious times to bathe here. It is held at Haridwar every twelve years when the planet Jupiter is in Aquarius and the Sun enters Aries. This festival is, indeed, timeless and dates back thousands of years. A previous festival was in April/May of 1998. Over two million people and sages attend this festival in Haridwar. After six years the Ardh Kumbha Mela is held at the six year interval, which is a much smaller festival. Other sacred bathing places include Neel Dhara at the main branch of the Ganges, and Gourikund, which is a small holy well.

Heading south from Har-ki-Pauri along the Ganges we will reach Gau Ghat, where it is said that bathers can be purified of sins, even up to the killing and eating of a cow. Vishnu Ghat marks the spot where Lord Vishnu once bathed. About a half kilometer south of Har-ki-Pauri is Kushavarta Ghat, where Dattatreya did penance many years ago by standing on one leg for a thousand years.

About half a kilometer upstream from Har-ki-Pauri is Bhimagoda Kund. This is said to have been created by a blow from the knee of Bhima, one of the five Pandavas, when he needed to provide water for his wife and brothers. Nearby is where we will go to get a ricksha to Rishikesh, unless we take a bus.

About six km north of Haridwar on the banks of the Ganges is Sapta Rishi Ashram where the Ganges divided itself and created seven small islands so it would not displease the Seven Rishis who were meditating there at the time.

Haridwar is known for having many ashramas and places of study. But if you want to stay at an ashrama to study yoga or Hinduism, Rishikesh is much more pleasant. Haridwar is a nice place to visit to see the temples and holy sites, but parts of it are like a typical big, noisy, and congested city.

RISHIKESH

Rishikesh, 24 kilometers away from Haridwar, is our next stop. From Haridwar we can take a bus or get a auto-ricksha from near Bimagoda Kund on the eastern side of Har ki-Pauri. With a population of around 75,000, it is a smaller, quieter, and fun place to go. It is a place in which you see the spiritual atmosphere and influence wherever you look. You will find good food, good water, clean air, a pleasant climate, plenty of temples, and many wandering *sadhus*, sages, and pilgrims. The town got its name from the time when Lord Hrishikesh, Vishnu, appeared here to grant *darshan* to Raibhya Rishi when he was performing austerities. The demons Madhu and Kaitabha were also killed here by Lord Vishnu.

One of the main temples is the Bharata temple in the central part of town, dedicated to the deity of Lord Narayana. This temple is only a half kilometer from Triveni Ghat, the main bathing *ghat* in town. This *ghat* is said to be where the subterranean Yamuna and Sarasvati meet the Ganges. This is also where the *shraddha* ceremonies are made to the forefathers, and where the funeral pyres are made. North of the Bharata temple beyond the Chandrabhaga River is the Balaji and Chandramouleswara temple. The architecture is in the South Indian style and it is managed by the board of the famous Tirupati temple in South India. The Shatrugna temple, dedicated to the youngest brother of Lord Rama, is about four-and-a-half kilometers from downtown Rishikesh.

One of the nicer places to stay is in the Swargashrama area on the east bank of the Ganges across the Sivanand or Ram Jhula suspension bridge. There are some very pleasant temples, ashramas, and guest accommodations here. The Divine Life Society, or Sivananda Ashrama, is just north of the bridge and offers many facilities for the spiritual aspirant from yoga classes and lectures that anyone can attend, to longer term programs for which you have to enroll beforehand. By the bridge, just after crossing it, is a small temple for Ganga Devi. You can watch the evening *arati* to the Ganges River here every evening around 6 or 7 P.M. Another nice temple is the Parmath temple. It is near the clock tower and has many diorama exhibits of the different incarnations of Krishna and Puranic legends. It has a lecture hall for Vedic discourses, spoken mostly in Hindi, and a variety of programs are held here attracting many pilgrims. It is headed by Swami Chidanand Saraswatiji Maharaja, who is a prominent guru in the area. It also has a nice central temple with a large deity of Visvarupa, Lord Krishna's universal form, which is one of the few I have seen in India. It also has 300 rooms for pilgrims. The kitchen also provides good and reasonably priced meals for those who sign up for them. They also have their own Ganga *puja*, which includes many nice devotional *bhajans*, and is attended by many people.

Beyond the Parmath temple going downstream along the Ganga you can find the International Vishwaguru Yoga-Vedanta Academy, or the Sri Ved Niketan Dham. It is a two-storey orange and yellow building in a courtyard surrounded by the ashrama rooms where you can stay. It offers a place for tourists on a low-budget, but also training in the practice of yoga if you are interested. The resident guru is Sri Vishwaguruji Maharaja Mahamandaleshwar, but most of the classes are given by Swami Dharmananda.

Also in the downstream area is the Maharishi Yogi Ashrama where the Beatles stayed for some time. However, it seems that if you don't have previous arrangements for visiting, the guard at the gate will not let you in. It is mostly for Indian pilgrims these days.

High on the side of a hill behind the Swargashrama area is the Bhutna Kailashanand Shiva temple, which has shrines on each of its several floors. You climb up the stairway to see them all, and from where you can get some nice views over the town of Rishikesh. The Tut Walla Baba Ashrama is beyond this temple. Continue going up the hill past a large ashrama on the left. After a bit you will come to a small bridge going over a stream, continue another 350 yards, until you see a small stone gravel path on your left. Climb the stone steps to a brick and tin-roofed building. This covers the entrance to a cave. Here Swami Shankardas, a humble bearded sage, gives informal teachings in yoga and meditation.

Another ashrama on the way to Rishikesh from Haridwar, just before we get to town, is that of Neem Karoli Baba. It is located under the forty-foot image of Hanuman.

Although there are no accommodations, you can visit. The Omkarananda Ashrama near the Rishikesh taxi stand can also provide courses in yoga studies. Aside from these ashramas are many others that you find out about by asking around. So there are plenty of places where you can learn about yoga or the Vedic culture of India. There are also traditional and orthodox schools that are only for the more seriously minded students, such as the Kailash Ashrama, which is a traditional institution strictly for sannyasis in the line of Shankaracharya.

The area around the Ganges River has got some nice sandy beaches for swims in the cold river. Large boulders are scattered along the shore on which you can sit and be warmed by the sun, or sit in meditation in the evening, which many people do. It can be a very mystical experience to sit near the flowing Ganges in these Himalayan foothills, under the stars and moon, especially as you see other sages also meditating in the twilight. There are also lots of nearby woods that you can walk through, past ashramas and residences of the local monks and renunciants. And the days are warm and the nights are cool. The best place to eat is the open air Chotiwala Restaurant. However, it may be really crowded around noon, so nearby restaurants are also good. Wandering cows will walk by looking for a little food. You can see the children on the bridge throwing bits of food into the river feeding the schools of large fish, which you can see when the water is clear. There are rows of holy beggars along some of the lanes, and foreigners and tourists are quite common. In the evening you can see some of the wandering mendicants who make a little cooking fire after they have taken whatever money they have received from their begging and purchased vegetables to cook for their meal. Later, they will be rolled up in their cloth bedding to take rest for the night along the Ganges or on the steps near the temples or shops. You can also walk along and see old *sadhus* in their rooms near the Ganges around Ved Niketan, maybe sitting on their small bed, with pictures of the deities on the wall, a few clothes hanging on a line, while they chant or read sacred books. Some of these old sages live permanently in Rishikesh, while others stay for a short while before continuing up into the mountains or elsewhere.

The Lakshmana Jhula area is only three kilometers upstream from Rishikesh, a pleasant walk away. This is where Lord Rama's brother, Lakshmana, performed penance, commemorated by the Lakshmana temple. And Rishi Kund is said to be where Lord Rama and Lakshmana took bath to purify themselves from killing the demon Ravana, who was also a brahmana. There are some small old temples as well as large modern ones in this area. Also, you will not want to miss the seven storied temple with the diorama exhibits. Up in the hills about 12 kilometers away from the Lakshmana Jhula bridge is the Neela Kantha Mahadeva temple. It's a four hour walk or a jeep ride up the hill. This is where Lord Shiva is supposed to have meditated after swallowing the poison that was manifested when the demigods and demons churned the ocean of milk in pursuit of the nectar that gave immortality.

So there is a lot to see and be a part of in the Rishikesh area that is certainly a part of the traditional culture of India.

DEHRA DUN

Dehra Dun, population 375,000 and growing, is only about 30 kilometres north of Rishikesh, a pleasant bus ride away. It is the capital of the newest state of Uttaranchal, so it is a growing and developing city. It has most of the conveniences that you may need after a stay in the mountains, such as internet cafes, medical facilities, post office, or for exchanging currency, or equipment to pick up for going into the mountains. Most of the main hops can be found along the busy Rajpur Road with the Clock Tower marking the cener of town at one end. It also has a nice climate when trying to escape the heat of the plains of India. It is not necessarily a holy place, but there are a number of small temples and Buddhist monasteries as well.

The places you may want to see include the Forest Reseach Institute Museum located in a large 500 hectare park and a beautiful building of the British Raj. You can see the institute's six galleries of exhibits and its museum by taking a six-seater from the clock tower to the institute. There is also the Wildlife Institute of India and the Survay of India, and the Rajaji National Park 5 kilometers southeast of Dehra Dun covering 800 square kilometers. The Wadia Institute of Himalayan Geology is also found here, which also has a museum of rocks and fossils. The city does have a strong military presence, not only because of its location but because of the military academy that is here. The Ram Rai Darbar is a mausoleum made on the order of the Muslim Aurangzeb for Ram Rai, son of Har Rai, the seventh Sikh guru. But Ram Rai did not follow his father and formed his own sect.

One of the interesting temples in Dehra Dun is the Tapakeshwar temple. This is a cave temple dedicated to Shiva. It is located on the banks of the Ton River. The cave has a low ceiling, which drips water, but has several shrines within it, including the central *lingam* which is bathed by water from a nearby stream which flows over it. By crossing the bridge over the river you can find another cave, though it is narrow, with a shrine to Vaishno Devi inside. Another temple in Dehra Dun is the Lakshman Sidh temple.

MUSSOORIE

With a population of about 29,000, it is a small but popular hill station just about 34 kilometers up from Dehra Dun. You can easily get a bus from Dehra Dun to either Gandhi Chowk, the Library bus stand, or Kulri Bazaar, the Picture Palace bus stand. The best attraction of Mussoorie is simply its location, especially being high up in the hills where people can get away from the heat of the plains during summer. It sits on top of a horse-shoe shaped ridge, 6560 feet above sea level. There is not that much to do here except relax and go for various walks or pony rides around the area that offer great views of the surrounding mountains and valleys. Treks and tours into the surrounding hills and mountains can also be arranged from here. There are plenty of hotels in various price ranges for tourists. The high tourist season is May to July, but it can be cloudy on an average day in the rainy season, which means you won't be able to see much of the surrounding hills during that time.

The Mall is the social center of town where you can find the usual shops with lots of Tibetan trinkets and jewelry. People come here to hang out. You can get the cable car here to the summit of Gun Hill, which is 7,000 feet above sea level, which offers great views of the neighboring mountains, and even those farther away such as Nanda Devi, and the Kedarnath and Badrinath peaks, which can be seen on a clear day. You can also take excursions to locations some distances away from Mussoorie for a day of adventure. One such place is the Surkhanda Devi temple, which is 28 miles (45 kilometers) outside of town. It is the highest point in the area at 9913 feet or 3021 meters in altitude. There is a steep two mile climb to the summit where you can get a great view over 124 miles of snows and hill tops on a clear day. According to legend, the temple marks the place where the head of Shiva's consort fell in order to stifle his cosmic dance that was shaking the whole universe. So this is a powerful Shakti-peeth. There are also churches of various denominations, a Radha-Krishna temple, a Sai Baba Temple, and a Muslim Jama Masjid. There is also a Tibetan community in Happy Valley with its Buddhist temple.

GOING TO SEE THE CHAR DHAM TEMPLES

From Rishikesh there are many important holy places we will want to visit, such as Badri-nath, Gangotri (near the source of the Ganges), Kedarnath, and Yamunotri (near the source of the Yamuna River). This is called the "Char Dhama" or four shrines pilgrimage tour. There will be many other holy towns you will travel through and where you may want to stop. There are also seven holy rivers in this area, which include the Alakananda, Bhagirathi, Dhauli Ganga, Mandakini, Pinder Ganga, the Nagar, and others. These rivers form five important *sangams* or confluences where they meet. Some pilgrims bathe in all five *sangams* before having *darshan* at Badrinath.

The best way to travel to these places is to hire a taxi or car so you can go when and where you want, but this is more expensive. The next best way to go is on a tour, of which there are several from which to choose, either leaving from Delhi, Haridwar, or Rishikesh. Rishikesh and Haridwar have tourist companies which can arrange tours for your visits to the northern holy places, or through which you can hire a taxi. The Nigam Tourist Office in Rishikesh can also make travel and accommodation arrangements for you, but do so several days in advance. There are several different tour packages from which to choose. Tours can also be arranged through the Garhwal Mandal Vikas Nigam Office in the Chandralok Building, 36 Janpath, Delhi.

Otherwise, just take the regular buses as best you can. To do this, I stay at the Surichi Hotel across from the Yatra Bus Stand when I'm ready to travel north. That way I can purchase my bus ticket the evening before, and then simply walk to the bus the next morning. It's easy to buy your ticket the day before, usually no later than 4:30 P.M. If you wait until the next morning, you might not be able to get a seat. The first bus of the day from Rishikesh leaves around 6:00 A.M., but without a previous reservation the bus is likely to be filled by the time you arrive at the Yatra Bus Stand at 5:30 A.M.

Before leaving on your tour, make sure you change all the money and travelers checks into rupees that you may need for the trip because some of the small towns that you will be visiting will have little facility for doing so.

The temples at the main places of interest, such as at Badrinath, open sometime during the last week of April to the first week of May, after consultations with astrologers and pundits. The opening is called the Akhand Jyoti Darshan. The temples stay open until the weather gets too severe, usually in the middle of November or by Diwali. Then the temples close for the season. The busiest time when most pilgrims visit this area is in May and June, and then again in September, which can create very crowded conditions when trying to find accommodations. The rainy season exists between the end of June to the beginning of September. During that period it can rain or get cold at any time, which can cause very muddy and uncomfortable conditions, as well as mud-slides and dangerous roads. Road service, meaning buses and taxis, can be stopped for days or even weeks if the conditions are too bad. By September, the hills are very lush and beautiful, which is why some people go at that time. At most times it is warm during the day and cool at night, but bring warm clothes and good walking shoes, especially if you plan to do any trekking to Gaumukh or other places.

Most pilgrims' priority is to at least visit Badrinath, but we will head to Yamunotri first. When we leave Rishikesh, the bus leaves at 6 A.M. and arrives at Hanuman Chatti at around 6 P.M., a long and adventurous bus ride. On the way, we will pass through such towns as Chamba (a small town on top of a hill which offers great views), Tehri (a dusty, dirty town I'd rather not have to go through, where they have built a large dam on the Ganges), Barkot, and then on to Hanuman Chatti where we spend the night at a guesthouse, or wherever we can get a room if the town is filled. Then it's by foot through Kharshal and Janki-chatti before reaching Yamunotri.

One thing that you will have to get used to is how the buses going through the mountains get so close to the edge of the road, which often has a sheer 200 or 300 foot drop down to the bottom of the gorge. Parts of the roads are often wide enough for only one vehicle, in which case they will have to back up to the closest area that is wide enough for two vehicles to get around each other. This certainly adds to the time it takes for the journey, and to its questionable safety. One time I was on a bus that was met by three buses approaching from the opposite direction on a narrow, rebuilt section of road. So our bus had to back up. Abruptly, the people in the back of the bus started getting excited and began jumping for the door and out of the bus. Suddenly, I thought maybe I better jump off as well. What happened was that the back of the bus was hanging over the side of the road. It would have been a long fall before the bus hit the hillside and rolled over until it landed in the river. Nonetheless, I stayed put, and soon everything was settled and the bus started on its way again. Then the people started scrambling back on the bus. We were on our way again, though hearts were pounding.

WARNING: If you go during the monsoon season, which generally starts at the end of June or early July and lasts until the middle of August, the steady rains can play havoc with the mountain sides, especially where the roads are located. When the mountains are cleared of trees to make way for the roads, landslides can take place, thus blocking the roads. Sometimes these landslides are just some rocks that have fallen and block the road, but at other times there can be a serious amount of rocks, soil, and mud that can take hours or days, sometimes even weeks to clear out of the way. Then buses and taxis will not be able to get through and you may be stuck on the road, or at whatever town you are situated for a length of time. Or, if you need to leave right away, you may have to walk by foot over the muddy landslide to the other side. Then you can catch some transportation the rest of the way out of the mountains. That is always challenging to say the least, especially if it is raining. However, in some years the monsoons simply do not show up, but do not expect that. Mountain weather is never predictable. Even when it is supposed to be the dry season, clouds can come in from nowhere and dump either rain or snow or both on the mountains. I have personally seen at a few places where a sunny day can turn into a brief but heavy snowstorm in minutes. Or where the weather of all four seasons happens in one day. So if you are doing any trekking up a mountain, or even just taking a bus to a holy site, you have to be prepared. But it is generally best not to go during the monsoon season in order to minimize the risks on the mountain roads.

YAMUNOTRI

Going to Yamunotri, Hanuman Chatti is the end of the road. There is not much to see here in this small town. Most people simply stop to get accommodations, which are very basic, and then continue on to Yamunotri. The best place to stay is the Nigam Tourist Rest House, which is where you will stay if you have booked a tour through their office. Otherwise, it is often booked up. The rest of the places are dirty, some without water, and over-priced. If you do not care for Hanuman Chatti, then as soon as you arrive you can begin the three hour walk to Janki-chatti which is a nicer but smaller town with cleaner places to stay. But since you will be walking, travel lite.

From Hanuman Chatti you reach Yamunotri by walking 14 kilometers, which takes a good five or six hours, so start early. It's a narrow uphill climb in most parts, which can be difficult, especially the last two or three kilometers to the top. It was too tough for me. I had walked ten kilometers up and just could not continue. I was out of breath and became too weak. My legs were shot. So I had to take a horse the last four kilometers up, and was very glad I did when I saw how steep the path can be. The route can also be quite narrow in parts, hardly room for two horses to pass each other, with sheer drops of 200 or 300 feet straight down. However, the views are quite splendid. Even as I was walking back down the mountain, I would pass by other people who were going up and who would ask me in a tired voice how much farther it was. I'd just try to be encouraging, however I could tell that for some people the climb was difficult.

About halfway there, you will pass by sulphur springs. You will also pass by Shiva Prayag, the confluence of the Nil Ganga and Yamuna rivers. Performing worship in the Shiva temple here is said to rid one of bad astrological influences.

The legend is that Yamuna was born from the wedding of Surya, the Sun god, and Sanjana, the daughter of Vishvakarma, the architect of the demigods. There was once a time when Surya became hopelessly in love with Sanjana and after some assistance from the demigod Vayu, the ruler of the winds, and other demigods, Vishvakarma agreed to the wedding of Sanjana and Surya. From this was born Yamuna who was graceful like Sanjana and glorious like Surya. However, Yamuna wearied of Surya's intensity after some time and had Chhaya, her sister river, take her place. Since then Yamuna has wandered through the mountains.

Yamunotri is considered to be where the sacred Yamuna River begins. The Hanuman Ganga and Tons River also begin here, both of which join the Yamuna. Yamunotri is located on the western side of Bandarpoonch Mountain, which has a height of 6,315 meters, so the peak is always snow covered. Also, nearby is a hot spring at Kalinda Parvata. Next to the main temple is Surya Kund, the most sacred of the hot springs. You can watch the pilgrims drop small cloth bags of rice or potatoes in the boiling water and pull them up in a few minutes fully cooked. You can also bathe in the Yamuna Bai Kund near the temple for a holy dip.

The main attraction at Yamunotri is, of course, the Yamunotri temple, built in 1839 and dedicated to the goddess Yamuna. Inside the temple you will find a black stone deity of Yamuna Devi and a white deity of Ganga Devi. Yamuna is the twin sister of Yamaraja, the lord of death. So if you bathe in her waters, it is said that you will be freed from a painful death. But before worshiping in the Yamuna temple, one is expected to visit the Dibya Shila, which is next to it.

Although many pilgrims come to Yamunotri (3,185 meters above sea level), the actual source of the Yamuna River is farther up at the Saptarishi Kund (4,421 meters above sea level). This is named as such because legend has it that the seven universal *rishis* performed austerities here in Satya-yuga. The *kund* is a glacial lake of dark blue water only about a half kilometer wide. However, there are six other *kunds* that are also located here. It takes a good 16 hours or more to go up to this lake and return. You have to make a 12 kilometer climb up hills and rocks, and walk through snow, ice, and water, as well as deal with the high altitude. You will need a guide to help find your way and a day in Yamunotri to get used to the high altitude before going. Since it is so difficult to reach, few people visit Saptarishi Kund.

GOING TO GANGOTRI

Once we are finished in Yamunotri, Gangotri is our next stop. You can take a 13 hour bus ride from Hanuman Chatti, which leaves at 5:30 A.M. You can also take a 12 hour bus ride directly from Rishikesh. Be sure to make reservations the day before. Other buses leave later as they fill up.

Dodital is one place worth noting, though it is out of the way as we go toward Gangotri. It is the place considered to be where Lord Ganesha had appeared or was born. It is a beautiful lake set in a lush forest with a temple nearby. It is said that it was here where Parvati bathed and created a boy from the dirt from her body. She then requested him not to let anyone approach while she was bathing. When Lord Shiva arrived, the boy blocked his way. Shiva, not knowing the boy was his son, cut off the boy's head. When Parvati heard what had happened, she became angry and explained the situation to Shiva.

Shiva then told his associates to bring the head of the first living being they saw. So they went searching and brought back the head of an elephant. Shiva fixed it onto the boy's body, who thus became Ganesh.

Uttarkashi, at an elevation of 1150 meters, is situated on the Bhagirathi River, and is surrounded by the Varanavat Mountains. It is another of the towns you will travel through, or even stop for the night if you take a late bus. Since it is a major stop-over place for pilgrims, there are numerous hotels here, many of which are small, but they tend to get booked up quickly, especially in the busy months of May and June. If you do stop here, there are a few temples to see. The Kashi Visvanatha temple is an ancient shrine of Lord Shiva with an ancient Shiva *lingam*. It is mentioned in the Vedic texts, such as the Kedarkhand of the *Skanda Purana*. Outside the Kashi Visvanatha temple is a large and old pole, its depth into the ground is unknown. You can attempt to make it sway and it will not budge, but try it with faith and it will move. The holiday of Makar Sakranti in January is a festival attended by thousands of devotees who come to pray, worship and offer Ganga water to the *lingam*. Different villages also bring their deities here on palanquins. The temple is only 200 meters from the Uttarkashi bus stand. The shrine to Kuteti Devi is another ancient temple linked to the motor road and is two kilometers from the Uttarkshi bus stand. Many visitors also come here. Other temples here include one for Annapurna, another for Parashurama, and one for Shakti, a Kali temple, and the Ekadash Rudra temple. You are also likely to see a number of *sadhus* here, some staying for a while and others traveling through as they go for other locations.

Bhairavghat, nine kilometers before reaching Gangotri, has the ancient temple of Bhairav Baba. One can stop here to see the deity in the temple. It is said that one will not receive complete spiritual reward for the pilgrimage to Gangotri if one does not worship Bhairav before going to Gangotri. However, if taking a bus to Gangotri, the buses do not stop here.

GANGOTRI

Gangotri is a major place of pilgrimage, 3140 meters above sea level, and easily reached by bus, which will take you right to the town, that is if the roads are open. One summer the roads had been closed for two months because of a major landslide. Pilgrims throng to this place from May to October. It is famous for its temple to the goddess Ganga Devi, the personality of the Ganges River. The present Gangotri temple was built in the early 19th century by a Nepalese general, Amar Singh Thapa. It was severely damaged by an avalanche and was renovated a hundred years later by the Maharaja of Jaipur. About 50 feet left of the temple, when facing the front of it, is the Bhagirathi Shila, the sacred stone where King Bhagiratha sat while worshiping Lord Shiva. He did this so Shiva would accept the force of the Ganga on his head from its descent from heaven to earth.

The reason why King Bhagiratha desired that the Ganga descend to earth was to purify the remains of the 60,000 sons of his great grandfather, King Sagar. What happened was that during Satya-yuga, King Sagar was going to perform an *ashvamedha-yajna* (a sacred horse ritual). This made the demigod Indra fearful that King Sagar may become more powerful than he. So Indra stole the horse and left it at the residence of Lord Kapila. King Sagar's 60,000 sons went to look for the horse and thought Kapiladeva stole it when they found it at his *ashrama*. Kapiladeva had been in deep meditation and when he was disturbed, he burned the 60,000 sons by the power of his glance. Only Asamanjas survived and went back to tell King Sagar what happened. Then the king's grandson, Asuman, returned to Kapiladeva and requested him to release the horse, which he did and explained that the king's sons could be saved if their remains could be bathed in the waters of the Ganga River. But in order for this to happen, Ganga Devi would have to descend from heaven to earth.

So King Bhagiratha pleased Ganga Devi to descend, but she explained that the force of her water descending from the heavenly region would destroy the earth. Therefore, King Bhagiratha pleased Lord Shiva to accept the powerful force of the river on his head. Thus, the Ganges descended to earth, landing on the head of the powerful Lord Shiva, and then followed King Bhagiratha who cut a deep gorge in the earth with his chariot. This gorge went all the way to the Bay of Bengal at Ganga Sagar, the island where Lord Kapiladeva resided. There, the Ganges purified the remains of the 60,000 sons of King Sagar so they could return to the spiritual world. Now, because of King Bhagiratha, so many other pilgrims can also take advantage of the holy Ganga, and visiting Gangotri is considered a most auspicious event. Worship is performed inside the temple, and the *arati* ceremony is also performed outside the temple to the Ganges River in the evening.

The Gangotri temple is opened on Akshaya Tritiya in April or May, a date calculated according to the Vedic calendar. Then it is closed around the time of Govardhana Puja in the month of Kartika (Oct-Nov). When the temple is closed, there is a grand ceremony in which the priests decorate a palanquin and take the deity of the Goddess Ganga while singing the Ganga Laheri and bring her to Mookhimath in a huge procession. Then the temple doors are closed for 6 months. The worship of Ganga Devi is continued in the temple at Mookhimath until the temple at Gangotri is ready to be opened again.

Gangotri is a pleasant town and also caters to foreigners who wish to make the trek to Gaumukh, the actual source of the Ganges, which is called the Bhagirathi here. As the river runs by the town, it is extremely loud and powerful as it flows in a northerly direction. This is what gives Gangotri (Ganga going north) its name. It is a peaceful town and a nice place to stay for a few days. However, it can be crowded and most hotels, although quite basic, can be booked up early. The Kedar Ganga also flows into the Ganges here, and 100 yards below this confluence is the loud Sahasradhara Falls, under which is said to be a natural Shiva *lingam*. Below the Sahasradhara Falls, only 100 meters from the bus stand, is Surya Kund. Lord Shiva was supposed to have been sitting at this Sahasradhara Falls when the Ganges came down from heaven. That is why this is considered the beginning of the river, according to tradition. From here, the water backed up into the mountains and froze because of the high altitude and became the glacier that extended up into the mountains.

From the Sahasradhara Falls the river squeezes into a gorge that is only about a meter wide, which shows how swift and powerful the river can be. Gauri Kund is only 300 meters farther downstream from the bus stand, where the Ganga can be seen flowing through narrow channels.

After Gauri Kund, one can find Patangna, which is two kilometers downstream from the bus stand, where it is believed the Pandavas performed their yagnas and austerities to redeem themselves from killing their relatives in their participation in the Kurukshetra war. After this along the path is a large cave, entered through a small door, called the Pandava Gupha or cave of the Pandavas.

Although the Ganges or Bhagirathi River starts from the glacier higher up in the mountains at Gaumukh, the glacier is said to have once extended all the way down to Gangotri many years ago, where Lord Shiva sat in meditation to receive it. However, now the glacier is receding higher into the mountains. One lady mentioned that after visiting Gaumukh nearly 20 years ago, the glacier had receded by almost a whole kilometer in that short time. Thus, it changes in appearance and location each year.

Gaumukh is the part of the glacier under which is the source of the Ganges. It is referred to as Gaumukh because it resembles a cow's face, and the ice cave from where the water rushes out resembles the mouth of a cow. However, because of the constant melting of the glacier, the shape is also always changing. The glacier is a wall of gray ice 328 feet tall. It spans an area of about 24 kilometers long by two kilometers wide, at an elevation of 14,000 feet. After the middle of October there is too much ice and snow for anyone to make the trek, in fact Gangotri itself shuts down until it opens the following April. Even without the snow it is not an easy climb.

It is 18 kilometers (though some now say 23) east from Gangotri to Gaumukh, the source of the Bhagirathi River. To reach Gaumukh you start by climbing the stairway up the hill by the Ganga Devi temple that leads you to the path. As you start out along the path through the trees, it is not too strenuous. It does not go too high or too low. You will first see Kanakgiri Ashrama, which is two kilometers from Gangotri. The first refreshment stop is Bhojgaddi, which is four kilometers out. There are many bhoj trees in the area.

Keep walking to Chirbasa, about eight kilometers out at a height of 3606 meters. This is nothing more than a little stop-over place with tea shops, tents, and mattresses provided by the local people. You can now get good views of the mountains if the weather is clear. Before you get to Chirbasa there is a small bridge over the Ganga, which should be three wooden planks wide. But I saw it when two planks had fallen away, leaving only one to walk on. This becomes extremely dangerous and makes it merely a balancing act to get across. So you must be cautious at some of these places. There are a few additional bridges like this at other places along the way.

From Chirbasa you take the path around a cliff face where the deterioration of the rock is blamed for a number of accidents. So you must be careful. After this, the path leads to a mountain desert.

Once you reach Bhojbasa, at a height of 3792 meters above sea level, you may prefer to spend the night, which most people do. It is tucked in a valley about 13 kilometers from Gangotri. The place is very basic with no electricity. There are a few huts, tents, and ashramas, such as the Lal Baba ashrama. The view of the Bhagirathi Mountains as they loom in the background is most impressive.

From Bhojbasa it is about five more kilometers or two hours to Gaumukh, which is 3892 meters above sea level. Of course, as the glacier melts, the distance to Gaumukh increases with time. Towering over Gaumukh is the beautiful Shivling Mountain, which summits at a height of 21,470 feet. After reaching Gaumukh, you may explore the area for a few hours, and take a holy bath in the icy waters. Watch out for rocks or even boulders that may come loose and roll down the hill. When we are ready we can head back to Bhojbasa for the night The next morning you can make the day's journey back to Gangotri.

If you want to go farther than Gaumukh, Tapovan is another five kilometers or four hours away, near Mount Shivling which is in clear view stretching up to 6501 meters tall. It is a dangerous climb and you should have warm clothing, food, and a tent. You should also have a guide since the snow can cover deep holes that you can fall into. Because of the decreased amount of oxygen in the air, one should also take it easy. Tapovan is 4460 meters in elevation. It is a lovely meadow with natural blooming flowers. The side of the meadow has the stream called the Akash Ganga, which fades into Gaumukh. At Tapovan you get a clear view of the Bhagirathi peaks (6512, 6456, and 6856 meters respectively) and you can also see the stretch of the Gaumukh glacier if you are up high enough. The famous Mount Sumeru is several more kilometers from Tapovan, which reaches a height of 6660 meters. For staying the night at Tapovan, you can pitch your tent, or find the huts of Bangali Maharaja or Nepali Maharaja.

On the other side of Tapovan are Nandanvan, Rakvan, and Sundarvan which can be seen. One can reach Kalandi through Nandanvan and from Kalandi one can reach Badrinath if taking the path through the mountains. Only well equipped mountaineers usually go past Tapovan.

Some of this may sound easy, however, as I pointed out, there are parts of this trek to Gaumukh that can be quite risky. The path cut out of the mountainside and the cliffs is often narrow in parts, with steep drops on the side and little support. There are also a few small bridges over the Ganga that can be quite narrow. The park service is supposed to help maintain the safety of the path, but they often do little. So the bridges that are supposed to be wide enough for one's stability may become in disrepair for long lengths of time. One bridge I came to was supposed to be three wooden planks wide, but two planks had fallen away, making it a balancing act to get across. Some people were crossing and others were turning back due to the excessive risk in crossing the fiercely flowing river. Even the small horses occasionally do not like to cross such a narrow bridge, and if anyone falls, the river takes them away quickly, and they drown, which has happened. There are a few such bridges that must be crossed on the way to Gaumukh, and then again on the way back.

ON THE WAY TO KEDARNATH

From Gangotri, Kedarnath is the next major holy sight to see. A bus from Gangotri to Gourikund, where the road ends, takes at least a day to reach it, or a day-and-a-half if you take a late bus. On our way, we will pass through the town of Uttarkashi again. At the time of this writing they no longer offer a direct bus from Gangotri to Kedarnath. It seems more people are hiring their own cars or jeeps. Nonetheless, you can take a morning bus, and there are a few, from Gangotri to Uttarkashi, spend the night and get a ticket for the next early morning bus to Kedarnath, which then arrives in the early evening at Gaurikund. Spend the night there and then in the morning you can climb or ride a horse up to the village of Kedarnath. The other way you can do this is to take a bus back to Rishikesh, and then take the next bus back up to Kedarnath.

Srinagar is another one of the towns we will travel through, which is good for an overnight stop if necessary. It is a small but bustling little town with a number of hotels. It has the Kamleshwar Mahadeva Shiva temple. There are also several small abandoned temples here in a cluster that was once used as a stronghold of tantrik practice. There is also a monastery and cave of Guru Goraknath, who lived here in the 6th century. If you go behind the monastery, you will find a cave where you can do meditation. There is a small image of Goraknath inside. If you sit quietly, the cave has such energy that you can be transported to a lofty state of consciousness very quickly. Nearby is the cemetery where yogis of this tradition have willingly cast off their bodies after entering deep *samadhi*.

The temple of Dari Devi, the Divine Mother, is also found here. She is worshiped as the Divine entity of nature.

Rudra Prayag is the next important town and is where the Mandakini River from Kedarnath flows into the Alakananda River. The Rudranatha and Jagdambi Devi temple are the main sites here, and nearby is a place where Narada Muni performed austerities for spiritual development.

In this area is also the shrine called Kali Math. To reach it you have to climb into the mountain. The Kali *shila* is a rock said to be the embodiment of Kali. You can see profiles of Shiva's face on the rock. According to *shastra*, or Vedic scripture, all nine forms of the Divine Mother, Kali, are said to reside in this rock. It is a powerful place for those who engage in tantrik practice.

Okhimath is just a little ways south of Guptakashi. It has a colorful temple and monastery, which has many small cells for meditation. The worship for Kedarnath is held here during the winter when it is too cold to stay in the mountains at higher elevations. Okhimath has all the different forms of Lord Shiva. So if you cannot visit Panch Kedar, the five main forms of Shiva in the temples of the area, then getting darshan of the deities at Okhimath is equal to being blessed by all of the forms of the Panch Kedar, as described later. This monastery is also the seat of the immortal sages, such as Parashurama and Visvamitra, as well as Varahi and Chandika, the tantrik goddesses.

Guptakashi, the next important town, is where Lord Shiva had fled to live incognito and even turned himself into a bull to hide from the Pandavas who later found him there. This is why this place is called Guptakashi, which means "hidden Kashi" or "hidden light". The Pandavas pursued Lord Shiva up to Kedarnath, where he gave up the disguise. There his bull hump became the *lingam*. The main temples here are for Ardhanareeswara (Gouri-Shankar) and Viswanath. In front of the Viswanath temple is the Manikarnika Kund which has water flowing from the head of Ganesh (water said to be from Yamunotri) and the head of a cow (water from Gangotri). Other than this, this city is another overnight stop if you are on a late bus, since they close the road here when it gets dark.

Another small town, Agastmuni, 25 km farther up the road, is where the Agastya Muni temple is and where he performed meditation.

Triyugi Narayana is another little place about five kilometers off the main road from Sonaprayag before you reach Gaurikund. You will not go through this by bus, but you must make a separate trip to reach it. So make sure the bus tour you take includes this place, or if you are traveling at your own pace, you can hire a taxi from Gaurikund to see this place. Legend has it that the marriage of Lord Shiva and Parvati happened here during Satya-yuga at Brahma Shila. Brahma acted as the priest and Parvati was given to Lord Shiva by her brother, Lord Narayana.

The main temple, the Akhand Dhuni temple, was built many years ago by Shankaracharya. Inside the front hall you will find the marriage ritual fire, which is said to have been kept burning for three *yugas*. Even today pilgrims can offer pieces of wood into the fire and take ashes as *prasada*, remnants from the ceremony. Thus, such pilgrims become participants in the wedding of Shiva and Parvati. Going past the fire and into the sanctum we find a silver deity of Lord Narayana standing two feet tall with Lakshmi and Sarasvati at His sides. Outside the temple and going around it clockwise, we first see a stone that marks the spot where the marriage of Shiva and Parvati took place. Nearby are four small holy *kunds* or water tanks, namely the Vishnu Kund, Rudra Kund, Brahma Kund, and the Sarasvati Kund. The temple is small, and it only takes a short time to see everything. From here we go back to Sonaprayag and on to Gaurikund, our stop to prepare for going to Kedarnath.

KEDARNATH

Gaurikund is the last stop before Kedarnath. This is where you may want to stay while visiting Kedarnath. There are a number of hotels or ashramas from which to choose. When you arrive, there will be numerous men from the hotels promoting what they have and willing to carry your bags to their place of business.

Gaurikund is where Parvati, Gaurimata, was born and did penance for hundreds of years in order to marry Lord Shiva. The exact spot is said to be at Gaurikund, the hot sulphur spring where you also can take a bath. There is one Gaurikund that you will see first which is sacred, then another at the far end of the street of hotels where everyone bathes. Nearby is also the small Gauri Devi temple.

Another significant temple not far away (about ½ km) is that of Sirkata Ganesh. This temple is said to mark the place where Lord Shiva beheaded his son Ganesh and gave him the elephant head, although there are other places that claim the same significance. As related in the *Skanda Purana*, this was when Ganesh was guarding Parvati who was bathing in Gaurikund. Ganesh, having not met his father before, forbade Shiva from coming closer. Shiva did not recognize Ganesh as his son and became angry and cut off his head when they fought. Parvati learned what happened when she returned and requested Shiva to revive Ganesh with another head. Shiva went off and returned with the head of the first creature he saw, which was that of an elephant.

The ashrama of Vyasadeva's father, Parashara Muni, is also located 40 km down from Gauri Kund in one of the villages. There is a big image of him there. You may have to ask the locals to find it if you are interested.

Kedarnatha, located along the Mandakini River, is a very significant place and is said to be the abode of Shiva. It is as sacred as Mount Kailash in Tibet. The village is located in a rich grassy area and surrounded by towering, white mountains. It is a beautiful view when the clouds are absent. The route to Kedarnath from Gaurikund, which is a steep incline of 14 kilometers, is dotted with small temples, forests, lush valleys, waterfalls, and colorful flowers. If you find that you cannot walk the whole distance, which may be likely after all the walking we have done, you can hire a horse to ride up. There are many people taking horses, which are located at the base of the hill, just outside of town. Sometimes even the horses slip on the stone path, which gets covered with horse manure in parts because of so many of them on this narrow lane. Usually you will have a guide walking with each horse, so it will not get too frisky or impatient to go up the path. I was on one horse without a guide, and at a few places the horse simply started galloping up the hill.

Over 100,000 pilgrims visit each year to have *darshan* in the temple dedicated to Lord Shiva as Kedareswara, also known as Sada Shiva, one of the 12 *jyotirlingas*, or spontaneously manifested Shiva *lingas*. It is one of the most important of all Shiva temples in India. The temple is situated at the end of a lane, which is surrounded by small hotels and restaurants. Along the lane is a barely decorated doorway amidst all the other shacks that shows the place where Sri Chaitanya once stayed while visiting this temple. They will not let you into the room itself but you can look in through the window. Inside are a few items and prints of Sri Chaitanya.

The Kedarnath temple building is a simple stone structure with a small tower over the sanctum. Inside the temple, the walls are carved with fine detailed images. There is also a large image of Nandi, Shiva's bull carrier, in the hall. Inside the sanctum, you will find a three-faced *linga*, which is about nine feet long, three feet high, and four feet wide. The sanctum is a small area, so it is often crowded with pilgrims, and you have to take your time. Then you circumambulate the *linga*, and then your priest will help guide you through the performance of the *puja* or worship. You can even touch the *lingam* or massage it with ghee as part of the ritual.

Other deities in the temple include Ganesh and Parvati in front of the altar door. Then there are Lord Krishna, the five Pandavas and their wife Draupadi, and their mother Kunti outside the second door. There is also a Lakshmi-Narayana deity believed to have been installed by Shankaracharya.

The unusual shape of the Shiva *linga* is because it represents the hump of the bull that Shiva turned into when the Pandavas found him at Guptakashi. Legend has it that the Pandavas wanted to purify themselves after the war at Kuruksetra and went to Kashi

(Varanasi, the city of Lord Shiva) to find Shiva to ask for his blessings. After a while, the Pandavas found him at Guptakashi and Bhima recognized him even though he was disguised as a bull. Bhima grabbed his tail and the bull sank into the ground, leaving only the hump above the earth. Shiva appeared before the Pandavas and instructed them to worship the hump. Thereafter, the temple was constructed around it and worship was begun and has continued to this day. However, when it gets too cold during winter, the priest from the Kedarnath temple continues the worship of Sri Kedarnatha at the Okhimath temple, which is farther south of Guptakashi. Okhimath also has temples of Shiva, Parvati, Usha Mandhata, and Aniruddha.

The Kedarnath temple is busy, so the waiting time to go in may be long, two hours in the morning and maybe only 15 minutes in the afternoon or evening. The temple is believed to have been originally constructed by the Pandavas thousands of years ago and reconstructed by Shankaracharya in the eighth century.

Kedarnath is also noted for being the place where Shankaracharya attained *samadhi* around 820 C.E., when he was barely 31 years of age. (However, some say he appeared around 500 B.C.E.) This is commemorated by the marble staff behind the temple that signifies the place where Shankaracharya left his body, although some people feel he left this world in Kanchipuram. This is another of those legends which seems to be shared by more than one place in India. Behind the temple is the Mahapanth Trail, or Gate to Heaven. This path is said to go north up to heaven, Swarga-rohini. Legend has it that this was the path the five Pandavas took after engaging in a big ceremony.

Also from behind the temple you can follow the walkway to the path that goes up the hill to the south side of the temple. Up on the hillside are the deities of Bhairavnath, the guardian deity over the temple. You can find this little cluster of deities outdoors standing on a little platform that overlooks the temple and town below. Flag poles mark the place, which can be seen from the temple. It also provides some nice views over the temple and little town with the mountains in the background, at least if the sky is clear.

During the winter when Kedarnatha closes, the worship continues at Okhimath (also spelled Ukhimat), where there is a very colorful temple similar in shape to that in Kedarnath but smaller. Inside are brass forms of Shiva. Visiting Okhimath is said to be equal to visiting the Panch (five) Kedars.

VISITING THE PANCH (FIVE) KEDAR TEMPLES

Along with the hump of Lord Shiva's body when he took the form of a bull, four other parts of his body also appeared in various places in the area. The Pandavas built temples in those spots as well. These places, altogether, are known as the Panch Kedars. These include the hump at Kedarnath, the arm at Tungnath, the face at Rudranath, the hair at Kalpeswara, and the navel at Madhyamaheswara.

To reach all of these places takes 14 days or so by making a long circular trek. There is a bus that leaves Gaurikund and will drop you off at access points so you can walk to the Panch Kedar temples. But it's for the more serious minded pilgrims.

You start, of course, at Kedarnath. After your *darshan* at Kedarnath is complete you go to Okhimath and on to the village of Mansuna. From there it is a hefty 24 kilometer trek to Madhyamaheswara, while stopping at Ransi overnight and Gondhar on the way. It is a small stone temple.

Farther down the road you get dropped off at Chopta to go to the highest temple in India, the Tungnath temple at an elevation of 12,065 feet. It's a seven kilometer or four hour climb to reach this temple located on a stone pavement near a cliff. All around it are the beautiful mountains of Neelkanth, Kedarnath, and Nanda Devi. Inside the temple are five silver faces that represent the five Pandavas. There are also images of Vyasadeva and Kalabhairava. Tungnath represents the arm of Shiva. Also nearby is a small Parvati temple.

Next we take a bus to the village of Helang, 14 kilometers south of Joshimath, to take the nine kilometer walk to the village of Urgam, and then a one-and-a-half kilometer walk to the Kalpeswara temple. This is a rock temple with the sanctum inside a cave.

Now we take a bus to Gopeswara and then to Sagar, from which we take a 24 kilometer trek to Rudranath, the last of the Panch Kedar temples. This temple represents Lord Shiva's face. The Rudraganga River is nearby, and there are good views of the surroundings below and the Trisul, Nanda Devi, and Parbat peaks.

IMPORTANT TOWNS ON THE WAY TO BADRINATH

Badrinath will be our next place of pilgrimage. From Kedarnatha we will take a bus south back to the main road at Rudraparayag, from where we will travel northeast up to Badrinath. On our way up, there are some significant towns we will be passing through that you may want to stop and visit if you have the time. Or you can wait and see them on your way back to Rishikesh after your visit to Badrinath.

Karna Prayag is one of the first noteworthy towns we will see after leaving Rudraprayag. This is where the Alakananda joins the Pinar Ganga, and where Karna, the Pandavas' half-brother, performed austerities to please Surya, the Sun-god, and Shiva.

Ranikhet is another place much farther east of Karna Prayag, from which you can take a hefty hike through the hills to the cave of Babaji, a master who used to live there and was mentioned by Paramahamsa Yogananda in his book, *Autobiography of a Yogi*. Some tours stop to make the climb to this cave temple. Make sure you go up and return before it gets dark.

Nanda Prayag is the next town, 21 kilometers farther along the road, which has the confluence of the Nandakini and Alakananda rivers. There is also a small Gopalji or Krishna temple here. This is also where Ravana is said to have performed austerities, and where Nanda Maharaja, Krishna's father, held a great ceremony. Also, as described in the *Puranas*, Dushyantha married Shakunthala, and Kanva Rishi had his ashrama in this location. From here we will continue on to Joshimath.

JOSHIMATH

This is a town that is nice to visit for its spiritual significance. You may have to spend the night here anyway if you take a late bus to Badrinath. They close the roads here in the evening until the next morning. This is also where they establish one-way traffic to Badrinatha. So you may have to wait a while as they stop traffic to allow all buses and cars to leave the road from Badrinatha before the long line of buses start from Joshimath.

Joshimath is significant for being the place where Shankaracharya established one of his four original centers. The name *joshimath* or *jyotimath* means "monastery of light." He also attained enlightenment while meditating in a cave under the Kalpavriksha (wish-fulfilling) tree. This mulberry tree is said to be over 2400 years old and is 125 feet tall with an enormous trunk. This is so big that the hollows in the trunk are large enough that a person could stay in them. On the other side of the tree trunk is a natural formation of Lord Ganesh, showing him sitting on a lotus. Pilgrims pray and do *puja* to this image. Next to this tree is the cave where Shankaracharya lived for several years.

This is where Shankaracharya got his realizations to write and defeat Buddhism and reestablish Vedic authority. Thereafter, Shankaracharya wrote his *Shankara Bhasya* here. The present Shankaracharya Math and temple is on a ridge above the town. You can find the cave where he meditated by entering the temple and following the signs. Plus, the Kalpavriksha tree is located up the stairs to the right of the temple entrance.

Another significant point about Joshimath is the temple of Lord Narasimhadeva, located in the lower part of town and over 1200 years old. It is not far from the road, so if you are taking a taxi, you can have your driver wait a little bit for you while you go to the temple complex. In fact, sometimes you can see this temple while they are holding up the vehicles before they begin the one-way traffic. You walk through the archway, and in the courtyard turn to the right to the temple sanctum, toward the back. This deity self-manifested from a *shalagram-shila* stone. He sits in a lotus position and is about ten inches tall and is very detailed. To the right are deities of Sita-Rama, Hanuman, and Garuda. On another altar to the right are deities of Kubera, Uddhava, and Badri Vishal. On the left wall is a deity of goddess Kali in her form as Chandika. And a deity of Lakshmi is found outside the temple door.

Shankaracharya is supposed to have originally installed this Narasimha *shalagram*. This means that in spite of his spreading an impersonalist philosophy to curb Buddhism in his day, he was very much a *bhakta*, a Vaishnava devoted to the personal form of the Supreme.

Another important point about the Lord Narasimhadeva deity is that the wrist is very thin and continuously getting thinner. You can get a good look at the wrist when the deity is being bathed between 7:30 and 8:30 A.M. It is said that the hand will finally break off the deity when the dark qualities of the age of Kali overcome the world. At that time, the nearby mountains of Jaya and Vijaya (appropriately named after the two guardians of the spiritual domain) near Vishnu Prayag will crumble and block the road leading to Badrinath. Then Bhavishya Badri (the Badri of the future) will become the new Badrinath, which is about 23 kilometers southeast of Joshimath. This will be the significant sign of the disappearance of spiritual culture in India as we have already described elsewhere.

One other important point about this temple is that the priests of Badrinath come here to continue their worship at the time when the Badrinath temple closes during winter.

Only thirty yards away from the Narasimha temple is the Vasudeva temple. This has a six foot tall, black stone deity of Lord Vasudeva, Krishna. He stands with Sri Bhu Devi (the personality of Mother Earth), Nila, and Kama. There is also a rare image of dancing Ganesh, considered to be only one of two in all of India. This temple is extremely old, no one knows how old, and is considered to be one of the 108 (Divya Desams) most important Vishnu temples in India.

On the other side of Joshimath is one of India's most beautiful ski resorts. It is reached by a cable car. The mountain range here is known for the many herbs found on its slopes, and for spiritual enlightenment. Hanuman was known to have found the legendary herb *sanjivani bhuti* from this area. From the hilltop you get a spectacular view of the mountains, including Nanda Devi, one of the highest in this range of peaks.

Vishnuprayag is the next town 10 kilometers farther up. This is where the confluence is for the Alakananda and Dhauli Ganga rivers.

Govind Ghat is another 10 kilometers up the road. If you are interested in seeing the Valley of Flowers, especially when it is in bloom after the rainy season, or in visiting Hemakund, this is where you start the trek into that region.

Hemakund is another place of pilgrimage for Hindus and Sikhs. This place is mentioned in the holy *Granth*, the Sikh scripture, as being where Guru Govind Singh meditated on the shores of a lake surrounded by seven snow-covered peaks. The water in the lake is clear and beautiful, and it is full of lotus flowers. You can reach it from Govind Ghat and by making a 20 kilometer trek east. This is also where you will find Ghangaria and the Valley of Flowers. The last five kilometers are most difficult, so dress warm and wear good walking shoes. The Sikh Gurudwara is next to the lake.

Pandukeswara is the next town known for the site of the Yogadhyan Badri temple. This is one of the Badri temples, which I'll explain shortly. Here is also where the priests of Badrinath bring the deity of Badri Vishal during the winter. Pandukeswar is where the Pandavas are believed to have been born.

Hanuman Chatti (different from the town of the same name near Yamunotri) is nine kilometers farther away. This area is significant because it was here in the Gandhamadhana Hills where Bhima of the Pandavas met Hanuman. While traveling on the road, Bhima met a very old monkey whose tail was in his way. Bhima asked if the monkey would move his tail, but the monkey replied that he did not have enough energy to do it, so Bhima could try if he liked. Bhima tried several times but could not move the monkey's tail. Then the monkey revealed himself to be Hanuman. Thus, Hanuman and Bhima realized they were brothers since they were both sons of Vayu. This area is also noted for being where Hanuman meditated and pleased Lord Badrinath.

BADRINATH (TIRUVADARIASHRAMA)

Now, another 15 kilometers farther away (35 km from Joshimath), we come to the holy town of Badrinath, or Badarikashrama, one of the most important and highly esteemed places of pilgrimage in India. Badrinath is 10,400 feet above sea level. The bus or taxi easily takes you up through the winding mountain road for the three hour drive to the town of Badrinath, as long as there are no landslides. However, it is about 12 hours from Rishikesh, which can be a long time to be on a bus.

Once we arrive at the bus station, there will be men who will want you to see their hotel. If you do not have one arranged, this can be helpful. There are many hotels and ashramas to choose from, and the months of June, July, and September are the busiest. Things slow down during the monsoon season because of wet and rainy roads, which can become dangerous, and then again as the weather gets cold. Badrinath closes completely during November and all but a few serious *sadhus* leave the town until next spring.

The present temple is about 400 years old, although the site goes back thousands of years. The *Skanda Purana* even mentions that it is one of the most sacred shrines even amongst all the shrines in heaven or hell. It is considered (in *Srimad-Bhagavatam* 3.4.22) the residence of the Supreme Being in His incarnation as the sages Nara-Narayana. It is also the ashrama of the compiler of the Vedic literature, Srila Vyasadeva. Such great devotees as Uddhava visited this place 5,000 years ago under the direction of Lord Krishna (*Bhagavatam* 11.29.44) so that he might purify himself by bathing in the holy waters there which emanated from Krishna's holy feet.

Badrinath is also known as "Narada Kshetram" because the sage Narada Muni attained liberation here in five days. Others who have visited include the great sages Gautama Rishi, Kapiladeva, Kashyapa Muni, and Shankaracharya who installed a temple here. This temple is the Jyotir Mutt, one of the five original temples he started. It has images of Adi Shankara and a crystal *lingam* that he worshiped. Also, great spiritual masters such as Ramanujacharya visited 955 years ago, and Madhavacharya visited a few times nearly 735 years ago. Also, Sri Nityananda visited on His tour of the holy places 500 years ago. And today up to nearly 2000 pilgrims visit Badrinath every day, thanks to the bus system which is a rather recent addition from only 30 years or so ago. Before the bus system was established, the only way to reach these mountainous holy sites was by walking.

One reason for its popularity is because it is considered to be one of the eight Svayam Vyakta Kshetras in India, or places where the spiritual realm manifests on earth. It is also one of the four holy *dhamas*, which include Ramesvaram, Jagannatha Puri, and Dwaraka, where pilgrims visit for spiritual merit and enlightenment. Badri is also the name of Maha-Lakshmi's favorite tree, the Ilandai.

The temple of Badrinatha is located across the Alaknanda River. To reach the bridge, we walk down the street where we find numerous shops selling all kinds of devotional paraphernalia, from beads, pictures, video CDs, music tapes and CDs, and many other things. We can easily see the temple from some distance away. After crossing the bridge over the Alaknanda River, we walk up the steps toward the temple. Sometimes there are long lines of people waiting to get in. So, to enter the temple, you wait in the line until it is your turn before going through the front door, across the small courtyard and into the *darshan* hall. The *darshan* hall is where the ceremonies are conducted, but which can accommodate only 15 to 20 people at a time. When it is your turn to enter the *garbha griha* or sanctum area, you can see the deity of Lord Badrinath. He is a black stone deity sitting in the lotus position, meditating, covered with silks and jewelry, barely visible underneath everything. To the right is His devotee Uddhava. Farther right are Nara and Narayana. Kneeling in front on the right is Narada Muni. Kneeling on the left is Garuda, His carrier. On the left side of Badrinath is Kubera, the treasurer of the demigods, and a silver Ganesh. Hanging over the deities is a canopy covered with a layer of pure gold. Outside the sanctum and in the courtyard there is also a shrine to Lakshmi on the left of the main temple which is painted red. Outside the exit door you will find the sitting place of Shankaracharya. Around the courtyard of the temple are other shrines that you will see. Behind the temple of Badrinarayan is the Lakshmi Narasimha mandir, with shrines to Desikacharyar and Ramanujacharya. Simply by accepting the *charanamrita* or bathing water of the deity and circumambulating the temple, it is said one will get the merit of performing an *ashvamedha* ritual.

The most auspicious time to have *darshan* of Lord Badrinath is in the early morning, so you can expect it to be crowded. The temple opens at 6:30 A.M. and closes between 1:00 P.M. and 3:00 P.M. It opens for the evening audiences and then closes for the day at 9:00 P.M. Since only a few people at a time can see the deity, there is a long waiting line all the time, but shorter in the afternoon than in the morning when it can take an hour or two to see the deity.

The deity of Badrinath is also called Badarinarayana or Badri Vishal. It is said to have self-manifested from a *shalagrama-shila* stone that was two feet tall. When Buddhism was in its prime, the deity somehow was neglected and thrown into Narada Kund where He stayed for several years. Later, Shankaracharya recovered the deity and reinstalled Him. This small Narada Kund is found a few feet from the Alaknanda River, and bathing in it is considered auspicious, especially before having *darshan* of Lord Badrinath. Another hot spring that pilgrims use is the Tapta Kund near the temple steps. It has a temperature of about 45 degrees centigrade (115 degrees Fahrenheit). Nearby are the Panch (Five) Shilas or rocks that represent Narada, Narasimha, Varaha, Garuda, and Markandeya.

A little upstream along the Alaknanda River is Brahma Kapal Ghat. This is where many people offer *pinda* to their ancestors in a *shraddha* ceremony. Local priests are ready to assist you, and you can see groups or families being instructed by the priests as they participate in such rites. The name of the *ghat* comes from the time when Lord Shiva cut off Lord Brahma's fifth head (Brahma Kapal) which fell here.

A place called Deva Darshini is where the *devas* or demigods come to have *darshan* of Badrinath. You can reach it by making a climb 600 feet up.

It is also said that Narada Muni and the demigods come here during the winter months to continue the worship of Badrinath when the other priests leave for the winter and go to Joshimath. In the middle of November the priests perform one last *puja*, leave the ghee lamps lit, and close the temple. Badrinath stays closed 6 months a year from

Deepavali all the way until the full moon day in the month of Chittirai (late spring in the Himalayas). Then in May they return, open the temple, and the ghee lamps are still burning, thanks to the demigods.

The tradition of this temple is explained as follows: Since the history of this temple is so old, the only way we can understand how it came to be is by the exlanations in the *Puranas*. In Satya-yuga, the Lord lived at Badarikashrama (Badrinatha) in a visible form. In Treta-yuga, the sages saw the Lord through the practice of yoga. Then during the age of Dvapara-yuga, it became difficult even for the sages to see the Lord. So then the sages and even the demigods prayed to the Lord, "You are our only supporter, please do not leave this place and ourselves."

Being pleased by their devotion, the Supreme said, "My dear ones and saints! After some time Kali-yuga will start. People in that age will be full of sins, wickedness, pride, and without any pious action. So I cannot stay in a visible form before them. But here under Narada Shila in the Alaknanda, there is a divine image of mine, which you may take and establish. If one sees that image, he will get the same reward of seeing me in visible form."

After that, Brahma and the other gods took that image out of the Narada Kund and asked Visvakarma, the architect of the gods, to build a temple, after which they established the deity there. Narada Muni was made their official priest, and a rule was made that the deity would be worshiped for six months by human beings, and the other six months by the gods. And this rule is still followed to this day.

In the *Skanda Purana* another story is told relating how the deity of Badrivishal was established. Therein it is explained that Lord Shankar (Shiva) told his son Skanda that in Kali-yuga, he would take the deity as a saint (Shankaracharya) from Narada Kund and install it. Thus, by seeing that deity, all the sins of a person will be removed in a moment, just as the heard of elephants run away by seeing a lion. So after some time, Lord Shakara took birth as Shankaracharya and established the deity of Sri Badrinathji for the general good of all people.

How this happened is further related. At the tender age of twelve, Shankaracharya went to Badarikashrama after a hard three months of travel up into the mountains with his pupils. He took bath in the hot springs of Taptakund and went into the temple, but the four-armed form of Narayana that had been established by the rishis in Satya-yuga was not there. In its place was a *shalagram-shila* stone, which is considered the same as the Lord. But Shankaracharya went outside the temple with a heavy heart, followed by the temple priests. He asked them, "Why is the temple without Narayana's form? I have heard that the Lord resides here in this pious place for the last four yugas."

The priests replied, "Because of the tyranny of Chinese robbers, our ancestors hid that form of the Lord in the nearby *kund*. But after that it was difficult to find. So from that time on we have allowed the *shalagram-shila* to reside on the altar." So Shankaracharya asked them if the form of the Lord could be found, would they install and worship it in the temple. The priests all agreed.

The Shankaracharya went to the *kund* and meditated, and then went into the water. The priests asked him not to go since there was a current below in which many people had lost their lives. But Shankaracharya did not listen. He went deep into the *kund* and pulled out a deity of Lord Narayana to everyone's astonishment. But the fingers on the right hand of the deity were broken, so he went back in and pulled out another deity, but the same fingers were broken. Then he did that a third time and became perplexed until a voice told him, "Shankara, you need not be confused. In this Kali-yuga, only this broken form will be worshiped." So in this way, Shankaracharya came out of the water with the deity and installed it in the temple in a solemn manner. He established one of his disciples, Nambudri Brahmana, for doing the worship. In this way, the deity and the temple were again established by Sri Shankaracharya. Today, people of all races, creeds, religions, and communities go there with respect to see the deity of Lord Narayana, Badrivishal.

There are additional noteworthy places in the area. There is also a temple to the beautiful Apsara Urvasi where she took away Indra's pride. And there is a boulder at Charanpaduka, two kilometers away, that has the footprints of Lord Vishnu. This is where He stepped when He once descended to earth. Near here is also Maninag Parvat Mountain, where Yudhisthira answered the *yaksha's* riddles as described in the *Mahabharata*.

You will also see many beautiful mountains surrounding the area. Across from the temple is the mountain Nara Parvata, behind the temple is Narayana Parvata, and to the left of that is Neelkantha, which rises almost 22,000 feet.

An interesting and large stone you might see or ask about is the Sesha Netra which has one eye of Ananta Sesha on it, who is said to be watching everyone. Guidebooks to Badrinatha are readily sold in the shops across the river from the temple. To get a more detailed description of the legends and stories behind this holy site, just purchase a copy and read it while visiting. I often do this when I travel to better absorb the significance of the holy place while I am here.

MANA

Mana is the little village about four kilometers past Badrinath, taking the path past Brahma Kapal. The is a paved path from the Badrinatha temple all the way to Mana. It is a pleasant walk through the fields and a few houses where local farmers live. You get some nice views of the local mountains on either side of the fields and the temple from a distance. Then it reaches the military camp. Unfortunately, Mana is near the border of China, which is only 48 kilometers away, so it has been a restricted area to foreigners. When I went the first time, I was met by a military man who simply asked me to come to a small cabin to have an officer ask me some questions and write down my passport number. It was all very cordial and only took a few minutes and I was again on my way. However, the last time I visited they did not do that. There was only one soldier along the path and he merely wanted to shake my hand after meeting someone from the United States. As you continue to walk along the path, you go over an area of white rocks near the water and cross the Alakananda River by the use of a rickety and narrow wooden bridge, since the larger suspension bridge has been wiped out by an avalanche or something. Then you go up the lengthy and sometimes steep path toward Bhima's Bridge. And if you do not want to walk, you can take a car or bus from the town of Badrinatha to the western edge of Mana. Then walk into town.

The villagers here are friendly, and often pay no attention to the hundreds of tourists and pilgrims who walk through their town. A little beyond the village is the Bridge of Bhima (Bhima Pul) which is a huge stone slab Bhima used so Draupadi and his brothers could easily cross the Sarasvati River. From there you can see the foaming milk-white water flowing out of a cave. This is the Sarasvati River, though not the original, which begins at a glacier north of Mana. The Sarasvati flows out of the cave a short distance to join the Alakananda at Keshava Prayag. The temple to the mother of Nara and Narayana, Mata Murti, is near Keshava Prayag.

Farther upstream and beyond Mana is Vasudhara Falls and Satopanth Lake. Take the path and walk across the flowering meadow and about three kilometers farther out you'll arrive at Vasudhara Falls, which is 135 feet high. The path is a little rough until you reach the starting place of the Alakananda near the Bhagirath Kharak and Satopanth glaciers. Keep going across the Chakra-tirtha meadow. This is near where Arjuna bathed and received the Pashupati Astra weapon from Lord Shiva, which he used in defeating the Kauravas during the battle of Kuruksetra. Finally, over the steep glacier, you'll reach Sato-panth Lake, 25 kilometers from Badrinath. This lake is called the Lake of Divine Trinity and at each of the three corners is where Lord Vishnu, Shiva, and Brahma meditate beside the crystal clear water. Lord Vishnu bathes in this lake on Ekadasi days. Here you can see the mountains of Neelkanth, Chaukhamba, and Swargarohini around you. The Swarga-rohan Mountain is also called the Stairway to Heaven because it is believed that the Pandavas ascended to the spiritual world while climbing this mountain, as described in the *Mahabharata*.

Above the town a few steep kilometers away is the place of Vyasadeva's cave, which is painted white with red stripes in front but is somewhat dark inside. A description above the doorway says that this cave is over 5000 years old, from the time when Vyasadeva lived here. Inside you will find a couple dark stone deities of Vyasadeva. You can certainly feel the energy in this cave as you sit here and meditate on the greatness of Vyasadeva and his writings. Many say that Srila Vyasadeva still lives here. You have to raise your consciousness to be able to see him. When I first visited this cave back in the early 90s, hardly anyone came here. There were only a few occasional visitors, and no priest was around. It was a most intimate setting to get into the higher vibration of the cave and residence of Srila Vyasadeva. I really liked it. But now, there is more emphasis for pilgrims to visit this site, so there are always people coming and going, and a priest is always there keeping guard. It's not quite the same, though I still recommend it for anyone.

The caves of Bhima and Muchukunda are located above Vyasadeva's cave. Not far away, back down the path, is Ganesh's cave, as noted by the sign on the hut. This is where Vyasadeva narrated to Ganesh the *Mahabharata* and *Srimad-Bhagavatam*. There are rocks that look like piles of papers that represent Ganesh's work of writing Vyasadeva's narrations. However, there are others who say that Vyasadeva wrote the *Mahabharata*, along with the *Vedas*, *Upanishads*, and some of the *Puranas* on the banks of the

Sarasvati River where long ago it flowed through Kuruksetra. Nearby is said to be where Lord Shiva narrated the *Skanda Purana* to the sage Skanda.

As with any mountain town, the weather here can be very unpredictable. One time when I was here, I arrived at night while it was cold and rainy. The next morning it became bright and sunny, but the clouds came in and it was snowing by noon. A few hours later it was sunny and warm again and melting the snow. But at night it was freezing. So be prepared for the way the weather changes.

THE FIVE BADRI TEMPLES

After we have completed our tour of Badrinath we can begin to head back to Rishikesh, but for some of the serious pilgrims, they may want to see the other Badri temples. Actually, there are five Badri temples scattered about in different places, which the serious pilgrim can see on his way back. The main temple is, of course, the Badri Vishal temple at Badrinath. Then there are the additional temples known as the Adi Badri, Vriddha Badri, Bhavishya Badri, and the Yogadhyan Badri. Naturally, these temples are not as popular, but some of the serious pilgrims visit them nonetheless. And some are easier to get to than others. For example, Yogadhyan Badri is in the town of Pandukeswara, 24 kilometers south of Badrinath. This is also the town where the Pandavas were born and where King Pandu did austerities for killing two mating deer who were actually two sages. King Pandu installed the bronze image of Yogadhyan Badri here.

The Vridha (or Bridha) Badri temple is in the little village of Animath, about 17 kilometers south of Joshimath. Vridha Badri appeared to Narada Muni when he performed penance here.

Bhavishya Badri is situated in the tiny village of Subhain, a three kilometer walk east of Tapovan, which is 15 kilometers or so east of Joshimath. This will be the main Badri temple in the future.

The Adi Badri Temple is the farthest away, located 18 kilometers south of Karna Prayag. Inside a small 16 temple complex, the main temple contains Adi Badri Narayana, a black stone deity that is three feet tall. In His hands He holds a mace, disc, and lotus.

Another place in the Badrinatha region is Dhudi Prayag, where the Pundavati River flows into the Alakananda. This is another place known as the birthplace of Ganesh.

DEVA PRAYAG (or DEOPRAYAG)

On our way back to Rishikesh, another town to take note of is Deva Prayag (or Deoprayag), 1700 feet above sea level. Devaprayag is considered to be Tirukkandam or Kadinagar. We may have already gone through this town if we went from Rishikesh to Kedarnatha or Badrinath. The tradition is that you stop here on your way up into the mountains to take a dip at the *sangam* and open your hearts to the great sages who have traveled and stayed at the holy sites in these mountains. However, if you have started your tour of the Char Dham sites in Yamunotri, and then gone to Gangotri, Kedarnath, and ending in Badrinatha, then you would have bypassed this town until now.

This is the first major town northeast of Rishikesh by about 70 kilometers and around 32 km southwest of Srinagar. It is also a resting point for pilgrims bound to (and from) Badrinath. It is where the confluence of the Bhagirathi and Alakananda rivers is located. This is where the river becomes the Ganga or Ganges, at least in name. This is a very important *sangam* or confluence, second only to Allahabad where the Yamuna, Ganges, and Sarasvati meet. Tradition has it that the town is named after Deosharma, a sage, who led a life of penance here and succeeded in having a glimpse of God.

At Deva Prayag, in Treta-yuga, Lord Rama and Lakshmana performed a *yajna*, spiritual ritual, here to purify themselves of killing the demon Ravana because he was a brahmana. You will find an old Raghunatha temple here, erected about 1250 years ago. It has a deity of Sri Rama that is 15 feet tall. Tradition is that the ancient temple was established by Adi Shankaracharya, enshrining Rama (Raghunathji). However, other legends say that the great temple was originally erected over ten thousand years ago and was built of massive uncemented stones. The temple, along with the other buildings of the town, was shattered by an earthquake in 1803 but the damage was subsequently repaired through the munificence of Daulat Rao Sindhia. There are also shrines to Hanuman, Badrinathji, Kaala Bhairavar, and Shiva here. Brahma, Dasaratha, and Rama are said to have prayed here. In light of this legend, the nearby Dasharathachal Peak contains a rock known as Dashrathshila on which King Dasharath is said to have done penance. A small stream, the *shanta* running down from the Dasarathachal, is named after Shanta, the daughter of King Dasharath and is considered to be sacred. Deoprayag is considered one of the Divya Desams, or one of the 108 most important Vishnu temples in India. You can also see Vamana's cave, which is behind the temple and up the hill a ways. And there is also the stone throne of Lord Rama not far away.

Once we are finished seeing Devaprayag, we can keep going down from the mountains and back to Rishikesh.

NAHAN

Once we are done with our tour of the Char Dham region, then from Rishikesh we may want to head farther north to see more of northern India. Going farther west from Dehra Dun, about 85 kilometers toward Chandigarh, is Nahan. It is a beautiful hill town settled on a wide ridge at an elevation of 3050 feet (930 Meters). To the south you can see the Haryana plains, and the Shivalik Mountains to the north. You enter the town through the Lytton Memorial gate. In the middle of town is the Ranital Park and the Pucca water tank. It also has a few palaces to see, and the Jagannatha temple in the bazaar. Near Kalamb, 10 km south of Nahan, is the interesting Saketi Fossil Park that displays fiberglass models of the prehistoric animals whose fossils had been found in the area. About 25 km out of Nahan is the Trilokpur temple which stands on a hill. It was built by Raja Deep Prakash in 1573. It is known for the colorful festival they hold in May and October which attracts thousands of pilgrims from the area.

Renuka Lake, formed by the surrounding hills, is about 45 km to the northeast of Nahan. This lake is connected with the legend of Renuka, the wife of the Vedic sage

Jamadagni and mother of the great Parashurama. It is said that taking bath here is most purifying for a person's spiritual development. There is an annual fair in November held around the lake and Parashurams Tal, a smaller lake next to the Renuka. People from the surrounding villages attend and join in the celebration with singing and dancing, vendors selling goods of all kinds, and of course worshipping and taking purifying dips in the water.

CHANDIGARH AND GOING NORTH

Chandigarh is one of the best transportation centers in the area. You can get buses going in any direction, and often times to the very town in the region that you want to reach. From Chandigarh we can decide which route we will take next. It is easy to take a direct bus from Chandigarh to Amritsar for a visit, or head northeast toward Manali. In this case we will first go toward Manali. Chandigarh really has little to offer the pilgrim, unless you want to stop and see the museum or art gallery. But while you are here, if you do want to stop for a visit, there are a few things you can see.

Chandigarh is a fairly modern city, built in the early 1950s and designed by the renowned architect Le Corbusier, and divided into 57 sectores. It is the capital of both Haryana and Punjab. It is built in a way where there is plenty of room for expansion and more development. Sector 17 is the main shopping area, with a plaza and fountain surrounded by shops. Nearby is the rose garden with a musical fountain, lovely lawns and over 1000 varieties of roses in multiple colors. In Sector 10 is the City Museum on the development of the town, the Natural History Museum, and the Art Gallery which has one of the best collections of sculptures, miniature paintings, and deities from various parts of India. Not far from the Capital Complex is the Rock Garden. This is a popular spot that has a collection of hills, waterfalls, caves, and artsy sculptures made from a variety of unlikely items. A short distance away is the Sukhna Lake, a man-made construction that draws many people for jogging or walking, boat paddling, or just enjoying the area, sunsets, or evening lights.

Once we start heading north, along the way there are a few small towns that we may want to see. **Pinjore** is not too far away from Chandigarh, about 45 minutes or 22 kilometers, and is where you can stop if you'd like to see the 17th century Moghul gardens and the Shish Mahal Palace, and the Rang and Jai Mahals. Then we go on to **Solan** where we find the Soloni Devi temple located on the southern side of town. The town of **Chail** is a little off the main road, and you will not go through it by bus, but here you can see the hilltop Chail Palace and an ancient Sikh temple.

If we want, we can take the bus from Chandigarh to Kalka where we can take the small gauge train through the hills straight up to Shimla.

SHIMLA

Shimla is a much larger town, population around 110,000, and crowded with lots of buildings, streets, and alleys packed onto the hillside. It is popular as a cool hill station during the summer with an altitude of 21,000 meters. However, when I was there in

June, it was still 30 degrees Centigrade, and I was sweating in the sun. So I did not think it was so cool. Nonetheless, it was especially used by the British when they would move here for the summer. There's not much of spiritual interest here, but you can certainly have a little fun exploring the town and walking to nearby points of interest, such as to Summer Hill, Prospect Hill, Chadwick Falls, the Hanuman temple at Sankat Mochan, or the Tara Devi temple seven kilometers out of town. Of course, that's if you still have the energy after everything else we have done so far.

According to tradition, Hanuman is said to have rested here while bringing the special *sanjeevani* herb from the Himalayan Mountains in order to save the life of Lakshmana, the brother of Lord Ramachandra. A temple dedicated to him is said to mark the spot on the summit of Jakhu Hill before the British became familiar with Shimla and turned it into their summer hill station. Monkeys are still found in the area of the temple as a manifestation of the deity. However, the village that was on the ridge of the Jakhu hill was named after the goddess Shyamla, an expansion of goddess Kali, the image of whom was worshipped by the villagers.

Narkanda is a town about 60 km east of Shimla. This small town, population 700, is a popular place for seeing the Himalayas, especially from Hattu peak at 3300 meters. This whole area is popular for ski resorts.

Rampur is a farther 52 km east, 140 km from Shimla, which is the site of a significant trade fair, the Lavi Mela, in November. It draws people from the area to trade their local goods. The town also has an interesting Buddhist monastery and an ancient Vedic temple.

Sarahan is 34 km farther east, the home of the Bhimkali temple which has a combination of Buddhist and Hindu architecture. From here we can go back to Shimla and then head northwest up to Bilaspur.

Bilaspur is about 67 km northwest of Shimla which has the Vyas Gufa cave, and the Lakshmi-Narayana and Radha Shyama temples. You can also find the temple of **Naina Devi** on top of a hill. This is a Shaktipeeth shrine to Sati, the consort of Lord Shiva, where it is considered the eyes of Sati fell to earth, the story of which is explained elsewhere. In this temple, when you go in you will see the deity in the form of a small, decorated black stone with golden eyes resting on a red backdrop. The eyes represent the graceful and constant gaze of Devi.

If we are going to continue our way north, then we will go through Bilaspur anyway, and then we can head up to the town of Mandi. If we are not interested in seeing Bilaspur, you can get a direct bus to Kullu or straight on toward Manali.

However, if we are heading south once our visit to Shimla is over, and if you do not want to see the little towns mentioned above, you can take a small train through the hills, going around forested curves and short tunnels, from Shimla to Kalka where we switch to the Himalayan Queen on the faster broad gauge line. This train goes directly to New Delhi but also stops at Kuruksetra, which is a very significant town in relation to Krishna if we want to stop there. But on this tour we will continue going north.

MANDI

This town, population about 30,000, is considered the gateway to the Kullu Valley. It is a pleasant town with the Beas River flowing through it. It has a popular Bhutanath Shiva temple, with its gold-plated pinnacle on its dome. This is an active temple and many things go on here for the local devotees. There are also the Triloknath (has a three-faced Shiva riding his bull Nandi, with Parvati standing at the side), Panchvaktra (for the five-faced image of Shiva) and Shayamalkoli temples at Tarna Hill. The Ardhanarishvara temple has an image that is half Shiva and half Parvati. The small Batuka Bhairon temple has a typical image found in Northern India of Shiva as Bhairava. Here he is seen as fierce, with protruding fangs and round eyes. Most of these temples are on the small size, yet some are beautifully carved stone examples of the Shikhara style architecture. The festival of Shivaratri is especially famous here. It lasts a week and deities are brought here from all over the area. Additional Vaishnava temples in Mandi include the Jagannatha, Ramachandra, Madho Rai Vishnu, and others. You can find an assortment just by wandering around.

KULLU

On our way to Kullu from Mandi we go through the town of **Bajaura**, about fifteen kilometers south of Kullu, where you will find the temple of Basheshar Mahadeva (Shiva) with ornate stone carvings.

Bijli Mahadeva Shiva temple is eight kilometers southeast of Kullu. This is reached by a difficult climb up a six kilometer incline. It has a 65-foot tall flagstaff that attracts lightning. When it's struck by lightning, the Shiva *linga* is broken, after which it is put back together with a paste made from roasted gram and wheat powder.

Bhekhli village is three kilometers out from Kullu and is where the Jagannatha Devi temple is located up a steep climb. And four kilometers out of Kullu toward Manali is a Vaishno Devi temple, with a representation of the goddess Vaishno in a small cave.

Kullu, population about 19,000, is a more mellow town and less crowded by tourists than Manali. In the ancient Sanskrit texts of the *Vishu Purana*, *Ramayana*, and *Mahabharata* Kullu is mentioned as Luluta. It was also known as Kulantapith, which indicated it was the end of the habitable world, up to the Rohtang pass where the landscape changes significantly from forested hillsides to barren moonscapes.

Kullu is particularly known for the Raghunathji temple, dedicated to Lord Rama. The deity was brought from Ayodhya in 1651 by King Raja Jagat Singh (1637-1672) after which he submitted the kingdom to the deity. Thus, the deity is considered to preside over the Kullu valley region. This was to make amends for having caused the death of a brahmana. From that time, the king and his successors accepted themselves as the agents of Raghunath. The temple is on a hill on the northern side of the Sarvari River behind the Kullu Raja's Rupi Palace that overlooks the city. It is reached by traversing a path from near the Kailash Cinema by the bus stand. It is best to visit before 9 A.M. or after 5 P.M.

The richly adorned deities lead the processions during the Dussehra festival, which celebrates the defeat of the demon Ravana by Lord Rama.

Other temples in the area of Kullu include those for Vaishno Devi, Jagannathi Devi, Basheshar Mahadev, and Bilji Mahadev, the last of which is found across from the town of Kullu.

Kullu is also well known for its Dussehra Festival in October. They have a huge festival here that celebrates the victory of Lord Rama over the demon Ravana. The deity of Raghunatha is brought into the valley on a chariot in a grand procession where He stays for a week. Then the other 200 or so deities in the area are brought to Him to offer worship. They assemble in the Dhalpur Maidan, the festival field. Vendors set up little shops to sell all kinds of things, and groups perform traditional dances. The town becomes very crowded with pilgrims at this time, so accommodations become quite limited.

PLACES ALONG THE WAY NORTH TO MANALI

Katrain is the town thirteen kilometers south of Manali. High above it is **Naggar**, which has the Naggar Castle hotel where you can get excellent views of the area. The castle used to be headquarters for the local Raja. The small old fort is built around a courtyard that has the Jagtipath temple. There is a story that a five by eight foot stone slab in the temple was cut from a stone at Deotiba and carried through the air by a swarm of honey bees. These bees had been transformed from a group of demigods. The stone was carried to Naggar Castle after it had been decided to be the seat of all the gods. Another aspect of the legend is that one of the rulers of Kullu took a girl from a village near the Rohtang Pass as a bride. The young Rani was so homesick that the deities of the area became bees and carried this rock from her village and placed it here as a reminder in her new home.

There are also a few old temples here, such as the Gauri Shankar Shiva temple that has deities of Shiva and Parvati. It is located at the small bazaar below the castle, and dates to the 11th or 12th century. Across from the front of the castle, off the main road, is the small Chatar Bhuj Vishnu temple, which has a beautiful Vishnu deity that stands four feet high. Higher up is the Tripura Sundri Devi temple, dedicated to Durga, with its pagoda-like structure. On the ridge higher up is the Murlidhar Krishna temple, reached after a tough 20-minute climb. Above the castle is the Roerich Art Gallery which displays the paintings of the Russian Nicholas Roerich.

Bhrigu Kund is a beautiful place where Bhrigu Muni is supposed to have performed austerities, but it takes a rugged, six hour walk to reach it. There is also the Beas Kund, source of the Beas River where Vyasadeva performed austerities.

Jagatsukh is the small village six kilometers south of Manali, off the main road. Here you'll find a small but old temple to Lord Shiva, the Gauri Shankara temple which has a *linga* in the sanctum, and is one of the more beautiful carved stone shikhara style temples. You can also see a temple of Murlidhar (Krishna). There is another temple to Sandhya Gayatri and Brahma that dates back to the 8th century. It has a number of images, such as Ganesh, Vishnu, Shiva, and Uma. There is also an image of a four-armed form of Mahishasuramardini, or Durga killing the Mahish demon. The Devi Sheravali temple has an image of Durga riding her lion carrier. The Pandavas are also said to have visited these temples.

Arjuna Gupha, or the cave of Arjuna, is about five kilometers south of Manali, not far from Jagatsukh near the Prime Cafe. This is where Arjuna underwent austerities to acquire the Pashupata Astra weapon from Lord Shiva. He fought and pleased Shiva, who was disguised as a Kirata, thus earning the weapon. To reach this place is a tough two hour climb with little to see upon reaching it. Furthermore, this may not be the exact place of the event since two other places in India claim the same history, unless Arjuna had continued his austerities in these places.

Vashisth is a small town three kilometers from Manali across the river. There are some small but interesting temples here. Tat Baba, located a short walk away from the Vashistha temple, is where the ashram of Vashistha, the spiritual master of Lord Rama, is said to have been. This is where he performed austerities. Legend has it that Vashistha once tied himself with ropes and jumped into the river when the *rakshasha* demon Kalmashped killed his 100 sons. But the river loosened the ropes and released him, which gave the river the name of Vipasha, or that which liberates one from bondage. There are also a number of sulphur hot springs around Vishisth, including some within the Vasistha temple grounds. The Manikaran hot springs is said to help one's spiritual progress as well as one's health. The legend is that a serpent stole the earrings of the goddess while she was bathing. Then while being threatened by Shiva, the serpent blew the earrings out of his underground residence, causing holes to be created through which the hot water now flows. Across from the Vashisth temple is a Mahadeva Shiva temple made of beautifully carved wood. It has a simple Shiva *lingam* inside. Up a stairway is a stone Rama temple, small but interesting, with deities of Sita-Rama and Lakshmana.

MANALI

Manali is a small resort town, population 4400, and is a good place to relax after our journey through Ladakh, or when getting ready to go to Ladakh. However, it gets really crowded in the months of May-June and through September. It has plenty of places to stay, but the prices may be high and hotels get quickly booked up in the tourist season. It also offers many nice walks, treks, and biking trips you can take through the nearby countryside and villages which are quaint but beautiful if you are into that. There are plenty of internet shops so you can catch up with emails, etc., before moving on if we want. But finding one without connection problems can be the challenge. People come for the cool atmosphere, but there are some spiritual points of interest here, too.

For example, the Manu temple, located three kilometers from downtown, marks where Manu first stepped onto dry land after saving the *Vedas* and the animals in his boat after the great flood. Manaligarh is the fort of Manu located in the village of the same name centered around the Manu Maharishi temple. In fact, the name Manali is in reference to this. The name "Manali" is short for the name "Manu-Alaya," which means the "home of Manu." It is one of the only temples to Manu in all of India. The simple temple has a tower over the sanctum, which enshrines a small deity within.

There is also the four-tiered pagoda-style Hidimba temple dedicated to the wife of Bhima in the Dhoongri forest, surrounded by deodar cedars. The present temple was built in 1553 around a small natural cave that houses the footprints of Hidimba. It was here that Bhima married Hidimba after he killed Hidimb, her man-eating brother. They had a son, Ghatotkatch, who was a great warrior who died in the Kuruksetra war. A tree temple for him is also nearby. In other words, this is not a temple structure, but a tree that has been turned into a temple. The Kullu royal family later adopted Hidimba as their patron goddess. Giving way to tourism, near the temple grounds you will now find plenty of carnival-like vendors offering the visitors such things as cotton candy, yak rides, pony rides, Tibetan ladies carrying large rabbits for the children to pet, and the typical snake charmers.

Manali also has the Museum of Traditional Himachal culture. It is a small but well-organized collection of arts and crafts from across the Kullu Valley. It is not far from the Hidimba temple, right across from the Ghatotkatch temple.

On the way down the hill from here, with a little diversion, you can stop and see the Siyali Mahadeva temple, newly built with a beautiful wood exterior covered with intricate carvings. However, they would not allow me to go inside.

Manali also has the largest settlement of Tibetan refugees in the Kullu Valley. The Gadhan Thekchokling Gompa was built in the 1960s by Tibetan refugees. It features a bright yellow roof and an image of Sakyamuni Buddha and the usual bright frescoes on the walls. In another location is the Himalayan Ngingmapa Buddhist monastery. This is a small *gompa* with a central temple with a few different images of Buddha, and a few other shrines.

One thing about Manali is that it seems that tourism is taking over. This is similar to many other places that were primarily spiritual sites. Where there was once open country is now covered with hotels and shops aimed at tourists. Like at the Manu temple, there were few buildings around it ten years ago, but now there are shops right next to it. This is an example of how India is losing its culture.

PLACES AROUND MANALI

There are a number of places around Manali which you can visit, if you have the time and energy. Some of these places are not easy to find or reach, yet I mention them since we are in the area.

The Tabo Buddhist Monastery is off the beaten path and a ways from any big towns. It is in Himachal Pradesh over 100 kilometers east of Manali. From Manali or Gramphu you take the road to Langja, and then the secondary road down to Tabo. There are also special travel packages available for pilgrims. So check with a travel agent once you reach Manali.

Architecturally it is quite impressive. It is one of the largest Buddhist complexes and holds a past that is being lost. It is an ancient seat of Buddhist religion. It contains nine temples, 23 *chortens*, and chambers for monks and nuns. You can find "The Temple of the Enlightened Gods" in the center of the complex. You can see the image of Vairocana turning the wheel of law. He is one of the five spiritual sons of the Adibuddha. Around him along the wall are 33 life-size stucco images of the Vajradhatu Mandala, with flaming circles around them.

There is also the Golden Temple, which is said to have been originally layered in gold, and has murals covering its walls and ceiling. Within the Mystic Mandala or Initiation Temple is a huge painting of Vairocana surrounded by the eight Bodhisattvas. Mystic mandalas cover the remaining spaces.

The temple of Bodhisattva Maitreya houses an image of Maitreya that is six meters tall. The temple has a hall and sanctum with vestibule, and has many murals within. The temple of Dromton, founded by Dromton (1008-1064), lies on the northern edge of the complex and has an intricately carved doorway. The large temple has a floor space of over 70 square meters, with another 42 square meters in the portico and niche. An image of Sakyamuni, with Sariputra and Maha Maugdalayana at his sides adorns the front wall. The other walls offer the eight Medicine Buddhas and guardian kings.

Newer additions to the complex include the Mahakala Vajra-bhairava temple, referred to as the temple of horror because it has the protective deity of the Geluk-pa sect, with other fierce deities in the room. It is supposed to be entered only after doing protective meditation.

The White Temple is also an attractive place to see. Above the enclave on the almost vertical cliff-face you can still find the caves that were once used by monks, and the traces of the paintings.

FROM MANALI TO LEH

Whether we can go to Leh from Manali will depend on the season and the snowfall. This road to Leh from Manali is usually open only from the end of June to September, depending on the weather. So if you are traveling outside of that season, don't expect the roads to be clear to go. If you are able to go to Leh, the bus stand at Manali has a booth with computerized service. It is a two day trip, leaving at 4-5 A.M., and going 297 miles or 476 km and reaching elevations up to 17,400 feet or 5304 meters. It stops for the night usually at Sarchu. Book your ticket as soon as you can since travelers can be numerous in the tourist season. Or use one of the many travel agents along the mall road. Or book through the Manali Luxury Coach Owner's Association. But you have to check the day before the bus is leaving because of the unpredictable nature of the weather. When available, you can also take taxis or share taxis for a 14-hour trip at a much higher cost.

We leave Manali early and we will head up through the pine forests along the Beas River. It is a fairly smooth ride at first. As we get near Mirhi, which is mostly a bunch of shacks that function as restaurants in front of steep grassy slopes that go up to the pass, the road begins to change.

Rohtang La pass is the first pass we go through at 3978 meters. You can also visit this place as a trip from Manali (50 miles, 32 km away), which is approached through a climb up some real hair pin turns. However, it offers some spectacular views of the local Himalayan mountains. It does require care in driving as "Rohtang" means "heaps of dead bodies" for the lives it has claimed over the years. If you have not bought winter clothes, there are plenty of shops along the way that can facilitate that need. At the pass, there are plenty of people playing in the mountain snow, partying and celebrating with friends. Some go for rides on horseback, or sleding through the snow. Traffic can be quite congested because of the number of people here, slowing any cars, busses, or trucks that are trying to get through. After the pass, the slopes get much barer of trees and vegetation. It is an exciting and exhilarating view as we look down over the mountains from the road. The road quickly descends through winding turns to Gramphu. The highway splits in two directions here, southeast to the Spiti Valley, or northwest to Keylong, where we will be going.

Khoksar or Kosar is the next town another 5 kilometers away. This is where you register at the police checkpoint as you start through this region. The town of Sissu is not far from here and has a lovely waterfall descending from the peaks. Also along the route is Gondhla which has an eight-storey tall castle of the Thakur of Gondhla, though it is in bad shape and viewed only from the outside. There is also a Buddhist *gompa* that has some historic importance.

Keylong is the next town after going through Tandi. Here a break from the drive is a usual custom. From the bus stand you go down the series of steps as you enter the town. If you spend the evening here, there are some decent places from which to choose for lodging. You can also find plenty of shops and several monasteries to see, which include the 900 year old Khardong *gompa*, one of the more prominent ones here. But it's a 4 km walk uphill after crossing the Bhaga River from the hospital. Another is the Shashur *gompa*, about 3 km out of Keylong. This belongs to the Gelugpa order, built in the 16th century, and is known for the masked dancers during the Chaam Festival in June-July.

From Keylong we go to Jispa and to Darcha where we stop at the police checkpoint and register again. From here we cross the river at Patseo which is where we see the last of any trees for the next 150 miles. We leave the forests for the barren rock and snows of the high ground and passes, starting with the Baralacha La pass at 4883 meters. The roads twist and turn through the rock. Then we head down through the Lingti plains to Sarchu for the usual night stop.

Sarchu is a tent city where you will find a number of tent encampments which dot an area 15 kilometers long, and where the bus will stop. You sleep in one of the chilly tents. The bus you are taking will determine in which tents you spend the night. They are all overpriced for what you get at about Rs 300-400 a tent, but you have to grin and bare it. Two bed tents come with bedding, but a good sleeping bag is still best to have when it gets close to September. Mountain weather is always unpredictable. There is plenty of food and tea here when needed, each encampment providing it from the makeshift kitchens they have. Another police checkpoint is on the northern end of Sarchu across from the HPTDC camp where you will need to register your passport number.

From Sarchu we soon cross into Ladakh. Ladakh was opened for tourism in 1974 and is still a peaceful place for trekking, exploring, and tasting what is here of Tibetan Buddhism. Along with its cultural and topographical similarities, that is one reason why it is called "Little Tibet."

The name Ladakh means "the land of high passes," which you will soon discover how true that is as we travel north. The land routes into Ladakh are only open a few months each year, May to October, and mostly only July to September. Other than that, only flights are possible into Leh, and they are unpredictable at best, dependant on the weather.

While visiting Ladakh there are many activities in which tourists can participate. These include trekking, rafting, camel safaris, mountaineering, and visiting the Buddhist *gompas*. However, the weather can fool you. It can be sunny and quickly burn your skin or suddenly turn cold in the shade. So be prepared with proper clothing.

Once we leave the Lingti Chu River Valley we begin to climb the winding road up to the Lachlang La pass at 5060 meters, which can be tough for both men and machines. The views of rock formations and snow peaks are quite impressive. After this we begin our descent through the Gorges of Pang. The tent town of Pang has another checkpost where we register our arrival, and is mostly just a few huts and tents.

Gradually we climb the Morey Plains, a huge plateau with an altitude of 15,000 feet or 4500 meters, until we reach Debring, another little shanty town. Then we go another 12 miles up to the next pass of Taglang La, at 17,469 feet or 5325 meters high. This is known for being the second highest road pass in the world, and certainly the highest point along this route. It is a slow climb up as you go over many miles of high altitude until the bus stops at the small temple that marks the summit. So it is quite chilly and windy, yet it offers some spectacular vistas. Thereafter, we make our way down to Lato, where you can see a huge Buddhist chorten on the roadside. Descending through a colorful ravine takes us to Upshi, where we find another police checkpost. Here the road enters the Indus Valley where we begin to leave the barren landscapes behind for more colorful scenery. We are now not so far away from Leh, testimony of which are the views of the Buddhist monasteries as we pass through Karu, Tikse, Shey, and Stok. Now we enter the town of Leh, which we will describe elsewhere in the book.

BACK FROM MANALI TO MANDI OR CHANDIGARH

If you are not going to Leh at this time, then you will need to backtrack back toward Mandi from Manali. A bus back to Mandi is easy to get, and from Mandi you can get a bus going to Dharamsala, if you want to continue on in a northwesterly direction. Or if you want to go farther west to places like Amritsar, and then farther north, you may want to take a bus to Chandigarh where it will be easy to get a bus or train to Amritsar. It will take several hours to reach Chandigarh from Manali, and it's another several hours from Chandigarh to Amritsar. So if you want to take a break, then a night stopover at Chandigarh may be good before taking the next bus or train to Amritsar.

AMRITSAR

On our way to Amritsar, however, or while we are in the area, we may want to take a side trip to the city of **Hoshiarpur**. This is where the *Bhrigu Samhita* is located. This is the great astrological text, said to have been written by Bhrigu Muni, the authority on Vedic astrology. This edition is said to have been written about 5,000 years ago and is now kept by the Bhrigus there. Presently, it is a 500 year old manuscript discovered in 1923 by Des Raj, grandfather of the Bhrigu Shastris. They are known to have everyone's horoscope either available or pending, which can be looked up if you can visit them. This is similar to the place in South India known as Vaithisvarankoil. By taking an early morning bus from Hoshiarpur, we'll arrive in Amritsar about six hours later.

We can also take a train or bus to Amritsar directly from Chandigar. There are plenty of hotels near the train station in Amritsar, which is fine since we will be leaving the city by train. I got one hotel on the hill to the east of the station, an easy cycle-ricksha ride away when taking the station's back entrance. When we are ready, we can take a 15-minute cycle-ricksha ride through the town to the Sikh Golden Temple, our main point of interest. Amritsar is a good sized town, and there are many stores and pedestrians in the downtown area.

As we approach the Golden Temple complex, we first see a huge white building with a clock tower in the middle. We first go to the shoe minder's stall to leave our shoes, and then we proceed after covering our head with a cloth. The head must be kept covered inside the temple complex. Outside the complex are many small shops that sell all sorts of Sikh religious paraphernalia and books. The temple also has a museum upstairs in the clock tower which displays a collection of historical paintings of many great Sikh persons and martyrs. The temple also provides free vegetarian food from its large kitchen. Free accommodations to all pilgrims who need it are also available. If you want, you can get a guide at the information office by the clock tower. Then, entering under the eastern clock tower, the stairways lead down to the large courtyard.

Amritsar, population 710,000, was developed in 1577 by the fourth Sikh guru, Ram Das. The name "Amritsar," or Amrita Sarovara, means the "Pool of Nectar," which is the sacred pool in the middle of the temple courtyard. After the pool was established, it was Ram Das' son, Arjun Dev, who built a temple in the middle of the pool in the late 16th century. He also installed the Sikh scripture in it, the *Adi Granth Sahib*. The *Granth* is a collection of verses and songs by revered saints, such as Ramananda, Namdev, Kabir, Nanak, etc., that Arjun Dev had compiled. It was Gobind Singh, the 10th Sikh guru, who established the principle that there would be no more successor gurus, but the *Granth* would be the guru.

As you circle the inner courtyard, going in a clockwise direction, there is a colonnade where there are many rooms where people can stay or rest. Next to the lake, the walkways are made of marble tiles. Some places have beautiful multicolored marble designs. Along the east side of the tank is the area of 68 holy places that Arjun Dev established as being equal to the 68 most holy places of the Hindus. On the south side are chains that lead into the lake so that the men can lower themselves into the water for a holy bath, which is done especially in the morning. As you continue to go around the lake, there are a few special trees and shrines that indicate special events, but the explanations are written in Hindi. On the northwest side of the pool is the Jubi tree, under which Baba Gujhaji, the temple High Priest, sat 450 years ago and oversaw the construction of the temple. Presently, the tree is believed to have powers to grant sons to women who hang strips of cloth from it. Beyond that on the north side is a *bhajan* band of four musicians singing as people sit and listen to the devotional music. You will also pass by other temple rooms and compartments where readings are going on of the *Granth.*

While I was walking around the temple during one of my visits here, one very nice Sikh man and his wife came up and explained that the tree we were standing near on the east side of the lake was in remembrance of the second Sikh guru. He had lived in a village and when Guru Nanak asked who he was, the boy replied, "I am the Dead One." His mother called him that because all of her sons had died young and he would probably die young as well. Then Guru Nanak blessed him and said, "Don't worry, now you will become the Old One." So later he became Guru Nanak's successor and lived to be 130 years old, long enough to see the fourth Sikh Guru.

The man went on to explain some of the tenets of Sikhism, most of which I already knew. He said that the basic principle of Sikhism is unity with God and universal brotherhood. They pray for health and prosperity, but not just for themselves or their community or other Sikhs, but for all people.

He continued to explain that there are four entrances into the Amrit Sarovara Lake and the Golden Temple itself. These represent the openness of Sikhism to all people of the four directions. There are also two temples: The central temple in the lake is for spiritual direction, while the temple on the land represents material instructions. It is by this unity of material and spiritual instructions that one can reach perfection in life and service to God and to humanity. The man went on to say that Sikhism is a world-wide community and since I was there at the Golden Temple, that meant I was also a member of their community. The man pleasantly pointed out that though we may be from different countries, because we were both at the Golden Temple, we were both brothers in spirit. And I firmly agree.

After circling the courtyard, it is time to enter the temple. The Golden Temple is called Hari Mandir, or Temple of the Lord. In 1761 the temple was destroyed by Ahmad Shah Durani. It was rebuilt in 1764 and then was roofed with copper-gilded plates by Ranjit Singh. Thereafter, it became known as the "Golden Temple." The dome of the temple is covered with 220 pounds of gold leaf.

The temple is reached by a causeway called the Guru's Bridge. You can take photos most everywhere except in the temple. Walking out to the temple, the Guru's Bridge is a beautiful walkway with brass railings. They have now built a roof over it with fans that greatly help those who use it to enter the temple, especially since the crowd on it moves very slowly because of the pace of people who move through the temple.

On the temple structure itself, the lower parts of the marble walls have beautiful inlaid flowers and designs, and the upper portion is gold plated. The temple also has beautiful embellished gold plates and doors. The first time I was there they were in the process of replacing the golden plates on the temple, which were about 250 years old. I returned a few years later when the renovations had been completed, and it is indeed a most beautiful building. Upon entering the temple, you can take a handful of halava that they give out, or take a handful when you walk back across the bridge after our visit to the temple. Inside you can see its wonderful design and interior. It is quite exquisite. As we enter the temple, some devotees stay and sit to listen to the songs, or bow down to offer respects to the holy Granth which is in the center of the sanctum. It is indeed inspiring to absorb the atmosphere and devotional mood within this holy monument that brings one closer to God.

The original *Granth* scripture is kept under a jeweled pink cloth on a decorated throne. To the left are several musicians playing and singing the verses of the *Granth* with harmonium, *karatala* hand cymbals, etc. This *kirtana* singing continuously goes out over the loudspeakers and helps produce a very devotional atmosphere. On the right side of the temple interior is an area where some people sit and listen. The top floor is the Hall of Mirrors where the Sikh gurus used to sit. Pilgrims are always walking through and then exiting in the back or side doors and then walk back across the bridge again when they are finished.

The Golden Temple and the courtyard around it is a beautiful place and has a calm and meditative atmosphere. It is especially peaceful at night when you can sit underneath the stars and listen to the soothing recitations of the *Granth* over the loudspeakers next to the pool, which reflects the image of the brightly lit temple on the surface. I will never forget that experience during which I had some very strong realizations in my own meditations. Other Sikhs will be observing prayers at that time, and even if you are not sure of what is happening, you are more than always welcome.

At night around 10 P.M. the *Granth* is ceremoniously taken from the temple to the Akal Takhat building where it spends the night. It is again returned to the temple in a short procession at 4 A.M. (5 A.M. in winter). If you are there at the time, you can watch the proceedings.

South of the temple complex is the temple gardens that cover 30 acres. The eight-storied tower of Babl-Atal, dedicated to Atal Rai, the son of Hargobind, the sixth guru, is at the southern end.

In spite of all the political turbulence that has gone on here over the years, the Sikhs are generally very friendly people and more than willing to share their culture with visitors. I actually had a very nice time on the occasions that I have visited the Golden Temple and met some genuinely friendly people who liked showing me around. It is also an example of an especially open and devotional community.

Not far from the Golden Temple is Jallianwala Bagh, the site where the British opened fire on a crowd of men, women, and children and killed some 2,000 Indians, including Hindus, Muslims, and Sikhs. This incident was a turning point in India's struggle for independence. You can still see the bullet holes in the well into which people jumped trying to escape the bullets.

Also, not far away is the Durgiana temple, dedicated to Lord Krishna. It is also in the middle of a small lake and reached by a bridge. As you enter the gateway leading to the Durgiana temple, there are two small altars, one on either side. One is for Ganesh and one for Durga, both of which are quite beautiful. Then you walk over the bridge out to the temple, which appears simple on the outside but is highly decorated on the inside. It has beautifully embossed silver plated doors with images of demigods and Puranic legends. There are many paintings and illustrations done in multicolored mirrors and lights and ribbons that hang throughout. It has three altars for the beautiful deities. One is for Radha-Krishna and a Govardhan-*shila* which sits on top of a male body, the only one I have ever seen like this. The center altar is for Lakshmi-Narayana, and the third altar is for Sita-Rama, Lakshmana, and Hanuman.

A short distance away from Amritsar, about 11 kilometers to the northwest, is Ram Tirtha Sarovara. This is a large sacred tank said to be dug by Hanuman. Valmiki is said to have had his ashrama here and was cured of leprosy by Rishi Chavan Prash by bathing in the waters. It is also said that Sita gave birth here to the sons of Lord Ramachandra, Kush and Luv.

GOING TO DHARAMSALA

Leaving Amritsar, I got up early to catch the 5:15 A.M. train to Pathankot, but this didn't leave until 6:30 A.M. This meant a lot of waiting around, which is not unusual while traveling in India. It can also take a lot of energy doing this kind of traveling, but once you arrive at these holy places it can be very exhilarating and rewarding.

This train provides a slow ride, stopping every ten minutes at every village. All you can do is sit back, relax, and watch the scenery and your fellow travelers. The train got to Pathankot around 10:00 A.M. We quickly get a cycle-ricksha and make it to the bus stop before the Dharamsala bus is filled up. Once the bus is full, we are off and rolling by 10:15. Soon we can begin to see the snow-capped mountains in the distance. Towards the end of this four hour long drive, we really start climbing up into the hills, and by 2:00 P.M. we arrive at the bus station at the southern end of Dharamsala.

While traveling up to Dharamsala, there are some other pilgrimage towns you may travel through which you may want to stop to see. Some of these places are best to see after arriving in Dharamsala, and using Dharamsala as a base for day trips. In this area are some of the Shaktipeeth temples, dedicated to Shakti, the consort of Lord Shiva. She is also considered the primordial embodiment of feminine energy and power. The Vedic texts relate how once Shakti went to the grand festival and ritual held by her father Daksha. However, Daksha disliked Shiva and insulted him by not inviting him and then talking badly about him. But rather than bearing such insults, Shakti immolated herself in flames and gave up her body, thus becoming Sati. Upon hearing about and then seeing the dead body of Sati, Shiva picked up her body and went into a rage and started a dance, the Tandava Nritya that could have destroyed everything. The other Vedic Gods, like Vishnu, severed the body into pieces and thus stifled Shiva's anger. The sites where the body parts of Sati's body fell on earth have been worshiped ever since as Shaktipeeths. There are such temples in other parts of India as well, but the sites in this area include the following:

Chintpurni is roughly 30 kilometers south of Kangra and has the temple to Chintpurni Devi, another form of Durga. This is the site where Sati's feet fell. Believers hold that worshiping at this shrine of Devi relieves you of all worries. Inside the temple is a golden *simhasan* or throne house with a gold umbrella over her. This shows the Devi in the form of a small vermillion-covered mound with conch shell eyes and bedecked with flowers. It is said that she appeared first to her devotee Mayidas in a dream who thereafter found her. Furthermore, the image of Devi is called Chhinnmastika or headless. Legend says that when Devi's two attendants had a desire to drink blood, Devi beheaded herself and quenched their thirst with her own blood. Since then Devi's headless form has been worshiped here.

Jawalamukhi temple is another Shaktipeeth pilgrimage site, 34 kilometers directly south of Kangra and not far from Chintpurni. It is built over a fissure at the top of the hills and is famous for its eternally burning flame, produced by natural gas that flows out of the rock in the sanctum. This is worshiped as the goddess in her fire aspect, called Jawalamukhi. The perennial flames emanating from the rocks are revered as the sacred place where Sati's tongue fell. Jwalamukhi is considered the most powerful Shaktipeeth. The temple is on a hill with a golden dome. The Sikh Maharaja Ranjit Singh is credited with having gold plated the temple's dome. The golden canopy housed at the temple complex was presented by the Mughal King, Akbar, who came barefooted to pay homage to the shrine in the sixteenth century. Inside are nine flames which give the blessings of the nine planets. Each small flame is in a niche, the main one being under a silver *sim-hasana* or throne where the pilgrims do worship. Mother Shakti is worshiped in nine forms of Durga, which are Mahakali, Annapurna, Chandi, Hinglaj, Vindya Vasini, Mahalakshmi, Saraswati, Ambika, and Anjana. In the temple at dusk a special bed is made with red decorated coverings, along with jewelry that is laid out, and the deity of Devi is invited to take rest, but her flame forms never extinguish.

Kangra, 18 kilometers south of Dharamsala, is known for its famous Bajreshwari Devi temple. This is said to be where Sati's breasts fell. Legend dates this place back 3500 years to Vedic times. This used to be a fabulously wealthy temple. Then in 1009 the notorious Mahmud of Ghazni stole a huge fortune in gold, silver, and jewels. Then Tughlag plundered it again in 1360. In fact, it was paved in plates of silver during Jehangir's reign. But the earthquake of 1905 destroyed it, and it has been rebuilt as we see it today. After each time the temple has been destroyed, it has been restored by the faithful devotees.

Many people still visit this temple. To reach it you will walk from the bus stand through narrow lanes filled with vendors selling many types of religious paraphernalia. Just follow these lanes until you reach the temple. Leave your shoes at a stall across the street and then go down the stairs and through the gates and you enter the courtyard with the temple in the center. You get in line with the rest of the pilgrims. When you finally have *darshan* you'll see the small altar of silver with multiple silver umbrellas hanging over the deity of the goddess. The deity, basically, is a small flat stone, the diameter about the size of a fist with eyes made of conch shells. A bright cloth and silver jewelry are draped around her. Behind the main deity are regular brass images of goddess Durga riding her lion carrier. Embossed silver walls are the backdrop behind the image. On each side of the center deity is a smaller mound or stone, three altogether. This is why Devi is also called Tripurmalini, representing Mahakali, Mahalakshmi, and Mahasarasvati. Many pilgrims come through and offer sweets, flowers, and incense for the temple priests to offer to the deity. The priests in turn give some of it out as *prasada*, sacred remnants.

Around the perimeter of the courtyard are offices, intermittent diorama exhibits, and a few other shrines. In the back and through the gate and down another stairway is a small temple shrine with a *lingam* in the center.

Legend is that to test her, Indra attacked her with his thunderbolt (Vajra), but it merged into her without harming her in any way. This is why she is called Vajreshwari.

A few other things to see here include the Kangra Fort, though mostly in ruins, which still stands above a cliff over the Banganga and Majhi rivers. You can reach it only by a narrow strip of land. Inside it has a few temples for Lakshmi-Narayana and Ambika Devi. There is also a Jain temple called the Indreshvara temple. To the west on a cliff is the temple to Jayanti Devi.

Masrur, 15 kilometers south of Kangra (22km by road), has 15 carved rock-cut temples similar to the large rock carved temples in Ellora, one of which has a stalagmite that is worshiped as a natural representation of Lord Shiva. These temples are ornately detailed in the Indo-Aryan style, although partly ruined. They are massive structures that offer a commanding view over the area. Due to their remote location, they have been freed from being damaged or defaced by Muslim invaders. The legend is that the five Pandava brothers carved these temples in one night while they were traveling during their exile.

Baijnath, 51 kilometers southeast of Dharamsala, 16 kilometers from Palampur, is known for its old Shiva temple that dates back to 804 C.E. It is dedicated to Vaidyanath, Shiva's aspect as Lord of Healing. It is a shikhara style with a tower over the sanctum, in which the main image is a Shiva *linga*. Other deities in the temple are enshrined in niches, which include Lakshmi-Vishnu, Brahma, Durga, Chamunda, Kartikeya, Mahishasuramardini, and Gajalakshmi. Baijnath also has the Siddhantatha temple.

Bilaspur has the final Shaktipeeth in the Himachal area with the temple of Naina Devi on top of a hill. This is considered where the eyes of Sati fell to earth. Bilaspur is much farther south of Daramsala, and 60 kilometers south of Mandi, and northwest of Shimla. More about Bilaspur is explained in connection with Shimla.

DHARAMSALA & MCLEOD GANJ

Once our bus arrives at Dharamsala, take the stairway up the hill and you will be right in the heart of town. With a population of about 26,000, it is another small but nice place to visit, especially to get away from the heat of the Indian plains in summer. There are plenty of small hotels to choose from in various price ranges. I settled on one hotel that was O.K. for 130 rupees a night. It had small rooms with attached bath and a little balcony that provided a wonderful view of the mountains above and the plains below.

Some people prefer to stay at Dharamsala where it is a little warmer at night than the colder McLeod Ganj 7 km farther up the hill. The weather can be very unpredictable at times. It can be pleasant one minute and then turn cloudy and rainy at any time. I also overheard a girl monk, a Westerner, talk of finding three or four scorpions in her room at the Tushita Buddhist retreat center, which is up in the woods above McLeod Ganj. This surprised me that there would be scorpions even at this altitude and in this cool climate, and this was in the month of March.

As we wander around the town, there are lots of small shops selling all kinds of things, from clothes, household goods, great Indian sweets, touring packages, and also vegetable and fruit markets. It's also easy to get bottled water here, which is now almost everywhere, but that was not always the case several years before this.

On sunny days the weather is great, the air is cool and the sun is warm which provides a great atmosphere for taking long walks. And there are plenty of hills and paths to explore farther up, especially from McLeod Ganj. You can take the roads up into the hills or take the trails through trees. On the northern end of town you can take the path that goes through the woods for a short-cut up to McLeod Ganj. It avoids most of the winding roads and joins the street only a short distance from the Central Tibetan Administration (C.T.A.) offices. This is a complex just off the road half way between Dharamsala and McLeod Ganj that takes care of many kinds of Tibetan affairs inside India as well as outside. It was established in 1960 soon after His Holiness the Dalai Lama escaped to India in 1959. Its main focus is to work towards the Tibetan people's struggle for independence and survival. They function according to the Charter of Tibetans in Exile, which is a constitution based on modern democratic principles.

There are departments of Religion and Culture, Education, Finance, Information and International Relations, Security, Health, and so on. It also has the Library of Tibetan Works and Archives where you can find out about classes in Tibetan Buddhism and meditation that are given by noted Lamas. These are especially popular when His Holiness the Dalai Lama conducts some of the classes in March. It is also where foreign students can enroll for courses or pick up their mail. Sometimes in the backyard behind a building across from the library you can see the monks practice their debates with one another. It can be very dramatic as they clap their hands at each philosophical point they make toward one another.

As we leave the C.T.A. complex, the main building near the driveway by the entrance is where you can get "A Guide to Little Lhasa in India," which is a small but very good and authoritative guide to Dharamsala and especially the McLeod Ganj area. The maps also show the many trails you can take for long walks in the hills and through the woods. This is a great adventure to see the countryside and the many little houses and retreats in the area. You could literally disappear from the world in this place. Not far from the C.T.A. is the Nechung Monastery. The Nechung Oracle helps locate new Dalai Lamas when required.

From the C.T.A. complex we can continue up the road or we can backtrack a little to another path which cuts through the woods again and takes us to a Buddhist shrine that has thousands of prayer flags flapping in the wind as they hang from high lines. This is located on the southern perimeter of the Lingkhor footpath which the Tibetans use to circumambulate the residence of the Dalai Lama. I believe this shrine is the Lhagyal-ri (Lhasol Ground) where the Tibetans perform their rituals and say their prayers to the protecting and guardian deities. It is a very quiet place and you can stay for a bit and watch as old Tibetan men and women alike walk by, chanting on their beads and turning the many prayer wheels you will find here.

Around the path to the right of the shrine are many boulders with prayers and mantras painted on them. The scene is as if it was taken out of a page of history from Tibet itself. Moving on to the left you may see a little shack with an old Tibetan who carves the names of patrons on to slate rocks, for a small fee, which are then placed along the route to this shrine.

Farther along the trail, the property on our right is securely fenced off. This is the area of the Dalai Lama's residence. It was here where he settled after fleeing Tibet, and the Indian government set this area, as well as a number of other areas throughout India, as a place for Tibetan refugees. Farther along we come to the Namgyal Monastery and the Tsuglagkhang (Central Cathedral) which is the focus of cultural and spiritual life in Dharamsala. There are many monks who study here, and the Tantrik college still performs rituals for and with the Dalai Lama. The Namgyal Monastery was originally founded by the Third Dalai Lama in the 16th century in Lhasa, and now, along with the Tsuglagkhang, has been reestablished during the exile here at McLeod Ganj.

The Tsuglagkhang Cathedral is a plain building, especially compared to the one in Lhasa, but it is nevertheless quite functional. You'll often see at least a few monks inside sitting and chanting from the texts. The Cathedral houses three important images. These are Sakyamuni Buddha, Padmasambhava, and Avalokiteshvara, the Buddha of compassion of whom the Dalai Lama is accepted as the recent incarnation. The central image is Sakyamuni Buddha which measures three meters high and is made of gilded bronze. The altar and image are very colorful.

The story of this particular image of Avalokiteshvara is quite moving. In the seventh century Songsten Gampo built and installed the jewel-encrusted image in the Lhasa Central Cathedral. It had become a major object of devotion for people throughout Central Asia. However, during the Cultural revolution, the Chinese Red Guards came and ransacked the temples in Lhasa and threw this and many other images into the streets. From what was tossed into the streets, some of the Tibetans managed to collect and then smuggle out of Tibet the wrathful and peaceful aspects of images of Avalokiteshvara, along with other artifacts. These relics passed through Nepal and then into India with the help of many people. Then another wrathful image of Avalokiteshvara and one of Amitabha, the Buddha of Boundless Light, also reached India. These were all assembled into the present image of the Buddha of Compassion in the Cathedral at McLeod Ganj. You'll now see this image encased as a precious relic and made of silver with eleven faces and a thousand arms and a thousand eyes.

The Tsuglagkhang also has full sets (100 volumes) of the Kagyur religious texts, the complete teachings of the Buddha, along with the 225 volumes of the Tengyur, which are later commentaries on the Kagyur by Indian Buddhist scholars.

In the afternoon you can watch the monks in the temple courtyard practice their debates, which is fascinating and quite theatrical at times. Across the courtyard from the temple are the security checkpoints at the entrance to the residence of the Dalai Lama, which is also where you'll most likely go if you have a private or public audience with him.

Nearby is the recently opened Namgyal cafe, which is a small but nice place to eat freshly made Tibetan foods. Be sure to ask for the vegetarian preparations, which they will cook fresh. A little book shop is just above it. At the café I met an elderly, retired Tibetan man who had taught about Tibet at Western Michigan College for two years in Kalamazoo, Michigan, which is not far from my hometown. He had also visited Detroit, taught two more years in Cleveland, and a few years in Oregon. It was quite interesting talking with him and unexpected to have met such a person in Dharamsala of all places who was familiar with Detroit, where I have been living.

Going the rest of the way into McLeod Ganj, we pass many shops and restaurants, as well as numerous vendors along the sides of the streets who sell all kinds of Tibetan items, such as jewelry, clothing, souvenirs, images, and nick-nacks. You can really feel the influence of the Tibetan culture and its people here at McLeod Ganj. The Tibetans are some of the friendliest people you could ever hope to meet. They seem to be ready to smile at any time, even with the simplest of greetings. They also seem to have a real zest for life, considering how they have all had to leave their homes, most of their possessions, and relatives in Tibet and enter India as refugees.

McLeod Ganj was named after David McLeod, the lieutenant governor of Punjab in 1848. It is a very small village composed of only two major streets that are only about two blocks long each. This forms a rectangular area around which are the major shops. At one end of the town is the Tibetan Handicraft center. You can walk in and see them in the process of making carpets, jackets, and other items on very simple equipment. These are sold to help support the Tibetan community here.

In the center of town is the Namgyalma *stupa*, which is a memorial to all those Tibetans who lost their lives fighting for a free Tibet. It represents the determination of Tibetans to preserve their own distinct way of life against overwhelming odds. The main shrine is a small chamber with an image of Sakyamuni Buddha and a large "wheel of law" that people turn as they leave. Around the outside of the rectangular shrine are many paintings of Buddhas and prayer wheels that the devotees turn as they circumambulate them while chanting mantras on their beads. You will see many monks walking about or eating at the restaurants in town.

At the other end of McLeod Ganj is the taxi and bus stand. The bus back to Dharamsala can fill up fast and costs five rupees. The 30-minute bus trip through the other neighboring towns is always a short but interesting adventure. Nearby is also the Nowrojees General Store which was one of the first stores to have been established in the bazaar at McLeod Ganj. From this part of town there are any number of retreat centers, paths to walk, temples or monasteries to visit, or other little towns and places to check out. The bus route will also take you past the church, St.-John-in-the-Wilderness. You can check your guidebook and map for further information.

For example, one place you may want to visit is the Bhagsu Shiva temple, reached by taking the mountain road north from the bus stand. The walk is pleasant and takes you through another little community of shops, restaurants, and residential houses. It's an area where many Westerners hang out or live in rented rooms in the houses offered by the locals. I happened to meet one American who lived in the area. He rented a nice room in a house owned and shared by a local Tibetan family. Although it was rustic with no modern amenities, it was only 30 rupees a night, or less than $30 a month. But he did say that it could be cold at night, rainy, and you need warm clothes at this altitude. And finding and using a toilet in the morning could be a little difficult.

A little farther is the small Bhagsu Shiva temple which is near some bathing pools fed by the cold mountain stream which flows through them. Many people, Indian and Tibetans alike, frolic in the water in spite of the sign that says no swimming or bathing. The temple has only a few little rooms, in which are rather small images of Shiva and other divinities.

A little past the pools there is a hole in the wall with an arrow next to a sign that says, "Waterfall." After you walk through the wall and begin going along the path, you can soon see in the distance on the hillside a nice waterfall. You take a lower path that is less risky or a higher path that is narrow with long, sheer drops on the side of it. Once you get there, you'll find plenty of people swimming in the cold mountain water, including hippies, tourists, and young Tibetan monks washing clothes, and others sunbathing after a swim. Off to the side is a little shack made with a tin roof which sits on piles of slate stone. This is a tiny café that offers only eggs, fire-brewed tea and stream cooled soda pop. Maybe by now they have a better building. So I had a drink and sat in its little seating area. It was a nice way to relax in the sun with the sound of the waterfall in the background and enjoy the mountain surroundings. After relaxing a bit, it was time to go back.

High in the hills above this Bhagsunath waterfall are the huts and caves of some of the Tibetan lamas and monks who seek this area for meditating in seclusion. Even though you may reach the waterfall, it is advised that you not disturb the recluses.

Coming back from the Bhagsu Shiva temple, while walking along the road, I heard the sound of drums and horns coming from a building on a hill. So I went up the drive and checked it out. I was quite fortunate to find a troupe of Tibetan dancers performing the ancient Tibetan mask dances. The place was a temple and lots of people had gathered in the courtyard to see the dancing. The members of the troupe primarily were from a Tibetan refugee camp in Mahendragada, Orissa. This type of mask dancing always depicts a story of good verses evil in the form of demons and Buddhist guardians. It was very interesting and quite colorful and full of tradition.

When I left it was starting to get cold. I stopped and had dinner at the Green Restaurant, a pleasant place that was filled mostly with Westerners, hippies, and those getting into the Tibetan Buddhist scene. Loud music from old Neil Young recordings was being played in the background.

That night I decided to walk back to Dharamsala after having taken the bus up. I hadn't taken the path back before so I was a little unfamiliar with it. I walked past the Dalai Lama's residence and when I came to the Lhagyal-ri shrine, I didn't know where to turn for the path down the hill. It had gotten dark sooner than I expected, and I hadn't dressed warmly and it was getting cold. The moonlight was all I had, and I was now getting lost. I kept walking faster along the path hoping to find some road. Then I ran into three Tibetans, one of which was a little old lady. She asked me (mostly in Tibetan) where I was going, and I said Dharamsala. Then she pointed out that the way I was going was no good. She physically turned me around and boldly tapped my arm to get me going back to the Buddhist shrine. She then got someone who spoke English to show me the right path to take and how to get started. Then I was on the right track. It was a humourous though much needed situation.

Thanks only for the full moon was I able to see all the rocks, bumps, and downed trees and other dangers to keep from falling or breaking a leg, and to keep from getting lost again. Finally, the path came out to the road and then I could see the lights of Dharamsala in the distance below to safely walk the rest of the way back. Later, I reached the well lit and still busy streets of Dharamsala where I picked up a few Indian sweets from a shop for a desert, and went back to my room to count my blessings. All in all, it was a great day.

There are also plenty of festivals at McLeod Ganj. One of the special ones is the Tibetan Opera and Folk Festival. This is held at T.I.P.A. (The Tibetan Institute of Performing Arts). This place is about a 15 minute walk out of McLeod Ganj. Simply take the road toward the Bhagsu temple and there soon will be a dirt road that breaks off to the left and goes up into the hills. After some walking you will come to the T.I.P.A. center. This is the home of Ihamo, a unique and very colorful Tibetan folk opera. The center preserves and trains its students in a number of musical dance and theatrical traditions of Tibet. It also makes its own costumes, masks, and musical instruments.

The Tibetan Folk Opera Festival is an annual event in April which lasts five days or so. It costs a nominal fee to attend, but is very interesting. Lots of families gather in the courtyard for picnics and celebration and to see the exhibits, dancing, plays, singing, and opera. The costumes are extremely colorful in the sunlight. The opera is, naturally, all in Tibetan, but it is also full of humor that almost anyone can understand. Even though the Tibetans are all refugees, having escaped from Communist Chinese occupied Tibet, they have a great joy in life and are quick to laugh and smile at the humor in the opera.

Late in the afternoon, after standing for hours where I could look over most everyone's head to view the opera, an old Tibetan lady in the crowd pointed to me and then pointed out a seat where I could sit. I didn't feel much like moving, suspecting that the opera would be over soon, but I thought fate was calling me and I should go. So I moved through the crowd and found the seat. Shortly after that the opera did end, and then the Dalai Lama, who attended, came out of his room that was a few storeys up in the building behind the crowd, and spoke to everyone. Where I happened to be was one of the best places to be situated to see and take a few photos of him, which I couldn't have gotten if I had remained where I was. Then after he spoke for about 10 minutes, he came down the stairway and walked through the crowd greeting people as he went, not far from where I was standing. The special relationship and respect between him and the Tibetan people is obvious.

One of the things you might want to do while you are in Dharamsala is ask for a public audience with the Dalai Lama. To get a private audience can take up to four months of waiting. But as long as he is in town, you can check to see when he plans to give the next public audience. To do this you must go to McLeod Ganj and take the road toward the Bhagsu temple from the bus stop. Go to the Branch Security Office in the same building (upstairs) as the Tibetan Welfare Office across from the Kokonor Hotel. This is where they'll let you know when the Dalai Lama is having his next public audience and how to sign up for it. If you are accepted, they will give you a permit and tell you not to bring any bags or cameras for security reasons. They will also tell you where and what time to go. You'll usually go to his residence and wait in the temple courtyard until everyone starts getting called, which will be around noon. They will call people in groups of ten according to your ticket number. Once inside the security gates, you get frisked twice and any cameras or bags people have are left in a room.

Beyond the security gates are the huts and quarters for servants and security personnel. Then there is a driveway that leads up the hill to a hall or reception building, and you wait outside along the driveway. Farther over is a house which is the actual residence of the Dalai Lama. Around 1:00 P.M. everyone is directed to get in a single line. I managed to be one of the first 25 in this group of around 300 people. Then the Dalai Lama and some of his assistants showed up and we circled around the driveway, as directed, to meet him. Each person approached and was able to shake his hand. When it was my turn, I took his hand in both of mine, bowed my head and looked up into his smiling face and said, "It is a pleasure to meet you." His hand was very soft but his handshake was firm. His face was so full of expression, with a big smile, that I thought he was about to say something. The exchange and moment was good enough. I then turned, accepted a piece of red string with a knot in it that the priest was handing out, and then I was on my way back out through the gates. The string is like a blessing and you tie the ends around your neck, which most of us were doing as a sign of having met the Dalai Lama. This indeed was a joyous occasion to have met the current incarnation of the compassionate Buddha, besides appreciating all the work he does for peace and the freedom of the Tibetan people. This made my visit to Dharamsala, Little Lhasa, as complete as it was going to be. And I certainly loved my visit here.

Now we can decide if we are going back south toward Ambala or Chandigarh or head farther north. To go south, we can easily take buses back to Chandigarh, or take a bus to Hoshiarpur and then take a train south. But on this tour we are heading north, so we get a bus to our next stop, which is Chamba.

CHAMBA

If we can handle the political hotspot and troubled land of Kashmir and are going to continue our way north to Jammu, then from Dharamsala we can take an 8-hour bus ride to visit the town of Chamba, which is a small town north of Dharamsala. Chamba, population 17,000, 56 kilometers from Dalhousie, has some temples that some people may want to visit. (This town also can be reached from Pathankot or Nurpur.) This town used to be the headquarters for the district. The old palace is now a hotel. The town is still a trading center, which is especially the focus during the Minjar festival in August which draws crowds from many of the surrounding towns. There is a colorful parade during the festival lead by the deity of Raghuvira, with other deities on palanquins following behind.

The Lakshmi-Narayana temple complex is near the palace and contains three Shiva temples and three Vishnu temples, the oldest of which dates to the 10th century while the most recent temple was built in 1828. It has temples of Lakshmi-Narayana, Radha-Krishna, and Lakshmi-Damodara all devoted to Vishnu. The Lakshmi-Narayana deities stand on a silver altar. The temples of Chandragupta (which has worn deities of Shiva-Parvati), Gauri-Shankar (which contain old deities of standing Shiva-Parvati and a four-headed Bhairav in a niche), and Trimuktesvara (with the Chaturmukha *linga*) are dedicated to Shiva. They have pitched roofs to let the snows drain off. Other shrines are also in this complex. Elsewhere is also a Hariraya Vishnu temple with a Sikhara form of architecture. This temple has a four-armed Vaikuntha form of Vishnu as the main deity. It is beautiful and uniquely fashioned with three heads—human, boar Varaha, and lion Narasimha. Near the palace is the Bansi Gopal temple, dedicated to Krishna with Radha-Krishna deities and a collection of other stone images, including Surya, Hari-Hara, Krishna with flute, Hanuman, Mahishasuramardini, Anantashayi Vishnu, Narasimha, Varaha, etc. A steep climb up the hill is the Chamunda temple, dedicated to the Devi Chamundra. This also offers grand views of Chamba, as well as the Ravi River below and the surroundings. Additional temples are also in this town. The Bhuri Singh Museum offers displays of silver jewelry and the miniature paintings that is an art that flourished in Chamba. From this side trip we go to Pathankot from where we catch the next bus or train to Jammu, if we wish to go there.

Bhramaur is a village 39 miles farther east of Chamba. Along the way a side road can take us to the Chatrari or Ghitrari temple which has one of the most lovely images of a bronze Shakti Devi. Bhramaur has the temple complex, built in the 10th century, called Chaurasi, which means eighty-four, after the 84 saints who had visited the town. There are not many left, but some of the temples you can see are dedicated to Ganesh, Narasimha, and the local deities of Manimahesh and Larkana Devi. The ornate wooden carvings on the temples and the images of the main deities are outstanding.

JAMMU

Jammu is a large city, population about 380,000, which for us may be little more than a stopover place on our way farther north. However, while we are here, there are a few very large and impressive temples we can see. Many historians and locals believe that Jammu was founded by King Jambu Lochan in the 14th century B.C.E. However, the name Jammu is also related to Jambavan who had lived in the cave temple called Peer Kho (also known as Jamawant Cave) located on Circular Road above the banks of the Tawi River. This cave is said to mark the area where Jambavan fought with Lord Krishna after Lord Krishna, who was investigating who had stolen His Syamantaka jewel, found Jambavati, Jambavan's beautiful daughter, playing with it in the cave. Suddenly, as Krishna entered the cave, there was a great roar that came from within and Jamabavan came out to defend his domain and wrestle with Lord Krishna, not knowing who He was. After 28 days of fighting, Jambavan finally realized that this was his Lord. Thus, Jambavan offered obeisances to Him, as well as the Syamantaka jewel, along with his daughter, Jambavati, who Lord Krishna married.

How this was destined to take place is that in Treta-yuga, the large and powerful Jambavan had seen the fight between Lord Rama and Ravana and desired to wrestle with the Lord. It was not possible at the time, but the Lord granted that in His next appearance as Lord Kirshna, his wish would be granted. So this is a very significant bit of ancient and spiritual history regarding Jammu.

When you go to visit the cave, you see the *babas* and the *pujari* priests who do the worship here. It is actually two caves that are situated about 20 to 30 feet below the surface of the temple complex. Going down a flight of marble stairs, you find the cave entrance with a height of about 5 feet. So you have to bend a little to enter it. It is about 3 feet wide and 15 feet deep. Going through this tunnel, you enter the larger, pentagonal cave which is about 12 feet high and 12 feet wide. Inside, there is a black Shiva *linga* that has been worshiped for many years. The Durga temple here also has images of Hanuman, Rama, Lakshmana, Janaki, Mahadeva (Shiva) and Parvati, as well as Vrinda Devi. There is also an eternal *dhuni* or flame that has been burning for thousands of years. It is said that this cave is (or was) the gateway to a tunnel system that lead to other caves and shrines outside India.

The next most important place to visit in Jammu is the Raghunatha Mandir in downtown Jammu. It is visited by many thousands of pilgrims, especially during the annual pilgrimage to the Vaishno Devi shrine. When you arrive, you have to go through heavy security checkpoints to enter, and no cameras, video equipment, cell phones, or bags are allowed inside. This is because this temple had been the target of Pakistani Muslim terrorists several years ago, but they were killed by security forces. It is presently a very nice and beautiful temple, and you will need at least two to three hours to see everything.

The main part of the present temple was constructed in 1835 by Maharaja Ranbir Singh of Jammu. This temple consists of seven main shrines, each with a tower of its own. It is also known for its library of numerous ancient texts. The interior of the temple is plated with gold, and there are as many as 125,000 *shalagrama-shilas* (stone representations of Lord Vishnu, Krishna) found all over the temple in different halls. As many as 365 deities are in this temple. You can also find many paintings that relate the pastimes as described in both the *Bhagavata Purana* and the *Ramayana*. There is also an eight foot tall, 400 kg Shiva *lingam* inside. There is another crystal Shiva *lingam* that stands five feet tall, made of transparent German crystal.

As we make our way through the temple to the inner sanctum, we can see the main deities of Sita-Rama and Lakshmana who reside on a golden altar. The smaller Rama deity is made of gold and taken out on a chariot every year for Ramanavami (Lord Rama's appearance celebration). On the right are golden Radha-Krishna deities who are also taken out on a chariot every Janmastami (Krishna's appearance day). Another black stone image of Bharata, the younger brother of Lord Rama, standing eight feet tall is also found in the temple. Large deities of Hanuman are at the first and second gates, and in the sanctum.

Once we have finished looking around this temple, we can make our way about half a kilometer to the large Rambireswara Shiva temple, built in 1883. It is unique in having one large, five foot tall *lingam* and ten smaller ones outside, and 125,000 Shiva *lingams* which come from the Narmada River in South India. It also has eleven rock crystals that have been formed into Shiva *lingams*, each measuring 12 to 18 inches tall. With its tower over the sanctum reaching up to 225 feet, it is the largest Shiva temple in North India.

Across from this temple is the the **Mubarak Mandi** Palace complex dating from 1824. It is a blend of Rajasthani, Mughal, and baroque architectural elements. It also houses the Dogra Art Gallery, which has a good collection of sculptures, manuscripts, and Pahari miniature paintings, terracottas, and other items. The Amar Mahal Palace Museum also has some paintings showing scenes from the *Mahabharata* along with portraits and items of royalty. Another historic but living monument is the **Ranbir Canals,** built by Maharaja Ranbir Singh, which conducts water from the Chenab in the reverse direction into the heart of the city from a distance of 32km.

Jammu also has the famous temple of Bawey Wali Mata inside the Bahu Fort where, every Tuesday and Sunday, pilgrims throng to worship the goddess. A little further away, on a spur opposite the Bahu Fort, overlooking the river Tawi, stands a temple dedicated to Mahamaya, a Dogra heroine who lost her life fourteen centuries ago fighting foreign invaders. The Panchbakhtar is another well known Shiva temple. Other important temples in Jammu are the Lakshmi Narayan temple, Duda Dhari temple, and the Panj Mandir in Gandhi Nagar.

You can also find a few Sikh temples and Muslim shrines, such as that of Peer Baba, the dargah of a legendary figure Peer Budhan Ali Shah. Situated behind the civil airport, it can be a very crowded destination for believers. It is the most famous and revered by people of all faiths. This Muslim Sufi saint is assumed to have lived up to 500 years old by supporting his life entirely on milk. The saint was a close friend of the tenth and the last guru of Sikhs, Guru Gobind Singh. Irrespective of caste and religion, whether Hindu, Muslim, or Sikhs, believers throng to this place on Thursdays to offer prayers and respect to the legendary saint.

Mansar Lake is another popular excursion destination 62 km out from Jammu, as well as a holy site sharing the legend of Lake Mansarovar. Newlyweds consider it auspicious to circumambulate around the lake to seek blessings of the Lord of Serpents, whose shrine is located on its bank at **Purmandal,** a town 40 km east of Jammu, situated on the banks of the sacred, mostly underground Devak River. It has a complex of ancient Kashmiri Shaivite temples and is often referred to as Chotta Kashi.

So if you stop at Jammu, there is enough to see to keep you busy for a couple days if you try to see everything.

VAISHNO DEVI

From Jammu we take a two-hour bus ride (48 kilometers) to Katra. This is where the road ends for the trek to the popular Vaishno Devi cave temple. Katra is the home of the Kalka Mata Mandir, a very old Shiva and Kali temple which has self-manifested deities. It is a very popular temple and visited by many traveling pilgrims. The care of the temple has now been given over to Iskcon, the Hare Krishna Movement, which is also building a new temple and guest house.

Twenty kilometers from Katra is the town of Raisi, which has a Sikh Gurudwara and another important cave temple. From Katra we continue to Vaishno Devi.

The reason why Vaishno Devi became so significant is that it is the place where Durga, as a girl, killed the demon Bhairon. The story is that around 700 years ago Bhairon and his guru, Goraknath, attended a festive feast for Kanya Puja that was arranged by Baba Shridar who lived in Hansali, a village about two kilometers from Katra. A divine girl appeared to him and told him to have a feast for the *puja*, and then she disappeared. Shortly thereafter, he met Gorakhnath and his 360 disciples and invited them to attend.

During the feast the divine girl again appeared and served all the guests whatever food they wanted from her Kamandal (wish fulfilling) pot. However, Gorakhnath and Bhairon wanted to make trouble for her and asked for meat and wine. She said she could not serve such things in the home of a brahmana. The demon Bhairon became furious. Then, while being chased by the angry demon Bhairon, the goddess turned into her subtle form and went toward Trikuta Hill. She then entered the Garbha Joon cave where she meditated for nine months. Bhairon finally reached the cave and the goddess used her trident to break through to the other side. Bhairon chased her to a cave at the peak of the mountain where the goddess Durga killed him. Thus, the cave is a place of the pastimes of the goddess, so many people visit this cave.

Vaishno Devi is reached by foot, pony, or palanquin. From the nearest motorable road, one can reach the pilgrim's complex called Bhawan in a few hours. Thereafter, from Katra, it is a steep and tough 13 kilometer climb. It takes about four hours to reach it, or longer if you're not in shape, and three hours to get back. So plan on starting early to get there and return in one day. Before you start, pick up a Yatra Slip at the tourist center by the Katra bus stand in order to go past the Ban Ganga temple, which you must reach within six hours of getting the slip. This is a checkpoint that monitors the people coming through, after which you get another slip at the Darbar Yatri Check Post.

The first important place we'll visit is the Bhumika temple, about one kilometer out from Katra. This is where the goddess disappeared. This place is also called Darshani Darwaza because you can see the three peaks of the Trikuta Parvat that is the dwelling of the goddess Vaishno Devi.

The next place we arrive at is the Ban Ganga temple. This is where the goddess shot an arrow into the ground which produced the sacred river, Ban Ganga, to satisfy the thirst of Langoor Vir. The goddess is supposed to have washed her hair at this place, which gives it the name Ban Ganga. Pilgrims usually take a sacred dip here. You must also show your checkpoint slip here in order to proceed.

Another one-and-a-half kilometers farther, and at an altitude of 3,380 feet, is the Charan Paduka temple. Her holy footprints, *charanpaduka*, are visible on a stone at this place where she rested for a time while being chased by Bhairon. Four-and-a-half kilometers more is Ardh Kuwari where there is the Garbha Joon cave where the goddess hid for nine months. When the demon, Bhairon, found the cave in his search for the goddess, she escaped by using her trident to make a new opening. The cave is 15 feet long and very narrow.

From here the path to Vaishno Devi gets quite steep for the next two-and-a-half kilometers. The mountain resembles the forehead of an elephant, therefore, this climb is called the Hathi Matha. You will find both a footpath and a stairway to make this climb, but the path is easier. After you climb to Sanjhi Chatt, there are four more kilometers to the Vaishno Devi cave, which has an altitude of 5,100 feet.

Once we reach the cave, before entering most pilgrims bathe in the water that comes out of the cave. Only 12 to 15 people are permitted in the cave at a time, so it can be a long wait to get in. You first get a number from the counter for the group with which you'll go in the cave. You'll wait at gate number two until your group is called. You then go through a low entrance for a couple yards and then walk in water that is from ankle to knee deep for 100 feet. This is called Charan Ganga. The cave ceiling is only about five feet high, so you cannot stand straight. Finally, you reach the end of the cave and walk up four steps to see the *pindies*, which are the consecrated rocks that represent the three deities of Maha-Sarasvati on the left, Maha-Lakshmi in the middle, and Maha-Kali on the right. Also inside is a lamp that never goes out.

The Vaishno Devi cave is the only temple in India where all three goddesses of Lakshmi (the goddess of fortune and wife of Lord Vishnu), Sarasvati (the goddess of learning), and Kali are worshiped together. This is also where the goddess Durga killed the demon Bhairon, so it is an important place. It is also believed that Sati's arm fell here after her immolation at Daksha's fire ceremony in Haridwar. So it is also a Shaktipeetha.

The best time to visit this temple is between March and July, as it can get cold the remainder of the year. The busiest time is during March-April and September-October. Between November and March the area can be cold and under snow. Even then many people visit. The pathway is completely lit up with lights for the pilgrims, and the shrine is open 24 hours except for two hours at both sunrise and sunset during the daily worship by the priests. There is always activity with the pilgrims, day and night. There can be up to 15 to 20 thousand pilgrims a day visiting this temple, and the line of people waiting to get in can be up to four kilometers long on holidays, such as the Kartika (Oct-Nov) full Moon. However, during the peak season when crowds can be as many as 25,000, and in spite of the effort that a pilgrim must undergo to reach the cave, *darshan* within the cave to see the goddess can be as short as only three seconds. Then you must turn to leave. And the priests there are not always the most diplomatic in the ways they deal with the pilgrims.

Before leaving Vaishno Devi, we can also visit the nearby Sri Ram temple and see the Shiva *lingam* in a cave 125 steps down. The Bhairon or Bhairav temple is about two-and-a-half kilometers and another 1600 feet up. It is traditional for pilgrims to visit this temple after visiting the Vaishno Devi cave. It is here where Bhairon's head landed when he was killed by the goddess, and the huge stone outside the cave represents his body. Legend has it that the demon prayed to the goddess after he was killed, and he was thus absolved of all sins by Durga. Also, tradition has it that Durga gave the benediction that all desires would be fulfilled for her devotees who visit this place.

Once our *darshan* is complete, we then make our way back and prepare for our return journey to Katra. If, however, we need to spend the night at Vaishno Devi, a town of 20,000, you may be able to find a place here or at Ardh Kuwari, which has basic rooms.

GOING TO KASHMIR

Unfortunately, the way things have gone in Kashmir, since 1994 or earlier, the region has been so unsettled that the U. S. Embassy has posted travel restrictions for U. S. citizens. This may be lifted in time, but until then if you go, they take no responsibility for you. So, if you decide not to go to Kashmir, then from Jammu we can head back to Ambala or Chandigarh and head northeast from there, or simply start back for Delhi.

If we do go to Srinagar, we need to be careful because there are also plenty of scams and methods of cheating tourists in Kashmir, especially for Westerners. (Read the "Introduction" to this book on "Being Cautious" and "Avoiding Scams" to review some of these techniques.) Some of these start with the Kashmiri tourist agents in Delhi. They are the only ones who will try to convince you that Kashmir is absolutely safe. Other Indians will never say that. Most Indians will tell you that Kashmir may be settled and safe one day, and then unsettled with outbreaks of violence the next. An example is that one time I was in India and I was thinking that things had been quiet in Srinagar, so maybe it would be safe to go. Three days later the war in Kargil broke out, which had strong connections with the militants in Srinagar. So you never know.

Another example of how things once were in the past, and hopefully will not again become in the future, is that while in Haridwar in 1994, I met a man who had to flee Kashmir, leaving his property, business, and money six years earlier. He said he loved Kashmir, it was the best place but he would never return because of the way the Muslims acted toward others in the region. Ethnic cleansing by militant Muslims toward others drove many away from the region, especially Hindu pundits, many of whom became refugees in their own country. Even western tourists had been kidnapped on occasion for ransom money, or even killed. So you need to take this into consideration if you go. Unfortunately, this was also a great setback for the other Muslims in Srinagar who were not militant in attitude and who depended on the tourist trade for their livelihood. Still, these days as things become more settled there, many Indians are again vacationing in Srinagar, renting houseboats and sightseeing with friends and family, especially to get a break from the heat of the Indian plains.

So, fortunately, things have gotten much safer in Kashmir at the time of this writing (2007) than they were even a few years ago, but there are still many military checkpoints and numerous soldiers all around the town. The head of the Department of Tourism in Kashmir also says there are now many foreigners who visit Srinagar. Nonetheless, things can change at any time, so you have to monitor the situation before you go and while you are there.

The best way to go to Kashmir seems to be to avoid the Kashmiri tourist agents in Delhi who ask for exhorbitant prices on facilities. Then when you get there, shop around for the accommodations that are most suitable for you. That way you can get the best deal rather than making reservations on something for which you are not aware of comparable prices. Do comparisons among the hotels or houseboats, if you are interested to stay on one. However, remember that the main tourist season is from June through August. So Srinagar can be busy at that time. Nonetheless, tourists are only rediscovering Srinagar these days, and it may still take time for people to feel comfortable to vacation there. Before 1990, the place would be packed up with few spare rooms or houseboats available anywhere. It was a thriving business. Yet, since then the tourist trade has faced a real set back due to the militant violence, but it is making a come back. If things stay peaceful there, tourism could increase dramatically, and prices will again go up on facilities. Then making prior reservations may become a necessity again. Even now, if you want the best houseboats or places to stay, prior reservations are recommended.

When I went to Srinagar I had a great time, and met other Westerners from various parts of the world who also had no problems. Yet, for many who had used the Kashmiri tourist agents in Delhi, it was the same story—their trip had been far more expensive than it needed to be. In other words, they had been cheated into paying far more for something that could have been done in a less expensive manner if only they would have known more about it, or waited to shop around once they arrived. Still, if you want to go, use the method that works best for you. Having prior reservations is certainly the way that often provides less hassle and a little more security.

TOWNS ALONG THE WAY TO SRINAGAR

If we can go to Srinagar from Katra and Jammu, we will continue north and travel either through or near many of the following towns that have sites of interest. However, if we are going to make a side trip to the famous Amarnath cave, 145 kilometers east of Srinagar, then we will want to turn at Khanabal and Anantnag, then go to Pahalgam, and from there make our pilgrimage to Amarnath, which we will describe shortly. Check at Jammu for a bus to Pahalgam.

Udhampur. As we travel this route, we will pass through this town. Ten kilometers from here is a town called **Krimchi** situated 20km off the National Highway which is the site of the region's three oldest temples that have fine carvings and sculptures, and which also reflects Greek influence in their architecture.

Ramnagar, a town southeast of Udhampur and reached by bus, has the Palace of Colors, known for the beautiful Pahari-style wall paintings.

Sudh Mahadeva is a little ways off the main road near Chinen, an eight kilometer walk will take you to Sudh Mahadev, a popular Shiva temple said to display portions of Shiva's trident. Many pilgrims visit for the three-day festival of singing, music, and dancing during the Asad Purnima festival in July-August. It is also thronged by pilgrims on full moon nights to worship the *trishul* and mace believed to belong to the Pandava hero Bhima. Also near Sudh Mahadev is **Gauri Kund**, the legendary spring where the Goddess

Parvati used to bathe before commencing her daily prayers at Sudh Mahadev. And **Mantalai,** set amidst lush deodar forests, is associated with the legend of the marriage of Lord Shiva with Goddess Parvati.

Kud, Patnitop, and Batote are the next towns we pass through as we continue. Kud, at 1738 meters, and Patnitop, 2024 meters, are both popular hill stations that offer simple places to stay and pleasant walks.

Kishtwar is a place that can be reached only if we are interested to turn off the main road at Batote and go on for a few hours to the east. It is a pleasant town surrounded by waterfalls and has sacred shrines to the Muslim saints (Hazrats) of Zainshah Sahib, Israr-ud-din Sahib, and Akhiyar Sahib. It also has a temple to the 18-armed Sarthala Devi.

If we keep going north from Batote, once we reach **Banihal**, we are 17 kilometers from the Jawarhar Tunnel (also called the Banihal Tunnel by some). It is 2500 meters long and once we exit the tunnel we are in the lush Valley of Kashmir. This is about 93 kilometers from Srinagar. In spite of the political violence of the region, this is one of the most beautiful areas of India. Before going into the tunnel there is a security checkpoint, so have your passports ready.

Verinag is another town not far from Banihal, to the east, and is the source of the Jhelum River. The spring is regarded as sacred, and Jehangir ordered an enclosure to be built around it. It has an octagonal walkway and brick halls, with honeycomb ceilings. The richly blue water runs out into a Mughal garden, which is the reception for the first few yards of the Jhelum River. Jehangir liked Verinag so much that he also had built a palace for himself here, but nothing of it remains.

Anantnag is on the way to Srinagar where we'll stop if we want to take a bus to Pahalgam, which is where most pilgrims begin their journey to Amarnath. South of Anantnag on a separate road is the town of **Achabal**, which has one of the many noteworthy Moghul gardens in Kashmir. This is said to have been built in 1620 by Jahanara, Shah Jahan's daughter. A little farther south is Kokarnag, famous for its rose gardens. At Mattan is a spring-fed pool filled with fish.

Martand, 60 kilometers (37 miles) southeast of Srinigar, which is a little ways north from Anantnag, has the large but ruined 18th century sun temple of Martand on the plateau above Mattan. This was built by King Lalitaditya Muktapida in the 7th to 8th century. Though in ruins, it is still impressive to view what once was there. It consists of a central shrine, and a pillared arcade with 84 columns around a courtyard. You can still see a few of the stone carved images, but some of the features have faded on them. From the hill you can see the valley below and the snowcapped mountains in the distance.

Avantipur, 28 kilometers (17 miles) southeast of Srinagar, the next town that we will pass through as we head north has the remains of two magnificent though ruined Hindu temples built from 855 to 883. The first and larger temple, dedicated to Avantiswara, is a Shiva temple. A half mile farther up is the smaller but better preserved Avantiswama temple, dedicated to Vishnu. There are still some interesting and detailed relief sculptures you can see. These were built during the reign of Avantivarman, the first ruler of the Utpala dynasty, after the Karkotas. The Utpalas were the last Hindu dynasty near the time of 856, before Islam came to Kashmir. There is little more than ruins of these temples to see at this point.

Parshaspur is another town on our way just outside of Srinagar. It has the massive ruins of an ancient temple, with huge blocks of stone scattered about a wide area.

Pandrethan, another town south of Srinagar, has the noteworthy Pandrethan Shiva temple. It is just after the military cantonment at Sonwar and dates back to 900. It is made of large blocks of limestone, built with a square plan in the center of a spring. It has a sloping roof, with stone slabs and adorned with typical sculpted figures.

If we do not stop to see these places on our way into Srinagar, it is easy to take a day trip to visit some of these closer sites after we arrive.

GOING TO AMARNATH

Pahalgam, at 2130 meters, is a good place to stay when planning a pilgrimage trek to Amarnath Cave. Today there are many hotels, lodges, restaurants, and shops for all price ranges, but rooms can be scarce during the pilgrimage season. Affluent families also come here, or even have second homes for holidays. It is surrounded by tree green mountains with snow caps in the background, and the lovely Lidder River flows through the town. Pahalgam does offer many walks through the hills to such places as the small Mamaleswara Shiva temple about one kilometer away. This is one of the oldest stone Hindu temples in Kashmir, from the 7th century, made of unhewn limestone boulders and mortar, with a water spring in front. Or you can go to Baisaran and Aru, 11 kilometers upstream for a day's walk. So there are various outfitters that can provide the facilities for whatever kind of trekking you want to do. There are many shepherds taking flocks of sheep here and there throughout the area. But save your walking energy if you are going to Amarnath.

Sheshnag, a beautiful mountain lake, has many stories and legends associated with it. It is a good trek 6 km from Pahalgam, past Hargam, and on past the villages of Fresluna and Chandanwari, 16 km from Pahalgam, where the Sheshnag is but a mountain stream. As a lake or beautiful green water, it is surrounded by seven peaks of steep mountains. The path is well marked and is traversed by tens of thousands during the pilgrimage when people go to Amarnath.

Over the years, this area has been a political hotbed with terrorists and militants that occasionally cause trouble for the pilgrims going to Amarnath. India has sent many police and army personnel to keep the peace. It is an especially sensitive area for foreign tourists who have been, at times, completely forbidden to make the pilgrimage. So check in advance if you want to go. Furthermore, the weather can be a serious factor in the pilgrimage to Amarnath. In 1996, 250 pilgrims died in the unexpected snow storms that occurred. Now the state governments will be using modern weather forecasting equipment and will restrict the pilgrimage period to 30 days only. Further regulations will be that pilgrims must be between the ages of 15 to 65 years old and no more than a maximum of 100,000 pilgrims can make the trek with a limit of 8,000 per day.

AMARNATH

Amarnath is a popular and sacred place of pilgrimage. Many thousands of people make this pilgrimage each year. Reaching Amarnath requires an arduous three to five day uphill trek through the mountains of Kashmir. It is situated in a narrow gorge at the farther end of the Lidder glacial valley at an elevation of 13,700 feet, and at a distance of 86 miles east of Srinagar. The Amravati stream that flows nearby is said to have formed from the elixir in Lord Shiva's hair, which is always the abode of the Ganga.

The present Kashmir valley, according to the *Nilamata Purana*, was once a huge lake, known as Satidesa, named after Shiva's consort Sati. It was surrounded by high mountains. To kill a demon, called Jalodhbava, who was "indestructible under water," Rishi Kashyap, the grandson of Brahma, with the blessings of Brahma, Vishnu, and Shiva, made a cut in the mountains and drained off the water. The land that emerged began to be inhabited and came to be called Kashmir, after Kashyap Rishi. At a few spots of rare beauty and seclusion, saints and gods carved out their hermitages for meditation.

Kashmir was a great Shaivite center in the 1st millennium C.E. Kashmiri Shaivism is referred to as Trika Mata and dates back to the 8th century C.E. Kalhana, a contemporary of King Jayasimha of Kashmir of the 12th century, describes Kashmir as Parvati incarnate.

The legend regarding the Amarnath Cave is that the cave was chosen by Bhole Shankar for narrating the secrets of immortality and the creation of the universe to Goddess Parvati. The story is that many centuries ago Parvati asked Shiva to let her know why and when he started wearing a garland of heads (Mund Mala). Bhole Shankar replied that whenever Parvati is born, he adds another head. Yet Parvati asked, "My Lord, my body is destroyed every time and I die again and again, but you are immortal. Please let me know the secret of this." Bhole Shankar replied that it is due to the eternal pastimes, Amar Katha. Goddess Parvati insisted that she be told the secret. For a long time, Shiva continued to delay telling her.

Finally, because of her consistent demand, Shiva made up his mind to tell her the secret. He first selected a lonely place where no living being could listen, which was the Amarnath Cave. In preparation to that, he left his carrier Nandi the bull at Pahalgam (Bailgaon). At Chandanwari he released the Moon from his hair (Jataon). At the banks of Lake Sheshnag he released the snakes that coiled around his arms and neck. He decided to leave his son Ganesha at Mahagunas Parvat (Mahaganesh Hill). At Panjtarni, Shivaji left the Five Elements behind (earth, water, air, fire, and sky). After leaving behind all these, Bhole Shankar entered the holy Amarnath Cave along with Parvati. To ensure that no living being would be able to hear this immortal tale, he created Rudra, named Kalagni, and ordered him to spread fire to eliminate every living thing in and around the Holy Cave. After this, he started narrating the secret of immortality to Parvati. However, by chance one bird's egg that was lying beneath Shiva's deerskin, upon which he was sitting, remained protected. It was believed to be non-living. Nonetheless, a pair of pigeons was born out of this egg and became immortal, having listened to the secret of immortality (Amar Katha). Many pilgrims report seeing the pair of pigeons when they trek the arduous route to pay their obeisance before the ice *lingam* of Shiva.

It is said that the cave was discovered by a Shepard named Buta Malik. A saint gave Buta Malik a bag full of coal, but on reaching his home, to his utter surprise when he opened the bag it was full of gold coins. This made him overwhelmed with joy. He ran to thank the Saint but what he found was that the Saint had disappeared. Instead, he found the cave and Shiva *lingam* therein. From that time on, it has been a sacred place of pilgrimage.

The ancient epics also narrate another story. It is related that many years ago the valley of Kashmir was under water. It was a big lake from which Kashyap Rishi drained the water through a number of rivers and outlets. Bhrigu Rishi once visited to have *darshan* of this holy cave and discovered the *lingam*. When people heard of the *lingam*, Amarnath became Shiva's abode and a place of pilgrimage.

The Pilgrimage to Amarnath traditionally starts on the 11th day after the new Moon (Ekadasi). The cave is only open between July and August, which is the rainy season. So the ground can be damp and slippery, and you can get plenty wet. But the area is snow-covered the rest of the time. You can also hire ponies and dandies for the trip. And many attend the annual Sravana (July-August) festival when it's said that Shiva first appeared.

When beginning the trek to Amarnath from Srinagar, we can start on the panchami day of the bright half of the month. The *Yatra* (pilgrimage) in its present religious form commences with the ceremony of "Chari Mubarak" at the Dashnami temple, Akhara, Srinagar. After the prayers, the *yatri* (pilgrim) acquires a special walking stick. It has both physical and religious significance; physically it helps the *yatri* in steadying himself on a snowy and slippery path; and spiritually it reminds him of his resolve made while at the temple if and when his faith begins to waver in the face of a long and arduous journey.

The next stop is at Pampur, 9 miles south east of Srinagar. Subsequent stops are at Avantipur, Brijbihara, and Martand. Martand is known for its ancient temple dedicated to the Sun god, now in ruins. Enroute to Martand are Anant Nag and Gautam Nag. Martand is known for its temple with a colonnade of 84 columns full of artistic work. This temple dates back to Lalitaditya of Kashmir of the 8th century. The next stop is at Aishmukam, and then Pahalgam, which is reached on the day of Dasami, the tenth day of the bright half of the month. Pahalgam has the confluence of the rivers Seshnag and Liddar.

The more common practice, however, is to simply begin our journey at Pahalgam, 96 km from Srinagar, and cover the distance to Amarnath and back in five days. The trek from Pahalgam to Amarnath cave is an ancient route and approaches the cave from the south. The 45 km distance is meant to be covered in four days, with night stops at Chandanwari, Sheshnag (Wawjan), and Panchtarni. The distance from Pahalgam to Chandanwari (12.8 km) is covered in about five to six hours, and the trail runs along the Lidder River. Pilgrims camp here on the first night. A major year round attraction here is a bridge covered with ice even though the surroundings are free from it. Chandanwadi is where we find the confluence of the rivers Asthan Marg and Seshnag.

At Chandanwari you can find beds and tents, food, and even mules and guides if you have the right price, all of which can be found at other places along the route. Autos and jeeps can go no farther than Chandanwari. From Chandanwari there begins a steep ascent to Pishu Ghati (3,171 meters), climbing 1500 feet over the course of 2 kilometers, and reminding the *yatris* that the path to salvation involves superhuman struggle and stamina. Pishu Ghati is believed to be the site where the demons were crushed by the gods.

The next day's trek of 13 km is through spectacular, primeval countryside. The main centre of attraction is Sheshnag, a mountain which derives its name from its seven peaks, resembling the heads of the servant of Lord Vishnu, the serpent Seshanaga from which its gets its name. Seshnag symbolizes the cosmic ocean in which Lord Vishnu, the preserver of this universe, reclines on His seven-headed serpent Seshanaga. Farther up and five miles farther away is the Seshnag Lake at a height of about 12,000 feet (3,570 meters) above sea level. The journey to Sheshnag follows steep inclines up the right bank of a cascading stream and wild scenery untouched by civilization. It takes about five more hours to reach it. The Seshnag River flows out of this lake. The second night's camp at Wawjan overlooks the deep blue waters of Sheshnag Lake and the glaciers beyond it.

The third day's 13 km trek steadily gains height, winding up across Mahagunas Pass at 4,600 meters and then descending to the meadow-lands of Panchtarni, the last camp before we reach the holy cave. So, after getting refreshed with the bath of ice-cold water at Seshnag, the *yatri* takes a steep climb to Panchatarni, 9 miles away, a confluence of five legendary streams. This is where we begin to feel the affects of the thin air and the need to pace ourselves so we can keep going. We climb to Wawjan before the steep climb to the Mahagunas Pass at a height of 14,000 feet (4,350 meters), after which there is a down slope where we begin to negotiate our short descent through ice and snow that leads to Poshpather (12,860 feet or 3920 meters). This area can be a large snowbed, and any precipitation, along with the constant traffic of pilgrims and mules, turns the route into a thick sludge that forces the pilgrim's concentration on maneuvering the path.

Once we reach Poshpather, we enter a green meadow festooned with wild flowers where ice and snow are no longer a factor in our walk. However, we still must cross the wide Sind River, which in the summer is easy to wade through by men and horses. Then we reach the Panchtarni (11,900 feet or 3627 meters) campsite where we spend the night.

The next morning we get ready for the final walk of another 3 miles to the cave of Amarnath. Traditionally, it is most auspicious to reach the Amarnath cave on the full moon day, and then our pilgrimage is complete. The area abounds with religious symbols and motifs, saffron-clad *sadhus*, vendors, and little shops selling all kinds of spiritual items. You can also find hot food served by the kitchens for the lines of hungry and tired pilgrims. Though Panchtarni to Amarnath is only 6 km, an early morning's start is recommended for there is a long queue waiting at the entrance to the cave. Furthermore, the final challenge is the last few thousand steps up to the cave itself.

As we reach the cave, pilgrims bathe in the Amaravati stream before going inside for *darshan*. Then, once the line of pilgrims gives way for us to enter the cave, we can stand with respect and devotion, if not wonder and a sense of accomplishment, before the ice formation of the *lingam*, the symbol of Shiva. The cave is large, about 90 feet long and 150 feet high. Once we get inside, the main attraction is the large ice formation made by many drops of water dripping on it. It looks like and is accepted as a naturally formed

Shiva *lingam*. Although it changes size according to the seasons, at its best it can be nearly six feet tall. It is largest usually on the full Moon day of July-August. Unfortunately, there have been times when it's been disappointingly small.

Nearby are several other ice formations that represent other demigods. On the left side of the Shiva *lingam* is another ice formation representing Ganesh, and on the right is one of Parvati and Bhairava. Inside the Amarnath cave is another small cave on the left of the image, from which a chalk-like substance is given out to pilgrims as Vibhuti. Legend has it that Shiva made the gods immortal by providing them with the celestial nectar, and resided here upon their request. This boon is what gave the name Amarnath, the place of immortality.

While visiting the sacred place, the devotees sing *bhajans*, chant mantras and prayers, and priests perform *arati* and *puja* ceremonies, invoking the blessings of Shiva. For those who journey with faith, it is a rewarding experience. This pilgrimage, though physically exerting, is also said to be one of the most sacred for Shiva worshipers. Recalling Swami Vivekananda's experience at the holy cave, sister Nivedita wrote: "Never had Swami felt such a spiritual exaltation. So saturated had he become with the presence of the Great God that for days after he could speak of nothing else. Shiva was all in all; Shiva, the eternal one, the great monk, rapt in meditation, aloof from the world." Later on, Swami Vivekananda himself recounted: "I have never been to anything so beautiful, so inspiring."

The pilgrim must understand that while making this pilgrimage, climatic conditions in the area are always uncertain. Rain or snowfall may happen at any time or place during the Yatra, along with abrupt temperature changes. Sunny weather may turn into rain or snow in a short time, and the temperature may fall to -5 degrees C, or 22 degrees Fahrenheit. It is not uncommon for pilgrims to get stranded in serious and life-threatening snowstorms at times.

The same day following *darshan* devotees can return to Panchtarni in time for lunch, and continue to Wawjan to spend the fourth night out, or continue farther to Zojibal, returning to Pahalgam on the fifth day. Once we are finished with our trek and *darshan* at Amarnath, we'll continue on our way to Srinagar if we want.

SRINAGAR

Srinagar, population of nearly a million people and an elevation of 5,675 feet (1,730m), is the capital of Kashmir and tourism in the area, and the stopover place for going to Ladakh. This has been and still is a great tourist place, although the political unrest in the area has certainly put a damper on things. So first check the level of political unrest before going to determine whether you should visit or just make a short stay, or forget about it altogether. For the serious spiritual pilgrim, however, Srinagar does not have so much to offer.

We will find Srinagar to be a crowded but colorful city that exudes a distinct Asian atmosphere. It is indeed different from the rest of India in language (Kashmiri and Dogri), climate, and in the way people look. The old city is the place to avoid and where most of the fighting has taken place, and where the attitude toward western tourists is still not always so friendly. There are plenty of soldiers, roadblocks at various places from time to time, and bunkers intermittently on the street corners. So if we visit Srinagar, stay near the lakes as much as possible for the safest places.

Dal Lake, one of the top tourist attractions in Srinagar, is actually three lakes divided into four parts, namely Gagribal, Lokut Dal, Bod Dal, and Nagin, which are separated by dikes or "floating gardens." Nagin Lake is considered the cleaner and quieter lake, and farther away from everything, which can be good in one way, and also riskier in another as you get farther away from town. The main area for the houseboats is at the southern end near the tourist district, not far from the main part of town. You'll find many shops, handicrafts, restaurants, hotels, and travel agents in this area. The bus stand where the Tourist Reception Centre used to be is also where you can get buses to and from Jammu and Leh. Srinagar is where you can stock up on the supplies you may need, or change money, or send parcels home before you head into Ladakh if you are going there. More about this later.

Srinagar is especially famous for its houseboats on Dal Lake. Of course, floating on the water and getting away from everything is a great experience in itself. To check out the boats to rent, which many people do here, you don't need to go to the Tourist Reception Centre (which has burned down leaving nothing left) or the Houseboat Owner's Association. You can go right to the lake and see what's there. The touts will try to sell you a boat as soon as you arrive, or even as you walk through town. Do not agree to anything without seeing the boat itself or you may regret it.

Most houseboats have a verandah where you can sit and watch the view of the lake, mountains, and other boats go by. Behind this is a living room, furnished, along with a dining room, two or three bedrooms, each with a bathroom. There are different categories for the level of facility, and prices that also include meals. The deluxe houseboats are like works of art, with finely carved teak paneling on the walls and ceilings, desk and chairs, and entranceway. You can rent a room with others or rent the entire boat. In some cases, you may be staying on the boat with the family who owns it and who will be taking care of you, if that is what you want. Make sure that the *shikara* boat trips to shore are free, and that they supply a bucket of warm water for bathing each morning. Also, don't be bothered by the many vendors who float by trying to sell you all kinds of things. They can be quite handy at times.

The water of the lake is fairly clear in most places, in spite of all the sewage from the city and houseboats. However, in other places the waterways are filled with debris and junk, and not clear at all. To take a leisurely cruise around the lake on a rented *shikara* boat can take all day to see most everything, but it is a great way to sit back, relax, and watch the changing views. In the lake, Silver Island and Gold Island are popular picnic spots, and your *shikara* boat can take you there. You can also bicycle around the lake if you are athletic

Seeing the Moghul gardens is also recommended while in town, but I suggest taking a taxi since some of them are little far away for a bicycle ride. Besides, a lonely guy or girl riding around asking people where a place is makes you an obvious target for cheaters or thieves who may want to take advantage of you. So, even though there are plenty of nice people here, be cautious.

To start our tour of the Moghul gardens, first we go out of town on the northeast side of the lake to the Kotar Khana (House of Pigeons), the once royal summer house. From the Kotar Khana we go on to the Chasma Shahi garden, or the Royal Spring, which is about nine kilometers out of Srinagar town. This is the smallest of the Moghul gardens, established in 1632 by Shah Jahan, located up a hillside with steep terraces and a spring of mineral water for its source of nutrients. The spring water gushes out cold and tasty, so everyone wants to get some. The water flows down a channel and there are a few flower beds around it. Lots of families visit this place, which presents a problem since the governor also lives in this area, so you have to go through a military checkpoint. And no video cameras are allowed. So on weekends, this can really slow things down.

Farther up the hill is Pari Mahal (Angels Palace). This is a small garden that rises up on the mountainside tier by tier. It is at or near the ruins of a 17th century Sufi religious college. It is nicely maintained and has arched verandas and secret nooks but crumbling stairways leading to various terraces. Each terrace is planted with beds of flowers. But what this does offer are spectacular views over Dal Lake with the mountains of the Pir Panjal range in the background.

A few kilometers farther north, about 4 kilometers out of town along Dal Lake, is Nishat Bagh, the gardens that were established in 1633 by Asaf Khan. The garden design follows a traditional Moghul plan with a central water channel flowing down the ten terraces lined with chinar trees that provide shade in which people can relax together. It has spacious lawns and formal flower beds. These offer great views over the lake with the Pir Panjal Mountains in the background.

On the northern side of the lake reached by road is Shalimar Bagh. This garden was built by Jehangir in 1616 for his wife, Nur Jahan, "light of the world." The top terrace used to be reserved strictly for the emperor and the court ladies during the Moghul period. Its central waterway, shaded by huge trees, gives a pleasant cooling effect as it flows down several terraces. The pavilions used to be in good shape, but one still has the paper mache interior with a painted ceiling that you can see. Along the sides of the garden are formal flower beds. This is one of the best gardens I've seen in all of India.

Farther down the same road is Harwan Bagh, a smaller garden at the base of the hill. It has a central walkway with small water channels flowing along the sides. The stairs lead up to a small water reservation where you can get good reflective views of the mountains. Small rows of flowers are lined in the garden. It's a good place for families since it has a playground for children.

Farther around the northern end of the lake we will arrive at Nasim Bagh. These are the oldest of the Moghul gardens in Kashmir, said to be established by Akbar in 1586. These are no longer maintained and are used by an engineering college.

Farther around and now on the west side of the lake is the Hazratbal Mosque, said to house a hair of the prophet which is displayed in a bottle a few times a year and on Fridays, though you can not get very close to it. At those times, the area becomes a bazaar with vendors selling all kinds of items or services. This is a new mosque on the shores of

Dal Lake with a white marble façade, with a single dome and minaret, which is beautifully reflected on the water. It has the snow-capped mountains in the background when viewed from the street. It is the only domed mosque in Srinagar.

Now we start going south, reaching the older area of Srinagar where we have to be more careful of the Islamic militant activity. There are a few other noteworthy sites. One that I will mention, although you can't visit it since the Army has moved in, is the Hari Parbat Fort on top of Sharika Hill on the west side of Nagin Lake. The early part of it was built between 1592 and 1598 during the reign of Akbar, while the newer parts date to the 18th century, developed by Ata Mohammad Khan. It has little of its former glory, but you can still see the strong walls. The inner apartments are dilapidated, but you can get a sense of how the early Muslims lived in Srinagar. Also on the hill, which makes it sacred for Hindus, is the temple to Sharika, a form of Durga. Around the hill are almond orchards which bloom in the spring.

Chatti Padshahi is a shrine to the sixth Sikh Guru, Guru Hargobind Singh, located at the southern gate at the foot of the Hari Parbat Fort near Kathi Darwaza in Rainawari. This is one of the most important Sikh Gurudwaras in Kashmir. The guru is said to have visited Kashmir while Emperor Aurangzeb reigned.

Also on the slopes of the hill is the mosque for Akhund Mulla Shah, the Sufi teacher of Akbar's great grandson, Dara Shikoh. It stands in a quiet garden and built of grey limestone. This is a unique feature of the hill, on each side is a structure for each of the main local religions. However, the fort itself was closed two days after it was open to the public for renovations, and there still is a plan to reopen it.

Sultan Arfaen's Shrine is also on the path up the hill and is an enchanting structure. It has an interior of marble, paper mache, and ornately carved wood. The road goes under a city gate and walls that were constructed by Akbar.

Another nearby shrine on the slopes of the hill is that of Makhdum Sahib, which draws interested people for the cures he is said to have developed. Views over the city here are quit nice, with the Jami Masjid dominating the skyline.

From here, a little farther south, we can see the local Jami Masjid Mosque. This was originally built in 1385 by Sultan Sikander and then expanded by his son, Zain-ul-Abidin. Then it burnt down in 1479, was rebuilt in 1503, and burnt down again. The present structure, built in 1674 during the reign of Maharaja Pratap Singh, is wooden with over 300 pillars which support the roof, each made of a single deodar tree. The expanse of its walls and four steeples certainly command attention in this area. It is 384 ft by 381 ft, which can hold over 40,000 people for prayers. Each wall has a large door that leads into its prayer halls. Thousands congregate here for Friday prayers. Though it is surrounded by the noisy and busy old bazaars, it is quiet inside.

The Pir Dastgir shrine is another important site in Kashmir. About 400 years old, it contains the relics of the great Muslim saint Pir Dastgir known for helping the people. Non-Muslims are allowed in, at least I was, by wearing a skull cap that they can supply. Photography is allowed of the general assembly hall, which is lovely with a paper mache interior painted in colorful detail.

Several blocks away is the Bulbul Shah Mosque, and also the tomb of Zain-ul-Abiden, the son of Sultan Sikander. The tomb is a brick, domed structure with glazed tiles in traditional Persian architecture, on the east side of the Jhelum River. However, it is said that it houses the remains of his mother and he is buried in the cemetery behind it.

Farther down the river, between the third and fourth bridge, is the Shah Hamdan Mosque (Khanqah-i-Mualla) with a pyramidal roof rising above the riverfront skyline. It was Shah Hamdan who first visited Kashmir in 1370 from Iran and converted many people from Hinduism to Islam. His real name was Mir Sayed Ali Hamadni, the surname being derived from the city name of Hamadan in Persia. The mosque, where he originally used to offer prayers, is made of wood carved into geometric designs, with an interior of paper mache paintings from floor to ceiling. This building was originally built in 1395 and burnt down a few times and rebuilt the last time in 1731. The pyramidal roof rises to a spire and besides the Islamic design it contains both regional Buddhist and Hindu styles. If you are a non-Muslim, you will have to stay outside, but you can still walk around it and see its fascinating architecture and paintings, as well as photograph the beautiful interior from a window near the front door. While wearing a skull cap, I found the Muslims there to be quite friendly and helped show me around. You may also want to cross the river to get a photo of this mosque with its reflection on the water, which makes a lovely site.

Across the river is the Pather Masjid Mosque, which is an unused and run-down stone structure, built by Nur Jahan in 1623. The Raghunath temple dedicated to Lord Rama is farther south from here.

We also can stroll along the Jhelum River where it flows through Srinagar. There are nine old bridges and a few newer ones that cross it, and, along with the buildings and mosques nearby, walking through this area provides for a very picturesque way of absorbing the cultural atmosphere. You can also visit the Shri Pratap Singh Museum just south of the Jhelum River, located between Raj Bhagh and Lal Mandi, but locally called the SPS Museum. This is the main storehouse of archeological discoveries in the area. It has a collection of sculptures from the old Hindu temples and archeologocial finds from sites throughout Kashmir. This includes large stone, sculpted deities of Vishnu, several of which have three heads for Vishnu, Varaha the boar, and Narasimha the lion. Deities of Devi and others like Buddha are also to be found, all from the Verinag and Anantnag area, dating back to the 6th century, showing that this region was once a strong part of the Vedic culture. Inside is poorly lit but is decked out like a palace with displays of textiles, local handicrafts, old coins, guns, a good collection of miniature paintings of Krishna's pastimes, and stuffed animals of the area.

Kashmir is well-known for the handicrafts you can buy here at the many emporiums in town or in the area. But if you buy anything of considerable size, ship it home before going on to Leh. There are also workshops you can visit to watch the workers in action. Things you can buy here include the famous Kashmir carpets, embroidery, shawls, sweaters, coats, along with paper mache items, wood carvings, saffron spice, and much more. And, of course, there are plenty of people who will expect you to buy something.

Behind the Boulevard near Dal Lake is Shankaracharya Hill which rises 1100 feet above the city. At the summit is a Hindu temple for Shiva, but an earlier temple was built here around 200 B.C.E. by Ashoka's son. One temple that had been built was by King Laltaditya in the 6th century C.E. was known as Gopadri. The road at the base of the hill where the State Government officials are located is still known as Gupkar road in connection with that temple. This is the oldest known site in Srinagar, believed to date back to 2500 B.C.E. when the original sandstone structure had been built by King Sandiman. It is also said that the philosopher Shankaracharya visited Kashmir about ten centuries ago and had stayed on the hilltop to meditate. The top of the hill also provides a great view over the lake. But due to security reasons cameras are not allowed through the final checkpoint. The temple as we find it today is built on a high octagonal plinth, reached by a flight of 270 steps, the side walls of which used to have inscriptions on them. The main interior shrine is a small circular room with a *lingam* about three feet tall. A new ceiling has inscriptions in Persian which connects its origin to the reign of Shah Jahan.

The hill used to be called Takht-i-Sulaiman, the Throne of Solomon, which definitely represents some of the history of this region, and why some people think that King Solomon had been here. Other factors to consider is that there is an inscription on the remnants of the old building which states that the new temple was restored in 78 C.E. by King Gopadatta (or Gopananda), who ruled Kashmir from 49-109 C.E. According to tradition, Solomon had visited the land of Kashmir. In fact, the local Muslims know Kashmir as "Bagh Suleiman," the Garden of Solomon. This would go in accord with the theory that some scholars believe that Kashmir was the "Promised Land," or the "Land of the Fathers" that the "ten lost tribes of Israel" wandered to in northern India where they found peace and tranquillity. This was after they had moved eastwards when they had been driven out of Israel by the Assyrians, never to be heard from again. Therefore, it may have indeed been Solomon, as tradition declares, who divided the Barehmooleh Mountain and created an outlet for the water that later formed Dal Lake. He also may have constructed the original building of the Takht-i-Suleiman on top of what is now Shankaracharya Hill.

ADDITIONAL SITES AROUND SRINAGAR

The **Khir Bhawani temple** is in the village of Tula Mula, 27 kms outside of Srinagar. It is a temple to goddess Ragnya Devi, symbolized as a sacred spring. The devotees of the goddess fast and gather here to pray on the eighth day of the full moon in the month of May-June (Jeshta Ashtami). On that day the goddess changes the colors of the spring waters. The name "Khir" or "Kheer" comes from the thousands of devotees who offer milk and "kheer" to the sacred spring. It is also said to turn black whenever there is a warning of an approaching calamity.

Burzahom is another historical site located outside of Srinagar to the east by 10 miles. It is found on a vast plateau that offers a great view of the countryside nearby. Its significance is the three pits and the oddly shaped megaliths found here that project out of the earth. A date as early as 2400 B.C.E. is connected with this site since the people who are said to have lived here are thought to predate the Nagas. These are the tribal people who are referred to in the local *Purana* known as the *Nilamata Purana* as being the earliest inhabitants of the Valley. Some of the findings from this site are now housed in the Shri Pratap Singh Museum.

Pattan, a town to the north of Srinagar on the road to Sopore, also has two temples, the remnants of which show a simple design. They were built of limestone blocks in the Karkota period or the ninth century by King Samkaravarman.

Yusmarg is another town that people see while in the area. It is about 25 miles (40 km) south of Srinagar. It is a colorful drive to reach the place, passing fruit tree groves, yellow mustard fields, spring flowers, and snow-capped mountains. We also pass the town of Cherar-e-Sharif, 19 miles out, which is now the burial place of the Sufi saint, Sheik Nur-ud-din, and why many visitors come to visit this place. Yusmarg is also called the meadow of Yus or Jesus, and some feel Jesus came here after he left the area of Palestine. It is a large meadow at an elevation of about 7,790 feet. Dark fir trees surround it and the snow-capped Pir Panjal mountain range is in the background. But there is not much else to see, with few hotels, restaurants, or shops to disturb the peace, or supply what you may need. So other than staying at a few tourist bungalows, you may want to bring whatever else you may need from Srinagar to tide you over during a visit here.

Gulmarg is yet another larger town, about 33 miles west of Srinagar. Again there is little of spiritual interest to see here, but it is well known for its snow skiing facilities. At an altitude of 8,950 feet, it stays cool year round. It is a large bowl-shaped meadow that has been laid out as a golf course, lined with fir trees and mountains on three sides, with views over the plains on the remaining side. There are great ski runs for all ranges of skiers, with skiing instructors and even week-long ski courses for those who need them. The price for such facility is a fraction of what you find elsewhere, so it has remained quite popular as a ski resort that attracts many Westerners. It is also known for the highest gondola that takes you up more than 400 meters to the top of Apharwat mountain which lets you see over the surrounding area. You can easily see both Yusmarg and Gulmarg as daytrips from Srinagar.

THE GRAVE OF JESUS

Another interesting and most controversial monument is the Rozabal, which means "tomb of the prophet." This is the burial place of Yuz Asaf, in the center of Srinagar's old part of town. The name Yuz Asaf relates to Jesus. Some people believe it is the grave of Jesus and others think it is all based on faulty premises, meaning it is merely a hoax. However, there is a complete line of logic behind this, so I will only give you the evidence and what people say and you can decide for yourself. That way, if you are ever in Srinagar, you can have some understanding of the significance of this place and check it out yourself.

To visit this grave of Jesus, you will find it in Anzimar next to a small Muslim cemetery in the Khanjar (Khanyar) quarter of Srinagar's old town. You find Rauzibal Khanyar down a narrow alley in an old, wooden mausoleum. The grave itself is in a building called

Roza bal, an abbreviation of *Rauza*, which means "tomb of a prophet." You enter the rectangular building through a small doorway. On your way in you'll see an inscription that explains that Yuz Asaf came to Kashmir many centuries ago and dedicated himself to the search for truth. The single inner chamber has two graves on the floor, each covered with heavy cloth and with wooden railings around them. The first and smaller grave is for the Islamic saint Syed Nasir-ud-Din, buried here in the 15th century. The larger grave behind it is for Yuz Asaf. Near the gravestone of Yuz Asaf are footprints carved in the stone showing the scars Jesus would have suffered during his crucifixion. It is the custom for pilgrims to place candles around the gravestones, and when years of wax was removed by Professor Hassnain, not only did he discover the footprints, but he also found a cross and rosary. As typical with Muslim mausoleums, these graves are a covering and the actual graves are in a crypt under the floor. However, some also say that due to age, the ground gave way and the original grave simply sank into the ground. A look into the real burial chamber is provided by a small opening. The grave which contains the remains of Yuz Asaf points east to west, according to Jewish tradition.

This all points to the conclusion that this could indeed be the burial place of Jesus. The grave has been maintained by attendants since its construction, which is established by ancient records to be as far back as 112 C.E.

The premise is that Jesus' Hebrew name was Yazu, similar to Yuz. In Arabic and the Koran his name was Hazrat Isa or Isa, and Issa in Tibetan, both of which are similar to the name Isha in Sanskrit. This tradition has been carried down through the *Far-hang-Asafia*, Volume One, which explains how Jesus healed some leper who then became *asaf*, meaning purified or healed. The word *yuz* means leader. Thus, Yuz Asaf became a common reference to Jesus as "leader of the healed."

There are other accounts of how Yuz Asaf preached throughout Persia, present-day Iran, converting many people. Some of these details can be found in Agha Mustafai's *Ahivali Ahaliau-i-Paras* which confirms that Jesus and Yuz Asaf are the same person. Even the well-known Emperor Akbar had a court poet who referred to Jesus as *Ai Ki Nam-i to: Yuz o Kristo*, which means, "Thou whose name is Yuz or Christ."

Other records and place names that relate to Jesus point to his presence in Afghanistan and Pakistan. The Acts of Thomas describe the journey of Jesus and Thomas in Pakistan (then Taxila) at the court of King Gundafor in the 26th year of his rule, which would be about 47 C.E.

Also, when Jesus came to Kashmir he came with a group of followers which included his mother, Mary, who must have been over 70 years old, and was no doubt weakened by the journey. Seventy kilometers east of Taxila, and 170 kilometers west of Srinagar on the border of Kashmir, is a small town called Mari, or Murree in English, near Rawalpindi. In that town is a very old grave called *Mai Mari da Asthan*, meaning "the final resting place of Mother Mary." Here is where she must have died before Jesus reached Kashmir, which was considered paradise, or heaven on earth. Even to this day this grave is maintained by Muslims as the resting place of Jesus' mother because he (Isa) is considered one of the main prophets of Islam.

Also near the villages of Naugam and Nilmag, about 40 kilometers south of Srinagar is a large plain called the Yuz-Marg, the meadow of Jesus. It is here that some of the tribes of Israel settled after 722 B.C.E. to live as shepherds, which is still a major occupation in the area today.

Even at Akbar's city, Fatehpur Sikri, near Agra, as you enter the main gate toward the mosque, there is an inscription which states: "Jesus (Peace be with him) has said: 'The world is a bridge. Pass over it, but do not settle down on it!'"

More evidence of Jesus in Kashmir is found in an inscription that was carved on the sides of the steps at the threshold on the Throne of Solomon in Srinagar. The meaning of this is described in detail by Mullah Nadiri, a historian during the rule of Sultan Zainul Aabidin, in 1413 in his book on the history of Kashmir, *Tarikh-i-Kashmir*. He relates that Gopananda, or Gopadatta, ruled Kashmir and had the Temple of Solomon refurbished by a Persian architect. During the renovation four sayings in ancient Persian were set in stone that said, in essence, that Bihishti Zagar is the constructor of these columns in the year of 54. Khwaja Rukun, son of Murjan, had these columns built. In the year 54, Yuz Asaf proclaimed his prophetic calling. He is Jesus, prophet of the sons of Israel.

Mullah Nadiri goes on to relate that during the rule of Gopadatta, Yuz Asaf came from the Holy Land to the Kashmir valley and proclaimed to be a prophet and preached to the people. Gopadatta ruled sixty years and two months before he died. It is calculated that Jesus came to Kashmir nearly 16 years after the crucifixion and lived to be around 80 years old. Even the *Koran* (23.50 or 52) intimates that Jesus did not die on the cross, but survived the crucifixion and ascended to live in a peaceful hill-side watered by a fresh spring.

All this means that not only did Jesus come to India to learn the spiritual knowledge of the brahmanas and Buddhists as other records have described, but after returning to his land of Israel to preach and was later crucified, he did not die on the cross but suffered and recovered. After that he ascended to Heaven, known as Kashmir, where, after some years, he died and was buried in Srinagar.

According to various records, during his missing years Jesus was supposed to have studied for four years at the temple of Jagannatha Puri. Then he traveled and studied with the Buddhists at Kapilavastu (present-day Lumbini), the birthplace of Buddha in Nepal. Then he went to Lhasa in Tibet for five years. After that he went homeward and then to Greece for sometime before going on to Egypt. Then at the age of 25 he went to Heliopolis and studied for five more years before returning to his homeland.

The story of Jesus' crucifixion is also interesting because, generally, most people die on the cross by starvation or suffocation when the ribs press down on the lungs so that the person can no longer breathe. This often takes several days. According to tradition, Jesus was nailed on the cross in the early afternoon of a Friday and taken down as dusk was approaching, after being nailed on the cross only four or five hours. So it is most unusual that a young and healthy person like Jesus died after only four hours on the cross. Thus, it is more likely that as a yogi he was able to enter an altered state and appear as if dead, only to be revived later. This is not uncommon with some yogis in India. Furthermore, there are modern commemorations of Jesus' crucifixion wherein people are crucified every year in the Phillippines and Mexico and survive quite easily. A person does not die of crucifixion after only four hours. Thus, it is quite likely that he survived the crucifixion and died elsewhere.

MOSES IN KASHMIR

While in Kashmir, another point of interest and controversy is that not only was Solomon and Jesus in Kashmir, but there is significant history that Moses was also here. In fact, Kashmir is considered to have the burial site of Moses as well. There is a grave-site that has been maintained for over 2700 years near the plains of Mowu, once called Moab, above Pishnag, once known as Pisga. This is on Mount Nebo and about 15 kilometers across from Bandipur, which was once known as Behat-poor and Beth-peor. This is considered to be the burial place of Moses.

The logic behind this is that the book of Deuteronomy (34.4-6) explains that Moses died in the land of Moab and was buried near Beth-peor. It is also explained elsewhere in the chapter that Mount Nebo in the Abarim Mountains, and Mount Pisga and Heshbon are in the vicinity. The biblical land of Moab is now called the plains of Mowu. Biblical Pisga is now called Pishnag. Beth-peor was later called Behat-pur near the Jhelum River, which is called the "Behat" River in Persian. Now Behat-pur is called Bandipur, and the village with the biblical name of Heshbon (*Deuteronomy* 4.46) is now called Hasba or Hasbal. This area is about 80 kilometers north of Srinagar.

If we travel to this area today, Bandipur (Beth-peor, meaning "the place that opens") is near where the Jhelum (Behat) River opens into the plains of Lake Wular. Another 18 kilometers north we find the village of Hasbal, both towns mentioned in the Bible. Mount Nebo, in the Abarim Mountain range, is across from Bandipur and above the village of Pishga. Mount Nebo offers a great view of the heavenly land of Kashmir.

Twelve kilometers north of Bandipur we come to the town of Aham-Sharif. From here we go by foot to reach the village of Booth at the base of Mount Nebo. We head west for an hour, taking a vague path up a steady slope. Several fields away is the tiny town of Booth with Mount Nebo rising behind it. Here we'll need to get the attendant of the grave, called the "Wali Rishi," or one of his friends who will guide us the rest of the way. He willingly leads us up to an open garden where there's a small mausoleum. This is the burial site of Sang Bibi, an Islamic female saint and two of her followers. Nearby is a stone column in the grass that stands about a meter tall which designates the grave of Moses.

Other places in Kashmir are also related to Moses. Near Shadipur north of Srinagar, the cliffs near the confluence of the Jhelum and Sindh rivers are called Kohna-i-Musa, "the cornerstone of Moses," where Moses is said to have rested. Three kilometers north of Bandipur is another of Moses' resting spots at Ayat-i-Maula.

About 46 kilometers south of Srinagar is a place called Bijbihara. This is a spot on the river bank referred to as Moses' Bath. The stone lion there is said to be about 5000 years old. The "Stone of Moses" or Ka-Ka-Bal is said to have been the subject of Moses' magic. It is also explained that, though it weighs 70 kilograms, the stone will rise a meter high of its own power if eleven people each touch it with a single finger and all properly recite the magic formula "ka-ka, ka-ka."

At Bijbihara's cemetery there is an inscription in Hebrew on an old grave. A few kilometers away you can see the Temple of Martand that resembles the steps, vestibule, pillared hall, and interior of a traditional Jewish temple, in spite of the Hindu demigods carved on the outside.

GOING INTO LADAKH FROM SRINIGAR

When our visit to Srinagar is complete, make sure you have gotten a bus ticket to Leh a day or two ahead of time because they are usually fully pre-booked. If you do not want to take a bus, flights to Leh are on Tuesdays and Thursdays, which offers quite spectacular views while flying over the mountains.

Other ways to get to Leh is to fly in from Delhi, Chandigarh, or Jammu, depending on availability, which can change quickly since flights are often over-booked and the weather may not permit the flight. You can also take a 485 kilometer, two-day bus ride from Manali. It is a very rough road which is open only from mid-June or later to mid-September, so plan accordingly.

If we were to go to Leh from Srinagar, it's a long 434 kilometers on a mostly paved road which travels along the Indus much of the way. The journey takes two days, and, although there are overnight accommodations in many towns, the buses stop overnight at Kargil. However, the military roadblocks and checkpoints do not help to speed things up. The road to Ladakh heads through the Sindh Valley, a beautiful area, and is the best way to go if you really want to see the landscape.

The Dachigan Wildlife Reserve is also along this route, which is to the northeast of Srinagar. This is the home to many species of wildlife, such as Black and Brown Bear, leopards, Musk Deer, and the Hangful Deer. It is a big reserve and requires permission from the Wildlife Authorities to explore it. There is also a beautiful view of a stream that flows through the forests that is fed by a glacier.

Sonamarg is reached after traveling for some 87 km northeast of Srinagar, which is at a height of 2740 meters. The drive offers some great views of the spectacular areas of the Kashmir countryside. The bus makes a stop here for tea and food, since this is the last major town before the Zoji La pass. It has pine trees and meadows everywhere with the beautiful snow-covered mountains in the distance. It is like a wild west town with wooden shacks and a truck stop. There are a few places to stay here but is a good base for trekking, which includes routes to the Himalayan lakes of Vishansar, Krishnasar, Gangabal and others. You can also hire ponies for the trip up to Thajiwas glacier, which is a beautiful attraction in the summer.

Baltal is the next stop, 15 km farther east, a tiny town at the base of Zoji La. Here is another town from where you can make the day's trek to the Amarnath Cave to see the natural Shiva *lingam* in the form of ice.

Zoji La, at 11,385 feet or 3529 meters, is the first mountain pass on our journey and is the first to be snowed over when it starts getting cold. It's only open from around mid-June to mid-September. So plan your trip accordingly. The road is unpaved here but offers breathtaking views. However, where the road has long, sheer drops along the edge will also take your breath away as you pray you don't get too close. But if you have already traveled to Badrinath, you should be a little used to this by now.

Approaching the pass you will encounter some dramatic hairpin turns called the Captain Bends in memory of a captain of the paramilitary Border Roads Organization who lost his life during the construction of this road. Landslides and the continuous work of maintaining the road has changed the face of the mountain over the years. At the top of the Bends the road flattens out as we approach the summit of the pass. Then, coming from the Kashmir side of the pass with trees and bushes, the landscape becomes desolate of all foliage. There is nothing but the grassy hillsides for the sheep and goats to graze during the summer. For the next hour until we get to Dras, even as we pass by a few settlements, there is little difference in the scenery of the barren, stony mountainsides.

Zoji La is like the entrance into Ladakh, which is called Little Tibet. It is just like a portion of Tibet in northern India. It is Tibetan in culture, religion, and its people. It has been open to outside visitors only since the mid-70s, so it can be and is called at times the "last Shangri-la." Ladakh is situated on a high plateau in the Himalayas, which form a barrier to the rain. This is why Ladakh is so barren and dry, except where the rivers flow from the distant glaciers. There can be drastic temperature changes, turning from warm to cold in minutes. The nights are usually very cold. So bring warm clothes, and a sleeping bag outside the summer season.

Drass is the first town we come to after the Zoji La pass. This can be a bitterly cold town in winter with lots of snowfall. We will have to stop here to register our names and passport numbers as we enter Ladakh from Srinagar.

We will pass by small villages that include Tasgam, Kharbu, and Chanigund as the road travels alongside the Dras River until it joins the Suru which flows from the south. Then we turn right along the Suru and we soon arrive at Kargil, the midway point between Srinagar and Leh.

Kargil is the next town and is the midpoint between Leh (231 km) and Srinagar (205 km). This is where the buses take an overnight stop. The Leh-Srinagar highway goes right next to the town. There are numerous shops, but no place to change traveler's checks. Yet you can change cash into rupees at the Hotel Siachen. It is best that you have enough rupees to make it through to Leh. There are a variety of hotels to choose from, and a few eateries, but not much of an assortment. Nonetheless, Zoji La Restaurant offers some vegetarian preps, and there is a fruit and vegetable market to get some basics. The buses arrive daily usually in the early evening. Thus, it is mostly a stopover place for travelers.

Kargil is built on a strip of land between the mountain and the river, so all traffic goes right through its main bazaar, which includes civil and military, since this is a main artery between Srinagar and Leh. Traffic is its mainstay, which is why there are a few new hotels and new houses up the hill. A leisurely walk across the footbridge will let you see the typical Ladakhi village of Puyin at the base of the mountainside. A walk up the hill can give you a view over the town and of the mountains towards the Suru River. The people who live here are predominantly Shiite Muslims, for which you will notice many more mosques, and even signs in Urdu. So be conservative in your dress and actions. Kargil has been an important link on this route for many years. However, if we are not spending an extra day here, we will not have much time for looking around since our bus, having arrived late at night, will be leaving early the next day.

Buses start for Leh around 4:30 A.M. for the 12 hour ride, so get yourself to the bus on time since they do not like to wait. Or if you have stayed here for more than a night, you can get the bus for Mulbekh at 7 A.M. or 2:30 P.M. for the one hour ride. You can also get taxis to Leh or to Srinagar. For Srinagar they need to leave between 11 P.M. and 2 A.M. to get into the one way traffic over the Zoji La pass. Buses from Kargil to Srinagar must start by 1 A.M. to clear the army checkpost for one-way traffic through Zoji La by 5 A.M. Furthermore, the Zoji La pass is closed one day a week for maintenance, which can cause a delay if you are not prepared.

IMPORTANT POINT

Kargil is also near the Line of Control between India and Pakistan. This was near the center of the war in 1999. So there is a strong military presence here and throughout the region, and if there are any difficulties in the relations between India and Pakistan, foreigners will not be allowed through army checkpoints and will be forced to return back.

At the time of this writing (mid-2007), the U. S. State Department recommends that U. S. citizens not travel to Jammu and Kashmir, especially around the Srinagar and Kargil areas. This is because a variety of terrorists groups operate in this region, sometimes targeting tourists. There is no problem for Ladakh. In spite of what has been said, I and the other tourists on the bus had no trouble traveling through the region, even with several checkpoints where we had to show our passports and fill out forms. But check the State Department's advice about Kashmir on their website if you are concerned.

ZANSKAR

Kargil is also the turning point for some people who may be going into Zanskar. They will be taking the route into the Suru Valley. This valley is also a great divide between the Himalaya and the Zanskar mountain ranges. The road goes south through various villages to Tangol and then takes an abrupt right, around which are great and beautiful mountains. The people in the villages of this area (population of over 12,000) are shy but friendly. And since there are few facilities for the traveler, be sure to take what you need with you.

The Zanskar landscape is treeless but grassy. There are areas of plains between the mountains for the cultivation of barley, peas, and some wheat, along with keeping yaks, goats, and sheep. Otherwise, Zanskar is known mostly for its trekking routes, which has become somewhat popular ever since the roads for jeeps and trucks were opened in 1980.

There are however various towns that have some noteworthy Buddhist *gompas*. In fact most villages have their own *gompas*, with interesting images and wall paintings, and even rock engravings done in a pre-Tibetan style. However, some of these villages are too small to be seen on a map. But I will describe a few of them anyway.

Sani is a village two hours' walk from Padum, which is a town deep in the Zanskar Valley on the sourthern end of the road, 230 km (143 miles) southeast of Kargil, with an altitude of 11,483 feet. Sani is one of the oldest Buddhist sites in Zanskar. It has a large *chorten* with a unique shape, called the Kanika Chorten, which is said to refer to the Kushan king Kanishka who ruled the empire around the 1st century C.E. that covered an area from Varanasi to Kabul. Legend says that the *chorten* was established by Padmasambhava. There is also a temple to Naropa, and a ring of monoliths that encloses an area that is particularly holy, and which bears inscriptions of a pre-Tibetan fashion. In the center of the rockface on the opposite side of the river can be seen a meditation cave and a footprint. It is said that Guru Nima Odzer stayed there practicing meditation for many years. Within the castle there are various beautiful wall paintings by Zadpa Dorje.

Karsha, another two hours from Padum, has a *gompa* and monastery that seems to cling to the hillside above the village. It is also connected with Padmasambhava. It has a Maitreya temple near the foot of the complex. The history is that it was first established by Phagspa Shesrab. The teacher Dorje Shesrab built the present monastery. There are shrines and wall paintings by Lama Dzadpa Dorje. The bone relics of Dorje Rinchen are also kept here. Two temples built by Rinchen Zangpo known as the Thugsjechenpoi Lhakhang and the Lhakhang Karpo are also here. A little ways away, across the gorge, is a temple to Avalokiteshwara known as Chuk-shik-jal which has detailed wall paintings in the old style as that seen in Alchi. Closer to the village of Karsha is the monastery of Khagsar. In the village of Langmi there is the Purang *gompa*, and in the village of Nangbaphal there is the Phagspa *gompa* and the Dorjezong nunnery at the top of the valley.

Stongde *Gompa* is about a three hours walk out from Padum, and was founded by the Tibetan master Marpa near the end of the 11th century. Nearby is a cave where it is said he went into meditation. The temple was taken over by the Gelugspa order during the 15th century, and has seven nicely decorated and preserved temples. This *gompa* is the home to around 60 lamas who owe their allegiance to Ngari Rinpoche who at present is embodied by the younger brother of the Dalai Lama. There are a number of shrines and beautiful wall paintings here.

Dzongkhul is a small *gompa* maintained by the Drugpa order in the western valley between Padum and the Pensi La. It is also attributed to Naropa. It is said that he meditated in the two caves that the *gompa* is built around. The temples have some beautiful large *thangka* paintings and life-like images of lamas of the order.

Other *gompas* can be found in Zanskar, such as at Phugtal, much farther south from Padum. But they are much less approachable and harder to reach. Some of them are situated on cliff faces of which the view is impressive, but to reach them can be dangerous. Besides, if you are going on to Leh, there will be plenty of easily reachable *gompas* and monasteries to fill your appetite for such adventures.

LADAKH AND THE GOMPAS WEST OF LEH

Ladakh is like a different world, and worth the endeavor to see. It offers strange scenery, spectacular sights, ancient hillside palaces, a colorful culture, and friendly people. However, during the tourist season, make sure you have small change in currency because many people in the smaller villages won't.

From Kargil, after crossing the Suru, the road rises to the Kharbathang Plateau. Once we cross the plateau, we now descend to Pashkyum, located in a beautiful valley surrounded by fields that are bordered by mountains. Then we will pass the settlements of Lotsum, Darket, and on to Shergol.

Shergol: By the time we reach the small village of Shergol, we will have entered the area of Buddhist influence and left the predominantly Muslim area behind. This will be noticed by the little *gompa* monastery on the eastern side of the mountain.

Mulbekh is the next town we come to. It has two *gompas* on the hillside known as the Serdung and Gandentse that offer great views over the beautiful valley, which may or may not be open. So check in town before climbing up to see them if you wish to visit since someone may know who has the keys. One thing to watch for a little ways beyond Mulbekh is a huge image of the future Buddha, Maitreya, carved into the face of the rock near the road standing 8 meters high, the lower part hidden by the small shrine built around it. This dates back to around 700 C.E. From here onward the signs of Buddhism are everywhere. You will see strings of prayer flags hanging from housetops, across gorges, or even bridges.

Now we encounter the Namika La pass at 4147 meters, the sign of which is on the west side of a valley with a pebble filled river bed below. Then there is the village of Kangrail which opens up for the Kanji River valley. We next approach the Bodh Kharbu military camp. Not too far ahead we can see across the river the ruined Stagtse Fort, and another at Heniskut. Then we ascend to the Fatu La pass, the highest on our journey at 13,450 feet, or 4094 meters. This offers a vista of amazing jagged peaks and barren mountainsides. Then the slope descends steeply for a while and then eases a bit until we see the next township on our right.

Coming to Mulbekh from Leh, the bus stops at Wakha, which is 2 kilometers before you get to Mulbekh. So to see any of Mulbekh, you have to be serious about making a stop before you can look through the town.

Lamayuru is the next village we come to with its houses along the slopes and the *gompas* on the hilltop, which is attended by 20 to 30 monks. The main *gompa* here was originally established before the 10th century, making it the oldest in Ladakh. It belongs to the Kagyupa order. It is located on a deteriorated hilltop and has spectacular mountains overlooking it, and a unique dried lake that you can also explore. Though the *gompa* has been damaged and rebuilt several times through the years, it still has worthwhile displays of carpets, images, frescoes, and *thangkas* that you can see, with a central image of Vairochana. However, the main temple is down a few alleys and steep flights of stairs, away from the main complex. The main shrine at the entrance is built around the cave where Naropa once meditated. This is where there are images of Naropa and his disciples Marpa and Mila-Respa. The main image is of the founder of the Dri-gung-pa order, Jigsten Gonbo. There is an impressive *puja* ceremony at 7 A.M. and 5 P.M. They hold their Yuru Kabgyat festival in July wherein they celebrate the destruction of evil and the bringing of peace.

The Wanla River deep in the valley has cut its way through the earth to form many stalagmites on the sides. Out from Lamayuru we begin to see through the breaks in the hills the numerous ranges of mountains that go off into the distance. A little farther, after a number of hairpin turns in the road, we cross the Wanla River, and then we drive out into the valley where we reach the descent of the Indus River. After this point we may take a break for lunch at a village such as Khalse, which has a few basic restaurants from which to choose. When we are ready to travel again, the road follows the route of the Indus all the way (62 miles, 100 km) into the city of Leh.

If coming from Leh for a visit at Lamayuru, this place is reached by using a bus for Kargil. So plan to stay the night. Guesthouses are decent, which have only shared bathrooms. The ride here has colorful and exciting hairpin turns through the mountains.

Rizong is the next town worth noting. It has the Rizong *gompa*, founded in 1831 by Lama Tsultim Nima, and the Julichen Nunnery. The *gompa* is small but has large Buddhas and a *stupa* in the three rooms open to visitors. These are found up a narrow road to the north of the highway. You will find the *gompa* on the other side of a natural amphitheatre. Therein are shrines, the wooden blocks of the biography of Lama Tsultim Nima, and various objects and books composed by the 1st Sras Rinpoche. About 40 monks reside here. The nunnery is a 45 minute or two kilometer walk from it, through fields and orchards. About 20 nuns stay here.

If coming from Leh, Rizong is about as far as you can go for a day trip. There is also no direct bus there, but you can get there by taxi or Kargil bus.

Saspol village is reached after Nyuria and Ule-Tokpe, which is the point where we cross the river if we want to visit the temples of Alchi.

Alchi is a small village with the Alchi *gompa*, a complex of five temples and numerous *chortens* scattered around the village. This is another 11th century *gompa*, noted for not being on a hill so we can easily reach it, a merciful change, at least for me compared to most of the hilltop *gompas* we see. It was established by Ringchen Zangpo, known for his translation work. Thus, it has Kashmiri influence in the architecture. Though no photos are allowed inside, the Sumtek and Du Khang halls are excellent displays of Indo-Tibetan paintings. It is noted for being in a fine state of preservation, especially its murals which include several superb mandalas. Not an inch of space is left unpainted with images, decorative designs or other elements. The temple also has three large Bodhisattva figures with their legs and torsos visible from the ground floor, and their heads sticking up through the ceiling to the next floor. These include Avalokiteshvara on the left, Maitreya, and then Manjushri. All of them have garments with such things as scenes of various holy places, events from the life of Buddha, and the 84 Masters of the Tantra respectively. There is an actual Kalachakra Mandala made of sand in a glass case, which they allow you to photograph without the use of flash, but not the wall paintings. The Bodhisattva alcove includes other gods and Buddhas, a six-armed green goddess, and a 22-armed Avalokiteshvara. The Dharma Wheel *gompa* has massive images of Buddha along with others made of clay. The central image is of Vairochana, the Resplendent Buddha. You can also see intricate wood carvings and Kashmiri murals.

However, I found the temple rooms rather small and cramped, and dimly lit. So you cannot see the artwork in some areas that well, and some paintings seemed quite faded. I personally felt that for the time and money you spend to get to Alchi, if coming from Leh, it is a poor value and there are better *gompas* to see than this one, in spite of what other guidebooks seem to say. Especially if you have been to Likir, Hemis, Thikse, and others where they also let you take photos.

Likir is the next place of importance. The highway climbs to a barren plateau and we come to the road where we turn if we are going to visit the Klu-kkhyil *gompa*. Coming from Kargil, this is not a place that we will see, since it is off the main highway. The access road takes you to it. It is said to be the first *gompa* in Ladakh to have been established by Tibetan monks. Established in the 11th century, it was dedicated to the Gelugpa order in the 15th century. It burned down and was rebuilt in the 18th century.

The history of this place is that the land for the monastery was first given to Lama Duwang Chosje during the time of the fifth king of Ladakh, Lhachen Gyalpo. The Lama blessed the site and thereafter the monastery was built in 1065. Tradition is that the monastery was encircled by two great serpent spirits, the *naga-rajas* (Nanda & Taksako), so its name became known as Likir (the *naga*-encircled). The monastery flourished under Lhawang Lodos Sangphu, the disciple of Khasdubje. Here the rituals of the three basic Pratimoksa disciplines are preserved.

What we find here is that outside in the back is an image of Maitreya that is 25 meters high. Though this place receives few visitors, it has a museum with displays of cultural and martial items, along with religious artifacts and *thangkas* dating 300-400 years old, labeled in English. It has a fine temple room with a few shrines and images behind glass, and a beautiful assembly hall with rows of seats and other Buddha images behind glass, a wall of manuscripts, numerous colorful hanging *thangkas*, along with detailed wall murals. It is a very nice place to visit and has good views from the roof. However, they close from 1 to 2 P.M. for lunch. From here, the highway then descends to a wide plain of Basgo.

Basgo has a few points of interest. At Basgo we can see the ruined fortifications that are along the red cliffs above the village. This once was a royal residence, and now the old palace has three temples. Up a winding and steep path we can visit the *gompa* (400 years old) and the citadel (500 years old), though it is mostly in ruins. The Gerzang temple is home to a large gold and copper image of Maitreya, the Buddha of the future, that is three storeys tall. The murals are the main source of interest here with depictions of Buddhas and Bodhisattvas, and decorative designs, details, and images in between these.

Nimmu is a few kilometers farther, noted for the *sangam* of the Indus and Zanskar rivers located 2 kilometers before you reach the town. You can look down and see the two rivers mixing their different colored waters. Just before the road turns away from the river, you can see where the Zanskar River joins the Indus. The two colors of the rivers remain distinct for a while until the silt of the Indus overpowers the clear waters of the Zanskar.

Phiyang We now cross another barren plateau to reach the small village of Taru, and then on toward the access road that takes us to the village of Phiyang. However, if we are taking a bus to Leh, we go right past it. If we do visit the Phyang *gompa*, mani walls will lead us along. Among its attractions is a large collection of Kashmiri bronzes and Buddhist deities dating back to the 13th century. It was built in the 16th century by King Tashi Namgyal and is home to about 45 monks.

Spituk *gompa* is 8 kilometers south of Leh on our approach to the town. This *gompa* sits on a hilltop overlooking the Indus, with the local village on one side and the military airport on the other. It belongs to the Gelugpa order and was built in the 15th century. It is the seat of the Kushok Bakula, which is a most important spiritual line in Ladakh. It is a typical *gompa* and the interior has some nice images of Buddha in the main prayer rooms. You will find dark halls and unexpected shrines in various corners. It has an image of Vajra-Bhairava, and one of the temples is to goddess Tara and contains beautifully sculpted images of her 23 manifestations. At the top of the hill is the Gankhang temple, which has a Buddha and other images similar to the fierce aspects of Durga. These are veiled and revealed only once a year for the Gu-Stor festival.

After this, we can see the increase in traffic, especially of the military, that marks the approach to Leh. Soon we can see the town of Leh with the 17th century palace that dominates the skyline. When we pass the Spituk *gompa* on a hill, we then travel through the village of Skara with its fields and houses, and then past a brightly painted *chorten* as we soon role into main bazaar of Leh.

Of course, if you go straight to Leh from Srinagar by bus and want to see some of these *gompas* that have been described, you can always visit several of the western *gompas* in a day trip by taxi. But start early. Furthermore, Rizong is about as far as you can go in one day. Going farther means that you may have to take a bus and spend the night at whatever place you intend to see and return by bus when you are ready.

LEH

Leh, population over 28,000 and capital of Ladakh, is not a large city and is small enough to easily find your way around. During the tourist season it is crowded with western travelers. It is mostly a military base, but it is still a very interesting town with fascinating sites and plenty of hotels and restaurants from which to choose. It's also a good town for arranging treks into the surrounding hills. It especially allows you to have a good look at the ancient Tibetan lifestyle without going to Tibet. Of course, we've already had a good taste of this when we visited Dharamsala, which is easier to get to and also very interesting.

The first day you get here it is best to take it easy due to the altitude (11,500 feet or 3500 meters). Too much activity the first day if you are not ready for it can take a lot out of you. So it is best to take one day for acclimatizing to the area, and even more days if you plan to do any trekking to higher altitudes.

The central bazaar goes way back in history in its importance in the lives of numerous travelers. Even the older Ladakhis can remember when it was busy with the arrival of caravans of camels and horses with great bundles of merchandise brought in from the area, such as Yarkand or from across the Karakoram in Sinkiang. It is easy to first get acquainted with Leh by spending some time wandering around the bazaar area. You can see the many vegetable vendors, bringing their produce from their farms, and spinning yarn or doing something else while talking amongst each other. There are also many shops that sell items such as soap, incense, household paraphernalia, Tibetan Buddhist religious items, *thangka* paintings, masks, Ladakhi clothes, and an assortment of other interesting merchandise. Jewelry shops also sell silver and semi-precious stones, such as turquoise, coral, and pearls. As you find your way through the alleys, you will also come across various dwellings, as well as *chortens* and walls made of the *mani* stones (stones with inscriptions such as the Om Mani Padme Hum mantra).

In the central part of town is the Leh Palace, which dates back to the 1630s and looks similar to Potala in Lhasa. It is the work of one of the great Ladakhi kings, Sengge Namgyal. From the roof you can get great views over the city and of the Zanskar Mountains across the Indus. The interior is worth exploring to see the prayer room with its Buddhist images and paintings, although it is a little dark, and the huge masks can make the place a little frightening, and which has the 1000-armed form of goddess Tara. Entry to tourists is available for a fee, and there is usually someone around who can make sure it is unlocked. But make your way through carefully as parts of it are not so well maintained. Carrying your own flash light or torch is helpful. The Palace has nine levels. The first three levels are used for storage. The fourth level has the Ketuk-Chepmo, or spacious courtyard. This is where the main religious ceremonies were performed. The next three levels have the royal living quarters, the main throne rooms and audience halls, along with more temple rooms. The outside terrace also takes up much of this floor, from which you can get great views over the town. The uppermost apartments are also above this on the top floor. Down the hill a bit, across the road from the palace are additional Buddhist temples you can visit.

Farther above the palace near the top of the hill is the Namgyal Tsemo *gompa*, which was built in 1430 by King Tashi Namgyal. This contains wall paintings and old manuscripts, a Gon-khang temple for the fierce guardian deities, and a large three-storey tall, solid gold image of a seated Maitreya Buddha, and a one-storied image of Avaloketeshvara and Manjushri. However, this is usually locked up, except in the morning and evening hours when a monk climbs up the hills from the Sankar *gompa* to take care of the butter lamps in front of the deities. Above it is the ruins of Tashi's fort *gompa*, ruined but worth the views over Leh. Once you climb up here, or take a vehicle up the road, the views are such that you may not want to come back down right away. You can see all of Leh and many of the hills and mountains in the disctance.

From the palace, it's a couple kilometers north of town through enjoyable country roads to the Sankar *gompa*. It is a branch of the Spitok *gompa* of the Gelugspa order. Its central courtyard is surrounded on three sides by the residences of the monks. This has a great image of Avalokitesvara with 1000 arms and heads, and bright wall paintings. This *gompa* is only open from 7 to 10 A.M. and 5 to 7 P.M., but it does have electricity. So you can visit it in early evening. Check with the local tourist office for any particular details about the places you want to visit. A good thing to do is go to the local book store and get yourself a map of Leh to plot the places you wish to visit.

North of Leh town is the village of Changspa, noted for its guesthouses and the Shanti Stupa. The Stupa was built by a Japanese Buddhist order and opened in 1985 by the Dalai Lama. Located up a hill, you can drive by road or walk up the long stairway to reach it. It's illuminated at night and offers impressive views over the area. You can also see old Buddhist carvings in Changspa, dating back to the time (8th–9th century) when Buddhism was adopted in Ladakh.

Walking through the small lanes of Leh is interesting, and if you want you can check out the Mahabodhi Society for meditation sessions and courses. You can also visit the Centre for Ecological Development which promotes the development of Ladakh through solar energy, organic farming, health education, and so on. If you want to stay in Ladakh for an extended visit with a Ladakhi family, the Student's Educational and Cultural Movement of Ladakh can provide some assistance. You can also check out The Cultural and Traditional Society for their cultural shows each evening. It's across from the Hotel Yak Tail behind the Shamshu complex. And if you are in the buying spirit, the handicrafts you can get here are rather expensive compared to similar items in Dharamsala or Kashmir.

The Leh Mosque stands in the main bazaar of Leh. It has green and white tile work of Turko and Iranian architecture. This was built in 1666-7 after an agreement between the Moghul Emperor Aurangzeb and Deldan Namgyal who ruled Ladakh at that time. The mosque is open only to men. Another mosque is found just down the street.

Festivals in Ladakh are also colorful if you are here the first part of September. You can see fine examples of cultural costumes that people wear, along with the singing and dancing.

TOWNS AND MONASTERIES SOUTH OF LEH

In seeing the various *gompas* in Ladakh, there are five main orders of Tibetan Buddhists to which the *gompas* belong. The Drugpa order is a branch of the Kagyupa order, or School of Oral Tradition. This was established in the 11th and 12th century by a line of Indian and Tibetan teachers, which include Tilopa, Naropa, Marpa, and Mila-Respa. The Gelugspa, or yellow hat order, was founded around 1400 by the reformer Tson-ka-pa. The Dalai Lama belongs to this order. Smaller sects include the Drigungpa, which also is a subsect of the Kagyupa order. The Nyingmapa is the most ancient order of all and bases its teachings directly on Padmasambhava. There is also the Saskyapa sect, which lost much influence in the 15th century by the Gelugspa order.

Choglamsar is farther south of Leh where there is a Tibetan refugee camp, which includes the SOS Children's Village. Some of the buildings here use solar technology. The hospital also is free from artificial heating systems, and a bakery uses solar power as well. You can also buy or order beautiful Tibetan carpets. This has become known as an important center for the study of Tibetan literature, history, and Buddhist culture. There is also the temporary residence of the Dalai Lama near the river.

Shey is the village along the main road, 15 kilometers south from Leh, above which is the 560 year old summer palace of the kings of Ladakh. It was the early capital of Ladakh, and was the birthplace of many princes and princesses. The palace, similar to the Leh Palace but smaller, is not in the best shape, but you can see the 12-meter-tall seated Sakyamani Buddha made of gold and copper in the palace *gompa*. It is the tallest in the area. Ancient wall murals are also seen here with beautifully rich colors of figures and landscapes. No photos are allowed, even with the Rs. 20 entry fee. It was under the direction of Queen Skalzang Dolma, widow of Sengge Namgyal, that it was built in 1647-9. Shey also has numerous *chortens* in the area and a number of rock engravings, especially one of the five Dhyani Buddhas at the base of the palace hill.

Another temple across the field by about 300 meters holds another large Buddha image. Traditionally it is said that it was built by Nepali craftsman brought over by Gyal Khatum, Sengge's mother. This is also a village that produces fine metal-ware. The wall murals show the 16 *arhats*, or the first disciples of the Buddha, along with such noted personalities as Padmasambhava, Atisa, and Tson-ka-pa. There are also another two Tantric shrines and a temple to Amitabha nearby.

The Tikse Gompa is farther south, 17 kilometers from Leh, which you can see a few kilometers past Shey. The access road takes you right up to the main building. There are numerous *chortens* along the way. This was first built at Stakmo by Sherab Zangpo of Stod. Later, his nephew, Spon Paldan Sherab, founded the Tikse *gompa* on the hill north of the Indus in 1430. There are about 80 monks in residence. Successive reincarnations of the Skyabsje Khanpo Rinpoche act as incumbents of the monastery. This is probably one of the nicer *gompas* to visit and is beautifully situated on the hilltop, 2 kilometers above the village and Indus River. It belongs to the Gelugpa order and is known for its library of Tibetan books. One whole wall is covered with the holes to house numerous volumes. Its artwork or wall paintings are also well-known, depicting many of the terrifying deities. You can observe the religious ceremonies in the early morning (around 6:30 A.M.) or at noon. You'll know when they start by the sounds of the long horns from the roof, which you can watch. Some great views over the Indus valley are available from the roof. As you enter the inner temple, you see the large head of a Maitreya Buddha, the Buddha of the future, who is two storeys tall, seated in the lotus position. This was dedicated by the Dalai Lama in 1980. The assembly hall is on the other side up the stairs, which has its own images and wall paintings to see. The old library is in a room on the roof. They hold the Gu-Stor festival in March. If you wish, spend the night at the hotel. Half-way down the hill is the White Du-khang temple, which also provides good views over the area from its roof. You can get a great view over Shey, Stackna on its lonely hillock, and Matho across the river.

Chemre is another place that has a small *gompa* we may want to visit. From Tikse we go farther south to Karu and then turn left to go northeast several kilometers away from the Indus. This is another Drugpa monastery founded by Stag-sang-ras-pa under the support of Sengge Namgyal in 1644. Again it is found on a hilltop, but approachable by road. The older Du-khang chapel has images of Stag-sang-ras-pa and other lamas. There is also a silver *chorten* and wall paintings including those of the Kalachakra and Akshobya mandalas. The top of the complex has a new temple for the image of Padmasambhava.

The *gompa* is also known for its 29 volume set of scriptures that have title pages lettered in solid silver with the text in pure gold.

Thak-Thak or Taktok (rock-roof) is a few kilometers beyond Chemre farther east above the village of Sakti. Its *gompa* is the only representative of the Nying-ma-pa order, founded in the 16th century. The inner shrine is a cave in which Padmasambhava is said to have stopped to meditate while traveling to Tibet. A kitchen is located in another cave. It has the usual paintings of the fierce deities. A new temple was consecrated outside the main complex by the Dalai Lama in 1980. From here we head back down toward Karu and cross the Indus to reach the Hemis *gompa*.

Stakna is a small *gompa* on a lonely hilltop 25 kilometers south of Leh, which we can see from the road. It is the earliest representation of the Drugpa sect, built by the step-brother of King Singge Namgyal. The place is nicely maintained and has a beautiful silver *chorten*. It has images, especially one of Avalokiteshvara from Assam (Kamrup), and paintings, but the lighting is so poor that you cannot see them very well. Going to the roof offers great views over the valley. There are about 30 monks in residence.

The Hemis Gompa is forty-five kilometers south from Leh, a half-day, bumpy bus ride past the Shey *gompa* and an hour beyond the Tikse Palace. It is located six kilometers off the main road and on the western side of the Indus River between two hills. If taking a bus, you can get off at Karu, and walk the several miles up to the Hemis Gompa, which, clings to the hillside and, being in a deep gorge, cannot be seen from the road. You walk up the long drive and to a narrow valley with a prayer wall and several Buddhist *stupas*, or just take a taxi to its door. It is one of the largest and most well-known of the Ladakh *gompas*. It also has nice copper images of sitting Buddhas, one about 20 feet tall, plus wall paintings, and a respectable library. Plus you can take photos but without flash. There is also a statue of an evil demon named Mirza, which commemorates the invasions of the Muslim chieftan, Mirza, in the 16th century. It is especially famous for its large Hemis Festival. The Cham or Setchu festival is when they have the mystery plays which honor the 8th century Buddhist saint and prophet, Padmasambhava, who took Buddhism to Tibet. These are performed in its large courtyard. This is a two-day event in late June or early July with mask dances and lots of spectators. The monks perform multiple dances and a drama depicting the victory of the forces evil, and culminates in the dismembering of an effigy molded from *tsampa* dough representing those who have committed serious crimes. Then the lords of the graveyard disperse the remains in all directions. During this festival they also unfurl the largest *thangka* in Tibet (12 meters wide and 4 storeys tall) every twelve years.

The Hemis Gompa, as it stands today, is over 400 years old, founded by Lama Stag-tsang-ras-pa under Sengge Namgyal in the 1630s, and belongs to the Drugpa order. However, the previous monastery, the Go San *gompa*, existed here for well over 1000 years earlier. Many inner rooms are filled with ancient writings, much of which are uncat-aloged. The Tshogs-khang temple also has some beautiful *chortens* and fine Buddha image, with wall paintings of the thousand Buddhas and fierce protective deities.

Above the monastery about 5 kilometers away is a hermitage founded by Gyalwa Kot-sang years before the Hemis monastery was built. It has four caves, including his meditation cave where he meditated continuously for 12 years. There are also his hand and footprints on the rock. It is a peaceful place for meditation retreat.

The Hemis Monastery is where, in 1886, Nicolas Notovitch is said to have discovered the ancient manuscript that describes the life and travels of Saint Issa, Jesus. This, as Notovitch explained, was a compilation of scrolls from the library in Lhasa that were brought from India, Nepal, and Magadha about 200 years after the time of Christ. It was originally written in the Pali language, and translated into Tibetan. The manuscript describes how Jesus traveled to India and to the north to Nepal and the Himalayan region. Swami Abhedananda also confirmed the existence of these texts at Hemis in 1922, and published his account of them in his book, *Kashmiri O Tibetti*. Nicholas Roerich also visited in 1925 and published his own account of the manuscripts in his book, *The Heart of Asia*.

Matho: The next noteworthy and 16th century *gompa* of the Sakya sect in the area is north of Hemis on the west-bank road along the Indus at the valley of Matho, about 26 kilometers south of Leh. This was founded about 500 years ago by Lama Dorje. There are shrines and a temple dedicated to the guardian deities here. They hold a significant festival where the monks go into trance and become possessed by spirits that will then answer questions regarding the welfare of Matho, Ladakh, or about the people who ask the questions. The museum offers some fine *thangkas* if you do visit.

Stok Palace is found by heading north of Matho, 15 kilometers south of Leh, up a deteriorated road from Hemis. Take the road that turns off the west-bank lane near the Choglamsar bridge. It had been the home of the Ladakh kings in the past, and is still used by the royal family. This 200 year old palace, built in 1825, is where the Rani of Stok, widow of the last king of Ladakh, still lives. They go to Manali in the winter. Her eldest son is likely to become the next king when he is of age. This was built by Tshespal Namgyal. He was the last king of independent Ladakh in the early 19th century. Now five of the 80 rooms are open to the public (8 A.M. to 7 P.M.) as a museum and have displays of rare ornaments, *thangkas*, crown jewels, traditional clothing, ritual objects that had been used by the kings of yore, and photos of the queen and her family. The monastery is a short distance away, which was founded by Lama Lhawang Lotus in the 14th century.

The best way to get to some of these *gompas* is to simply take a few day trips out from Leh by hiring a taxi or car, or rent a jeep. These can be booked by the trip or for half- or full-day journeys to the *gompas*.

LEAVING LEH FOR MANALI

When our visit to Leh is complete, we may head south toward Manali. If we take a bus, it is a good idea to get our ticket a day or more before we leave since there may be a long queue in the high tourist season. The bus leaves at 5 A.M. for the 2-day journey, but we must be ready to stay in Leh another night in case the bus doesn't show up, which occasionally happens due to ever-changing weather conditions. It can easily change from sunny and warm to rain or snow quickly. It plays havoc on the road conditions as well. The upkeep is a constant endeavor from landslides or washouts.

The 485 kilometer road is open from mid-June or later to mid-September, depending on the level of winter snows. The road also reaches heights of 5328 meters at Taglang La pass, the second highest pass in the world. So if you have not gotten used to the altitude in Leh, you may get headaches or nausea along the way. Only about half of the road is paved, so it is a rough ride.

As we head south, it is a most interesting ride, quite an adventure. Traveling up to the Taglang La pass offers some great views. If the bus stops at the summit, you can visit the little temple at the top of the pass. After a while you'll go through Pang Camp, which is where most buses stop for lunch at the few restaurant shops in tents by the river. Prices are good for the food. Farther along is the Lachlung La pass, the second highest pass along this route at 5065 meters.

Once we arrive at Sarchu, we are back in the state of Himachal Pradesh, and it is another stop for registering our passport numbers at the military checkpoint. Most buses stop here for the night. Prices are too high for the accommodations in tents, which average Rs. 300 to Rs. 400, but this is all that is available if you stop here. The next pass is Baralacha La at 4883 meters, where the road soon starts to accompany the Chenab River.

After some time we arrive at Tandi where the road meets the Chenab and Chandrabagha Rivers. Then Keylong, or Kvelang, is the first major town on our route, and then on to Kosar, or Khoksar, for a lunch stop, as well as registering our passport numbers at the checkpoint again. A lovely waterfall is located in the nearby town of Sissu. Finally, we start the slow drive up winding hair-pin turns as we climb Rohtang La Pass, which gives great views of the surrounding mountains the higher we get. After we cross the Rohtang La Pass at 3978 meters, we'll make our descent into Manali. While going over the pass, we get into a traffic jam in which numerous Indian tourists have traveled up here to play in the snow. It is quite a site to see. People going on sled rides, Yak rides, horse rides, hang gliding, and partying in the cold. From Rohtang La Pass it takes about another two hours or so to arrive in Manali.

At Manali we can spend the night here and prepare to continue our travel south the next day, if we have already visited this place, as described earlier. We can go south to Mandi where you can travel northwest up to the Buddhist center of Dharamsala, and from there over to Amritsar or points farther north, if you have not already done that. Or simply take a bus straight to Chandigarh and then to Delhi. Or you can travel to Shimla for a visit where, as a change of pace, you can take a small train south through the hills, going around forested curves and into short tunnels, to Kalka where we switch to the Himalayan Queen on the faster broad gauge line. This train goes directly to New Delhi but also stops at Kuruksetra, which is certainly worth seeing as one of the important holy places in northern India. It is a town with strong connections with the ancient history of India, and with Lord Krishna who spoke the *Bhagavad-gita* here during the *Mahabharata* war. So we will make this our last stop in this northern region, if we did not see it on our way going north.

KURUKSETRA

Kuruksetra is a spiritually important and peaceful town which no pilgrim should miss. It is 118 kilometers north of Delhi, or about a four hour train ride away. It is most noted for being the place where Lord Krishna sang the *Bhagavad-gita*, which means the "song of God," to his friend Arjuna. The *Bhagavad-gita* is a classic text of India and Vedic thought. Every December there is the festival of Gita Jayanti, which is the celebration of Krishna relating the *Bhagavad-gita*.

Although there are plenty of *dharmshalas* in town and more hotels than there used to be, there is one hotel located about a 30 minute cycle-ricksha ride away from the train station, located near some of the holy sites: The Nilkantha Tourist Complex. It is a simple affair with two floors of rooms surrounding a courtyard. It is not far from the Brahma Sarovara, Sannihit Sarovara, and other temples. So it is conveniently located. Rooms here are fairly nice and not so expensive. From my room I could hear the holy recitations coming from the loudspeaker at a temple across the field which I could see from my balcony. In the evening there are also plenty of fireflies that look like stars in the grass.

The Iskcon temple is in the older part of town. If you can get there in the morning you can have *darshan* of the beautiful Radha-Krishna deities, which stand about two feet tall, and the smaller Gaura-Nitai deities. You can also attend the *arati* and have a nice *prasadam* breakfast. The temple is quite nice and expanding. They also have guest quarters on the top floor where visitors can stay. The number of devotees is small, but they are very friendly and helpful. In fact, they helped arrange my motor ricksha transportation to see the holy places in town.

Not only was the *Bhagavad-gita* sung by Lord Krishna in Kuruksetra, but other spiritually important events also took place here. Krishna met his friends and residents of Vrindavana here during an eclipse while He was living in Dwaraka. He also took bath in Brahma Sarovara and the Sannihit Sarovara water tanks. It is said that the Brahma Sarovara tank is one of the most important in all of India, and that all the holy waters of India are found in the Brahma Sarovara during an eclipse, which is why millions of pilgrims come here to bathe during such an event. It is also said that those who bathe here, live here, visit, or die in Kuruksetra go to heaven after death. In the *Kuruksetra Mahatmya* of the *Mahabharata* the sage Pulastya says that even the dust of Kuruksetra will cause one to reach the highest goal. This is the benefit for all who died in the battle of Kuruksetra 5,000 years ago, and one reason why the battle took place here. It is another reason why every pilgrim should visit this holy place.

Furthermore, it is said that Manu wrote the *Manu-samhita* here. Some people also believe that Vyasadeva wrote some of the Vedic texts, such as the *Mahabharata*, at his ashrama along the banks of the Sarasvati River when the Sarasvati used to flow through Kuruksetra. This is not to contradict the premise that he also wrote Vedic texts in his ashrama near Badrinatha. The *Rig* and *Sama Vedas* may have been written here as well. Even Lord Buddha is said to have visited Kuruksetra.

While we are here, there are several places we want to visit. First of all, Jyotisar is the place where Krishna related the *Bhagavad-gita* to His devotee Arjuna. This is about 10 kilometers north of town. It is a pleasant motor-ricksha ride away, and it provides a time to meditate on the occasion when the huge armies gathered on these plains thousands of years ago. Jyotisar is now a small park with a central banyan tree over a small marble chariot that marks where Krishna sang the *Bhagavad-gita* and showed Arjuna His universal form. The banyan tree is said to be the same tree as when Krishna and Arjuna were present and, thus, the only living witness to the event. There is a large pond of water here that provides for a refreshing atmosphere. There are also a few other small shrines, like an old Shiva temple. It is most pleasant to sit and meditate on the significance of the area and read some of the *Bhagavad-gita* while visiting.

The history of the Battle of Kuruksetra and the speaking of the *Bhagavad-gita* can be told briefly. The five Pandava brothers, born of King Pandu, were the legitimate heirs to the kingdom of India. However, when the Pandavas were still young, Pandu died untimely and Dhritarashtra, the head of the Kuru family, assumed control until the Pandavas were grown. However, due to his love for his own sons, Dhritarashtra engaged in many plots and intrigues to eliminate the Pandavas so his sons, the Kauravas, could inherit the kingdom. After many years of tribulations, close escapes from death, and fourteen years of exile, the Pandavas returned to reclaim their rights to the throne. However, the Kurus were not inclined to honor the Pandavas in any way. Even after asking for only five villages, one for each of the Pandavas to rule, Duryodhana, the chief of the Kauravas, said he would not give them enough land with which to stick in a pin.

After all peaceful negotiations were exhausted, the Pandavas agreed that there was no other choice than to fight. Even Lord Krishna went and personally asked the Kauravas to settle the matter in a peaceful way, but this was not what was destined to be. Each side then amassed huge armies from all over India and beyond. In fact, the Kurus had a much larger army and far greater warriors than the Pandavas. However, the greatest ally of the Pandavas was their great moral and spiritual character, and their friend Sri Krishna, the most powerful personality.

When it was time for the huge armies to face each other on the plains of Kuruksetra, there were many millions of warriors, horses, chariots, and elephants ready to fight. Before the battle, Krishna, who was serving as Arjuna's chariot driver and advisor, drove Arjuna's chariot between the two great armies. Seeing the number of friends and relatives on each side ready to fight each other, Arjuna hesitated and felt much grief over the situation. He felt it was useless to fight. He preferred to retire to the forest and live as a recluse and meditate. It was then that Krishna took the opportunity to sing the *Bhagavad-gita* to Arjuna to show him that action for devotional service and to protect *Sanatana-dharma* is a higher standard.

The *Bhagavad-gita* is the essence of all Vedic philosophy and is composed of 720 verses and explains such topics as the nature of the soul, God, the material universe, activities and karma, reincarnation, the process of yoga, the purpose of life, and more. After all this was explained to Arjuna, he took courage with proper understanding and fought. Thereafter, the war of Kuruksetra lasted for 18 days in which several million warriors died in the fierce fighting. Then the Pandavas were rightfully established in their kingdom, and Sri Krishna had provided His eternal instructions in the form of the *Bhagavad-gita*

for all of humanity. This is all elaborated in the *Mahabharata* which is composed of
100,000 verses, making it the longest poem in literary history.

When we leave Jyotisar, our next stop is at Bana Ganga. This is where Grandfather
Bhisma left this world on the 11th day of the Battle of Kuruksetra. The battle was so fierce
that Bhisma's back was covered with arrows. Finally, he fell on his back and laid on what
appeared as a bed of arrows. Then Krishna and the Pandavas, hearing the news, gathered
around him as he prepared to leave this world. Bhisma was one of the greatest and most
respected of the warriors on the battlefield. As he lay there, he became thirsty and Arjuna
shot an arrow into the ground from which sprang Ganges water to quench Bhisma's
thirst. This later formed into what is now a small *kund* or water tank called Bana Ganga,
or Bhisma Kund. Bathing in it is said to give the benefits of bathing at all the holy *tirthas*.

Next to the *kund* is a small temple that has images of Bhisma on the bed of arrows sur-
rounded by Krishna and the Pandavas in the act of listening to Bhisma as he instructs
Yudhisthira on the path of *dharma*, or spiritual merit. There is also a deity of Krishna in
His universal form. At one end of the *kund* is a huge 26-foot tall deity of Hanuman.
There is also a little temple here of Sita-Rama, Lakshmana, Hanuman, and Durga. When
we are finished here, next we'll go to the large Brahma Sarovara tank.

Brahma Sarovara is one of the holiest tanks in India and is where millions of pilgrims
gather to bathe during an eclipse. One who bathes here is said to receive the merit of performing an *ashvamedha* ritual, and one is freed from all sins by bathing here during an
eclipse. This is where Lord Brahma performed a large sacrificial ceremony and also from
where he manifested the earth planet in the process of creation. Legend has it that
Brahma Sarovara was excavated first by King Kuru long before the epic battle of Kuruksetra. It is a huge tank (half a kilometer wide and one kilometer long) with an island in the
middle connected by a road that cuts through it. On the island is a water well called the
Chandra Kupa Well, one of the oldest sacred wells. Tradition has it that in ancient times
the water in the well would change to milk during the solar eclipse. Next to the well is a
small Radha-Krishna temple where Yudhisthira is said to have built a victory pillar after
the successful culmination of the war. This lake is also where Krishna, His brother Balarama, and His sister Subhadra came from Dwaraka to bathe during an eclipse. Along the
side of the tank is a smaller island with the Sarveshwar Mahadeva (Shiva) temple on it.

The streets nearby have a number of other temples that we can visit, such as the Birla
Gita Mandir. This has a deity of Krishna in the act of explaining the *Bhagavad-gita* to
Arjuna. Outside is a chariot with images of Krishna and Arjuna on it. Down the road
along Brahma Sarovara are other temples and ashramas, many of which are quite nice.
You can simply ride down the street and stop to see the ones you want to visit.

Nearby is Sannihit Sarovara, another lake or water tank that is very significant. It is
not as large as Brahma Sarovara, but it is fairly big (1500 by 450 feet). Sannihit means the
assembly of the entire range of holy *tirthas* or sacred sites, which is said to happen every
Amavas, or eclipse, especially the Somavati Amavas (lunar eclipse). It is also said that all
of the sacred holy places gather here on the new Moon day, and that this is where the
seven sacred Sarasvatis meet. Performing the *shraddha* ceremony for the benefit of the
ancestors and bathing during the eclipse is said to purify you of all your sins and give you

the merit of having performed 1,000 *ashvamedha* ceremonies. Lord Krishna also bathed here and met the *gopis* and residents of Vrindavana when He was present.

On the eastern end of the tank are several small temples to Vishnu, Dhruva, Hanuman, Durga, Lakshmi-Narayana, etc. Across the road is a large, beautiful temple to Lakshmi-Narayana. There are also numerous *sadhus* found here, and those who merely *look* like *sadhus*. In fact, as I walked around the lake on one occasion, I came upon a group of *sadhus* who, instead of engaging in meditation or reading scriptures, etc., were sitting and playing a game of cards. When I asked them if I could take a photo, a few instantly said no. Playing like a naive tourist, I asked why not, and one answered, "What do you think?" They thought I was going to take a photo and then give it to the newspapers. Of course, I knew why they didn't want their photo taken: They didn't want to be seen that way because they would lose their credibility. This made me realize how few real *sadhus* actually exist.

Not far from here is a very impressive, government operated Krishna Museum. Every aspect of this museum is related to the pastimes of Krishna and the various ways to express devotion to Him. The museum has a wide assortment of brass, metal, and wood deities of Krishna, Jagannatha, along with paintings, drawings, sculptures, and artwork from all over India. There was also a life-size image of Mother Yasoda with Krishna and Balarama. It also has an assortment of costumes and dress from different eras of Indian history. This museum is very nicely done and well worth the visit, but don't take any photos or, as I was told, that may take away your camera.

Our next stop is Kamal Nabha or Nabhi, which is a water *kund* said to mark the place where Brahma was born out of the lotus flower that arose from the *nabhi* or navel of Lord Vishnu. This is located in the old town of Thanesar. The water tank here is not that large and is green with algae, but is very significant. There is only a small shrine with Lakshmi-Narayana deities and a picture on the wall of Vishnu with Brahma on the lotus coming from Vishnu's navel. In the entranceway are a few other small deities.

Another short ride to a different part of town takes us to the Sthaneswara temple and tank. This is also quite interesting and is where the Pandavas prayed to Lord Shiva for blessings to be victorious in the war of Kuruksetra. The water from the tank is considered sacred and to have healing powers. A few drops of the water from the tank is said to have cured King Ban or Vena of leprosy. The temples around the tank have very beautiful deities of Krishna, Radha-Govinda, Sita-Rama and Lakshmana, Shiva, Durga, etc., and an ancient Shiva *lingam*.

Down the road is the Bhadra Kali temple. This is another Shaktipeeth which marks the place where Sati's ankle fell when Lord Vishnu cut her dead body into pieces as it was being held by Lord Shiva. This was after she left her body when she had been insulted by her father, Daksha, in Haridwar for having Shiva as her husband.

There is an assortment of other noteworthy places around Kuruksetra, some of which you may want to visit if you have time. The mound called Amin, eight miles outside of town, is where Arjuna's son, Abhimanyu, was caught in the Chackra Vyuha military formation and killed during the battle of Kuruksetra, as described in the *Mahabharata*. And the Karna Vadha trench is where Karna, the Pandavas half-brother who fought against them, was killed when his chariot got stuck there. And Jind and Safidon are towns where you'll find such *tirthas* as Ram Hridaya where Parashurama performed a spiritual ceremony. At Birhi Kalan near Jind is Varaha Tirtha where Lord Varaha appeared in order to save the earth. Sarp Damam, in Safidon, is where Janamejaya, the son of Maharaja Pariksit, performed a fire sacrifice in order to destroy all the snakes after his father was bitten by the snake bird Takshaka from a curse by Shringi, as described in the *Srimad-Bhagavatam*. This is in connection with the holy town of Shukratal. If you have the time to do some research, the library at Kuruksetra has a good collection of Vedic literature in Sanskrit and English. In this way, Kuruksetra has much to offer the sincere pilgrim and also elaborates the significance of the *Bhagavad-gita*.

BACK TO DELHI

After our visit to Kuruksetra, we can easily take the train, having previously purchased our tickets, and travel down to New Delhi where we can decide what is next on our agenda: More traveling or a return home. Even in New Delhi we can see some of the important temples, which have been described elsewhere. This can continue to uplift our consciousness even within the environs of the city, and before we move on with the adventure of our lives.

So now we have completed our pilgrimage to all of the major holy places in Northern India. Though there are many more that could have been included, the ones we saw or heard about are the holy sites of several major religions in many locations, along with places that are related to the Vedic legends and even the creation of the world. We have now also been to places that have provided inspiration and deep realizations for many sages and holy men, not to mention ourselves. And by visiting these places and witnessing and feeling the atmosphere of the various cultures, we also have been able to expand our consciousness and realizations about life in this world and beyond. Many of these places are like jumping-off points that can help propel us into the higher dimensions and realities of life. This can certainly play a very important part of our spiritual development, which can help catapult us back to the spiritual dimension. This, after all, is the main purpose of life. And if we have traveled with a seeker's humility and quest for higher experiences, then some of us who have gone on this journey, or even parts of it, have certainly attained glimpses into the same visions of the sages that have gone on before us, and viewed similar levels of higher reality. The effects and memories of such encounters will stay with us forever and, thus, change our lives. This is priceless experience.

The area of Har-ki-Pauri in Haridwar, where the Ganga meets the plains of India.

Pilgrims happily bathing in the Ganga (Ganges) at Har-ki-Pauri.

The smooth and calm Ganga River flowing past the eastern part of Rishikesh, with the foothills of the Himalayas in the background.

The Lakshmana Jula suspension bridge overlooking the Ganga River with both new and old temples nearby.

A Vaishnava devotee of Lord Ramachandra, one of many who visit or pass through the holy town of Rishikesh.

Crowds gather to enter the Badrinatha temple to get *darshan* of Lord Badrinatha who is Lord Vishnu in a sitting position. Other deities and smaller shrines are also found within the temple and back courtyard.

A happy Buddhist monk enjoying a refreshment in town at Mcleod Ganj.

A Tibetan girl at the Shoton Festival at Mcleod Ganj.

A Tibetan mask dancer at one of the numerous Buddhist temples in Mcleod Ganj.

The Dalai Lama walking through the crowds who respectfully and gladly greet him at the Shoton Festival in Mcleod Ganj.

The beautiful Sikh Golden Temple at Amritsar, the holiest of all Sikh shrines.

A Tibetan lady making textile handicrafts at one of the craft centers in Mcleod Ganj.

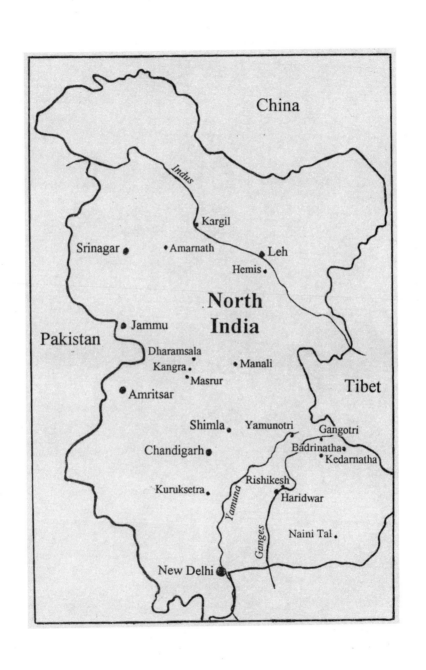

▼

The Major Holy Sites
and Temples of
Far Northeast India

Far Northeast India presently consists of seven separate states. These are all fairly small, and some tourists never hear of them because they do not know where they are. But the largest state, certainly in population, is Assam. North of the western part of Assam is the small country of Bhutan. Around the eastern leg of Assam is the state of Arunachal Pradesh. South of Arunachal is Nagaland, followed by Manipur, Mizoram, and Tripura. Southwest of Assam is Meghalaya. And this whole area is on the east side of Bangladesh, which makes it a little more difficult to reach. Besides, permits are also required to enter this region. Some permits, such as those for Sikhim, are relatively easy to get at the border as you enter the state. Other permits for areas such as Arunachal Pradesh, Nagaland, Tripura, etc., are much more difficult to acquire and take some advance preparation. Otherwise, the only way you can get permits is if you know someone in high places.

The people in India's Northeast region begin to show their oriental appearances. The Northeast is still the homeland of many indigenous tribes who still practice their own culture. However, the way certain religious groups are trying to infiltrate the area and convert people by one means or another is becoming a threat to the continued existence of the natural traditions of the people. And this is something that has been dividing the people in ways in which they were never divided before, and is reducing their culture to a mere museum piece. However, there are those who have recognized this threat, and can see how conversion is not something that really has been a cause for social advancement. Therefore, such people are working for the preservation of the indigenous cultures of the area. It is a pity that the culture is being threatened since the people of this region are very nice for the most part, very sincere, and also most hospitable. I have had many memorable experiences with the people on my tours of this region, and met some incredibly sweet and caring people. They have unique cultural dances, lovely traditional dress, exceptional artwork and skills with crafts, and beautifully produced textiles. I have a whole collection of attractive traditional scarves and shawls that have been given to me by the people of the area. And the different colors in the fabrics are often a sign of which tribe of people produced it. This is what makes it unique.

Far Northeast India has been a big part of the Vedic culture and tradition of India. For example, when we look back at the history of the region, we find that Lord Krishna's friend Arjuna had married a Naga wife, Ulupi, in Nagaland. Arjuna's brother Bhima also married a Bachari tribal girl from the area of Nagaland. The city of Dimapur has the ruins of the Bachari tribe known as Bhima's palace. In fact, Dimapur is one of the oldest cities in the northeast, being 2,000 or 3,000 years old, if not older, and was once known as Hidimbipur after the name of Bhima's wife, Hidimbi. She was a member of the Dimasa Bachari tribe. Their son was Ghatotkacha, a great warrior as explained in the *Mahabharata*.

Furthermore, Krishna married Rukmini in Arunachal Pradesh. The area of Agninagar is where the story of Usha and Anirudha took place. Anirudha was the grandson of Krishna and the son of Pradyumna. It is where the huge battle happened between Anirudha and the army of Usha's father. Landmarks in the area can be seen of this episode of Vedic history. This is described in the *Srimad-Bhagavatam*. So there is much of India's ancient tradition that connects the area. Probably Assam has the most interesting of holy sites and temples to see. But Sikhim has most of the Tibetan Buddhist monasteries to see.

ENTERING THE NORTHEAST REGION

As we enter Northeast India, there are a few ways we can go. If we have gone to Kathmandu, we can continue our travels by going to Darjeeling rather than going back to Patna or Varanasi. We can travel by bus, across the flat lands of Nepal, to the border town of Kakarbhitta. This is a bus ride that will take about 14 hours, so you will get here in the evening if we depart in the morning. (Of course, if you are not interested in seeing the landscape, you can also take the night bus.) Once you arrive, you can either spend the night here and start out in the morning, or you can still cross the border and stay the night at Naksalbari, the Indian border town, or go on to Siliguri.

For me, it is easier to spend the night at Kakarbhitta, where there are inexpensive hotels offering simple rooms, and plenty of travel agents to accommodate any further travel arrangements you need. After spending the night, we get up and go through Nepali customs and immigration, cross the border, go through Indian immigration to get our passport stamped, and then get a motor ricksha or taxi to Siliguri. Siliguri is not as far away, and once there we can get a bus to Darjeeling, or take a share taxi. The trip to Darjeeling takes only about 4 to 5 hours.

If, however, you are crossing into Nepal from Darjeeling, the whole process is just the opposite. You take your morning bus or a share taxi down to Siliguri. I took a share taxi, which is a jeep that picks up customers along the way and charges each rider about 100 rupees for the ride. They put your luggage on the roof and when they get enough customers, then they start out, always ready to pick up more if they are not full. A full load would be about 3 people in the front, counting the driver, four people in the back seat, and as many as will fit in the back compartment. We left Darjeeling about 7 A.M., and I was in Kakarbhitta by 1 P.M. In Siliguri, it is easier to spend the extra money for a motor ricksha to take you to the border town than it is to get a cheaper bus. There is no waiting around and you go right to the border. Then you go through Indian immigration, cross the border, check into Nepal immigration and fill in the form, give them a passport photo, pay your $30, and get a three month visa. Then through a travel agent I booked a ticket for the next morning's bus which leaves at 4.30 A.M. I then checked into an inexpensive hotel room for the night. I also booked a hotel at Kathmandu for at least the first night so that by the time I arrived in the evening, I would not have to shop around for a place to stay in Kathmandu. I could easily do that the next day if I wanted. So, with all that settled, I spent the rest of the afternoon reading, writing, taking a walk, and getting caught up with plans for the next part of my trip. (Of course, once again, if you are not interested in seeing the Nepali landscape, then you can immediately book a seat on the night bus, which leaves at 3, 4, and 5 P.M., whichever works best for you.)

The other way many people go to Darjeeling is to take a bus or a train up from Kolkatta to Siliguri. Then from Siliguri you can take a bus, share taxi, or the "Toy Train" to Darjeeling. On your way up from Kolkatta, if you have not already seen it and are interested, you can also stop in to see the small town of Ramakeli, as described in connection with Mayapur. Some people say the best way to go is to fly from Kolkata to Bagdogra and then continue by bus or train. The miniature railway or "Toy Train" is a famous experience that many tourists like when going up to this mountain resort. But it takes longer and some people have said that the seven hours of continual winding through the hills gets repetitious.

Siliguri does not have much of interest, but it does have a beautiful Iskcon Krishna temple, said to be the largest temple in the northeast. And it is big and beautiful, not to be missed if you are in the area. It has beautiful grounds and fountains, a large temple room with altars of Sri Sri Radha-Madhava, and another of Lord Chaitanya and His associates, plus a restaurant, gift shop, and ashrama. There is also a separate shrine for Sita-Rama and Lakshmana, another for Durga, and another for Shiva. So it has something for everyone and was quite busy with people and families during the evening I went.

DARJEELING

Once you arrive in Darjeeling, you will see that it is mostly a town of hotels and tourist shops. It is not really a temple town or pilgrimage site. The view of the mountains is actually the main attraction of Darjeeling, aside from being an escape from the heat of the plains, especially in the summer. It is also where people come to see the snow, which is a special novelty for the people of the lower elevations of India. I'm from Michigan where we grew up with the not uncommon harsh winter snows. So it can be amusing to see Indian families come to Darjeeling in the winter who get out of their jeeps to oogle over nothing more than a thick layer of frost. The hotels are somewhat reasonably priced in the winter, but a simple room for 300 rupees in winter can go for 900 or more in the summer when the town gets really packed up with tourists. The general tourist may like the atmosphere and feeling of this town with all its little shops and a variety of local people from the Himalayan region. And some come here to go on treks into the mountains. But if touring is your main interest, then a better place is Kathmandu, as I have already described.

The town of Darjeeling sits on a narrow mountain ridge standing 2134 meters high, and was once the summer headquarters of the Bengal government. The British established this as one of their favorite summer places for their troops in the mid-1800s. On Observatory Hill, where there is now a small Shiva shrine, there used to be a monastery of the Buddhist Red Hat sect before it was destroyed in the 19th century by the Nepali Gorkhas. The monastery was called Dorjeling (the place of the thunderbolt) from which Darjeeling got its name.

Darjeeling is a friendly town and an interesting place to wander the streets to look around. If you are cold, which it gets in the winter, just climbing up and down the hillside streets of the town will warm you up. As you look around, you will see a fair number of pure vegetarian restaurants. So being a vegetarian here is easy. Bakeries are also easy to find. Tourists shops, some of which have been here for many years, also provide a way to see and buy many types of art work from this area. You can also visit the Tibetan Refugee Self Help Center, where the Tibetan people live and learn how to make various crafts, from dolls, weaving tapestries and textiles, painting *thankas*, etc. Any items bought here goes to help support the Tibetan people and its center.

There are many areas of town from which you can get a great view of some of the Himalayan mountains. At North Point in Darjeeling's northwest corner, you can get a good view of the mountains. This is also where India's first cable car system was built to connect Darjeeling to Singla Bazaar in the Little Rangeet Valley. From Observatory Hill, or a better view from Tiger Hill 10 km south of Darjeeling, one can easily see Mount Kanchenjunga (8580 meters, 28,150 feet) flanked by Kabru and Pandim. To the right you can also see Mount Everest, Makalu, and Lhotse if the weather is good. I went to see the sunrise at Tiger Hill, at which time I was lucky enough to be there on a morning when there were absolutely no clouds in the sky. So I got some great photos of Kachenjunga and the surrounding mountains in the morning sun light. However, this was in January when the air is often crisp and clear, and it was really cold that morning. When you reach Tiger Hill, they offer tickets for a higher price to go into the heated lounge. But the heat was only from two small space heaters which did next to nothing. It was still worth getting the beautiful mountain photos, but I was shivering by the time I left.

For those who are interested, there is also a zoological park on a hill. It is one of the nicer ones that I have been to in India, quiet and peaceful, with a selection of Himalayan animals to see. South of the zoo is Lloyd's Botanical Gardens with an interesting collection of Himalayan flora. There is also the Himalayan Institute and the Mountaineering Museum next to the zoo that honors the noted mountain climbers of the world, many of whom have come through Darjeeling on their way to Mount Everest. It also has a display of various mountain climbing equipment, and also has the resting place of the Sherpa Tenzing Norgay on the hilltop. He is a hero of the region, having accompanied Sir Edmond Hillary to the summit of Everest in 1953. He lived here and was the director of the Institute for many years.

One thing you will see plenty of are the numerous tea fields. You can easily reach a tea farm on the outskirts of Darjeeling, where you can also buy a packet of tea for later. They will also brew you a cup on the spot from freshly picked leaves. Darjeeling tea is especially noted for its flavor and its natural organic qualities. Buying it here is cheap if you are a tea lover, and you can buy the tea made from the leaves, or the higher quality tea made strictly from the buds.

There are some Hindu temples in Darjeeling like the Dhirdham temple near the train station. This is styled after the Pashupatinatha temple in Bhaktapur near Kathmandu, though smaller in size. There are also Buddhist monasteries such as the Ghoom and the Aloobari monasteries, which are interesting to visit. The Goom monastery has an image of the Maitreya Buddha of the future. You can take photos of the Goom monastery and its altar with the large image of Maitreya, the Buddha of the future, as well as the walls which are covered with beautiful murals. Other than these temples, Darjeeling has little spiritual significance.

There was, however, one interesting underground Durga temple that I visited quite by chance. It was off a country road at the northern end of town, reached by a walkway down the hillside. You climb down the steps and into a corner of the hill. It was really quiet and peaceful. No one was there, but you could tell some worship was going on everyday. There were Shiva *lingams*, a large image of Hanuman, and a small cave. Down a stairway near the bottom was a small shrine to Durga where there was a little ghee lamp still burning. This must have been a place that was established by a hermit a long time ago. I knew nothing more about it, but felt privileged for having been given the chance to visit this little temple.

Other than these few things to see, there is really not much to do or visit in Darjeeling, except just hang out and wander around town. So we do not stay long here since there is more to do elsewhere. However, while we are on our way to other places like Sikhim, Assam, or Arunachal Pradesh, we can come through this area for a brief visit.

KALIMPONG

As we get ready to enter or leave Sikhim, we will pass the road that leads to Kalimpong. This is another city based on a ridge in the rolling foothills of the Himalayas at an altitude of 1250 meters, 50 km from Darjeeling. It is a bustling town, though somewhat small. It used to be part of the Sikhim kingdom and the Tibetan mule caravan route, but was passed over to the British in the 19th century and became part of West Bengal. There is not much here, but it is still known for its bazaars where villagers arrive every week to sell their farm produce and handicrafts. So, as you are passing through the area, if you are interested to visit it, or cannot get a permit for Sikhim, it has a few things you might like to see.

There is the Tharpa Choling Monastery that belongs to the Yellow Hat sect of Tibetan Buddhism. Not far away, or just down the hill from it, is the Thongsa Gompa or Bhutanese Monastery, the oldest in the area, founded in 1692. There is also the Zong Dog Palri Fo-Brang Monastery, built in the 1970s. There are also some flower nurseries that grow orchids. Crafts are also made here to help support the people, such as at the Gauripur House for destitute women that was started by Rabindranath Tagore. He used to spend his summers here. The trip to Kalimpong is quite fascinating from Darjeeling or the Teesta River Bridge, which you cross on the way to Gangtok anyway.

PERMITS FOR SIKHIM

Most of the far eastern states of India are restricted areas and foreigners are given entrance only with the proper permits. So plan accordingly if you want to go. Getting a permit to visit Sikhim is easy (as described below), but for other parts of the Northeast it may take more endeavor. The thing to remember is that there has been much disunion, violence, and many deaths in the Northeast, primarily due to the force and fanaticism of the militant Christian groups, insurgents, and separatists. There are also disturbances felt against outsiders who come in and take needed jobs. This is why a system of control has been put in place in an attempt to regulate the movement of people and foreigners who cross the state lines of this region. This is especially for Arunachal Pradesh, Nagaland, Tripura, etc. Much more could be said here about this from my experience in this region.

The best way to try and get a permit to travel in India's Northeast is to take the help from friends, if you have any, that live in this area. Otherwise, you may also try any overseas consular offices before you leave for India. Or you may try to contact the Foreigners' Registration Office, Hans Bhavan (near Tilak Bridge), Bahadur Shah, Zafar Marg, New Delhi 110002. Or try Trade Adviser, Government of Assam, 8 Russell Street, Kolkata 700071.

GANGTOK

When we are ready to leave Darjeeling, we head farther north to Gangtok, Sikhim. You can take a bus if you want, but this will take more time. It travels back down the main highway to Siliguri and then back up to Gangtok. The best way to travel is by a share taxi, which are easy to get in Darjeeling. The central taxi stand in Darjeeling has many taxis waiting for customers to Gangtok. The destination signs will be on the hood of the jeep. Yet, it can be best to book your taxi the night before to be assured you get an early start. The share taxi goes up through the hilly and narrow country roads where the buses cannot go. So they cut right through the woods up toward Kalimpong where they connect with the main roads again and then drive up to Gangtok. This is worth it for the views alone. It is a fantastic drive through some great landscapes and beautiful hills and mountains in the distance. I was impressed to think that some people live up here and see these sights everyday. So it is an exciting little journey through the back roads.

The eastern part of the state of Sikhim is closed to tourists, but you can still visit the capital, Gangtok, and other parts of western Sikhim with a proper permit. Your permit will state what cities in Sikhim you are permitted to visit.

So as you cross the border from West Bengal to Sikhim, your share taxi will stop at the border. It will wait for you as you enter the border office, which checks your passport and takes down your essential information. But then you have to go up the hill to the police office, a short walk away and located on the left under an arch. You enter an office on the left side and go to the desk where the officer will give you a permit to enter Sikhim. This is often a two-day permit, but once you get to Gangtok you can go to the Foreigners' Regional Registration Office where you can quite easily get your permit extended for another three weeks or so. Anyway, once you get your permit, you have to go back down the hill to the border office where they stamp your passport and let you go on your way. Remember to keep your paper permit with you because someone may ask for it during your travels here, and they will ask you to give it back on your way out of Sikhim.

Once you get into town, the share taxi stand is quite busy and confusing, but local taxis are nearby, up one street level higher on the hill or on the main street of town. From here you can also find various hotels if you are not sure of where to stay. Also, on this main street are the banks for changing money, as well as internet cafes, and numerous shops for various things you may want besides tourist items or crafts and art work of the area. Lall's Market is just up an alley. It offers just about anything you may want, from shoulder bags and suitcases, shoes, kitchen utensils, and fruits and vegetables.

Sikhim is a Buddhist state and has many monasteries, which some pilgrims and travelers may want to visit. Some are reached only by trekking to them, and others are visited more easily. Some of the places you can see in Gangtok include the Tsuk-La-Khang, which is the primary place of Buddhist worship here, also called the Royal chapel. Many of the older people in town come here on a regular basis to chant on their beads and do their religious practice. This temple holds a large collection of Buddhist scriptures. It is the assembly place for the local Buddhist community and where the coronations and royal weddings used to take place. I did not find the building itself to be all that beautiful, but its interior is covered with colorful murals. The altars are also wonderfully decorated with many images of the Buddha, Bodhisattvas, and other deities. You may have to approach one of the army officers for permission to enter, as this is designated as being a place for no sightseeing, and no photography inside. The festival to the god of Kanchenjunga is performed here in September. The famous Black Hat dance symbolizing the conquest of good over evil is also performed here for the New Year's festival. I found the best way to reach this temple was to use the southern gate. You go up to the Tashi Ling gate and turn right, go about 30 feet, take a left and enter a small door through the fenced gate and go up the slope until you see the temple. The northern gate is patrolled by guards who simply said this was no entranceway. Not far away is the Deer Park which provides a viewpoint and holds some deer, and an image of Buddha as he was seen at Sarnath.

The Namgyal Institute of Tibetology is also worth a visit. It has a traditional style of architecture, and contains one of the largest collections of books on Tibetan culture, languages, and Mahayana Buddhism. It also has a large collection of art, such as detailed silk embroidered *thankas*, deities, and sells a few items of religious arts, crafts, and books. It is well worth the visit. They had just finished some renovation on the place when I was there, and a friend of mine had one of the officers show me around and explain everything.

The Chorten Monastery is a short walk away farther up the hill. It is recognized by its gold point over its white *chorten*, and the numerous prayer flags attached to poles. Here is the monastery for training new lamas. Inside the courtyard and down the steps is a shrine with huge images of Padmasambava and his manifestation of Guru Snang-Sid Zilzon. This is situated within the area of the Orchid Sanctuary, which is said to contain as many as 454 different species of Sikhim orchids.

On the other side of town there is the Enchey Monastery. This small but 200 year old place provides some nice views over the town and to Kanchenjunga. It also hosts religious dances here in December. The annual *chaam* or mask dance is held here every January. It is an important seat of the Nyingmapa order, built on the site blessed by Lama Druptab Karpo, whose mystic powers enabled him to master flight. It is only open in the morning up to 11A.M.

There is also a place called Hanuman Tok located on a hill at the north end of Gangtok. There is a small Hanuman temple here, managed by the military since it is now an outpost for the area. It has a nice Hanuman deity inside, and from this point you can get some of the best views of the Kachenjunga and nearby mountains beyond the valley below. However, these are still not views that are quite as good as at Darjeeling. Ganesh Tok is a little farther down the hills and has a small shrine to Ganesh. This place also offers closer views over Gantok city and the mountains in the distance. Another place that offers some good views, not as nice as the others, is Tashi View Point.

If you are into shopping for crafts and local arts, visit the Institute of Cottage industries. Here you can see an assortment of crafts, including handwoven blankets, shawls, carpets, and other items.

RUMTEK

To the west of Gangtok by 24 km, reached by bus or taxi, is the Rumtek Monastery. This has the Dharma Chakra Center, a monastery in the lower valleys of Sikkim that is the headquarters of the Mahayana Kagyupa (Black Hat) sect of Tibetan Buddhism, and location of its chief, the Gyala Karmipa. This sect was founded by Lama Marpa, disciple of Naropa, in the 11th century. There are now several divisions of this sect, of which the most important are the Drukpa, Kagyupa, and Karmapa sects. This has quite a history, which has helped develop this place.

What you can see here now are gorgeous Buddhist temples. As you enter the Rumtek compound through the doorway under the arch, you will notice the Buddhist symbol Ridhag Chokhor on top of it. This shows the Dharma Wheel and the pair of male and female deer, which is a common symbol in Buddhist monasteries. The legend behind this symbol is that after attaining enlightenment, Buddha retired to an isolated place. When he meditated, Lord Brahma holding a golden wheel of 1000 spokes and Lord Indra holding a white conch appeared before him and offered them in exchange of the holy Dharma. Buddha announced that he would turn the wheel of Dharma three times. At this point, two deer emerged from the forest and gazed directly at the wheel. Since then, it is known that the wheel symbolizes the teachings of the Buddha and the deer symbolize Brahma and Indra, who in turn symbolize students. The upward turned faces of the deer signify attentiveness, their direct gaze shows reflection and their reclining posture demonstrates meditation.

As you enter the spacious courtyard, quarters for the monks surround this beautiful four-storey monastery. It is in this courtyard where the famous lama dance ritual takes place. At the center of the courtyard stands a pillar on which the entire history of the Rumtek monastery is inscribed in Tibetan. Regular festivals are held here. These include Losar, the Tibetan New Year, and the Dubchen and Tsechu *pujas* every alternative year when the mask dances are performed. Around the temple doorways are beautiful murals of the four guardians. It is believed that after Buddha attained enlightenment, the four guardians promised to protect every Buddhist monastery. The monastery also has a painting of Lord Ganesh. This is significant because the 16th Gyalwa Karmapa had dreamt that Lord Ganesh was assisting him in the construction of the monastery.

Entering the temple, you will see victory banners, wall murals, and red pillars that are enrobed with long silk *thankas*. Here the image of Sakyamani Buddha is present, which is flanked by Shariputra and Mangalputra on either side. Sakyamuni Buddha has 100 small images of Buddha on either side that are made of clay and painted gold. In front of the image are the thrones of the 16th Gyalwa Karmapa, his regents and other Rinpoches. The Vajra master, chant master, and the disciplinary master sit on the red-carpeted benches that are in the hall. The shrines of the Mahakal and Mahakali occupy the rear right of the main hall. To the left are the shrines of Tshering Mchenga Gongkhang, the female Dharma protector of the Kagyu lineage, and the Drolod Gongkhang, the wrathful emanation of the Guru Padmasambhava.

This monastery was built from the personal resources of the Gyalwa Karmapa, along with assistance from the Sikhimese Chogyal, individual donors, and the Indian Government.

If we go around the main temple building and take the walkway on the right side of it, we go up the stairs to the back of the building behind the temple. Entering through the hallway and around to the right we come into the room that holds the Golden Stupa, or the Lhabab Chorten. It is 13 feet tall and stands at the center of the temple. It contains the remains of His Holiness the 16th Gyalwa Karmapa who fled Tibet in 1959 after the Chinese invasions. He built a replica here of his monastery at Tsurpha in Tibet. He died in 1981. The Chorten or urn is gold plated and embedded with jewels, mostly ancient turquoise and coral. The main image of the Vajradhara or Dorje Chang is five feet tall. It is located at the center rear with the other images of the eminent gurus. The *stupa* also consists of the sixteen successive Gyalwa Karmapas.

Across from this building is the Karmae Shri Nalanda Institute for Higher Buddhist Studies. This is for the propagation of the Buddhist Dharma as envisioned by the 16th Gyalwa Karmapa. Just outside the walls of the compound is the Lakhang, a temple for the ladies, which allows entry for anyone. It is for all those who are not monks and the residents who live nearby and wish to come here for their practice.

Another three kilometers beyond Rumek is a smaller monastery. The best way to see the area of Gangtok and Rumtek at the same time is to take an organized bus tour, or simply take a taxi van to the monastery. The monastery also offers excellent views back over Gangtok and the valleys around it.

PEMAYANGTSE

Farther west from Gangtok (about 120 km) is another noted Buddhist temple, the Pemayangtse monastery. It is located on a long ridge with good views of the Kanchenjunga mountain range. It is said to be the oldest monastery in Sikkim, founded in 1705, and is the headquarters of the Mahayana Nyingmapa or red cap sect of Tibetan Buddhism. It is a three-storied structure enclosing many murals and images, particularly Padmasambhava, who started this sect in the 8th century. The most noteworthy is the seven-tiered painted model in wood of a complete view from heaven to hell, and everything in-between. It was built in five years exclusively by the late Dungzin Rinpoche. Only two kilometers away is the nice little town of Pelling, a place that can be used as a base for trekking, or as a place to stay during your visit here.

To visit other parts of Sikhim may require a permit. So check before you start traveling much, since changes are developing in this regard.

PHODANG & LABRANG MONASTERIES

About 38 km north of Gangtok are a few smaller monasteries. The Phodang is certainly not as ornate as the Rumtek, after which it may not seem like it is worth the trip. But it is peaceful and timeless in its atmosphere. You can take the bus to reach this monastery along the road to Mangam, but the really winding road feels better if you take a jeep. It is easy to look around the monastery and the monks will help explain things. If you go to the back room, you will see unusually dark murals showing demonic beings dismembering the occupants of hell. The Labrang Monastery is a 2 km climb farther up the hill, which is an older structure.

TASHIDING MONASTERY

The Tashiding Monastery stands on the summit of a heart-shaped hill. It was built in 1717. The legend behind this place is that Guru Padmasambhava once shot an arrow into the air and then meditated at this place where it landed. The main temple was rebuilt in 1987. It is a mystical place with many chortens, mani stones, and prayer-wheels driven by streams, along with the Ratong and Rangeet rivers nearby, and the Kanchenjunga mountain in the background. Large crowds of pilgrims visit this place during the Bumchu festival. It is during this festival when the priests take sacred water that was placed in a sealed jar by a 17th century Buddhist saint and mix it with the river water and distribute it to the pilgrims for its special potency. Each year oracle priests can predict the future of Sikhim by how the water is too full or too low. Tashiding also has the Thongwa Rangdol Chorten, which is said to purify the sins of anyone who merely glimpses it.

Many other monasteries and temples are in Sikhim, many of which are smaller or do not provide facilities for tourists. So the ones I have described are the main monasteries that can give you a good experience of this culture.

ASSAM

To visit Assam, we take a bus back to Siliguri and book a train to Guahati (or Guwahati). Guahati can also be reached by flying up from Kolkata. Assam has a few places that the serious pilgrim may want to see. Building temples in Assam goes back to early times. There were numerous shrines to Vishnu, Shiva, Durga, and others, but due to the changing waters of the Brahmaputra River, earthquakes, or invaders, most of these older temples no longer exist. Now many of them are mere mounds in the jungles at such places as Guahati, Tezpur, Sadiya, Nowgong, etc.

Assam used to be known in ancient times as Pragijyotisha in such texts as the *Mahabharata*, *Ramayana*, and other *Puranas*. The name Assam is connected with the Shan invaders who entered the Brahmaputra valley from Thailand near the start of the 13th century, and who were known as the Ahoms at the time. Their tradition relates that the name was derived from the word *Asama*, which meant "peerless" or "unequaled." They ruled for 600 years.

Many other tribes came into the region. After the Ahoms was a wave of Indo-Chinese people called the Bodo tribe. They form an important section of non-Aryan people in Assam. Even within this race or tribe there are sub-tribes such as the Koc, Kachari, Lalung, Dimacha, Garo, Rabha, Tipura, Chutiya, and Maran. The modern language of Assamese developed out of Sanskrit back in the 10th century.

Assam has been viewed as a land of magic and astrology, from where it gets its name, Pragijyotisha. Others also have considered Assam to be where the Tantrik form of Hinduism originated. The area of Kamarupa, now Guahati, especially became a center for Tantrik worship. Popular belief says that it was the home of Shaktism, along with the area of Bengal. This is also where you find many of the *shakti-pithas*. These are the places where the parts of Sati's body fell. This is in relation to the tradition that after Parvati gave up her body after the insults she heard from her father Daksha toward her husband Lord Shiva, she decided to give up her body. Thus, while in meditation her body burst into flames, and she committed Sati. Afterwards, Shiva was so remorseful that he picked up the body of Sati and carried it with him. Then the body was cut into pieces which fell to different locations known as *shakti-pithas*, which also became very powerful.

The *Kalika Purana* describes these locations as follows: 1) Devikuta is where Sati's two feet fell, and where the Devi is represented as Mahabhaga; 2) Uddiyana is where the two thighs fell and where the Devi is Katyayini, 3) Kamagiri in Kamarupa (present day Guahati) is where the yoni fell and where the Devi is Kamakhya; 4) the locality near the eastern border of Kamarupa is where the navel fell and where the Devi is Dikkaravasini; 5) Jalandhara is where the two breasts fell and the Devi there is Chandi; 6) Purnagiri is where the neck and shoulders fell and where the Devi is Purnesvari; 7) the place where the head fell is on the border of Kamarupa where the Devi is known as Lalitakanta. More of the *pithas* exist elsewhere.

GUAHATI

The **Kamakhya Devi Mandir** is on top of Nilachal Hill, 10 km from Guahati. Pilgrims from all over India visit this temple. Nilachal Hill is said to be a form of Lord Shiva's *lingam*. This temple is one of the main centers of the Shakti and Tantrik philosophy in India and enshrines an image of a *yoni* of Devi, Shiva's wife. When Shiva carried away his wife, Sati, after the calamitous attempt of Daksha's fire ritual, this was where her *yoni* fell. Thus, it is a *shakti-pitha*. It is a center of a widely practiced and powerful Tantrik following in India.

It is said that many years ago this temple had up to 5,000 dancers affiliated with it, which can give you some idea of how big and important it once was. The original structure, the ruins of which can still be seen, was destroyed in 1553 by a brahmana, Kalapahar, who had been rejected from his brahmana status for marrying a Muslim princess. After having been destroyed by Muslim invaders, the temple was again rebuilt in 1665.

When you visit this temple, you get in line for *darshan* with the other pilgrims, or have a local priest prepare your offering and then guide you through when it is your turn. As you enter the sanctum, there are a few small altars that you will pass, then climb down a short stairway to a small mysterious chamber. This is in the natural cave that also has a spring that provides water over the main image, which is a symbol of the *yoni*. This temple is unique in that it enshrines no image of the goddess. Then you offer flowers to the *matra yoni*, which is kept covered with a silk sari and flowers. After you have made your offering and accepted a little *prasada*, newly energized by the atmosphere, you climb back up the stairway and make your way out of the temple.

Outside the temple we can see another aspect of its importance because it has great examples of sculptural art. On the western end of the temple we can see decorative panels that depict such content as a mother suckling her child, a man blowing a conch, dancing figures, a dancing Ganesh, and a fearful looking but emaciated Chamunda.

Asvakranta in the northern part of Guahati is an important Vaishnava shrine. This is across from Guahati and reached by motorboats from the Suklesvar Ghat. *Asvakranta* means to ascend by horses, and is reference to when Lord Krishna camped with His army before he killed Narakasura. Naraka, thousands of years earlier, had been placed as one of the kings of Pragjyotisha by Lord Vishnu. In the beginning he ruled well and was pious, but after his association with King Bana of Sonitpur, Naraka became wicked. Bana, who was also known as Banasura, became powerful after receiving blessings from Shiva, but he misused those blessings. Then Naraka began to give trouble to the brahmanas and neglected goddess Kamakhya, who was greatly favored by Vishnu. Even when the sage

Vasistha came to Kamarupa to worship Kamakhya, Naraka refused to give permission, which earned his being cursed by the sage to be killed by his own father, Vishnu, within the form of Lord Krishna.

Finally, Lord Krishna invaded Pragjyotisha. He stopped with His army on the rock opposite Guahati, on the north bank of the Brahmaputra River. He killed Narakasura and installed his son Bhagadatta on the throne. The place where Krishna stopped is where a temple was installed.

As described further by the legend, when Narakasura was slain, being remorseful, the demon pleaded with Krishna that his death would be celebrated with fanfare in the early hours of the morning of the new moon in the month of Libra, which is in accord with the holiday of Deepawali.

The temple contains the image of a reclining Vishnu on Anantadeva, called Anantasayin Vishnu. The sculpture is of great artistic excellence. A tortoise, frog, and waterweed support the form of Ananta. The lower left of Vishnu's four arms is on the body of the serpent Ananta, while the lower right is resting on His right thigh. A four-faced Brahma is shown sitting on the lotus that has sprung out of the navel of Lord Vishnu. Two rows of Nagakanyas are seen kneeling with folded hands at the feet of Vishnu. Vishnu is also flanked by Mahalakshmi and the demons Madhu and Kaitaba. Outside the temple a number of small holes in the rock on the bank of the river are said to be the footprints of Krishna's horses.

This place is considered to be a great holy *tirtha*. One who visits it gets released from all kinds of karma and sins, and merely by touching a speck of the dust from this place even a hardened sinner can attain salvation, liberation from *samsara*, or the rounds of birth and death.

The **Sukresvara temple** is on the bank of the Brahmaputra in Guahati on the Hasti hill, according to the *Kalika Purana*. It is also said to be the ashrama of the sage Sukra. This had the Sukrasvara *linga*. It is one of the largest *lingas* in India. The present temple was built in 1744 by King Pramatta Singh of the Ahom dynasty.

The **Navagraha Mandir**, temple of nine planets on Chitrachala Hill, was once a center for the study of astrology. You enter the temple by walking under an archway and climb the short stairway up to the main temple, which has a dome with a beehive shape. It is fairly dark inside the temple and there is a separate *lingam* or form for each planet. These are Surya (Sun), Chandra (Moon), Mangala (Mars), Budha (Mercury), Brahaspati (Jupiter), Sukra (Venus), Sani (Saturn), and Rahu and Ketu (the north and south nodes of the moon). You go to the particular planet that you need assistance with, and a priest will come and help you with the necessary ritual. The temple we see today was built in 1752 during the time of King Rajesvar Singh. This is the temple from which Guahati's original name may have come from, which was Pragjyotishapura, indicating the place for the study of astrology, *jyotish*.

The **Umananda temple** is a Shiva temple on Peacock Island in the middle of the Brahmaputra River, reached by ferry. Lord Shiva is said to have dwelt here for a time in the form of Bhayananda. The little hill where the temple is located is also called Bhasmachala. The *Kalika Purana* explains that Shiva sprinkled ashes here and gave knowledge to

Parvati. Once when Shiva was in meditation on the hill, Kamadeva (Cupid) interrupted his yoga. Thus, Shiva, in anger, burnt Kamadeva to ashes (*bhasma*) by the fire of his glance, which gave the hill the name of Bhasmachala.

Another legend is that the heavenly goddess Urvasi resides here, or once resided here, to bring nectar for the enjoyment of Kamakhya from the small *kund* there. This is called Urvasi Kund.

To reach the temple you take a ferry across the river and arrive at the dock and climb up the rocky stairway to an area where you can purchase *puja* paraphernalia, like flowers, incense, etc. These are used when you reach the temple. If you walk to the left along the sidewalk, you first visit a small Hanuman temple. Out by the water, there are some carvings of Ganesh in the rocks. Then we proceed up the stairs to the main temple on top of the island. At the entrance is a shrine to Ganesh, which is usual for saying a few prayers to remove whatever obstacle we may have in the process of our *puja*. A few other shrines to Shiva are also nearby. In the main temple is a stairway leading down to a cavern where there is a small basement sanctuary. The main shrine is in a small pit where there looks to be a *lingam* covered with flowers, but on the side is a conch that is said to be a self-manifested sign of Parvati, or Umananda. When they do the *puja*, the priest also pours water over it, and there is a drain that takes the liquid away, which is also said to be self-manifested. So this is a special shrine. After the *puja* the priest gives you some of the offering as *prasada*, or remnants to be honored. The most important day to perform the *puja* is the Amavasya (new moon) when it falls on a Monday. The Shiva-Caturdasi is also a very important festival held once a year.

There is also a **Janardhana temple** in the center of Guahati which has an image of Buddha.

The **Ugra Tara temple** in Uzan Bazaar in the eastern part of Guahati is another important Shakta shrine. Ugra Tara is generally accepted as part of the Buddhist pantheon, and is identified as Tiksna-Kanta, Eka-Jata, etc. But the *Yogini Tantra* explains that Tara is the same as Kali and Kamakhya, the embodiment of supreme love. Yet, it is said that those who think they are different will go to hell. The temple we see now was built by king Siva Singh in 1725. It has a front hall with a typical Shikhara over the sanctum.

Ugra Tara, however, was worshiped according to the Vamachara rites (the dark left hand path) because of a curse by Vasistha. This is because once the goddess Ugra Tara drove away the residents from Kamarupa because of a complaint by Brahma, that all of the residents of Kamarupa were going to heaven because of the sacredness of the place, and no one was going to his realm. So Shiva ordered Ugra Tara to change things. Yet when her hosts placed their hands on Vasistha to drive him away as well, he was in meditation on Shiva and upon being disturbed in this way pronounced a curse that since they were also expelling him, she should be worshiped according to the Vamachara system. He also stated that since she and Shiva both wished to expel him, they would receive the worship of the *mlecchas*, and Shiva will always be covered with ashes and carry bones. Even the land of Kamarupa would be ruled over by *mlecchas* and all Shaivite scriptures would become rare until the advent of Lord Vishnu. Thus, according to the curse, the worship that was offered was conducted according to the Vamachara system, which included the slaughter of a wide variety of animals at the altar of Shiva and Tara, some of which still goes on today at certain temples and at specific times.

The modern **Tirupati Balaji Mandir** is a little south of Guahati. Its architecture is styled after the temple in Tirupati with ornately carved temple walls, and beautiful tall *gopurams* of the South India fashion. There are separate temple shrines to Balaji, Lakshmi, Ganesh, Durga, and a *homa* pit.

The **Vasistha Ashrama**, in a town just 12 km southeast of Guahati, is where he lived his last 15 years. There is the Vasistha temple that preserves the place from which he left his body. It is located along three streams that flow down the hill, which are the Sandhya, Lalita, and Kanta. This place is said to be where he used to clean and gather water for his *sadhana,* and where he meditated on Lord Shiva. A temple of Shiva is also found here. It is located between two forested hills where other sages have lived, and is now a nice picnic spot and place of pilgrimage for visitors.

The finely decorated **Hayagriva Madhava Mahdap temple** is about 14 miles northwest of Guahati, on the other side of the Brahmaputra River, on the Manikuta Hill at Hajo. This is a beautiful Vaishnava temple, and one of the pre-Ahom temples in Assam. The Deity inside is accepted to be one of Narasimha, although the name Hayagriva is in reference to the *avatara* form of Lord Vishnu with a head of a horse. It was Vishnu as Hayagriva who took back the *Vedas* that had been stolen from Brahma by the demons Madhu and Kaitabha. Buddhists also hold this temple in reverence and accept the deity inside as one of Lord Buddha.

The present structure dates back to King Raghudeva Narayana of the 16th century. The temple is an octagonal stone structure, about 30 feet in diameter with a pyramidal roof. It is sculpted with finely carved elephants on a molding about two feet above the plinth. The upper walls have life-sized sculpted figures, including the ten *avataras* of Vishnu. The sanctum or *garbhagriha* is a chamber about 14 feet square which is reached after descending a stairway of stone steps. Therein you will find a pedestal with the main image. Another legend is that King Indradyumna from Orissa had a dream in which a big tree came floating in the sea and he was to cut it into seven pieces. When the dream came true, two of the pieces were brought to Kamarupa Desa in this district, and one of the pieces of wood was fashioned into Hayagriva.

Another temple here is the Kedaresvara temple. This place is also where the Bhotias believe Buddha left this world and attained *nirvana*. This was once a great center of culture and learning. And taking a pilgrimage to the Pao Mecca mosque near Hajo is believed to equal one-fourth of a pilgrimage to Mecca.

Guahati also has the Assam State Museum. It is just east of the railway station and has a large collection of local handicrafts, a gallery of stone and bronze deities and sculptures excavated from the area, and reconstructions of tribal villages.

The **Bhimapur Hill** near Guahati has a Bhimashankar Shiva temple. Legend holds that a demon of the name of Bhima inflicted trouble and problems on the beings in the region. Thus, he was finally slain by Shiva when Bhima tried to kill a king who was a devotee of Shiva and who was engaged in worship.

Madan Kamdev is the spectacular temple ruins about 31 miles (50 km) northwest of Guahati. These date back to the 10th to 12th centuries when the area was ruled by the Pala dynasty. These include stone carvings of deities, erotic images, celestial nymphs, and other articles which are found on the hill.

Kaziranga is the 430 square km wildlife reserve that you may likely drive through if you travel to the east side of Assam. It is known for being a home for rhinoceros. It also has wild buffalo, tigers, elephants, deer, bears, and numerous kinds of birds.

Silghat, in the district of Nowgong in Assam, has the **Hatimura temple** dedicated to the Goddess as Mahishasuramardini. It has been a center for Shakti worship for several centuries. The present temple is built on the ruins of an ancient structure, which dates back to the 18th century and built by the Ahom ruler Pramatta Singh.

Tezpur is where we find the **Dah Parbatiya temple** to the west of the town. Tezpur was called Sonithpur, or the city of blood, in the pre-historic times when it was the capital of Banasura. He was a great devotee of Shiva. Bana had many sons and one daughter who secretly married Aniruddha, the grandson of Krishna. A mighty battle took place here between Sri Krishna and the demon Banasura and his men. This temple is basically the ruins of the oldest shrine in Assam. It is what is left of a Shiva temple that was built on the ruins of a previous temple that had been destroyed during the earthquake of 1897.

Tezpur also has remains of other temples in the area, such as those preserved in the park and at the Planters' Association or Club. There is also the ruins of a massive temple where the office of the Deputy Commission has been built. There is little to go on for uncovering legends associated with this temple, but it appears to have been a large temple dedicated to Surya.

Sibsagar (Sivasagar) is a modern district in Assam, which was the former capital of Ahom, and came to prominence with the Ahom rulers who governed the area for over 600 years from the time of their arrival in 1228. It was the Ahoms who cut through all the smaller principalities in Assam as well as the surrounding tribal areas and made it into the one political union of Assam. The Ahom kings were known for building temples. And most of the ruins are from that time. They were defeated by the Burmese in 1817 and their kingdom became part of the British Indian Empire in 1826.

The **Negriting temple** is in this Sibsagar district about 17 miles from Jorhat and 14 from Golaghat. This is a Shiva temple on a small hill surrounded on three sides by tea plantations and open country to the Brahmaputra on the other. The present temple was built by King Rajesvar Singh (1751-1769) after the previous temple that was built by Pratap Singh in the 17th century was damaged by the flooded Brahmaputra River. The origin of the site is based on a legend that the sage Aurvya Muni, in the Puranic age, wanted to make this into a new Kashi. He had gathered a number of Shiva *lingams* that are now all buried in a parcel of land called the Sital Pathar.

The Shiva temple here is quite attractive in the Shikhara style with a tower over the sanctum. This enshrines a large Bana *linga* which is on a flat stone upon which is carved a number of additional Shiva *lingas*. On the outside walls there are niches that hold lovely sculptures. Around the main temple are additional shrines for Ganesh, Surya, Durga, and

Vishnu, which are like smaller versions of the main temple. This temple is reached only by taxi service since no buses stop nearby.

The **Sib Dol temples** (Sivadol) are on the bank of the Sibsagar tank. These are also lovely and large temples of the Shikhara style of architecture, which include Vishnu and Devi temples.

Gaurisagar has the **Devi Dol temple**, about two and a half miles from Sibsagar. It is also of the style of the Sib Dol temple. It has bands of sculptured panels on the outside, with niches that contain sculpted images. The Assam Tai Museum is around the lake.

At Sadiya the **Tamresvari temple** is one of the oldest of this region. It means "goddess of the copper temple." It is about seven miles from Sadiya in a ruined condition in over-grown jungles. It is a small temple that once had a copper roof before it caved in. The interior is only about eight feet square. So it is not all that worth seeing for most people, and not easily reached. However, the significance of this temple is in the legends of the region. Sadiya was the capital of the Chutiyas, a Mongolian tribe who were here since the beginning of the 13th century. The Chutiya dynasty claims descent from Bhismak (or Bhishmaka) who was the father of Rukmini, the consort of Lord Krishna.

Golapara has the **Sri Surya Pahar ruins** about seven miles from town near Dobapara Road. The mandir is a small structure that enshrines a circular tablet, four-and-a-half feet around with carved images representing the various celestial bodies including Surya. The center figure in the sculpture is enclosed within a circle, surrounded by 12 smaller seated figures. The center figure is said to be Kasyapa Muni surrounded by 12 Suryas who are considered the sons of Kasypapa and Aditi.

Gargaon, about 13 km east of Sibsagar, has Ahom ruins, and the pyramidal mausoleums of the Ahom Kings are another 15 km east at Charaideo. You can also find a number of Shiva temples along the way to Jorhat.

The ruins here are significant in that they represent sculptural remains of the three sects of Hindus, namely the Shaivites, Vaishnavas, and Shaktas. Several rock-cut figures can be found here. There are images of Durga, Shiva, and Manasa, which is a twelve-armed deity cut from a single rock. It shows seven serpents using their hoods to provide an umbrella for her, and each of her arms holds a weapon. This is one of the only examples of a twelve-armed image in Assam. The foot of the hill also has many Shiva *lingas* cut from the granite. On the hill is another shrine of more modern origin. Ruins of several old temples are scattered over the hill. A small modern sun temple is also located here.

There are also a number of Vaishnava centers which were started by a person locally called Sankaradeva (1449-1569). He was born in a Bhuyan family in Alipukhuri, a town about 16 miles from Nowgong. He was the source and motivation for the Vaishnava movement in Assam. He was a great philosophical genius, poet, writer, and seer, and wrote his *Bhakti-ratnakara* and several other books, and numerous poems and songs. He and his followers started several of the main Vaishnava schools and temples that still exist in the area, called Satras. He also started what are called Namghars, which are temples or places (*ghar*) of the Lord's holy name (*nama*). Therein the main emphasis of worship is the singing of the Lord's holy names and *bhajans*. Sankaradeva, different from Adi Sankara, did not try to present any new philosophy, but merely brought new ways to present the Vaishnava tradition to Assam. It is quite a story to read about his life and development. The main Satras, which are actually complexes of study and worship with ashramas for students, can be found at Bardowa (near Nowgong), Barpeta (in Kamrupa district about 60 miles from Guahati), and Majuli Island (in the Brahmaputra not far from Jorhat).

ARUNACHAL PRADESH

Surrounding the eastern wing of Assam is the state of Arunachal Pradesh. This is an area with many of the old tribes still intact. It is especially interesting to interact with the tribal people and see their old cultural dances, costumes, and rituals. Most of these have strong affiliations and carry-overs with the ancient Vedic culture. I feel that many of these tribal customs and legends are like tributaries of the main river of *Sanatana-dharma* which flows through India and all of southeast Asia, all of which hold much in common when one looks into them.

There are numerous features of Arunachal Pradesh, one of which is India's largest Buddhist monastery at Tawang, located at an altitude of 10,000 feet. This is where the sixth Dalai Lama was born and where his footprint is still honored. There are more than 250 lamas of the Tibetan Gelugpa sect that reside here. The monastery shrine has bronze images of the Mahayana Buddhist pantheon and a gilded deity of a seated Buddha that is 26 feet tall. Many pilgrims attend the New Year's festival to watch the masked dancers.

Parashurama Kund is one of the holy places in Arunachal, located several miles from Wakro, or 24 kilometers from Tezu, and not far from the border of China and about 40 km from Myanmar. It is reached by a jeep ride up into the hills to the tributary of the Brahmaputra called the Lohit River. This is where Parashurama performed penance to attain freedom from sin. The history of this place is that one day Renuka, mother of Parashurama, went to the Ganga for having bath and bringing water. A delay in bringing the water made *rishi* Jamadagni, her husband, very angry as it was getting late for the mid-day worship, and she had let lusty desires develop for someone she saw. So he asked his sons to kill her for this offense. None of the six sons obliged except for Parashurama.

Parashurama then chopped off the head of his mother, but as a result of the sin, the handle of his axe would not leave his hand. Jamadagni was very pleased with him for carrying out his order and granted him a boon. Parashurama then prayed that his mother could be brought back to life, and then asked how to be freed from the sin. Jamadagni granted the boon and brought his wife back to life and told Parashurama to bathe in the Brahma Kund to attain freedom from the sin. Parashurama went to this *kund* and bathed there and performed penances, which is now called Parashurama Kund. Then his axe left his hand, which can still be seen sitting across the river in the form of a rock formation that resembles a large axe.

When you arrive here, you follow a path up from the road to a few temples, but keep walking to visit the *kund* first and visit the temples after a holy dip in the water. You walk 331 steps up a stairway into the forested hill, and then back down to the hillside to the river bank. Here is a beautiful site, with clear flowing water coming from the mountains. Pilgrims take a quick bath here and then can walk back up the hill and to the temples. The main temple is for Parashurama, one of the few that you will find anywhere. Inside are a few deities of Shiva, Durga, a Shiva *linga*, and small and large images of Parashurama. Once we have offered our respects at the temple, then our visit is complete and we can walk the rest of the way to the road.

Many pilgrims come here during the Makarsankranti festival, which takes place on January 14 each year. At that time thousands of people climb up and down the narrow stairway to visit the *kund* and pay respects at the temples to acquire spiritual merit.

Bhismak Nagar is a city established by a king named Bhismak, according to the *Mahabharata*. The story relates how Lord Krishna married Rukmini, the daughter of Bhismak, against the king's wishes. The ruins of the historical Bhismak Nagar are located at a distance of 40 kilometers from Tezu near Sunpura circle. The surrounding of the Bhismak Nagar is maintained by the Archeological Survey of India.

Tawang, northwest of Tezpur, has the largest Buddhist monastery in India. It has over 500 monks. Inside the temple you will find a 26-feet tall image of the Buddha. The ancient library also has many beautiful *thangkas* and manuscripts. Tawang is also the area where the Dalai Lama came through when he fled Tibet. The Bramdungchung Nunnery is located 12 km northwest of Tawang. The road along the way allows for wonderful views of landscapes and snow-capped mountains.

MEGHALAYA

Just south of Assam is Meghalaya. Shillong is the popular center and capital of Meghalaya, which means "abode of the clouds," which hints at how much rainfall they receive here. The place of Cherrapunji, 56 kilometers from Shillong, is one of the wettest places in the world with over 413 inches of rain every year. Shillong is another hill station situated at 1496 meters or 4,908 feet, surrounded by rolling hills with pine trees and waterfalls. The drive through the hilly roads through this area is quite lovely and scenic.

The town does have a tourist office in the Police Bazaar to help you arrange your travel, which is also one of the main shopping areas. The Laitumkrah and Bara Bazaar are two more shopping areas where you can still find the old market atmosphere and the local products for sale from the people of the Khasi tribe. Not far away is Ward Lake, known for its garden and boating facility. Lady Hydari Park is another noted garden in town. North of this park you will find the Meghalaya State Museum which is good for a quick look through. There are also some Hindu and Buddhist temples and prayer halls of the Khasi tribe here, but they are outnumbered by Christian churches.

TRIPURA

The town of Unakoti is considered an important place of pilgrimage in Tripura. It is 180 kilometers south of Agartala. The word *unakoti* means "one less than a crore." A crore is 10 million. Legends relate that an inspired, religious sculptor wanted to provide some service to the gods by creating "one less than a crore" of images in a day. There are no records regarding how many of such images still exist, or when they were made. But estimates place them around the 11th and 12th centuries.

The most imposing sculpture is the huge bust of Lord Shiva, which is around 30 feet high. It is locally called Unakotiswara Kal Bhairav. It is carved in a vertical rock-face of grey stone and has an elaborate embroidered head-dress, which is flanked by full-sized female figures of Ganga and Gouri. A small stream flows nearby.

About 50 meters downstream are three imposing images of Ganesh among the scattered rocks. One of the images is a huge, four-armed, seated Ganesh flanked by two standing figures of Sarabhuja Ganesh with three tusks, along with Asthabhuja Ganesh with four tusks. Numerous images, both big and small, are scattered on the hillside and in the jungle in an area of one kilometer. These include two Chaturmukha and one Trimukha *lingas*. Other images are of Vishnu, Ravana, Hanuman, Narasimha, Hara-Gauri, along with many tribal deities. The large spring fair held here during Ashokastami attracts numerous pilgrims from both near and far.

NAGALAND

Some areas of the Northeast are very particular about any foreigner registering for a permit. I was there on a lecture tour visiting with many tribal people and giving talks and interviews with the newspapers and so on. We were so busy that we forgot or did not take the time to register with the local police station in Dimapur. It is not enough to have a permit, but you must still register with the police upon entrance into the state. So, because we had not done that yet, they were already formulating the papers to have us deported. The chief of police said we were acting like we owned the place but had not registered with them yet. Anyway, we registered in time to avoid getting kicked out, but this shows that if you can get a permit to enter the state, you also have to register with the police before proceeding with your journey.

Nagaland is an attractive area. You will find lovely hills in this land, and the capital of Kohima is another typical hilltop city, beautifully spread out over several hills. It is a fairly modern city with a number of shopping areas with lots of stores.

In Dimapur there are the ruins called Bhima's Palace, which are the ruins of the Bachari tribe. These are the contemporaries of the Ahom kingdom, before it became Assam. These are remnants of structures that are now scattered blocks of stone and brick pieces that show carvings of various designs. It is known that these date back to the 13th century and show much Vedic influence on most of them.

The Naga tribes here are known for having been fierce fighters. And many of them still have pride in their old traditions, which has kept their people together and united for so many years. One strange thing is that through most of Nagaland, you will find that there are no birds, except for a few chickens in the farmyard. There was one joke I heard that related how the people used to be so fierce that there are no birds in Nagaland because they ate them all. But when I got there I found that it was actually a fact, that for whatever reason, there are no birds in Nagaland.

MANIPUR

This state is one of the most beautiful in the northeast and still preserves much of its Vedic traditions. According to the Manipur census, about 62% are followers of the Vedic tradition, primarily Vaishnava, while 26% are Christian, 8% Muslim, and 4% are still following the tribal customs. However, the tribal customs are also held in much respect throughout most of the area. So it is not like there is a serious campaign to stop the tribal traditions, which in many ways are similar to the Vedic culture. So you will find a wide range of customs and respect for nature and the higher beings.

Since the Manipur Hindu community is primarily Vaishnava, you will see many ladies wearing both a red *bindi* plus the Vaishnava "V" style *tilok* on their foreheads. The Vedic holidays like Holi (which goes on for six days) and Lord Krishna's appearance day are especially observed in Manipur, and it is a great place to participate and watch the festivities when they happen. Many people participate in *sankirtana* groups, all chanting the Lord's holy names, especially the Hare Krishna mantra during these holidays.

Manipur is also known for its style of martial arts and dance. The dancing style is unique, especially the Manipur drummers who swirl in various ways and drum intricate beats at the same time. The dance portraying the Rasa-lila of Lord Krishna is a special feature, which can go on for hours. The costumes are also of a high caliber of beauty and design, and the expressions the dancers use to signify emotion and attraction for Lord Krishna can melt anyone's heart and certainly put one in a transcendental mood.

The Manipur style of martial arts is especially known for its fierceness, yet gracefulness at the same time. To see a couple of martial artists swinging swords with such speed at each other, but with such choreography, the required precision is amazing. Even the girl martial artists are not to be missed, nor underestimated.

At Imphal, the capital of Manipur, "Mother's Market" is a unique feature. It is a market covering over two city blocks where the vendors are only women. They sell everything you may want here, from handlooms, shawls, seasonings, household utensils, food, etc. It was something that was set up to help the women of the area find a means of survival and income.

The Iskcon temple is also beautiful, with lovely Radha-Krishna deities, friendly devotees, and people who work for the preservation of the other cultures and unity of the religions. This is very much appreciated by the Manipur people.

How Manipur became a Vaishnav country is also an interesting story. I will provide a short version of it here. The Vedic texts explain that Manipur, as well as all of India and Southeast Asia, has always been a Vedic country. But it has especially rekindled that interest since the 17th century. It was during the reign of King Kyamba when he received a Vishnu chakra from king Khekhomba of the Shan kingdom, and set it in a temple in which the worship has continued by his descendants. Of course, the Vaishnava philosophy of Sri Chaitanya Mahaprabhu also reached Manipur in the seventeenth century by such Vaishnavas as the disciples of the great Srila Narottama Dasa Thakur, whose songs are still sung there. King Garibniwaja also worshiped Lord Ramachandra. But his grandson, Rajarshi Bhagyachandra, really influenced the sway toward Vaishnavism.

In 1762, the Burmese invaded Manipur. So the king and queen had to flee into neighboring Ahom, now called Assam. Rajeshvara heard about the greatness of Bhagyachandra and gave him shelter, and they became good friends. But Bhagyachandra's envious uncle wrote to King Rajeshvara saying that this person was not the real Bhagyachandra, but an imposter. So Rajashvara devised a plan to find out. On the advice of his ministers, the king made a plan to bring Bhagyachandra into a public arena, without any weapons, and force him to tame a wild elephant.

When Bhagyachandra found out about this, he prayed to Lord Krishna for guidance and was informed by Lord Krishna in a dream that he should enter the arena with nothing more than *japa* beads and a flower garland. Then victory would be his. However, Lord Krishna also told him that one day he would be the only leader of Manipur, at which time he should install a deity of Govinda that looked in the same way as he was seeing Krishna right now in his dream. The deity also should be carved from a particular jackfruit tree growing on the Kaina hillside. Then the king should arrange for an installation festival with Rasa-lila dancers and special devotional songs.

The next morning the crowds had gathered to see what would happen to the king. When the king entered the arena, the elephant soon charged toward him, but as he moved, it appeared that it was being hit by some unseen force. So as it charged, the elephant slowed and went to its knees before the king. Only King Bhagyachandra could see that it was Lord Krishna who was riding on the elephant's head like a mahout. Then the king offered the garland to Lord Krishna, and mounted the elephant and rode it to the sound of the cheering crowds. King Rajeshvara was then convinced of King Bhagyachandra's qualities and offered apologies. He then went back to Manipur with the forces of King Rajeshvara and regained the thrown.

He then set out to bring his kingdom back to normalcy and to preserve cultural diversity. However, in his management of things, he forgot to install the deity of Govinda as was requested in the dream by Lord Krishna. But one day the king granted an audience to an old farm lady. She said that she had been taking care of her field when a young boy came to her and began amusingly playing tricks on her. This attracted the lady. Then the young boy asked her to deliver a message to the king, and to tell him that he had promised to install the deity of Govinda, but he was neglecting this and he was now quite angry. When the king heard this, he realized it was Lord Krishna. So he followed the lady back to her village, located the jackfruit tree on the Kaina hill, and arranged to have it brought back to Langthabal, his capital, where carvers would make the deity.

However, even though he described the appearance of the deity as best he could, the carvers made a beautiful deity several times, but none matched the way the king had seen Lord Krishna. Each time the deity was gorgeously installed in a newly built temple. Finally, as the carvers were nearing the end of the wood they had of the tree, they made an image that matched the vision of the king. Then this deity was installed in a joyous festival. The king, his court, and the whole country was dedicated to Lord Govinda. The king did not force others to give up their own culture, but simply set the example of devotion and inspired the rest of the people to become Vaishnavas. It is also from this festival, during November of 1779, which gave prominence to the special Manipuri style of the

Rasa-lila dances, done for the pleasure of the deity and the upliftment of the audience to focus on the Lord's pastimes.

This, therefore, will provide a little insight into the cause for the beauty of the area of Manipur and the Northeast region of India.

The lovely Rumtek Monastery just south of Gangtok.

The Bodo tribe's Bagrumba or butterfly dance in colorful and customary outfits.

The large Chorten Stupa and monastery on the southern side of Gangtok, Sikhim.

Young monks learning the art of painting Buddhist *thankas* at the Gangtok Institute of Cottage Industries where people are trained in a skill for self-sufficiency.

The miraculous Khari dance of the Bodos, in which the dancer performs on sharp knife blades without getting cut, in northern Assam.

Rongmei Tribe dancers from the Chingmei Rong village near the city of Imphal, Manipur wearing customary clothes of the culture.

One of the women vendors in "Mother's Market" in Imphal, Manipur where you can get vegetables, textiles, utensils, etc. The market is only for women vendors, made to help women support themselves.

One of the dancers posing as Lord Krishna in the Manipur style of dance known as the Rasa-lila.

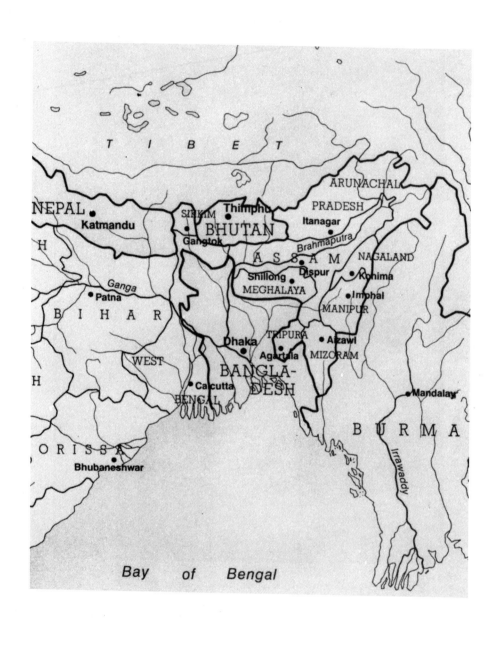

Conclusion

If you have toured any of these areas of India, you will never forget the many sights, sounds, places, and the people you have met or may have traveled with, and the profound experiences, both material and spiritual, that this tour will have provided for you. In some ways, perhaps in many ways, you will never be quite the same. Perhaps your whole view of life and how you fit into this universe will have changed. India has a way of doing that to a person. Perhaps you have gained a whole new appreciation for life and what matters most to you. However, it will only affect you positively to the degree in which you are open to it. But no matter whether you have changed a little or a lot, from this point onward you will never be exactly the same.

Quite honestly, that is why I love to go on these journeys and pilgrimages in India. When I feel too cramped and stifled in whatever it is I have been doing, and when the day to day humdrum is getting too much for me, or I begin to feel like I am forgetting who I really am, I set sail on an open journey to a land that may force me to take a different and closer look at myself, this world, and where I fit into it materially and spiritually. And when I'm done, I feel greatly rewarded for it. In some ways, it's hard to explain, but I feel 100 percent richer afterwards. It's an experience and a change in consciousness that you can get in no other way. And I will take the best of the experience with me for the rest of my life.

There have been times when I've finished a tour of the holy places of part of India and felt so spiritualized at the end of it that I thought even if for some reason I died right now, everything would be just fine. After visiting so many temples, seeing so many deities, sacred sites, or participating in ancient and divine festivals, I have felt so spiritual, so close to God, that I thought my consciousness could not get any better. What a great state of mind to leave this world, or to continue going on with this life. At least I will be highly charged for a long while. Be it good or bad, high or low, up or down, beautiful as well as ugly, there is always something that helps me understand more about who I am when I visit India. It is always more than merely seeing some tourist attractions. It is as if it reaches into your core and shows you who you are, whether you always like what you see or not.

In the same way, if you visit the right places, and experience the spiritual aspects of this exotic land, that is what India can do for you a as well. However, whether it does that to you or not may depend on how open you are to it, what you see, your attitude, how flexible you are to the conditions you will find in India, and whether you follow the recommended precautions as outlined in this book. But if the right combination of mental adjustments and the connection with the proper places to observe and absorb in India takes place, you will definitely have a rich and rewarding experience. And I hope this book will help take you to the same conclusion that keeps me coming back to India time and time again. There is always something new that India and the people have to offer with each and every journey I take through it. So, cast your fate to the open road, sing out Hari, Hari, and be ready for all the best that can happen to you.

APPENDIX A

▼

Preparing for Your Trip to India
A Short Guide

I often get questions about how to prepare for a trip to India and what to do, what to bring, and how to go about having a safe trip. So to help those who wish to have a pleasant journey, I am preparing this article to guide you through the basics. Naturally, traveling to India is an extremely individualistic experience. What you may love in your trip someone else may dislike. Someone may have life-changing experiences and insights, while another may simply want to leave and go home. So it can vary tremendously.

Anyway, be sure to do your homework before you go. By that I mean try to figure out where or what cities and towns you will be visiting before you arrive so that you can adjust your schedule accordingly. However, if you are traveling alone leave room for changes in your plans because once you start traveling, you may meet other travelers who will tell you about places that you hadn't planned to see, but will then want to visit. This is actually part of the fun. Of course, it's always safer to travel with someone else, especially if they have been to India before, and especially if you are a woman. Or you may be traveling with a group tour, which can greatly simplify things, especially if you are not used to traveling in India. However, I have traveled alone throughout India on most of my trips, and met many others who have done the same with great success. But often times such people are serious pilgrims, like myself, or serious travelers who have specific things they want to see, or are familiar in the ways of traveling by themselves. India is not always a place in which it is easy to travel. Nonetheless, for those who are not familiar with traveling in India, let me get you started. The first thing you need to do is to:

GET A PASSPORT AND A VISA

Most of you probably have a passport. For those of you who don't, you can get all the information you need by looking up "Passports" in your phone book in the "US Government Offices" section. There will also be a listing of how to obtain this information online for those of you with online capabilities. There are also rush services available for passports.

All tourists to India are required to have a visa. If you are receiving visa information by mail, a visa application and instructions are included. If you want to receive this information by email, please go to the website, http://www.indiacgny.org/for the application and instructions. You can also check these sites for information about visas and applications that are listed on my links page, such as: http://www.indianembassy.org, and, http://chicago.indianconsulate.com/VISAINSN.html. Also check, http://www.indianembassy.org/consular/visa.pdf, for downloadable visa application forms in Adobe Acrobat Reader.

It is best to apply for the 6-month tourist visa, which should be enough for most tourists. This will cost about $60 for a US citizen, plus postage. However, I go to India on a regular basis, so I have a ten year visa, which costs $150. It allows me to go as often as I like as long as each visit is no longer than six months.

If you apply for a visa by express mail to the Indian Consulate, your visa will be processed in 5 days. If you live in a city with an Indian Consulate and submit your application at the counter, the visa will be processed the same day. The listing of Consulate offices is given in the visa instructions. Apply to the one designated for your area. It is best to send it by certified or registered mail, and add a return envelope with prepaid postage by certified or registered mail as well.

In the visa application, you will be asked to list the areas of India you plan to travel to. So list a few places that you may be visiting. When I'm traveling, I'm usually visiting so many places that it would be difficult to list them all. So I merely list a few. You will also be asked to give 2 references for people residing in India. List a couple of friends if you have any there, or call the Consulate about this if you have no one in particular that you know. Or if you are affiliated with a temple and have friends there, there are bound to be some people who can help you out with a few names and addresses.

IMMUNIZATIONS

If this is your first trip to India, you may be worried about diseases. Contact your doctor or the Disease Control Center in the local hospital if you would like professional immunization advice. They will let you know of any outbreaks of diseases in India, or any for which you should be prepared. From personal experience, malaria medication may create discomfort, and may not be worthwhile, and you may not need it. It is always helpful to ensure that your tetanus shot is updated, as you are walking barefooted through old structures. Otherwise, typhoid and cholera may also be of some concern.

The first time I went to India, I got shots and medicine for everything. Later I learned that most of them are only good to a certain percentage anyway. Now I don't bother with it, but only take along herbs and anti-diarrhea medicine, like Imodium A-D. Another very good Ayurvedic medicine that will help, if you can find it once you get to India, is Sudha Sindhu. This is quite good for stomach problems and diarrhea. I use it whenever I start getting an upset stomach to keep it from developing into anything further. However, it is not so easy to find.

A very helpful medication is a low-grade antibiotic called "Doxycycline", which kills bacteria in the Gastro Intestinal tract. It can be taken on a daily basis to ensure that you don't have stomach problems during your stay. Ask your doctor for advice regarding this medication.

PACKING LIST

Following the suggested list for what you will need to bring will help you make sure that you are prepared for whatever may happen. Because you will be moving from place to place, please ensure you have 4 changes of clothes, some of which need to be appropriate for temples, if that is a place where you will be visiting. And going to India should mean visiting temples. And remember that the hotel laundry service, when available, may not always be convenient. So this is what you want to bring along:

1. Particular clothes, which can include:

A. Modest light-weight summer attire, unless you are going into the northern regions during the winter months. This would include:

B. a couple pair of pants,

C. shorts if you want (for a man),

D. three or four simple T-shirts,

E. A hat for warmth when going into the mountains, and a sunhat for protection from the sun, which you can also get in India. In the winter the days will be warm but the nights can be cool.

F. A coat or warm sweatshirt. In the winter, or if you are going up into the mountains even in summer, you need to bring a winter coat as well. A lightweight wrap or sweater can be good for heavily air-conditioned buses or trains, or cool evenings as well.

G. Raincoat & umbrella, a necessity in the monsoon season, and the umbrella can help protect you from the sun in the summer.

H. Additional clothes can include something you may need for visiting temples. Once you get to India, you can also shop around for these. I usually bring two kurtas and two dhotis with me, while you may bring or buy two kurtas and two pair of loose fitting white pants, or pajamas as they are often called in India. Women can bring or buy a few blouses and a couple of saris or long skirts or dresses. Shorts for women are inappropriate in India. Such an outfit can cost anywhere from $20-$30 in India. Pants or jeans can also be acceptable in most other places.

2. Socks. These can help against hot temple stones, especially during the heat of the summer or in the south. However, I usually don't bring socks since they get dirty quickly and become just another item to wash everyday. If you visit the temples in the morning, then the stones will likely not be overly hot from the sun. However, during the summer in the south, the outdoor stone floors and courtyards can draw in the heat from the summer sun quickly, and can burn your feet by 11 AM.

3. Sandals that can be easily removed, or simple and cool jogging shoes

4. Sunscreen

5. Mosquito repellent

6. Over the counter diarrhea medication, as previously mentioned.

7. A small packet of Kleenex.

8. A small flashlight, especially one that can fit in your purse or shoulder bag, because in the small villages the lights can go out at any time, and it is better to be equipped.

9. Snacks like granola bars, dried fruit, or nuts if you want, otherwise there are plenty of snacks you can buy in the stores in India.

10. Cold medicine, and aspirin or Tylenol, or herbs to help maintain your health.

11. A water bottle carrier if you want. I always buy bottled water from the shops.

12. A lite shoulder bag to carry your things while on the bus, and a smaller fanny pack or purse to carry your valuables into the temples or while you shop, especially for women.

13. Pens for yourself and to give to the children that you will meet everywhere—they love brightly-colored pens. However, requests for pens have greatly diminished over the years because the quality of Indian pens have improved. Yet in some areas, they still ask for American pens.

14. A good alarm clock, and a traveler's watch. I often bring a cheap Casio watch with a built in calculator, which is great for figuring currency exchange rates on prices.

15. Camera, the one of your choice, and plenty of film, although you can buy good film in the bigger Indian cities. Bring the film in a lead bag that you can purchase at your local camera store to protect it from airport X-ray machines. However, in this day and age of higher security, it can help if the plastic film containers are see-thru, like those Fuji Film makes. Then the airport security people can easily see what is inside if they have any questions, which should not be the case if it is in your check-in luggage. Of course, as digital cameras become more popular, this arrangement is not so necessary. But then make sure you bring enough memory for storing your photos.

16. Also consider Q-Tips or cotton swabs for cleaning your ears, some band aid bandages, a role of medical tape, and a tube of anti-septic ointment, just in case. These can also help if you get blisters on your feet from walking or any small cuts. A small container of Vaseline may also be helpful.

17. Don't forget your finger nail clippers, and any other small toiletries that you like, such as soap, toothpaste, toothbrush, and razor & blades, or hair shampoo, yet many of these are readily available in India if you forget or run out.

18. You may also want to bring a money belt, or thin wallet to keep in your front pocket.

19. Make copies of your passport and visa, and your list of travelers checks, to keep in various places amongst your belongings.

20. Bring a good but not overly large shoulder bag or backpack to put all of this stuff in. I usually bring nothing more than I can handle at any one time. So that includes a shoulder bag and my camera bag, since I'm always photographing the temples and holy sites. And that's it. Of course, once you begin shopping around and picking up things to take back home with you, additional bags or suitcases can easily be purchased to pack all the stuff you want to bring back home. However, I usually wait to do my souvenir shopping until near the end of my trip so I don't have to be lugging a bunch of stuff around wherever I go. Although I am often going to many out of the way places where many other tourists wouldn't consider.

You don't want to lug too much stuff with you because some places don't always have nearby ricksha or taxi services. This happened when I was in Sanchi, which only had horse-drawn carts, I think one or two in the whole village, and the train station was in the next town. In Badami I had the same problem. So even though many places will have service to help you, some places are so small, depending on where you go, that you don't want to be stuck with too many things to carry.

21. Traveler's checks and enough cash, keep them in separate places. An ATM card is also convenient. There are often more ATM machines than banks who can cash traveler's checks, especially in smaller towns.

22. Other helpful items that I bring include:

A. Bottles (for holy soil or water), B. Indian train schedule, C. Guidebook, D. Maps, E. Itinerary of places I'm considering visiting, F. Small notebook for photo notes, etc., G. Journal to write in, H. Extra pair of glasses, I. Combination lock for places where you stay, J. Lock & keys for bag and house, K. Some plastic bags for storage or separating dirty clothes, L. Handkerchief or wash cloths, for wiping away the sweat, M. List of India contacts, N. Tilok, O. Japa beads, P. 2 gamchas, Q. 2 kaupinas or underpants, and R. a towel.

23. An electrical adapter to change voltage for any appliances brought from America to be used in India is also a good idea, like hairdryers, recharging batteries for digital cameras, etc.

24. Plane tickets, by all means don't forget these, and make an extra copy of them.

APPENDIX B

▼

Suggested Routes for Short Pilgrimages

If your time is limited, you may not have the means to take one of the tours as described in this book. So a shorter pilgrimage may be necessary. So here are a few suggestions:

If you come into India through New Delhi, you may first see the city of New Delhi, then go to Mathura and Vrindavana to see the land of Lord Krishna, which has many sites to see. Agra is not far from there if you want to see the Taj Mahal, along with Fatehpur Sikri an hour west. But while in the area, Jaipur is another most interesting place to see, only six hours away from Mathura or Delhi, with many more temples and holy sites. A quick bus trip up to Haridwar and Rishikesh from either Vrindavana or New Delhi is also a nice location to include. And Kurukshetra, three hours north of Delhi can also easily be included.

If you are spending time near Kolkata, you can see that city for a day or two. Then go to Mayapur, about three hours away to see the birthplace of Sri Chaitanya, where there are many temples and holy sites. If you are going to stay in this area for a while, you can also arrange a bus or taxi ride to Ekachakra to see the birthplace of Sri Nityananda. Otherwise, you can take a jaunt down to Jagannatha Puri to see the temples there, as well as in Bhubaneswara and the Konarka Sun temple. You can also stop at Remuna along the way to Puri to see the Kshira-chora-Gopinatha temple.

If you are near Chennai, then there are some temples in that town worth seeing, plus be sure to go to Tirupati, one of the most sacred places in the area. From there Kanchipuram is not far away, and points farther south are easily reachable, depending on how much time you have.

If you are in the Mumbai area, there are some temples and sites to see there, and you can also make some trips out to Nasik, or to Pune, stopping at Lonavla along the way for the Karla and Bhaja caves.

THE TWELVE SHIVA JYOTIRLINGA SHRINES IN INDIA

If you want to see the main Shiva temples, meaning the *jyotirlingas*, they are not located together, but all over various parts of India. I've met some people who try to visit all of thse temples, which are listed as follows:

1. Kedarnath, located in the mountains of Uttaranchal

2. Somnath, found at Prabhas Patan in along the west coast of Gujarat.

3. Sri Sailam, near Kurnool in Andhra Pradesh.

4. Mahakaleshwar, in Ujjain.

5. Omkareshwar and Mamleshwara in Madhya Pradesh.

6. Bhimashankar, in the Sahyadri Hills of Maharashtra.

7. Viswanatha in Varanasi.

8. Tryambakeshwar, near Nasik in Maharashtra.

9. Vaidyanath, in Deoghar, Jarkhand, some feel in Parali in Maharasthra north of Mumbai.

10. Nageshwar, near Dwarka in Gujarat.

11. Rameswaram, along the east coast in southern Tamil Nadu.

12. Grishneshwar, not far from the Ellora Caves, north of Aurangabad.

A PPENDIX   C

▼

About the Photographs

One problem I have when making decisions on which photographs to include in a book is that I have so many from which to choose. I have over 15,000 color slides or images of India that I have taken over the years, and I am always returning to India and bringing back more photographs. Many of them are unique, or capture certain things about the people or places that I could never get again. So the question is often, which photos to include? So I hope that the ones that have been chosen for this book will convey some of the atmosphere and experience of what India is like.

Another point is that my style of photography is what I call "cultural photojournalism." I do not like to set up scenes to photograph. I like to keep a low profile and walk around taking photographs of things as they happen, or of people when they do not know that I am there. I think it adds much more realism to the experience, as if the viewer of the photograph gets a sense of being there. Of course, this also means that, as a photographer, you have to take your chances in getting the scenes you want, regardless of weather or other circumstances that create constant change in the venue. Or you must have the patience in waiting for certain scenes to develop. At other times, I am merely documenting buildings and holy places the way they are today, knowing that things always change. What you see today may not be there in the future. This itself can have some importance.

I have also presented the photographs in this book in black and white to help keep the cost of the book down. This is not meant to be a coffee table art book, but a practical guide in understanding the most spiritually significant places and how to reach them. Some people like black and white prints more than color. They say it adds a deeper sense of drama to the photograph. But India also is known for its colorful landscapes, people, festivals, clothes, and food. So that part of it you will see when you get there, or you can also see some more of my photography in color on my website, or by ordering the DVD with some of the collections of photos that I have taken. Or maybe someday I will be able to offer a large book of color photographs of India.

Travel Books That Were Helpful

These are some general books that had been helpful to my research on the holy places of India. However, as I traveled, I picked up numerous small books or booklets on the cities, holy places, or regions where I traveled. I don't list these because they are generally available only in India at the places they describe and tend to come and go out of circulation quickly. You can have the same experience and find additional books and information as you travel. They can be quite helpful and informative.

GENERAL BOOKS

India, by Lonely Planet, ISBN: 1-74059-694-3, www.lonelyplant.com. One of the best and most popular books for general information on getting around India.

Holy Places and Temples of India, Jada Bharat Dasa (John Howley), Spiritual Guides, 1996. A very nice book that mostly covers Vedic and Vaishnava temples all over India.

India, Eyewitness Travel Guides, D. K. Publishing, 375 Hudson St., New York, NY 10014, 2002, ISBN: 07894-8395-5. A good book for general information on all aspects of India with numerous small photos of everything.

India, by Insight Guides, Prentice Hall Press, APA Publications, New York, NY. ISBN: 0-13-456856-7. A great book with lots of photos and general information on India.

Insight Guides has also published books on:

Rajasthan, ISBN: 013-467861-3.

India's Western Himalaya, ISBN: 0-13-472291-4.

Nepal, ISBN: 0-395-66208-7.

Nepal, by Lonely Planet, 1990, ISBN: 0-86442-189-3. Another of the best on general information for getting around Nepal.

India Unveiled, by Robert Arnett, published by Atman Press, PMB #345, 2525 Auburn Ave., Columbus, Georgia 31906-1376, 1996. www.atmanpress.com. A great book, one of the best for coffee table photographic books on India. Robert is a personal friend of mine and continues to update and improve this book. If you want a volume with good large photos of India, this is the book. This is also the book that the government of India gave to Bill Clinton on one of his visits to India.

On Pilgrimage in Holy India, H. H. Bhakti Vikas Swami, Bhakti Vikas Books, c/o Iskcon, Jahangirpura, Surat, Gujarat, India, 2005.

The Penguin Guide to the Monuments of India, 2 volumes, by George Michell, published by the Penguin Group, London, England, 1989. A great set of books on the various monuments, temples, and buildings of India.

BOOKS ON SPECIAL AREAS
ON MAYAPUR

Sri Navadvipa Dhama and Jagannatha Puri, A Practical Guide, by Jada Bharata Dasa (John Howley), Spiritual Guides, 1997, ISBN: 0-9653858-2-5. This is a great and practical book on seeing most of the holy places in the area of Navadvipa.

Gauradesa: The Place of Gauranga Mahaprabhu, by Manjari Devi Dasi, Spiritual Frontiers Publications. This is a beautiful book with numerous photos giving the background and pastimes of the local regions.

Appreciating Navadvipa Dhama, by Mahanidhi Swami, 1996. This is all about the significance and pastimes of Lord Chaitanya and His associates in Navadvipa.

ON VRINDAVANA

Many of the following books are found only at book stands or shops associated with Iskcon temples at the particular locations they cover, or on Iskcon website bookstores.

Vrindavana and Braja Mandala—A Practical Guide, Jada Bharata dasa (John Howley), Spiritual Guides, 1997, ISBN: 0-9653858-1-7. This has maps and all the information so you know how and what you will find in visiting the numerous temples and holy places in around Vrindavana. Available at most Iskcon outlets or at the Vridavana temple.

Vraja Mandala Darshan, Touring the Land of Krishna, A Complete Guide to Mathura, Vrindavana and Jaipur, by Miles Davis, Ph.D., (Patita Pavana Das), International Institute of Indology, 1984. I don't know if this book is still available, but it was and still is one of my favorites. Gives you easy directions on how to find places and temples, legends and what you will find at the place when you get there.

Vrindavana Dhama Ki Jaya, by Dhruva Maharaja dasa, Entourage Publishing International, 1988, ISBN: 0-945475-00-4. Great on stories and small photos of the holy places of Vrindavana.

Radha Kunda Mahima Madhuri, The Sweet Glories of Radha Kunda, Mahanidhi Swami. All about the significance and finding the holy sites around Radha Kunda near Vrindavana.

Gaudiya Vaishnavana Samadhis in Vrindavan, Mahanidhi Swami, 1993. A guide to finding and the significance of various Samadhi tombs of Vaishnava saints in the area of Vrindavana.

Appreciating Sri Vrindavana Dhama, Mahanidhi Swami, 1991. All about the philosophical significance of Radha-Krishna and the pastimes in Vrindavana.

The Complete Guide to Vrndavana, by Rajasekhara Dasa Brahmacari, Vedanta Vision Publications. A small book that has the essential details for getting around the holy sites.

The Color Guide to Govardhana Hill, by Rajasekhara Dasa Brahmacari, Vedanta Vision Publications. A pictorial guide that shows you around the area of Govardhana Hill in Vrindavana area.

The Color Guide to Radha Kunda, by Rajasekhara Dasa Brahmacari, Vedanta Vision Publications. A pictorial guide around the area of Radha Kunda.

Glossary

Acharya—the spiritual master who sets the proper standard by his own example.

Achaleshvara—Shiva as Lord of the Hill.

Adinatha—the first of the 24 Jain *Tirthankaras*.

Advaita—nondual, meaning that the Absolute Truth is one, and that there is no individuality between the Supreme Being and the individual souls which merge into oneness, the Brahman, when released from material existence. The philosophy taught by Sankaracharya.

Agastya Muni—a sage who was the knower of the *Vedas*.

Agni—fire, or Agni the demigod of fire.

Agnihotra—the Vedic sacrifice in which offerings were made to the fire, such as ghee, milk, sesame seeds, grains, etc. The demigod Agni would deliver the offerings to the demigods that are referred to in the ritual.

Ahankara—false ego, identification with matter.

Ahimsa—nonviolence.

Akarma—actions which cause no *karmic* reactions.

Akasha—the ether, or etheric plane; a subtle material element in which sound travels.

Amba, Ambika—name of Mother Durga.

Amrita—the nectar of immortality derived from churning the ocean of milk.

Amriteshvara—Shiva as Lord of Ambrosia.

Ananda—spiritual bliss.

Ananta—unlimited

Annapurna—Parvati a name meaning Filled with Food.

Aranyaka—sacred writings that are supposed to frame the essence of the *Upanishads*.

Arati—the ceremony of worship when incense and ghee lamps are offered to the Deities.

Arca-vigraha—the worshipable Deity form of the Lord made of stone, wood, etc.

Ardhanarishvara—Shiva as half Shiva and half Parvati.

Aryan—a noble person, one who is on the Vedic path of spiritual advancement.

Asana—postures for meditation, or exercises for developing the body into a fit instrument for spiritual advancement.

Asat—that which is temporary.

Ashrama—one of the four orders of spiritual life, such as *brahmacari* (celibate student), *grihastha* (married householder), *vanaprastha* (retired stage), and *sannyasa* (renunciate); or the abode of a spiritual teacher or *sadhu*. Also a spiritual training center or school.

Ashvamedha—a Vedic ritual involving offerings to God made by brahmana priests.

Atma—the self or soul. Sometimes means the body, mind, and senses.

Atman—usually referred to as the Supreme Self.

Avadhuta—a person who is so transcendental that he is beyond the normal rules and regulations of spiritual life.

Avatara—an incarnation of the Lord who descends from the spiritual world.

Avidya—ignorance or nescience.

Aum—*om* or *pranava*

Ayurveda—the original wholistic form of medicine as described in the Vedic literature.

Babaji—wandering mendicant holy man.

Betel—a mildly intoxicating nut.

Bhagavan—one who possesses all opulences, God.

Bhagiratha—a king who brought the Ganges down from heaven by the austerities he performed.

Bhairava—Shiva as the terrifying destroyer.

Bhajan—song of worship.

Bhajan kutir—a small dwelling used for one's worship and meditation.

Bhakta—a devotee of the Lord who is engaged in *bhakti-yoga*.

Bhakti—love and devotion for God.

Bhakti-yoga—the path of offering pure devotional service to the Supreme.

Bhang—pronounced bong, a sweet mixed with hashish.

Bhava—preliminary stage of love of God.

Bidi—an Indian cigarette.

Bodhi—the tree under which Buddha became enlightened.

Brahma—the demigod of creation who was born from Lord Vishnu, the first created living being and the engineer of the secondary stage of creation of the universe when all the living entities were manifested.

Brahmacari—a celebate student, usually five to twenty-five years of age, who is trained by the spiritual master. One of the four divisions or *ashramas* of spiritual life.

Brahmani—consort of Brahma.

Brahmajyoti—the great white light or effulgence which emanates from the body of the Lord.

Brahmaloka—the highest planet or plane of existence in the universe; the planet where Lord Brahma lives.

Brahman—the spiritual energy; the all-pervading impersonal aspect of the Lord; or the Supreme Lord Himself.

Brahmana or brahmin—one of the four orders of society; the intellectual class of men who have been trained in the knowledge of the *Vedas* and initiated by a spiritual master.

Brahmana—the supplemental books of the four primary *Vedas*. They usually contained instructions for performing Vedic *agnihotras*, chanting the *mantras*, the purpose of the rituals, etc. The *Aitareya* and *Kaushitaki Brahmanas* belong to the *Rig-veda*, the *Satapatha Brahmana* belongs to the *White Yajur-veda*, and the *Taittiriya Brahmana* belongs to the *Black Yajur-veda*. The *Praudha* and *Shadvinsa Brahmanas* are two of the eight *Brahmanas* belonging to the *Atharva-veda*.

Brahmarsis—great rishis or sages who are also knowledgeable brahmanas.

Brahminical—to be clean and upstanding, both outwardly and inwardly, like a *brahmana* should be.

Brijbasi—a resident of Vraja, Vrindavan.

Buddha—Lord Buddha or a learned man.

Caranamrita—the water that has been used to bathe the Deity and is offered in small spoonfuls to visitors in the temple.

Causal Ocean or Karana Ocean—is the corner of the spiritual sky where Maha-Vishnu lies down to create the material manifestation.

Chaitanya Mahaprabhu—the most recent incarnation of the Lord who appeared in the 15th century in Bengal and who originally started the *sankirtana* movement, based on congregational chanting of the holy names.

Chakra—a wheel, disk, or psychic energy center situated along the spinal column in the subtle body of the physical shell.

Chandra—the moon.

Chandrashekara—Shiva as Moon Crested.

Chaturbhuja—Shiva as Four-armed.

Chorten—Buddhist dome-like structure that are often built to commemorate a great lama or hold sacred relics within.

Cit—eternal knowledge.

Darshan—the devotional act of seeing and being seen by the Deity in the temple.

Dakshinamurti—Shiva as teacher of yoga and universal knowledge.

Dashavatara—the ten incarnations of Lord Vishnu: Matsya, Kurma, Varaha, Narasimha, Vamana, Parashurama, Rama, Krishna, Buddha, and Kalki.

Deity—the *arca-vigraha*, or worshipful form of the Divinity in the temple.

Deva—a demigod, or higher being.

Devaloka—the higher planets or planes of existence of the devas.

Devas—demigods or heavenly beings from higher levels of material existence, or a godly person.

Dham—a holy place.

Dharma—the essential nature or duty of the living being.

Dharmachakra—Buddhist wheel of law, the first sermon given by Buddha at Sarnath.

Dharmashala—a shelter or guesthouse for pilgrims at temples or holy towns.

Digambara—one of the two main Jain sects, sky-clad.

Diksha—spiritual initiation.

Divya Desam—One of the 108 most important Vishnu temples in India.

Diwali—festival of lights, marks the end of the rainy season.

Dualism—as related in this book, it refers to the Supreme as both an impersonal force (Brahman) as well as the Supreme Person.

Durga—the form of Parvati, Shiva's wife, as a warrior goddess known by many names according to her deeds, such as Simhavahini when riding her lion, Mahishasurama-rdini for killing the demon Mahishasura, Jagaddhatri as the mother of the universe, Kali when she killed the demon Raktavija, Tara when killing Shumba, etc. She assumes or incarnates in as many as 64 different forms, depending on her activities. Dvapara-yuga—the third age which lasts 864,000 years.

Dwaita—dualism the principle that the Absolute Truth consists of the infinite Supreme Being along with the infinitesimal, individual souls.

Ekadasi—a fast day on the eleventh day of the waxing and waning moon.

Gana—Shiva's dwarf attendants.

Ganapati—Ganesh as Lord of the *ganas*.

Gandharvas—the celestial angel-like beings who have beautiful forms and voices, and are expert in dance and music, capable of becoming invisible and can help souls on the earthly plane.

Ganesh—a son of Shiva, said to destroy obstacles (as Vinayaka) and offer good luck to those who petition him.

Gangapuja—the *arati* ceremony for worshiping the Ganges.

Ganges—the sacred and spiritual river which, according to the *Vedas*, runs throughout the universe, a portion of which is seen in India. The reason the river is considered holy is that it is said to be a drop of the Karana Ocean outside of the universe that leaked in when Lord Vishnu, in His incarnation as Gangeshvara—Shiva as Lord of Ganga.

Gangotri—the source of the Ganges River in the Himalayas.

Garbhodakasayi Vishnu—the expansion of Lord Vishnu who enters into each universe.

Garuda—Lord Vishnu's bird carrier.

Gaudiya—a part of India sometimes called Aryavarta or land of the Aryans, located south of the Himalayas and north of the Vindhya Hills.

Gaudiya *sampradaya*—the school of Vaishnavism founded by Sri Caitanya.

Gauri—name of Parvati meaning Fair One.

Gaurishankara—Shiva and Parvati together.

Gayatri—the spiritual vibration or *mantra* from which the other *Vedas* were expanded and which is chanted by those who are initiated as *brahmanas* and given the spiritual understanding of Vedic philosophy.

Ghat—a bathing place along a river or lake with steps leading down to the water.

Godasa—one who serves the senses.

Goloka Vrindavana—the name of Lord Krishna's spiritual planet.

Gompa—Buddhist monastery.

Gopuram—the tall ornate towers that mark the gates to the temples, often found in south India.

Gosvami—one who is master of the senses.

Govardhana-shila—a sacred stone from Govardhana Hill, considered as a direct form or expansion of Lord Krishna.

Govinda—a name of Krishna which means one who gives pleasure to the cows and senses.

Govindaraja—Krishna as Lord of the Cowherds.

Grihastha—the householder order of life. One of the four *ashramas* in spiritual life.

Gunas—the modes of material nature of which there is *sattva* (goodness), *rajas* (passion), and *tamas* (ignorance).

Guru—a spiritual master.

Hanuman—the popular monkey servant of Lord Rama.

Hare—the Lord's pleasure potency, Radharani, who is approached for accessibility to the Lord.

Hari—a name of Krishna as the one who takes away one's obstacles on the spiritual path.

Haribol—a word that means to chant the name of the Lord, Hari.

Harinam—refers to the name of the Lord, Hari.

Har Ki Pauri—the holy bathing *ghats* in Hardwar where the Ganges leaves the mountains and enters the plains. It is at this spot where the Kumbha Mela is held every twelve years.

Hayagriva—Lord Vishnu as the giver of knowledge.

Hinayana—Lesser Vehicle, the Buddhist school that stresses achieving one's own enlightenment.

Hiranyagarbha—another name of Brahma who was born of Vishnu in the primordial waters within the egg of the universe.

Hiranyakashipu—the demon king who was killed by Lord Vishnu in His incarnation as Narasimha.

Hrishikesa—a name for Krishna which means the master of the senses.

Impersonalism—the view that God has no personality or form, but is only an impersonal force (Brahman) which the individual souls merge back into when released from material existence.

Impersonalist—those who believe God has no personality or form.

Incarnation—the taking on of a body or form.

ISKCON—International Society for Krishna Consciousness.

Jagadambi—Parvati as Mother of the World.

Jagannatha—Krishna as Lord of the Universe, especially as worshipped in Jagannatha Puri.

Jagat Kishora—name of Krishna.

Jai or *Jaya*—a term meaning victory, all glories.

Japa—the chanting one performs, usually softly, for one's own meditation.

Japa-mala—the string of beads one uses for chanting.

Jiva—the individual soul or living being.

Jivanmukta—a liberated soul, though still in the material body and universe.

Jiva-shakti—the living force.

Jyotirlinga—the luminous energy of Shiva manifested as a self-manifested *lingam* at one of 12 places, such as Kedarnatha, Patan, Ujjain, and Varanasi.

Kali—the demigoddess who is the fierce form of the wife of Lord Shiva. The word *kali* comes from *kala*, the Sanskrit word for time: the power that dissolves or destroys everything.

Kali-yuga—the fourth and present age, the age of quarrel and confusion, which lasts 432,000 years and began 5,000 years ago.

Kalki—future incarnation of Lord Vishnu who appears at the end of Kali-yuga.

Kalpa—a day in the life of Lord Brahma which lasts a thousand cycles of the four *yugas*.

Kama—lust or inordinate desire.

Kama sutra—a treatise on sex enjoyment.

Karanodakasayi Vishnu (Maha-Vishnu)—the expansion of Lord Krishna who created all the material universes.

Karma—material actions performed in regard to developing one's position or for future results which produce *karmic* reactions. It is also the reactions one endures from such fruitive activities.

Karma-yoga—system of yoga for using one's activities for spiritual advancement.

Karttikeya—son of Shiva and Parvati, also known as Skanda, Subramanya, Keshava— Krishna with long hair.

Kirtana—chanting or singing the glories of the Lord.

Krishna—the name of the original Supreme Personality of Godhead which means the most attractive and greatest pleasure. He is the source of all other incarnations, such as Vishnu, Rama, Narasimha, Narayana, Buddha, Parashurama, Vamanadeva, Kalki at the end of Kali-yuga, etc.

Krishnaloka—the spiritual planet where Lord Krishna resides.

Kshatriya—the second class of *varna* of society, or occupation of administrative or protective service, such as warrior or military personel.

Ksirodakasayi Vishnu—the Supersoul expansion of the Lord who enters into each atom and the heart of each individual.

Kumbha Mela—the holy festival in which millions of pilgrims and sages gather to bathe in the holy and purifying rivers for liberation at particular auspicious times that are calculated astrologically. The Kumbha Mela festivals take place every three years alternating between Allahabad, Nasik, Ujjain, and Hardwar.

Kuruksetra—the place of battle 5,000 years ago between the Pandavas and the Kauravas ninety miles north of New Delhi, where Krishna spoke the *Bhagavad-gita*.

Lakshmi—the goddess of fortune and wife of Lord Vishnu.

Lila—pastimes

Lilavataras—the many incarnations of God who appear to display various spiritual pastimes to attract the conditioned souls in the material world.

Linga—the formless symbol of Lord Shiva, often represents universal space.

Madana-mohana—name of Krishna as one who fills the mind with love.

Madhava—Krishna.

Mahabharata—the great epic of the Pandavas, which includes the *Bhagavad-gita*, by Vyasadeva.

Maha-mantra—the best *mantra* for self-realization in this age, called the Hare Krishna *mantra*.

Mahatma—a great soul or devotee.

Maha-Vishnu or Karanodakasayi Vishnu—the Vishnu expansion of Lord Krishna from whom all the material universes emanate.

Mahayana—Great Vehicle, the Buddhist school that stresses giving aid to all living beings toward enlightenment.

Mahishamardini—Durga as the slayer of the buffalo demon.

Mandapa or *Mandapam*—the front hallway of a Vedic temple.

Mandir—a temple.

Mantra—a sound vibration which prepares the mind for spiritual realization and delivers the mind from material inclinations. In some cases a *mantra* is chanted for specific material benefits.

Maya—illusion, or anything that appears to not be connected with the eternal Absolute Truth.

Mayavadi—the impersonalist or voidist who believes that the Supreme has no form, or that any form of God is but a product of *maya*.

Mohini—Lord Vishnu's incarnation as the most beautiful woman.

Moksha—liberation from material existence.

Murti—a deity of the Lord or an image of a demigod or spiritual master that is worshiped.

Murugan—means the divine child, the Tamil name for Subramaniya, one of the sons of Shiva and Parvati, especially worshiped in South India. It is said that he was born to destroy the demon Tarakasura.

Nandi—Shiva's bull carrier.

Narasimha—Lord Vishnu's incarnation as the half-man half-lion who killed the demon Hiranyakashipu.

Narayana—the four-handed form of the Supreme Lord.

Nataraja—King of Dance, usually referring to Shiva, but also Krishna.

Nirguna—without material qualities.

Nirvana—the state of no material miseries, usually the goal of the Buddhists or voidists.

Nityananda—the brother of Sri Chaitanya, and *avatara* of Lord Balarama.

Om or *Omkara*—*pranava*, the transcendental *om mantra*, generally referring to the attributeless or impersonal aspects of the Absolute.

Pan—a concoction of ground betel nut and spices that acts as a mild stimulant or intoxicant. It is very popular and often leaves the teeth stained red.

Pandal—a large tent where religious gatherings are held.

Paramahamsa—the highest level of self-realized devotees of the Lord.

Paramatma—the Supersoul, or localized expansion of the Lord.

Parampara—the system of disciplic succession through which transcendental knowledge descends.

Parashurama—incarnation of Vishnu with an axe who cleansed the world of the deviant *kshatriya* warriors.

Parsvanatha—one of the prominent Jain *thirthankaras*.

Prana—the life air or cosmic energy.

Pranayama—control of the breathing process as in *astanga* or *raja-yoga*.

Prasada—food or other articles that have been offered to the Deity in the temple and then distributed amongst people as the blessings or mercy of the Deity.

Prema—matured love for Krishna.

Puja—the worship offered to the Deity.

Pujari—the priest who performs worship, *puja*, to the Deity.

Purusha or *Purusham*—the supreme enjoyer.

Radha—Krishna's favorite devotee and the personification of His bliss potency.

Rahu—deity representation of the planetary node that causes solar eclipses.

Rajarsi—a Raja or great *rishi* or sage.

Raja-yoga—the eightfold yoga system.

Rajo-guna—the material mode of passion.

Ramachandra—an incarnation of Krishna as He appeared as the greatest of kings.

Ramanuja—Vaishnava philosopher.

Ramayana—the great epic of the incarnation of Lord Ramachandra.

Rasa—an enjoyable taste or feeling, a relationship with God.

Ravana—demon king of the *Ramayana*.

Rishi—saintly person who knows the Vedic knowledge.

Sacrifice—in this book it in no way pertains to human sacrifice, as many people tend to think when this word is used. But it means to engage in an austerity of some kind for a higher, spiritual purpose.

Sati—Shiva's wife who killed herself by immolation in fire.

Sac-cid-ananda-vigraha—the transcendental form of the Lord or of the living entity which is eternal, full of knowledge and bliss.

Sadhana—a specific practice or discipline for attaining God realization.

Sadhu—Indian holy man or devotee.

Saguna Brahman—the aspect of the Absolute with form and qualities.

Samadhi—trance, the perfection of being absorbed in the Absolute.

Samsara—rounds of life; cycles of birth and death; reincarnation.

Sanatana-dharma—the eternal nature of the living being, to love and render service to the supreme lovable object, the Lord.

Sangam—the confluence of two or more rivers.

Sankhya—analytical understanding of material nature, the body, and the soul.

Sankirtana-yajna—the prescribed sacrifice for this age: congregational chanting of the holy names of God.

Sannyasa—the renounced order of life, the highest of the four *ashramas* on the spiritual path.

Sarasvati—the goddess of knowledge and intelligence.

Sattva-guna—the material mode of goodness.

Sati—the name of Durga after she sacrificed herself.

Satya-yuga—the first of the four ages which lasts 1,728,000 years.

Shabda-brahma—the original spiritual vibration or energy of which the *Vedas* are composed.

Shaivites—worshipers of Lord Shiva.

Shakti—energy, potency or power, the active principle in creation. Also the active power or wife of a deity, such as Shiva/Shakti.

Shaktipeeth or *shaktipith*—a great holy place, usually marked by a temple, where a part of the body of Sati or Durga fell to the earth.

Shalagrama-shila—the sacred stone that is accepted as a direct form of Lord Vishnu.

Shastra—the authentic revealed Vedic scripture.

Shiva—the benevolent one, the demigod who is in charge of the material mode of ignorance and the destruction of the universe. Part of the triad of Brahma, Vishnu, and Shiva who continually create, maintain, and destroy the universe. He is known as Rudra when displaying his destructive aspect.

Sikha—a tuft of hair on the back of the head signifying that one is a Vaishnava.

Skanda—son of Shiva and Parvati, leader of the army of the gods; also known as Karttikeya and Subramanya or Murugan.

Srimad-Bhagavatam—the most ripened fruit of the tree of Vedic knowledge compiled by Vyasadeva.

Sruti—scriptures that were received directly from God and transmitted orally by *brahmanas* or *rishis* down through succeeding generations. Traditionally, it is considered the four primary *Vedas*.

Stupa—a Buddhist hemispherical or dome monument that often housed ashes or relics of great Buddhist teachers.

Sudra—the working class of society, the fourth of the *varnas*.

Surya—Sun or solar deity.

Svami—one who can control his mind and senses.

Svetambara—one of the two main Jain sects, white robed.

Swayambhu or *svayambhu*—a deity or image that is self-manifested, without being carved or produced by man.

Tamo-guna—the material mode of ignorance.

Tapasya—voluntary austerity for spiritual advancement.

Thanka—Tibetan cloth painting, usually based on Buddhist philosophy.

Tilok—the clay markings that signify a person's body as a temple, and the sect or school of thought of the person.

Tirtha—a holy place of pilgrimage.

Tirthankara—a person who is a perfected spiritual guide or teacher in Jainism.

Treta-yuga—the second of the four ages which lasts 1,296,000 years.

Tulasi—the small tree that grows where worship to Krishna is found. It is called the embodiment of devotion, and the incarnation of Vrinda-devi.

Upanishads—the portions of the *Vedas* which primarily explain philosophically the Absolute Truth. It is knowledge of Brahman which releases one from the world and allows one to attain self-realization when received from a qualified teacher. Except for the *Isa Upanishad*, which is the 40th chapter of the *Vajasaneyi Samhita* of the *Sukla (White) Yajur veda*, the *Upanishads* are connected to the four primary *Vedas*, generally found in the *Brahmanas*.

Vaikunthas—the planets located in the spiritual sky.

Vaishnava—a worshiper of the Supreme Lord Vishnu or Krishna and His expansions or incarnations.

Vaishnava-*aparadha*—an offense against a Vaisnava or devotee, which can negate all of one's spiritual progress.

Vaisya—the third class of society engaged in business or farming.

Vajra—thunderbolt.

Vamana—dwarf incarnation of Vishnu who covered the universe in three steps.

Vanaprastha—the third of the four *ashramas* of spiritual life in which one retires from family life in preparation for the renounced order.

Varaha—Lord Vishnu's boar incarnation.

Varna—sometimes referred to as caste, a division of society, such as *brahmana* (a priestly intellectual), a *kshatriya* (ruler or manager), *vaisya* (a merchant, banker, or farmer), and *sudra* (common laborer).

Varnashrama—the system of four divisions of society and four orders of spiritual life.

Vayu—demigod of the air.

Vedanta-sutras—the philosophical conclusion of the four *Vedas*.

Vedas—generally means the four primary *samhitas; Rig, Yajur, Sama, Atharva.*

Venktateshvara—Vishnu as Lord of the Venkata Hills, worshiped in Tirumala.

Vidya—knowledge.

Vishnu—the expansion of Lord Krishna who enters into the material energy to create and maintain the cosmic world.

Vishvakarma—demigod architect of the heavens.

Vishvanatha—Shiva as Lord of the universe, worshiped in Varanasi as a *linga*.

Vishvarupa—universal form of Lord Vishnu.

Vrindavana—the place where Lord Krishna displayed His village pastimes 5,000 years ago, and is considered to be part of the spiritual abode.

Vyasadeva—the incarnation of God who appeared as the greatest philosopher who compiled the main portions of the Vedic literature into written form.

Yajna—a ritual or austerity that is done as a sacrifice for spiritual merit, or ritual worship of a demigod for good *karmic* reactions.

Yamaraja—the demigod and lord of death who directs the living entities to various punishments according to their activities.

Yamuna—goddess personification of the Yamuna River.

Yatra—a spiritual pilgrimage to a holy site.

Yatri—a person who goes on a yatra.

Yoga—linking up with the Absolute.

Yoga-*siddhi*—mystic perfection.

Yoni—sexual emblem of Devi or Durga or Shakti, the universal female energy, often represented as a pedestal for the *Linga*.

Index

About Stephen Knapp

Stephen Knapp grew up in a Christian family, during which time he seriously studied the Bible to understand its teachings. In his late teenage years, however, he sought answers to questions not easily explained in Christian theology. So he began to search through other religions and philosophies from around the world and started to find the answers for which he was looking. He also studied a variety of occult sciences, ancient mythology, mysticism, yoga, and the spiritual teachings of the East. After his first reading of the *Bhagavad-gita*, he felt he had found the last piece of the puzzle he had been putting together through all of his research. Therefore, he continued to study all of the major Vedic texts of India to gain a better understanding of the Vedic science.

It is known amongst all Eastern mystics that anyone, regardless of qualifications, academic or otherwise, who does not engage in the spiritual practices described in the Vedic texts cannot actually enter into understanding the depths of the Vedic spiritual science, nor acquire the realizations that should accompany it. So, rather than pursuing his research in an academic atmosphere at a university, Stephen directly engaged in the spiritual disciplines that have been recommended for hundreds of years. He continued his study of Vedic knowledge and spiritual practice under the guidance of a spiritual master. Through this process, and with the sanction of His Divine Grace A. C. Bhaktivedanta Swami Prabhupada, he became initiated into the genuine and authorized spiritual line of the Brahma-Madhava-Gaudiya *sampradaya*, which is a disciplic succession that descends back through Sri Caitanya Mahaprabhu and Sri Vyasadeva, the compiler of Vedic literature, and further back to Sri Krishna. Through this initiation he has taken the spiritual name of Sri Nandanandana dasa. Besides being *brahminically* initiated, Stephen has also been to India numerous times and traveled extensively throughout the country, visiting all but three small states, and most of the major holy places, thus gaining a wide variety of spiritual experiences that only such places can give.